BRITISH HIT ALBUMS

PAUL GAMBACCINI · TIM RICE · JONATHAN RICE

GRR Editorial Associate: TONY BROWN

GUINNESS

ACKNOWLEDGEMENTS

Special thanks to Eileen Heinink, Jan Rice, Tom Rice and Tony Vickers. We also want to thank *New Musical Express* and *CIN* for their charts and many record companies for their patient help.

Editor: David Roberts
Deputy Editor and Picture Researcher: Paola Simoneschi
Editorial Assistant: Sallie Collins
Design: Stonecastle Graphics Ltd
Layout: Kathy Aldridge

First edition 1983
Second edition 1986
Third edition 1988
Fourth edition 1990
Fifth edition 1992
Sixth edition 1994

Published in Great Britain by
Guinness Publishing Ltd,
33 London Road, Enfield,
Middlesex

Typeset in Bembo and Gill Sans by
Ace Filmsetting Ltd, Frome, Somerset

Printed and bound in Great Britain by
The Bath Press, Bath, Avon

A catalogue record for this book is available from the British Library

ISBN 0–85112–725–5

INTRODUCTION

MICK AND MEAT LOAF SET RECORDS; WHITNEY AND LIONEL SELL THEM

We should not be surprised if a lot of this edition's readers are four-legged and horned. We are in a bull market. Gallup announced in January 1994 that album sales in 1993 had increased during the year by 6.9%, approximately double the rise for general retail sales. Nearly every music business expert, bona fide or bogus, has pronounced that the LP chart is now a more reliable indicator of mass audience taste than the singles survey. And, to read the measurement closest to home, sales of the last edition of *Hit Albums* were up 25%, while *Hit Singles* held steady.

The increased focus on the album chart is predominantly due to changes in the record business that have been discussed in previous issues of this book. Since the precedent set by Michael Jackson's *Thriller*, record companies have viewed the single as a promotional tool for a major artist's album, rather than as a separate artistic statement. The singles chart has come to be dominated by artists who are too new to have albums or who work in a style such as dance that favours the individual track over the full-length set. These trends have continued in the last two years, and the albums market has evolved in further ways that deserve mention.

The first is that the aforemen-  tioned dance artists do reach the album chart, but in an invisible way. Since 1989 multi-artist compilations have been segregated from the main chart and put into their own list. This separation has the virtue of giving readers and listeners of the artists chart an uninterrupted flow of individual and identifiable acts, rather than a sequence punctuated by titles ending with absurdly high numbers, such as the number two best-selling compilation of 1993, *Now! That's What I Call Music 26*. But isolating multi-artist anthologies in this way keeps them from view and gives the impression they are not registering significant sales. In fact, the top 50 compilations of 1993 were all contained in the top 171 of the overall chart prepared by Gallup, which is presented to the trade but rarely seen by the public. Not only were the majority of the tracks on the top 30 compilations of the year from clubland, 12 of the top 30 actually had the word 'dance' in their titles. This made 'dance' the most used word in the names of the top 30 compilations, even ahead of '93' (11), 'the' (10), and 'hits' (7).

It is evident that devotees of dance music enjoy collections of their favourite hits rather than single artist LPs, but this does not mean that they do not buy albums. The dance share of the compilation market is increasing, the compilation piece of the music pie is getting bigger, and the sheer number of compilations is on the up. Nineteen ninety-three was the first year in which *Music Week* tallied the release of over 2,000 multi-artist compilations.

INTRODUCTION

The activity in the compilation field can be followed in our Various Artists section. Buried there forever will be the greatest sales achievement of Whitney Houston, which can only be noted this once. The decision to pad out her contributions to the soundtrack of the film *The Bodyguard* with numbers by other Arista artists took the disc out of the artists chart and into the compilations. Overall, the CD, which included the historically successful single 'I Will Always Love You', was the number two seller of 1993, behind Meat Loaf's *Bat Out Of Hell II – Back Into Hell*, but for the public record it was removed from the artists countdown and considered the number one compilation of the year. Not only did Meat nip 'Nippy', as Whitney was nicknamed in childhood, but the original *Bat Out Of Hell* overtook *Rumours* to reclaim its position as the longest running chart album of all time.

Another signpost on the long and winding road of album-chart history was the appearance of *Stars* by Simply Red, led by Mick Hucknall, as the best seller of both 1991 and 1992. This was the first time the same disc had held the top sales spot for two years, although Dire Straits' *Brothers In Arms* had come close in the mid-80s. Major albums have recently enjoyed prolonged periods of significant sales. One reason is the aforementioned mining of LPs for singles, which enjoy radio play that is basically a year or two's free commercials for the album. Another is the lack of urgency the wider audience feels for major new releases: whether the work is bought tomorrow, next week or next month doesn't really matter as much as it did 30 years ago, when Beatles albums sold phenomenal amounts in short periods of time.

Because sales of an act's latest work can be spread out over time, the gaps between projects have become longer. R.E.M. and U2, who released *Automatic For The People* and *Zooropa* respectively less than two years after *Out Of Time* and *Achtung Baby*, seemed prolific, while Prince, who – until his announced retirement/rechristening – put out a new work each year, appeared promiscuous in his musical favours. One consequence of this is that annual sales and Most Weeks on Chart lists lose their ability to reflect the long-term public standing of an artist. The act may be absent from one year's lists simply because it has nothing current to sell.

When Elton John was informed in late December 1993 that his *Duets* had slipped in the United States from its debut position of 25 to 26, he might have been distressed at the premature peak, but actually he should have taken heart. *Duets* was the number one British album in America that week, narrowly outpacing Rod Stewart's *Unplugged . . . And Seated* and Phil Collins' *Both Sides*. This statistic was glum news indeed for the British record industry. That the country which once ruled the sound waves internationally had been pushed out

of the top 25 in the world's biggest market was a staggering setback. Furthermore, the three artists named were all industry legends, indicating that UK labels had failed dismally in their attempt to develop new transcendent stars.

It was not time for the hemlock yet, though, because the news was almost as bad for the American record companies. The Billboard charts have recently been dominated by rap and country artists who have made little or no impact on the international scene, and some pop and rock acts who have registered abroad have done so on only a limited scale. Though some of the American performers who did best in Britain during the last two years had comparable success at home, such as Meat Loaf, many actually were far better off in the United Kingdom than the United States. Former 'Endless Love' duettists Lionel Richie and Diana Ross both had year-end top five anthologies in the UK without anything approaching comparable success in the US. R.E.M. did far better with *Automatic For The People* here, where it was the number two artist album of 1993, than there, where it was 24th. Tina Turner continued her phase of greatest retail success in Europe as a whole and Britain in particular, while k.d. lang suddenly emerged to be bigger on this side of the Atlantic than the other. When the *Greatest Hits* of Doris Day is a sales smash in the UK, as it was in 1993, and *The Chronic* by Dr. Dre isn't, as it wasn't, we must realize that American artists are still doing well, but not necessarily the same ones who are going gold and platinum in their native country. The regionalization of repertoire continues to be a *bête noire* of the music business.

What all this means is that British record buyers are buying more albums by more of the artists they want, rather than those multinationals would like them to support. They are also purchasing a larger volume of compilations, even though they may be kept in ignorance of this fact. Considering as well those Gallup statistics reporting real increases in the number of units sold, we really do present this sixth edition of *Hit Albums* to a bull market. We have therefore made sure the cover is not red.

Good reading and good listening.

PAUL GAMBACCINI   JONATHAN RICE   TIM RICE

1958

In 1948 CBS introduced the long-playing microgroove recording to America. It was devised by Peter Goldmark who, it is said, had had enough of getting up several times during one piece of music to change several 78s. He thought there had to be a market for a single disc that could contain an entire symphony or sonata.

The 18 albums that hit the chart in the last eight weeks of 1958, the first weeks of *Melody Maker*'s Top Ten chart (the first LP chart published in the UK), demonstrated that Goldmark's invention had other applications. None of the 18 best-sellers was a classical orchestral performance! Thirteen were by adult male performers with wide audience appeal and five were of show business origin – that is, stage, screen or television.

The soundtrack to *South Pacific* was number one for each of the eight weeks, a prelude to its equally total domination of the 1959 lists. The man with the most LPs to chart was Frank Sinatra, who touched the Top Ten four times. Elvis Presley had the most total weeks on chart, that is to say a sum of the runs of each of his hit LPs. Both *Elvis' Golden Records* and *King Creole* were on every one of the eight charts.

The other artists who contributed to the all-male domain were Perry Como, Russ Conway, Mario Lanza, the American satirist Tom Lehrer, and Johnny Mathis. Perhaps Lanza was the closest to what Goldmark had in mind: one side of his disc was the soundtrack to the film about the classical tenor Enrico Caruso, *The Great Caruso*.

1959

It can be whispered in reverent awe or shouted from the rooftops, but the achievement is so great that it cannot be conveyed in casual conversation: the original soundtrack to the film *South Pacific* was at number one for the entire year 1959. This family favourite led the list for every one of the 52 weeks, a feat which has never been matched, though later discs would surpass it in sales. *South Pacific* boasted a wide range of memorable music, from the love ballad *Some Enchanted Evening* (an American number one for Perry Como) to the novelty tune *Happy Talk* (eventually a UK number one for Captain Sensible).

Film soundtracks were still the leading money-spinners in the LP market of 1959. The form was only a decade old, and soundtracks, Broadway cast performances and classical works were still the most logical initial uses of Peter Goldmark's invention, requiring the additional space a long player could provide. The movie versions of *Gigi* and *The King And I* were notable winners in 1959, as was the New York stage production of *West Side Story*.

Rock-and-roll vocalists, previously content with singles, made further inroads into the album field, but Frank Sinatra still scored the most weeks on chart for a solo singer. Elvis Presley was a close second, registering an impressive success with *Elvis' Golden Records*. The chart appearance of two LPs by Cliff Richard was the best 1959 showing by a young Briton.

Curtain Up!, a compilation of stars from the London Palladium hosted by Bruce Forsyth, enjoyed a 13-week run, but the most impressive performance by a show business star was that of Peter Sellers, who spent 32 weeks in the Top Ten with two solo LPs and a further five with his colleagues the Goons.

1960

South Pacific dominated the album charts one more time in 1960, though not to the extent it had in 1959. It was in the best-sellers for every one of the 53 charts of the year, the only title to achieve that run, but it did occasionally let other discs take the top spot. Number one on the very first *Record Retailer* album chart, that of 10 March, was *The Explosive Freddy Cannon*, which fell in fragments the following week after giving Cannon the distinction of being the first rock-and-roll singer to have a number one LP in the UK. Even the second, Elvis Presley, who had been a more likely contender for that honour, only managed one week at the summit, scoring with *Elvis Is Back*. The other disc to interrupt the *South Pacific* streak was *Down Drury Lane To Memory Lane*, a nostalgic effort by the studio group 101 Strings.

Rock-and-roll made great progress in the long playing market in 1960. The previous year only four rockers had charted in the entire 12 months. This time five of the top six acts were rock stars, though the majority of chart artists were still not of this nature. Presley pipped Peter Sellers as the individual with most weeks on the chart, though Sellers would have ranked above Presley if the computation included his additional appearances with the Goons and Sophia Loren, not, one must add, on the same disc.

American guitarist Duane Eddy's surprisingly strong showing in fourth place should not be overlooked.

1961

Commercial success does not guarantee artistic immortality, as the George Mitchell Minstrels have proved. Their *Black And White Minstrel Show* was an enormous success on television, record and stage, but an entire generation has grown up in, shall we say, the dark about their achievements.

The Black And White Minstrel Show was the only album to stay in the chart for the whole of 1961. It accumulated seven weeks at number one in four separate visits, while *Another Black And White Minstrel Show* had a single mighty eight-week run at the top. Mass audiences loved the old-time performances of The Minstrels, many of whom blacked up to sing vintage popular songs. It was the dated nature of their material, as well as increased sophistication concerning racial matters, which spelled an end to large scale interest in the group in the late sixties.

Elvis Presley was the outstanding artist for the second consecutive year, enjoying 22 weeks at number one with the soundtrack to *GI Blues*. The granddaddy of film favourites, *South Pacific*, put in a final nine weeks at the peak before retiring. It was a bumper year for original cast recordings of stage musicals, with a strong emphasis on the London stage. *Oliver*, *Sound Of Music* and *Stop The World I Want To Get Off* all had lengthy runs with British rosters. The year saw hit honours for the well-remembered *Beyond The Fringe* and the completely forgotten *King Kong*. Even the London cast of *Bye Bye Birdie* flew out of the wings and into the charts.

Frank Sinatra continued his series of fine years, entering the Top Twenty with seven titles on four different labels. Cliff Richard had three new top two successes and one happy hangover from 1960, *Me And My Shadows*. *21 Today* was his first number one, though his mates beat him to the top by six weeks with their debut disc *The Shadows*.

1962

Elvis Presley and the George Mitchell Minstrels overachieved again in 1962. The King of rock and roll notched up 18 weeks at number one with his *Blue Hawaii* soundtrack, more time at the top than any other long player that year, and he ruled the roost for six more weeks with *Pot Luck*. The Minstrels led the list with their new release, *On Stage With The George Mitchell Minstrels*, and then encored with their 1960 issue, the original *Black And White Minstrel Show*. Their three albums tallied a total of 109 weeks in the chart, the first time any act had hit the century.

Compared to these two artists the rest of the field failed to flame, though *South Pacific* again managed to appear in every one of the 52 charts. The new film sensation was *West Side Story*, surpassing its significant stage sales to pace the pack for 12 weeks. Four other multi-media successes were the soundtrack to *It's Trad Dad*, the original cast album of the London production *Blitz*, and two Dorothy Provine sets inspired by her television series *The Roaring 20s*. Further evidence of the taste for trad was the appearance of a budget album, *The Best Of Ball, Barber And Bilk*, at number one for two weeks. Chris Barber and Acker Bilk had appeared together on two fast-selling packages in 1961, sans Kenny Ball.

The Shadows achieved the fabulous feat of nabbing their second number one with their second effort, *Out Of The Shadows*. They shared credit on Cliff Richard's table-topping *The Young Ones*. Cliff managed to top the Shads in weeks on chart thanks to his subsequent release, the literally timed and titled *32 Minutes And 17 Seconds*.

8

1963

Beatlemania spread like a flash fire in 1963, and the album chart showed its effects. The Fab Four's *Please Please Me* seized the top spot on 11 May and held it for 30 consecutive weeks, to be replaced only by *With The Beatles*, which kept clear for a further 21. The Liverpudlians had come from nowhere to hold the premier position for one week shy of a full year. It was nothing short of a musical revolution: from their arrival until 1968, only one non-rock album would have a look in at number one. A field that had been the domain of the soundtrack and cast album overnight became ruled by rock. It was hard to believe that 1963 had begun with *The Black And White Minstrel Show* still in the lead. With a couple of notable exceptions, the film and stage market dried up.

Cliff Richard was the weeks on chart champ this time, his total fed by three new successes. The second highest figures were achieved equally by Elvis Presley and Buddy Holly. The Pelvis began twitching in anxiety as the soundtracks to three bad films did progressively worse. Holly, dead for four years, had always been a strong album seller, but really surged in 1963 when the poignantly-titled collection *Reminiscing* joined the list of his other posthumous best sellers.

Frank Ifield proved a one-year though not a one-hit wonder, reaching number three with two releases. He never came close again. Frank Sinatra rebounded with three top tenners, including a team-up with Count Basie that went to number two.

1964

T he Beatles and Rolling Stones monopolized the number one position during 1964, making it the purest year for rock music in terms of holding the top spot. The only 12 weeks John, Paul, George and Ringo were not ahead with either *With The Beatles, A Hard Day's Night* or *Beatles For Sale*, their chief competition was in front with the debut disc *The Rolling Stones*. The fresh triumphs of *A Hard Day's Night* and *Beatles For Sale* gave the Beatles four number ones in four releases, a 100 per cent success ratio they maintained through all of their 11 official international outings, though two other issues, a 1966 UK compilation and the *Yellow Submarine* soundtrack on which they played only a part, fell short of the top. No other act has hit number one every time with as many records.

The Fab Four's quartet of hit LPs gave them 104 weeks on chart, the first time a century had been achieved by a rock act. But even they were outdistanced by Jim Reeves. The American country singer had enjoyed two big albums to accompany his two strong singles in the first half of the year. After he died in a plane crash in July, nine further packages made the chart, six in a four-week period. Gentleman Jim accumulated 115 weeks on chart in all, a record that would stand until 1968.

Third in the weeks on chart category was Roy Orbison, who enjoyed the distinction of seeing his *In Dreams* set on every chart of the year, a feat attained for the second consecutive year by *West Side Story*. Cliff Richard had only one new album, below average for his early years, and Elvis Presley slipped seriously as none of his three long players reached the top three.

1965

F or the three middle years of the 60s only the Beatles, Rolling Stones, Bob Dylan and *The Sound Of Music* reached number one, trading off in a seemingly endless sequence. The first three were the rock artists who came to represent the spirit of the decade, while the last was a show business phenomenon that came, saw, conquered, and wouldn't go away.

The Beatles began the year on top with *Beatles For Sale* and ended it there with *Rubber Soul*, having spent much of the summer there as well with *Help*. Bob Dylan had the second highest total of chart-toppers, two, succeeding *The Freewheelin' Bob Dylan* with his own *Bringing It All Back Home*, but his most impressive statistic was his 112 weeks on chart. Much of his back catalogue charted in late 1964 and 1965. Though primarily considered an album artist, he also logged five Top Thirty singles in 1965, his peak year.

Dylan's dear friend Joan Baez shared his success, with three charters to follow her 1964 debut. Her winners included *Joan Baez, Joan Baez No. 5* and *Farewell Angelina*, but no sign of Joan Baez Nos. 2, 3 or 4.

Though Miss Baez was the front-running credited female vocalist, Julie Andrews accounted for the greatest grosses with her soundtracks. *Mary Poppins* spent the most weeks on chart of any 1965 title, 50, and *The Sound Of Music* began a run to rival that of *South Pacific*, accumulating its first 20 weeks at number one.

Sir Winston Churchill, who had died early in the year, had a posthumous Top Ten LP, *The Voice Of Sir Winston Churchill*.

1966

ash register tills were still alive to *The Sound Of Music* in 1966. If the Beatles or Rolling Stones didn't have a new album, the star soundtrack of the 60s kept the number one position warm. It followed *Rubber Soul* and preceded *Aftermath*; it moved back in the aftermath of *Aftermath* and before *Revolver*. When the latter Beatles album had shot its bolt, Julie Andrews and company skipped back to the top for the last three months of the year.

The Sound Of Music was the only album to spend all of 1966 in the best sellers. It was as big an international phenomenon as a UK success. *Time* reported that it had sold seven million copies by Christmas, outmoving all other stage or screen sets, even the legendary *South Pacific*.

The musical version of the Von Trapp family story was a timely purchase in any season, not linked to fad or fashion. The Beatles' unprecedented popularity, on the other hand, had made every one of their new discs an immediate must purchase. A short period of colossal concentrated sale would then be followed by a chart decline. Hence *Revolver*, a summer number one, was almost gone by Christmas. Parlophone, wanting a Beatles product for the major marketing month of the year, issued *A Collection Of Beatles Oldies* in December. However, the fans weren't fooled. It peaked at seven, a commercial miscalculation.

The Beach Boys spent more weeks on the chart than anyone in 1966, with five long players accumulating 95 weeks between them. This success reflected their four consecutive top three singles. One album, the classic *Pet Sounds*, did much better in Britain than America, reaching number two.

The other album artist of note was Herb Alpert, who garnered 89 weeks, but while his Tijuana Brass LPs loitered on the list they did not reach the highest chart positions.

10

1967

istory remembers 1967 as the year of flower power and psychedelia. The only real evidence of this in the upper echelons of the LP charts was the tremendous success of the Beatles' landmark *Sergeant Pepper's Lonely Hearts Club Band* and the considerable achievement of *Are You Experienced* by the Jimi Hendrix Experience.

Sergeant Pepper, chosen the best rock album of all time in two international critics' polls, spent exactly half the year at number one. The other 26 weeks were divided between the recurrent *The Sound Of Music* and the first-time sets by the distinctly unpsychedelic

Monkees. In a year when they had six hit singles and a cult television show, the 'fabricated four' reached the top with *The Monkees* and *More Of The Monkees*.

With only those four albums going all the way in 1967, it was a major achievement to get to number two. Hendrix and band did. Cream did respectably but not quite as well, earning Top Ten placings with their first two cartons of *Fresh Cream* and *Disraeli Gears*. The Rolling Stones surprisingly peaked at three with *Between The Buttons*.

It was a fine year for easy listening and soul. In addition to *Best Of The Beach Boys*, records that rode the roster for all 52 weeks included the soundtracks of *The Sound Of Music* and *Dr Zhivago* and *Going Places* by Herb Alpert and the Tijuana Brass. Alpert led overall by a toot with 101 weeks on chart, though the Beach Boys were a close second with 97. Tom Jones had three Top Ten issues and the Dubliners, Irish singers enjoying a year of British popularity, had two.

This was the best year on record for Geno Washington, an outstanding live soul attraction. Otis Redding and the Four Tops also had strong chart performances, but they would do even better in 1968.

1968

The album chart lost its sense of discipline in 1968. In previous years the number of different artists who had reached number one, not counting performers on film soundtracks, could be counted on the fingers of a sawmill operator's hand. This time no fewer than a dozen different acts went all the way, with occasional further appearances by *The Sound Of Music*.

The nature of the chart-toppers changed, too. Recently the number one spot had been the property of the world's outstanding rock talents. In 1968 Val Doonican, Tom Jones and Andy Williams managed to head the hordes. The Small Faces and Scott Walker enjoyed their only number one LPs, and Simon and Garfunkel their first. The Four Tops, Otis Redding, and Diana Ross and the Supremes broke the all-white stranglehold on the top spot. The only black faces to have been there before were the made-up ones of the George Mitchell Minstrels. Sadly, Redding's number one was achieved posthumously. Four albums charted after his death, two studio sets, a compilation, and a live LP.

For the fifth time in six seasons, the Fab Four had the Christmas number one, this year with the double disc *The Beatles*, often referred to as *The White Album*. The Rolling Stones could reach no higher than three for the second straight year. Bob Dylan, on the other hand, had a marvellous comeback from his motorcycle mishap, spending 13 weeks at number one with *John Wesley Harding*.

Tom Jones had 135 weeks on the chart, the highest total yet achieved in any calendar year. Otis Redding also broke the previous high, set by another aeroplane casualty, Jim Reeves, by tallying 121 weeks. In the How Great Thou Were department, Elvis Presley only had one week on the chart in 1968, as did the George Mitchell Minstrels. Even the Mothers Of Invention did better than both of them put together.

1969

For the third time the Beatles began and ended a year with different albums at number one. Their double LP *The Beatles* ushered 1969 in and *Abbey Road* showed it out. The 11 straight weeks the latter disc spent on top just before Christmas was the longest consecutive stint by any record since *Sergeant Pepper*. *Abbey Road* returned in the last week of the year, marking the fifth occasion in 1969 when a former number one encored at that position. This statistic demonstrates the instability of the chart during these 12 months.

Familiar faces atop the heap included Bob Dylan, who successfully flirted with country music in *Nashville Skyline*, the Rolling Stones, who managed a week out front with *Let It Bleed*, and Elvis Presley, who scored a glorious comeback with *From Elvis In Memphis*. Other rock luminaries who led the list included Cream, whose farewell set *Goodbye* had three separate appearances at number one, the Moody Blues, who scored the first of their three toppers, and Jethro Tull, making their only standout stint with *Stand Up*.

But one cannot overlook the achievement of the easy listening mogul Ray Conniff, who spent three weeks ahead of the herd without the benefit of a hit single. Jim Reeves astonished all by registering the only number one of his career five years after his death. It should be noted, however, that his *According To My Heart* was a budget album.

Best Of The Seekers bested all competition on five separate occasions. The Australians had the most weeks on chart with a comparatively feeble total of 66, three ahead of Simon and Garfunkel, who tallied their total without the benefit of a new release.

One LP most chartologists might not have remembered as a number one which did get there was *Diana Ross And The Supremes Join The Temptations*. One LP most chartologists might have thought of as a number one which did not get there was the Who's rock opera *Tommy*, which had to settle for the second spot.

1970

Simon and Garfunkel were the mighty men of the new decade's first year. Britain's bestselling album of the 70s, *Bridge Over Troubled Water*, dominated the chart, spending 23 weeks at number one. The closest competitors, *Abbey Road* and *Led Zeppelin III*, managed five weeks each. The S&G catalogue also sold handsomely in the wake of *Water*, giving the duo an astonishing 167 weeks on the chart in a single year, easily smashing Tom Jones' record of 135.

With the exception of the compilations *Motown Chartbusters Vol 3 & 4* and the Christmas number one, *Andy Williams' Greatest Hits*, every chart-topper was by a rock artist. The Beatles began their break-up year with *Abbey Road* and parted with their spring smash *Let It Be*. Fab Four fans obviously didn't want to say goodbye, buying enough various Beatle albums to give the group 122 weeks in the chart, the highest total of any year in their career. In parallel fashion, the greatest American star of the 60s, Bob Dylan, also had his last two number one LPs in 1970, *Self Portrait* and *New Morning*.

It was a banner year for what was then called progressive music. The Moody Blues had a number one and an admirable 115 weeks on the chart. Led Zeppelin flew over all followers with both *II* and *III*. Pink Floyd exploded with a real mother, *Atom Heart Mother*, and Black Sabbath won hosannas for heavy metal with their powerful *Paranoid*.

The outstanding performance by an artist in a supporting role was by Johnny Cash. Though he did not get to number one, the former Sun star did notch up 125 weeks on the chart as four albums entered on the heels of his phenomenally successful *Johnny Cash At San Quentin*.

Bridge Over Troubled Water was the outstanding album of yet another year, accumulating 17 weeks at number one, more than any other title. It was the only LP to appear on every one of the year's weekly tabulations.

Simon and Garfunkel works spent a total of 102 weeks on the chart during 1971, a sum exceeded only by the product of the prolific Andy Williams. The long-time hitmaker was at the peak of his career courtesy of his popular television series, and two different titles, *Greatest Hits* and *Home Loving Man*, reached number one for him during the 12-month period. No other artist had more than one chart-topper this year, although three lots of uncredited session singers and instrumentalists did go all the way with budget compilations of cover versions. If anyone was involved with more than one of these productions, they have wisely remained silent.

Two ex-Beatles fronted the flock with solo albums, Paul McCartney with *Ram* and John Lennon with *Imagine*, though additional credits were given to Linda McCartney and the Plastic Ono Band, respectively. *Sticky Fingers*, the Rolling Stones' first effort on their eponymous label, gave them a one-for-one record. They continued their 100 per cent performance until their 1974 issue, *It's Only Rock And Roll*, only hit number two. The Stones' competitors for the title of the World's Greatest Live Rock and Roll Band, the Who, scored their only chart-topper ever, *Who's Next*, while after a year of dominating the singles scene T. Rex managed an album number one in *Electric Warrior*. Other acts enjoying outstanding years included Led Zeppelin, Rod Stewart, James Taylor, and the veteran Frank Sinatra. Only the *My Way* man and Elvis Presley were still going strong from the original crew of 1958.

13

1972

Marc Bolan and a load of other people dominated the album charts in 1972. The T. Rex phenomenon was a manifestation of genuine fan fervour. The appearance of five Various Artist LPs at number one was a triumph of marketing.

The year began with *Electric Warrior* retaining the top spot. In May a double re-issue, *My People Were Fair/Prophets Seers And Sages*, grabbed the glory for a week, bearing the original label credit of Tyrannosaurus Rex. That an artist's old material released under an obsolete name could get to number one indicated the frenzied following T. Rex had at the time. The following set, *Bolan Boogie*, also went all the way.

Bolan's boys were one of four attractions to spend between 80 and 90 weeks on the chart in 1972. Cat Stevens did best with 89 in a year when no one hit the century.

Rod Stewart had his second good year as *Never A Dull Moment* went to number one and *Every Picture Tells A Story* continued a long run. These were the first two of six consecutive toppers by the leader of the Faces. That group's *A Nod's As Good As A Wink* reached the second slot in 1972, narrowly missing an unusual double for Stewart. No artist had ever scored number ones as a soloist and a group member in the same year, though Cliff Richard had made it on his own and with the Shadows backing him. Paul Simon came close, touching the top with his solo debut in 1972, but *Bridge Over Troubled Water* had, by then, finished making occasional appearances at number one.

Outside of the *Concert For Bangladesh* triple album, the Various Artists compilations that led the list for 27 weeks, over half the year, were assembled by marketing firms for television advertising. This innovation in merchandising started a packaging trend that has stayed strong ever since. Sales of this type of disc generally offered no indication of how popular taste in music was changing, as success was attributable to the impact of the commercial rather than the music itself.

Rod Stewart (*Pictorial Press*)

1973

David Bowie and Max Bygraves have never shared the concert stage, but they certainly were together in the 1973 album charts. The innovatory space rocker had six hit LPs that year, the singalong star five. Two of Bowie's efforts, *Aladdin Sane* and *Pin Ups*, were number ones, while the resuscitated *Hunky Dory* soared to three. Bygraves scored three Top Ten entries with his everybody-join-in approach to medleys of old favourites.

The Rise And Fall Of Ziggy Stardust And The Spiders From Mars had broken Bowie big in '72. Now he ruled the album chart, accumulating an unprecedented 182 weeks on the list during '73 with the six different titles. This sum shattered the mark of 167 weeks set by Simon and Garfunkel in 1970. Ironically, the defunct duo still managed to total 104 weeks in 1973, three years after their break-up, with the potent pairing of *Greatest Hits* and *Bridge Over Troubled Water*.

The siblings from the States, the Carpenters, managed 88 weeks in the list to tie Max Bygraves for third, though the positions reached were less impressive. Elton John and Slade both achieved two number ones, Gilbert O'Sullivan his only one and Roxy Music their first. Rod Stewart nabbed one as a soloist and another as a member of the Faces, completing the odd double that had eluded him in 1972.

Perhaps the most telling statistic of the year is that 20 different albums reached number one. This new high suggested that even the outstanding artists were not dominating the charts as firmly as in the 60s, and that marketing departments had learned how to achieve great sales in a limited time period.

1974

15

Two artists who were already strong in 1973, the Carpenters and Elton John, surged in 1974. Richard and Karen accumulated 17 weeks at number one in four summit visits with *The Singles 1969–73*, the highest total since *Bridge Over Troubled Water*. The bespectacled pianist, who had scored two number ones the previous 12 months, bagged another brace this time, reigning with *Caribou* and the Christmas number one *Elton John's Greatest Hits*.

Another keyboard wizard did a double. For the second successive year the previously unknown feat of hitting the heights both as a soloist and a group member was achieved. Rick Wakeman's last album with Yes, *Tales From Topographic Oceans* was the year's first number one. That spring the synthesizer star topped the table again with his own *Journey To The Centre Of The Earth*.

Dramatic evidence that the album and singles charts had grown far apart was offered in September. Mike Oldfield held the first two long player disc positions with his new release, *Hergest Ridge*, and his 1973 classic, *Tubular Bells*. Simultaneously the Osmonds were at one and two in the seven-inch stakes with their own *Love Me For A Reason* and Donny and Marie's *I'm Leaving It (All) Up To You*. Oldfield and Osmonds – two more contrasting acts could hardly be imagined.

David Bowie narrowly nudged the Carpenters in the weeks on chart table in 1974, 107 to 106. In the process he picked up his third career number one, *Diamond Dogs*.

The Beatles were close behind with 104, thanks to the year-long persistence of their 1973 compilations, *1962–66* and *1967–70*. Paul McCartney was doubtless more pleased by the seven-week tenure at the top by Wings' *Band On The Run*.

1975

The album and singles charts showed greater similarities in 1975 than in the immediate past. The three best-selling singles of the year were by the Bay City Rollers, Rod Stewart and the Stylistics, and all three artists also achieved number one LPs. *Best Of The Stylistics* spent more weeks in the Top Ten than any other disc, a statistic that startles until one recalls it benefited from a mighty marketing campaign that included considerable television advertising.

Other greatest hits albums that went to the summit courtesy of blurbs on the box included anthologies by Perry Como, Engelbert Humperdinck, Tom Jones and Jim Reeves; mass appeal singers logically benefited most from mass advertising. The one collection that went to number one naturally as a result of the artist's current popularity rather than artificial stimulus was *Elton John's Greatest Hits*. By landing the laurels for the last five weeks of 1974 and the first five of 1975, the Pinner prodigy matched the Stylistics' ten weeks over two calendar years. Elton was out front on his own with his total of 105 weeks on the chart, approached only by the slow-to-fade Simon and Garfunkel, whose back catalogue stayed around for one hundred more seven-day spells.

The year ended with Queen's *A Night At The Opera* ruling. It included the Christmas number one single, *Bohemian Rhapsody*. Status Quo, Led Zeppelin and Pink Floyd all lent the number one spot a heavier touch during the course of '75. Max Boyce translated his Welsh superstardom into disc sales with the first ever comedy number one.

1976

Beware of Greeks bearing gift tokens. There must have been a lot of them about in 1976, because Demis Roussos came from out of the Aegean blue to spend more weeks in the album chart than any other artist. The man-mountain scaled the survey with two top five entries, *Happy To Be* and *Forever And Ever*, in reaching his total of 84 weeks, one more than Queen, two more than John Denver, and three more than Pink Floyd. Roussos also topped the singles chart with his *Roussos Phenomenon* EP, the first time an Extended Play disc triumphed in that table.

The low magnitude of the leading weeks on chart total suggests that no artist stood out as David Bowie had only recently. This was indeed the case, as only Led Zeppelin zapped two number ones in 1976, both of which stayed on top for only one week. Were there a trend it would appear to have been in Greatest Hits compilations, with number one packages coming from Perry Como, Roy Orbison, Slim Whitman, Abba, the Beach Boys, and Glen Campbell. The legendary guitar star Bert Weedon actually made it all the way with a set of other people's hits. This information should not suggest that Weedon, Whitman, Como, Campbell or even the Beach Boys were enjoying a renaissance in singles sales, merely that television advertising of the Greatest Hits LP had reached the peak of its success. Only the 11 weeks spent at number one by *Abba's Greatest Hits*, the highest sum of list leading weeks in 1976, reflected fame on 45. Indeed, the SuperSwedes were enjoying their best year on the singles chart.

Rock Follies and *Stupidity* (by Dr Feelgood) both reached the top without benefit of a hit single. For *Rock Follies* the feat was doubly distinctive: the Andy Mackay–Howard Schuman score was the first television soundtrack ever to top the album chart.

Marketing was the main matter when it came to getting to number one in 1977. Clever campaigns, with a heavy emphasis on television advertising, succeeded in helping several artists who had gone cold back to glory.

Slim Whitman, who had registered one hit single in 20 years, was once again brilliantly promoted to the premier long player position by United Artists marketing. The Beatles had their first weeks of supremacy since *Let It Be* with an extremely after-the-fact live album. Connie Francis and Bread, both of whom had fallen flat for some time, had number one compilations. The roll call of artists who vaulted to Valhalla with TV anthologies reads like a Hall of Fame: Johnny Mathis, Elvis Presley, Cliff Richard, Diana Ross and the Supremes, the Shadows, and Frank Sinatra. By its very nature this plethora of platters could only be issued once, so 1977 was the peak of this kind of catalogue culling.

Abba were on top for a total of ten weeks, more than any other act or compilation. The Sex Pistols made history with their debut disc, *Never Mind The Bollocks Here's The Sex Pistols*, number one for two weeks in November despite some retail reluctance to display the provocative title. It was the first New Wave number one.

Pink Floyd bested Abba for most weeks on chart, 108 to 106, on the basis of their new number two, *Animals*, and their still-selling back list. In the year of his death Elvis Presley accumulated 95 weeks with an unprecedented 18 titles, almost all re-entries.

Two film soundtracks proved it was still possible for albums to achieve lengthy runs at number one, television advertising campaigns and a diverging market notwithstanding. *Saturday Night Fever* stayed on top for 18 weeks, the longest uninterrupted reign since that of *Sergeant Pepper's Lonely Hearts Club Band*, and indeed there were fewer number one LPs in 1978, eight, than in any year since 1967, the time of the classic Beatles release.

Grease was the other movie megahit, spending 13 weeks atop the greasy pole. Since John Travolta starred in both films, one might assume he was on the number one for 31 weeks of the year, the most by any artist since the cast of *The Sound Of Music* achieved the same figure in 1966. But though Travolta was shown on the cover of *Fever*, earning a royalty, he did not figure in the music. The Bee Gees, whose tunes dominated the motion picture, did not appear on the screen. The real winner was the Robert Stigwood Organisation, which issued both films and discs.

Boney M, who enjoyed a pair of chart topping singles in 1978, also enjoyed their most successful LP, *Nightflight To Venus*. Abba earned seven more number one weeks with *The Album* and managed 112 weeks on chart during the year, clearly outdistancing all competition. Fleetwood Mac's *Rumours*, America's top record of 1977, finally managed seven days at the summit in Britain.

1979

Nineteen different albums played musical chairs with the number one position in 1979, more than twice the total of toppers the previous year. No piece of product could compete with RSO's 1978 soundtracks in terms of length of stay there. *The Best Disco Album In The World*, a Warner Brothers compilation released at the height of the disco craze and supported by television advertising, managed the longest stint, six weeks. Indeed, Warners as a company may have been the sales star of the year, managing to place three consecutive number ones at the top in their first week of release. Certainly the artists involved – Led Zeppelin, Gary Numan and Boney M – could not have been appealing to the same buyers.

The real star performers of 1979 were Abba, Blondie and the Electric Light Orchestra. The first two names each achieved two number ones, spending totals of seven and five weeks ahead respectively. Gary Numan did nab one winner under his own name and another in his group identity, Tubeway Army, but each of those only stayed in the lead for one week.

ELO's mark of merit was the 112 weeks spent on the chart by their various albums, including the number one *Discovery*. The Jeff Lynne-led ensemble had their finest 12 months, enjoying four Top Ten singles as well. The only act to approach ELO in weeks on chart was Blondie with an exact century; Earth Wind and Fire trailed in third with 68.

Bat Out Of Hell by Meat Loaf and Jeff Wayne's *War Of The Worlds* each spent the entire year on the chart as they headed for two of the longest runs in recent times. Neither album ever reached number one, but both ultimately outsold almost every disc that did in 1979.

1980

Twenty-three different albums led the list at some point during 1980, the most in any single year to date. The number one position was like New England's fabled weather: if you didn't like it, you could stick around for an hour and it would change. Johnny Mathis, Genesis and Rose Royce appeared in quick succession, and if the rapid variation from easy listening to rock to soul wasn't enough for the catholic consumer, Sky followed with a kind of classical and pop hybrid that was impossible to categorize.

With more number one albums in a year than David Bowie has had images in a career, staying in front for even a month was an achievement. The Pretenders made it with their eponymous debut disc, and Roxy Music were champs for four weeks in two stints with *Flesh And Blood*. The star performers of the year were Police and Abba. The Bleach Boys had their second number one LP, *Zenyatta Mondatta*, and scored 116 on chart in total, far in front of the 70-week sum of runner-up AC/DC. The Scandinavian sensations once again had chart-toppers early and late in a year, registering in January with *Greatest Hits Volume 2* and beginning a nine-week rule in November with *Super Trouper.*

An extremely odd circumstance characterized the spring. For the entire season, albums had two-week runs at number one and were then replaced. Seven LPs were in the spring string. The previous record for consecutive two-week reigns had been a mere two, so this development was certainly curious if ultimately unimportant.

1981

To find the top album artists of 1981 one didn't have to look far beyond the letter 'A' in alphabetical browser bins. Abba began and ended the year at number one with *Super Trouper* and *The Visitors*, extending their string of chart-topping LPs to seven. Adam and the Ants were the breakout act of the year, accumulating 12 weeks at the very top with *Kings Of The Wild Frontier*, the longest leading stint. *Kings* was also one of five long players to stay the course for the entire year. It was joined by previous Adam material and the end-of-year release *Prince Charming* to give the Ants 87 weeks on the chart, a total topped only by Barry Manilow. The American balladeer bettered the Ant total by five weeks. Personal appearances and heavy promption gave him a career peak in Britain several years after he had done his best at home.

One had to look hard to find evidence of the growth of technopop, the synthesized sound making great inroads in the singles market. *Dare* by the Human League was the nation's best-seller for one week, but this was before the fourth single from the set, *Don't You Want Me,* became the year's Christmas number one and propelled its parent back up the charts in 1982. Ultravox, important pioneers of technopop, re-entered for another 48 weeks with *Vienna* on the strength of the single of the same name.

There were oddities, as always. *The Royal Wedding* of Prince Charles to Lady Diana Spencer was number one for a fortnight, twice as long as Motorhead managed with their equally live *No Sleep Till Hammersmith,* but the Royals never challenged the heavy metal merchants to a battle of the bands.

1982

'Remember my name', Irene Cara advised in the title tune of the film *Fame,* 'I'm gonna live forever.' Well, almost. *Fame* itself proved to be more enduring than any of the young people in it.

When the BBC began broadcasting the American television series *Fame,* a spin-off from the Alan Parker movie, Cara's original version of the song, a US hit in 1980, zoomed to the top of the UK singles chart. It was actually only the beginning of a phenomenon.

BBC Records' *The Kids From Fame* television cast collection proceeded to lead the list itself. Fuelled by two Top Ten singles, this album sold over 850,000 copies by December, surpassing even the previous year's *Royal Wedding* to become the BBC's best-selling long player.

RCA had leased the album because BBC1 could only plug vinyl with the BBC label, and they needed to establish the singing actors as a recording act. Mission accomplished, RCA issued a second TV platter, *The Kids From Fame Again*, and this also made the top three.

The sales success of the *Kids From Fame* was peculiar to Britain. In contrast, the only LP that outsold theirs in the UK in 1982 was by a worldwide star. *Love Songs* by Barbra Streisand was the year's best seller. That it did so well was perhaps surprising, since it was a make-do collection with only two new songs assembled in lieu of new product.

ABC distinguished themselves by spending their first-ever week on the chart at number one with *The Lexicon Of Love*. The debut marked another first, the initial joint number one on the album chart. *The Lexicon Of Love* shared the spotlight with – yes – *Fame*.

1983

Two of the greatest stars of the early Seventies stood out this year, but whereas one, David Bowie, had already set album chart standards, Michael Jackson had previously been best known as a singles artist. He managed to reach number five in 1979 with *Off The Wall*, his solo album start on Epic, but nothing prepared the world for what happened in 1983.

Thriller first entered the sweepstakes in December 1982, but by the end of its first month of release had only climbed to 15. It was only with the release of the second single from the set, *Billie Jean*, that the platter peaked. It went all the way three times for a total of seven weeks and was the year's best seller. Michael enjoyed three further weeks at number one when Motown's repackaged *18 Greatest Hits* proved popular during the summer. The llama lover totalled 123 weeks on chart.

This year, however, David Bowie achieved a total eclipse of the chart, setting a new mark with 198. This staggering sum beat his old record of 182, established a full decade earlier in 1973. Nearly all his success this year came in the wake of *Let's Dance*, which entered at number one. Thirteen Bowie titles in all appeared in the 53 charts of 1983. Ten Bowie albums were in the week of 16 July, the year's greatest monopoly.

Phil Collins racked up 78 weeks on chart on his own and also did very well with Genesis. Meat Loaf followed closely with 76. Mighty sales figures were accumulated by Paul Young and Lionel Richie. Richard Clayderman, the French pianist cleverly promoted in both print and television, enjoyed two of the year's Top 100 and amassed 66 weeks on chart. He was far and away 1983's most successful instrumentalist.

Thirteen of the year's twenty top albums were by groups. Culture Club were number one for five weeks with *Colour By Numbers* and Men At Work toiled the same time at the top with *Business As Usual*. Duran Duran only managed one week ahead of the field with *Seven And The Ragged Tiger* but did stockpile 105 weeks on chart, more than any group save Dire Straits, who garnered 107 without issuing any new material. Twenty-three different titles reached number one during 1983, more than in any previous calendar year.

Bonnie Tyler was the only female artist to spend even a single week ahead of the field, though Alison 'Alf' Moyet was the featured vocalist with two-week champs Yazoo. Barbra Streisand was the woman winner in weeks on chart with 57, but most of these were the final flings of 1982's list leader, *Love Songs*. The most noteworthy variety of female achievement from a chart-watcher's point of view was the faddish popularity of a new form – the workout album. Two of the year's Top 100 were of this sort, *Jane Fonda's Workout Record* and Felicity Kendal's *Shape Up And Dance (Volume 1).* Jackie Genova also charted with an exercise exemplar.

Barbra Streisand (Pictorial Press)

1984

The face that dominated music advertising on television in George Orwell's dreaded year turned out not to be Big Brother but a pig. The porker was the meaty mascot of the EMI/Virgin anthologies *Now That's What I Call Music.* The first *Now* ended 1983 and began 1984 at number one. The second moved into the sty in the sky in April and the third checked in during August. The three double albums spent a total of 15 of the year's 52 weeks on top, more than any individual act managed to achieve. *Now 4* did well enough in its mere month of release to be one of 1984's Top Ten but was kept out of number one by CBS/WEA's even more lucrative imitative compilation *The Hits Album/The Hits Tape.*

Television advertising also played a prominent part in the success of the longest-running number one of the year, the late Bob Marley and the Wailers' *Legend* (12 weeks). The top-selling album of 1984 was *Can't Slow Down* by Lionel Richie. Though it was only number one for a fortnight it was near the top most of the year. The Motown marvel was one of an astonishing seven albums to stay on the chart for the entire year along with *Can't Slow Down,* Michael Jackson's *Thriller,* Paul Young's *No Parlez,* Meat Loaf's *Bat Out Of Hell,* Queen's *Greatest Hits* and U2's *Live – Under A Blood Red Sky.*

Billy Joel had the most albums on chart in a single week, six. Nik Kershaw managed two of the year's Top Fifty, Elton John two of the Top 100. Michael Jackson had a trio of best sellers, *Off The Wall* continuing its revival and *18 Greatest Hits* being a compilation shared with the Jackson Five. Jackson wound up with 136 weeks on chart. He was the year's top weekly act.

Other groups with noteworthy performances included U2, who totalled an even 100 weeks on chart; Queen, who had two of the year's Top Fifty; and Wham!, whose *Make It Big* was one of the year's Top Five. The Smiths scored two Top Tens on the independent Rough Trade label and *Welcome To The Pleasuredome* by Frankie Goes To Hollywood gave ZTT its first week at number one.

It was not a great year for female soloists. None reached number one, though women did make the top spot as members of Eurythmics and the Thompson Twins. Sade had the biggest seller by a woman, *Diamond Life*, while Elaine Paige had two of the year's Top 100. Barbra Streisand accumulated 67 weeks on chart to lead the ladies.

Instrumentalists fared poorly. Richard Clayderman was the only non-vocalist in the year's Top 100. The independent compilation company Street Sounds attained 15 charters during the year. The devotional artist Bryn Yemm had three new albums in, more than any other British act. 1984 was itself a star. It was the first year to have three hit LPs named after it. The artists were Eurythmics, Van Halen and Rick Wakeman.

1985

The long distance runner wasn't lonely in 1985. Nine albums remained on the chart for the entire 52 weeks, and four acts accumulated totals in excess of one hundred weeks on chart. Astonishing records were set. After a series of UK stadium dates Bruce Springsteen placed his entire catalogue of seven albums in the Top Fifty. Never before had an artist with that large a body of work got the lot that high. Springsteen finished the year with a total of 177 weeks on chart, the third best figure ever. *Born In The U.S.A.* was one of the nine discs that saw the year through. It wound up the number four seller of 1985. Competing with The Boss for the title of Male Artist of the Year, Phil Collins finished with fewer weeks on chart, a still spectacular 131, but managed to nab the number two spot of the year-end tabulation with *No Jacket Required.*

Madonna was clearly the female artist of 1985; her *Like A Virgin* (the third best-selling set of the year) and her retitled first album both entered the Top Fifty. As noteworthy as her own success was the extremely strong showing by female artists in general. Seven of the year's Top Twenty were either by female soloists or outfits with female vocalists. Sade's two albums both finished in the Top Twenty.

Dire Straits and U2 vied for Group of Year honours. Mark Knopfler's lot put in a special claim with the year's number one, *Brothers In Arms*. 1985 was the third successive year in which Dire Straits exceeded 100 weeks on chart, a feat previously performed only by Simon and Garfunkel. During the three-year period 1983–85, Mark's men leapt from 33rd to 8th on the all-time list. Despite their achievements they were slightly pipped in weeks on chart by U2, 168 to 158. The Irish band were also on a prolonged hot streak, having vaulted from 20 to 375 weeks on chart in three years.

Richard Clayderman retained his laurels as leading solo instrumentalist, but James Last bounced back as the top orchestra. It was also a good year for what might be called up-market material, with Andrew Lloyd Webber's *Requiem*, Leonard Bernstein's operatic version of *West Side Story* and the Anderson/Rice/Ulvaeus *Chess* all in 1985's Top 100.

The most successful broadcasting and charity event of all time, Live Aid, achieved another distinction as the single happening that has most influenced the album chart. In the 27 July chart nine albums by acts in the concert re-entered the Top 100, four after a long absence, and 21 previously peaked packages suddenly surged.

The craze of 1984, the TV compilations of recent and current hits, abated only slightly, with three EMI/Virgin *Now* packages in the year-end Top Ten and two CBS/WEA *Hits* collections in the Top Twenty.

Meat Loaf's *Bat Out Of Hell* fell from favour, but still managed to add 31 weeks on chart to equal *The Sound Of Music* as the all-time longest-running chart LP.

ere there a pinball machine of the album chart it would have tilted this year as Dire Straits amassed an unprecedented 217 listed weeks, an average of over four placings per week.

That *Brothers In Arms* was the year's number two in sales, slipping down just one place from 1985's top spot, was remarkable enough. That Mark Knopfler's band was so popular that a substantial part of Dire Straits' back catalogue resided in the best sellers was astounding.

There was another artist, however, who accounted for three of the Top 100 of 1986. Madonna sold stacks of all three of her releases, and *True Blue* was the year's number one. All told she spent 125 weeks on chart, by far the highest figure ever achieved by a woman. 1985 debutante Whitney Houston's first album was 1986's number five set of the year.

In the rich-get-richer category old friends Phil Collins and Queen excelled themselves, Collins moving up to third in the annual weeks on chart listing. Though his total fell from 131 to 113 he made amends by sharing Genesis' 28 weeks. Queen broke through the century mark for the first time while staying in the Top Ten artists list for the third consecutive year. Paul Simon's *Graceland* was the year's number four.

Madonna and Collins were the only two solo artists in the year-end weeks on chart Top Ten. The LP list seemed the province of the big groups in 1986, with Simple Minds enjoying their biggest year and U2 finishing in the charmed circle for the fourth year in succession, even though they had no new issues. Talking Heads put in their finest career outing, while A-Ha and Five Star cut impressive figures in their first full year of activity. The *Now* and *Hits* series stayed strong.

1987

hatever you thought of the charts in 1987, you had to agree it was a *Bad* year. Lightning struck a second time for Michael Jackson as he once again achieved a year-end number one. The main difference was that whereas the champ of 1983, *Thriller*, had started slowly in 1982 and grown gradually, *Bad* was a massive number one in its first week and retained its edge to finish several lengths in front. The new set was only the second package in history to debut at number one in both the UK and US charts. The first was another of this year's giants, *Whitney*, which wound up at number three for 1987.

Bad, in contrast, seemed to pose no threat to *Thriller*, far and away the most successful LP ever released. Its global sales at about forty million were well ahead of the immediate runners-up, including *Rumours* by Fleetwood Mac, but that 1977 phenomenon had its own reason to celebrate ten years later. During the course of 1987 it overtook *Bat Out Of Hell* to become the longest-runner in chart chronicles.

The reappearance of *Rumours* can be largely attributed to the continued growth of the compact disc market which gave a new lease of life to many classic albums. Collectors who already had black vinyl copies bought CD versions for their superior sound. The Beatles benefited most clearly from this. All of their original studio sets were issued on CD in 1987, and all charted. The 20th anniversary of *Sergeant Pepper's Lonely Hearts Club Band* attracted massive media attention and boosted the classic package back to the Top Three.

Though Madonna did not have one of the year's Top Ten sellers she was the most charted artist of 1987, her albums making 127 appearances. This tally exceeded the record for a female artist she herself set only the previous year.

U2 and Queen followed the champ with 126 and 117 weeks respectively, both continuing their lengthy run of strong showings and improving on their fine 1986 figures. Dire Straits did well, too, their 84 weeks giving them a career total of exactly 900, the top total of acts still recording.

The Phantom Of The Opera made history by becoming the first original cast recording to top the UK chart. In this respect *My Fair Lady* may have been unlucky. In the very first chart of 1958 and peaking at number two, it may have been a number one had its earlier sales been tabulated.

For the sixth consecutive year the three acts with the most weeks on chart totalled at least 100. Seven of 1988's ten top stars had been in the charmed circle before, six of them the previous year. Michael Jackson, who paced the pack with 116 weeks, was returning to the leaders for the first time since 1984.

Jacko's joyride came courtesy of *Bad*, on the chart all year, and a variety of back items including *Thriller* and Motown repackages. In his case the progress from one year to the next looked like a week-to-week sequence, with 1987's number one slipping two places to number three on the 1988 year end tally. Bad was constantly in the public eye thanks to Jackson's personal appearances at open air venues and a steady stream of hit singles. The promotion paid off. Britain was the one major country where *Bad* outsold *Thriller*, and the artist topped the table of weeks on chart for the first time.

The second place finishers on both the sales and weeks on chart list were vinyl veterans. Cliff Richard, who had the year's number one single, *Mistletoe And Wine*, also had the runner-up album, *Private Collection*. It was the first time he had finished in the top two in both chart categories. Fleetwood Mac, who had undergone a telephone book's worth of personnel changes since their album chart breakthrough in 1968, scored their first annual century with 107 weeks, second only to Jackson. They, too, were helped by touring, and scored two of the year's 30 best sellers, *Tango In The Night* and *Greatest Hits*. The Pet Shop Boys were the third act to accumulate 100 weeks on chart, doing best with *Introspective*.

In addition to the two groups mentioned above, U2, Dire Straits, Whitney Houston and Luther Vandross repeated in the year's Top Ten acts. Whitney now had 200 weeks on chart with only two albums for an astonishing average of 100 weeks per release. This was still unlikely to impress U2 and Dire Straits, who continued their winning ways and seemed to guarantee they would finish ahead of Queen as the top album acts of the 80s.

The most amazing achievement by a new artist belonged to Kylie Minogue. Before January 1988 she had never released an album in Britain. At the end of the year she had the top title of the 12 months, *Kylie*. This was the first time a solo artist had scored the year's top seller with a debut disc. The teen market didn't just support Stock-Aitken-Waterman acts. The fresh-faced trio Bros wound up at number four with their debut issue, *Push*. Another new act who came in the Top Ten sellers in famous fashion was Tracy Chapman, whose career took off after she appeared before a live global television audience at the Nelson Mandela Birthday Concert.

Compilations took up so many of the top positions in the album chart that the industry decided they would be segregated in future and have their own list in 1989. This meant that the performance of the *Now! That's What I Call Music* series in placing editions 11, 12 and 13 in the year-end top 15 would never be repeated. Even compilation soundtracks like the phenomenal *Dirty Dancing* would be separated out. As the year ended observers wondered if new artists would actually benefit from the new order, in which product by individual acts would overnight chart higher than it would have in 1988. Would the illusion of success become a reality?

25

1989

The cosy feeling old friends gave the album chart in 1988 was displaced by the excitement of new acquaintances a year later. Jason Donovan, a co-star of Kylie Minogue on television's soap opera *Neighbours*, repeated his fellow Australian's feat of having the best selling LP of the year with a premiere performance. His *Ten Good Reasons* outshone even Simply Red's long-burning *A New Flame*.

The continued shift in sales from singles to albums was dramatically underscored this year when four LPs but no 45s sold over a million copies. Including sales in all configurations, the year's number one single, *Ride On Time* by Black Box, managed 849,116 units. *Ten Good Reasons* shifted 1,450,500. Indeed, the seven top albums of the year outsold every single. It was thus important financially as well as for image that the young Stock-Aitken-Waterman favourites did well on both sides. Kylie and Jason were each in the 1989 Top Ten on both charts, with Miss Minogue enjoying the year's number six album, *Enjoy Yourself*.

Kylie was one of eight acts to finish in the year's Top Ten acts who had not been in the previous list. Recalling that in 1988 only four names were non-repeaters gives an indication of the progress of new talent in 1989. Guns N' Roses made the most impressive showing, leading the lot with 85 weeks on chart. This figure, achieved by *Appetite For Destruction* and *GN'R Lies*, was admittedly below the century, the first time since 1982 that the year's top tally was short of 100. Nonetheless it was a major achievement for a heavy metal act. Strong sellers in this genre had traditionaly opened strongly and faded quickly.

Erasure finished second in the weeks-on-chart sweepstakes, moving up from fourth the year before. Third in the table was what might be called a veteran newcomer, Gloria Estefan. In a masterful piece of public relations her group Miami Sound Machine groomed her as its focal point and then gave her joint and finally sole billing. The strategy succeeded spectacularly with the year's number four seller *Anything For You* by Gloria Estefan and Miami Sound Machine, and the number five, *Cuts Both Ways*, credited merely to Gloria Estefan.

Another notable newcomer to the top acts list was the Scottish band Deacon Blue, who finished fourth. Bobby Brown, 1989's top singles star, made his album table bow at number ten. The late Roy Orbison experienced a phenomenal posthumous comeback, appearing in the Top Ten acts list for the first time since 1964. A quarter of a century was by far the longest gap between visits to this charmed circle.

The fastest selling work in 1989 was released late in the year. Phil Collins' . . . *But Seriously* managed to chalk up sales of over one million in only six weeks, beginning a long run at number one and setting itself up for continued chart domination in early 1990. Here was a case where the change of decades would be bridged by a single strong record. This had not been the case when the 70s met the 80s, when Greatest Hits acts by Abba and Rod Stewart took turns at the top. The *South Pacific* film soundtrack had welded 1959 and 1960 together, and the Beatles' *Abbey Road* had both seen out 1969 and welcomed 1970. . . . *But Seriously* now joined these giants.

1990

26

Classic stars and classical music dominated 1990. Phil Collins spent a further ten weeks at number one at the beginning of the year with his late 1989 smash . . . *But Seriously*. Its total of 15 weeks at the top was the thirteenth longest run at number one in chart history. . . . *But Seriously* remained on the register all year long and wound up 1990's best seller. Collins had another of the year's Top Ten, *Serious Hits Live*, and discs by the singing drummer from Genesis spent more weeks on chart (85) than those of any other artist.

Collins was the outstanding male star to have dominated the field. Elton John was the only other artist to have two of the year's ten best sellers. His *Very Best Of Elton John* and *Sleeping With The Past* were both number ones, making him the only act to have two chart toppers in 1990.

Luciano Pavarotti followed with 1¹/₃ number ones, pacing the pack with his own *Essential Pavarotti* and as one of the 'three tenors' *In Concert*. José Carreras and Placido Domingo joined the inimitable Italian on the latter live recording. It was the first time three chart acts had joined forces to achieve a number one album as a trio. Jazzmen Kenny Ball, Chris Barber and Acker Bilk had gone to the top in 1962, but this was before Ball had charted on his own. By beating *In Concert* to number one with his own compilation, Luciano Pavarotti became the first classical artist to achieve a number one.

The top instrumentalist of the year was Nigel Kennedy, whose performance of Vivaldi's *Four Seasons* gave him the year's twelfth best seller and was the main factor in his finishing fourth on the Most Weeks On Chart list. His total of 66 was the highest ever by a classical artist.

The year's standout female star, Madonna, added to her historic achievements. Her *Immaculate Collection* was 1990's number two in sales. By leading the list for the last six weeks of the year, she took her career total to 16 weeks in pole position, overtaking Barbra Streisand as the woman with the most weeks at number one. Various Madonna titles accumulated 53 weeks on chart to regain for her the distinction as most charted woman that she had last enjoyed in 1987. Tina Turner shared her weeks on chart total, thanks to the long-running *Foreign Affair*, but trailed her in sales.

UB40 were the group with most weeks on chart, due in large measure to *Labour Of Love II*, but they were surpassed in sales by the Carpenters. Richard and Karen's *Only Yesterday* was one of the year's ten best sellers. The success of this catalogue promotion surprised the music business, especially since much of the material had been included in the 1974 number one *The Singles 1969–73*. The seven-week list-leading leasehold of *Only Yesterday* moved the Carpenters to a tie with Cliff Richard for eighth position on the Most Weeks At Number One list.

David Bowie also made noteworthy career progress. *ChangesBowie* was his seventh album to enter the chart at number one. Nobody else had debuted at the top as often. Bowie moved into a three-way tie for fifth in the Most Number One Albums category.

Special note should be taken of the achievement of Michael Bolton, whose *Soul Provider* never got higher than number four in any weekly chart, yet finished fifth for the year. In contrast, Prince was number one first week out with *Graffiti Bridge*, yet didn't even finish in the top 75 sellers of 1991. The American number one of the year, MC Hammer's *Please Hammer Don't Hurt 'Em*, was Britain's number 36, as good evidence as any that the massive sales enjoyed by rap artists in the US were not being duplicated in the UK.

1991

The brightest stars this year were the ones in the title of Simply Red's album, the best seller of the year and their fourth top two hit in as many releases. As exciting as the achievements of Mick Hucknall's group were, with *Stars* enjoying a long Top Five run and returning to number one as *A New Flame* had done two years earlier, Simply Red could not be said to have loomed large over the year. No act did. The weeks on chart winner for 1991, Michael Bolton, amassed the lowest total, 63, since Elvis Presley triumphed with 51 in 1960.

Whereas both Phil Collins and Elton John had each scored two of the year's Top Ten sellers in 1990, no artist achieved the feat in the following 12 months. Queen came closest, with three out of the Top Forty. Even before Freddie Mercury's death the quartet had tallied two number ones this calendar year, making them the only act to have more than one. *Innuendo* led the list for a fortnight in February and *Greatest Hits II* debuted at number one in November. The double gave Queen a career total of eight number ones, the third highest total in history, tying them with Abba and Led Zeppelin behind the Beatles (12) and the Rolling Stones (9).

Greatest Hits II returned to the top after Mercury passed away and stayed there through the holidays for a total of five weeks as head of the hits. It was the second highest figure for the year, Eurythmics' *Greatest Hits* having been number one for ten weeks. The latter disc was the year's best seller until the holiday period, when it was finally eclipsed by *Stars*.

Simply Red, Eurythmics and Queen had 1991's best sellers, but other groups merited attention. Roxette had most weeks on chart by a duo or group (62), just one shy of Michael Bolton's winning figure. After their first half dozen chart albums peaked short of the

Top Ten, R.E.M. got lucky with number seven, going all the way with *Out Of Time* and winding up with one of the Top Ten of the year. The Doors broke on through with four items when Oliver Stone's film biography of Jim Morrison was released.

The year's greatest chart disappointments were also most registered by groups. Simple Minds and U2 broke their strings of consecutive number one releases at four and three, respectively. Dire Straits opened at number one with *On Every Street*, but its solitary seven days at the summit were a fleeting moment compared to the 14 weeks their preceding studio set, *Brothers In Arms*, had enjoyed.

The only one of 1990's Top Ten to repeat in '91 was Madonna's *Immaculate Collection*. She again accumulated the Most Weeks On Chart By A Female Artist. However, in a reversal of their 1990 two-woman race, Tina Turner outsold her, with *Simply The Best* finishing the year at number four, the best showing by any soloist. Cher was also in the year-end Top Ten. She nabbed the first number one of her 26-year chart career, *Love Hurts*.

The memory of the slow start by *Thriller* warmed one from hasty judgment of Michael Jackson's work, but it certainly appeared from its first five weeks on the market that *Dangerous* was truly in peril compared to its immediate predecessors. After debuting at number one the set made way for the return of *Queen's Greatest Hits II*. By Christmas Jackson had the odd distinction of also being outsold by another Michael – Crawford.

No instrumentalists were in the year-end Top Fifty. Luciano Pavarotti was there with *Essential Pavarotti II* and as part of the 'three tenors' *In Concert*. For the second consecutive year Michael Bolton had one of the year's Top Ten sellers without ever getting to number one. Proving that there are always new records to be set, *Circle Of One* by Oleta Adams was the first album to re-enter the chart at number one.

28

Michael Jackson (Pictorial Press)

1992

T his year cash registers joined the lead vocalists of rock bands in singing. Seventies groups, 80s outfits and newly emerging bands came together to give metal music in various forms its greatest domination of the Weeks On Chart table to date.

The leader of the list was Queen, who tallied 128 weeks on chart with various titles. The reason for their resurgence was, of course, the death in December 1991 of front man Freddie Mercury. Public affection for him and respect for the group could not be overestimated. There have been several tragic demises in rock history, but one has to go back to 1964 to find a deceased artist leading the Weeks On Chart list. In that instance the star, Jim Reeves, presented a very different form of material, country and western. It is worth noting that the top American star of the early 90s, Garth Brooks, specialized in a genre of modern country that did not initially make a massive impact in Britain.

With their 1992 performance Queen moved to within a tiara's distance of the King, Elvis Presley, for fourth place in the all-time Most Weeks On Chart list. They had managed to rank that high in the countdown without ever having previously topped the 12-month table. Despite being dead for 15 years Presley was still putting up a good fight, scoring yet another posthumous hit.

The special and sad circumstances of Queen's success did not keep any particular pop singer from leading the list. The number two act was another rock band, Guns N' Roses, who accumulated 121 weeks in the tally they had led in 1989 with a mere 85. Their *Use Your Illusion II* slightly outperformed *Use Your Illusion I*, mainly because, at the time of their original release in late 1991, the second set had included a track that had recently been a top three single, 'You Could Be Mine'. Top Ten singles from the two albums continued to be issued during 1992.

There were four other rock acts in the year-end Top Ten. U2 returned to the list for the first time since 1989. R.E.M. climbed to seventh from their 1991 debut position of ten. Nirvana brought the Seattle sound to the UK in blissful fashion with *Nevermind* in the best sellers list all 53 chart weeks of the year. Genesis also saw the year through with their number one hit *We Can't Dance*. Simple Minds did not finish in the top ten Weeks On Chart but were in the top ten for sales, with their *Glittering Prize 81/92* winding up the year's number four.

The top-selling disc of the year was *Stars* by Simply Red. For the first time in history, one album managed to be the best seller of two consecutive years. Back catalogue sales gave the group 77 weeks on chart, the third-highest total behind Queen and Guns N' Roses. Simply Red were one of seven acts with a figure higher than Michael Bolton's 1991 winning total of 63.

Bolton was not inactive in 1992, finishing at seven in the sales survey with *Timeless (The Classics)*, but he could not beat the top two male vocalists of the year, who had both begun their careers at Motown. Lionel Richie was still there, returning from a six-year break with a case study of making a little go a long way. *Back To Front*, a collection of greatest hits with new material, was the second-highest selling album of the year and his first number one since 1984. Michael Jackson's *Dangerous* was the year's number five in sales. He did outdistance Richie in terms of weeks on chart, as his other albums contributed to his constant presence.

Anyone guessing the identity of the top female vocalist of the year would probably have started with Annie Lennox, whose award-winning *Diva* was a number one that sold well enough to finish as the year's number six hit and even returned to the top spot after a half-

29

year absence. Enya would also be a reasonable guess, as she was the woman with the most weeks on chart. However, the actual best-selling female artist was Cher, whose *Greatest Hits* was the third biggest record of the year. It was a comment on her star status in Britain that this CD was not a factor in America, just as 'The Shoop Shoop Song' was a number one in the UK and not even a Top Twenty hit in the US.

Every year produces its own oddities. Nineteen ninety two was the tenth anniversary of Madness' only number one album, *Complete Madness*, so it was appropriate they should come out of retirement to visit the top spot again with another compilation, *Divine Madness*. Abba also managed the ten-year trick with *Gold*, their first number one since 1982's *The Singles – The First Ten Years.*

One had to go back even further for the first half of Mike Oldfield's feat. *Tubular Bells II* was the number one follow-up to his 1973 original, which had reached the top the following year after the success of *Hergest Ridge*. The 18-year gap between a number one album and its number one sequel was by far the longest time between chart-topping numerically related albums of original material. Indeed, the only previous such exercise in titles to result in a brace of number ones, *Rolling Stones* and *Rolling Stones No. 2*, involved only a seven-month wait.

1993

30

Meat Loaf swooped like a bat out of chart hell this year, scoring his first number one in a dozen years. *Bat Out Of Hell II – Back Into Hell* was the official sequel to the 1978 classic *Bat Out Of Hell* and reached the top spot denied the original. (Although many trivia contest competitors might be caught out on this point, Meat Loaf's only previous number one was *Dead Ringer*.) *Bat Out Of Hell II* overtook hits from earlier in the year, including the leading compilation, *The Bodyguard*, to become the best-selling title of 1993. The *Bat* man also rejuvenated sales of his back catalogue, with both the 15-year-old album and the anthology *Hits Out Of Hell* winding up in the year's top 100 sellers.

Unusually for this era, the availability of the single 'I'd Do Anything For Love (But I Won't Do That)' on *Bat Out Of Hell II* did not seem to diminish sales of either CD. It has become customary for singles to plummet when they appear on album, but this one stayed at number one for seven weeks and gave Meat Loaf the number one single as well as album of the year.

The Meat treats all came in the final third of the year, but they still managed to combine for 58 weeks on chart. This total, the highest number for a male vocalist, was also achieved by works of Eric Clapton, most notably his *Unplugged* hit. R.E.M. continued their progress in the annual table, leading the list for the first time with 97 weeks. Their biggest hit was *Automatic For The People*, the year's second-best seller. By any account, R.E.M. were the leading group of 1993. Guns N' Roses and Nirvana were also repeaters from the previous year's winners' circle.

If one included Tina Turner, the leading female artist on this table, as a rock artist, then eight of the top ten, indeed eight of the top nine, were of this musical style. This was the greatest domination any musical style had achieved in the Weeks On Chart computation. When one considers that the ninth act in the top nine was Abba, charting strictly with collections of old hits, one could be excused for thinking that rock was the only form of music that was selling. In fact considerable sales were being enjoyed by rave and other forms of dance music, but these were via anthologies that were listed in the compilation chart. Though they might be experiencing strong singles sales, most record makers in these styles were either not making albums or not selling them in large numbers.

Although Tina Turner was the first female in the Weeks On Chart list, several women enjoyed better-selling albums. Dina Carroll was a Top Ten stalwart with her debut disc, *So Close*, then number three hit of the year. Diana Ross came in fifth in the 1993 sales chart with *One Woman – The Ultimate Collection* and Mariah Carey anchored the Top Ten with *Music Box*. Annie Lennox managed another year in the best sellers with *Diva*, which climbed back to number one the week of 6 March. Twenty-five other discs had occupied the peak place since *Diva* debuted there on 18 April 1992, giving it the distinction of longest gap between weeks at number one.

Special note must be made of the achievement of Take That, who were the only act to place two titles in the Top Twenty. Simply Red earned further plaudits this year when their *Stars* passed the three million mark in sales. Cliff Richard won congratulations again when his new work debuted at number one, 32 years after his first appearance at the summit with *21 Today*. This was far and away the longest spread of number ones, although Cliff did appear to be running out of titles: the 1993 issue was simply called *The Album*.

An unusual feature of the album chart late in the year was the presence of two albums called *Duets*. Both releases, by Elton John and Frank Sinatra with various vocal partners, made the top five of the weekly chart, with Elton doing best overall. Several stars charted with *Unplugged* soundtracks from MTV programmes, though Rod Stewart had the wit to expand his title to include . . . *And Seated*.

If ever a week went by without a chart being compiled, the previous week's chart was used again for the purposes of all the statistics and information contained in this book. The dates used throughout correspond to the Saturday ending the week in which the chart was published. So, for example, Abba's *Waterloo* album entered the chart in the week ending 8 June 1974, making their first day of chart action 2 June 1974.

THE CHARTS USED IN COMPILING THIS BOOK ARE:

8 Nov 58 ..... First album chart published by *Melody Maker*. It is a Top Ten.

27 Jun 59 ..... Newspaper strike. No chart published until 8 August, so the 20 June chart is repeated throughout.

26 Mar 60 ..... First *Record Retailer* chart published, a Top 20. We have taken our information from the *Record Retailer* from this date onwards, although the *Melody Maker* chart continued.

14 Apr 66 ..... Chart becomes a Top 30.

8 Dec 66 ..... Chart becomes a Top 40.

12 Feb 69 ..... Chart drops back to a Top 15.

8 Mar 69 ..... Incorrect chart published. Correct chart calculated by back tracking from the following week's listings.

11 Jun 69 ..... Chart becomes a Top 20 again.

25 Jun 69 ..... Chart becomes a Top 40 again.

9 Aug 69 ..... Chart is a Top 32 (!) for this one week only.

11 Oct 69 ..... Chart drops back to a Top 25.

8 Nov 69 ..... Chart varies from a Top 20 to a Top 24 until 24 January 70.

31 Jan 70 ..... Chart lists between 47 and 77 albums each week until 9 January 1971.

9 Jan 71 ..... *Record Retailer* becomes *Record And Tape Retailer*.

16 Jan 71 ..... Chart stabilizes as a Top 50.

6 Feb 71 ..... Postal strike means no chart published until 3 April 71. 30 January chart repeated throughout.

7 Aug 71 ..... The Full Price chart (the one we've been using) is combined with the previously separate Budget chart. This means there is a sudden influx of budget-label albums onto the chart.

8 Jan 72 ..... Chart reverts to full-price albums only, so the budget albums disappear as suddenly as they appeared.

18 Mar 72 ..... *Record and Tape Retailer* becomes *Music Week*.

13 Jan 73 ..... Chart is a Top 24 for this week only.

5 Jan 74 ..... Chart is a Top 42 for this week only.

5 Jul 75 ..... Chart becomes a Top 60.

14 Jan 78 ..... Chart is a Top 30 for this week only

2 Dec 78 ..... Chart becomes a Top 75.

13 Oct 79 ..... Two consecutive weeks' charts published simultaneously as a result of a speedy new chart compilation system which enables *Music Week* to catch up a week. Until this date, the publication of the chart had been more than a week after the survey period. Both charts of this date are included in our calculations.

8 Aug 81 ..... Chart becomes a Top 100.

14 Jan 89 ..... Chart splits in two, and becomes a Top 75 'Artist Albums' and a Top 20 'Compilation Albums'. For this book, the Artist Albums chart is considered the main chart, but we record separately the activities of the Compilations chart.

HIT ALBUMS

ALPHABETICALLY BY ARTIST

*Kurt Cobain (centre), lead singer of **Nirvana**, who popularised grunge rock in Britain, took his life in April 1994.*

The information given in this part of the book is as follows:

DATE the album first hit the chart, the album **TITLE**, **LABEL**, **CATALOGUE NUMBER**, the **HIGHEST POSITION** it reached on the chart, and the **TOTAL WEEKS** it remained on the chart. Number one albums are highlighted with a **STAR** ★ and Top 10 albums with a **DOT** ●. A **DAGGER** † indicates the album is still on the chart on 25 December 1993, the final chart included in our calculations for this edition.

For the purposes of this book, an album is considered a re-issue if it hits the chart for a second time with a new catalogue number. From the time when albums began to be produced in both mono and stereo versions (around 1966), we list only the stereo catalogue number. Cassette sales and – since the mid-80s – CD sales, have become rapidly more significant in the compilation of the album charts, and the catalogue numbers listed reflected this.

Describing a recording act in one sentence is often fraught with danger, but we have attempted to do so above each act's list of hits. Although we are aware that many of the 'vocalists' thus described also play an instrument, we have only mentioned this fact where the artist's instrumental skills were an important factor in the album's success.

In this edition, for the first time, we have credited hit albums in combination with other chart acts to both artists' lists. So, for example, you will find *The Cream Of Eric Clapton* listed twice, once under Eric Clapton and once under Cream. There is no separate entry for them as a combined act, and the weeks that record spent on the chart are credited to both acts.

AARONSON – *See HAGAR, SCHON, AARONSON, SHRIEVE*

ABBA
Sweden/Norway, male/female vocal/instrumental group   *584 wks*

8 Jun	74	**WATERLOO** *Epic EPC 80179*	28	2 wks
31 Jan	76	**ABBA** *Epic EPC 80835*	13	10 wks
10 Apr	76 ★	**GREATEST HITS** *Epic EPC 69218*	1	130 wks
27 Nov	76 ★	**ARRIVAL** *Epic EPC 86108*	1	92 wks
4 Feb	78 ★	**THE ALBUM** *Epic EPC 86052*	1	61 wks
19 May	79 ★	**VOULEZ-VOUS** *Epic EPC 86086*	1	43 wks
10 Nov	79 ★	**GREATEST HITS VOL.2** *Epic EPC 10017*	1	63 wks
22 Nov	80 ★	**SUPER TROUPER** *Epic EPC 10022*	1	43 wks
19 Dec	81 ★	**THE VISITORS** *Epic EPC 10032*	1	21 wks
20 Nov	82 ★	**THE SINGLES – THE FIRST TEN YEARS** *Epic ABBA 10*	1	22 wks
19 Nov	83	**THANK YOU FOR THE MUSIC** *Epic EPC 10043*	17	12 wks
19 Nov	88	**ABSOLUTE ABBA** *Telstar STAR 2329*	70	7 wks
3 Oct	92 ★	**GOLD – GREATEST HITS** *Polydor 5170072*	1†	64 wks
5 Jun	93	**MORE ABBA GOLD – MORE ABBA HITS**		
		Polydor 5193532 .:	14	14 wks

Russ **ABBOT** *UK, male vocalist*   *16 wks*

5 Nov	83	**RUSS ABBOT'S MADHOUSE** *Ronco RTL 2096*	41	7 wks
23 Nov	85	**I LOVE A PARTY** *K-Tel ONE 1313*	12	9 wks

Gregory **ABBOTT** *US, male vocalist*   *5 wks*

10 Jan	87	**SHAKE YOU DOWN** *CBS 450061–1*	53	5 wks

ABC *UK, male vocal/instrumental group*   *90 wks*

3 Jul	82 ★	**THE LEXICON OF LOVE** *Neutron NTRS 1*	1	50 wks
26 Nov	83	**BEAUTY STAB** *Neutron NTRL 2*	12	13 wks
26 Oct	85	**HOW TO BE A ZILLIONAIRE** *Neutron NTRH 3*	28	3 wks
24 Oct	87 ●	**ALPHABET CITY** *Neutron NTRH 4*	7	10 wks
28 Oct	89	**UP** *Neutron 838646 1*	58	1 wk
21 Apr	90 ●	**ABSOLUTELY** *Neutron 8429671*	7	12 wks
24 Aug	91	**ABRACADABRA** *Parlophone PCS 7355*	50	1 wk

Group was UK/US, male/female for third album.

Paula **ABDUL** *US, female vocalist*   *50 wks*

15 Apr	89 ●	**FOREVER YOUR GIRL** *Siren SRNLP 19*	3	39 wks
10 Nov	90	**SHUT UP AND DANCE (THE DANCE MIXES)**		
		Virgin America VUSLP 28	40	2 wks
27 Jul	91 ●	**SPELLBOUND** *Virgin America VUSLP 33*	4	9 wks

A.B.'S *Japan, instrumental group*   *2 wks*

14 Apr	84	**DEJA VU** *Street Sounds XKHAN 503*	80	2 wks

ACADEMY of ANCIENT MUSIC conducted by Christopher HOGWOOD *UK, male conductor/*
instrumentalist – harpsichord, UK chamber orchestra   *2 wks*

16 Mar	85	**THE FOUR SEASONS (VIVALDI)** *L'Oiseau Lyre 4101261* .	85	2 wks

ACADEMY OF ST MARTIN IN THE FIELDS – *See Neville MARRINER and the ACADEMY OF ST MARTIN IN THE FIELDS*

A
35

ACCEPT *Germany, male vocal/instrumental group*   *5 wks*

7 May 83	**RESTLESS AND WILD** *Heavy Metal Worldwide HMILP 6* ...	98	2 wks
30 Mar 85	**METAL HEART** *Portrait PRT 26358*	50	1 wk
15 Feb 86	**KAIZOKU-BAN** *Portrait PRT 5916*	91	1 wk
3 May 86	**RUSSIAN ROULETTE** *Portrait PRT 26893*	80	1 wk

AC/DC *Australia/UK, male vocal/instrumental group*   *243 wks*

5 Nov 77	**LET THERE BE ROCK** *Atlantic K 50366*	17	5 wks
20 May 78	**POWERAGE** *Atlantic K 50483*	26	9 wks
28 Oct 78	**IF YOU WANT BLOOD YOU'VE GOT IT** *Atlantic K 50532*	13	58 wks
18 Aug 79 ●	**HIGHWAY TO HELL** *Atlantic K 50628*	8	32 wks
9 Aug 80 ★	**BACK IN BLACK** *Atlantic K 50735*	1	40 wks
5 Dec 81 ●	**FOR THOSE ABOUT TO ROCK** *Atlantic K 50851*	3	29 wks
3 Sep 83 ●	**FLICK OF THE SWITCH** *Atlantic 78-0100-1*	4	9 wks
13 Jul 85 ●	**FLY ON THE WALL** *Atlantic 781263*	7	10 wks
7 Jun 86	**WHO MADE WHO** *Atlantic WX 57*	11	12 wks
13 Feb 88 ●	**BLOW UP YOUR VIDEO** *Atlantic WX 144*	2	14 wks
6 Oct 90 ●	**THE RAZOR'S EDGE** *Atco WX 364*	4	18 wks
7 Nov 92 ●	**LIVE** *Atco 7567922152*	5	7 wks

ACE OF BASE *Sweden, male/female vocal/instrumental group* *7 wks*

19 Jun 93	**HAPPY NATION** *London 5177492*	21	7 wks

Bryan ADAMS
Canada, male vocalist/instrumentalist – guitar   *207 wks*

2 Mar 85 ●	**RECKLESS** *A & M AMA 5013*	7	115 wks
24 Aug 85	**YOU WANT IT, YOU GOT IT** *A & M AMLH 64864*	78	5 wks
15 Mar 86	**CUTS LIKE A KNIFE** *A & M AMLH 64919*	21	6 wks
11 Apr 87 ●	**INTO THE FIRE** *A & M AMA 3907*	10	21 wks
5 Oct 91 ★	**WAKING UP THE NEIGHBOURS** *A & M 3971641*	1	54 wks
20 Nov 93 ●	**SO FAR SO GOOD** *A & M 5401572*	2†	6 wks

Oleta ADAMS *US, female vocalist/instrumentalist – piano*   *33 wks*

26 May 90 ★	**CIRCLE OF ONE** *Fontana 8427441*	1	26 wks
7 Aug 93 ●	**EVOLUTION** *Fontana 5149652*	10	7 wks

Cliff ADAMS SINGERS *UK, male/female vocal group*   *20 wks*

16 Apr 60	**SING SOMETHING SIMPLE** *Pye MPL 28013*	15	4 wks
24 Nov 62	**SING SOMETHING SIMPLE** *Pye Golden Guinea GGL 0150*	15	2 wks
20 Nov 76	**SING SOMETHING SIMPLE '76** *Warwick WW 5016/17* ..	23	8 wks
25 Dec 82	**SING SOMETHING SIMPLE** *Ronco RTD 2087*	39	6 wks

All the identically titled albums are different.

ADAMSKI *UK, male multi-instrumentalist/producer*   *16 wks*

9 Dec 89	**LIVE AND DIRECT** *MCA MCL 1900*	47	11 wks
13 Oct 90 ●	**DOCTOR ADAMSKI'S MUSICAL PHARMACY** *MCA MCG 6107*	8	5 wks

King Sunny ADE and his AFRICAN BEATS
Nigeria, male vocalist and male vocal/instrumental group   *1 wk*

9 Jul 83	**SYNCHRO SYSTEM** *Island ILPS 9737*	93	1 wk

ADEVA *US, female vocalist*   *24 wks*

9 Sep 89 ● **ADEVA** *Cooltempo ICTLP 13* .... **6** 24 wks

ADICTS *UK, male vocal/instrumental group*   *1 wk*

4 Dec 82 **SOUND OF MUSIC** *Razor RAZ 2* .... **99** 1 wk

ADORABLE *UK, male vocal/instrumental group*   *1 wk*

13 Mar 93 **AGAINST PERFECTION** *Creation CRECD 138* .... **70** 1 wk

ADVENTURES *UK, male/female vocal/instrumental group* *11 wks*

21 May 88 **THE SEA OF LOVE** *Elektra EKT 45* .... **30** 10 wks
17 Mar 90 **TRADING SECRETS WITH THE MOON** *Elektra EKT 63* **64** 1wk

ADVERTS *UK, male/female vocal/instrumental group*   *1 wk*

11 Mar 78 **CROSSING THE RED SEA WITH THE ADVERTS**
Bright BRL 201 .... **38** 1 wk

AEROSMITH *US, male vocal/instrumental group*   *54 wks*

5 Sep 87 **PERMANENT VACATION** *Geffen WX 126* .... **37** 14 wks
23 Sep 89 **PUMP** *Geffen WX 304* .... **3** 24 wks
1 May 93 ● **GET A GRIP** *Geffen GED 24444* .... **2** 16 wks

AFGHAN WHIGS *US, male vocal/instrumental group*   *1 wk*

16 Oct 93 **GENTLEMEN** *Blast First BFFP 90CD* .... **58** 1 wk

AFTER THE FIRE *UK, male vocal/instrumental group*   *4 wks*

13 Oct 79 **LASER LOVE** *CBS 83795* .... **57** 1 wk
1 Nov 80 **80 F** *Epic EPC 84545* .... **69** 1 wk
3 Apr 82 **BATTERIES NOT INCLUDED** *CBS 85566* .... **82** 2 wks

AFRICAN BEATS – See King Sunny ADE and his AFRICAN BEATS

A-HA *Norway, male vocal/instrumental group*   *142 wks*

9 Nov 85 ● **HUNTING HIGH AND LOW** *Warner Bros. WX 30* .... **2** 77 wks
18 Oct 86 ● **SCOUNDREL DAYS** *Warner Bros. WX 62* .... **2** 29 wks
14 May 88 ● **STAY ON THESE ROADS** *Warner Bros. WX 166* .... **2** 19 wks
2 Nov 90 **EAST OF THE SUN WEST OF THE MOON**
Warner Bros. WX 378 .... **12** 4 wks
16 Nov 91 **HEADLINES AND DEADLINES – THE HITS OF A-HA**
Warner Bros. WX 450 .... **12** 10 wks
26 Jun 93 **MEMORIAL BEACH** *Warner Bros. 9362452292* .... **17** 3 wks

AIRHEAD *UK, male vocal/instrumental group*   *7 wks*

1 Feb 92 **BOING** *Korova 9031746792* .... **29** 7 wks

ALARM *UK, male vocal/instrumental group*   *29 wks*

25 Feb 84 ● **DECLARATION** *IRS IRSA 7044* .... **6** 11 wks
26 Oct 85 **STRENGTH** *IRS MIRF 1004* .... **18** 6 wks

14 Nov 87	**EYE OF THE HURRICANE** *IRS MIRG 1023*	**23**	4 wks
5 Nov 88	**ELECTRIC FOLKLORE LIVE** *IRS MIRMC 5001*	**62**	2 wks
30 Sep 89	**CHANGE** *IRS EIRSAX 1020*	**13**	3 wks
24 Nov 90	**STANDARDS** *IRS EIRSA 1043*	**47**	1 wk
4 May 91	**RAW** *IRS EIRSA 1055*	**33**	2 wks

JOHN ALDISS – *See LONDON PHILHARMONIC CHOIR*

ALEXANDER BROTHERS UK, *male vocal duo*   *1 wk*

10 Dec 66	**THESE ARE MY MOUNTAINS** *Pye GGL 0375*	**29**	1 wk

ALLEN – *See FOSTER and ALLEN*

ALICE IN CHAINS US, *male vocal/instrumental group*   *13 wks*

24 Oct 92	**DIRT** *Columbia 4723302*	**42**	13 wks

ALIEN SEX FIEND
UK, *male/female vocal/instrumental group*   *1 wk*

12 Oct 85	**MAXIMUM SECURITY** *Anagram GRAM 24*	**100**	1 wk

ALL ABOUT EVE
UK, *male/female vocal/instrumental group*   *37 wks*

27 Feb 88 ●	**ALL ABOUT EVE** *Mercury MERH 119*	**7**	29 wks
28 Oct 89 ●	**SCARLET AND OTHER STORIES** *Mercury 838965 1* ...	**9**	4 wks
7 Sep 91	**TOUCHED BY JESUS** *Vertigo 510461*	**17**	3 wks
7 Nov 92	**ULTRAVIOLET** *MCA MCD 10712*	**46**	1 wk

Mose ALLISON US, *male vocalist/instrumentalist – piano*   *1 wk*

4 Jun 66	**MOSE ALIVE** *Atlantic 587–007*	**30**	1 wk

ALLMAN BROTHERS BAND
US, *male vocal/instrumental group*   *4 wks*

6 Oct 73	**BROTHERS AND SISTERS** *Warner Bros. K 47507*	**42**	3 wks
6 Mar 76	**THE ROAD GOES ON FOREVER** *Capricorn 2637 101* ...	**54**	1 wk

ALMIGHTY UK, *male vocal/instrumental group*   *9 wks*

20 Oct 90	**BLOOD FIRE AND LIVE** *Polydor 8471071*	**62**	1 wk
30 Mar 91	**SOUL DESTRUCTION** *Polydor 8479611*	**22**	4 wks
17 Apr 93 ●	**POWERTRIPPIN'** *Polydor 5191042*	**5**	4 wks

Marc ALMOND UK, *male vocalist*   *25 wks*

16 Oct 82	**UNTITLED** *Some Bizzare BZA 13★*	**42**	4 wks
20 Aug 83	**TORMENT AND TORREROS** *Some Bizzare BIZL 4★*	**28**	5 wks
10 Nov 84	**VERMIN IN ERMINE** *Some Bizzare BIZL 8*	**36**	2 wks
5 Oct 85	**STORIES OF JOHNNY** *Some Bizzare FAITH 1*	**22**	3 wks
18 Apr 87	**MOTHER FIST AND HER FIVE DAUGHTERS** *Some Bizzare FAITH 2★★*	**41**	2 wks
8 Oct 88	**THE STARS WE ARE** *Parlophone PCS 7324*	**41**	5 wks
16 Jun 90	**ENCHANTED** *Some Bizzare PCS 7344*	**52**	1 wk
26 Oct 91	**TENEMENT SYMPHONY** *Some Bizzare WX 442*	**39**	3 wk

★*Marc and the Mambas.*
★★*Marc Almond and the Willing Sinners.*

A
38

Herb ALPERT and the TIJUANA BRASS
US, male band leader/instrumentalist − trumpet   *312 wks*

29 Jan	66 ●	**GOING PLACES** *Pye NPL 28065*	**4**	138 wks
23 Apr	66 ●	**WHIPPED CREAM AND OTHER DELIGHTS**		
		Pye NPL 28058	**2**	42 wks
28 May	66	**WHAT NOW MY LOVE** *Pye NPL 28077*	**18**	17 wks
11 Feb	67 ●	**S.R.O.** *Pye NSPL 28088*	**5**	26 wks
15 Jul	67	**SOUNDS LIKE** *A & M AMLS 900*	**21**	10 wks
3 Feb	68	**NINTH** *A & M AMLS 905*	**26**	9 wks
29 Jun	68 ●	**BEAT OF THE BRASS** *A & M AMLS 916*	**4**	21 wks
9 Aug	69	**WARM** *A & M AMLS 937*	**30**	4 wks
14 Mar	70	**THE BRASS ARE COMIN'** *A & M AMLS 962*	**40**	1 wk
30 May	70 ●	**GREATEST HITS** *A & M AMLS 980*	**8**	27 wks
27 Jun	70	**DOWN MEXICO WAY** *A & M AMLS 974*	**64**	1 wk
13 Nov	71	**AMERICA** *A & M AMLB 1000*	**45**	1 wk
12 Nov	77	**40 GREATEST** *K-Tel NE 1005*	**45**	2 wks
17 Nov	79	**RISE** *A & M AMLH 64790*★	**37**	7 wks
4 Apr	87	**KEEP YOUR EYE ON ME** *Breakout AMA 5125*★	**79**	3 wks
28 Sep	91	**THE VERY BEST OF HERB ALPERT** *A & M 3971651*★ .	**34**	3 wks

★*Herb Alpert.*
On 29 Jun 67 Going Places *and* What Now My Love *changed labels and numbers to A & M AMLS 965 and AMLS 977 respectively.*

ALTERED IMAGES
UK, female/male vocal/instrumental group   *40 wks*

19 Sep	81	**HAPPY BIRTHDAY** *Epic EPC 84893*	**26**	21 wks
15 May	82	**PINKY BLUE** *Epic EPC 85665*	**12**	10 wks
25 Jun	83	**BITE** *Epic EPC 25413*	**16**	9 wks

ALTERN 8   *UK, male instrumental/production duo*   *4 wks*

25 Jul	92	**FULL ON ... MASK HYSTERIA** *Network TOPCD 1*	**11**	4 wks

AMAZULU   *UK, female vocal group*   *1 wk*

6 Dec	88	**AMAZULU** *Island ILPS 9851*	**97**	1 wk

AMEN CORNER   *UK, male vocal/instrumental group*   *8 wks*

30 Mar	68	**ROUND AMEN CORNER** *Deram SML 1021*	**26**	7 wks
1 Nov	69	**EXPLOSIVE COMPANY** *Immediate IMSP 023*	**19**	1 wk

AMERICA   *US, male vocal/instrumental group*   *22 wks*

22 Jan	72	**AMERICA** *Warner Bros. K 46093*	**14**	13 wks
9 Dec	72	**HOMECOMING** *Warner Bros. K 46180*	**21**	5 wks
10 Nov	73	**HAT TRICK** *Warner Bros. K 56016*	**41**	3 wks
7 Feb	76	**HISTORY – AMERICA'S GREATEST HITS**		
		Warner Bros. K 56169	**60**	1 wk

AMERICAN MUSIC CLUB
US, male vocal/instrumental group   *2 wks*

27 Mar	93	**MERCURY** *Virgin CDV 2708*	**41**	2 wks

Tori AMOS   *US, female vocalist*   *16 wks*

18 Jan	92	**LITTLE EARTHQUAKES** *East West 7567823582*	**14**	16 wks

AND WHY NOT *UK, male vocal group*   *3 wks*

10 Mar 90   **MOVE YOUR SKIN** *Island ILPS 9935* ....   **24**   3 wks

Carleen ANDERSON *UK, female vocalist*   *1 wk*

13 Nov 93   **DUSKY SAPPHO EP** *Circa YRCDG 108* ....   **38**   1 wk

Ian ANDERSON *UK, male vocalist/instrumentalist – flute*   *1 wk*

26 Nov 83   **WALK INTO LIGHT** *Chrysalis CDL 1443* ....   **78**   1 wk

Jon ANDERSON *UK, male vocalist*   *19 wks*

24 Jul   76 ● **OLIAS OF SUNHILLOW** *Atlantic K 50261* ....   **8**   10 wks
15 Nov 80   **SONG OF SEVEN** *Atlantic K 50756* ....   **38**   3 wks
5 Jun   82   **ANIMATION** *Polydor POLD 5044* ....   **43**   6 wks

See also Jon and Vangelis; Anderson Bruford Wakeman Howe.

Laurie ANDERSON
US, female vocalist/multi-instrumentalist   *8 wks*

1 May 82   **BIG SCIENCE** *Warner Bros. K 57002* ....   **29**   6 wks
10 Mar 84   **MISTER HEARTBREAK** *Warner Bros. 92–5077–1* ....   **93**   2 wks

Lynn ANDERSON *US, female vocalist*   *1 wk*

17 Apr 71   **ROSE GARDEN** *CBS 64333* ....   **45**   1 wk

Moira ANDERSON *UK, female vocalist*   *6 wks*

20 Jun 70   **THESE ARE MY SONGS** *Decca SKL 5016* ....   **50**   1 wk
5 Dec 81   **GOLDEN MEMORIES** *Warwick WW 5107★* ....   **46**   5 wks

★ *Harry Secombe and Moira Anderson.*

ANDERSON BRUFORD WAKEMAN HOWE
UK, male vocal/instrumental group   *6 wks*

8 Jul   89   **ANDERSON BRUFORD WAKEMAN HOWE** *Arista 209970*   **14**   6 wks

See also Jon Anderson; Rick Wakeman; Steve Howe.

Julie ANDREWS *UK, female vocalist*   *5 wks*

16 Jul   83   **LOVE ME TENDER** *Peach River JULIE 1* ....   **63**   5 wks

ANGELIC UPSTARTS
UK, male vocal/instrumental group   *20 wks*

18 Aug 79   **TEENAGE WARNING** *Warner Bros. K 50634* ....   **29**   7 wks
12 Apr 80   **WE'VE GOTTA GET OUT OF THIS PLACE**
              Warner Bros. K 56806 ....   **54**   3 wks
7 Jun   81   **2,000,000 VOICES** *Zonophone ZONO 104* ....   **32**   3 wks
26 Sep 81   **ANGELIC UPSTARTS** *Zonophone ZEM 102* ....   **27**   7 wks

ANIMAL NIGHTLIFE *UK, male vocal/instrumental group* *6 wks*

24 Aug 85   **SHANGRI-LA** *Island ILPS 9830* ....   **36**   6 wks

The artist with the most weeks on chart in 1967 was the very unpsychedelic **Herb Alpert**.

Tori Amos (top right) was launched in Britain before her homeland with the reasoning that the British market was more sympathetic to her sound. She could then be promoted in the States as an American who had enjoyed success abroad. The strategy worked in both countries. (Pictorial Press)

Rick Astley was number one in his first chart week, dropped down in his second and never regained the position. (Pictorial Press)

The American co-author of this book promoted this line-up of **The Animals** at his high school in Connecticut in early 1966.

ANIMALS UK, male vocal/instrumental group — 86 wks

14 Nov 64 ●	**THE ANIMALS**	Columbia 33SX 1669	**6**	20 wks
22 May 65 ●	**ANIMAL TRACKS**	Columbia 33SX 1708	**6**	26 wks
16 Apr 66 ●	**MOST OF THE ANIMALS**	Columbia 33SX 6035	**4**	20 wks
28 May 66 ●	**ANIMALISMS**	Decca LK 4797	**4**	17 wks
25 Sep 71	**MOST OF THE ANIMALS (re-issue)**	MFP 5218	**18**	3 wks

ANNIHILATOR UK, male vocal/instrumental group — 1 wk

11 Aug 90	**NEVER NEVERLAND**	Road Runner RR 93741	**48**	1 wk

Adam ANT UK, male vocalist — 150 wks

15 Nov 80 ★	**KINGS OF THE WILD FRONTIER**	CBS 84549★	**1**	66 wks
17 Jan 81	**DIRK WEARS WHITE SOX**	Do It RIDE 3★	**16**	29 wks
14 Nov 81 ●	**PRINCE CHARMING**	CBS 85268★	**2**	21 wks
23 Oct 82 ●	**FRIEND OR FOE**	CBS 25040	**5**	12 wks
19 Nov 83	**STRIP**	CBS 25705	**20**	8 wks
14 Sep 85	**VIVE LE ROCK**	CBS 26533	**42**	3 wks
24 Mar 90	**MANNERS AND PHYSIQUE**	MCA MCG 6068	**19**	3 wks
28 Aug 93 ●	**ANTMUSIC – THE VERY BEST OF ADAM ANT**			
	Arcade ARC 3100052		**6**	8 wks

★Adam and the Ants.

A
42

ANTHRAX US, male vocal/instrumental group — 22 wks

18 Apr 87	**AMONG THE LIVING**	Island ILPS 9865	**18**	5 wks
24 Sep 88	**STATE OF EUPHORIA**	Island ILPS 9916	**12**	4 wks
8 Sep 90	**PERSISTENCE OF TIME**	Island ILPS 9967	**13**	5 wks
20 Jul 91	**ATTACK OF THE KILLER B'S**	Island ILPS 9980	**13**	5 wks
29 May 93	**SOUND OF WHITE NOISE**	Elektra 7559614302	**14**	3 wks

ANTI-NOWHERE LEAGUE
UK, male vocal/instrumental group — 12 wks

22 May 82	**WE ARE . . . THE LEAGUE**	WXYZ LMNOP 1	**24**	11 wks
5 Nov 83	**LIVE IN YUGOSLAVIA**	I.D. NOSE 3	**88**	1 wk

ANTI-PASTI UK, male vocal/instrumental group — 7 wks

15 Aug 81	**THE LAST CALL**	Rondelet ABOUT 5	**31**	7 wks

ANTS – See Adam ANT

APACHE INDIAN UK, male rapper — 2 wks

6 Feb 93	**NO RESERVATIONS**	Island CID 8001	**36**	2 wks

Carmine APPICE – See Jeff BECK, Tim BOGERT and Carmine APPICE

Kim APPLEBY UK, female vocalist — 13 wks

8 Dec 90	**KIM APPLEBY**	Parlophone PCS 7348	**23**	13 wks

See also Mel and Kim.

APRIL WINE Canada, male vocal/instrumental group — 8 wks

15 Mar 80	**HARDER . . . FASTER**	Capitol EST 12013	**34**	5 wks
24 Jan 81	**THE NATURE OF THE BEAST**	Capitol EST 12125	**48**	3 wks

ARCADIA *UK, male vocal/instrumental group* *10 wks*

7 Dec 85	**SO RED THE ROSE** Parlophone Odeon PCSD 101	30	10 wks

Tasmin ARCHER *UK, female vocalist* *42 wks*

31 Oct 92 ●	**GREAT EXPECTATIONS** EMI CDEMC 3624	8	42 wks

ARGENT *UK, male vocal/instrumental group* *9 wks*

29 Apr 72	**ALL TOGETHER NOW** Epic EPC 64962	13	8 wks
31 Mar 73	**IN DEEP** Epic EPC 65475	49	1 wk

Joan ARMATRADING *UK, female vocalist* *191 wks*

4 Sep 76	**JOAN ARMATRADING** A & M AMLH 64588	12	27 wks
1 Oct 77 ●	**SHOW SOME EMOTION** A & M AMLH 68433	6	11 wks
14 Oct 78	**TO THE LIMIT** A & M AMLH 64732	13	10 wks
24 May 80 ●	**ME MYSELF I** A & M AMLH 64809	5	23 wks
12 Sep 81 ●	**WALK UNDER LADDERS** A & M AMLH 64876	6	29 wks
12 Mar 83 ●	**THE KEY** A & M AMLX 64912	10	14 wks
26 Nov 83	**TRACK RECORD** A & M JA 2001	18	32 wks
16 Feb 85	**SECRET SECRETS** A & M AMA 5040	14	12 wks
24 May 86	**SLEIGHT OF HAND** A & M AMA 5130	34	6 wks
16 Jul 88	**THE SHOUTING STAGE** A & M AMA 5211	28	10 wks
16 Jun 90	**HEARTS AND FLOWERS** A & M 3952981	29	4 wks
16 Mar 91 ●	**THE VERY BEST OF JOAN ARMATRADING**		
	A & M 3971221	9	11 wks
20 Jun 92	**SQUARE THE CIRCLE** A & M 3953882	34	2 wks

ARMOURY SHOW *UK, male vocal/instrumental group* *1 wk*

21 Sep 85	**WAITING FOR THE FLOODS** Parlophone ARM 1	57	1 wk

Louis ARMSTRONG
US, male band leader vocalist/instrumentalist − trumpet/cornet *14 wks*

22 Oct 60	**SATCHMO PLAYS KING OLIVER**		
	Audio Fidelity AFLP 1930	20	1 wk
28 Oct 61	**JAZZ CLASSICS** Ace of Hearts AH 7	20	1 wk
27 Jun 64	**HELLO DOLLY** London HAR 8190	11	6 wks
16 Nov 68	**WHAT A WONDERFUL WORLD** Stateside SSL 10247 ...	37	3 wks
20 Feb 82	**THE VERY BEST OF LOUIS ARMSTRONG**		
	Warwick WW 5112	30	3 wks

ARRESTED DEVELOPMENT
US, male/female vocal/instrumental group *37 wks*

31 Oct 92 ●	**3 YEARS, 5 MONTHS AND 2 DAYS IN THE LIFE OF ...**		
	Cooltempo CCD 1929	3	34 wls
10 Apr 93	**UNPLUGGED** Cooltempo CTCD 33	40	3 wks

Steve ARRINGTON *US, male vocalist* *11 wks*

13 Apr 85	**DANCIN' IN THE KEY OF LIFE** Atlantic 781245	41	11 wks

Davey ARTHUR − See FUREYS and Davey ARTHUR

ART OF NOISE *UK, male/female instrumental duo* *37 wks*

3 Nov 84	**(WHO'S AFRAID OF) THE ART OF NOISE**		
	ZTT ZTTIQ 2	27	17 wks
26 Apr 86	**IN VISIBLE SILENCE** Chrysalis WOL 2	18	15 wks
10 Oct 87	**IN NO SENSE/NONSENSE** China WOL 4	55	2 wks
3 Dec 88	**THE BEST OF THE ART OF NOISE** China 837 367 1 ..	55	3 wks

Act was a group for first two albums.

A

43

ASAP *UK, male vocal/instrumental group* — *1 wk*

4 Nov 89	**SILVER AND GOLD** *EMI EMC 3566*	....	70	1 wk

ASHFORD and SIMPSON *US, male/female vocal duo* — *6 wks*

16 Feb 85	**SOLID** *Capitol SASH 1*	....	42	6 wks

ASIA *UK, male vocal/instrumental group* — *50 wks*

10 Apr 82	**ASIA** *Geffen GEF 85577*	....	11	38 wks
20 Aug 83 ●	**ALPHA** *Geffen GEF 25508*	....	5	11 wks
14 Dec 85	**ASTRA** *Geffen GEF 26413*	....	68	1 wk

ASSOCIATES *UK, male vocal/instrumental group* — *28 wks*

22 May 82 ●	**SULK** *Associates ASCL 1*	....	10	20 wks
16 Feb 85	**PERHAPS** *WEA WX 9*	....	23	7 wks
31 Mar 90	**WILD AND LONELY** *Circa CIRCA 11*	....	71	1 wk

Act was a duo for the first album.

Rick ASTLEY *UK, male vocalist* — *62 wks*

28 Nov 87 ★	**WHENEVER YOU NEED SOMEBODY** *RCA PL 71529*	.	1	34 wks
10 Dec 88 ●	**HOLD ME IN YOUR ARMS** *RCA PL 71932*	....	8	19 wks
2 Mar 91 ●	**FREE** *RCA PL 74896*	....	9	9 wks

A
44

ASWAD *UK, male vocal/instrumental group* — *52 wks*

24 Jul 82	**NOT SATISFIED** *CBS 85666*	....	50	6 wks
10 Dec 83	**LIVE AND DIRECT** *Island IMA 6*	....	57	16 wks
3 Nov 84	**REBEL SOULS** *Island ILPS 9780*	....	48	2 wks
28 Jun 86	**TO THE TOP** *Simba SIMBALP 2*	....	71	3 wks
9 Apr 88 ●	**DISTANT THUNDER** *Mango ILPS 9895*	....	10	15 wks
3 Dec 88	**RENAISSANCE** *Stylus SMR 866*	....	52	8 wks
22 Sep 90	**TOO WICKED** *Mango MLPS 1054*	....	51	2 wks

ATHLETICO SPIZZ 80
UK, male vocal/instrumental group — *5 wks*

26 Jul 80	**DO A RUNNER** *A & M AMLE 68514*	....	27	5 wks

Chet ATKINS *US, male instrumentalist – guitar* — *16 wks*

18 Mar 61	**THE OTHER CHET ATKINS** *RCA RD 27194*	....	20	1 wk
17 Jun 61	**CHET ATKINS' WORKSHOP** *RCA RD 27214*	....	19	1 wk
30 Feb 63	**CARIBBEAN GUITAR** *RCA RD 7519*	....	17	3 wks
24 Nov 90	**NECK AND NECK** *CBS 4674351★*	....	41	11 wks

★ Chet Atkins and Mark Knopfler.

Rowan ATKINSON *UK, male comedian* — *9 wks*

7 Feb 81	**LIVE IN BELFAST** *Arista SPART 1150*	....	44	9 wks

ATLANTIC STARR
US, male/female vocal/instrumental group — *15 wks*

15 Jun 85	**AS THE BAND TURNS** *A & M AMA 5019*	....	64	3 wks
11 Jul 87	**ALL IN THE NAME OF LOVE** *WEA WX 115*	....	48	12 wks

ATOMIC ROOSTER *UK, male vocal/instrumental group 13 wks*

13 Jun	70	**ATOMIC ROOSTER** *B & C CAS 1010*	49	1 wk
16 Jan	71	**DEATH WALKS BEHIND YOU** *Charisma CAS 1026*	12	8 wks
21 Aug	71	**IN HEARING OF ATOMIC ROOSTER** *Pegasus PEG 1* ..	18	4 wks

ATTRACTIONS – *See Elvis COSTELLO and the ATTRACTIONS*

AU PAIRS *UK, female/male vocal/instrumental group 10 wks*

| 6 Jun | 81 | **PLAYING WITH A DIFFERENT SEX** *Human HUMAN 1* | 33 | 7 wks |
| 4 Sep | 82 | **SENSE AND SENSUALITY** *Kamera KAM 010* .... | 79 | 3 wks |

Brian AUGER TRINITY – *See Julie DRISCOLL and the Brian AUGER TRINITY*

Patti AUSTIN *US, female vocalist 1 wk*

| 26 Sep | 81 | **EVERY HOME SHOULD HAVE ONE** *Quest K 56931* ... | 99 | 1 wk |

AUTEURS *UK, male/female vocal/instrumental group 2 wks*

| 6 Mar | 93 | **NEW WAVE** *Hut CDHUT 7* .... | 35 | 2 wks |

AVERAGE WHITE BAND
UK, male vocal/instrumental group 47 wks

1 Mar	75	● **AVERAGE WHITE BAND** *Atlantic K 50058*	6	14 wks
5 Jul	75	**CUT THE CAKE** *Atlantic K 50146*	28	4 wks
31 Jul	76	**SOUL SEARCHING TIME** *Atlantic K 50272*	60	1 wk
10 Mar	79	**I FEEL NO FRET** *RCA XL 13063*	15	15 wks
31 May	80	**SHINE** *RCA XL 13123*	14	13 wks

Roy AYERS *US, male vocalist/instrumentalist – vibraphone 2 wks*

| 26 Oct | 85 | **YOU MIGHT BE SURPRISED** *CBS 26653* .... | 91 | 2 wks |

Pam AYRES *UK, female vocalist 29 wks*

| 27 Mar | 76 | **SOME OF ME POEMS AND SONGS** *Galaxy GAL 6003* .. | 13 | 23 wks |
| 11 Dec | 76 | **SOME MORE OF ME POEMS AND SONGS**
Galaxy GAL 6010 .... | 23 | 6 wks |

Charles AZNAVOUR *France, male vocalist 21 wks*

29 Jun	74	**AZNAVOUR SINGS AZNAVOUR VOL. 3** *Barclay 80472* .	23	7 wks
7 Sep	74	● **A TAPESTRY OF DREAMS** *Barclay 90003*	9	13 wks
2 Aug	80	**HIS GREATEST LOVE SONGS** *K-Tel NE 1078*	73	1 wk

AZTEC CAMERA *UK, male vocal/instrumental group 76 wks*

23 Apr	83	**HIGH LAND HARD RAIN** *Rough Trade ROUGH 47*	22	18 wks
29 Sep	84	**KNIFE** *WEA WX 8*	14	6 wks
21 Nov	87	● **LOVE** *WEA WX 128*	10	43 wks
16 Jun	90	**STRAY** *WEA WX 350*	22	7 wks
29 May	93	**DREAMLAND** *WEA 4509924922*	21	2 wks

Derek B *UK, male rapper* *9 wks*

| 28 May 88 | **BULLET FROM A GUN** *Tuff Audio DRKLP 1* .... | **11** | 9 wks |

Eric B. and RAKIM *US, male vocal/instrumental duo* *10 wks*

12 Sep 87	**PAID IN FULL** *Fourth & Broadway BRLP 514*	**85**	4 wks
6 Aug 88	**FOLLOW THE LEADER** *MCA MCG 6031*	**25**	4 wks
7 Jul 90	**LET THE RHYTHM HIT 'EM** *MCA MCG 6097*	**58**	1 wk
11 Jul 92	**DON'T SWEAT THE TECHNIQUE** *MCA MCAD 10594*	**73**	1 wk

B BOYS *US, male vocal/instrumental group* *1 wk*

| 28 Jan 84 | **CUTTIN' HERBIE** *Streetwave X KHAN 501* .... | **90** | 1 wk |

BABES IN TOYLAND
US, female vocal/instrumental group *3 wks*

| 5 Sep 92 | **FONTANELLE** *Southern 185012* .... | **24** | 2 wks |
| 3 Jul 93 | **PAINKILLER** *Southern 185122* .... | **53** | 1 wk |

BABY ANIMALS *Australia, male vocal/instrumental group* *1 wk*

| 14 Mar 92 | **BABY ANIMALS** *Imago PD 90580* .... | **70** | 1 wk |

BACCARA *Spain, female vocal duo* *6 wks*

| 4 Mar 78 | **BACCARA** *RCA PL 28316* .... | **26** | 6 wks |

Burt BACHARACH *US, orchestra and chorus* *43 wks*

22 May 65	● **HIT MAKER – BURT BACHARACH** *London HAR 8233* .	**3**	18 wks
28 Nov 70	**REACH OUT** *A & M AMLS 908*	**52**	3 wks
3 Apr 71	● **PORTRAIT IN MUSIC** *A & M AMLS 2010*	**5**	22 wks

BACHELORS *Ireland, male vocal group* *103 wks*

27 Jun 64	● **THE BACHELORS AND 16 GREAT SONGS** *Decca LK 4614*	**2**	44 wks
9 Oct 65	**MORE GREAT SONG HITS FROM THE BACHELORS** *Decca LK 4721*	**15**	6 wks
9 Jul 66	**HITS OF THE SIXTIES** *Decca TXL 102*	**12**	9 wks
5 Nov 66	**BACHELORS' GIRLS** *Decca LK 4827*	**24**	8 wks
1 Jul 67	**GOLDEN ALL TIME HITS** *Decca SKL 4849*	**19**	7 wks
14 Jun 69	● **WORLD OF THE BACHELORS** *Decca SPA 2*	**8**	18 wks
23 Aug 69	**WORLD OF THE BACHELORS VOL. 2** *Decca SPA 22* ..	**11**	7 wks
22 Dec 79	**25 GOLDEN GREATS** *Warwick WW 5068*	**38**	4 wks

BACHMAN-TURNER OVERDRIVE
Canada, male vocal/instrumental group *13 wks*

| 14 Dec 74 | **NOT FRAGILE** *Mercury 9100 007* .... | **12** | 13 wks |

BACK TO THE PLANET
UK, male vocal/instrumental group   *2 wks*

| 18 Sep | 93 | MIND AND SOUL COLLABORATORS   *Parallel ALLCD 2* | 32 | 2 wks |

BAD COMPANY   *UK, male vocal/instrumental group*   *87 wks*

15 Jun	74 ●	BAD COMPANY *Island ILPS 9279*	3	25 wks
12 Apr	75 ●	STRAIGHT SHOOTER *Island ILPS 9304*	3	27 wks
21 Feb	76 ●	RUN WITH THE PACK *Island ILPS 9346*	4	12 wks
19 Mar	77	BURNIN' SKY *Island ILPS 9441*	17	8 wks
17 Mar	79 ●	DESOLATION ANGELS *Swansong SSK 59408*	10	9 wks
28 Aug	82	ROUGH DIAMONDS *Swansong SSK 59419*	15	6 wks

BAD ENGLISH   *UK/US, male vocal/instrumental group*   *2 wks*

| 16 Sep | 89 | BAD ENGLISH   *Epic 4634471* .... | 74 | 1 wk |
| 19 Oct | 91 | BACKLASH   *Epic 4685691* .... | 64 | 1 wk |

BAD MANNERS   *UK, male vocal/instrumental group*   *44 wks*

26 Apr	80	SKA 'N' B *Magnet MAG 5033*	34	13 wks
29 Nov	80	LOONEE TUNES *Magnet MAG 5038*	36	12 wks
24 Oct	81	GOSH IT'S BAD MANNERS *Magnet MAGL 5043*	18	12 wks
27 Nov	82	FORGING AHEAD *Magnet MAGL 5050*	78	1 wk
7 May	83	THE HEIGHT OF BAD MANNERS *Telstar STAR 2229* ..	23	6 wks

BAD NEWS   *UK, male vocal group*   *1 wk*

| 24 Oct | 87 | BAD NEWS   *EMI EMC 3535* .... | 69 | 1 wk |

BAD SEEDS – *See Nick CAVE featuring the BAD SEEDS*

Angelo BADALAMENTI   *Italy, male arranger*   *25 wks*

| 17 Nov | 90 | MUSIC FROM 'TWIN PEAKS'   *Warner Bros.   7599263161* . | 27 | 25 wks |

BADLANDS   *UK, male vocal/instrumental group*   *3 wks*

| 24 Jun | 89 | BADLANDS   *WEA 7819661* .... | 39 | 2 wks |
| 22 Jun | 91 | VOODOO HIGHWAY   *Atlantic 7567822511* .... | 74 | 1 wk |

Joan BAEZ   *US, female vocalist*   *88 wks*

18 Jul	64 ●	JOAN BAEZ IN CONCERT VOL. 2 *Fontana TFL 6033* ..	8	19 wks
15 May	65 ●	JOAN BAEZ NO. 5 *Fontana TFL 6043*	3	27 wks
19 Jun	65 ●	JOAN BAEZ *Fontana TFL 6002*	9	13 wks
27 Nov	65 ●	FAREWELL ANGELINA *Fontana TFL 6058*	5	23 wks
19 Jul	69	JOAN BAEZ ON VANGUARD *Vanguard SVXL 100*	15	5 wks
3 Apr	71	FIRST TEN YEARS *Vanguard 6635 003*	41	1 wk

Philip BAILEY   *US, male vocalist*   *17 wks*

| 30 Mar | 85 | CHINESE WALL   *CBS 26161* .... | 29 | 17 wks |

Anita BAKER   *US, female vocalist*   *76 wks*

3 May	86	RAPTURE *Elektra EKT 37*	13	47 wks
29 Oct	88 ●	GIVING YOU THE BEST THAT I GOT *Elektra EKT 49* .	9	20 wks
14 Jul	90 ●	COMPOSITIONS *Elektra EKT 72*	7	9 wks

B
47

Anita Baker *charted with her first UK release, but this was preceded by The Songstress, a successful title on an independent label.*

Part of the Aspects Of Love cast that reached number one, **Michael Ball** *went on to a top five success of his own while starring in his own TV series.* (Pictorial Press)

Bananarama *are shown with gold discs awarded for their biggest album success,* The Greatest Hits Collection.

This is the first edition of this book in which **Shirley Bassey** *is no longer the female soloist with the most hit albums.*

BAKER-GURVITZ ARMY
UK, male vocal/instrumental group   *5 wks*

22 Feb 75 **BAKER-GURVITZ ARMY** *Vertigo 9103 201* .... **22** 5 wks
See also Ginger Baker's Air Force.

Ginger BAKER'S AIR FORCE
UK, male vocal/instrumental group   *1 wk*

13 Jun 70 **GINGER BAKER'S AIR FORCE** *Polydor 266 2001* ...... **37** 1 wk
See also Baker-Gurvitz Army.

BALAAM AND THE ANGEL
UK, male/vocal instrumental group   *2 wks*

16 Aug 86 **THE GREATEST STORY EVER TOLD** *Virgin V 2377* .. **67** 2 wks

Kenny BALL *UK, male vocalist/instrumentalist – trumpet*   *50 wks*

25 Aug 62 ★ **BEST OF BALL, BARBER AND BILK**
                   Pye Golden Guinea GGL 0131★ .... **1** 24 wks
7 Sep 63 ● **KENNY BALL'S GOLDEN HITS**
                   Pye Golden Guinea GGL 0209 .... **4** 26 wks

★ *Kenny Ball, Chris Barber and Acker Bilk.*

Michael BALL *UK, male vocalist*   *21 wks*

30 May 92 ★ **MICHAEL BALL** *Polydor 5113302* .... **1** 10 wks
17 Jul 93 ● **ALWAYS** *Polydor 5196662* .... **3** 11 wks

BANANARAMA *UK, female vocal group*   *97 wks*

19 Mar 83 ● **DEEP SEA SKIVING** *London RAMA 1* .... **7** 16 wks
28 Apr 84 **BANANARAMA** *London RAMA 2* .... **16** 11 wks
19 Jul 86 **TRUE CONFESSIONS** *London RAMA 3* .... **46** 5 wks
19 Sep 87 **WOW!** *London RAMA 4* .... **27** 26 wks
22 Oct 88 ● **THE GREATEST HITS COLLECTION** *London RAMA 5* . **3** 37 wks
25 May 91 **POP LIFE** *London 8282461* .... **42** 1 wk
10 Apr 93 **PLEASE YOURSELF** *London 8283572* .... **46** 1 wk

BAND *Canada/US, male vocal/instrumental group*   *18 wks*

31 Jan 70 **THE BAND** *Capitol EST 132* .... **25** 11 wks
3 Oct 70 ● **STAGE FRIGHT** *Capitol EA SW 425* .... **15** 6 wks
27 Nov 71 **CAHOOTS** *Capitol EA–ST 651* .... **41** 1 wk

BAND AID – *See MIDGE URE*

BANDERAS *UK, female vocal/instrumental duo*   *3 wks*

13 Apr 91 **RIPE** *London 8282471* .... **40** 3 wks

BANGLES *US, female vocal/instrumental group*   *93 wks*

16 Mar 85 **ALL OVER THE PLACE** *CBS 26015* .... **86** 1 wk
15 Mar 86 ● **DIFFERENT LIGHT** *CBS 26659* .... **3** 47 wks
10 Dec 88 ● **EVERYTHING** *CBS 4629791* .... **5** 26 wks
9 Jun 90 ● **GREATEST HITS** *CBS 4667691* .... **4** 19 wks

B
49

Tony BANKS *UK, male instrumentalist – keyboards*　　*7 wks*

20 Oct 79	**A CURIOUS FEELING** *Charisma CAS 1148*	21	5 wks
25 Jun 83	**THE FUGITIVE** *Charisma TBLP 1*	50	2 wks

BANSHEES – *See SIOUXSIE and the BANSHEES*

Chris BARBER
UK, male vocalist/instrumentalist – trombone　　*88 wks*

24 Sep 60	**CHRIS BARBER BAND BOX NO. 2**		
	Columbia 33SCX 3277	17	1 wk
5 Nov 60	**ELITE SYNCOPATIONS** *Columbia 33SX 1245*	18	1 wk
12 Nov 60	**BEST OF CHRIS BARBER** *Ace Of Clubs ACL 1037*	17	1 wk
27 May 61 ●	**BEST OF BARBER AND BILK VOL. 1**		
	Pye Golden Guinea GGL 0075*	4	43 wks
11 Nov 61 ●	**BEST OF BARBER AND BILK VOL. 2**		
	Pye Golden Guinea GGL 0096*	8	18 wks
25 Aug 62 ★	**BEST OF BALL, BARBER AND BILK**		
	Pye Golden Guinea GGL 0131**	1	24 wks

* *Chris Barber and Acker Bilk.*
** *Kenny Ball, Chris Barber and Acker Bilk.*

BARCLAY JAMES HARVEST
UK, male vocal/instrumental group　　*42 wks*

14 Dec 74	**BARCLAY JAMES HARVEST LIVE** *Polydor 2683 052* ...	40	2 wks
18 Oct 75	**TIME HONOURED GHOST** *Polydor 2383 361*	32	3 wks
23 Oct 76	**OCTOBERON** *Polydor 2442 144*	19	4 wks
1 Oct 77	**GONE TO EARTH** *Polydor 2442 148*	30	7 wks
21 Oct 78	**BARCLAY JAMES HARVEST XII** *Polydor POLD 5006* ...	31	2 wks
23 May 81	**TURN OF THE TIDE** *Polydor POLD 5040*	55	2 wks
24 Jul 82	**A CONCERT FOR THE PEOPLE (BERLIN)**		
	Polydor POLD 5052	15	11 wks
28 May 83	**RING OF CHANGES** *Polydor POLH 3*	36	4 wks
14 Apr 84	**VICTIMS OF CIRCUMSTANCE** *Polydor POLD 5135*	33	6 wks
14 Feb 87	**FACE TO FACE** *Polydor POLD 5209*	65	1 wk

Daniel BARENBOIM – *See John WILLIAMS and Daniel BARENBOIM*

Syd BARRETT *UK, male vocalist/instrumentalist – guitar*　　*1 wk*

7 Feb 70	**MADCAP LAUGHS** *Harvest SHVL 765*	40	1 wk

Wild Willy BARRETT – *See John OTWAY and Wild Willy BARRETT*

BARRON KNIGHTS *UK, male vocal/instrumental group* *22 wks*

2 Dec 78	**NIGHT GALLERY** *Epic EPC 83221*	15	13 wks
1 Dec 79	**TEACH THE WORLD TO LAUGH** *Epic EPC 83891*	51	4 wks
13 Dec 80	**JUST A GIGGLE** *Epic EPC 84550*	45	5 wks

John BARRY *UK, male arranger/conductor*　　*17 wks*

29 Jan 72	**THE PERSUADERS** *CBS 64816*	18	9 wks
20 Apr 91	**DANCES WITH WOLVES (film soundtrack)** *Epic 4675911*	45	8 wks

BASIA *Poland, female vocalist*　　*4 wks*

13 Feb 88	**TIME AND TIDE** *Portrait 4502631*	61	3 wks
3 Mar 90	**LONDON WARSAW NEW YORK** *Epic 4632821*	68	1 wk

Count BASIE *US, male orchestra leader/instrumentalist – piano* *24 wks*

16 Apr 60	**CHAIRMAN OF THE BOARD** *Columbia 33SX 1209*	17	1 wk
23 Feb 63 ●	**SINATRA – BASIE** *Reprise R 1008**	2	23 wks

* *Frank Sinatra and Count Basie.*

**B
50**

Toni BASIL   US, *female vocalist*   16 wks

6 Feb 82	**WORD OF MOUTH** *Radialchoice BASIL 1*	**15** 16 wks

Shirley BASSEY   UK, *female vocalist*   273 wks

28 Jan 61	**FABULOUS SHIRLEY BASSEY** *Columbia 33SX 1178*	**12** 2 wks
25 Feb 61 ●	**SHIRLEY** *Columbia 33SX 1286*	**9** 10 wks
17 Feb 62	**SHIRLEY BASSEY** *Columbia 33SX 1382*	**14** 11 wks
15 Dec 62	**LET'S FACE THE MUSIC** *Columbia 33SX 1454★*	**12** 7 wks
4 Dec 65	**SHIRLEY BASSEY AT THE PIGALLE** *Columbia 33SX 1787*	**16** 7 wks
27 Aug 66	**I'VE GOT A SONG FOR YOU** *United Artists ULP 1142* ...	**26** 1 wk
17 Feb 68	**TWELVE OF THOSE SONGS** *Columbia SCX 6204*	**38** 3 wks
7 Dec 68	**GOLDEN HITS OF SHIRLEY BASSEY** *Columbia SCX 6294*	**28** 40 wks
11 Jul 70	**LIVE AT THE TALK OF THE TOWN**	
	United Artists UAS 29095	**38** 6 wks
29 Aug 70 ●	**SOMETHING** *United Artists UAS 29100*	**5** 28 wks
15 May 71 ●	**SOMETHING ELSE** *United Artists UAG 29149*	**7** 9 wks
2 Oct 71	**BIG SPENDER** *Sunset SLS 50262*	**27** 8 wks
30 Oct 71	**IT'S MAGIC** *Starline SRS 5082*	**32** 1 wk
6 Nov 71	**THE FABULOUS SHIRLEY BASSEY** *MFP 1398*	**48** 1 wk
4 Dec 71	**WHAT NOW MY LOVE** *MFP 5230*	**17** 5 wks
8 Jan 72	**THE SHIRLEY BASSEY COLLECTION**	
	United Artists UAD 60013/4	**37** 1 wk
19 Feb 72	**I CAPRICORN** *United Artists UAS 29246* ....`..	**13** 11 wks
29 Nov 72	**AND I LOVE YOU SO** *United Artists UAS 29385*	**24** 9 wks
2 Jun 73 ●	**NEVER NEVER NEVER** *United Artists UAG 29471*	**10** 10 wks
15 Mar 75 ●	**THE SHIRLEY BASSEY SINGLES ALBUM**	
	United Artists UAS 29728	**2** 23 wks
1 Nov 75	**GOOD, BAD BUT BEAUTIFUL** *United Artists UAS 29881*	**13** 7 wks
15 May 76	**LOVE, LIFE AND FEELINGS** *United Artists UAS 29944* ...	**13** 5 wks
4 Dec 76	**THOUGHTS OF LOVE** *United Artists UAS 30011*	**15** 9 wks
25 Jun 77	**YOU TAKE MY HEART AWAY** *United Artists UAS 30037*	**34** 5 wks
4 Nov 78 ●	**25TH ANNIVERSARY ALBUM** *United Artists SBTV 601 4748*	**3** 12 wks
12 May 79	**THE MAGIC IS YOU** *United Artists UATV 30230*	**40** 5 wks
17 Jul 82	**LOVE SONGS** *Applause APKL 1163*	**48** 5 wks
20 Oct 84	**I AM WHAT I AM** *Towerbell TOWLP 7*	**25** 18 wks
18 May 91	**KEEP THE MUSIC PLAYING** *Dino DINTV 21*	**25** 7 wks
5 Dec 92	**THE BEST OF SHIRLEY BASSEY** *Dino DINCD 49*	**27** 5 wks
4 Dec 93	**SHIRLEY BASSEY SINGS ANDREW LLOYD WEBBER**	
	Premier CDDPR 114	**56** 2 wks

★ *Shirley Bassey with the Nelson Riddle Orchestra.*

BASS-O-MATIC   UK, *male multi-instrumentalist*   2 wks

13 Oct 90	**SET THE CONTROLS FOR THE HEART OF THE BASS**	
	Virgin V 2641	**57** 2 wks

Mike BATT – *See Justin Hayward*

BAUHAUS   UK, *male vocal/instrumental group*   24 wks

15 Nov 80	**IN THE FLAT FIELD** *4AD CAD 13*	**72** 1 wk
24 Oct 81	**MASK** *Beggars Banquet BEGA 29*	**30** 5 wks
30 Oct 82 ●	**THE SKY'S GONE OUT** *Beggars Banquet BEGA 42*	**4** 6 wks
23 Jul 83	**BURNING FROM THE INSIDE** *Beggars Banquet BEGA 45* .	**13** 10 wks
30 Nov 85	**1979–1983** *Beggars Banquet BEGA 64*	**36** 2 wks

BAY CITY ROLLERS
UK, *male vocal/instrumental group*   127 wks

12 Oct 74 ★	**ROLLIN'** *Bell BELLS 244*	**1** 62 wks
3 May 75 ★	**ONCE UPON A STAR** *Bell SYBEL 8001*	**1** 37 wks
13 Dec 75 ●	**WOULDN'T YOU LIKE IT** *Bell SYBEL 8002*	**3** 12 wks
25 Sep 76 ●	**DEDICATION** *Bell SYBEL 8005*	**4** 12 wks
13 Aug 77	**IT'S A GAME** *Arista SPARTY 1009*	**18** 4 wks

B
51

BBC SYMPHONY ORCHESTRA, SINGERS and CHORUS *UK, orchestra/choir and audience*   *6 wks*

4 Oct	69	**LAST NIGHT OF THE PROMS** *Philips SFM 23033*	**36**	1 wk
11 Dec	82	**HIGHLIGHTS – LAST NIGHT OF THE PROMS '82**		
		K-Tel NE 1198	**69**	5 wks

Last Night Of The Proms *was conducted by Colin Davis and* Highlights – Last Night Of The Proms '82 *by James Loughran.*

BBC WELSH CHORUS – *See Aled JONES*

BEACH BOYS *US, male vocal/instrumental group*   *547 wks*

B
52

25 Sep	65	**SURFIN' USA** *Capitol T 1890*	**17**	7 wks
19 Feb	66 ●	**BEACH BOYS PARTY** *Capitol T 2398*	**3**	14 wks
16 Apr	66 ●	**BEACH BOYS TODAY** *Capitol T 2269*	**6**	25 wks
9 Jul	66 ●	**PET SOUNDS** *Capitol T 2458*	**2**	39 wks
16 Jul	66 ●	**SUMMER DAYS** *Capitol T 2354*	**4**	22 wks
12 Nov	66 ●	**BEST OF THE BEACH BOYS** *Capitol T 20865*	**2**	142 wks
11 Mar	67	**SURFER GIRL** *Capitol T 1981*	**13**	14 wks
21 Oct	67 ●	**BEST OF THE BEACH BOYS VOL. 2** *Capitol ST 20956* .	**3**	39 wks
18 Nov	67 ●	**SMILEY SMILE** *Capitol ST 9001*	**9**	8 wks
16 Mar	68 ●	**WILD HONEY** *Capitol ST 2859*	**7**	15 wks
21 Sep	68	**FRIENDS** *Capitol ST 2895*	**13**	8 wks
23 Nov	68 ●	**BEST OF THE BEACH BOYS VOL. 3** *Capitol ST 21142*	**9**	12 wks
29 Mar	69 ●	**20/20** *Capitol EST 133*	**3**	10 wks
19 Sep	70 ●	**GREATEST HITS** *Capitol T 21628*	**5**	30 wks
5 Dec	70	**SUNFLOWER** *Stateside SSL 8251*	**29**	6 wks
27 Nov	71	**SURF'S UP** *Stateside SLS 10313*	**15**	7 wks
24 Jun	72	**CARL AND THE PASSIONS/SO TOUGH** *Reprise K 44184*	**25**	1 wk
17 Feb	73	**HOLLAND** *Reprise K 54008*	**20**	7 wks
10 Jul	76 ★	**20 GOLDEN GREATS** *Capitol EMTV 1*	**1**	86 wks
24 Jul	76	**15 BIG ONES** *Reprise K 54079*	**31**	3 wks
7 May	77	**THE BEACH BOYS LOVE YOU** *Brother/Reprise K 54087* .	**28**	1 wk
21 Apr	79	**LA (LIGHT ALBUM)** *Caribou CRB 86081*	**32**	6 wks
12 Apr	80	**KEEPING THE SUMMER ALIVE** *Caribou CRB 86109* ...	**54**	3 wks
30 Jul	83 ★	**THE VERY BEST OF THE BEACH BOYS**		
		Capitol BBTV 1867193	**1**	17 wks
22 Jun	85	**THE BEACH BOYS** *Caribou CRB 26378*	**60**	2 wks
23 Jun	90 ●	**SUMMER DREAMS** *Capitol EMTVD 51*	**2**	23 wks

BEASTIE BOYS *US, male vocal group*   *42 wks*

31 Jan	87 ●	**LICENCE TO ILL** *Def Jam 450062*	**7**	40 wks
5 Aug	89	**PAUL'S BOUTIQUE** *Capitol EST 2102*	**44**	2 wks

BEAT *UK, male vocal/instrumental group*   *69 wks*

31 May	80 ●	**JUST CAN'T STOP IT** *Go-Feet BEAT 001*	**3**	32 wks
16 May	81	**WHA'PPEN** *Go-Feet BEAT 3*	**3**	18 wks
9 Oct	82	**SPECIAL BEAT SERVICE** *Go-Feet BEAT 5*	**21**	6 wks
11 Jun	83 ●	**WHAT IS BEAT? (THE BEST OF THE BEAT)**		
		Go-Feet BEAT 6	**10**	13 wks

BEATLES *UK, male vocal/instrumental group*   *1116 wks*

6 Apr	63 ★	**PLEASE PLEASE ME** *Parlophone PMC 1202*	**1**	70 wks
30 Nov	63 ★	**WITH THE BEATLES** *Parlophone PMC 1206*	**1**	51 wks
18 Jul	64 ★	**A HARD DAY'S NIGHT** *Parlophone PMC 1230*	**1**	38 wks
12 Dec	64 ★	**BEATLES FOR SALE** *Parlophone PMC 1240*	**1**	46 wks
14 Aug	65 ★	**HELP** *Parlophone PMC 1255*	**1**	37 wks
11 Dec	65 ★	**RUBBER SOUL** *Parlophone PMC 1267*	**1**	42 wks
13 Aug	66 ★	**REVOLVER** *Parlophone PMC 7009*	**1**	34 wks
10 Dec	66 ●	**A COLLECTION OF BEATLES OLDIES**		
		Parlophone PMC 7016	**7**	34 wks
3 Jun	67 ★	**SERGEANT PEPPER'S LONELY HEARTS CLUB BAND**		
		Parlophone PCS 7027	**1**	148 wks

13 Jan	68	**MAGICAL MYSTERY TOUR (import)** *Capitol SMAL 2835*	**31**	2 wks
7 Dec	68 ★	**THE BEATLES** *Apple PCS 7067/8*	**1**	22 wks
1 Feb	69 ●	**YELLOW SUBMARINE** *Apple PCS 7070*	**3**	10 wks
4 Oct	69 ★	**ABBEY ROAD** *Apple PCS 7088*	**1**	81 wks
23 May	70 ★	**LET IT BE** *Apple PXS 1*	**1**	59 wks
16 Jan	71	**A HARD DAY'S NIGHT (re-issue)** *Parlophone PCS 3058* .	**30**	1 wk
24 Jul	71	**HELP (re-issue)** *Parlophone PCS 3071*	**33**	2 wks
5 May	73 ●	**THE BEATLES 1967–1970** *Apple PCSP 718*	**2**	113 wks
5 May	73 ●	**THE BEATLES 1962–1966** *Apple PCSP 717*	**3**	148 wks
25 Jun	76	**ROCK 'N' ROLL MUSIC** *Parlophone PCSP 719*	**11**	15 wks
21 Aug	76	**THE BEATLES TAPES** *Polydor 2683 068*	**45**	1 wk
21 May	77 ★	**THE BEATLES AT THE HOLLYWOOD BOWL**		
		Parlophone EMTV 4	**1**	17 wks
17 Dec	77 ●	**LOVE SONGS** *Parlophone PCSP 721*	**7**	17 wks
3 Nov	79	**RARITIES** *Parlophone PCM 1001*	**71**	1 wk
15 Nov	80	**BEATLES BALLADS** *Parlophone PCS 7214*	**17**	16 wks
30 Oct	82 ●	**20 GREATEST HITS** *Parlophone PCTC 260*	**10**	30 wks
7 Mar	87	**PLEASE PLEASE ME (re-issue)** *Parlophone CDP 746 435–2*	**32**	4 wks
7 Mar	87	**WITH THE BEATLES (re-issue)** *Parlophone CDP 746 436–2*	**40**	2 wks
7 Mar	87	**A HARD DAY'S NIGHT (2nd re-issue)**		
		Parlophone CDP 746 437–2	**30**	4 wks
7 Mar	87	**BEATLES FOR SALE (re-issue)** *Parlophone CDP 746 438–2*	**45**	2 wks
9 May	87	**HELP (2nd re-issue)** *Parlophone CDP 746 439–2*	**61**	2 wks
9 May	87	**RUBBER SOUL (re-issue)** *Parlophone CDP 746 440–2*	**60**	3 wks
9 May	87	**REVOLVER (re-issue)** *Parlophone CDP 746 441–2*	**55**	5 wks
6 Jun	87 ●	**SERGEANT PEPPER'S LONELY HEARTS CLUB BAND**		
		(re-issue) *Parlophone CDP 746 442–2*	**3**	24 wks
5 Sep	87	**THE BEATLES (re-issue)** *Parlophone CDS 746 443–9*	**18**	2 wks
5 Sep	87	**YELLOW SUBMARINE (re-issue)**		
		Parlophone CDP 746 445–2	**60**	1 wk
3 Oct	87	**MAGICAL MYSTERY TOUR (re-issue)**		
		Parlophone PCTC 255	**52**	1 wk
31 Oct	87	**ABBEY ROAD (re-issue)** *Parlophone CDP 746 446–2*	**30**	2 wks
31 Oct	87	**LET IT BE (re-issue)** *Parlophone CDP 746 447–2*	**50**	1 wk
19 Mar	88	**PAST MASTERS VOLUME 1** *Parlophone CDBPM 1*	**49**	1 wk
19 Mar	88	**PAST MASTERS VOLUME 2** *Parlophone CDBPM 2*	**46**	1 wk
2 Oct	93 ●	**THE BEATLES 1962–1966 (re-issue)**		
		Parlophone BEACD 2511	**3†**	13 wks
2 Oct	93 ●	**THE BEATLES 1967–1970 (re-issue)**		
		Parlophone BEACD 2512	**4†**	13 wks

Yellow Submarine *featured several tracks by the George Martin Orchestra. The albums recharted in 1987 and 1993 after being made available as compact discs. The label numbers are the CD catalogue numbers of these re-issues.*

BEATMASTERS *UK, male/female instrumental group* *10 wks*

1 Jul	89	**ANYWAYAWANNA** *Rhythm King LEFTLP 10*	**30**	10 wks

BEATS INTERNATIONAL
UK, male/female vocal/instrumental group *15 wks*

14 Apr	90	**LET THEM EAT BINGO** *Go Beat 8421961*	**17**	15 wks

BEAUTIFUL SOUTH
UK, male/female vocal/instrumental group *62 wks*

4 Nov	89 ●	**WELCOME TO THE BEAUTIFUL SOUTH**		
		Go! Discs AGOLP 16	**2**	23 wks
10 Nov	90 ●	**CHOKE** *Go! Discs 8282331*	**2**	22 wks
11 Apr	92 ●	**0898** *Go! Discs 8283102*	**4**	17 wks

BE-BOP DELUXE *UK, male vocal/instrumental group* *28 wks*

31 Jan	76	**SUNBURST FINISH** *Harvest SHSP 4053*	**17**	12 wks
25 Sep	76	**MODERN MUSIC** *Harvest SHSP 4058*	**12**	6 wks
6 Aug	77 ●	**LIVE! IN THE AIR AGE** *Harvest SHVL 816*	**10**	5 wks
25 Feb	78	**DRASTIC PLASTIC** *Harvest SHSP 4091*	**22**	5 wks

B
53

Jeff BECK UK, male vocal/instrumentalist – guitar   14 wks

13 Sep	69	**BECK-OLA** Columbia SCX 6351	39	1 wk
28 Apr	73	**JEFF BECK, TIM BOGERT AND CARMINE APPICE**		
		Epic EPC 65455★	28	3 wks
24 Jul	76	**WIRED** CBS 86012	38	5 wks
19 Jul	80	**THERE AND BACK** Epic EPC 83288	38	4 wks
17 Aug	85	**FLASH** Epic EPC 26112	83	1 wk

★ Jeff Beck, Tim Bogert and Carmine Appice.

BEE GEES UK/Australia, male vocal/instrumental group   224 wks

12 Aug	67 ●	**BEE GEES FIRST** Polydor 583–012	8	26 wks
24 Feb	68	**HORIZONTAL** Polydor 582–020	16	15 wks
28 Sep	68 ●	**IDEA** Polydor 583–036	4	18 wks
5 Apr	69 ●	**ODESSA** Polydor 583–049/50	10	1 wk
8 Nov	69 ●	**BEST OF THE BEE GEES** Polydor 583–063	7	22 wks
9 May	70	**CUCUMBER CASTLE** Polydor 2383–010	57	2 wks
17 Feb	79 ★	**SPIRITS HAVING FLOWN** RSO RSBG 001	1	33 wks
10 Nov	79 ●	**BEE GEES GREATEST** RSO RSDX 001	6	25 wks
7 Nov	81	**LIVING EYES** RSO RSBG 002	73	8 wks
3 Oct	87 ●	**E.S.P.** Warner Bros. WX 83	5	24 wks
29 Apr	89	**ONE** Warner Bros. WX 252	29	3 wks
17 Nov	90 ●	**THE VERY BEST OF THE BEE GEES** Polydor 8473391 ..	8	38 wks
6 Apr	91	**HIGH CIVILISATION** Warner Bros. WX 417	24	5 wks
25 Sep	93	**SIZE ISN'T EVERYTHING** Polydor 5199452	33†	4 wks

All albums from Cucumber Castle onwards group were UK only.

B
54

Sir Thomas BEECHAM UK, conductor   2 wks

26 Mar	60	**CARMEN** HMV ALP 1762/4	18	2 wks

Full credit on sleeve reads 'Orchestre National de la Radio Diffusion Française, conducted by Sir Thomas Beecham'.

BELL BIV DEVOE US, male vocal group   5 wks

1 Sep	90	**POISON** MCA MCG 6094	35	5 wks

BELLAMY BROTHERS US, male vocal duo   6 wks

19 Jun	76	**BELLAMY BROTHERS** Warner Bros. K 56242	21	6 wks

Regina BELLE US, female vocalist   5 wks

1 Aug	87	**ALL BY MYSELF** CBS 450 998–1	53	4 wks
16 Sep	89	**STAY WITH ME** CBS 465132 1	62	1 wk

BELLE STARS UK, female vocal/instrumental group   12 wks

5 Feb	83	**THE BELLE STARS** Stiff SEEZ 45	15	12 wks

BELLY US, male/female vocal/instrumental group   10 wks

13 Feb	93 ●	**STAR** 4AD 3002CD	2	10 wks

Pierre BELMONDE
France, male instrumentalist – panpipes   10 wks

7 Jun	80	**THEMES FOR DREAMS** K-Tel ONE 1077	13	10 wks

BELMONTS – See DION and the BELMONTS

Björk Gudmundsdottir of the Sugarcubes dropped her surname for her solo career. (One Little Indian Records)

Last in the chart on his own in 1977, **Tony Bennett** recently won a Grammy Award for his Frank Sinatra tribute album and then appeared on Sinatra's Duets.

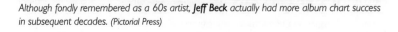

Although fondly remembered as a 60s artist, **Jeff Beck** actually had more album chart success in subsequent decades. (Pictorial Press)

BELOVED *UK, male vocal/instrumental duo* *29 wks*

3 Mar	90	**HAPPINESS** East West WX 299	**14**	14 wks
1 Dec	90	**BLISSED OUT** East West WX 383	**38**	2 wks
20 Feb	93 ●	**CONSCIENCE** East West 4509914832	**2**	13 wks

Pat BENATAR *US, female vocalist* *83 wks*

25 Jul	81	**PRECIOUS TIME** Chrysalis CHR 1346	**30**	7 wks
13 Nov	82	**GET NERVOUS** Chrysalis CHR 1396	**73**	6 wks
15 Oct	83	**LIVE FROM EARTH** Chrysalis CHR 1451	**60**	5 wks
17 Nov	84	**TROPICO** Chrysalis CHR 1471	**31**	25 wks
24 Aug	85	**IN THE HEAT OF THE NIGHT** Chrysalis CHR 1236	**98**	1 wk
7 Dec	85	**SEVEN THE HARD WAY** Chrysalis CHR 1507	**69**	4 wks
7 Nov	87 ●	**BEST SHOTS** Chrysalis PATV 1	**6**	19 wks
16 Jul	88	**WIDE AWAKE IN DREAMLAND** Chrysalis CDL 1628 ...	**11**	13 wks
4 May	91	**TRUE LOVE** Chrysalis CHR 1805	**40**	3 wks

Cliff BENNETT and the REBEL ROUSERS
UK, male vocal/instrumental group *3 wks*

22 Oct	66	**DRIVIN' ME WILD** MFP 1121	**25**	3 wks

Tony BENNETT *US, male vocalist* *63 wks*

29 May	65	**I LEFT MY HEART IN SAN FRANCISCO** CBS BPG 62201	**13**	14 wks
19 Feb	66 ●	**A STRING OF TONY'S HITS** CBS DP 66010	**9**	13 wks
10 Jun	67	**TONY'S GREATEST HITS** CBS SBPG 62821	**14**	24 wks
23 Sep	67	**TONY MAKES IT HAPPEN** CBS SBPG 63055	**31**	3 wks
23 Mar	68	**FOR ONCE IN MY LIFE** CBS SBPG 63166	**29**	5 wks
26 Feb	77	**THE VERY BEST OF TONY BENNETT –** **20 GREATEST HITS** Warwick PA 5021	**23**	4 wks

George BENSON *US, male vocalist/instrumentalist – guitar* *270 wks*

19 Mar	77	**IN FLIGHT** Warner Bros. K 56237	**19**	23 wks
18 Feb	78	**WEEKEND IN L.A.** Warner Bros. K 66074	**47**	1 wk
24 Mar	79	**LIVING INSIDE YOUR LOVE** Warner Bros. K 66085	**24**	14 wks
26 Jul	80 ●	**GIVE ME THE NIGHT** Warner Bros. K 56823	**3**	40 wks
14 Nov	81	**GEORGE BENSON COLLECTION** Warner Bros. K 66107	**19**	35 wks
11 Jun	83 ●	**IN YOUR EYES** Warner Bros. 92–3744–1	**3**	53 wks
26 Jan	85 ●	**20/20** Warner Bros. 92–5178–1	**9**	19 wks
19 Oct	85 ★	**THE LOVE SONGS** K-Tel NE 1308	**1**	27 wks
6 Sep	86	**WHILE THE CITY SLEEPS . . .** Warner Bros. WX 55	**13**	27 wks
11 Jul	87	**COLLABORATION** Warner Bros WX 91★	**47**	6 wks
10 Sep	88	**TWICE THE LOVE** Warner Bros. WX 160	**16**	10 wks
8 Jul	89	**TENDERLY** Warner Bros. WX 263	**52**	3 wks
26 Oct	91	**MIDNIGHT MOODS – THE LOVE COLLECTION** Telstar STAR 2450	**25**	12 wks

★ *George Benson and Earl Klugh.*

BERLIN *US, male/female vocal/instrumental group* *11 wks*

17 Jan	87	**COUNT THREE AND PRAY** Mercury MER 101	**32**	11 wks

BERLIN PHILHARMONIC ORCHESTRA – *See Herbert VON KARAJAN*

Leonard BERNSTEIN *US, male conductor* *2 wks*

10 Feb	90	**BERNSTEIN IN BERLIN – BEETHOVEN'S 9TH** Deutsche Grammophon	**54**	2 wks

Leonard BERNSTEIN'S WEST SIDE STORY – *See Studio Cast Recordings*

B
56

Shelley BERMAN *US, male vocalist – comedian* *4 wks*

19 Nov 60	**INSIDE SHELLEY BERMAN** *Capitol CLP 1300*	12	4 wks

Chuck BERRY *US, male vocalist/instrumentalist – guitar* *53 wks*

25 May 63	**CHUCK BERRY** *Pye International NPL 28024*	12	16 wks
5 Oct 63 ●	**CHUCK BERRY ON STAGE** *Pye International NPL 28027* ..	6	11 wks
7 Dec 63 ●	**MORE CHUCK BERRY** *Pye International NPL 28028*	9	8 wks
30 May 64 ●	**HIS LATEST AND GREATEST** *Pye NPL 28037*	8	7 wks
3 Oct 64	**YOU NEVER CAN TELL** *Pye NPL 29039*	18	2 wks
12 Feb 77 ●	**MOTORVATIN'** *Chess 9288 690*	7	9 wks

Mike BERRY *UK, male vocalist* *3 wks*

24 Jan 81	**THE SUNSHINE OF YOUR SMILE** *Polydor 2383 592*	63	3 wks

Nick BERRY *UK, male vocalist* *8 wks*

20 Dec 86	**NICK BERRY** *BBC REB 618*	99	1 wk
21 Nov 92	**NICK BERRY** *Columbia 4727182*	28	7 wks

The two identically titled albums are different.

BEVERLEY-PHILLIPS ORCHESTRA
UK, orchestra *9 wks*

9 Oct 76	**GOLD ON SILVER** *Warwick WW 5018*	22	9 wks

Frankie BEVERLY *– See MAZE featuring Frankie BEVERLY*

B-52s *US, male/female vocal/instrumental group* *69 wks*

4 Aug 79	**B-52s** *Island ILPS 9580*	22	12 wks
13 Sep 80	**WILD PLANET** *Island ILPS 9622*	18	4 wks
11 Jul 81	**THE PARTY MIX ALBUM** *Island IPM 1001*	36	5 wks
27 Feb 82	**MESOPOTAMIA** *EMI ISSP 4006*	18	6 wks
21 May 83	**WHAMMY!** *Island ILPS 9759*	33	4 wks
8 Aug 87	**BOUNCING OFF THE SATELLITES** *Island ILPS 9871* ..	74	2 wks
29 Jul 89 ●	**COSMIC THING** *Reprise WX 283*	8	27 wks
14 Jul 90	**THE BEST OF THE B-52s – DANCE THIS MESS AROUND** *Island ILPS 9959*	36	3 wks
11 Jul 92 ●	**GOOD STUFF** *Reprise 7599269432*	8	6 wks

BIBLE *UK, male vocal/instrumental group* *2 wks*

2 Jan 88	**EUREKA** *Cooltempo CHR 1646*	71	1 wk
7 Oct 89	**THE BIBLE** *Ensign CHEN 12*	67	1 wk

BIG AUDIO DYNAMITE
UK, male vocal/instrumental group *43 wks*

16 Nov 85	**THIS IS BIG AUDIO DYNAMITE** *CBS 26714*	27	27 wks
8 Nov 86	**No. 10 UPPING STREET** *CBS 450 137-1*	11	8 wks
9 Jul 88	**TIGHTEN UP VOL. 88** *CBS 4611991*	33	3 wks
16 Sep 89	**MEGATOP PHOENIX** *CBS 4657901*	26	3 wks
2 Nov 90	**KOOL-AID** *CBS 4674661*	55	1 wk
17 Aug 91	**THE GLOBE** *Columbia 4677061*	63	1 wk

BIG BEN BANJO BAND *UK, male instrumental group* *1 wk*

17 Dec 60	**MORE MINSTREL MELODIES** *Columbia 33SX 1254*	20	1 wk

B
57

BIG COUNTRY UK, male vocal/instrumental group   144 wks

6 Aug 83 ●	**THE CROSSING** *Mercury MERH 27*	**3**	80 wks
27 Oct 84 ★	**STEELTOWN** *Mercury MERH 49*	**1**	21 wks
12 Jul 86 ●	**THE SEER** *Mercury MERH 87*	**2**	16 wks
8 Oct 88 ●	**PEACE IN OUR TIME** *Mercury MERH 130*	**9**	6 wks
26 May 90 ●	**THROUGH A BIG COUNTRY – GREATEST HITS**		
	Mercury 8460221	**2**	17 wks
28 Sep 91	**NO PLACE LIKE HOME** *Vertigo 5102301*	**28**	2 wks
3 Apr 93	**THE BUFFALO SKINNERS** *Compulsion CDNOIS 2*	**25**	2 wks

BIG DADDY KANE US, male vocalist   3 wks

30 Sep 89	**IT'S A BIG DADDY THING** *Cold Chillin' WX 305*	**37**	3 wks

BIG DISH UK, male vocal/instrumental group   3 wks

11 Oct 86	**SWIMMER** *Virgin V 2374*	**85**	1 wk
23 Feb 91	**SATELLITES** *East West WX 400*	**43**	2 wks

BIG FUN UK, male vocal group   11 wks

12 May 90 ●	**A POCKETFUL OF DREAMS** *Jive FUN 1*	**7**	11 wks

BIG ROLL BAND – *See Zoot MONEY and the BIG ROLL BAND*

BIG SOUND – *See Simon DUPREE and the BIG SOUND*

B
58

Mr. Acker BILK
UK, male band leader, vocalist/instrumentalist – clarinet   *161 wks*

19 Mar 60 ●	**SEVEN AGES OF ACKER** *Columbia 33SX 1205*	**6**	6 wks
9 Apr 60	**ACKER BILK'S OMNIBUS** *Pye NJL 22*	**14**	3 wks
4 Mar 61	**ACKER** *Columbia 33SX 1248*	**17**	1 wk
1 Apr 61	**GOLDEN TREASURY OF BILK** *Columbia 33SX 1304* ...	**11**	6 wks
27 May 61 ●	**BEST OF BARBER AND BILK VOL. 1**		
	Pye Golden Guinea GGL 0075★	**4**	43 wks
11 Nov 61 ●	**BEST OF BARBER AND BILK VOL. 2**		
	Pye Golden Guinea GGL 0096★	**8**	18 wks
26 May 62 ●	**STRANGER ON THE SHORE** *Columbia 33SX 1407*	**6**	28 wks
25 Aug 62 ★	**BEST OF BALL, BARBER AND BILK**		
	Pye Golden Guinea GGL 0131★★	**1**	24 wks
4 May 63	**A TASTE OF HONEY** *Columbia 33SX 1493*	**17**	4 wks
9 Oct 76	**THE ONE FOR ME** *Pye NSPX 41052*	**38**	6 wks
4 Jun 77 ●	**SHEER MAGIC** *Warwick WW 5028*	**5**	8 wks
11 Nov 78	**EVERGREEN** *Warwick PW 5045*	**17**	14 wks

★ *Chris Barber and Acker Bilk.*
★★ *Kenny Ball, Chris Barber and Acker Bilk.*

BIRDLAND UK, male vocal/instrumental group   1 wk

2 Mar 91	**BIRDLAND** *Lazy LAZY 25*	**44**	1 wk

BIRTHDAY PARTY
Australia, male vocal/instrumental group   *3 wks*

24 Jul 82	**JUNKYARD** *4AD CAD 207*	**73**	3 wks

Stephen BISHOP US, male instrumentalist – piano   3 wks

1 Apr 72	**GRIEG AND SCHUMANN PIANO CONCERTOS**		
	Philips 6500 166	**34**	3 wks

BIZARRE INC *UK, male/female vocal instrumental group* — 2 wks

| 7 Nov 92 | **ENERGIQUE** *Vinyl Solution STEAM 47CD* .... | 41 | 2 wks |

BJORK *Iceland, female vocalist* — 24 wks

| 17 Jul 93 ● | **DEBUT** *One Little Indian TPLP 31CD* .... | 3† | 24 wks |

BLACK *Ireland, male vocalist/instrumentalist, Colin Vearncombe* — 29 wks

26 Sep 87 ●	**WONDERFUL LIFE** *A & M AMA 5165*	3	23 wks
29 Oct 88	**COMEDY** *A & M AMA 5222*	32	4 wks
1 Jun 91	**BLACK** *A & M 3971261*	42	2 wks

Cilla BLACK *UK, female vocalist* — 63 wks

13 Feb 65 ●	**CILLA** *Parlophone PMC 1243*	5	11 wks
14 May 66 ●	**CILLA SINGS A RAINBOW** *Parlophone PMC 7004*	4	15 wks
13 Apr 68 ●	**SHER-OO** *Parlophone PCS 7041*	7	11 wks
30 Nov 68	**BEST OF CILLA BLACK** *Parlophone PCS 7065*	21	11 wks
25 Jul 70	**SWEET INSPIRATION** *Parlophone PCS 7103*	42	4 wks
29 Jan 83	**THE VERY BEST OF CILLA BLACK** *Parlophone EMTV 38*	20	9 wks
2 Oct 93	**THROUGH THE YEARS** *Columbia 4746502*	41	2 wks

Mary BLACK *UK, female vocalist* — 2 wks

| 3 Jul 93 | **THE HOLY GROUND** *Grapevine GRACD 11* .... | 58 | 2 wks |

BLACK BOX *Italy, male/female vocal/instrumental group* — 30 wks

| 5 May 90 | **DREAMLAND** *deConstruction PL 74572* .... | 14 | 30 wks |

BLACK CROWES *US, male vocal/instrumental group* — 18 wks

| 24 Aug 91 | **SHAKE YOUR MONEY MAKER** *Def American 8425151* .. | 36 | 11 wks |
| 23 May 92 ● | **SOUTHERN HARMONY AND MUSICAL COMPANION** *Def American 5122632* .... | 2 | 7 wks |

BLACK LACE *UK, male vocal/instrumental group* — 26 wks

8 Dec 84 ●	**PARTY PARTY – 16 GREAT PARTY ICEBREAKERS** *Telstar STAR 2250*	4	14 wks
7 Dec 85	**PARTY PARTY 2** *Telstar STAR 2266*	18	6 wks
6 Dec 86	**PARTY CRAZY** *Telstar STAR 2288*	58	6 wks

BLACK, ROCK and RON *US, male rap group* — 1 wk

| 22 Apr 89 | **STOP THE WORLD** *Supreme SU 5* .... | 72 | 1 wk |

BLACK SABBATH
UK/US, male vocal/instrumental group — 211 wks

7 Mar 70 ●	**BLACK SABBATH** *Vertigo VO 6*	8	42 wks
26 Sep 70 ★	**PARANOID** *Vertigo 6360 011*	1	27 wks
21 Aug 71 ●	**MASTER OF REALITY** *Vertigo 6360 050*	5	13 wks
30 Sep 72 ●	**BLACK SABBATH VOL. 4** *Vertigo 6360 071*	8	10 wks
8 Dec 73 ●	**SABBATH BLOODY SABBATH** *WWA WWA 005*	4	11 wks
27 Sep 75 ●	**SABOTAGE** *NEMS 9119 001*	7	7 wks
7 Feb 76	**WE SOLD OUR SOUL FOR ROCK 'N' ROLL** *NEMS 6641 335*	35	5 wks

6 Nov 76		**TECHNICAL ECSTASY** *Vertigo 9102 750*	**13**	6 wks
14 Oct 78		**NEVER SAY DIE** *Vertigo 9102 751*	**12**	6 wks
26 Apr 80	●	**HEAVEN AND HELL** *Vertigo 9102 752*	**9**	22 wks
5 Jul 80	●	**BLACK SABBATH LIVE AT LAST** *NEMS BS 001*	**5**	15 wks
27 Sep 80		**PARANOID (re-issue)** *NEMS NEL 6003*	**54**	2 wks
14 Nov 81		**MOB RULES** *Mercury 6V'02119*	**12**	14 wks
22 Jan 83		**LIVE EVIL** *Vertigo SAB 10*	**13**	11 wks
24 Sep 83	●	**BORN AGAIN** *Vertigo VERL 8*	**4**	7 wks
1 Mar 86		**SEVENTH STAR** *Vertigo VERH 29★*	**27**	5 wks
28 Nov 87		**THE ETERNAL IDOL** *Vertigo VERH 51*	**66**	1 wk
29 Apr 89		**HEADLESS CROSS** *IRS EIRSA 1002*	**31**	2 wks
1 Sep 90		**TYR** *IRS EIRSA 1038*	**24**	3 wks
4 Jul 92		**DEHUMANIZER** *IRS EIRSCD 1064*	**28**	2 wks

★ *Black Sabbath featuring Tony Iommi.*

BLACK UHURU
Jamaica, male/female vocal/instrumental group   *22 wks*

13 Jun 81	**RED** *Island ILPS 9625*	**28**	13 wks
22 Aug 81	**BLACK UHURU** *Virgin VX 1004*	**81**	2 wks
19 Jun 82	**CHILL OUT** *Island ILPS 9701*	**38**	6 wks
25 Aug 84	**ANTHEM** *Island ILPS 9773*	**90**	1 wk

Band of the BLACK WATCH   *UK, military band*   *13 wks*

7 Feb 76	**SCOTCH ON THE ROCKS** *Spark SRLM 503*	**11**	13 wks

BLACK WIDOW   *UK, male vocal/instrumental group*   *2 wks*

4 Apr 70	**SACRIFICE** *CBS 63948*	**32**	2 wks

BLACKFOOT   *US, male vocal/instrumental group*   *22 wks*

18 Jul 81		**MARAUDER** *Atco K 50799*	**38**	12 wks
11 Sep 82		**HIGHWAY SONG – BLACKFOOT LIVE** *Atco K 50910* ..	**14**	6 wks
21 May 83		**SIOGO** *Atco 79–0080–1*	**28**	3 wks
29 Sep 84		**VERTICAL SMILES** *Atco 790218*	**82**	1 wk

BLACKHEARTS – *See Joan JETT and the BLACKHEARTS*

Ritchie BLACKMORE'S RAINBOW – *See RAINBOW*

Howard BLAKE conducting the SINFONIA OF LONDON   *UK, conductor and orchestra*   *12 wks*

22 Dec 84	**THE SNOWMAN** *CBS 71116*	**54**	12 wks

Narration by Bernard Cribbins.

BLANCMANGE   *UK, male vocal/instrumental duo*   *57 wks*

9 Oct 82		**HAPPY FAMILIES** *London SH 8552*	**30**	38 wks
26 May 84	●	**MANGE TOUT** *London SH 8554*	**8**	17 wks
26 Oct 85		**BELIEVE YOU ME** *London LONLP 10*	**54**	2 wks

Mary J. BLIGE   *US, female vocalist*   *1 wk*

20 Mar 93	**WHAT'S THE 411** *Uptown UPTD 10681*	**53**	1 wk

BLIND FAITH   *UK, male vocal/instrumental group*   *10 wks*

13 Sep 69	★	**BLIND FAITH** *Polydor 583–059*	**1**	10 wks

BLITZ *UK, male vocal/instrumental group* *3 wks*

6 Nov 82 **VOICE OF A GENERATION** *No Future PUNK 1* .... 27 3 wks

BLIZZARD OF OZ – *See Ozzy OSBOURNE*

BLOCKHEADS – *See Ian DURY and the BLOCKHEADS*

BLODWYN PIG *UK, male vocal/instrumental group* *11 wks*

16 Aug 69 ● **AHEAD RINGS OUT** *Island ILPS 9101* .... 9 4 wks
23 Apr 70 ● **GETTING TO THIS** *Island ILPS 9122* .... 8 7 wks

BLONDIE *US/UK, female/male vocal/instrumental group* *292 wks*

 4 Mar 78 ● **PLASTIC LETTERS** *Chrysalis CHR 1166* .... 10 54 wks
23 Sep 78 ★ **PARALLEL LINES** *Chrysalis CDL 1192* .... 1 105 wks
10 Mar 79 **BLONDIE** *Chrysalis CHR 1165* .... 75 1 wk
13 Oct 79 ★ **EAT TO THE BEAT** *Chrysalis CDL 1225* .... 1 38 wks
29 Nov 80 ● **AUTOAMERICAN** *Chrysalis CDL 1290* .... 3 16 wks
31 Oct 81 ● **BEST OF BLONDIE** *Chrysalis CDLTV 1* .... 4 40 wks
 5 Jun 82 ● **THE HUNTER** *Chrysalis CDL 1384* .... 9 12 wks
17 Dec 88 **ONCE MORE INTO THE BLEACH** *Chrysalis CJB 2★* .... 50 4 wks
16 Mar 91 ● **THE COMPLETE PICTURE – THE VERY BEST OF**
　　　　　　 DEBORAH HARRY AND BLONDIE
　　　　　　 Chrysalis CHR 1817★ .... 3 22 wks

★ *Deborah Harry and Blondie.*

BLOOD SWEAT AND TEARS
US/Canada, male vocal/instrumental group *21 wks*

13 Jul 68 **CHILD IS FATHER TO THE MAN** *CBS 63296* .... 40 1 wk
12 Apr 69 **BLOOD SWEAT AND TEARS** *CBS 63504* .... 15 8 wks
 8 Aug 70 **BLOOD SWEAT AND TEARS 3** *CBS 64024* .... 14 12 wks

BLOW MONKEYS *UK, male vocal/instrumental group* *27 wks*

19 Apr 86 **ANIMAL MAGIC** *RCA PL 70910* .... 21 8 wks
25 Apr 87 **SHE WAS ONLY A GROCER'S DAUGHTER**
　　　　　　 RCA PL 71245 .... 20 8 wks
11 Feb 89 **WHOOPS! THERE GOES THE NEIGHBOURHOOD**
　　　　　　 RCA PL 71858 .... 46 2 wks
26 Aug 89 ● **CHOICES** *RCA PL 74191* .... 5 9 wks

BLUE AEROPLANES
UK, male/female vocal/instrumental group *4 wks*

24 Feb 90 **SWAGGER** *Ensign CHEN 13* .... 54 1 wk
17 Aug 91 **BEATSONGS** *Ensign CHEN 21* .... 33 3 wks

BLUE MURDER *US, male vocal/instrumental group* *3 wks*

 6 May 89 **BLUE MURDER** *Geffen WX 245* .... 45 3 wks

BLUE NILE *UK, male vocal/instrumental group* *6 wks*

19 May 84 **A WALK ACROSS THE ROOFTOPS** *Linn LKH 1* ...... 80 2 wks
21 Oct 89 **HATS** *Linn LKH 2* .... 12 4 wks

BLUE OYSTER CULT
US, male vocal/instrumental group *40 wks*

 3 Jul 76 **AGENTS OF FORTUNE** *CBS 81385* .... 26 10 wks
 4 Feb 78 **SPECTRES** *CBS 86050* .... 60 1 wk

B

61

28 Oct	78	**SOME ENCHANTED EVENING** *CBS 86074*	**18**	4 wks
18 Aug	79	**MIRRORS** *CBS 86087*	**46**	5 wks
19 Jul	80	**CULTOSAURUS ERECTUS** *CBS 86120*	**12**	7 wks
25 Jul	81	**FIRE OF UNKNOWN ORIGIN** *CBS 85137*	**29**	7 wks
22 May	82	**EXTRATERRESTRIAL LIVE** *CBS 22203*	**39**	5 wks
19 Nov	83	**THE REVOLUTION BY NIGHT** *CBS 25686*	**95**	1 wk

BLUE PEARL *UK/US, male/female vocal/instrumental group* *2 wks*

| 1 Dec | 90 | **NAKED** *Big Life BLR LP4* .... | **58** | 2 wks |

BLUE RONDO A LA TURK
UK, male vocal/instrumental group *2 wks*

| 6 Nov | 82 | **CHEWING THE FAT** *Diable Noir V 2240* .... | **80** | 2 wks |

BLUEBELLS *UK, male vocal/instrumental group* *15 wks*

| 11 Aug | 84 | **SISTERS** *London LONLP 1* .... | **22** | 10 wks |
| 17 Apr | 93 | **THE SINGLES COLLECTION** *London 8284052* .... | **27** | 5 wks |

BLUES BAND *UK, male vocal/instrumental group* *18 wks*

8 Mar	80	**OFFICIAL BOOTLEG ALBUM** *Arista BBBP 101*	**40**	9 wks
18 Oct	80	**READY** *Arista BB 2*	**36**	6 wks
17 Oct	81	**ITCHY FEET** *Arista BB 3*	**60**	3 wks

BLUR *UK, male vocal/instrumental group* *9 wks*

| 7 Sep | 91 | ● **LEISURE** *Food FOODLP 6* .... | **7** | 6 wks |
| 22 May | 93 | **MODERN LIFE IS RUBBISH** *Food FOODCD 9* .... | **15** | 3 wks |

B M EX *UK, male production/instrumental group* *2 wks*

| 30 Jan | 93 | **APPOLONIA** *Union City UCRCD 14* .... | **17** | 2 wks |

BODINES *UK, male vocal/instrumental group* *1 wk*

| 29 Aug | 87 | **PLAYED** *Pop BODL 2001* .... | **94** | 1 wk |

Tim BOGERT – *See Jeff BECK*

Suzy BOGGUSS *US, female vocalist* *1 wk*

| 25 Sep | 93 | **SOMETHING UP MY SLEEVE** *Liberty CDEST 221* ...... | **69** | 1 wk |

Marc BOLAN – *See T. REX*

BOLSHOI *UK, male vocal/instrumental group* *1 wk*

| 3 Oct | 87 | **LINDY'S PARTY** *Beggars Banquet BEGA 86* .... | **100** | 1 wk |

Michael BOLTON *US, male vocalist* *162 wks*

17 Mar	90	● **SOUL PROVIDER** *CBS 4653431*	**4**	72 wks
11 Aug	90	**THE HUNGER** *CBS 4601631*	**44**	5 wks
18 May	91	● **TIME LOVE AND TENDERNESS** *Columbia 4678121*	**2**	57 wks
10 Oct	92	● **TIMELESS (THE CLASSICS)** *Columbia 4723022*	**3**	23 wks
27 Nov	93	● **THE ONE THING** *Columbia 4743552*	**4†**	5 wks

B

62

BOMB THE BASS UK, male producer, Tim Simenon   14 wks

22 Oct 88	**INTO THE DRAGON** *Rhythm King DOOD 1*	**18**	10 wks
31 Aug 91	**UNKNOWN TERRITORY** *Rhythm King 4687740*	**19**	4 wks

BOMBALURINA featuring Timmy MALLETT
UK, male vocalist   *5 wks*

15 Dec 90	**HUGGIN' AN' A KISSIN'** *Polydor 8476481*	**55**	5 wks

BON JOVI US, male vocal/instrumental group   225 wks

28 Apr 84	**BON JOVI** *Vertigo VERL 14*	**71**	3 wks
11 May 85	**7800° FAHRENHEIT** *Vertigo VERL 24*	**28**	12 wks
20 Sep 86 ●	**SLIPPERY WHEN WET** *Vertigo VERH 38*	**6**	109 wks
1 Oct 88 ★	**NEW JERSEY** *Vertigo VERH 62*	**1**	45 wks
14 Nov 92 ★	**KEEP THE FAITH** *Jambco 5141972*	**1†**	56 wks

See Jon Bon Jovi.

Jon BON JOVI US, male vocalist   23 wks

25 Aug 90 ●	**BLAZE OF GLORY/YOUNG GUNS II** *Vertigo 8464731* ..	**2**	23 wks

See Bon Jovi.

Graham BOND UK, male vocalist/instrumentalist – keyboards 2 wks

20 Jun 70	**SOLID BOND** *Warner Bros. WS 3001*	**40**	2 wks

Gary U.S. BONDS US, male vocalist   8 wks

22 Aug 81	**DEDICATION** *EMI America AML 3017*	**43**	3 wks
10 Jul 82	**ON THE LINE** *EMI America AML 3022*	**55**	5 wks

BONEY M
Jamaica/Montserrat/Antilles, male/female vocal group   *140 wks*

23 Apr 77	**TAKE THE HEAT OFF ME** *Atlantic K 50314*	**40**	15 wks
6 Aug 77	**LOVE FOR SALE** *Atlantic K 50385*	**60**	1 wk
29 Jul 78 ★	**NIGHT FLIGHT TO VENUS** *Atlantic/Hansa K 50498*	**1**	65 wks
29 Sep 79 ★	**OCEANS OF FANTASY** *Atlantic/Hansa K 50610*	**1**	18 wks
12 Apr 80 ★	**THE MAGIC OF BONEY M** *Atlantic/Hansa BMTV 1*	**1**	26 wks
6 Sep 86	**THE BEST OF 10 YEARS** *Stylus SMR 621*	**35**	5 wks
27 Mar 93	**THE GREATEST HITS** *Telstar TCD 2656*	**14**	10 wks

BONFIRE Germany, male vocal/instrumental group   1 wk

21 Oct 89	**POINT BLANK** *MSA ZL 74249*	**74**	1 wk

Graham BONNET UK, male vocalist   3 wks

7 Nov 81	**LINE UP** *Mercury 6302151*	**62**	3 wks

BONNIE – *See DELANEY and BONNIE and FRIENDS*

BONZO DOG DOO-DAH BAND
UK, male vocal/instrumental group   *4 wks*

18 Jan 69	**DOUGHNUT IN GRANNY'S GREENHOUSE**		
	Liberty LBS 83158	**40**	1 wk
30 Aug 69	**TADPOLES** *Liberty LBS 83257*	**36**	1 wk
22 Jun 74	**THE HISTORY OF THE BONZOS**		
	United Artists UAD 60071	**41**	2 wks

B
63

Betty BOO *UK, female vocalist*   *25 wks*

22 Sep	90 ●	**BOOMANIA** *Rhythm King LEFTLP 12*	**4**	24 wks
24 Oct	92	**GRRR! IT'S BETTY BOO** *WEA 4509909082*	**62**	1 wk

BOO RADLEYS *UK, male vocal/instrumental group*   *5 wks*

4 Apr	92	**EVERYTHING'S ALRIGHT FOREVER**		
		Creation CRECD 120	**55**	1 wk
28 Aug	93	**GIANT STEPS** *Creation CRECD 149*	**17**	4 wks

BOOGIE DOWN PRODUCTIONS
US, male rapper   *9 wks*

18 Jan	88	**BY ALL MEANS NECESSARY** *Jive HIP 63*	**38**	3 wks
22 Jul	89	**GHETTO MUSIC** *Jive HIP 80*	**32**	4 wks
25 Aug	90	**EDUTAINMENT** *Jive HIP 100*	**52**	2 wks

BOOKER T. and the MG'S
US, male instrumental group   *5 wks*

25 Jul	64	**GREEN ONIONS** *London HAK 8182*	**11**	4 wks
11 Jul	70	**McLEMORE AVENUE** *Stax SXATS 1031*	**70**	1 wk

B
64

BOOMTOWN RATS
Ireland, male vocal/instrumental group   *93 wks*

17 Sep	77 ●	**BOOMTOWN RATS** *Ensign ENVY 1*	**18**	11 wks
8 Jul	78 ●	**TONIC FOR THE TROOPS** *Ensign ENVY 3*	**8**	44 wks
3 Nov	79 ●	**THE FINE ART OF SURFACING** *Ensign ENROX 11*	**7**	26 wks
24 Jan	81 ●	**MONDO BONGO** *Mercury 6359 042*	**6**	7 wks
3 Apr	82	**V DEEP** *Mercury 6359 082*	**64**	5 wks

Pat BOONE *US, male vocalist*   *12 wks*

22 Nov	58 ●	**STARDUST** *London HAD 2127*	**10**	1 wk
28 May	60	**HYMNS WE HAVE LOVED** *London HAD 2228*	**12**	2 wks
25 Jun	60	**HYMNS WE LOVE** *London HAD 2092*	**14**	1 wk
24 Apr	76	**PAT BOONE ORIGINALS** *ABC ABSD 301*	**16**	8 wks

BOOTZILLA ORCHESTRA – *See Malcolm McLAREN*

BOO-YAA T.R.I.B.E. *US, male rap group*   *1 wk*

14 Apr	90	**NEW FUNKY NATION** *Fourth + Broadway*	**74**	1 wk

BOSTON *US, male vocal/instrumental group*   *43 wks*

5 Feb	77	**BOSTON** *Epic EPC 81611*	**11**	20 wks
9 Sep	78 ●	**DON'T LOOK BACK** *Epic EPC 86057*	**9**	10 wks
4 Apr	81	**BOSTON** *Epic EPC 32038*	**58**	2 wks
18 Oct	86	**THIRD STAGE** *MCA MCG 6017*	**37**	11 wks

The two eponymous albums are different.

Judy BOUCHER *UK, female vocalist*   *1 wk*

25 Apr	87	**CAN'T BE WITH YOU TONIGHT** *Orbitone OLP 024* ...	**95**	1 wk

BOW WOW WOW
UK, female/male vocal/instrumental group 38 wks

24 Oct 81	SEE JUNGLE! SEE JUNGLE! GO JOIN YOUR GANG YEAH CITY ALL OVER! GO APE CRAZY *RCA RCALP 0027 3000*	26	32 wks
7 Aug 82	I WANT CANDY *EMI EMC 3416*	26	6 wks

David BOWIE *UK, male vocalist* 889 wks

1 Jul	72 ●	THE RISE AND FALL OF ZIGGY STARDUST AND THE SPIDERS FROM MARS *RCA Victor SF 8287*	5	106 wks
23 Sep	72 ●	HUNKY DORY *RCA Victor SF 8244*	3	69 wks
29 Nov	72	SPACE ODDITY *RCA Victor LSP 4813*	17	37 wks
29 Nov	72	THE MAN WHO SOLD THE WORLD *RCA Victor LSP 4816*	26	22 wks
5 May	73 ★	ALADDIN SANE *RCA Victor RS 1001*	1	47 wks
3 Nov	73 ★	PIN-UPS *RCA Victor RS 1003*	1	21 wks
8 Jun	74 ★	DIAMOND DOGS *RCA Victor APLI 0576*	1	17 wks
16 Nov	74 ●	DAVID LIVE *RCA Victor APL 2 0771*	2	12 wks
5 Apr	75 ●	YOUNG AMERICANS *RCA Victor RS 1006*	2	12 wks
7 Feb	76 ●	STATION TO STATION *RCA Victor APLI 1327*	5	16 wks
12 Jun	76 ●	CHANGESONEBOWIE *RCA Victor RS 1055*	2	28 wks
29 Jan	77 ●	LOW *RCA Victor PL 12030*	2	18 wks
29 Oct	77 ●	HEROES *RCA Victor PL 12522*	3	18 wks
14 Oct	78 ●	STAGE *RCA Victor PL 02913*	5	10 wks
9 Jun	79 ●	LODGER *RCA BOW LP 1*	4	17 wks
27 Sep	80 ★	SCARY MONSTERS AND SUPER CREEPS *RCA BOW LP 2*	1	32 wks
10 Jan	81 ●	VERY BEST OF DAVID BOWIE *K-Tel NE 1111*	3	20 wks
17 Jan	81	HUNKY DORY (re-issue) *RCA International INTS 5064*	32	51 wks
31 Jan	81	THE RISE AND FALL OF ZIGGY STARDUST AND THE SPIDERS FROM MARS (re-issue) *RCA International INTS 5063*	33	62 wks
28 Nov	81	CHANGESTWOBOWIE *RCA BOW LP 3*	24	17 wks
6 Mar	82	ALADDIN SANE (re-issue) *RCA International INTS 5067*	49	24 wks
14 Jan	83	RARE *RCA PL 45406*	34	11 wks
23 Apr	83 ★	LETS DANCE *EMI America AML 3029*	1	56 wks
30 Apr	83	PIN-UPS (re-issue) *RCA International INTS 5236*	57	15 wks
30 Apr	83	THE MAN WHO SOLD THE WORLD (2nd re-issue) *RCA International INTS 5237*	64	8 wks
14 May	83	DIAMOND DOGS (re-issue) *RCA International INTS 5068*	60	14 wks
11 Jun	83	HEROES (re-issue) *RCA International INTS 5066*	75	8 wks
11 Jun	83	LOW (re-issue) *RCA International INTS 5065*	85	5 wks
20 Aug	83	GOLDEN YEARS *RCA BOWLP 4*	33	5 wks
5 Nov	83	ZIGGY STARDUST – THE MOTION PICTURE *RCA PL 84862*	17	6 wks
28 Apr	84	FAME AND FASHION (ALL TIME GREATEST HITS) *RCA PL 84919*	40	6 wks
19 May	84	LOVE YOU TILL TUESDAY *Deram BOWIE 1*	53	4 wks
6 Oct	84 ★	TONIGHT *EMI America DB 1*	1	19 wks
2 May	87 ●	NEVER LET ME DOWN *EMI America AMLS 3117*	6	16 wks
24 Mar	90 ★	CHANGESBOWIE *EMI DBTV 1*	1	29 wks
14 Apr	90	HUNKY DORY (2nd re-issue) *EMI EMC 3572*	39	2 wks
14 Apr	90	THE MAN WHO SOLD THE WORLD (2nd re-issue) *EMC 3573*	66	1 wk
14 Apr	90	SPACE ODDITY (2nd re-issue) *EMI EMC 3571*	64	1 wk
23 Jun	90	THE RISE AND FALL OF ZIGGY STARDUST AND THE SPIDERS FROM MARS (2nd re-issue) *EMC 3577*	25	4 wks
28 Jul	90	ALADDIN SANE (2nd re-issue) *EMI EMC 3579*	43	1 wk
28 Jul	90	PIN-UPS (re-issue) *EMI EMC 3580*	52	1 wk
27 Oct	90	DIAMOND DOGS (2nd re-issue) *EMI EMC 3584*	67	1 wk
4 May	91	YOUNG AMERICANS (2nd re-issue) *EMI EMD 1021*	54	1 wk
4 May	91	STATION TO STATION (2nd re-issue) *EMI EMD 1020*	57	1 wk
7 Sep	91	LOW (2nd re-issue) *EMI EMD 1027*	64	1 wk
17 Apr	93 ★	BLACK TIE WHITE NOISE *Arista 74321136972*	1	11 wks
20 Nov	93 ●	THE SINGLES COLLECTION *EMI CDEM 1512*	9†	6 wks

B
65

BOXCAR WILLIE *US, male vocalist* 12 wks

31 May	80 ●	KING OF THE ROAD *Warwick WW 5084*	5	12 wks

Max BOYCE *UK, male vocalist/comedian* · *105 wks*

5 Jul	75	**LIVE AT TREORCHY** *One Up OU 2033*	21	32 wks
1 Nov	75 ★	**WE ALL HAD DOCTORS' PAPERS** *EMI MB 101*	1	17 wks
20 Nov	76 ●	**THE INCREDIBLE PLAN** *EMI MB 102*	9	12 wks
7 Jan	78	**THE ROAD AND THE MILES** *EMI MB 103*	50	3 wks
11 Mar	78	**LIVE AT TREORCHY (re-issue)** *One Up OU 54043*	42	6 wks
27 May	78 ●	**I KNOW COS I WAS THERE** *EMI MAX 1001*	6	14 wks
13 Oct	79	**NOT THAT I'M BIASED** *EMI MAX 1002*	27	13 wks
15 Nov	80	**ME AND BILLY WILLIAMS** *EMI MAX 1003*	37	8 wks

BOY GEORGE *UK, male vocalist* · *11 wks*

27 Jun	87	**SOLD** *Virgin V 2430*	29	6 wks
2 Oct	93	**AT WORST ... THE BEST OF BOY GEORGE AND**		
		CULTURE CLUB *Virgin VTCD 19★*	24	5 wks

★ *Boy George and Culture Club.*
See also Jesus Loves You.

BOY MEETS GIRL *US, male/female vocal/instrumental duo* · *1 wk*

4 Feb	89	**REEL LIFE** *RCA PL 88414*	74	1 wk

BOYS *UK, male vocal/instrumental group* · *1 wk*

1 Oct	77	**THE BOYS** *NEMS NEL 6001*	50	1 wk

BOYZ II MEN *US, male vocal group* · *18 wks*

31 Oct	92 ●	**COOLEYHIGHHARMONY** *Motown 5300892*	7	18 wks

BRAD *US, male vocal/instrumental group* · *1 wk*

15 May	93	**SHAME** *Epic 4735962*	72	1 wk

Paul BRADY *Ireland, male vocalist/instrumentalist – guitar* · *1 wk*

6 Apr	91	**TRICK OR TREAT** *Fontana 8484541*	62	1 wk

Billy BRAGG *UK, male vocalist* · *77 wks*

21 Jan	84	**LIFE'S A RIOT WITH SPY VS SPY**		
		Go! Discs UTILITY UTIL 1	30	30 wks
20 Oct	84	**BREWING UP WITH BILLY BRAGG**		
		Go! Discs AGOLP 4	16	21 wks
4 Oct	86 ●	**TALKING WITH THE TAXMAN ABOUT POETRY**		
		Go! Discs AGOLP 6	8	8 wks
13 Jun	87	**BACK TO BASICS** *Go! Discs AGOLP 8*	37	4 wks
1 Oct	88	**WORKERS PLAYTIME** *Go! Discs AGOLP 15*	17	4 wks
12 May	90	**THE INTERNATIONALE** *Utility UTIL 11*	34	4 wks
28 Sep	91 ●	**DON'T TRY THIS AT HOME** *Go! Discs 8282791*	8	6 wks

Wilfred BRAMBELL and Harry H. CORBETT
UK, male comic duo · *34 wks*

23 Mar	63 ●	**STEPTOE AND SON** *Pye NPL 18081*	4	28 wks
11 Mar	64	**STEPTOE AND SON** *Pye GGL 0217*	14	5 wks
14 Mar	64	**MORE JUNK** *Pye NPL 18090*	19	1 wk

First two albums are different.

David Bowie first got to the head of the chart in 1973. *(Pictorial Press)*

Boyz II Men won Best Rhythm and Blues Vocal, Duo or Group, at the 34th annual Grammy Awards. *(Pictorial Press)*

BRAND NEW HEAVIES
US, male/female vocal/instrumental group   18 wks

| 14 Mar | 92 | **BRAND NEW HEAVIES** London 8283002 .... | 25 | 16 wks |
| 5 Sep | 92 | **HEAVY RHYME EXPERIENCE** Acid Jazz 8283352 ...... | 38 | 2 wks |

BRAND X UK, male vocal/instrumental group   6 wks

| 21 May | 77 | **MOROCCAN ROLL** Charisma CAS 1126 .... | 37 | 5 wks |
| 11 Sep | 82 | **IS THERE ANYTHING ABOUT?** CBS 85967 .... | 93 | 1 wk |

Laura BRANIGAN US, female vocalist   18 wks

| 18 Aug | 84 | **SELF CONTROL** Atlantic 780147 .... | 16 | 14 wks |
| 24 Aug | 85 | **HOLD ME** Atlantic 78–1265–1 .... | 64 | 4 wks |

BRASS CONSTRUCTION
US, male vocal/instrumental group   12 wks

| 20 Mar | 76 ● | **BRASS CONSTRUCTION** United Artists UAS 29923 ..... | 9 | 11 wks |
| 30 Jun | 84 | **RENEGADES** Capitol EJ 24 0160 .... | 94 | 1 wk |

BREAD US, male vocal/instrumental group   179 wks

26 Sep	70	**ON THE WATERS** Elektra 2469–005	34	5 wks
18 Mar	72 ●	**BABY I'M A WANT-YOU** Elektra K 42100	9	19 wks
28 Oct	72 ●	**BEST OF BREAD** Elektra K 42115	7	100 wks
27 Jul	74	**THE BEST OF BREAD VOL. 2** Elektra K 42161	48	1 wk
29 Jan	77	**LOST WITHOUT YOUR LOVE** Elektra K 52044	17	6 wks
5 Nov	77 ★	**THE SOUND OF BREAD** Elektra K 52062	1	46 wks
28 Nov	87	**THE VERY BEST OF BREAD** Telstar STAR 2303	84	2 wks

B
68

BREAK MACHINE US, male vocal/dance group   16 wks

| 9 Jun | 84 | **BREAK MACHINE** Record Shack SOHO LP 3 .... | 17 | 16 wks |

BREATHE UK, male vocal/instrumental group   5 wks

| 8 Oct | 88 | **ALL THAT JAZZ** Siren SRNLP 12 .... | 22 | 5 wks |

BREEDERS US, female/male vocal/instrumental group   8 wks

| 9 Jun | 90 | **POD** 4AD CAD 0006 .... | 22 | 3 wks |
| 11 Sep | 93 ● | **LAST SPLASH** 4AD CAD 3014CD .... | 5 | 5 wks |

Maire BRENNAN Ireland, female vocalist   2 wks

| 13 Jun | 92 | **MAIRE** RCA PD 75358 .... | 53 | 2 wks |

Adrian BRETT UK, male instrumentalist – flute   11 wks

| 10 Nov | 79 | **ECHOES OF GOLD** Warwick WW 5062 .... | 19 | 11 wks |

Paul BRETT UK, male instrumentalist – guitar   7 wks

| 19 Jul | 80 | **ROMANTIC GUITAR** K-Tel ONE 1079 .... | 24 | 7 wks |

Edie BRICKELL and the NEW BOHEMIANS
US, female/male vocal/instrumental group   *18 wks*

4 Feb 89	**SHOOTING RUBBERBANDS AT THE STARS**		
	Geffen WX 215	**25**	17 wks
10 Nov 90	**GHOST OF A DOG** *Geffen WX 386*	**63**	1 wk

BRIGHOUSE AND RASTRICK BRASS BAND
UK, male brass band   *11 wks*

28 Jan 78 ●	**FLORAL DANCE** *Logo 1001*	**10**	11 wks

Sarah BRIGHTMAN   *UK, female vocalist*   *6 wks*

17 Jun 89	**THE SONGS THAT GOT AWAY** *Really Useful 839116 1* .	**48**	2 wks
8 Aug 92	**AMIGOS PARA SIEMPRE** *East West 4509902562★*	**53**	4 wks

★ *José Carreras and Sarah Brightman.*
See also Andrew Lloyd Webber.

BRILLIANT   *UK, male/female vocal/instrumental group*   *1 wk*

20 Sep 86	**KISS THE LIPS OF LIFE** *Food BRILL 1*	**83**	1 wk

Johnny BRISTOL   *US, male vocalist*   *7 wks*

5 Oct 74	**HANG ON IN THERE BABY** *MGM 2315 303*	**12**	7 wks

BRODSKY QUARTET – *See Elvis Costello and the ATTRACTIONS*

June BRONHILL and Thomas ROUND
Australia/UK, female/male vocal duo   *1 wk*

18 Jun 60	**LILAC TIME** *HMV CLP 1248*	**17**	1 wk

BRONSKI BEAT   *UK, male vocal/instrumental group*   *65 wks*

20 Oct 84 ●	**THE AGE OF CONSENT** *Forbidden Fruit BITLP 1*	**4**	53 wks
21 Sep 85	**HUNDREDS AND THOUSANDS** *Forbidden Fruit BITLP 2*	**24**	6 wks
10 May 86	**TRUTHDARE DOUBLEDARE** *Forbidden Fruit BITLP 3* ...	**18**	6 wks

Elkie BROOKS   *UK, female vocalist*   *212 wks*

18 Jun 77	**TWO DAYS AWAY** *A & M AMLH 68409*	**16**	20 wks
13 May 78	**SHOOTING STAR** *A & M AMLH 64695*	**20**	13 wks
13 Oct 79	**LIVE AND LEARN** *A & M AMLH 68509*	**34**	6 wks
14 Nov 81 ●	**PEARLS** *A & M ELK 1981*	**2**	79 wks
13 Nov 82 ●	**PEARLS II** *A & M ELK 1982*	**5**	25 wks
14 Jul 84	**MINUTES** *A & M AML 68565*	**35**	7 wks
8 Dec 84	**SCREEN GEMS** *EMI SCREEN 1*	**35**	11 wks
6 Dec 86 ●	**NO MORE THE FOOL** *Legend LMA 1*	**5**	23 wks
27 Dec 86 ●	**THE VERY BEST OF ELKIE BROOKS** *Telstar STAR 2284*	**10**	18 wks
11 Jun 88	**BOOKBINDER'S KID** *Legend LMA 3*	**57**	3 wks
18 Nov 89	**INSPIRATIONS** *Telstar STAR 2354*	**58**	3 wks
13 Mar 93	**ROUND MIDNIGHT** *Castle Communications CTVCD 113* ..	**27**	4 wks

Garth BROOKS   *US, male vocalist*   *2 wks*

15 Feb 92	**ROPIN' THE WIND** *Capitol CDESTU 2162*	**41**	2 wks'

Nigel BROOKS SINGERS
UK, male/female vocal choir   *17 wks*

29 Nov 75 ● SONGS OF JOY *K-Tel NE 706*	**5**	16 wks
5 Jun 76 **20 ALL TIME EUROVISION FAVOURITES** *K-Tel NE 712*	**44**	1 wk

BROS   *UK, male vocal/instrumental duo*   *69 wks*

9 Apr 88 ● **PUSH** *CBS 460629 1*	**2**	54 wks
28 Oct 89 ● **THE TIME** *CBS 465918 1*	**4**	13 wks
12 Oct 91 **CHANGING FACES** *Columbia 4688171*	**18**	2 wks

Act was a group for first album.

BROTHER BEYOND
UK, male vocal/instrumental group   *24 wks*

26 Nov 88 ● **GET EVEN** *Parlophone PCS 7327*	**9**	23 wks
25 Nov 89 **TRUST** *Parlophone PCS 7337*	**60**	1 wk

BROTHERHOOD OF MAN
UK, male/female vocal group   *40 wks*

24 Apr 76 **LOVE AND KISSES FROM** *Pye NSPL 18490*	**20**	8 wks
12 Aug 78 **B FOR BROTHERHOOD** *Pye NSPL 18567*	**18**	9 wks
7 Oct 78 ● **BROTHERHOOD OF MAN** *K-Tel BML 7980*	**6**	15 wks
29 Nov 80 **SING 20 NUMBER ONE HITS** *Warwick WW 5087*	**14**	8 wks

B
70

BROTHERS JOHNSON
US, male vocal/instrumental duo   *22 wks*

19 Aug 78 **BLAM!!** *A & M AMLH 64714*	**48**	8 wks
23 Feb 80 **LIGHT UP THE NIGHT** *A & M AMLK 63716*	**22**	12 wks
18 Jul 81 **WINNERS** *A & M AMLK 63724*	**42**	2 wks

Edgar BROUGHTON BAND
UK, male vocal/instrumental group   *6 wks*

20 Jun 70 **SING BROTHER SING** *Harvest SHVL 772*	**18**	4 wks
5 Jun 71 **THE EDGAR BROUGHTON BAND** *Harvest SHVL 791* ..	**28**	2 wks

Crazy World Of Arthur BROWN
UK, male vocal/instrumental group   *16 wks*

6 Jul 68 ● **CRAZY WORLD OF ARTHUR BROWN** *Track 612005* ..	**2**	16 wks

Bobby BROWN   *US, male vocalist*   *62 wks*

28 Jan 89 ● **DON'T BE CRUEL** *MCA MCF 3425*	**3**	41 wks
5 Aug 89 **KING OF STAGE** *MCA MCL 1886*	**40**	6 wks
2 Dec 89 **DANCE! . . . YA KNOW IT!** *MCA MCG 6074*	**26**	10 wks
5 Sep 92 **BOBBY** *MCA MCAD 10695*	**11**	5 wks

Dennis BROWN   *Jamaica, male vocalist*   *6 wks*

26 Jun 82 **LOVE HAS FOUND ITS WAY** *A & M AMLH 64886*	**72**	6 wks

James BROWN *US, male vocalist*　　　*51 wks*

18 Oct	86	**GRAVITY** *Scotti Bros. SCT 57108*	**85**	3 wks
2 Jan	88	**BEST OF JAMES BROWN – GODFATHER OF SOUL**		
		K-Tel NE 1376	**17**	21 wks
25 Jun	88	**I'M REAL** *Scotti Brothers POLD 5230*	**27**	5 wks
16 Nov	91	**SEX MACHINE – THE VERY BEST OF JAMES BROWN**		
		Polydor 8458281	**19**	22 wks

Joe BROWN *UK, male vocalist/instrumentalist – guitar*　　*47 wks*

1 Sep	62	● **A PICTURE OF YOU** *Pye Golden Guinea GGL 0146*	**3**	39 wks
25 May	63	**JOE BROWN – LIVE** *Piccadilly NPL 38006*	**14**	8 wks

Sam BROWN *UK, female vocalist*　　*30 wks*

11 Mar	89	● **STOP** *A & M AMA 5195*	**4**	18 wks
14 Apr	90	**APRIL MOON** *A & M AMA 9014*	**38**	12 wks

Jackson BROWNE *US, male vocalist*　　*36 wks*

4 Dec	76	**THE PRETENDER** *Asylum K 53048*	**26**	5 wks
21 Jan	78	**RUNNING ON EMPTY** *Asylum K 53070*	**28**	7 wks
12 Jul	80	**HOLD OUT** *Asylum K 52226*	**44**	5 wks
13 Aug	83	**LAWYERS IN LOVE** *Asylum 96–0268–1*	**37**	7 wks
8 Mar	86	**LIVES IN THE BALANCE** *Asylum EKT 31*	**36**	7 wks
17 Jun	89	**WORLD IN MOTION** *Elektra EKT 50*	**39**	2 wks
6 Nov	93	**I'M ALIVE** *Elektra 7559615242*	**35**	3 wks

Dave BRUBECK *US, male instrumental group*　　*17 wks*

25 Jun	60	**TIME OUT** *Fontana TFL 5085★*	**11**	1 wk
7 Apr	62	**TIME FURTHER OUT** *Fontana TFL 5161*	**12**	16 wks

★ *Dave Brubeck Quartet.*

Jack BRUCE *UK, male vocalist/instrumentalist – bass*　　*9 wks*

27 Sep	69	● **SONGS FOR A TAILOR** *Polydor 583–058*	**6**	9 wks

BRUFORD – *See ANDERSON BRUFORD WAKEMAN HOWE*

Peabo BRYSON – *See Roberta FLACK*

Lindsey BUCKINGHAM *US, male vocalist*　　*1 wk*

8 Aug	92	**OUT OF THE CRADLE** *Mercury 5126582*	**51**	1 wk

BUCKS FIZZ *UK, male/female vocal group*　　*80 wks*

8 Aug	81	**BUCKS FIZZ** *RCA RCALP 5050*	**14**	28 wks
18 May	82	● **ARE YOU READY?** *RCA RCALP 8000*	**10**	23 wks
19 Mar	83	**HAND CUT** *RCA RCALP 6100*	**17**	13 wks
3 Dec	83	**GREATEST HITS** *RCA RCA PL 70022*	**25**	13 wks
24 Nov	84	**I HEAR TALK** *RCA PL 70397*	**66**	2 wks
13 Dec	86	**THE WRITING ON THE WALL** *Polydor POHL 30*	**89**	1 wk

Harold BUDD/Liz FRASER/Robin GUTHRIE/ Simon RAYMOND
UK, male/female vocal/instrumental group　　*2 wks*

22 Nov	86	**THE MOON AND THE MELODIES** *4AD CAD 611*	**46**	2 wks

B

BUDGIE UK, male vocal/instrumental group 10 wks

8 Jun	74	**IN FOR THE KILL** MCA MCF 2546	29	3 wks
27 Sep	75	**BANDOLIER** MCA MCF 2723	36	4 wks
31 Oct	81	**NIGHT FLIGHT** RCA RCALP 6003	68	2 wks
23 Oct	82	**DELIVER US FROM EVIL** RCA RCALP 6054	62	1 wk

BUFFALO TOM US, male vocal/instrumental group 4 wks

14 Mar	92	**LET ME COME OVER** Situation Two SITU 36CD	49	1 wk
9 Oct	93	**(BIG RED LETTER DAY)** Beggars Banquet BBQCD 142 ...	17	3 wks

BUGGLES UK, male vocal/instrumental duo 6 wks

16 Feb	80	**THE AGE OF PLASTIC** Island ILPS 9585	27	6 wks

BUNNYMEN – See ECHO and the BUNNYMEN

Eric BURDON and WAR
UK, male vocalist and US, male vocal/instrumental group 2 wks

3 Oct	70	**ERIC BURDON DECLARES WAR** Polydor 2310–041	50	2 wks

Jean-Jacques BURNEL
UK, male vocalist/instrumentalist – bass guitar 10 wks

21 Apr	79	**EUROMAN COMETH** United Artists UAG 30214	40	5 wks
3 Dec	83	**FIRE AND WATER** Epic EPC 25707★	40	5 wks

★ Dave Greenfield and Jean-Jacques Burnel.

B
72

Kate BUSH UK, female vocalist 260 wks

11 Mar	78 ●	**THE KICK INSIDE** EMI EMC 3223	3	70 wks
25 Nov	78 ●	**LIONHEART** EMI EMA 787	6	36 wks
20 Sep	80 ★	**NEVER FOR EVER** EMI EMA 7964	1	23 wks
25 Sep	82 ●	**THE DREAMING** EMI EMC 3419	3	9 wks
28 Sep	85 ★	**HOUNDS OF LOVE** EMI KAB 1	1	51 wks
22 Nov	86 ★	**THE WHOLE STORY** EMI KBTV 1	1	44 wks
28 Oct	89 ●	**THE SENSUAL WORLD** EMI EMD 1010	2	20 wks
13 Nov	93 ●	**THE RED SHOES** EMI CDEMD 1047	2†	7 wks

Jonathan BUTLER
South Africa, male vocalist/instrumentalist – guitar 14 wks

12 Sep	87	**JONATHAN BUTLER** Jive HIP 46	12	11 wks
4 Feb	89	**MORE THAN FRIENDS** Jive HIP 70	29	3 wks

BUTTHOLE SURFERS
UK, male vocal/instrumental group 2 wks

16 Mar	91	**PIOUHGD** Rough Trade R 20812601	68	1 wk
3 Apr	93	**INDEPENDENT WORM SALOON** Capitol CDEST 2192 .	73	1 wk

BUZZCOCKS UK, male vocal/instrumental group 23 wks

25 Mar	78	**ANOTHER MUSIC IN A DIFFERENT KITCHEN**		
		United Artists UAG 30159	15	11 wks
7 Oct	78	**LOVE BITES** United Artists UAG 30184	13	9 wks
6 Oct	79	**A DIFFERENT KIND OF TENSION**		
		United Artists UAG 30260	26	3 wks

BY ALL MEANS *US, male/female vocal group*　　　*1 wk*

16 Jul	88	**BY ALL MEANS** *Fourth & Broadway BRLP 520*	80	1 wk

Max BYGRAVES *UK, male vocalist*　　　*176 wks*

23 Sep	72 ●	**SING ALONG WITH MAX** *Pye NSPL 18361*	4	44 wks
2 Dec	72	**SING ALONG WITH MAX VOL. 2** *Pye NSPL 18383*	11	23 wks
5 May	73 ●	**SINGALONGAMAX VOL. 3** *Pye NSPL 18401*	5	30 wks
29 Sep	73 ●	**SINGALONGAMAX VOL. 4** *Pye NSPL 18410*	7	12 wks
15 Dec	73	**SINGALONGPARTY SONG** *Pye NSPL 18419*	15	6 wks
12 Oct	74	**YOU MAKE ME FEEL LIKE SINGING A SONG** *Pye NSPL 18436*	39	3 wks
7 Dec	74	**SINGALONGAXMAS** *Pye NSPL 18439*	21	6 wks
13 Nov	76 ●	**100 GOLDEN GREATS** *Ronco RTDX 2019*	3	21 wks
28 Oct	78	**LINGALONGAMAX** *Ronco RPL 2033*	39	5 wks
16 Dec	78	**THE SONG AND DANCE MEN** *Pye NSPL 18574*	67	1 wk
19 Aug	89 ●	**SINGALONGAWARYEARS** *Parkfield Music PMLP 5001* ...	5	19 wks
25 Nov	89	**SINGALONGAWARYEARS VOLUME 2** *Parkfield Music PMLP 5006*	33	6 wks

Charlie BYRD – *See Stan GETZ and Charlie BYRD*

Donald BYRD *US, male vocalist/instrumentalist – trumpet*　　　*3 wks*

10 Oct	81	**LOVE BYRD** *Elektra K 52301*	70	3 wks

BYRDS *US, male vocal/instrumental group*　　　*42 wks*

28 Aug	65 ●	**MR. TAMBOURINE MAN** *CBS BPG 62571*	7	12 wks
9 Apr	66	**TURN, TURN, TURN** *CBS BPG 62652*	11	5 wks
1 Oct	66	**5TH DIMENSION** *CBS BPG 62783*	27	2 wks
22 Apr	67	**YOUNGER THAN YESTERDAY** *CBS SBPG 62988* ...	37	4 wks
4 May	68	**THE NOTORIOUS BYRD BROTHERS** *CBS 63169*	12	11 wks
24 May	69	**DR. BYRDS AND MR. HYDE** *CBS 63545*	15	1 wk
14 Feb	70	**BALLAD OF EASY RIDER** *CBS 63795*	41	1 wk
28 Nov	70	**UNTITLED** *CBS 66253*	11	4 wks
14 Apr	73	**BYRDS** *Asylum SYLA 8754*	31	1 wk
19 May	73	**HISTORY OF THE BYRDS** *CBS 68242*	47	1 wk

David BYRNE *UK, male vocalist*　　　*15 wks*

21 Feb	81	**MY LIFE IN THE BUSH OF GHOSTS** *Polydor EGLP 48★*	29	8 wks
21 Oct	89	**REI MOMO** *Warner Bros. WX 319*	52	2 wks
14 Mar	92	**UH-OH** *Luaka Bop 7599267992*	26	5 wks

★ *Brian Eno and David Byrne.*

C&C MUSIC FACTORY/CLIVILLES and COLE
US, male production duo; US, male/female vocal/instrumental group　　　*14 wks*

9 Feb	91 ●	**GONNA MAKE YOU SWEAT** *Columbia 4678141★*	8	13 wks
28 Mar	92	**GREATEST REMIXES VOL. 1** *Columbia 4694462★★*	45	1 wk

★ *C&C Music Factory.*
★★ *Clivilles and Cole.*

Belinda Carlisle is shown in the autumn of
1989, when her Runaway Horses *album*
was galloping into the top five. *(Pictorial Press)*

The only hit album by *Charlene* was wisely
titled after her only hit single, a number one.
(Motown Records)

Kate Bush has hit the top ten with each of
her eight releases.

Montserrat CABALLE *Spain, female vocalist*　　　*11 wks*

22 Oct 88	**BARCELONA** *Polydor POLH 44★*	15	8 wks
8 Aug 92	**FROM THE OFFICIAL BARCELONA GAMES**		
	CEREMONY *RCA Red Seal 09026612042★★*	41	3 wks

★ Freddie Mercury and Montserrat Caballe.
★★ Placido Domingo, José Carreras and Montserrat Caballe.

CABARET VOLTAIRE
UK, male vocal/instrumental group　　　*11 wks*

26 Jun 82	**2 X 45** *Rough Trade ROUGH 42*	98	1 wk
13 Aug 83	**THE CRACKDOWN** *Some Bizzare CV 1*	31	5 wks
10 Nov 84	**MICRO-PHONIES** *Some Bizzare CV 2*	69	1 wk
3 Aug 85	**DRINKING GASOLINE** *Some Bizzare CVM 1*	71	2 wks
26 Oct 85	**THE COVENANT, THE SWORD AND THE ARM OF**		
	THE LORD *Some Bizzare CV 3*	57	2 wks

CACTUS WORLD NEWS
Ireland, male vocal/instrumental group　　　*2 wks*

24 May 86	**URBAN BEACHES** *MCA MCG 6005*	56	2 wks

J.J. CALE *US, male vocalist/instrumentalist – guitar*　　　*24 wks*

2 Oct 76	**TROUBADOUR** *Island ISA 5011*	53	1 wk
25 Aug 79	**5** *Shelter ISA 5018*	40	6 wks
21 Feb 81	**SHADES** *Shelter ISA 5021*	44	7 wks
20 Mar 82	**GRASSHOPPER** *Shelter IFA 5022*	36	5 wks
24 Sep 83	**#8** *Mercury MERL 22*	47	3 wks
26 Sep 92	**NUMBER 10** *Silvertone ORECD 523*	58	2 wks

John CALE – *See Lou REED*

Maria CALLAS *Greece, female vocalist*　　　*7 wks*

20 Jun 87	**THE MARIA CALLAS COLLECTION** *Stylus SMR 732* ..	50	7 wks

CAMEL *UK, male vocal/instrumental group*　　　*47 wks*

24 May 75	**THE SNOW GOOSE** *Decca SKL 5207*	22	13 wks
17 Apr 76	**MOON MADNESS** *Decca TXS 115*	15	6 wks
17 Sep 77	**RAIN DANCES** *Decca TXS 124*	20	8 wks
14 Oct 78	**BREATHLESS** *Decca TXS 132*	26	1 wk
27 Oct 79	**I CAN SEE YOUR HOUSE FROM HERE** *Decca TXS 137*	45	3 wks
31 Jan 81	**NUDE** *Decca SKL 5323*	34	7 wks
15 May 82	**THE SINGLE FACTOR** *Decca SKL 5328*	57	5 wks
21 Apr 84	**STATIONARY TRAVELLER** *Decca SKL 5334*	57	4 wks

CAMEO *US, male vocal/instrumental group*　　　*47 wks*

10 Aug 85	**SINGLE LIFE** *Club JABH 11*	66	12 wks
18 Oct 86 ●	**WORD UP** *Club JABH 19*	7	34 wks
26 Nov 88	**MACHISMO** *Club 836002 1*	86	1 wk

Glen CAMPBELL *US, male vocalist*　　　*184 wks*

31 Jan 70	**GLEN CAMPBELL LIVE** *Capitol SB 21444*	16	14 wks
28 Feb 70	**BOBBIE GENTRY AND GLEN CAMPBELL**		
	Capitol ST 2928★	50	1 wk
30 May 70	**TRY A LITTLE KINDNESS** *Capitol ESW 389*	37	10 wks

C
75

12 Dec 70	**THE GLEN CAMPBELL ALBUM** *Capitol ST 22493*	**16**	5 wks
27 Nov 71 ●	**GREATEST HITS** *Capitol ST 21885*	**8**	113 wks
25 Oct 75	**RHINESTONE COWBOY** *Capitol E-SW 11430*	**38**	9 wks
20 Nov 76 ★	**20 GOLDEN GREATS** *Capitol EMTV 2*	**1**	27 wks
23 Apr 77	**SOUTHERN NIGHTS** *Capitol E-ST 11601*	**51**	1 wk
22 Jul 89	**THE COMPLETE GLEN CAMPBELL** *Stylus SMR 979* ...	**47**	4 wks

★ *Bobbie Gentry and Glen Campbell.*

CANNED HEAT US, *male vocal/instrumental group* 40 wks

29 Jun 68 ●	**BOOGIE WITH CANNED HEAT** *Liberty LBL 83103*	**5**	21 wks
14 Feb 70 ●	**CANNED HEAT COOKBOOK** *Liberty LBS 83303*	**8**	12 wks
4 Jul 70	**CANNED HEAT '70 CONCERT** *Liberty LBS 83333*	**15**	3 wks
10 Oct 70	**FUTURE BLUES** *Liberty LBS 83364*	**27**	4 wks

Freddy CANNON US, *male vocalist* 11 wks

27 Feb 60 ★	**THE EXPLOSIVE FREDDY CANNON** *Top Rank 25/108* .	**1**	11 wks

CAPERCAILLIE
UK/Ireland, *male/female vocal/instrumental group* 3 wks

25 Sep 93	**SECRET PEOPLE** *Arista 74321162742*	**40**	3 wks

CAPTAIN SENSIBLE UK, *male vocalist* 3 wks

11 Sep 82	**WOMEN AND CAPTAIN FIRST** *A & M AMLH 68548* ..	**64**	3 wks

CAPTAIN and TENNILLE
US, *male instrumentalist – keyboards and female vocalist* 6 wks

22 Mar 80	**MAKE YOUR MOVE** *Casablanca CAL 2060*	**33**	6 wks

CAPTAIN BEEFHEART and his MAGIC BAND
US, *male vocal/instrumental group* 16 wks

6 Dec 69	**TROUT MASK REPLICA** *Straight STS 1053*	**21**	1 wk
23 Jan 71	**LICK MY DECALS OFF BABY** *Straight STS 1063*	**20**	10 wks
29 May 71	**MIRROR MAN** *Buddah 2365 002*	**49**	1 wk
19 Feb 72	**THE SPOTLIGHT KID** *Reprise K 44162*	**44**	2 wks
18 Sep 82	**ICE CREAM FOR CROW** *Virgin V 2337*	**90**	2 wks

CARAVAN UK, *male vocal/instrumental group* 2 wks

30 Aug 75	**CUNNING STUNTS** *Decca SKL 5210*	**50**	1 wk
15 May 76	**BLIND DOG AT ST. DUNSTAN'S** *BTM BTM 1007*	**53**	1 wk

CARCASS UK, *male vocal/instrumental group* 1 wk

6 Nov 93	**HEARTWORK** *Earache MOSH 097CD*	**67**	1 wk

Mariah CAREY US, *female vocalist* 102 wks

15 Sep 90 ●	**MARIAH CAREY** *CBS 4668151*	**6**	36 wks
26 Oct 91 ●	**EMOTIONS** *Columbia 4688511*	**4**	40 wks
18 Jul 92 ●	**MTV UNPLUGGED EP** *Columbia 4718692*	**3**	10 wks
11 Sep 93 ★	**MUSIC BOX** *Columbia 4742702*	**1†**	16 wks

Since her immediate and uninterrupted success began in 1990 **Mariah Carey** has been meeting a galaxy of fellow stars, including Gladys Knight, Michael Bolton, Gloria Estefan and James Brown. (Pictorial Press)

Belinda CARLISLE US, female vocalist   136 wks

2 Jan 88 ● HEAVEN ON EARTH *Virgin V 2496*	4	54 wks
4 Nov 89 ● RUNAWAY HORSES *Virgin V 2599*	4	39 wks
26 Oct 91 ● LIVE YOUR LIFE BE FREE *Virgin V 2680*	7	16 wks
19 Sep 92 ★ THE BEST OF BELINDA VOL. 1 *Virgin BELCD 1*	1	22 wks
23 Oct 93 ● REAL *Virgin CDV 2725*	9	5 wks

CARMEL UK, female/male vocal/instrumental group   11 wks

1 Oct 83 CARMEL *Red Flame RFM 9*	94	2 wks
24 Mar 84 THE DRUM IS EVERYTHING *London SH 8555*	19	8 wks
27 Sep 86 THE FALLING *London LONLP 17*	88	1 wk

Eric CARMEN US, male vocalist   1 wk

15 May 76 ERIC CARMEN *Arista ARTY 120*	58	1 wk

Kim CARNES US, female vocalist   16 wks

20 Jun 81 MISTAKEN IDENTITY *EMI America AML 3018*	26	16 wks

CARPENTERS US, male/female vocal/instrumental duo   564 wks

23 Jan 71 CLOSE TO YOU *A & M AMLS 998*	23	82 wks
30 Oct 71 THE CARPENTERS *A & M AMLS 63502*	12	36 wks
15 Apr 72 TICKET TO RIDE *A & M AMLS 64342*	20	3 wks
23 Sep 72 A SONG FOR YOU *A & M AMLS 63511*	13	37 wks
7 Jul 73 ● NOW AND THEN *A & M AMLH 63519*	2	65 wks
26 Jan 74 ★ THE SINGLES 1969–1973 *A & M AMLH 63601*	1	125 wks
28 Jun 75 ★ HORIZON *A & M AMLK 64530*	1	27 wks
23 Aug 75 TICKET TO RIDE (re-issue) *Hamlet AMLP 8001*	35	2 wks
3 Jul 76 ● A KIND OF HUSH *A & M AMLK 64581*	3	15 wks
8 Jan 77 LIVE AT THE PALLADIUM *A & M AMLS 68403*	28	3 wks
8 Oct 77 PASSAGE *A & M AMLK 64703*	12	12 wks
2 Dec 78 ● THE SINGLES 1974–1978 *A & M AMLT 19748*	2	27 wks
27 Jun 81 MADE IN AMERICA *A & M AMLK 63723*	12	10 wks
15 Oct 83 ● VOICE OF THE HEART *A & M AMLX 64954*	6	19 wks
20 Oct 84 ● YESTERDAY ONCE MORE *EMI/A & M SING 1*	10	26 wks
13 Jan 90 LOVELINES *A & M AMA 3931*	73	1 wk
31 Mar 90 ★ ONLY YESTERDAY *A & M AMA 1990*	1	74 wks

Vikki CARR US, female vocalist   12 wks

22 Jul 67 WAY OF TODAY *Liberty SLBY 1331*	31	2 wks
12 Aug 67 IT MUST BE HIM *Liberty LBS 83037*	12	10 wks

José CARRERAS Spain, male vocalist   101 wks

1 Oct 88 JOSE CARRERAS COLLECTION *Stylus SMR 860*	90	4 wks
23 Dec 89 JOSE CARRERAS SINGS ANDREW LLOYD WEBBER *WEA WX 325*	42	6 wks
1 Sep 90 ★ IN CONCERT *Decca 4304331★*	1	70 wks
23 Feb 91 THE ESSENTIAL JOSE CARRERAS *Philips 4326921*	24	9 wks
6 Apr 91 HOLLYWOOD GOLDEN CLASSICS *East West WX 416*	47	3 wks
8 Aug 92 FROM THE BARCELONA GAMES CEREMONY *RCA Red Seal 09026612042★★*	41	3 wks
8 Aug 92 AMIGOS PARA SIEMPRE *East West 4509902562★★★*	53	4 wks
16 Oct 93 WITH A SONG IN MY HEART *Teldec 4509923692*	73	1 wk
25 Dec 93 CHRISTMAS IN VIENNA *Sony Classical SK 53358★★★★*	71†	1 wk

★ *Luciano Pavarotti, Placido Domingo and José Carreras.*
★★ *Placido Domingo, José Carreras and Montserrat Caballé.*
★★★ *José Carreras and Sarah Brightman.*
★★★★ *Placido Domingo, Diana Ross and José Carreras.*

Dina CARROLL UK, *female vocalist* 46 wks

30 Jan	93 ● SO CLOSE *A & M 5400342*	2†	46 wks

Jasper CARROTT UK, *male comedian* 66 wks

18 Oct	75 ● RABBITS ON AND ON *DJM DJLPS 462*	10	7 wks
6 Nov	76 CARROTT IN NOTTS *DJM DJF 20482*	56	1 wk
25 Nov	78 THE BEST OF JASPER CARROTT *DJM DJF 20549*	38	13 wks
20 Oct	79 THE UNRECORDED JASPER CARROTT		
	DJM DJF 20560	19	15 wks
19 Sep	81 BEAT THE CARROTT *DJM DJF 20575*	13	16 wks
25 Dec	82 CARROTT'S LIB *DJM DJF 20580*	80	3 wks
19 Nov	83 THE STUN (CARROTT TELLS ALL) *DJF 20582*	57	8 wks
7 Feb	87 COSMIC CARROTT *Portrait LAUGH 1*	66	3 wks

CARS US, *male vocal/instrumental group* 72 wks

2 Dec	78 CARS *Elektra K 52088*	29	15 wks
7 Jul	79 CANDY-O *Elektra K 52148*	30	6 wks
6 Oct	84 HEARTBEAT CITY *Elektra 960296*	25	30 wks
9 Nov	85 THE CARS GREATEST HITS *Elektra EKT 25*	27	19 wks
5 Sep	87 DOOR TO DOOR *Elektra EKT 42*	72	2 wks

CARTER – THE UNSTOPPABLE SEX MACHINE
UK, *male vocal/instrumental duo* 32 wks

2 Mar	91 ● 30 SOMETHING *Rough Trade R2011 2702*	8	9 wks
21 Sep	91 101 DAMNATIONS *Big Cat ABB 101*	29	6 wks
1 Feb	92 30 SOMETHING (re-issue) *Chrysalis CHR 1897*	21	4 wks
16 May	92 ★ 1992 – THE LOVE ALBUM *Chrysalis CCD 1946*	1	9 wks
18 Sep	93 ● POST HISTORIC MONSTERS *Chrysalis CDCHR 7090* ..	5	4 wks

Johnny CASH US, *male vocalist* 285 wks

23 Jul	66 EVERYBODY LOVES A NUT *CBS BPG 62717*	28	1 wk
4 May	68 FROM SEA TO SHINING SEA *CBS 62972*	40	1 wk
6 Jul	68 OLD GOLDEN THROAT *CBS 63316*	37	2 wks
24 Aug	68 ● FOLSOM PRISON *CBS 63308*	8	53 wks
23 Aug	69 ● JOHNNY CASH AT SAN QUENTIN *CBS 63629*	2	114 wks
4 Oct	69 GREATEST HITS VOL. 1 *CBS 63062*	23	25 wks
7 Mar	70 ● HELLO I'M JOHNNY CASH *CBS 63796*	6	16 wks
15 Aug	70 ● WORLD OF JOHNNY CASH *CBS 66237*	5	31 wks
12 Dec	70 THE JOHNNY CASH SHOW *CBS 64089*	18	6 wks
18 Sep	71 MAN IN BLACK *CBS 64331*	18	7 wks
13 Nov	71 JOHNNY CASH *Hallmark SHM 739*	43	2 wks
20 May	72 ● A THING CALLED LOVE *CBS 64898*	8	11 wks
14 Oct	72 STAR PORTRAIT *CBS 67201*	16	7 wks
10 Jul	76 ONE PIECE AT A TIME *CBS 81416*	49	3 wks
9 Oct	76 THE BEST OF JOHNNY CASH *CBS 10000*	48	2 wks
2 Sep	78 ITCHY FEET *CBS 10009*	36	4 wks

CASHFLOW US, *male vocal/instrumental group* 3 wks

28 Jun	86 CASHFLOW *Club JABH 17*	33	3 wks

CASHMERE US, *male vocal/instrumental group* 5 wks

2 Mar	85 CASHMERE *Fourth & Broadway BRLP 503*	63	5 wks

David CASSIDY US, *male vocalist* 94 wks

20 May	72 ● CHERISH *Bell BELLS 210*	2	43 wks
24 Feb	73 ● ROCK ME BABY *Bell BELLS 218*	2	20 wks
24 Nov	73 ★ DREAMS ARE NOTHIN' MORE THAN WISHES		
	Bell BELLS 231	1	13 wks

C
79

3 Aug	74 ●	**CASSIDY LIVE** *Bell BELLS 243*	**9**	7 wks
9 Aug	75	**THE HIGHER THEY CLIMB** *RCA Victor RS 1012*	**22**	5 wks
8 Jun	85	**ROMANCE** *Arista 206 983*	**20**	6 wks

CATHERINE WHEEL UK, male vocal/instrumental group 2 wks

| 29 Feb | 92 | **FERMENT** *Fontana 5109032* .... | **36** | 1 wk |
| 31 Jul | 93 | **CHROME** *Fontana 5180392* .... | **58** | 1 wk |

Nick CAVE featuring the BAD SEEDS
Australia, male vocalist with male vocal/instrumental group   10 wks

2 Jun	84	**FROM HER TO ETERNITY** *Mute STUMM 17*	**40**	3 wks
15 Jun	85	**THE FIRST BORN IS DEAD** *Mute STUMM 21*	**53**	1 wk
30 Aug	86	**KICKING AGAINST THE PRICKS** *Mute STUMM 28*	**89**	1 wk
1 Oct	88	**TENDER PREY** *Mute STUMM 52*	**67**	1 wk
28 Apr	90	**THE GOOD SON** *Mute STUMM 76*	**47**	1 wk
9 May	92	**HENRY'S DREAM** *Mute CDSTUMM 92*	**29**	2 wks
18 Sep	93	**LIVE SEEDS** *Mute CDSTUMM 122*	**67**	1 wk

CAVEMAN UK, male rap duo   2 wks

| 13 Apr | 91 | **POSITIVE REACTION** *Profile FILER 406* .... | **43** | 2 wks |

C.C.S. UK, male vocal/instrumental group   5 wks

| 8 Apr | 72 | **C.C.S.** *RAK SRAK 503* .... | **23** | 5 wks |

CENTRAL LINE UK, male vocal/instrumental group   5 wks

| 13 Feb | 82 | **BREAKING POINT** *Mercury MERA 001* .... | **64** | 5 wks |

CERRONE France, male producer/multi-instrumentalist   1 wk

| 30 Sep | 78 | **SUPERNATURE** *Atlantic K 50431* .... | **60** | 1 wk |

A CERTAIN RATIO UK, male vocal/instrumental group 3 wks

| 30 Jan | 82 | **SEXTET** *Factory FACT 55* .... | **53** | 3 wks |

Peter CETERA US, male vocalist   4 wks

| 13 Sep | 86 | **SOLITUDE/SOLITAIRE** *Full Moon 925474–1* .... | **56** | 4 wks |

Richard CHAMBERLAIN US, male vocalist   8 wks

| 16 Mar | 63 ● | **RICHARD CHAMBERLAIN SINGS** *MGM C 923* ...... | **8** | 8 wks |

CHAMELEONS UK, male vocal/instrumental group   4 wks

25 May	85	**WHAT DOES ANYTHING MEAN? BASICALLY**		
		Statik STAT LP 22	**60**	2 wks
20 Sep	86	**STRANGE TIMES** *Geffen 924 119–1*	**44**	2 wks

CHAMPAIGN US, male/female vocal/instrumental group   4 wks

| 27 Jun | 81 | **HOW 'BOUT US** *CBS 84927* .... | **38** | 4 wks |

CHANGE US, male/female vocal/instrumental group   23 wks

| 19 May 84 | **CHANGE OF HEART** WEA WX 5 | 34 | 17 wks |
| 27 Apr 85 | **TURN ON THE RADIO** Cooltempo CHR 1504 | 39 | 6 wks |

Michael CHAPMAN UK, male vocalist   1 wk

| 21 Mar 70 | **FULLY QUALIFIED SURVIVOR** Harvest SHVL 764 | 45 | 1 wk |

Tracy CHAPMAN US, female vocalist   94 wks

21 May 88 ★	**TRACY CHAPMAN** Elektra EKT 44	1	75 wks
14 Oct 89 ★	**CROSSROADS** Elektra EKT 61	1	16 wks
9 May 92	**MATTERS OF THE HEART** Elektra 7559612152	19	3 wks

CHAPTERHOUSE UK, male vocal/instrumental group   3 wks

| 11 May 91 | **WHIRLPOOL** Dedicated DEDLP 001 | 23 | 3 wks |

CHAQUITO ORCHESTRA
UK, orchestra arranged and conducted by Johnny Gregory   2 wks

| 24 Feb 68 | **THIS IS CHAQUITO** Fontana SFXL 50★ | 36 | 1 wk |
| 4 Mar 72 | **THRILLER THEMES** Philips 6308 087 | 48 | 1 wk |

★ *Chaquito and Quedo Brass.*

CHARGE GBH UK, male vocal/instrumental group   6 wks

| 14 Aug 82 | **CITY BABY ATTACKED BY RATS** Clay CLAYLP 4 | 17 | 6 wks |

CHARLATANS UK, male vocal/instrumental group   21 wks

| 20 Oct 90 ★ | **SOME FRIENDLY** Situation Two SITU 30 | 1 | 17 wks |
| 4 Apr 92 | **BETWEEN 10TH AND 11TH** Situation Two SITU 37CD | 21 | 4 wks |

CHARLENE US, female vocalist   4 wks

| 17 Jul 82 | **I'VE NEVER BEEN TO ME** Motown STML 12171 | 43 | 4 wks |

Ray CHARLES US, male vocalist/instrumentalist – piano   45 wks

28 Jul 62 ●	**MODERN SOUNDS IN COUNTRY AND WESTERN MUSIC** HMV CLP 1580	6	16 wks
23 Feb 63	**MODERN SOUNDS IN COUNTRY AND WESTERN MUSIC VOL. 2** HMV CLP 1613	15	5 wks
20 Jul 63	**GREATEST HITS** HMV CLP 1626	16	5 wks
5 Oct 68	**GREATEST HITS VOL. 2** Stateside SSL 10241	24	8 wks
19 Jul 80	**HEART TO HEART – 20 HOT HITS** London RAY TV 1	29	5 wks
24 Mar 90	**THE COLLECTION** Arcade RCLP 101	36	3 wks
13 Mar 93	**RAY CHARLES – THE LIVING LEGEND** Arcade ARC 94642	48	3 wks

CHARLES and EDDIE US, male vocal duo   15 wks

| 12 Dec 92 | **DUOPHONIC** Capitol CDESTU 2186 | 19 | 15 wks |

Tina CHARLES UK, female vocalist   7 wks

| 3 Dec 77 | **HEART 'N' SOUL** CBS 82180 | 35 | 7 wks |

C
81

CHAS and DAVE UK, male vocal/instrumental duo   96 wks

5 Dec 81	**CHAS AND DAVE'S CHRISTMAS JAMBOREE BAG**		
	Warwick WW 5166	25	15 wks
17 Apr 82	**MUSTN'T GRUMBLE** *Rockney 909*	35	11 wks
8 Jan 83	**JOB LOT** *Rockney ROC 910*	59	15 wks
15 Oct 83 ●	**CHAS AND DAVE'S KNEES UP – JAMBOREE BAG**		
	NO 2 *Rockney ROC 911*	7	17 wks
11 Aug 84	**WELL PLEASED** *Rockney ROC 912*	27	10 wks
17 Nov 84	**CHAS AND DAVE'S GREATEST HITS** *Rockney ROC 913*	16	10 wks
15 Dec 84	**CHAS AND DAVE'S CHRISTMAS JAMBOREE BAG**		
	(re-issue) *Rockney ROCM 001*	87	1 wk
9 Nov 85	**JAMBOREE BAG NUMBER 3** *Rockney ROC 914*	15	13 wks
13 Dec 86	**CHAS AND DAVE'S CHRISTMAS CAROL ALBUM**		
	Telstar STAR 2293	37	4 wks

CHEAP TRICK US, male vocal/instrumental group   15 wks

24 Feb 79	**CHEAP TRICK AT BUDOKAN** *Epic EPC 86083*	29	9 wks
6 Oct 79	**DREAM POLICE** *Epic EPC 83522*	41	5 wks
5 Jun 82	**ONE ON ONE** *Epic EPC 85740*	95	1 wk

CHECK 1-2 – *See Craig McLACHLAN and CHECK 1-2*

Chubby CHECKER US, male vocalist   7 wks

27 Jan 62	**TWIST WITH CHUBBY CHECKER** *Columbia 33SX 1315*	13	4 wks
3 Mar 62	**FOR TWISTERS ONLY** *Columbia 33SX 1341*	17	3 wks

CHER US, female vocalist   200 wks

2 Oct 65 ●	**ALL I REALLY WANT TO DO** *Liberty LBY 3058*	7	9 wks
7 May 66	**SONNY SIDE OF CHER** *Liberty LBY 3072*	11	11 wks
16 Jan 88	**CHER** *Geffen WX 132*	26	22 wks
22 Jul 89 ●	**HEART OF STONE** *Geffen GEF 24239*	7	84 wks
29 Jun 91 ★	**LOVE HURTS** *Geffen GEF 24427*	1	51 wks
21 Nov 92 ★	**GREATEST HITS 1965–1992** *Geffen GED 24439*	1	23 wks

The catalogue number for Heart Of Stone *changed from* WX 262 *during the album's run. See also Sonny and Cher.*

CHERELLE US, female vocalist   9 wks

25 Jan 86	**HIGH PRIORITY** *Tabu TBU 26699*	17	9 wks

Neneh CHERRY US, female vocalist   44 wks

17 Jun 89 ●	**RAW LIKE SUSHI** *Circa CIRCA 8*	2	42 wks
7 Nov 92	**HOMEBREW** *Circa CIRCD 25*	27	2 wks

CHIC US, male/female vocal/instrumental group   47 wks

3 Feb 79 ●	**C'EST CHIC** *Atlantic K 50565*	2	24 wks
18 Aug 79	**RISQUE** *Atlantic K 50634*	29	12 wks
15 Dec 79	**THE BEST OF CHIC** *Atlantic K 50686*	30	8 wks
5 Dec 87	**FREAK OUT** *Telstar STAR 2319★*	72	3 wks

★ *Chic and Sister Sledge.*
See also Compilation Albums – Dino.

CHICAGO US, male vocal/instrumental group   106 wks

27 Sep 69 ●	**CHICAGO TRANSIT AUTHORITY** *CBS 66221★*	9	14 wks
4 Apr 70 ●	**CHICAGO** *CBS 66233*	6	27 wks
3 Apr 71	**CHICAGO 3** *CBS 66260*	31	1 wk
30 Sep 72	**CHICAGO 5** *CBS 69108*	24	2 wks

Cher endured the longest gap between chart debut and first number one, 26 years.
(Pictorial Press)

23 Oct 76	**CHICAGO X** *CBS 86010*	21	11 wks
2 Oct 82	**CHICAGO 16** *Full Moon K 99235*	44	9 wks
4 Dec 82	**LOVE SONGS** *TV Records TVA 6*	42	8 wks
1 Dec 84	**CHICAGO 17** *Full Moon 925060*	24	20 wks
25 Nov 89	**THE HEART OF CHICAGO** *Reprise WX 328*	15	14 wks

★ *Chicago Transit Authority.*

CHICKEN SHACK
UK, male/female vocal/instrumental group   *9 wks*

22 Jul 68	**40 BLUE FINGERS FRESHLY PACKED**		
	Blue Horizon 7–63203	12	8 wks
15 Feb 69 ●	**OK KEN?** *Blue Horizon 7–63209*	9	1 wk

CHIEFTAINS – *See James GALWAY; Van MORRISON*

Toni CHILDS *US, female vocalist*   *1 wk*

29 Apr 89	**UNION** *A & M AMA 5175*	73	1 wk

CHIMES *UK, male/female vocal/instrumental group*   *19 wks*

23 Jun 90	**THE CHIMES** *CBS 4664811*	17	19 wks

CHINA CRISIS *UK, male vocal/instrumental group*   *68 wks*

20 Nov 82	**DIFFICULT SHAPES AND PASSIVE RHYTHMS**		
	Virgin V 2243	21	18 wks
12 Nov 83	**WORKING WITH FIRE AND STEEL –**		
	POSSIBLE POP SONGS VOL 2 *Virgin V 2286*	20	16 wks
11 May 85 ●	**FLAUNT THE IMPERFECTION** *Virgin V 2342*	9	22 wks
6 Dec 86	**WHAT PRICE PARADISE** *Virgin V 2410*	63	6 wks
13 May 89	**DIARY OF A HOLLOW HORSE** *Virgin V 2567*	58	2 wks
15 Sep 90	**CHINA CRISIS COLLECTION** *Virgin V 2613*	32	4 wks

CHORDS *UK, male vocal/instrumental group*   *3 wks*

24 May 80	**SO FAR AWAY** *Polydor POLS 1019*	30	3 wks

CHRISTIANS *UK, male vocal/instrumental group*   *94 wks*

31 Oct 87 ●	**THE CHRISTIANS** *Island ILPS 9876*	2	68 wks
27 Jan 90 ★	**COLOUR** *Island ILPS 9948*	1	17 wks
10 Oct 92	**HAPPY IN HELL** *Island CID 9996*	18	3 wks
20 Nov 93	**THE BEST OF THE CHRISTIANS** *Island CIDTV 6*	22†	6 wks

Tony CHRISTIE *UK, male vocalist*   *10 wks*

24 Jul 71	**I DID WHAT I DID FOR MARIA** *MCA MKPS 2016*	37	1 wk
17 Feb 73	**WITH LOVING FEELING** *MCA MUPS 468*	19	2 wks
31 May 75	**TONY CHRISTIE – LIVE** *MCA MCF 2703*	33	3 wks
6 Nov 76	**BEST OF TONY CHRISTIE** *MCA MCF 2769*	28	4 wks

CHRON GEN *UK, male vocal/instrumental group*   *3 wks*

3 Apr 82	**CHRONIC GENERATION** *Secret SEC 3*	53	3 wks

Sir Winston CHURCHILL *UK, male statesman*   *8 wks*

13 Feb 65 ●	**THE VOICE OF CHURCHILL** *Decca LXT 6200*	6	8 wks

CINDERELLA US, male vocal/instrumental group   8 wks

| 23 Jul | 88 | **LONG COLD WINTER** Vertigo VERH 59 .... | **30** | 6 wks |
| 1 Dec | 90 | **HEARTBREAK STATION** Vertigo 8480181 .... | **36** | 2 wks |

CITY BEAT BAND – *See PRINCE CHARLES and the CITY BEAT BAND*

Gary CLAIL ON-U SOUND SYSTEM
UK, male vocalist/producer   2 wks

| 4 May | 91 | **EMOTIONAL HOOLIGAN** Perfecto PL 74965 .... | **35** | 2 wks |

CLANCY BROTHERS and Tommy MAKEM
Ireland, male vocal/instrumental group and male vocalist   5 wks

| 16 Apr | 66 | **ISN'T IT GRAND BOYS** CBS BPG 62674 .... | **22** | 5 wks |

CLANNAD Ireland, male/female vocal/instrumental group   134 wks

2 Apr	83	**MAGICAL RING** RCA RCALP 6072	**26**	21 wks
12 May	84	**LEGEND (MUSIC FROM ROBIN OF SHERWOOD)**		
		RCA PL 70188	**15**	40 wks
2 Jun	84	**MAGICAL RING (re-issue)** RCA PL 70003	**91**	1 wk
26 Oct	85	**MACALLA** RCA PL 70894	**33**	24 wks
7 Nov	87	**SIRIUS** RCA PL 71513	**34**	4 wks
11 Feb	89	**ATLANTIC REALM** BBC REB 727	**41**	3 wks
6 May	89 ●	**PASTPRESENT** RCA PL 74074	**5**	23 wks
20 Oct	90	**ANAM** RCA PL 74762	**14**	7 wks
15 May	93 ●	**BANBA** RCA 74321139612	**5**	11 wks

Eric CLAPTON UK, male vocalist/instrumentalist – guitar 432 wks

30 Jul	66 ●	**BLUES BREAKERS** Decca LK 4804★	**6**	17 wks
5 Sep	70	**ERIC CLAPTON** Polydor 2383–021	**17**	8 wks
26 Aug	72	**HISTORY OF ERIC CLAPTON** Polydor 2659 2478 027 ..	**20**	6 wks
24 Mar	73	**IN CONCERT** RSO 2659020★★	**36**	1 wk
24 Aug	74 ●	**461 OCEAN BOULEVARD** RSO 2479 118	**3**	19 wks
12 Apr	75	**THERE'S ONE IN EVERY CROWD** RSO 2479 132	**15**	8 wks
13 Sep	75	**E.C. WAS HERE** RSO 2394 160	**14**	6 wks
11 Sep	76 ●	**NO REASON TO CRY** RSO 2479 179	**8**	7 wks
26 Nov	77	**SLOWHAND** RSO 2479 201	**23**	13 wks
9 Dec	78	**BACKLESS** RSO RSD 5001	**18**	12 wks
10 May	80 ●	**JUST ONE NIGHT** RSO RSDX 2	**3**	12 wks
7 Mar	81	**ANOTHER TICKET** RSO RSD 5008	**18**	8 wks
24 Apr	82	**TIME PIECES – THE BEST OF ERIC CLAPTON**		
		RSO RSD 5010	**20**	14 wks
19 Feb	83	**MONEY & CIGARETTES** Duck W 3773	**13**	17 wks
9 Jun	84	**BACKTRACKIN'** Starblend ERIC 1	**29**	16 wks
23 Mar	85 ●	**BEHIND THE SUN** Duck 92–5166–1	**8**	14 wks
6 Dec	86 ●	**AUGUST** Duck WX 71	**3**	42 wks
26 Sep	87 ●	**THE CREAM OF ERIC CLAPTON** Polydor ECTV 1★★★ ..	**3**	105 wks
18 Nov	89 ●	**JOURNEYMAN** Duck WX 322	**2**	32 wks
26 Oct	91	**24 NIGHTS** Duck WX 373	**17**	7 wks
12 Sep	92 ●	**UNPLUGGED** Duck 9362450242	**2†**	67 wks

★ *John Mayall and Eric Clapton.*
★★ *Derek and the Dominos.*
★★★ *Eric Clapton and Cream.*
From 9 Jul 93 The Cream Of Eric Clapton *was repackaged and was available as* The Best Of Eric Clapton.

Gary CLARK UK, male vocalist   2 wks

| 8 May | 93 | **TEN SHORT SONGS ABOUT LOVE** Circa CIRCD 23 .. | **25** | 2 wks |

C
85

Petula CLARK *UK, female vocalist*   *43 wks*

30 Jul	66	**I COULDN'T LIVE WITHOUT YOUR LOVE**			
		Pye NPL 18148	**11**	10 wks
4 Feb	67	**HIT PARADE** *Pye NPL 18159*	**18**	13 wks
18 Feb	67	**COLOUR MY WORLD** *Pye NPL 18171*	**16**	9 wks
7 Oct	67	**THESE ARE MY SONGS** *Pye NSPL 18197*	**38**	3 wks
6 Apr	68	**THE OTHER MAN'S GRASS IS ALWAYS GREENER**			
		Pye NSPL 18211	**37**	1 wk
5 Feb	77	**20 ALL TIME GREATEST** *K-Tel NE 945*	**18**	7 wks

Dave CLARK FIVE
UK, male vocal/instrumental group   *31 wks*

18 Apr	64 ●	**A SESSION WITH THE DAVE CLARK FIVE**			
		Columbia 33SX 1598	**3**	8 wks
14 Aug	65 ●	**CATCH US IF YOU CAN** *Columbia 33SX 1756*	**8**	8 wks
4 Mar	78 ●	**25 THUMPING GREAT HITS** *Polydor POLTV 7*	**7**	10 wks
17 Apr	93	**GLAD ALL OVER AGAIN** *EMI CDEMTV 75*	**28**	5 wks

Louis CLARK – *See ROYAL PHILHARMONIC ORCHESTRA*

John Cooper CLARKE *UK, male vocalist*   *9 wks*

19 Apr	80	**SNAP CRACKLE AND BOP** *Epic EPC 84083*	**26**	7 wks
5 Jun	82	**ZIP STYLE METHOD** *Epic EPC 85667*	**97**	2 wks

Stanley CLARKE *US, male vocal/instrumentalist – bass*   *2 wks*

12 Jul	80	**ROCKS PEBBLES AND SAND** *Epic EPC 84342*	**42**	2 wks

CLASH *UK, male vocal/instrumental group*   *107 wks*

30 Apr	77	**CLASH** *CBS 82000*	**12**	16 wks
25 Nov	78 ●	**GIVE 'EM ENOUGH ROPE** *CBS 82431*	**2**	14 wks
22 Dec	79 ●	**LONDON CALLING** *CBS CLASH 3*	**9**	20 wks
20 Dec	80	**SANDINISTA** *CBS FSLN 1*	**19**	9 wks
22 May	82 ●	**COMBAT ROCK** *CBS FMLN 2*	**2**	23 wks
16 Nov	85	**CUT THE CRAP** *CBS 26601*	**16**	3 wks
2 Apr	88 ●	**THE STORY OF THE CLASH** *CBS 460244 1*	**7**	20 wks
16 Nov	91	**THE SINGLES** *Columbia 4689461*	**68**	2 wks

CLASSIX NOUVEAUX
UK, male vocal/instrumental group   *6 wks*

30 May	81	**NIGHT PEOPLE** *Liberty LBG 30325*	**66**	2 wks
24 Apr	82	**LA VERITE** *Liberty LBG 30346*	**44**	4 wks

Richard CLAYDERMAN
France, male instrumentalist – piano   *200 wks*

13 Nov	82 ●	**RICHARD CLAYDERMAN** *Decca SKL 5329*	**2**	64 wks
8 Oct	83	**THE MUSIC OF RICHARD CLAYDERMAN**			
		Decca SKL 5333	**21**	28 wks
24 Nov	84	**THE MUSIC OF LOVE** *Decca SKL 5340*	**28**	21 wks
1 Dec	84	**CHRISTMAS** *Decca SKL 5337*	**53**	5 wks
23 Nov	85	**THE CLASSIC TOUCH** *Decca SKL 5343*	**17**	18 wks
22 Nov	86	**HOLLYWOOD AND BROADWAY** *Decca SKL 5344*	**28**	9 wks
28 Nov	87	**SONGS OF LOVE** *Decca SKL 5345*	**19**	13 wks
3 Dec	88	**A LITTLE NIGHT MUSIC** *Decca Delphine 8281251*	**52**	5 wks
25 Nov	89	**THE LOVE SONGS OF ANDREW LLOYD WEBBER**			
		Decca Delphine 8281751	**18**	10 wks
24 Nov	90	**MY CLASSIC COLLECTION** *Decca Delphine 8282281*	**29**	7 wks

Eric Clapton is shown during his 1992 residency at the Royal Albert Hall. (Pictorial Press)

9 Nov 91	**TOGETHER AT LAST** *Delphine/Polydor 5115251★*		14	15 wks
14 Nov 92	**THE VERY BEST OF RICHARD CLAYDERMAN**			
	Decca Delphine 8283362★★		47	5 wks

★ *Richard Clayderman and James Last.*
★★ *Richard Clayderman with the Royal Philharmonic Orchestra.*

CLAYTOWN TROUPE
UK, male vocal/instrumental group   *1 wk*

21 Oct 89	**THROUGH THE VEIL** *Island ILPS 9933*	72	1 wk

CLIMAX BLUES BAND
UK, male vocal/instrumental group   *1 wk*

13 Nov 76	**GOLD PLATED** *BTM 1009*	56	1 wk

CLIMIE FISHER   *UK, male vocal/instrumental duo*   *38 wks*

13 Feb 88	**EVERYTHING** *EMI EMC 3538*	14	36 wks
21 Oct 89	**COMING IN FOR THE KILL** *EMI EMC 3565*	35	2 wks

Patsy CLINE   *US, female vocalist*   *22 wks*

19 Jan 91	**SWEET DREAMS** *MCA MCG 6003*	18	10 wks
19 Jan 91	**DREAMING** *Platinum Music PLAT 303*	55	4 wks
5 Sep 92	**THE DEFINITIVE PATSY CLINE** *Arcade ARC 94992* ...	11	8 wks

CLIVILLES & COLE – *See C&C MUSIC FACTORY/CLIVILLES & COLE*

Luis COBOS   *Spain, male orchestra leader*   *1 wk*

21 Apr 90	**OPERA EXTRAVAGANZA** *Epic MOOD 12*	72	1 wk

Eddie COCHRAN
US, male vocalist/instrumentalist – guitar   *47 wks*

30 Jul 60	**SINGING TO MY BABY** *London HAU 2093*	19	1 wk
1 Oct 60 ●	**EDDIE COCHRAN MEMORIAL ALBUM**		
	London HAG 2267	9	12 wks
12 Jan 63	**CHERISHED MEMORIES** *Liberty LBY 1109*	15	3 wks
20 Apr 63	**EDDIE COCHRAN MEMORIAL ALBUM** (re–issue)		
	Liberty LBY 1127	11	18 wks
19 Oct 63	**SINGING TO MY BABY** (re–issue) *Liberty LBY 1158*	20	1 wk
9 May 70	**VERY BEST OF EDDIE COCHRAN** *Liberty LBS 83337* ..	34	3 wks
18 Aug 79	**THE EDDIE COCHRAN SINGLES ALBUM**		
	United Artists UAK 30244	39	6 wks
16 Apr 88	**C'MON EVERYBODY** *Liberty ECR 1*	53	3 wks

Brenda COCHRANE   *Ireland, female vocalist*   *14 wks*

14 Apr 90	**THE VOICE** *Polydor 8431411*	14	11 wks
6 Apr 91	**IN DREAMS** *Polydor 8490341*	55	3 wks

Joe COCKER   *UK, male vocalist*   *47 wks*

26 Sep 70	**MAD DOGS AND ENGLISHMEN** *A & M AMLS 6002* ...	16	8 wks
6 May 72	**JOE COCKER/WITH A LITTLE HELP FROM**		
	MY FRIENDS *Double Back TOOFA 1/2*	29	4 wks
30 Jun 84	**A CIVILISED MAN** *Capitol EJ 24 0139 1*	100	1 wk
11 Apr 92	**NIGHT CALLS** *Capitol CDESTU 2167*	25	14 wks
27 Jun 92 ●	**THE LEGEND – THE ESSENTIAL COLLECTION**		
	PolyGram TV 5154112	4	20 wks

COCKNEY REBEL – *See Steve HARLEY and COCKNEY REBEL*

COCKNEY REJECTS UK, male vocal/instrumental group 17 wks

15 Mar 80	**GREATEST HITS VOL. 1** *Zonophone ZONO 101*	**22**	11 wks
25 Oct 80	**GREATEST HITS VOL. 2** *Zonophone ZONO 102*	**23**	3 wks
18 Apr 81	**GREATEST HITS VOL. 3 (LIVE AND LOUD)**		
	Zonophone ZEM 101	**27**	3 wks

COCONUTS – *See Kid CREOLE and the COCONUTS*

COCTEAU TWINS
UK, male/female vocal/instrumental group   *42 wks*

29 Oct 83	**HEAD OVER HEELS** *4AD CAD 313*	**51**	15 wks
24 Nov 84	**TREASURE** *4AD CAD 412*	**29**	8 wks
26 Apr 86 ●	**VICTORIALAND** *4AD CAD 602*	**10**	7 wks
1 Oct 88	**BLUE BELL KNOLL** *4AD CAD 807*	**15**	4 wks
22 Sep 90 ●	**HEAVEN OR LAS VEGAS** *4AD CAD 0012*	**7**	5 wks
30 Oct 93	**FOUR CALENDAR CAFE** *Fontana 5182592*	**13**	3 wks

See also Harold Budd/Liz Fraser/Robin Guthrie/Simon Raymond.

Leonard COHEN Canada, male vocalist   *146 wks*

31 Aug 68	**SONGS OF LEONARD COHEN** *CBS 63241*	**13**	71 wks
3 May 69 ●	**SONGS FROM A ROOM** *CBS 63587*	**2**	26 wks
24 Apr 71 ●	**SONGS OF LOVE AND HATE** *CBS 69004*	**4**	18 wks
28 Sep 74	**NEW SKIN FOR THE OLD CEREMONY** *CBS 69087* ...	**24**	3 wks
10 Dec 77	**DEATH OF A LADIES' MAN** *CBS 86042*	**35**	5 wks
16 Feb 85	**VARIOUS POSITIONS** *CBS 26222*	**52**	6 wks
27 Feb 88	**I'M YOUR MAN** *CBS 460642 1*	**48**	13 wks
6 Aug 88	**GREATEST HITS** *CBS 32644*	**99**	1 wk
5 Dec 92	**THE FUTURE** *Columbia 4724982*	**36**	3 wks

Marc COHN UK, male vocalist/instrumentalist – piano   *23 wks*

29 Jun 91	**MARC COHN** *Atlantic 7567821781*	**27**	20 wks
12 Jun 93	**THE RAINY SEASON** *Atlantic 7567824912*	**24**	3 wks

COLDCUT UK, male production duo   *4 wks*

29 Apr 89	**WHAT'S THAT NOISE** *Ahead Of Our Time CCUTLP 1* ...	**20**	4 wks

Lloyd COLE UK, male vocalist   *86 wks*

20 Oct 84	**RATTLESNAKES** *Polydor LCLP 1★*	**13**	30 wks
30 Nov 85 ★	**EASY PIECES** *Polydor LCLP 2★*	**5**	18 wks
7 Nov 87 ●	**MAINSTREAM** *Polydor LCLP 3★*	**9**	20 wks
8 Apr 89	**1984–1989** *Polydor 837736 1★*	**14**	7 wks
3 Mar 90	**LLOYD COLE** *Polydor 8419071*	**11**	6 wks
28 Sep 91	**DON'T GET WEIRD ON ME BABE** *Polydor 5110931*	**21**	3 wks
23 Oct 93	**BAD VIBES** *Fontana 5183182*	**38**	2 wks

★Lloyd Cole and the Commotions.

Nat 'King' COLE US, male vocalist   *126 wks*

19 Aug 61	**STRING ALONG WITH NAT 'KING' COLE**		
	Encore ENC 102	**12**	9 wks
20 Oct 62 ●	**NAT 'KING' COLE SINGS AND THE GEORGE**		
	SHEARING QUINTET PLAYS *Capitol W 1675★*	**8**	7 wks
27 Mar 65	**UNFORGETTABLE NAT 'KING' COLE** *Capitol W 20664*	**19**	8 wks
7 Dec 68 ●	**BEST OF NAT 'KING' COLE** *Capitol ST 21139*	**5**	18 wks
5 Dec 70	**BEST OF NAT 'KING' COLE VOL. 2** *Capitol ST 21687* ..	**39**	2 wks
27 Nov 71	**WHITE CHRISTMAS** *MFP 5224★★*	**45**	1 wk
8 Apr 78 ★	**20 GOLDEN GREATS** *Capitol EMTV 9*	**1**	37 wks
20 Nov 82 ●	**GREATEST LOVE SONGS** *Capitol EMTV 35*	**7**	26 wks

C
89

| 26 Nov 88 | CHRISTMAS WITH NAT 'KING' COLE | *Stylus SMR 868* . | **25** | 9 wks |
| 23 Nov 91 | UNFORGETTABLE NAT 'KING' COLE | *EMI EMTV 61* . | **23** | 9 wks |

★ *Nat 'King' Cole and the George Shearing Quintet.* ★★ *Nat 'King' Cole and Dean Martin.*
The two Unforgettable Nat 'King' Cole *albums are different.*

Natalie COLE *US, female vocalist* *65 wks*

17 Sep	83 ●	UNFORGETTABLE: A MUSICAL TRIBUTE TO NAT 'KING' COLE *CBS 10042*★	**5**	16 wks
7 May	88	EVERLASTING *Manhattan MTL 1012*	**62**	4 wks
20 May	89 ●	GOOD TO BE BACK *EMI-USA MTL 1042*	**10**	12 wks
27 Jul	91	UNFORGETTABLE – WITH LOVE *Elektra EKT 91*	**11**	29 wks
26 Jun	93	TAKE A LOOK *Elektra 7559614962*	**16**	4 wks

★ *Johnny Mathis and Natalie Cole.*

Dave and Ansil COLLINS *Jamaica, male vocal duo* *2 wks*

| 7 Aug 71 | DOUBLE BARREL | *Trojan TBL 162* | **41** | 2 wks |

Joan COLLINS – *See Anthony NEWLEY, Peter SELLERS, Joan COLLINS*

Judy COLLINS *US, female vocalist* *18 wks*

10 Apr	71	WHALES AND NIGHTINGALES *Elektra EKS 75010*	**37**	2 wks
31 May	75 ●	JUDITH *Elektra K 52019*	**7**	12 wks
14 Dec	85	AMAZING GRACE *Telstar STAR 2265*	**34**	4 wks

Phil COLLINS *UK, male vocalist/instrumentalist – drums* *739 wks*

21 Feb	81 ★	FACE VALUE *Virgin V 2185*	**1**	274 wks
13 Nov	82 ●	HELLO I MUST BE GOING *Virgin V 2252*	**2**	164 wks
2 Mar	85 ★	NO JACKET REQUIRED *Virgin V 2345*	**1**	176 wks
2 Dec	89 ★	. . . BUT SERIOUSLY *Virgin V 2620*	**1**	69 wks
17 Nov	90 ●	SERIOUS HITS . . . LIVE! *Virgin PCLP 1*	**2**	50 wks
20 Nov	93 ★	BOTH SIDES *Virgin CDV 2800*	**1†**	6 wks

Willie COLLINS *US, male vocalist* *1 wk*

| 14 Jun 86 | WHERE YOU GONNA BE TONIGHT? *Capitol EST 2012* | **97** | 1 wk |

COLOR ME BADD *US, male vocal group* *22 wks*

| 24 Aug 91 ● | C.M.B. *Giant WX 425* | **3** | 22 wks |

COLOSSEUM *UK, male vocal/instrumental group* *14 wks*

17 May	69	COLOSSEUM *Fontana S 5510*	**15**	1 wk
22 Nov	69	VALENTYNE SUITE *Vertigo VO 1*	**15**	2 wks
5 Dec	70	DAUGHTER OF TIME *Vertigo 6360 017*	**23**	5 wks
26 Jun	71	COLOSSEUM LIVE *Bronze ICD 1*	**17**	6 wks

COLOURBOX *UK, male vocal/instrumental group* *2 wks*

| 24 Aug 85 | COLOURBOX *4AD CAD 508* | **67** | 2 wks |

COLOUR FIELD *UK, male vocal/instrumental group* *8 wks*

| 4 May | 85 | VIRGINS AND PHILISTINES *Chrysalis CHR 1480* | **12** | 7 wks |
| 4 Apr | 87 | DECEPTION *Chrysalis CDL 1546* | **95** | 1 wk |

Alice COLTRANE – *See SANTANA*   **COMETS** – *See Bill HALEY and his COMETS*

COMIC RELIEF UK, charity ensemble of comedians *8 wks*

10 May 86 ●	UTTERLY UTTERLY LIVE!	*WEA WX 51*	**10**	8 wks

COMMITMENTS
Ireland, male/female vocal/instrumental group *111 wks*

26 Oct 91 ●	**THE COMMITMENTS (film soundtrack)**		
	MCA MCA 10286	**4**	100 wks
25 Apr 92	**THE COMMITMENTS VOL. 2** *MCA MCAD 10506*	**13**	11 wks

COMMODORES US/UK, male vocal/instrumental group *126 wks*

13 May 78	**LIVE** *Motown TMSP 6007*	**60**	1 wk
10 Jun 78 ●	**NATURAL HIGH** *Motown STML 12087*	**8**	23 wks
2 Dec 78	**GREATEST HITS** *Motown STML 12100*	**19**	16 wks
18 Aug 79	**MIDNIGHT MAGIC** *Motown STMA 8032*	**15**	25 wks
28 Jun 80	**HEROES** *Motown STMA 8034*	**50**	5 wks
18 Jul 81	**IN THE POCKET** *Motown STML 12156*	**69**	5 wks
14 Aug 82 ●	**LOVE SONGS** *K-Tel NE 1171*	**5**	28 wks
23 Feb 85	**NIGHTSHIFT** *Motown ZL 72343*	**13**	10 wks
9 Nov 85	**THE VERY BEST OF THE COMMODORES**		
	Telstar STAR 2249	**25**	13 wks

Group were US only for first seven albums.

COMMOTIONS – See Lloyd COLE

COMMUNARDS UK, male vocal/instrumental duo *74 wks*

2 Aug 86 ●	**COMMUNARDS** *London LONLP 18*	**7**	45 wks
17 Oct 87 ●	**RED** *London LONLP 39*	**4**	29 wks

Perry COMO US, male vocalist *191 wks*

8 Nov 58 ●	**DEAR PERRY** *RCA RD 27078*	**6**	5 wks
31 Jan 59 ●	**COMO'S GOLDEN RECORDS** *RCA RD 27100*	**4**	5 wks
10 Apr 71	**IT'S IMPOSSIBLE** *RCA Victor SF 8175*	**13**	13 wks
7 Jul 73 ★	**AND I LOVE YOU SO** *RCA Victor SF 8360*	**1**	109 wks
24 Aug 74	**PERRY** *RCA Victor APLI 0585*	**26**	3 wks
19 Apr 75	**MEMORIES ARE MADE OF HITS** *RCA Victor RS 1005* .	**14**	16 wks
25 Oct 75 ★	**40 GREATEST HITS** *K-Tel NE 700*	**1**	34 wks
3 Dec 83	**FOR THE GOOD TIMES** *Telstar STAR 2235*	**41**	6 wks

COMPILATION ALBUMS – See *VARIOUS ARTISTS*

COMSAT ANGELS UK, male vocal/instrumental group *9 wks*

5 Sep 81	**SLEEP NO MORE** *Polydor POLS 1038*	**51**	5 wks
18 Sep 82	**FICTION** *Polydor POLS 1075*	**94**	2 wks
8 Oct 83	**LAND** *Jive HIP 8*	**91**	2 wks

Harry CONNICK Jr
US, male vocalist/instrumentalist – piano *64 wks*

22 Sep 90 ●	**WE ARE IN LOVE** *CBS 4667361*	**7**	46 wks
26 Oct 91	**BLUE LIGHT RED LIGHT** *Columbia 4690871*	**16**	11 wks
30 Jan 93	**25** *Columbia 4728092*	**35**	2 wks
12 Jun 93	**FOREVER FOR NOW** *Columbia 4738732*	**32**	5 wks

Ray CONNIFF US, male orchestra leader *96 wks*

28 May 60	**IT'S THE TALK OF THE TOWN** *Philips BBL 7354*	**15**	1 wk
25 Jun 60	**S'AWFUL NICE** *Philips BBL 7281*	**13**	1 wk
26 Nov 60 ●	**HI-FI COMPANION ALBUM** *Philips BET 101*	**3**	44 wks

C
91

20 May 61	MEMORIES ARE MADE OF THIS *Philips BBL 7439*	14	4 wks
29 Dec 62	WE WISH YOU A MERRY CHRISTMAS		
	CBS BPG 62092	12	1 wk
29 Dec 62	'S WONDERFUL 'S MARVELLOUS *CBS DPG 66001* ...	18	3 wks
16 Apr 66	HI-FI COMPANION ALBUM (re-issue) *CBS DP 66011* .	24	4 wks
9 Sep 67	SOMEWHERE MY LOVE *CBS SBPG 62740*	34	3 wks
21 Jun 69 ★	HIS ORCHESTRA, HIS CHORUS, HIS SINGERS,		
	HIS SOUND *CBS SPR 27*	1	16 wks
23 May 70	BRIDGE OVER TROUBLED WATER *CBS 64020*	30	14 wks
12 Jun 71	LOVE STORY *CBS 64294*	34	1 wk
19 Feb 72	I'D LIKE TO TEACH THE WORLD TO SING *CBS 64449*	17	4 wks

Billy CONNOLLY *UK, male vocalist*   *108 wks*

20 Jul 74 ●	SOLO CONCERT *Transatlantic TRA 279*	8	33 wks
18 Jan 75 ●	COP YER WHACK OF THIS *Polydor 2383 310*	10	29 wks
20 Sep 75	WORDS AND MUSIC *Transatlantic TRA SAM 32*	34	10 wks
6 Dec 75 ●	GET RIGHT INTAE HIM *Polydor 2383 368*	6	14 wks
11 Dec 76	ATLANTIC BRIDGE *Polydor 2383 419*	20	9 wks
28 Jan 78	RAW MEAT FOR THE BALCONY *Polydor 2383 463*	57	3 wks
5 Dec 81	PICK OF BILLY CONNOLLY *Polydor POLTV 15*	23	8 wks
5 Dec 87	BILLY AND ALBERT *10 DIX 65*	81	2 wks

Russ CONWAY *UK, male instrumentalist – piano*   *69 wks*

22 Nov 58 ●	PACK UP YOUR TROUBLES *Columbia 33SX 1120*	9	5 wks
2 May 59 ●	SONGS TO SING IN YOUR BATH *Columbia 33SX 1149* .	8	10 wks
19 Sep 59 ●	FAMILY FAVOURITES *Columbia 33SX 1169*	3	16 wks
19 Dec 59 ●	TIME TO CELEBRATE *Columbia 33SX 1197*	3	7 wks
26 Mar 60	MY CONCERTO FOR YOU *Columbia 33SX 1214*	5	17 wks
17 Dec 60 ●	PARTY TIME *Columbia 33SX 1279*	7	11 wks
23 Apr 77	RUSS CONWAY PRESENTS 24 PIANO GREATS		
	Ronco RTL 2022	25	3 wks

Ry COODER *US, male vocalist/instrumentalist – guitar*   *30 wks*

11 Aug 79	BOP TILL YOU DROP *Warner Bros. K 56691*	36	9 wks
18 Oct 80	BORDER LINE *Warner Bros. K 56864*	35	6 wks
24 Apr 82	THE SLIDE AREA *Warner Bros. K 56976*	18	12 wks
14 Nov 87	GET RHYTHM *Warner Bros. WX 121*	75	3 wks

Peter COOK and Dudley MOORE
UK, male comedy duo   *34 wks*

21 May 66	ONCE MOORE WITH COOK *Decca LK 4785*	25	1 wk
18 Sep 76	DEREK AND CLIVE LIVE *Island ILPS 9434*	12	25 wks
24 Dec 77	COME AGAIN *Virgin V 2094*	18	8 wks

See also Dudley Moore.

Sam COOKE *US, male vocalist*   *27 wks*

26 Apr 86 ●	THE MAN AND HIS MUSIC *RCA PL 87127*	8	27 wks

COOKIE CREW *UK, female vocal duo*   *4 wks*

6 May 89	BORN THIS WAY! *London 828134 1*	24	4 wks

Rita COOLIDGE *US, female vocalist*   *44 wks*

6 Aug 77 ●	ANYTIME ANYWHERE *A & M AMLH 64616*	6	28 wks
6 May 78	NATURAL ACT *A & M AMLH 64690★*	35	4 wks
8 Jul 78	LOVE ME AGAIN *A & M AMLH 64699*	51	1 wk
14 Mar 81 ●	VERY BEST OF *A & M AMLH 68520*	6	11 wks

★ *Kris Kristofferson and Rita Coolidge.*

COOL NOTES UK, male/female vocal/instrumental group   2 wks

9 Nov 85   **HAVE A GOOD FOREVER** Abstract Dance ADLP 1   66   2 wks

Alice COOPER US, male vocalist   122 wks

5 Feb	72	**KILLER** Warner Bros. K 56005	27	18 wks
22 Jul	72 ●	**SCHOOL'S OUT** Warner Bros. K 56007	4	20 wks
9 Sep	72	**LOVE IT TO DEATH** Warner Bros. K 46177	28	7 wks
24 Mar	73 ★	**BILLION DOLLAR BABIES** Warner Bros. K 56013	1	23 wks
12 Jan	74	**MUSCLE OF LOVE** Warner Bros. K 56018	34	4 wks
15 Mar	75	**WELCOME TO MY NIGHTMARE** Anchor ANCL 2011 ..	19	8 wks
24 Jul	76	**ALICE COOPER GOES TO HELL** Warner Bros. K 56171 .	23	7 wks
28 May	77	**LACE AND WHISKY** Warner Bros. K 56365	33	3 wks
23 Dec	78	**FROM THE INSIDE** Warner Bros. K 56577	68	3 wks
17 May	80	**FLUSH THE FASHION** Warner Bros. K 56805	56	3 wks
12 Sep	81	**SPECIAL FORCES** Warner Bros. K 56927	96	1 wk
12 Nov	83	**DADA** Warner Bros. 92–3969–1	93	1 wk
1 Nov	86	**CONSTRICTOR** MCA MCF 3341	41	2 wks
7 Nov	87	**RAISE YOUR FIST AND YELL** MCA MCF 3392	48	3 wks
26 Aug	89 ●	**TRASH** Epic 465130 1	2	12 wks
13 Jul	91 ●	**HEY STOOPID** Epic 4684161	4	7 wks

Alice Cooper was US, male vocal/instrumental group for first five albums.

Julian COPE UK, male vocalist   29 wks

3 Mar	84	**WORLD SHUT YOUR MOUTH** Mercury MERL 37	40	4 wks
24 Nov	84	**FRIED** Mercury MERL 48	87	1 wk
14 Mar	87	**SAINT JULIAN** Island ILPS 9861	11	10 wks
29 Oct	88	**MY NATION UNDERGROUND** Island ILPS 9918	42	2 wks
16 Mar	91	**PEGGY SUICIDE** Island ILPSD 9977	23	7 wks
15 Aug	92	**FLOORED GENIUS – THE BEST OF JULIAN COPE**		
		Island CID 8000★	22	3 wks
31 Oct	92	**JEHOVAKILL** Island 5140522	20	2 wks

★ *Julian Cope and the Teardrop Explodes.*

Harry H. CORBETT – See Wilfred BRAMBELL and Harry H. CORBETT

Hugh CORNWELL UK, male vocalist   1 wk

18 Jun   88   **WOLF** Virgin V 2420   98   1 wk

CORRIES UK, male vocal/instrumental duo   5 wks

9 May	70	**SCOTTISH LOVE SONGS** Fontana 6309–004	46	4 wks
16 Sep	72	**SOUND OF PIBROCH** Columbia SCX 6511	39	1 wk

Elvis COSTELLO and the ATTRACTIONS
UK, male vocalist and male vocal/instrumental group   185 wks

6 Aug	77	**MY AIM IS TRUE** Stiff SEEZ 3★	14	12 wks
1 Apr	78 ●	**THIS YEAR'S MODEL** Radar RAD 3★	4	14 wks
20 Jan	79 ●	**ARMED FORCES** Radar RAD 14	2	28 wks
23 Feb	80 ●	**GET HAPPY** F-Beat XXLP 1	2	14 wks
31 Jan	81 ●	**TRUST** F-Beat XXLP 11★	9	7 wks
31 Oct	81 ●	**ALMOST BLUE** F-Beat XXLP 13	7	18 wks
10 Jul	82 ●	**IMPERIAL BEDROOM** F-Beat XXLP 17	6	12 wks
6 Aug	83 ●	**PUNCH THE CLOCK** F-Beat XXLP 19	3	13 wks
7 Jul	84 ●	**GOODBYE CRUEL WORLD** F-Beat ZL 70317	10	10 wks
20 Apr	85 ●	**THE BEST OF ELVIS COSTELLO – THE MAN**		
		Telstar STAR 2247★	8	17 wks
1 May	86	**KING OF AMERICA** F-Beat ZL 70496★★	11	9 wks
27 Sep	86	**BLOOD AND CHOCOLATE** Imp XFIEND 80	16	5 wks
18 Feb	89 ●	**SPIKE** Warner Bros. WX 238★	5	16 wks
28 Oct	89	**GIRLS GIRLS GIRLS** Demon DFIEND 160★	67	1 wk

C

93

| 25 May 91 ● MIGHTY LIKE A ROSE | Warner Bros. WX 419★ | 5 | 6 wks |
| 30 Jan 93 THE JULIET LETTERS | Warner Bros 9362451802★★★ | 18 | 3 wks |

★ *Elvis Costello.* ★★ *Costello Show.* ★★★ *Elvis Costello and the Brodsky Quartet.*

John COUGAR – *See John Cougar MELLENCAMP*

Phil COULTER
Ireland, male orchestra leader/instrumentalist – piano   *15 wks*

| 13 Oct 84 | SEA OF TRANQUILLITY | K-Tel Ireland KLP 185 | 46 | 14 wks |
| 18 May 85 | PHIL COULTER'S IRELAND | K-Tel ONE 1296 | 86 | 1 wk |

David COVERDALE UK, *male vocalist*   *1 wk*

| 27 Feb 82 | NORTHWINDS | Purple TTS 3513 | 78 | 1 wk |

COVERDALE PAGE UK, *male vocal/instrumental duo*   *8 wks*

| 27 Mar 93 ● COVERDALE PAGE | EMI CDEMD 1041 | 4 | 8 wks |

COWBOY JUNKIES
US, male/female vocal/instrumental group   *7 wks*

| 24 Mar 90 | THE CAUTION HORSES | RCA PL 90450 | 33 | 4 wks |
| 15 Feb 92 | BLACK EYED MAN | RCA PD 90620 | 21 | 3 wks |

CRAMPS US, *male/female vocal/instrumental group*   *13 wks*

25 Jun 83	OFF THE BONE	Illegal ILP 012	44	4 wks
26 Nov 83	SMELL OF FEMALE	Big Beat NED 6	74	2 wks
1 Mar 86	A DATE WITH ELVIS	Big Beat WIKA 46	34	6 wks
24 Feb 90	STAY SICK!	Enigma ENVLP 1001	62	1 wk

CRANBERRIES Ireland, *male/female vocal/instrumental group 1 wk*

| 13 Mar 93 | EVERYBODY ELSE IS DOING IT, SO WHY CAN'T WE | | |
| | Island CID 8003 | 64 | 1 wk |

CRANES UK, *male vocal/instrumental group*   *2 wks*

| 28 Sep 91 | WINGS OF JOY | Dedicated DEDLP 003 | 52 | 1 wk |
| 8 May 93 | FOREVER | Dedicated DEDCD 009 | 40 | 1 wk |

CRASS UK, *male vocal/instrumental group*   *2 wks*

| 28 Aug 82 | CHRIST THE ALBUM | Crass BOLLOX 2U2 | 26 | 2 wks |

Beverley CRAVEN
UK, female vocalist/instrumentalist – piano   *64 wks*

| 2 Mar 91 ● BEVERLEY CRAVEN | Columbia 4670531 | 3 | 52 wks |
| 9 Oct 93 ● LOVE SCENES | Epic 4745172 | 4† | 12 wks |

Michael CRAWFORD UK, *male vocalist*   *63 wks*

28 Nov 87	SONGS FROM THE STAGE AND SCREEN		
	Telstar STAR 2308★	12	13 wks
2 Dec 89	WITH LOVE Telstar STAR 2340	31	7 wks
9 Nov 91 ● PERFORMS ANDREW LLOYD WEBBER		
	Telstar STAR 2544	3	36 wks
13 Nov 93	A TOUCH OF MUSIC IN THE NIGHT Telstar TCD 2676	12†	7 wks

★ *Michael Crawford and the London Symphony Orchestra.*

Randy CRAWFORD US, female vocalist   147 wks

28 Jun	80 ●	**NOW WE MAY BEGIN** Warner Bros. K 56791	10	16 wks
16 May	81 ●	**SECRET COMBINATION** Warner Bros. K 56904	2	60 wks
12 Jun	82 ●	**WINDSONG** Warner Bros. K 57011	7	17 wks
22 Oct	83	**NIGHTLINE** Warner Bros. 92–3976–1	37	4 wks
13 Oct	84 ●	**MISS RANDY CRAWFORD – THE GREATEST HITS**		
		K-Tel NE 1281	10	17 wks
28 Jun	86	**ABSTRACT EMOTIONS** Warner Bros. WX 46	14	10 wks
10 Oct	87	**THE LOVE SONGS** Telstar STAR 2299	27	13 wks
21 Oct	89	**RICH AND POOR** Warner Bros. WX 308	63	1 wk
27 Mar	93 ●	**THE VERY BEST OF RANDY CRAWFORD**		
		Dino DINCD 58	8	9 wks

Robert CRAY BAND US, male vocal/instrumental group 52 wks

12 Oct	85	**FALSE ACCUSATIONS** Demon FIEND 43	68	1 wk
15 Nov	86	**STRONG PERSUADER** Mercury MERH 97	34	28 wks
3 Sep	88	**DON'T BE AFRAID OF THE DARK** Mercury MERH 129	13	12 wks
22 Sep	90	**MIDNIGHT STROLL** Mercury 8466521	19	7 wks
12 Sep	92	**I WAS WARNED** Mercury 5127212	29	3 wks
16 Oct	93	**SHAME AND SIN** Mercury 5185172	48	1 wk

CRAZY HORSE – See Neil YOUNG

CRAZY WORLD – See Crazy World of Arthur BROWN

CREAM UK, male vocal/instrumental group   287 wks

24 Dec	66 ●	**FRESH CREAM** Reaction 593–001	6	17 wks
18 Nov	67 ●	**DISRAELI GEARS** Reaction 594–003	5	42 wks
17 Aug	68 ●	**WHEELS OF FIRE (double)** Polydor 583–031/2	3	26 wks
17 Aug	68 ●	**WHEELS OF FIRE (single)** Polydor 583–033	7	13 wks
8 Feb	69 ●	**FRESH CREAM (re-issue)** Reaction 594–001	7	2 wks
15 Mar	69 ★	**GOODBYE** Polydor 583–053	1	28 wks
8 Nov	69 ●	**BEST OF CREAM** Polydor 583–060	6	34 wks
4 Jul	70 ●	**LIVE CREAM** Polydor 2383–016	4	15 wks
24 Jun	72	**LIVE CREAM VOL. 2** Polydor 2383 119	15	5 wks
26 Sep	87 ●	**THE CREAM OF ERIC CLAPTON**		
		Polydor ECTV★	3	105 wks

★ *Eric Clapton and Cream.*
From *9 Jul 93* The Cream Of Eric Clapton *was repackaged and was available as* The Best Of Eric Clapton.

CREATURES UK, male/female vocal/instrumental duo   9 wks

28 May	83	**FEAST** Wonderland SHELP 1	17	9 wks

CREEDENCE CLEARWATER REVIVAL
US, male vocal/instrumental group   65 wks

24 Jan	70	**GREEN RIVER** Liberty LBS 83273	20	6 wks
28 Mar	70 ●	**WILLY AND THE POOR BOYS** Liberty LBS 83338	10	24 wks
2 May	70	**BAYOU COUNTRY** Liberty LBS 83261	62	1 wk
12 Sep	70 ★	**COSMO'S FACTORY** Liberty LBS 83388	1	15 wks
23 Jan	71	**PENDULUM** Liberty LBG 83400	23	12 wks
30 Jun	79	**GREATEST HITS** Fantasy FT 558	35	5 wks
19 Oct	85	**THE CREEDENCE COLLECTION** Impression IMDP 3 . . .	68	2 wks

CREME – See GODLEY and CREME

Kid CREOLE and the COCONUTS
US, male/female vocal/instrumental group   54 wks

22 May	82 ●	**TROPICAL GANGSTERS** Ze ILPS 7016	3	40 wks
26 Jun	82	**FRESH FRUIT IN FOREIGN PLACES** Ze ILPS 7014 . . .	99	1 wk
17 Sep	83	**DOPPELGANGER** Island ILPS 9743	21	6 wks
15 Sep	84	**CRE-OLE** Island IMA 13	21	7 wks

An unusual group of stars watches as **Lou Christie** meets Princess Margaret. Can that be David Bowie waiting patiently?

Cream suggest that they, not the Pet Shop Boys, should have covered 'Go West'. (Pictorial Press)

THANKS FOR VOTING ME THE #1
ORCHESTRA FOR 1967

BEST WISHES
FOR 1968

RAY
CONNIFF

Ray Conniff might not have been so excited about 1967–68 if he knew what was coming up in 1969.

Patsy Cline made her British breakthrough 28 years after her death in a plane crash.

Bernard CRIBBINS – *See Howard BLAKE conducting the SINFONIA OF LONDON*

CRICKETS   US, male vocal/instrumental group   34 wks

25 Mar 61	**IN STYLE WITH THE CRICKETS** *Coral LVA 9142*	13 7 wks
27 Oct 62 ●	**BOBBY VEE MEETS THE CRICKETS** *Liberty LBY 1086★*	2 27 wks

★ *Bobby Vee and the Crickets.*
See also Buddy Holly and the Crickets.

Bing CROSBY   US, male vocalist   42 wks

8 Oct 60 ●	**JOIN BING AND SING ALONG** *Warner Brothers WM 4021*	7 11 wks
21 Dec 74	**WHITE CHRISTMAS** *MCA MCF 2568*	45 3 wks
20 Sep 75	**THAT'S WHAT LIFE IS ALL ABOUT**	
	United Artists UAG 2973	28 6 wks
5 Nov 77	**THE BEST OF BING** *MCA MCF 2540*	41 7 wks
5 Nov 77 ●	**LIVE AT THE LONDON PALLADIUM** *K-Tel NE 951* . .	9 2 wks
17 Dec 77	**SEASONS** *Polydor 2442 151*	25 7 wks
5 May 79	**SONGS OF A LIFETIME** *Philips 6641 923*	29 3 wks
14 Dec 91	**CHRISTMAS WITH BING CROSBY** *Telstar STAR 2468* .	66 3 wks

David CROSBY   US, male vocalist   12 wks

24 Apr 71	**IF ONLY I COULD REMEMBER MY NAME**	
	Atlantic 2401–005	12 7 wks
13 May 72	**GRAHAM NASH AND DAVID CROSBY**	
	Atlantic K 50011★	13 5 wks

★ *Graham Nash and David Crosby.*
See also Crosby, Stills, Nash and Young.

CROSBY, STILLS, NASH and YOUNG
US/UK/Canada, male vocal/instrumental group   93 wks

23 Aug 69	**CROSBY, STILLS AND NASH** *Atlantic 588189★*	25 5 wks
30 May 70 ●	**DEJA VU** *Atlantic 2401–001*	5 61 wks
22 May 71 ●	**FOUR-WAY STREET** *Atlantic 2956 004*	5 12 wks
21 May 74	**SO FAR** *Atlantic K 50023*	25 6 wks
9 Jul 77	**CSN** *Atlantic K 50369★*	23 9 wks

★ *Crosby, Stills and Nash.*

CROSS   UK/US, male vocal/instrumental group   2 wks

6 Feb 88	**SHOVE IT** *Virgin V 2477*	58 2 wks

Christopher CROSS   US, male vocalist   93 wks

21 Feb 81	**CHRISTOPHER CROSS** *Warner Bros. K 56789*	14 77 wks
19 Feb 83 ●	**ANOTHER PAGE** *Warner Bros. W 3757*	4 16 wks

CROWDED HOUSE
Australia/New Zealand, male vocal/instrumental group   66 wks

13 Jul 91 ●	**WOODFACE** *Capitol EST 2144*	6 56 wks
23 Oct 93 ●	**TOGETHER ALONE** *Capitol CDESTU 2215*	4† 10 wks

CROWN HEIGHTS AFFAIR
US, male vocal/instrumental group   3 wks

23 Sep 78	**DREAM WORLD** *Philips 6372 754*	40 3 wks

CRUSADERS *US, male vocal/instrumental group*   *30 wks*

21 Jul	79 ●	STREET LIFE *MCA MCF 3008*	10	16 wks
19 Jul	80	RHAPSODY AND BLUE *MCA MCG 4010*	40	5 wks
12 Sep	81	STANDING TALL *MCA MCF 3122*	47	5 wks
7 Apr	84	GHETTO BLASTER *MCA MCF 3176*	46	4 wks

Bobby CRUSH *UK, male instrumentalist – piano*   *12 wks*

29 Nov	72	BOBBY CRUSH *Philips 6308 135*	15	7 wks
18 Dec	82	THE BOBBY CRUSH INCREDIBLE DOUBLE DECKER		
		Warwick WW 5126/7	53	5 wks

CUD *UK, male vocal/instrumental group*   *1 wk*

| 11 Jul | 92 | ASQUARIUS *A & M 3953902* .... | 30 | 1 wk |

CUDDLES – *See Keith HARRIS, ORVILLE and CUDDLES*

CULT *UK, male vocal/instrumental group*   *83 wks*

18 Jun	83	SOUTHERN DEATH CULT *Beggars Banquet BEGA 46★* ...	43	3 wks
8 Sep	84	DREAMTIME *Beggars Banquet BEGA 57*	21	8 wks
26 Oct	85 ●	LOVE *Beggars Banquet BEGA 65*	4	22 wks
18 Apr	87 ●	ELECTRIC *Beggars Banquet BEGA 80*	4	27 wks
22 Apr	89 ●	SONIC TEMPLE *Beggars Banquet BEGA 98*	3	11 wks
5 Oct	91 ●	CEREMONY *Beggars Banquet BEGA 122*	9	4 wks
13 Feb	93 ★	PURE CULT *Beggars Banquet BEGACD 130*	1	8 wks

★ *Southern Death Cult.*

CULT JAM – *See LISA LISA and CULT JAM with FULL FORCE*

CULTURE *Jamaica, male vocal/instrumental group*   *1 wk*

| 1 Apr | 78 | TWO SEVENS CLASH *Lightning LIP 1* .... | 60 | 1 wk |

CULTURE BEAT
UK/US/Germany male/female vocal/instrumental group   *1 wk*

| 25 Sep | 93 | SERENITY *Dance Pool 4741012* .... | 56 | 1 wk |

CULTURE CLUB *UK, male vocal/instrumental group*   *149 wks*

16 Oct	82 ●	KISSING TO BE CLEVER *Virgin V 2232*	5	59 wks
22 Oct	83 ★	COLOUR BY NUMBERS *Virgin V 2285*	1	56 wks
3 Nov	84 ●	WAKING UP WITH THE HOUSE ON FIRE *Virgin V 2330*	2	13 wks
12 Apr	86 ●	FROM LUXURY TO HEARTACHE *Virgin V 2380*	10	6 wks
18 Apr	87 ●	THIS TIME *Virgin VTV 1*	8	10 wks
2 Oct	93	AT WORST ... THE BEST OF BOY GEORGE AND		
		CULTURE CLUB *Virgin VTCD 19★*	24	5 wks

★ *Boy George and Culture Club.*

CURE *UK, male vocal/instrumental group*   *192 wks*

2 Jun	79	THREE IMAGINARY BOYS *Fiction FIX 001*	44	3 wks
3 May	80	17 SECONDS *Fiction FIX 004*	20	10 wks
25 Apr	81	FAITH *Fiction FIX 6*	14	8 wks
15 May	82 ●	PORNOGRAPHY *Fiction FIX D7*	8	9 wks
3 Sep	83	BOYS DON'T CRY *Fiction SPELP 26*	71	7 wks
24 Dec	83	JAPANESE WHISPERS *Fiction FIXM 8*	26	14 wks
12 May	84 ●	THE TOP *Fiction FIXS 9*	10	10 wks

98

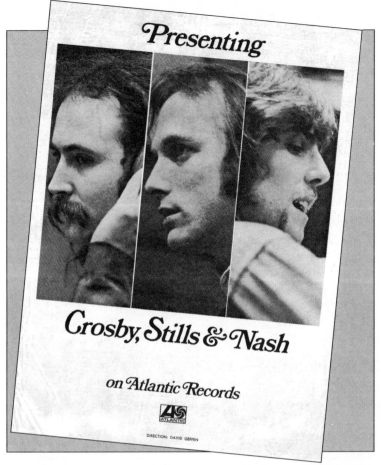

Crosby, Stills and Nash are introduced to the music business in June 1969. Less than a year later, Neil Young was added to the line-up.

3 Nov 84	**CONCERT – THE CURE LIVE** *Fiction FIXH 10*	**26**	4 wks
7 Sep 85 ●	**THE HEAD ON THE DOOR** *Fiction FIXH 11*	**7**	13 wks
31 May 86 ●	**STANDING ON A BEACH – THE SINGLES**		
	Fiction FIXH 12	**4**	35 wks
6 Jun 87 ●	**KISS ME KISS ME KISS ME** *Fiction FIXH 13*	**6**	15 wks
13 May 89 ●	**DISINTEGRATION** *Fiction FIXH 14*	**3**	26 wks
17 Nov 90 ●	**MIXED UP** *Fiction 8470991*	**8**	17 wks
6 Apr 91 ●	**ENTREAT** *Fiction FIXH 17*	**10**	5 wks
2 May 92 ★	**WISH** *Fiction FIXCD 20*	**1**	13 wks
25 Sep 93	**SHOW** *Fiction FIXCD 25*	**29**	2 wks
6 Nov 93	**PARIS** *Fiction FIXCD 26*	**56**	1 wk

The compact disc version of FIXH 12 was titled Staring At The Sea.

CURIOSITY KILLED THE CAT
UK, male vocal/instrumental group　　　　　　　　*27 wks*

9 May 87 ★	**KEEP YOUR DISTANCE** *Mercury CATLP 1*	**1**	24 wks
4 Oct 89	**GETAHEAD** *Mercury 842010 1*	**29**	3 wks

CURVE *UK, male/female vocal/instrumental duo*　　*6 wks*

21 Mar 92	**DOPPELGANGER** *Anxious ANXCD 77*	**11**	3 wks
19 Jun 93	**RADIO SESSIONS** *Anxious ANXCD 80*	**72**	1 wk
25 Sep 93	**CUCKOO** *Anxious ANXCD 81*	**23**	2 wks

CURVED AIR *UK, male/female vocal/instrumental group*　*32 wks*

5 Dec 70 ●	**AIR CONDITIONING** *Warner Bros. WSX 3012*	**8**	21 wks
9 Oct 71	**CURVED AIR** *Warner Bros. K 46092*	**11**	6 wks
13 May 72	**PHANTASMAGORIA** *Reprise K 46158*	**20**	5 wks

Adge CUTLER – *See WURZELS*

CUTTING CREW
UK/Canada, male vocal/instrumental group　　　　*6 wks*

29 Nov 86	**BROADCAST** *Siren SIRENLP 7*	**41**	6 wks

CYPRESS HILL *US, male rap group*　　　*21 wks*

7 Aug 93	**BLACK SUNDAY** *Ruffhouse 4740752*	**13†**	21 wks

Billy Ray CYRUS *US, male vocalist*　　　*10 wks*

29 Aug 92 ●	**SOME GAVE ALL** *Mercury 5106352*	**9**	10 wks

Holgar CZUKAY – *See David SYLVIAN*

Heavy D and the BOYZ
US, male vocal/instrumental group　　　　　　　*3 wks*

10 Aug 91	**A PEACEFUL JOURNEY** *MCA MCA 10289*	**40**	3 wks

D. MOB *UK, male producer, Danny D*   *11 wks*

11 Nov 89   **A LITTLE BIT OF THIS A LITTLE BIT OF THAT**
            FFRR 8281591 .... **46**   11 wks

DAINTEES – *See Martin STEPHENSON and the DAINTEES*

DAISY CHAINSAW
UK, male/female vocal/instrumental group   *1 wk*

10 Oct 92   **ELEVENTEEN** *Deva TPLP 100CD* .... **62**   1 wk

DAKOTAS – *See Billy J. KRAMER and the DAKOTAS*

DALEK I *UK, male vocal/instrumental group*   *2 wks*

9 Aug 80   **COMPASS KUMPAS** *Backdoor OPEN 1* .... **54**   2 wks

DALI'S CAR *UK, male vocal/instrumental duo*   *1 wk*

1 Dec 84   **THE WAKING HOUR** *Paradox DOXLP 1* .... **84**   1 wk

Roger DALTREY *UK, male vocalist*   *24 wks*

26 Jul   75   **RIDE A ROCK HORSE** *Polydor 2660 111* .... **14**   10 wks
4 Jul   77   **ONE OF THE BOYS** *Polydor 2442 146* .... **45**   1 wk
23 Aug   80   **McVICAR (film soundtrack)** *Polydor POLD 5034* .... **39**   11 wks
2 Nov   85   **UNDER A RAGING MOON** *10 DIX 17* .... **52**   2 wks

Glen DALY *UK, male vocalist*   *2 wks*

20 Nov 71   **GLASGOW NIGHT OUT** *Golden Guinea GGL 0479* ...... **28**   2 wks

D
101

DAMNED *UK, male vocal/instrumental group*   *54 wks*

12 Mar   77   **DAMNED DAMNED DAMNED** *Stiff SEEZ 1* .... **36**   10 wks
17 Nov   79   **MACHINE GUN ETIQUETTE** *Chiswick CWK 3011* ..... **31**   5 wks
29 Nov   80   **THE BLACK ALBUM** *Chiswick CWK 3015* .... **29**   3 wks
28 Nov   81   **BEST OF** *Chiswick DAM 1* .... **43**   12 wks
23 Oct   82   **STRAWBERRIES** *Bronze BRON 542* .... **15**   4 wks
27 Jul   85   **PHANTASMAGORIA** *MCA MCF 3275* .... **11**   17 wks
13 Dec   86   **ANYTHING** *MCA MCG 6015* .... **40**   2 wks
12 Dec   87   **LIGHT AT THE END OF THE TUNNEL** *MCA MCSP 312*   **87**   1 wk

Vic DAMONE *US, male vocalist*   *8 wks*

25 Apr   81   **NOW!** *RCA INTS 5080* .... **28**   7 wks
2 Apr   83   **VIC DAMONE SINGS THE GREAT SONGS** *CBS 32261* .   **87**   1 wk

DANA *Ireland, female vocalist*   *2 wks*

3 Jan   81   **EVERYTHING IS BEAUTIFUL** *Warwick WW 5099* ...... **43**   2 wks

Suzanne DANDO *UK, female exercise instructor*   *1 wk*

17 Mar 84   **SHAPE UP AND DANCE WITH SUZANNE DANDO**
            Lifestyle LEG 21 .... **87**   1 wk

Charlie DANIELS BAND
US, male vocal/instrumental group   *1 wk*

10 Nov 79   **MILLION MILE REFLECTIONS** *Epic EPC 83446* .... **74**   1 wk

Crowded House *play a crowded stage at C.B.G.B. in New York. (Pictorial Press)*

Kiki Dee *is joined backstage during her 1974 engagement at New York City's Bottom Line by (left to right): Pete Townshend, Elton John and Nona Hendryx. (Pictorial Press)*

DANNY WILSON *UK, male vocal/instrumental group* *11 wks*

30 Apr	88	**MEET DANNY WILSON** *Virgin V 2419*	**65**	5 wks
29 Jul	89	**BEEBOP MOPTOP** *Virgin V 2594*	**24**	5 wks
31 Aug	91	**SWEET DANNY WILSON** *Virgin V 2669*	**54**	1 wk

DANSE SOCIETY *UK, male vocal/instrumental group* *4 wks*

| 11 Feb | 84 | **HEAVEN IS WAITING** *Society 205 972* .... | **39** | 4 wks |

Stephen DANTE *UK, male vocalist* *1 wk*

| 3 Sep | 88 | **FIND OUT** *Cooltempo CTLP 6* .... | **87** | 1 wk |

Terence Trent D'ARBY *US, male vocalist* *89 wks*

25 Jul	87	★ **INTRODUCING THE HARDLINE ACCORDING TO TERENCE TRENT D'ARBY** *CBS 450 911–1*	**1**	65 wks
4 Nov	89	**NEITHER FISH NOR FLESH** *CBS 4658091*	**12**	5 wks
15 May	93	● **SYMPHONY OR DAMN** *Columbia 4735612*	**4**	19 wks

DARE *UK, male vocal/instrumental group* *1 wk*

| 14 Sep | 91 | **BLOOD FROM STONE** *A & M 3953601* .... | **48** | 1 wk |

Bobby DARIN *US, male vocalist* *15 wks*

19 Mar	60	● **THIS IS DARIN** *London HA 2235*	**4**	8 wks
9 Apr	60	**THAT'S ALL** *London HAE 2172*	**15**	1 wk
5 Oct	85	**THE LEGEND OF BOBBY DARIN – HIS GREATEST HITS** *Stylus SMR 8504*	**39**	6 wks

DARLING BUDS
UK, male/female vocal/instrumental group *3 wks*

| 18 Feb | 89 | **POP SAID** *Epic 462894 1* .... | **23** | 3 wks |

DARTS *UK, male/female vocal/instrumental group* *57 wks*

3 Dec	77	● **DARTS** *Magnet MAG 5020*	**9**	22 wks
3 Jun	78	**EVERYONE PLAYS DARTS** *Magnet MAG 5022*	**12**	18 wks
18 Nov	78	● **AMAZING DARTS** *K-Tel/Magnet DLP 7981*	**8**	13 wks
6 Oct	79	**DART ATTACK** *Magnet MAG 5030*	**38**	4 wks

F.R. DAVID *France, male vocalist* *6 wks*

| 7 May | 83 | **WORDS** *Carrere CAL 145* .... | **46** | 6 wks |

Windsor DAVIES – *See Don ESTELLE and Windsor DAVIES*

Colin DAVIS – *See BBC SYMPHONY ORCHESTRA*

Carl DAVIS and the ROYAL LIVERPOOL PHILHARMONIC ORCHESTRA
US, male conductor and orchestra *4 wks*

| 19 Oct | 91 | **PAUL McCARTNEY'S LIVERPOOL ORATORIO** *EMI Classics PAUL 1* .... | **36** | 4 wks |

Miles DAVIS *US, male instrumentalist – trumpet*   *6 wks*

11 Jul	70	**BITCHES BREW** *CBS 66236*	**71**	1 wk
15 Jun	85	**YOU'RE UNDER ARREST** *CBS 26447*	**88**	1 wk
18 Oct	86	**TUTU** *Warner Bros. 925490 1*	**74**	2 wks
3 Jun	89	**AMANDLA** *Warner Bros. WX 250*	**49**	2 wks

Sammy DAVIS Jr *US, male vocalist*   *1 wk*

13 Apr	63	**SAMMY DAVIS JR. AT THE COCONUT GROVE** *Reprise R 6063/2*	**19**	1 wk

Spencer DAVIS GROUP
UK, male vocal/instrumental group   *47 wks*

8 Jan	66	● **THEIR 1ST LP** *Fontana TL 5242*	**6**	9 wks
22 Jan	66	● **THE 2ND LP** *Fontana TL 5295*	**3**	18 wks
11 Sep	66	● **AUTUMN '66** *Fontana TL 5359*	**4**	20 wks

DAWN *US, male/female vocal group*   *2 wks*

4 May	74	**GOLDEN RIBBONS** *Bell BELLS 236*	**46**	2 wks

Doris DAY *US, female vocalist*   *28 wks*

6 Jan	79	**20 GOLDEN GREATS** *Warwick PR 5053*	**12**	11 wks
11 Nov	89	**A PORTRAIT OF DORIS DAY** *Stylus SMR 984*	**32**	9 wks
6 Nov	93	**GREATEST HITS** *Telstar TCD 2659*	**14†**	8 wks

Taylor DAYNE *US, female vocalist*   *17 wks*

5 Mar	88	**TELL IT TO MY HEART** *Arista 208898*	**24**	17 wks

Chris DE BURGH *Ireland, male vocalist*   *252 wks*

12 Sep	81	**BEST MOVES** *A & M AMLH 68532*	**65**	4 wks
9 Oct	82	**THE GETAWAY** *A & M AMLH 68549*	**30**	16 wks
19 May	84	**MAN ON THE LINE** *A & M AMLX 65002*	**11**	24 wks
29 Dec	84	● **THE VERY BEST OF CHRIS DE BURGH** *Telstar STAR 2248*	**6**	70 wks
24 Aug	85	**SPANISH TRAIN AND OTHER STORIES** *A & M AMLH 68343*	**78**	3 wks
7 Jun	86	● **INTO THE LIGHT** *A & M AM 5121*	**2**	59 wks
4 Oct	86	**CRUSADER** *A & M AMLH 64746*	**72**	1 wk
15 Oct	88	★ **FLYING COLOURS** *A & M AMA 5224*	**1**	30 wks
4 Nov	89	● **FROM A SPARK TO A FLAME – THE VERY BEST OF CHRIS DE BURGH** *A & M CDBLP 100*	**4**	29 wks
22 Sep	90	**HIGH ON EMOTION – LIVE FROM DUBLIN** *A & M 3970861*	**15**	6 wks
9 May	92	● **POWER OF TEN** *A & M 3971882*	**3**	10 wks

DE LA SOUL *US, male rap/sampling group*   *70 wks*

25 Mar	89	**3 FEET HIGH AND RISING** *Big Life DLSLP 1*	**13**	57 wks
25 May	91	● **DE LA SOUL IS DEAD** *Big Life BLRLP 8*	**7**	11 wks
9 Oct	93	**BUHLOONE MINDSTATE** *Big Life BLRCD 25*	**37**	2 wks

Waldo DE LOS RIOS *Argentina, orchestra*   *26 wks*

1 May	71	● **SYMPHONIES FOR THE SEVENTIES** *A & M AMLS 2014*	**6**	26 wks

Manitas DE PLATA *Spain, male instrumentalist – guitar* *1 wk*

29 Jul	67	**FLAMENCO GUITAR** *Philips SBL 7786*	40	1 wk

DEACON BLUE *UK, male/female vocal/instrumental group* *176 wks*

6 Jun	87	**RAINTOWN** *CBS 4505491*	14	77 wks
15 Apr	89 ★	**WHEN THE WORLD KNOWS YOUR NAME**		
		CBS 4633211	1	54 wks
22 Sep	90 ●	**OOH LAS VEGAS** *CBS 4672421*	3	8 wks
15 Jun	91 ●	**FELLOW HOODLUMS** *Columbia 4685501*	2	27 wks
13 Mar	93 ●	**WHATEVER YOU SAY SAY NOTHING** *Columbia 4735272*	4	10 wks

DEAD CAN DANCE
Australia, male/female vocal/instrumental duo *1 wk*

25 Sep	93	**INTO THE LABYRINTH** *4AD CAD 3013CD*	47	1 wk

DEAD KENNEDYS *US, male vocal/instrumental group* *8 wks*

13 Sep	80	**FRESH FRUIT FOR ROTTING VEGETABLES**		
		Cherry Red BRED 10	33	6 wks
4 Jul	87	**GIVE ME CONVENIENCE** *Alternative Tentacles VIRUS 5* ..	84	2 wks

DEAD OR ALIVE *UK, male vocal/instrumental group* *22 wks*

D
105

28 Apr	84	**SOPHISTICATED BOOM BOOM** *Epic EPC 25835*	29	3 wks
25 May	85 ●	**YOUTHQUAKE** *Epic EPC 26420*	9	15 wks
14 Feb	87	**MAD, BAD AND DANGEROUS TO KNOW**		
		Epic 450 257–1	27	4 wks

DEAN – *See JAN and DEAN*

Hazell DEAN *UK, female vocalist* *3 wks*

22 Oct	88	**ALWAYS** *EMI EMC 3546*	38	3 wks

DeBARGE *US, male/female vocal group* *2 wks*

25 May	85	**RHYTHM OF THE NIGHT** *Gordy ZL 72340*	94	2 wks

Kiki DEE *UK, female vocalist* *9 wks*

26 Mar	77	**KIKI DEE** *Rocket ROLA 3*	24	5 wks
18 Jul	81	**PERFECT TIMING** *Ariola ARL 5050*	47	4 wks

Dave DEE, DOZY, BEAKY, MICK and TICH
UK, male vocal/instrumental group *15 wks*

2 Jul	66	**DAVE DEE, DOZY, BEAKY, MICK AND TICH**		
		Fontana STL 5350	11	10 wks
7 Jan	67	**IF MUSIC BE THE FOOD OF LOVE . . . PREPARE FOR**		
		INDIGESTION *Fontana STL 5388*	27	5 wks

DEEE-LITE *US, male/female vocal/instrumental group* *19 wks*

8 Sep	90	**WORLD CLIQUE** *Elektra EKT 77*	14	18 wks
4 Jul	92	**INFINITY WITHIN** *Elektra 7559613132*	37	1 wk

DEEP PURPLE *UK, male vocal/instrumental group*   *274 wks*

24 Jan	70	**CONCERTO FOR GROUP AND ORCHESTRA** *Harvest SHVL 767*	26	4 wks
20 Jun	70 ●	**DEEP PURPLE IN ROCK** *Harvest SHVL 777*	4	68 wks
18 Sep	71 ★	**FIREBALL** *Harvest SHVL 793*	1	25 wks
15 Apr	72 ★	**MACHINE HEAD** *Purple TPSA 7504*	1	24 wks
6 Jan	73	**MADE IN JAPAN** *Purple TPSP 351*	16	14 wks
17 Feb	73 ●	**WHO DO WE THINK WE ARE** *Purple TPSA 7508*	4	11 wks
2 Mar	74 ●	**BURN** *Purple TPA 3505*	3	21 wks
23 Nov	74 ●	**STORM BRINGER** *Purple TPS 3508*	6	12 wks
5 Jul	75	**24 CARAT PURPLE** *Purple TPSM 2002*	14	17 wks
22 Nov	75	**COME TASTE THE BAND** *Purple TPSA 7515*	19	4 wks
27 Nov	76	**DEEP PURPLE LIVE** *Purple TPSA 7517*	12	6 wks
21 Apr	79	**THE MARK II PURPLE SINGLES** *Purple TPS 3514*	24	6 wks
19 Jul	80 ★	**DEEPEST PURPLE** *Harvest EMTV 25*	1	15 wks
13 Dec	80	**IN CONCERT** *Harvest SHDW 4121/4122*	30	8 wks
4 Sep	82 ●	**DEEP PURPLE LIVE IN LONDON** *Harvest SHSP 4124* ..	23	5 wks
10 Nov	84 ●	**PERFECT STRANGERS** *Polydor POLH 16*	5	15 wks
29 Jun	85	**THE ANTHOLOGY** *Harvest PUR 1*	50	3 wks
24 Jan	87 ●	**THE HOUSE OF BLUE LIGHT** *Polydor POLH 32*	10	9 wks
16 Jul	88	**NOBODY'S PERFECT** *Polydor PODV 10*	38	2 wks
2 Nov	90	**SLAVES AND MASTERS** *RCA PL 90535*	45	2 wks
7 Aug	93	**THE BATTLE RAGES ON ...** *RCA 74321154202*	21	3 wks

DEF LEPPARD *UK, male vocal/instrumental group*   *159 wks*

22 Mar	80	**ON THROUGH THE NIGHT** *Vertigo 9102 040*	15	8 wks
25 Jul	81	**HIGH 'N' DRY** *Vertigo 6359 045*	26	8 wks
12 Mar	83	**PYROMANIA** *Vertigo VERS 2*	18	8 wks
29 Aug	87 ★	**HYSTERIA** *Bludgeon Riffola HYSLP 1*	1	101 wks
11 Apr	92 ★	**ADRENALIZE** *Bludgeon Riffola 5109782*	1	30 wks
16 Oct	93 ●	**RETRO ACTIVE** *Bludgeon Riffola 5183052*	6	4 wks

DEFINITION OF SOUND *US, male rap group*   *4 wks*

29 Jun	91	**LOVE AND LIFE** *Circa CIRCA 14*	38	3 wks

Desmond DEKKER *Jamaica, male vocalist*   *4 wks*

5 Jul	69	**THIS IS DESMOND DEKKER** *Trojan TTL 4*	27	4 wks

DEL AMITRI *UK, male vocal/instrumental group*   *63 wks*

24 Feb	90 ●	**WAKING HOURS** *A & M AMA 9006*	6	44 wks
13 Jun	92 ●	**CHANGE EVERYTHING** *A & M 3953852*	2	19 wks

DELANEY and BONNIE and FRIENDS
US/UK, male/female vocal/instrumental group   *3 wks*

6 Jun	70	**ON TOUR** *Atlantic 2400–013*	39	3 wks

DEMON *UK, male vocal/instrumental group*   *5 wks*

14 Aug	82	**THE UNEXPECTED GUEST** *Carrere CAL 139*	47	3 wks
2 Jul	83	**THE PLAGUE** *Clay CLAY LP 6*	73	2 wks

Chaka DEMUS and PLIERS
Jamaica, male vocal/instrumental duo   *9 wks*

10 Jul	93	**TEASE ME** *Mango CIDM 1102*	26	9 wks

Cathy DENNIS   UK, female vocalist   35 wks

10 Aug 91 ● **MOVE TO THIS** *Polydor 8495031*	**3**	31 wks
23 Jan 93 ● **INTO THE SKYLINE** *Polydor 5139352*	**8**	4 wks

Sandy DENNY   UK, female vocalist   2 wks

2 Oct 71 **THE NORTH STAR GRASSMAN AND THE RAVENS**		
Island ILPS 9165	**31**	2 wks

John DENVER   US, male vocalist   240 wks

17 Mar 73 **ROCKY MOUNTAIN HIGH** *RCA SF 2308*	**11**	15 wks
2 Jun 73 **POEMS, PRAYERS AND PROMISES**		
RCA SF 8219	**19**	5 wks
23 Jun 73 **RHYMES AND REASONS** *RCA Victor SF 8348*	**21**	5 wks
30 Mar 74 ● **THE BEST OF JOHN DENVER** *RCA Victor APLI 0374* ..	**7**	69 wks
7 Sep 74 ● **BACK HOME AGAIN** *RCA Victor APLI 0548*	**3**	29 wks
22 Mar 75 **AN EVENING WITH JOHN DENVER**		
RCA Victor LSA 3211/12	**31**	4 wks
11 Oct 75 **WIND SONG** *RCA Victor APLI 1183*	**14**	21 wks
15 May 76 ● **LIVE IN LONDON** *RCA Victor RS 1050*	**2**	29 wks
4 Sep 76 ● **SPIRIT** *RCA Victor APLI 1694*	**9**	11 wks
19 Mar 77 ● **BEST OF JOHN DENVER VOL. 2** *RCA Victor PL 42120* .	**9**	9 wks
11 Feb 78 **I WANT TO LIVE** *RCA PL 12561*	**25**	5 wks
21 Apr 79 **JOHN DENVER** *RCA Victor PL 13075*	**68**	1 wk
28 Nov 81 **PERHAPS LOVE** *CBS 73592*★	**17**	21 wks
22 Oct 83 **IT'S ABOUT TIME** *RCA RCALP 6087*	**90**	2 wks
1 Dec 84 **JOHN DENVER COLLECTION** *Telstar STAR 2253*	**20**	11wks
23 Aug 86 **ONE WORLD** *RCA PL 85811*	**91**	3 wks

★ *Placido Domingo and John Denver.*

D
107

Karl DENVER   UK, male vocalist   27 wks

23 Dec 61 ● **WIMOWEH** *Ace Of Clubs ACL 1098*	**7**	27 wks

DEPECHE MODE   UK, male vocal/instrumental group   156 wks

14 Nov 81 ● **SPEAK AND SPELL** *Mute STUMM 5*	**10**	33 wks
9 Oct 82 ● **A BROKEN FRAME** *Mute STUMM 9*	**8**	11 wks
3 Sep 83 ● **CONSTRUCTION TIME AGAIN** *Mute STUMM 13*	**6**	12 wks
6 Sep 84 ● **SOME GREAT REWARD** *Mute STUMM 19*	**5**	12 wks
26 Oct 85 ● **THE SINGLES 81–85** *Mute MUTEL 1*	**6**	22 wks
29 Mar 86 ● **BLACK CELEBRATION** *Mute STUMM 26*	**4**	11 wks
10 Oct 87 ● **MUSIC FOR THE MASSES** *Mute STUMM 47*	**10**	4 wks
25 Mar 89 ● **101** *Mute STUMM 101*	**5**	8 wks
31 Mar 90 ● **VIOLATOR** *Mute STUMM 64*	**2**	30 wks
3 Apr 93 ★ **SONGS OF FAITH AND DEVOTION**		
Mute CDSTUMM 106	**1†**	13 wks

DEREK AND CLIVE – *See Peter COOK and Dudley MOORE*

DES'REE   UK, female vocalist   5 wks

29 Feb 92 **MIND ADVENTURES** *Dusted Sound 4712632*	**26**	5 wks

DEREK and the DOMINOS – *See Eric CLAPTON*

DESTROYERS – *See George THOROGOOD and the DESTROYERS*

DETROIT SPINNERS   US, male vocal group   3 wks

14 May 77 **DETROIT SPINNERS' SMASH HITS** *Atlantic K 50363* ..	**37**	3 wks

Sidney DEVINE   UK, male vocalist   11 wks

| 10 Apr 76 | DOUBLE DEVINE   *Philips 6625 019* .... | 14 | 10 wks |
| 11 Dec 76 | DEVINE TIME   *Philips 6308 283* .... | 49 | 1 wk |

DEVO   US, male vocal/instrumental group   22 wks

16 Sep 78	Q: ARE WE NOT MEN? A: NO WE ARE DEVO!		
	Virgin V 2106	12	7 wks
23 Jun 79	DUTY NOW FOR THE FUTURE *Virgin V 2125*	49	6 wks
24 May 80	FREEDOM OF CHOICE *Virgin V 2162*	47	5 wks
5 Sep 81	NEW TRADITIONALISTS *Virgin V 2191*	50	4 wks

Howard DEVOTO   UK, male vocalist   2 wks

| 6 Aug 83 | JERKY VERSIONS OF THE DREAM   *Virgin V 2272* .... | 57 | 2 wks |

DEXY'S MIDNIGHT RUNNERS
UK, male/female vocal/instrumental group   93 wks

26 Jul 80 ●	SEARCHING FOR THE YOUNG SOUL REBELS		
	Parlophone PCS 7213	6	10 wks
7 Aug 82 ●	TOO-RYE-AY *Mercury MERS 5*	2	46 wks
26 Mar 83	GENO *EMI EMS 1007*	79	2 wks
21 Sep 85	DON'T STAND ME DOWN *Mercury MERH 56*	22	6 wks
8 Jun 91	THE VERY BEST OF DEXY'S MIDNIGHT RUNNERS		
	Mercury 8464601	12	15 wks

Group was all male for first album.

Jim DIAMOND   UK, male vocalist   5 wks

| 22 May 93 | JIM DIAMOND   *PolyGram TV 8438472* .... | 16 | 5 wks |

Neil DIAMOND   US, male vocalist   536 wks

3 Apr 71	TAP ROOT MANUSCRIPT *Uni UNLS 117*	19	12 wks
3 Apr 71	GOLD *Uni UNLS 116*	23	11 wks
11 Dec 71	STONES *Uni UNLS 121*	18	14 wks
5 Aug 72 ●	MOODS *Uni UNLS 128*	7	19 wks
12 Jan 74	HOT AUGUST NIGHT *Uni ULD 1*	32	2 wks
16 Feb 74	JONATHAN LIVINGSTON SEAGULL *CBS 69047*	35	1 wk
9 Mar 74	RAINBOW *MCA MCF 2529*	39	5 wks
29 Jul 74	HIS 12 GREATEST HITS *MCA MCF 2550*	13	78 wks
9 Nov 74	SERENADE *CBS 69067*	11	14 wks
10 Jul 76 ●	BEAUTIFUL NOISE *CBS 86004*	10	26 wks
12 Mar 77 ●	LOVE AT THE GREEK *CBS 95001*	3	32 wks
6 Aug 77	HOT AUGUST NIGHT (re-issue) *MCA MCSP 255*	60	1 wk
17 Dec 77	I'M GLAD YOU'RE HERE WITH ME TONIGHT		
	CBS 86044	16	12 wks
25 Nov 78 ●	20 GOLDEN GREATS *MCA EMTV 14*	2	29 wks
6 Jan 79	YOU DON'T BRING ME FLOWERS *CBS 86077*	15	23 wks
19 Jan 80	SEPTEMBER MORN *CBS 86096*	14	11 wks
22 Nov 80 ●	THE JAZZ SINGER (film soundtrack) *Capitol EAST 12120*	3	110 wks
28 Feb 81	LOVE SONGS *MCA MCF 3092*	43	6 wks
5 Dec 81	THE WAY TO THE SKY *CBS 85343*	39	13 wks
19 Jun 82	12 GREATEST HITS VOL. 2 *CBS 85844*	32	8 wks
13 Nov 82	HEARTLIGHT *CBS 25073*	43	10 wks
10 Dec 83	THE VERY BEST OF NEIL DIAMOND *K-Tel NE 1265* .	33	11 wks
28 Jul 84 ●	PRIMITIVE *CBS 86306*	7	10 wks
24 May 86	HEADED FOR THE FUTURE *CBS 26952*	36	8 wks
28 Nov 87	HOT AUGUST NIGHT 2 *CBS 460 408–1*	74	4 wks
25 Feb 89	THE BEST YEARS OF OUR LIVES *CBS 463201 1*	42	6 wks
9 Nov 91	LOVESCAPE *Columbia 4688901*	36	13 wks
4 Jul 92 ★	THE GREATEST HITS 1966–1992 *Columbia 4715022*	1	30 wks
28 Nov 92	THE CHRISTMAS ALBUM *Columbia 4724102*	50	6 wks
9 Oct 93	UP ON THE ROOF – SONGS FROM THE BRILL		
	BUILDING *Columbia 4743562*	28	11 wks

DIAMOND HEAD UK, male vocal/instrumental group   9 wks

23 Oct	82	**BORROWED TIME** MCA DH 1001	24	5 wks
24 Sep	83	**CANTERBURY** MCA DH 1002	32	4 wks

DICKIES US, male vocal/instrumental group   19 wks

17 Feb	79	**THE INCREDIBLE SHRINKING DICKIES**		
		A & M AMLE 64742	18	17 wks
24 Nov	79	**DAWN OF THE DICKIES** A & M AMLE 68510	60	2 wks

Bruce DICKINSON UK, male vocalist   9 wks

19 May	90	**TATTOOED MILLIONAIRE** EMI EMC 3574	14	9 wks

Barbara DICKSON UK, female vocalist   140 wks

18 Jun	77	**MORNING COMES QUICKLY** RSO 2394 188	58	1 wk
12 Apr	80 ●	**THE BARBARA DICKSON ALBUM** Epic EPC 84088 ...	7	12 wks
16 May	81	**YOU KNOW IT'S ME** Epic EPC 84551	39	6 wks
6 Feb	82 ●	**ALL FOR A SONG** Epic 10030	3	38 wks
24 Sep	83	**TELL ME IT'S NOT TRUE** Legacy LLM 101	100	1 wk
23 Jun	84	**HEARTBEATS** Epic EPC 25706	21	8 wks
12 Jan	85 ●	**THE BARBARA DICKSON SONGBOOK** K-Tel NE 1287	5	19 wks
23 Nov	85	**GOLD** K-Tel ONE 1312	11	18 wks
15 Nov	86	**THE VERY BEST OF BARBARA DICKSON**		
		Telstar STAR 2276	78	8 wks
29 Nov	86	**THE RIGHT MOMENT** K-Tel ONE 1335	39	8 wks
6 May	89	**COMING ALIVE AGAIN** Telstar STAR 2349	30	7 wks
15 Aug	92	**DON'T THINK TWICE IT'S ALL RIGHT**		
		Columbia MOODCD 25	32	5 wks
28 Nov	92	**THE BEST OF ELAINE PAIGE AND BARBARA**		
		DICKSON Telstar TCD 2632★	22	9 wks

★ *Elaine Paige and Barbara Dickson.*
Tell Me It's Not True *is a mini-album featuring songs from the musical* Blood Brothers.

Bo DIDDLEY US, male vocalist/instrumentalist – guitar   16 wks

5 Oct	63	**BO DIDDLEY** Pye International NPL 28026	11	8 wks
9 Oct	63	**BO DIDDLEY IS A GUNSLINGER** Pye NJL 33	20	1 wk
30 Nov	63	**BO DIDDLEY RIDES AGAIN** Pye International NPL 28029	19	1 wk
15 Feb	64	**BO DIDDLEY'S BEACH PARTY** Pye NPL 28032	13	6 wks

DIESEL PARK WEST UK, male vocal/instrumental group 3 wks

11 Feb	89	**SHAKESPEARE ALABAMA** Food FOODLP 2	55	2 wks
15 Feb	92	**DECENCY** Food FOODCD 7	57	1 wk

DIFFORD and TILBROOK
UK, male vocal/instrumental duo   3 wks

14 Jul	84	**DIFFORD AND TILBROOK** A & M AMLX 64985	47	3 wks

DIGITAL UNDERGROUND
US, male vocal/instrumental group   2 wks

7 Apr	90	**SEX PACKETS** BCM BCM 377LP	59	1 wk
30 Jun	90	**DOWUTCHYALIKE/PACKET MAN** BCM BCM 463X ..	59	1 wk

Richard DIMBLEBY UK, male broadcaster   5 wks

4 Jun	66	**VOICE OF RICHARD DIMBLEBY** MFP 1087	14	5 wks

DINOSAUR JR US, male vocalist   5 wks

| 2 Mar 91 | GREEN MIND blanco y negro BYN 24 | 36 | 2 wks |
| 20 Feb 93 ● | WHERE YOU BEEN blanco y negro 4509916272 | 10 | 3 wks |

DIO UK/US, male vocal/instrumental group   48 wks

11 Jun 83	HOLY DIVER Vertigo VERS 5	13	15 wks
21 Jul 84 ●	THE LAST IN LINE Vertigo VERL 16	4	14 wks
7 Sep 85 ●	SACRED HEART Vertigo VERH 30	4	6 wks
5 Jul 86	INTERMISSION Vertigo VERB 40	22	5 wks
22 Aug 87 ●	DREAM EVIL Vertigo VERH 46	8	5 wks
26 May 90	LOCK UP THE WOLVES Vertigo 8460331	28	3 wks

DION and the BELMONTS US, male vocal group   5 wks

| 12 Apr 80 | 20 GOLDEN GREATS K-Tel NE 1057 | 31 | 5 wks |

DIRE STRAITS UK, male vocal/instrumental group   1058 wks

22 Jul 78 ●	DIRE STRAITS Vertigo 9102 021	5	130 wks
23 Jun 79 ●	COMMUNIQUE Vertigo 9102 031	5	32 wks
25 Oct 80 ●	MAKIN' MOVIES Vertigo 6359 034	4	249 wks
2 Oct 82 ★	LOVE OVER GOLD Vertigo 6359 109	1	198 wks
24 Mar 84 ●	ALCHEMY – DIRE STRAITS LIVE Vertigo VERY 11	3	163 wks
25 May 85 ★	BROTHERS IN ARMS Vertigo VERH 25	1	196 wks
29 Oct 88 ★	MONEY FOR NOTHING Vertigo VERH 64	1	48 wks
21 Sep 91 ★	ON EVERY STREET Vertigo 5101601	1	35 wks
22 May 93 ●	ON THE NIGHT Vertigo 5147662	4	7 wks

D
110

DISCHARGE UK, male vocal/instrumental group   5 wks

| 15 May 82 | HEAR NOTHING, SEE NOTHING, SAY NOTHING Clay CLAYLP 3 | 40 | 5 wks |

DISCIPLES OF SOUL – See LITTLE STEVEN

DISPOSABLE HEROES OF HIPHOPRISY
US, male rap/instrumental duo   3 wks

| 16 May 92 | HYPOCRISY IS THE GREATEST LUXURY 4th + B'way BRCD 584 | 40 | 3 wks |

Sacha DISTEL France, male vocalist   14 wks

| 2 May 70 | SACHA DISTEL Warner Bros. WS 3003 | 21 | 14 wks |

DIVINYLS Australia, male/female vocal/instrumental duo   1 wk

| 20 Jul 91 | DIVINYLS Virgin America VUSLP 30 | 59 | 1 wk |

DJ JAZZY JEFF and FRESH PRINCE
US, male rap duo   7 wks

28 Feb 87	ROCK THE HOUSE Champion CHAMP 1004	97	1 wk
21 May 88	HE'S THE DJ, I'M THE RAPPER Jive HIP 61	68	2 wks
14 Sep 91	HOMEBASE Jive HIP 116	69	1 wk
11 Dec 93	CODE RED Jive CHIP 140★	50†	3 wks

★ Jazzy Jeff and Fresh Prince.

Karl Denver (above, centre) went all the
wimoweh to the top ten in 1962.

DJ Jazzy Jeff and the Fresh Prince (Will
Smith, the Fresh Prince, is leaning on Jeff
Townes) have, as a duo, survived Smith's
success in television and films.

Since his emergence in 1964, **Bob Dylan** has
been the American artist with the most
weeks at number one.

The original
'**Just Like
a Woman**'
—written by Bob Dylan

From his sensational new album...

DOCTOR and the MEDICS
UK, male/female vocal/instrumental group   *3 wks*

| 21 Jun | 86 | LAUGHING AT THE PIECES MCA MIRG 1010 .... | 25 | 3 wks |

DR. FEELGOOD *UK, male vocal/instrumental group*   *33 wks*

18 Oct	75	MALPRACTICE *United Artists UAS 29880*	17	6 wks
2 Oct	76 ★	STUPIDITY *United Artists UAS 29990*	1	9 wks
4 Jun	77 ●	SNEAKIN' SUSPICION *United Artists UAS 30075*	10	6 wks
8 Oct	77	BE SEEING YOU *United Artists UAS 30123*	55	3 wks
7 Oct	78	PRIVATE PRACTICE *United Artists UAG 30184*	41	5 wks
2 Jun	79	AS IT HAPPENS *United Artists UAK 30239*	42	4 wks

DR. HOOK *US, male vocal/instrumental group*   *146 wks*

25 Jun	76 ●	A LITTLE BIT MORE *Capitol E-ST 23795*	5	42 wks
29 Oct	77	MAKING LOVE AND MUSIC *Capitol EST 11632*	39	4 wks
27 Oct	79	PLEASURE AND PAIN *Capitol EAST 11859*	47	6 wks
17 Nov	79	SOMETIMES YOU WIN *Capitol EST 12018*	14	44 wks
29 Nov	80	RISING *Mercury 6302 076*	44	5 wks
6 Dec	80 ●	DR. HOOK'S GREATEST HITS *Capitol EST 26037*	2	28 wks
14 Nov	81	DR. HOOK LIVE IN THE UK *Capitol EST 26706*	90	1 wk
13 Jun	92 ●	COMPLETELY HOOKED – THE BEST OF DR. HOOK *Capitol CDESTV 2*	3	16 wks

D

112

Ken DODD *UK, male vocalist*   *36 wks*

25 Dec	65 ●	TEARS OF HAPPINESS *Columbia 33SX 1793*	6	12 wks
23 Jul	66	HITS FOR NOW AND ALWAYS *Columbia SX 6060*	14	11 wks
14 Jan	67	FOR SOMEONE SPECIAL *Columbia SCX 6224*	40	1 wk
29 Nov	80 ●	20 GOLDEN GREATS OF KEN DODD *Warwick WW 5098*	8	12 wks

DODGY *UK, male vocal/instrumental group*   *1 wk*

| 5 Jun | 93 | THE DODGY ALBUM *A & M 5400822* .... | 75 | 1 wk |

DOGS D'AMOUR *UK, male vocal/instrumental group*   *12 wks*

22 Oct	88	IN THE DYNAMITE JET SALOON *China WOL 8*	97	1 wk
25 Mar	89	A GRAVEYARD OF EMPTY BOTTLES *China 8390740* .	16	4 wks
30 Sep	89	ERROL FLYNN *China 8397001*	22	3 wks
6 Oct	90	STRAIGHT *China 8437961*	32	2 wks
7 Sep	91	DOG'S HITS AND THE BOOTLEG ALBUM *China WOL 1020*	58	1 wk
15 May	93	... MORE UNCHARTED HEIGHTS OF DISGRACE *China WOLCD 1032*	30	1 wk

DOKKEN *US, male vocal/instrumental group*   *1 wk*

| 21 Nov | 87 | BACK FOR THE ATTACK *Elektra EKT 43* .... | 96 | 1 wk |

Thomas DOLBY
UK, male vocalist/instrumentalist – keyboards   *29 wks*

22 May	82	THE GOLDEN AGE OF WIRELESS *Venice In Peril VIP 1001*	65	10 wks
18 Feb	84	THE FLAT EARTH *Parlophone Odeon PCS 2400341*	14	14 wks
7 May	88	ALIENS ATE MY BUICK *Manhattan MTL 1020*	30	3 wks
8 Aug	92	ASTRONAUTS AND HERETICS *Virgin CDV 2701*	35	2 wks

DOLLAR UK, male/female vocal duo   28 wks

15 Sep	79	**SHOOTING STARS** Carrere CAL 111	36	8 wks
24 Apr	82	**THE VERY BEST OF DOLLAR** Carrere CAL 3001	31	9 wks
30 Oct	82	**THE DOLLAR ALBUM** WEA DTV 1	18	11 wks

Placido DOMINGO Spain, male vocalist   152 wks

28 Nov	81	**PERHAPS LOVE** CBS 73592★	17	21 wks
21 May	83	**MY LIFE FOR A SONG** CBS 73683	31	8 wks
27 Dec	86	**PLACIDO DOMINGO COLLECTION** Stylus SMR 625	30	14 wks
23 Apr	88	**GREATEST LOVE SONGS** CBS 44701	63	2 wks
17 Jun	89	**GOYA . . . A LIFE IN A SONG** CBS 463294 1	36	4 wks
17 Jun	89	**THE ESSENTIAL DOMINGO** Deutsche Grammophon PDTV 1	20	8 wks
1 Sep	90 ★	**IN CONCERT** Decca 4304331★★	1	70 wks
24 Nov	90	**BE MY LOVE . . . AN ALBUM OF LOVE** EMI EMTV 54★★★	14	12 wks
7 Dec	91	**THE BROADWAY I LOVE** East West 9031755901	45	6 wks
13 Jun	92	**DOMINGO: ARIAS AND SPANISH SONGS** Deutsche Grammophon 4371122	47	3 wks
8 Aug	92	**FROM THE OFFICIAL BARCELONA GAMES CEREMONY** RCA Red Seal 09026612042★★★★	41	3 wks
25 Dec	93	**CHRISTMAS IN VIENNA** Sony Classical SK 53358★★★★★	71†	1 wk

★ *Placido Domingo and John Denver.*
★★ *José Carreras, Placido Domingo and Luciano Pavarotti.*
★★★ *Placido Domingo featuring The London Symphony Orchestra.*
★★★★ *Placido Domingo, José Carreras and Montserrat Caballe.*
★★★★★ *Placido Domingo, Diana Ross and José Carreras.*
See also Andrew Lloyd Webber.

Fats DOMINO
US, male vocalist/instrumentalist – piano   1 wk

16 May	70	**VERY BEST OF FATS DOMINO** Liberty LBS 83331	56	1 wk

Lonnie DONEGAN UK, male vocalist   29 wks

1 Sep	62 ●	**GOLDEN AGE OF DONEGAN** Pye Golden Guinea GGL 0135	3	23 wks
9 Feb	63	**GOLDEN AGE OF DONEGAN VOL. 2** Pye Golden Guinea GGL 0170	15	3 wks
25 Feb	78	**PUTTING ON THE STYLE** Chrysalis CHR 1158	51	3 wks

DONOVAN UK, male vocalist   73 wks

5 Jun	65 ●	**WHAT'S BIN DID AND WHAT'S BIN HID** Pye NPL 18117	3	16 wks
6 Nov	65	**FAIRY TALE** Pye NPL 18128	20	2 wks
8 Jul	67	**SUNSHINE SUPERMAN** Pye NPL 18181	25	7 wks
14 Oct	67 ●	**UNIVERSAL SOLDIER** Marble Arch MAL 718	5	18 wks
11 May	68	**A GIFT FROM A FLOWER TO A GARDEN** Pye NSPL 20000	13	14 wks
12 Sep	70	**OPEN ROAD** Dawn DNLS 3009	30	4 wks
24 Mar	73	**COSMIC WHEELS** Epic EPC 65450	15	12 wks

Jason DONOVAN
Australia, male vocalist   99 wks

13 May	89 ★	**TEN GOOD REASONS** PWL HF 7	1	54 wks
9 Jun	90 ●	**BETWEEN THE LINES** PWL HF 14	2	26 wks
28 Sep	91 ●	**GREATEST HITS** PWL HF 20	9	17 wks
11 Sep	93	**ALL AROUND THE WORLD** Polydor 8477452	27	2 wks

See also Stage Cast Recordings – Joseph And The Amazing Technicolour Dreamcoat.

DOOBIE BROTHERS US, male vocal/instrumental group 30 wks

30 Mar 74	**WHAT WERE ONCE VICES ARE NOW HABITS**		
	Warner Bros. K 56206	19	10 wks
17 May 75	**STAMPEDE** Warner Bros. K 56094	14	11 wks
10 Apr 76	**TAKIN' IT TO THE STREETS** Warner Bros. K 56196	42	2 wks
17 Sep 77	**LIVING ON THE FAULT LINE** Warner Bros. K 56383	25	5 wks
11 Oct 80	**ONE STEP CLOSER** Warner Bros. K 56824	53	2 wks

DOOLEYS UK, male/female vocal/instrumental group 27 wks

30 Jun 79 ●	**THE BEST OF THE DOOLEYS** GTO GTTV 038	6	21 wks
3 Nov 79	**THE CHOSEN FEW** GTO GTLP 040	56	4 wks
25 Oct 80	**FULL HOUSE** GTO GTTV 050	54	2 wks

Val DOONICAN Ireland, male vocalist 170 wks

12 Dec 64 ●	**LUCKY 13 SHADES OF VAL DOONICAN**		
	Decca LK 4648	2	27 wks
3 Dec 66 ●	**GENTLE SHADES OF VAL DOONICAN** Decca LK 4831	5	52 wks
2 Dec 67 ★	**VAL DOONICAN ROCKS BUT GENTLY**		
	Pye NSPL 18204	1	23 wks
30 Nov 68 ●	**VAL** Pye NSPL 18236	6	11 wks
14 Jun 69 ●	**WORLD OF VAL DOONICAN** Decca SPA 3	2	31 wks
13 Dec 69	**SOUNDS GENTLE** Pye NSPL 18321	22	9 wks
19 Dec 70	**THE MAGIC OF VAL DOONICAN** Philips 6642 003	34	3 wks
27 Nov 71	**THIS IS VAL DOONICAN** Philips 6382 017	40	1 wk
22 Feb 75	**I LOVE COUNTRY MUSIC** Philips 9299261	37	2 wks
21 May 77	**SOME OF MY BEST FRIENDS ARE SONGS**		
	Philips 6641 607	29	5 wks
24 Mar 90	**SONGS FROM MY SKETCH BOOK** Parkfield PMLP 5014	33	6 wks

D

114

DOORS US, male vocal/instrumental group 84 wks

28 Sep 68	**WAITING FOR THE SUN** Elektra EKS7 4024	16	10 wks
11 Apr 70	**MORRISON HOTEL** Elektra EKS 75007	12	8 wks
26 Sep 70	**ABSOLUTELY LIVE** Elektra 2665 002	69	1 wk
31 Jul 71	**L.A. WOMAN** Elektra K 42090	28	4 wks
1 Apr 72	**WEIRD SCENES INSIDE THE GOLD MINE**		
	Elektra K 62009	50	1 wk
29 Oct 83	**ALIVE, SHE CRIED** Elektra 96–0269–1	36	5 wks
4 Jul 87	**LIVE AT THE HOLLYWOOD BOWL** Elektra EKT 40 ...	51	3 wks
6 Apr 91	**THE DOORS (soundtrack)** Elektra EKT 85	11	17 wks
20 Apr 91	**BEST OF THE DOORS** Elektra EKT 21	17	18 wks
20 Apr 91	**THE DOORS** Elektra K 42012	43	12 wks
1 Jun 91	**IN CONCERT** Elektra EKT 88	24	5 wks

Lee DORSEY US, male vocalist 4 wks

17 Dec 66	**NEW LEE DORSEY** Stateside SSL 10192	34	4 wks

DOUBLE Switzerland, male vocal/instrumental duo 4 wks

8 Mar 86	**BLUE** Polydor POLD 5187	69	4 wks

DOUBLE TROUBLE UK, male production duo 1 wk

4 Aug 90	**AS ONE** Desire LULP 6	73	1 wk

DOUBLE TROUBLE – See Stevie Ray VAUGHAN and DOUBLE TROUBLE

Craig DOUGLAS UK, male vocalist 2 wks

6 Aug 60	**CRAIG DOUGLAS** Top Rank BUY 049	17	2 wks

Will DOWNING *US, male vocalist* — *28 wks*

26 Mar 88	**WILL DOWNING** *Fourth & Broadway BRLP 518*	**20**	23 wks
18 Nov 89	**COME TOGETHER AS ONE** *Fourth & Broadway BRLP 538*	**36**	2 wks
6 Apr 91	**A DREAM FULFILLED** *Fourth & Broadway BRLP 565*	**43**	3 wks

DREAD ZEPPELIN *UK, male vocal/instrumental group* — *2 wks*

11 Aug 90	**UN-LED-ED** *IRS EIRSA 1042*	**71**	2 wks

D:REAM *UK, male vocal/instrumental duo* — *2 wks*

30 Oct 93	**D:REAM ON VOL. 1** *Magnet 4509933712*	**44**	2 wks

DREAM ACADEMY
UK, male/female vocal/instrumental group — *2 wks*

12 Oct 85	**THE DREAM ACADEMY** *blanco y negro BYN 6*	**58**	2 wks

DREAM WARRIORS *Canada, male rap group* — *7 wks*

16 Feb 91	**AND NOW THE LEGACY BEGINS** *Fourth & Broadway BRLP 560*	**18**	7 wks

DREAMERS – *See FREDDIE and the DREAMERS*

D
115

DRIFTERS *US, male vocal group* — *88 wks*

18 May 68	**GOLDEN HITS** *Atlantic 588–103*	**27**	7 wks
10 Jun 72	**GOLDEN HITS (re-issue)** *Atlantic K 40018*	**26**	8 wks
8 Nov 75 ●	**24 ORIGINAL HITS** *Atlantic K 60106*	**2**	34 wks
13 Dec 75	**LOVE GAMES** *Bell BELLS 246*	**51**	1 wk
18 Oct 86	**THE VERY BEST OF THE DRIFTERS** *Telstar STAR 2280*	**24**	15 wks
14 Mar 87	**STAND BY ME (THE ULTIMATE COLLECTION)** *Atlantic WX 90★*	**14**	8 wks
20 Oct 90	**THE BEST OF BEN E. KING AND THE DRIFTERS** *Telstar STAR 2373★*	**15**	16 wks

★ *Ben E. King and the Drifters.*

Julie DRISCOLL and the Brian AUGER
TRINITY *UK, female/male vocal/instrumental group* — *13 wks*

8 Jun 68	**OPEN** *Marmalade 608–002*	**12**	13 wks

D-TRAIN *US, male vocalist/multi-instrumentalist, Hubert Eaves* — *4 wks*

8 May 82	**D-TRAIN** *Epic EPC 85683*	**72**	4 wks

DUBLINERS *Ireland, male vocal/instrumental group* — *88 wks*

13 May 67 ●	**A DROP OF THE HARD STUFF** *Major Minor MMLP 3* ..	**5**	41 wks
9 Sep 67	**BEST OF THE DUBLINERS** *Transatlantic TRA 158*	**25**	11 wks
7 Oct 67 ●	**MORE OF THE HARD STUFF** *Major Minor MMLP 5*	**8**	23 wks
2 Mar 68	**DRINKIN' AND COURTIN'** *Major Minor SMLP 14*	**31**	3 wks
25 Apr 87	**THE DUBLINERS 25 YEARS CELEBRATION** *Stylus SMR 731*	**43**	10 wks

Stephen 'Tin Tin' DUFFY *UK, male vocalist* — *7 wks*

20 Apr 85	**THE UPS AND DOWNS** *10 DIX 5*	**35**	7 wks

George DUKE *US, male vocalist/instrumentalist – keyboards*   *4 wks*

26 Jul 80   **BRAZILIAN LOVE AFFAIR** *Epic EPC 84311*   33   4 wks

DUKES – *See Steve EARLE*

Candy DULFER
Holland, female instrumentalist – saxophone   *11 wks*

18 Aug 90   **SAXUALITY** *RCA PL 74661*   27   9 wks
13 Mar 93   **SAX-A-GO-GO** *Ariola 4321111812*   56   2 wks

Simon DUPREE and the BIG SOUND
UK, male vocal/instrumental group   *1 wk*

13 Aug 67   **WITHOUT RESERVATIONS** *Parlophone PCS 7029*   39   1 wk

DURAN DURAN *UK, male vocal/instrumental group*   *366 wks*

27 Jun 81 ● **DURAN DURAN** *EMI EMC 3372* . . . .   3 118 wks
22 May 82 ● **RIO** *EMI EMC 3411* . . . .   2 109 wks
 3 Dec 83 ★ **SEVEN AND THE RAGGED TIGER** *EMI DD 1*   1   47 wks
24 Nov 84 ● **ARENA** *Parlophone DD 2*   6   31 wks
 6 Dec 86   **NOTORIOUS** *EMI DDN 331*   16   16 wks
29 Oct 88   **BIG THING** *EMI DDB 33*   15   5 wks
25 Nov 89 ● **DECADE** *EMI DDX 10*   5   15 wks
 1 Sep 90 ● **LIBERTY** *Parlophone PCSD 112*   8   4 wks
27 Feb 93 ● **DURAN DURAN (THE WEDDING ALBUM)**
              Parlophone CDDB 34   4   21 wks

Group were UK/US from 1990 and were billed as Duranduran on EMI DDB 33.   ●

Deanna DURBIN *Canada, female vocalist*   *4 wks*

30 Jan 82   **THE BEST OF DEANNA DURBIN**
              MCA International MCL 1634   84   4 wks

Ian DURY and the BLOCKHEADS
UK, male vocal/instrumental group   *118 wks*

22 Oct 77 ● **NEW BOOTS AND PANTIES!!** *Stiff SEEZ 4*   5   90 wks
 2 Jun 79 ● **DO IT YOURSELF** *Stiff SEEZ 14*   2   18 wks
 6 Dec 80   **LAUGHTER** *Stiff SEEZ 30*   48   4 wks
10 Oct 81   **LORD UPMINSTER** *Polydor POLD 5042*   53   4 wks
 4 Feb 84   **4,000 WEEKS HOLIDAY** *Polydor POLD 5112★*   54   2 wks

★ *Ian Dury and the Music Students.*

Bob DYLAN *US, male vocalist*   *568 wks*

23 May 64 ★ **THE FREEWHEELIN' BOB DYLAN** *CBS BPG 62193* . . .   1   49 wks
11 Jul   64 ● **THE TIMES THEY ARE A-CHANGIN'** *CBS BPG 62251*   4   20 wks
21 Nov 64 ● **ANOTHER SIDE OF BOB DYLAN** *CBS BPG 62429*   8   19 wks
 8 May 65   **BOB DYLAN** *CBS BPG 62022*   13   6 wks
15 May 65 ★ **BRINGING IT ALL BACK HOME** *CBS BPG 62515*   1   29 wks
 9 Oct 65 ● **HIGHWAY 61 REVISITED** *CBS BPG 62572*   4   15 wks
20 Aug 66 ● **BLONDE ON BLONDE** *CBS DDP 66012*   3   15 wks
14 Jan 67 ● **GREATEST HITS** *CBS SBPG 62847*   6   82 wks
 2 Mar 68 ★ **JOHN WESLEY HARDING** *CBS SBPG 63252*   1   29 wks
17 May 69 ★ **NASHVILLE SKYLINE** *CBS 63601*   1   42 wks
11 Jul   70 ★ **SELF PORTRAIT** *CBS 66250*   1   15 wks
28 Nov 70 ★ **NEW MORNING** *CBS 69001*   1   18 wks
25 Dec 71   **MORE BOB DYLAN GREATEST HITS** *CBS 67238/9* . .   12   15 wks
29 Sep 73   **PAT GARRETT AND BILLY THE KID (film soundtrack)**
              CBS 69042   29   11 wks

23 Feb	74 ●	**PLANET WAVES** *Island ILPS 9261*	7	8 wks
13 Jul	74 ●	**BEFORE THE FLOOD** *Asylum IDBD 1*	8	7 wks
15 Feb	75 ●	**BLOOD ON THE TRACKS** *CBS 69097*	4	16 wks
26 Jul	75 ●	**THE BASEMENT TAPES** *CBS 88147*	8	10 wks
31 Jan	76 ●	**DESIRE** *CBS 86003*	3	35 wks
9 Oct	76 ●	**HARD RAIN** *CBS 86016*	3	7 wks
1 Jul	78 ●	**STREET LEGAL** *CBS 86067*	2	20 wks
26 May	79 ●	**BOB DYLAN AT BUDOKAN** *CBS 96004*	4	19 wks
8 Sep	79 ●	**SLOW TRAIN COMING** *CBS 86095*	2	13 wks
28 Jun	80 ●	**SAVED** *CBS 86113*	3	8 wks
29 Aug	81 ●	**SHOT OF LOVE** *CBS 85178*	6	8 wks
12 Nov	83 ●	**INFIDELS** *CBS 25539*	9	12 wks
15 Dec	84	**REAL LIVE** *CBS 26334*	54	2 wks
22 Jun	85	**EMPIRE BURLESQUE** *CBS 86313*	11	6 wks
2 Aug	86	**KNOCKED OUT LOADED** *CBS 86326*	35	5 wks
23 Apr	88	**GREATEST HITS** *CBS 460907 1*	99	1 wk
25 Jun	88	**DOWN IN THE GROOVE** *CBS 460267 1*	32	3 wks
18 Feb	89	**DYLAN AND THE DEAD** *CBS 463381 1★*	38	3 wks
14 Oct	89 ●	**OH MERCY** *CBS 465800 1*	6	7 wks
22 Sep	90	**UNDER THE RED SKY** *CBS 4671881*	13	3 wks
13 Apr	91	**THE BOOTLEG SERIES VOLS 1–3** *Columbia 4680861* ...	32	5 wks
14 Nov	92	**GOOD AS I BEEN TO YOU** *Columbia 4727102*	18	3 wks
20 Nov	93	**WORLD GONE WRONG** *Columbia 474 8572*	35	2 wks

★ *Bob Dylan and the Grateful Dead.*
The two Greatest Hits *collections are different.*

E

E STREET BAND – *See Bruce SPRINGSTEEN*

EAGLES *US, male vocal/instrumental group*   *293 wks*

27 Apr	74	**ON THE BORDER** *Asylum SYL 9016*	28	9 wks
12 Jul	75 ●	**ONE OF THESE NIGHTS** *Asylum SYLA 8759*	8	40 wks
12 Jul	75	**DESPERADO** *Asylum SYLL 9011*	39	9 wks
6 Mar	76 ●	**THEIR GREATEST HITS 1971–1975** *Asylum K 53017* ...	2	77 wks
25 Dec	76 ●	**HOTEL CALIFORNIA** *Asylum K 53051*	2	63 wks
13 Oct	79 ●	**THE LONG RUN** *Asylum K 52181*	4	16 wks
22 Nov	80	**LIVE** *Asylum K 62032*	24	13 wks
18 May	85 ●	**BEST OF THE EAGLES** *Asylum EKT 5*	8	66 wks

Steve EARLE and the DUKES
US, male vocal/instrumental group   *15 wks*

4 Jul	87	**EXIT 0** *MCA MCF 3379★*	77	2 wks
19 Nov	88	**COPPERHEAD ROAD** *MCA MCF 3426*	44	8 wks
7 Jul	90	**THE HARD WAY** *MCA MCG 6095*	22	4 wks
19 Oct	91	**SHUT UP AND DIE LIKE AN AVIATOR** *MCA MCA 10315*	62	1 wk

★ *Steve Earle.*

EARTH WIND AND FIRE
US, male vocal/instrumental group   *160 wks*

21 Jan	78	**ALL 'N' ALL** *CBS 86051*	13	23 wks
16 Dec	78 ●	**THE BEST OF EARTH WIND AND FIRE VOL. 1** *CBS 83284*	6	42 wks
23 Jun	79 ●	**I AM** *CBS 86084*	5	41 wks
1 Nov	80 ●	**FACES** *CBS 88498*	10	6 wks
14 Nov	81	**RAISE** *CBS 85272*	14	22 wks
19 Feb	83	**POWERLIGHT** *CBS 25120*	22	7 wks
10 May	86 ●	**THE COLLECTION** *K-Tel NE 1322*	5	13 wks
28 Nov	92	**THE VERY BEST OF EARTH WIND AND FIRE** *Telstar TCD 2631*	40	6 wks

EAST 17   *UK, male vocal group*   *23 wks*

27 Feb	93 ★	**WALTHAMSTOW** *London 8283732*	1	14 wks
17 Jul	93	**WALTHAMSTOW (re-issue)** *London 8284262*	17†	9 wks

EASTERHOUSE   *UK, male vocal/instrumental group*   *1 wk*

28 Jun	86	**CONTENDERS** *Rough Trade ROUGH 94*	91	1 wk

EAST OF EDEN   *UK, male vocal/instrumental group*   *2 wks*

14 Mar	70	**SNAFU** *Deram SML 1050*	29	2 wks

Sheena EASTON   *UK, female vocalist*   *37 wks*

31 Jan	81	**TAKE MY TIME** *EMI EMC 3354*	17	19 wks
3 Oct	81	**YOU COULD HAVE BEEN WITH ME** *EMI EMC 3378* .	33	6 wks
25 Sep	82	**MADNESS, MONEY AND MUSIC** *EMI EMC 3414*	44	4 wks
15 Oct	83	**BEST KEPT SECRET** *EMI EMC 1077951*	99	1 wk
4 Mar	89	**THE LOVER IN ME** *MCA MCG 6036*	30	7 wks

Clint EASTWOOD and General SAINT
Jamaica, male vocal duo   *3 wks*

6 Feb	82	**TWO BAD DJ** *Greensleeves GREL 24*	99	2 wks
28 May	83	**STOP THAT TRAIN** *Greensleeves GREL 53*	98	1 wk

EAT STATIC   *UK, male instrumental duo*   *1 wk*

15 May	93	**ABDUCTION** *Ultimate BARKCD 1*	62	1 wk

Hubert EAVES – *See D-TRAIN*

ECHO and the BUNNYMEN
UK, male vocal/instrumental group   *89 wks*

26 Jul	80	**CROCODILES** *Korova KODE 1*	17	6 wks
6 Jun	81 ●	**HEAVEN UP HERE** *Korova KODE 3*	10	16 wks
12 Feb	83 ●	**PORCUPINE** *Korova KODE 6*	2	17 wks
12 May	84 ●	**OCEAN RAIN** *Korova KODE 8*	4	26 wks
23 Nov	85 ●	**SONGS TO LEARN & SING** *Korova KODE 13*	6	15 wks
18 Jul	87 ●	**ECHO AND THE BUNNYMEN** *WEA WX 108*	4	9 wks

EDDIE and the HOT RODS
UK, male vocal/instrumental group   *5 wks*

18 Dec	76	**TEENAGE DEPRESSION** *Island ILPS 9457*	43	1 wk
3 Dec	77	**LIFE ON THE LINE** *Island ILPS 9509*	27	3 wks
24 Mar	79	**THRILLER** *Island ILPS 9563*	50	1 wk

Duane EDDY   *US, male instrumentalist – guitar*   *88 wks*

6 Jun	59 ●	**HAVE TWANGY GUITAR WILL TRAVEL** *London HAW 2160*	6	3 wks
31 Oct	59 ●	**SPECIALLY FOR YOU** *London HAW 2191*	6	8 wks
19 Mar	60 ●	**THE TWANG'S THE THANG** *London HAW 2236*	2	25 wks
26 Nov	60	**SONGS OF OUR HERITAGE** *London HAW 2285*	13	5 wks
1 Apr	61 ●	**A MILLION DOLLARS' WORTH OF TWANG** *London HAW 2325*	5	19 wks
9 Jun	62	**A MILLION DOLLARS' WORTH OF TWANG VOL. 2** *London HAW 2435*	18	1 wk

21 Jul	62 ●	**TWISTIN' AND TWANGIN'** *RCA RD 27264*	**8**	12 wks
8 Dec	62	**TWANGY GUITAR – SILKY STRINGS** *RCA RD 7510* .	**13**	11 wks
16 Mar	63	**DANCE WITH THE GUITAR MAN** *RCA RD 7545*	**14**	4 wks

EDMONTON SYMPHONY ORCHESTRA – *See PROCOL HARUM*

Dave EDMUNDS *UK, male vocalist/instrumentalist – guitar*   21 wks

23 Jun	79	**REPEAT WHEN NECESSARY** *Swansong SSK 59409*	**39**	12 wks
18 Apr	81	**TWANGIN'** *Swansong SSK 59411*	**37**	4 wks
3 Apr	82	**DE7** *Arista SPART 1184*	**60**	3 wks
30 Apr	83	**INFORMATION** *Arista 205 348*	**92**	2 wks

---

Dennis EDWARDS *US, male vocalist*   1 wk

14 Apr	84	**DON'T LOOK ANY FURTHER** *Gordy ZL 72148*	**91**	1 wk

---

EEK-A-MOUSE *Jamaica, male vocalist*   3 wks

14 Aug	82	**SKIDIP** *Greensleeves GREL 41*	**61**	3 wks

---

801 *UK, male vocal/instrumental group*   2 wks

20 Nov	76	**801 LIVE** *Island ILPS 9444*	**52**	2 wks

---

808 STATE *UK, male instrumental group*   18 wks

16 Dec	89	**NINETY** *ZTT ZTT 2*	**57**	5 wks
16 Mar	91 ●	**EX:EL** *ZTT ZTT 6*	**4**	10 wks
13 Feb	93	**GORGEOUS** *ZTT 4509911002*	**17**	3 wks

---

EIGHTH WONDER
UK, male/female vocal/instrumental group   4 wks

23 Jul	88	**FEARLESS** *CBS 460628 1*	**47**	4 wks

---

ELECTRIBE 101
UK/Germany, male/female vocal/instrumental group   4 wks

20 Oct	90	**ELECTRIBAL MEMORIES** *Mercury 8429651*	**26**	3 wks

---

ELECTRIC BOYS *Sweden, male vocal/instrumental group*   1 wk

6 Jun	92	**GROOVUS MAXIMUS** *Vertigo 5122552*	**61**	1 wk

---

ELECTRIC LIGHT ORCHESTRA
UK, male vocal/instrumental group   370 wks

12 Aug	72	**ELECTRIC LIGHT ORCHESTRA** *Harvest SHVL 797*	**32**	4 wks
31 Mar	73	**ELO 2** *Harvest SHVL 806*	**35**	1 wk
11 Dec	76 ●	**A NEW WORLD RECORD** *United Artists UAG 30017*	**6**	100 wks
12 Nov	77 ●	**OUT OF THE BLUE** *United Artists UAR 100*	**4**	108 wks
6 Jan	79	**THREE LIGHT YEARS** *Jet JET BX 1*	**38**	9 wks
16 Jun	79 ★	**DISCOVERY** *Jet JET LX 500*	**1**	46 wks
1 Dec	79 ●	**ELO'S GREATEST HITS** *Jet JET LX 525*	**7**	18 wks
8 Aug	81 ★	**TIME** *Jet JETLP 236*	**1**	32 wks
2 Jul	83 ●	**SECRET MESSAGES** *Jet JET LX 527*	**4**	15 wks
15 Mar	86 ●	**BALANCE OF POWER** *Epic EPC 26467*	**9**	12 wks

E
119

16 Dec 89	**THE GREATEST HITS** *Telstar STAR 2370*	**23**	21 wks
1 Jun 91	**ELECTRIC LIGHT ORCHESTRA PART 2**		
	Telstar STAR 2503★	**34**	4 wks

★ *ELO Part 2.*
A New World Record *changed label number to JET LP 200 and* Out Of The Blue *changed to JET DP 400 during their chart runs.* The Greatest Hits *was also issued under the title* The Very Best Of Electric Light Orchestra, *with the same track listings and catalogue number.*

ELECTRIC SUN – *See Uli Jon ROTH and ELECTRIC SUN*

ELECTRIC WIND ENSEMBLE
UK, male instrumental group   *9 wks*

18 Feb 84	**HAUNTING MELODIES** *Nouveau Music NML 1007*	**28**	9 wks

ELECTRONIC *UK, male vocal/instrumental duo*   *16 wks*

8 Jun 91 ●	**ELECTRONIC** *Factory FACT 290*	**2**	16 wks

Danny ELFMAN *US, male orchestra leader*   *6 wks*

12 Aug 89	**BATMAN** *Warner Bros. WX 287*	**45**	6 wks

Duke ELLINGTON *US, orchestra*   *2 wks*

8 Apr 61	**NUT CRACKER SUITE** *Philips BBL 7418*	**11**	2 wks

Ben ELTON *UK, male comedian*   *2 wks*

14 Nov 87	**MOTORMOUTH** *Mercury BENLP 1*	**86**	2 wks

EMERSON, LAKE and PALMER
UK, male instrumental group   *135 wks*

5 Dec 70 ●	**EMERSON, LAKE AND PALMER** *Island ILPS 9132*	**4**	28 wks
19 Jun 71 ★	**TARKUS** *Island ILPS 9155*	**1**	17 wks
4 Dec 71 ●	**PICTURES AT AN EXHIBITION** *Island HELP 1*	**3**	5 wks
8 Jul 72 ●	**TRILOGY** *Island ILPS 9186*	**2**	29 wks
22 Dec 73 ●	**BRAIN SALAD SURGERY** *Manticore K 53501*	**2**	17 wks
24 Aug 74 ●	**WELCOME BACK MY FRIENDS TO THE SHOW THAT**		
	NEVER ENDS – LADIES AND GENTLEMEN:		
	EMERSON, LAKE AND PALMER *Manticore K 63500* ..	**5**	5 wks
9 Apr 77 ●	**WORKS** *Atlantic K 80009*	**9**	25 wks
10 Dec 77	**WORKS VOL. 2** *Atlantic K 50422*	**20**	5 wks
9 Dec 78	**LOVE BEACH** *Atlantic K 50552*	**48**	4 wks

See also Greg Lake; Emerson, Lake and Powell.

EMERSON, LAKE and POWELL
UK, male vocal/instrumental group   *5 wks*

14 Jun 86	**EMERSON, LAKE AND POWELL** *Polydor POLD 5191* ...	**35**	5 wks

See also Greg Lake; Cozy Powell; Emerson, Lake and Palmer.

EMF *UK, male vocal/instrumental group*   *21 wks*

18 May 91 ●	**SCHUBERT DIP** *Parlophone PCS 7353*	**3**	19 wks
10 Oct 92	**STIGMA** *Parlophone CDPCSD 122*	**19**	2 wks

An EMOTIONAL FISH
UK, male vocal/instrumental group   *3 wks*

25 Aug 90	**AN EMOTIONAL FISH** *East West WX 359*	**40**	3 wks

EN VOGUE US, female vocal group   42 wks

| 2 Jun | 90 | **BORN TO SING** Atlantic 7567820841 .... | **23** | 13 wks |
| 23 May | 92 ● | **FUNKY DIVAS** East West America 7567921212 .... | **4** | 29 wks |

ENERGY ORCHARD
Ireland, male vocal/instrumental group   2 wks

| 12 May | 90 | **ENERGY ORCHARD** MCA MCG 6083 .... | **53** | 2 wks |

ENGLAND FOOTBALL WORLD CUP
SQUAD UK, male football team vocalists   18 wks

| 16 May | 70 ● | **THE WORLD BEATERS SING THE WORLD BEATERS** Pye NSPL 18337 .... | **4** | 8 wks |
| 15 May | 82 | **THIS TIME** K-Tel NE 1169 .... | **37** | 10 wks |

ENGLISH CHAMBER ORCHESTRA – *See John WILLIAMS; Nigel KENNEDY; Andrew LLOYD WEBBER; Kiri TE KANAWA*

ENIGMA UK, male vocal/instrumental group   3 wks

| 5 Sep | 81 | **AIN'T NO STOPPIN'** Creole CRX 1 .... | **80** | 3 wks |

ENIGMA Romania, male producer   57 wks

| 22 Dec | 90 ★ | **MCMXC AD** Virgin International VIR 11 .... | **1** | 57 wks |

Brian ENO UK, male instrumentalist – keyboards   13 wks

9 Mar	74	**HERE COME THE WARM JETS** Island ILPS 9268	**26**	2 wks
21 Oct	78	**MUSIC FOR FILMS** Polydor 2310 623	**55**	1 wk
21 Feb	81	**MY LIFE IN THE BUSH OF GHOSTS** Polydor EGLP 48★	**29**	8 wks
8 May	82	**AMBIENT FOUR ON LAND** EG EGED 20	**93**	1 wk
12 Sep	92	**NERVE NET** Opal 9362450332	**70**	1 wk

★ *Brian Eno and David Byrne.*

ENUFF Z'NUFF US, male vocal/instrumental group   1 wk

| 13 Apr | 91 | **STRENGTH** Atco 7567916381 .... | **56** | 1 wk |

ENYA Ireland, female vocalist/instrumentalist – keyboards   186 wks

6 Jun	87	**ENYA** BBC REB 605	**69**	4 wks
15 Oct	88 ●	**WATERMARK** WEA WX 199	**5**	87 wks
16 Nov	91 ★	**SHEPHERD MOONS** WEA WX 431	**1**	77 wks
28 Nov	92 ●	**THE CELTS** WEA 4509911672	**10**	18 wks

The Celts is a repackaged and re-issued version of Enya.

EPMD US, male rap duo   1 wk

| 16 Feb | 91 | **BUSINESS AS USUAL** Def Jam 4676971 .... | **69** | 1 wk |

EQUALS UK, male vocal/instrumental group   10 wks

| 18 Nov | 67 ● | **UNEQUALLED EQUALS** President PTL 1006 .... | **10** | 9 wks |
| 9 Mar | 68 | **EQUALS EXPLOSION** President PTLS 1015 .... | **32** | 1 wk |

E
121

Gloria Estefan touches her star on the Hollywood Walk of Fame. (Pictorial Press)

En Vogue are shown at the Soul Train music awards. (Pictorial Press)

ERASURE *UK, male vocal/instrumental duo* *284 wks*

14 Jun	86 ★	WONDERLAND *Mute STUMM 25*		71	7 wks
11 Apr	87 ●	THE CIRCUS *Mute STUMM 35*		6	107 wks
30 Apr	88 ★	THE INNOCENTS *Mute STUMM 55*		1	78 wks
28 Oct	89 ★	WILD! *Mute STUMM 75*		1	48 wks
26 Oct	91 ★	CHORUS *Mute STUMM 95*		1	25 wks
28 Nov	92 ★	POP! – THE FIRST 20 HITS *Mute CDMUTEL 2*		1	19 wks

David ESSEX *UK, male vocalist* *158 wks*

24 Nov	73 ●	ROCK ON *CBS 65823*		7	22 wks
19 Oct	74 ●	DAVID ESSEX *CBS 69088*		2	24 wks
27 Sep	75 ●	ALL THE FUN OF THE FAIR *CBS 69160*		3	20 wks
5 Jun	76	ON TOUR *CBS 95000*		51	1 wk
30 Oct	76	OUT ON THE STREET *CBS 86017*		31	9 wks
8 Oct	77	GOLD AND IVORY *CBS 86038*		29	4 wks
6 Jan	79	DAVID ESSEX ALBUM *CBS 10011*		29	7 wks
31 Mar	79	IMPERIAL WIZARD *Mercury 9109 616*		12	9 wks
12 Jun	80	HOT LOVE *Mercury 6359 017*		75	1 wk
19 Jun	82	STAGE-STRUCK *Mercury MERS 4*		31	15 wks
27 Nov	82	THE VERY BEST OF DAVID ESSEX *TV Records TVA 4* .		37	11 wks
15 Oct	83	MUTINY *Mercury MERH 30*		39	4 wks
17 Dec	83	THE WHISPER *Mercury MERH 34*		67	6 wks
6 Dec	86	CENTRE STAGE *K-Tel ONE 1333*		82	4 wks
19 Oct	91	HIS GREATEST HITS *Mercury 5103081*		13	13 wks
10 Apr	93 ●	COVER SHOT *PolyGram TV 5145632*		3	8 wks

Mutiny is a studio recording of a musical that was not staged until 1985. Both this album and the eventual stage production starred David Essex and Frank Finlay.

Gloria ESTEFAN *US, female vocalist* *197 wks*

19 Nov	88 ★	ANYTHING FOR YOU *Epic 4631251*★		1	54 wks
5 Aug	89 ★	CUTS BOTH WAYS *Epic 4651451*		1	64 wks
16 Feb	91 ●	INTO THE LIGHT *Epic 4677821*		2	36 wks
14 Nov	92 ●	GREATEST HITS *Epic 4723322*		2	32 wks
10 Jul	93	MI TIERRA *Epic 4737992*		11	11 wks

★ *Miami Sound Machine.*

Don ESTELLE and Windsor DAVIES
UK, male vocal duo *8 wks*

10 Jan	76 ●	SING LOFTY *EMI EMC 3102*		10	8 wks

ETERNAL *UK, female vocal group* *3 wks*

11 Dec	93	ALWAYS AND FOREVER *EMI CDEMD 1053*		33†	3 wks

Melissa ETHERIDGE *US, female vocalist* *2 wks*

30 Sep	89	BRAVE AND CRAZY *Island ILPS 9939*		63	1 wk
9 May	92	NEVER ENOUGH *Island CID 9990*		56	1 wk

EUROPE *Sweden, male vocal/instrumental group* *43 wks*

22 Nov	86 ●	THE FINAL COUNTDOWN *Epic EPC 26808*		9	37 wks
17 Sep	88	OUT OF THIS WORLD *Epic 4624491*		12	5 wks
19 Oct	91	PRISONERS IN PARADISE *Epic 4687551*		61	1 wk

EUROPEANS *UK, male vocal/instrumental group* *1 wk*

11 Feb	84	LIVE *A & M SCOT 1*		100	1 wk

E
123

EURYTHMICS UK, female/male vocal/instrumental duo 423 wks

12 Feb	83 ●	**SWEET DREAMS (ARE MADE OF THIS)**			
		RCA RCALP 6063	**3**	60 wks
26 Nov	83 ★	**TOUCH** RCA PL 70109	**1**	48 wks
9 Jun	84	**TOUCH DANCE** RCA PG 70354	**31**	5 wks
24 Nov	84	**1984 (FOR THE LOVE OF BIG BROTHER)** Virgin V 1984	**23**	17 wks
11 May	85 ●	**BE YOURSELF TONIGHT** RCA PL 70711	**3**	80 wks
12 Jul	86 ●	**REVENGE** RCA PL 71050	**3**	52 wks
21 Nov	87 ●	**SAVAGE** RCA PL 71555	**7**	33 wks
23 Sep	89 ★	**WE TOO ARE ONE** RCA PL 74251	**1**	32 wks
30 Mar	91 ★	**GREATEST HITS** RCA PL 74856	**1**	91 wks
27 Nov	93	**EURYTHMICS LIVE 1983–1989** RCA 74321171452	**22†**	5 wks

Phil EVERLY US, male vocalist 1 wk

7 May	83	**PHIL EVERLY** Capitol EST 27670	**61**	1 wk

See also the Everly Brothers.

EVERLY BROTHERS US, male vocal duo 123 wks

2 Jul	60 ●	**IT'S EVERLY TIME** Warner Bros. WM 4006	**2**	23 wks
15 Oct	60 ●	**FABULOUS STYLE OF THE EVERLY BROTHERS**		
		London HAA 2266	**4**	11 wks
4 Mar	61 ●	**A DATE WITH THE EVERLY BROTHERS**		
		Warner Bros. WM 4028	**3**	14 wks
21 Jul	62	**INSTANT PARTY** Warner Bros. WM 4061	**20**	1 wk
12 Sep	70 ●	**ORIGINAL GREATEST HITS** CBS 66255	**7**	16 wks
8 Jun	74	**THE VERY BEST OF THE EVERLY BROTHERS**		
		Warner Bros. K 46008	**43**	1 wk
29 Nov	75 ●	**WALK RIGHT BACK WITH THE EVERLYS**		
		Warner Bros. K 56118	**10**	10 wks
9 Apr	77	**LIVING LEGENDS** Warwick WW 5027	**12**	10 wks
18 Dec	82	**LOVE HURTS** K-Tel NE 1197	**31**	22 wks
7 Jan	84	**EVERLY BROTHERS REUNION CONCERT**		
		Impression IMDP 1	**47**	6 wks
3 Nov	84	**THE EVERLY BROTHERS** Mercury MERH 44	**36**	4 wks
29 May	93	**GOLDEN YEARS OF THE EVERLY BROTHERS –**		
		THEIR 24 GREATEST HITS Warner Bros. 9548319922 ..	**26**	5 wks

See also Phil Everly.

E
124

EVERYTHING BUT THE GIRL
UK, male/female vocal/instrumental group 74 wks

16 Jun	84	**EDEN** blanco y negro BYN 2	**14**	22 wks
27 Apr	85 ●	**LOVE NOT MONEY** blanco y negro BYN 3	**10**	9 wks
6 Sep	86	**BABY THE STARS SHINE BRIGHT** blanco y negro BYN 9	**22**	9 wks
12 Mar	88	**IDLEWILD** blanco y negro BYN 14	**13**	9 wks
6 Aug	88	**IDLEWILD (re-issue)** blanco y negro BYN 16	**21**	6 wks
17 Feb	90 ●	**THE LANGUAGE OF LOVE** blanco y negro BYN 21	**10**	6 wks
5 Oct	91	**WORLDWIDE** blanco y negro BYN 25	**29**	5 wks
22 May	93 ●	**HOME MOVIES – THE BEST OF EVERYTHING BUT**		
		THE GIRL blanco y negro 4509923192	**5**	8 wks

EXODUS US, male vocal/instrumental group 1 wk

11 Feb	89	**FABULOUS DISASTER** Music For Nations MFN 90	**67**	1 wk

EXPLOITED UK, male vocal/instrumental group 26 wks

16 May	81	**PUNK'S NOT DEAD** Secret SEC 1	**20**	11 wks
14 Nov	81	**EXPLOITED LIVE** Superville EXPLP 2001	**52**	3 wks
19 Jun	82	**TROOPS OF TOMORROW** Secret SEC 8	**17**	12 wks

Eurythmics enjoyed unexpected chart action in 1993 with a live album released after their break-up. *(Pictorial Press)*

Vocalist Gary Charone and guitarist Nuno Bettencourt were the high-profile half of **Extreme**, described by Brian May at the Freddie Mercury Tribute Concert at Wembley as the band who best understood and carried on what Queen were all about. *(Pictorial Press)*

EXTREME *US, male vocal/instrumental group* *72 wks*

| 1 Jun | 91 | EXTREME II PORNOGRAFFITI *A & M 3953131* .... | 12 | 61 wks |
| 26 Sep | 92 ● | III SIDES TO EVERY STORY *A & M 5400062* .... | 2 | 11 wks |

F

FAB *UK, male producers* *3 wks*

| 10 Nov | 90 | POWER THEMES 90 *Telstar STAR 2430* .... | 53 | 3 wks |

FACES *UK, male vocal/instrumental group* *57 wks*

4 Apr	70	FIRST STEP *Warner Bros. WS 3000*	45	1 wk
8 May	71	LONG PLAYER *Warner Bros. W 3011*	31	7 wks
25 Dec	71 ●	A NOD'S AS GOOD AS A WINK ... TO A BLIND HORSE *Warner Bros. K 56006*	2	22 wks
21 Apr	73 ★	OOH-LA-LA *Warner Bros. K 56011*	1	13 wks
26 Jan	74 ●	OVERTURE AND BEGINNERS *Mercury 9100 001★*	3	7 wks
21 May	77	THE BEST OF THE FACES *Riva RVLP 3*	24	6 wks
7 Nov	92	THE BEST OF ROD STEWART AND THE FACES 1971–1975 *Mercury 5141802★*	58	1 wk

★ *Rod Stewart and the Faces.*
See also Rod Stewart.

Donald FAGEN *US, male vocalist* *25 wks*

| 20 Oct | 82 | THE NIGHTFLY *Warner Bros. 923696* .... | 44 | 16 wks |
| 5 Jun | 93 ● | KAMAKIRIAD *Reprise 9362452302* .... | 3 | 9 wks |

FAIRGROUND ATTRACTION
UK, male/female vocal/instrumental group *54 wks*

| 28 May | 88 ● | THE FIRST OF A MILLION KISSES *RCA PL 71696* .... | 2 | 52 wks |
| 30 Jun | 90 | AY FOND KISS *RCA PL 74596* .... | 55 | 2 wks |

Group were male only on last album.

FAIRPORT CONVENTION
UK, male/female vocal/instrumental group *41 wks*

2 Aug	69	UNHALFBRICKING *Island ILPS 9102*	12	8 wks
17 Jan	70	LIEGE AND LIEF *Island ILPS 9115*	17	15 wks
18 Jul	70	FULL HOUSE *Island ILPS 9130*	13	11 wks
3 Jul	71 ●	ANGEL DELIGHT *Island ILPS 9162*	8	5 wks
12 Jul	75	RISING FOR THE MOON *Island ILPS 9313*	52	1 wk
28 Jan	89	RED AND GOLD *New Routes RUE 002*	74	1 wk

FAITH BROTHERS *UK, male vocal/instrumental group* *1 wk*

| 9 Nov | 85 | EVENTIDE *Siren SIRENLP 1* .... | 66 | 1 wk |

FAITH NO MORE *US, male vocal/instrumental group* *64 wks*

17 Feb	90	THE REAL THING *Slash 8281541*	30	35 wks
16 Feb	91	LIVE AT THE BRIXTON ACADEMY *Slash 8282381*	20	4 wks
20 Jun	92 ●	ANGEL DUST *Slash 8283212*	2	25 wks

Adam FAITH *UK, male vocalist*   *46 wks*

19 Nov	60 ●	**ADAM** *Parlophone PMC 1128*	6	36 wks
11 Feb	61	**BEAT GIRL (film soundtrack)** *Columbia 33SX 1225*	11	3 wks
24 Mar	62	**ADAM FAITH** *Parlophone PMC 1162*	20	1 wk
25 Sep	65	**FAITH ALIVE** *Parlophone PMC 1249*	19	1 wk
19 Dec	81	**20 GOLDEN GREATS** *Warwick WW 5113*	61	3 wks
27 Nov	93	**MIDNIGHT POSTCARDS** *PolyGram TV 8213982*	43	2 wks

Marianne FAITHFULL *UK, female vocalist*   *19 wks*

5 Jun	65	**COME MY WAY** *Decca LK 4688*	12	7 wks
5 Jun	65	**MARIANNE FAITHFULL** *Decca LK 4689*	15	2 wks
24 Nov	79	**BROKEN ENGLISH** *Island M1*	57	3 wks
17 Oct	81	**DANGEROUS ACQUAINTANCES** *Island ILPS 9648*	45	4 wks
26 Mar	83	**A CHILD'S ADVENTURE** *Island ILPS 9734*	99	1 wk
8 Aug	87	**STRANGE WEATHER** *Island ILPS 9874*	78	2 wks

FALCO *Austria, male vocalist*   *15 wks*

26 Apr	86	**FALCO 3** *A & M AMA 5105*	32	15 wks

FALL *UK, male vocal/instrumental group*   *29 wks*

20 Mar	82	**HEX ENDUCTION HOUR** *Kamera KAM 005*	71	3 wks
20 Oct	84	**THE WONDERFUL AND FRIGHTENING WORLD OF** *Beggars Banquet BEGA 58*	62	2 wks
5 Oct	85	**THE NATION'S SAVING GRACE** *Beggars Banquet BEGA 67*	54	2 wks
11 Oct	86	**BEND SINISTER** *Beggars Banquet BEGA 75*	36	3 wks
12 Mar	88	**THE FRENZ EXPERIMENT** *Beggars Banquet BEGA 91* ...	19	4 wks
12 Nov	88	**I AM KURIOUS, ORANJ** *Beggars Banquet BEGA 96*	54	2 wks
8 Jul	89	**SEMINAL LIVE** *Beggars Banquet BBL 102*	40	2 wks
3 Mar	90	**EXTRICATE** *Cog Sinister 8422041*	31	3 wks
15 Sep	90	**458489** *Beggars Banquet BEGA 111*	44	2 wks
4 May	91	**SHIFT WORK** *Cog Sinister 8485941*	17	2 wks
28 May	92	**CODE: SELFISH** *Cog Sinister 5121622*	21	1 wk
8 May	93 ●	**INFOTAINMENT SCAN** *Permanent PERMCD 12*	9	3 wks

Agnetha FALTSKOG *Sweden, female vocalist*   *17 wks*

11 Jun	83	**WRAP YOUR ARMS AROUND ME** *Epic EPC 25505* ...	18	13 wks
4 May	85	**EYES OF A WOMAN** *Epic EPC 26446*	38	3 wks
12 Mar	88	**I STAND ALONE** *WEA WX 150*	72	1 wk

Georgie FAME *UK, male vocalist*   *72 wks*

17 Oct	64	**FAME AT LAST** *Columbia 33SX 1638*	15	8 wks
14 May	66 ●	**SWEET THINGS** *Columbia SX 6043*	6	22 wks
15 Oct	66 ●	**SOUND VENTURE** *Columbia SX 6076*	9	9 wks
11 Mar	67	**HALL OF FAME** *Columbia SX 6120*	12	18 wks
1 Jul	67	**TWO FACES OF FAME** *CBS SBPG 63018*	22	15 wks

FAMILY *UK, male vocal/instrumental group*   *41 wks*

10 Aug	68	**MUSIC IN THE DOLLS HOUSE** *Reprise RLP 6312*	35	3 wks
22 Mar	69 ●	**FAMILY ENTERTAINMENT** *Reprise RSLP 6340*	6	3 wks
7 Feb	70 ●	**A SONG FOR ME** *Reprise RSLP 9001*	4	13 wks
28 Nov	70 ●	**ANYWAY** *Reprise RSX 9005*	7	7 wks
20 Nov	71	**FEARLESS** *Reprise K 54003*	14	2 wks
30 Sep	72	**BANDSTAND** *Reprise K 54006*	15	10 wks
29 Sep	73	**IT'S ONLY A MOVIE** *Raft RA 58501*	30	3 wks

FAMILY CAT *UK, male vocal/instrumental group*   *1 wk*

4 Jul	92	**FURTHEST FROM THE SUN** *Dedicated DEDCD 007*	55	1 wk

F

127

Faith No More were from San Francisco, but Live At The Brixton Academy *was a UK-only success. (Pictorial Press)*

The *4 Non Blondes* were *(clockwise from bottom left) lead singer and writer of 'What's Up' Linda Perry, Christa Hillhouse, Roger Rocha and Dawn Richardson.*

Marianne Faithfull constructed one of the longest spans of chart albums by a female vocalist, 22 years. *(Pictorial Press)*

FAMILY STAND *US, male/female vocal/instrumental group* *3 wks*

19 May 90	**CHAIN** *Atlantic WX 349*	....	**52**	3 wks

FAMILY STONE – *See SLY and the FAMILY STONE*

Chris FARLOWE *UK, male vocalist* *3 wks*

2 Apr 66	**14 THINGS TO THINK ABOUT** *Immediate IMLP 005*	....	**19**	1 wk
10 Dec 66	**THE ART OF CHRIS FARLOWE** *Immediate IMLP 006*	...	**37**	2 wks

FARM *UK, male vocal/instrumental group* *17 wks*

16 Mar 91 ★	**SPARTACUS** *Produce MILKLP 1*	....	**1**	17 wks

FARMERS BOYS *UK, male vocal/instrumental group* *1 wk*

29 Oct 83	**GET OUT AND WALK** *EMI EMC 1077991*	....	**49**	1 wk

John FARNHAM *Australia, male vocalist* *9 wks*

11 Jul 87	**WHISPERING JACK** *RCA PL 71224*	....	**35**	9 wks

FARRAR – *See MARVIN, WELCH and FARRAR*

FASHION *UK, male vocal/instrumental group* *17 wks*

3 Jul 82 ●	**FABRIQUE** *Arista SPART 1185*	....	**10**	16 wks
16 Jun 84	**TWILIGHT OF IDOLS** *De Stijl EPC 25909*	....	**69**	1 wk

FASTER PUSSYCAT *US, male vocal/instrumental group* *3 wks*

16 Sep 89	**WAKE ME WHEN IT'S OVER** *Elektra EKT 64*	....	**35**	2 wks
22 Aug 92	**WHIPPED** *Elektra 7559611242*	....	**58**	1 wk

FASTWAY *UK, male vocal/instrumental group* *2 wks*

30 Apr 83	**FASTWAY** *CBS 25359*	....	**43**	2 wks

FAT BOYS *US, male rap group* *5 wks*

3 Oct 87	**CRUSHIN'** *Urban URBLP 3*	....	**49**	4 wks
30 Jul 88	**COMING BACK HARD AGAIN** *Urban URBLP 13*	......	**98**	1 wk

FAT LADY SINGS *UK, male vocal/instrumental group* *1 wk*

18 May 91	**TWIST** *East West WX 418*	....	**50**	1 wk

FAT LARRY'S BAND *US, male vocal/instrumental group* *4 wks*

9 Oct 82	**BREAKIN' OUT** *Virgin V 2229*	....	**58**	4 wks

FATBACK BAND *US, male vocal/instrumental group* *7 wks*

6 Mar 76	**RAISING HELL** *Polydor 2391 203*	....	**19**	6 wks
4 Jul 87	**FATBACK LIVE** *Start STL 12*	....	**80**	1 wk

F
129

FATHER ABRAHAM and the SMURFS
Holland, male vocalist as himself and Smurfs   *11 wks*

25 Nov 78   **FATHER ABRAHAM IN SMURFLAND**   *Decca SMURF 1* .   **19**   11 wks

FATIMA MANSIONS
Ireland, male vocal/instrumental group   *1 wk*

6 Jun 92   **VALHALLA AVENUE**   *Radioactive KWCD 18* ....   **52**   1 wk

FBI – *See Redhead KINGPIN and the FBI*

Phil FEARON and GALAXY
UK, male/female vocal/instrumental group   *9 wks*

25 Aug 84 ● **PHIL FEARON AND GALAXY**   *Ensign ENCL 2* ....   **8**   8 wks
14 Feb 85   **THIS KIND OF LOVE**   *Ensign ENCL 4* ....   **98**   1 wk

Wilton FELDER   *US, male instrumentalist – tenor sax*   *3 wks*

23 Feb 85   **SECRETS**   *MCA MCF 3237* ....   **77**   3 wks
Also featuring Bobby Womack and introducing Alltrina Grayson.

José FELICIANO   *US, male vocalist/instrumentalist – guitar*   *40 wks*

2 Nov 68 ● **FELICIANO**   *RCA Victor SF 7946* ....   **6**   36 wks
29 Nov 69   **JOSE FELICIANO**   *RCA Victor SF 8044* ....   **29**   2 wks
14 Feb 70   **10 TO 23**   *RCA SF 7946* ....   **38**   1 wk
22 Aug 70   **FIREWORKS**   *RCA SF 8124* ....   **65**   1 wk

F

130

FELIX   *UK, male producer*   *4 wks*

10 Apr 93   **#1**   *Deconstruction 74321137002* ....   **26**   4 wks

Julie FELIX   *US, female vocalist*   *4 wks*

11 Sep 66   **CHANGES**   *Fontana TL 5368* ....   **27**   4 wks

Bryan FERRY   *UK, male vocalist*   *272 wks*

3 Nov 73 ● **THESE FOOLISH THINGS**   *Island ILPS 9249* ....   **5**   42 wks
20 Jul 74 ● **ANOTHER TIME, ANOTHER PLACE**   *Island ILPS 9284* .   **4**   25 wks
2 Oct 76   **LET'S STICK TOGETHER**   *Island ILPSX 1* ....   **19**   5 wks
5 Mar 77 ● **IN YOUR MIND**   *Polydor 2302 055* ....   **5**   17 wks
30 Sep 78   **THE BRIDE STRIPPED BARE**   *Polydor POLD 5003* .....   **13**   5 wks
15 Jun 85 ★ **BOYS AND GIRLS**   *EG EGLP 62* ....   **1**   44 wks
26 Apr 86 ★ **STREET LIFE – 20 GREAT HITS**   *EG EGTV 1★* ....   **1**   77 wks
14 Nov 87 ● **BETE NOIRE**   *Virgin V 2474* ....   **9**   16 wks
19 Nov 88 ● **THE ULTIMATE COLLECTION**   *EG EGTV 2★* ....   **6**   27 wks
3 Apr 93 ● **TAXI**   *Virgin CDV 2700* ....   **2**   14 wks

★ *Bryan Ferry and Roxy Music.*

Brad FIDEL   *Germany, male arranger*   *7 wks*

31 Aug 91   **TERMINATOR 2**   *Vareses Sarabande VS 5335* ....   **26**   7 wks

Gracie FIELDS   *UK, female vocalist*   *3 wks*

20 Dec 75   **THE GOLDEN YEARS**   *Warwick WW 5007* ....   **48**   3 wks

FIELDS OF THE NEPHILIM
UK, male vocal/instrumental group   *9 wks*

30 May	87	**DAWNRAZOR** *Situation 2 SITU 18*	62	2 wks
17 Sep	88	**THE NEPHILIM** *Situation 2 SITU 22*	14	3 wks
6 Oct	90	**ELIZIUM** *Beggars Banquet BEGA 115*	22	2 wks
6 Apr	91	**EARTH INFERNO** *Beggars Banquet BEGA 120*	39	2 wks

52ND STREET *UK, male/female vocal/instrumental group*   *1 wk*

19 Apr	86	**CHILDREN OF THE NIGHT** *10 DIX 25*	71	1 wk

FINE YOUNG CANNIBALS
UK, male vocal/instrumental group   *96 wks*

21 Dec	85	**FINE YOUNG CANNIBALS** *London LONLP 16*	11	27 wks
18 Feb	89 ★	**THE RAW AND THE COOKED** *London 8280691*	1	68 wks
15 Dec	90	**FYC** *London 8282211★*	61	1 wk

★ *FYC.*
FYC *is a remix album of* The Raw And The Cooked.

Tim FINN *New Zealand, male vocalist*   *2 wks*

10 Jul	93	**BEFORE AND AFTER** *Capitol CDEST 2202*	29	2 wks

FIRM *UK, male vocal/instrumental group*   *8 wks*

2 Mar	85	**THE FIRM** *Atlantic 78–1239–1*	15	5 wks
5 Apr	86	**MEAN BUSINESS** *Atlantic WX 35*	46	3 wks

FIRST CIRCLE *US, male vocal/instrumental group*   *2 wks*

2 May	87	**BOYS' NIGHT OUT** *EMI America AML 3118*	70	2 wks

FISCHER-Z *UK, male vocal/instrumental group*   *1 wk*

23 Jun	79	**WORD SALAD** *United Artists UAG 30232*	66	1 wk

FISH *UK, male vocalist*   *11 wks*

10 Feb	90 ●	**VIGIL IN A WILDERNESS OF MIRRORS** *EMI EMD 1015*	5	6 wks
9 Nov	91	**INTERNAL EXILE** *Polydor 5110491*	21	3 wks
30 Jan	93	**SONGS FROM THE MIRROR** *Polydor 5174992*	46	2 wks

FISHBONE *US, male vocal/instrumental group*   *1 wk*

13 Jul	91	**THE REALITY OF MY SURROUNDINGS** *Columbia 4676151*	75	1 wk

Ella FITZGERALD *US, female vocalist*   *23 wks*

11 Jun	60	**ELLA SINGS GERSHWIN** *Brunswick LA 8648*	13	3 wks
18 Jun	60	**ELLA AT THE OPERA HOUSE** *Columbia 3SX 10126*	16	1 wk
23 Jul	60	**ELLA SINGS GERSHWIN VOL. 5** *HMV CLP 1353*	18	2 wks
10 May	80	**THE INCOMPARABLE ELLA** *Polydor POLTV 9*	40	7 wks
27 Feb	88	**A PORTRAIT OF ELLA FITZGERALD** *Stylus SMR 847* .	42	10 wks

F
131

FIVE PENNY PIECE
UK, male/female vocal/instrumental group   *6 wks*

| 24 Mar | 73 | **MAKING TRACKS** *Columbia SCX 6536* .... | 37 | 1 wk |
| 3 Jul | 76 ● | **KING COTTON** *EMI EMC 3129* .... | 9 | 5 wks |

FIVE STAR *UK, male/female vocal group*   *153 wks*

3 Aug	85	**LUXURY OF LIFE** *Tent PL 70735*	12	70 wks
30 Aug	86 ★	**SILK AND STEEL** *Tent PL 71100*	1	58 wks
26 Sep	87 ●	**BETWEEN THE LINES** *Tent PL 71505*	7	17 wks
27 Aug	88	**ROCK THE WORLD** *Tent PL 71747*	17	5 wks
21 Oct	89	**GREATEST HITS** *Tent PL 74080*	53	3 wks

FIVE THIRTY *UK, male vocal/instrumental group*   *1 wk*

| 31 Aug | 91 | **BED** *East West WX 530* .... | 57 | 1 wk |

FIXX *UK, male vocal/instrumental group*   *7 wks*

| 22 May | 82 | **SHUTTERED ROOM** *MCA FX 1001* .... | 54 | 6 wks |
| 21 May | 83 | **REACH THE BEACH** *MCA FX 1002* .... | 91 | 1 wk |

Roberta FLACK *US, female vocalist*   *35 wks*

15 Jul	72	**FIRST TAKE** *Atlantic K 40040*	47	2 wks
13 Oct	73	**KILLING ME SOFTLY** *Atlantic K 50021*	40	2 wks
7 Jun	80	**ROBERTA FLACK AND DONNY HATHAWAY**		
		Atlantic K 50696★	31	7 wks
17 Sep	83	**BORN TO LOVE** *Capitol EST 7122841★★*	15	10 wks
31 Mar	84	**GREATEST HITS** *K-Tel NE 1269*	35	14 wks

★ *Roberta Flack and Donny Hathaway.*
★★ *Peabo Bryson and Roberta Flack.*

F
132

FLASH AND THE PAN
Australia, male vocal/instrumental group   *2 wks*

| 16 Jul | 83 | **PAN-ORAMA** *Easy Beat EASLP 100* .... | 69 | 2 wks |

FLEETWOOD MAC
UK/US, male/female vocal/instrumental group   *766 wks*

2 Mar	68 ●	**FLEETWOOD MAC** *Blue Horizon BPG 7–63200*	4	37 wks
7 Sep	68 ●	**MR. WONDERFUL** *Blue Horizon 7–63205*	10	11 wks
30 Aug	69	**PIOUS BIRD OF GOOD OMEN** *Blue Horizon 7–63215* ...	18	4 wks
4 Oct	69 ●	**THEN PLAY ON** *Reprise RSLP 9000*	6	11 wks
10 Oct	70	**KILN HOUSE** *Reprise RSLP 9004*	39	2 wks
19 Feb	72	**GREATEST HITS** *CBS 6901*	36	12 wks
6 Nov	76	**FLEETWOOD MAC** *Reprise K 54043*	23	20 wks
26 Feb	77 ★	**RUMOURS** *Warner Bros. K 56344*	1	443 wks
27 Oct	79 ★	**TUSK** *Warner Bros. K 66088*	1	26 wks
13 Dec	80	**FLEETWOOD MAC LIVE** *Warner Bros. K 66097*	31	9 wks
10 Jul	82 ●	**MIRAGE** *Warner Bros. K 56592*	5	39 wks
25 Apr	87 ★	**TANGO IN THE NIGHT** *Warner Bros. WX 65*	1	100 wks
3 Dec	88 ●	**GREATEST HITS** *Warner Bros. WX 221*	3	31 wks
21 Apr	90 ★	**BEHIND THE MASK** *Warner Bros. WX 335*	1	21 wks

Group were UK and male only for first 6 albums. All the above albums are different, although some are identically titled.

Berni FLINT *UK, male vocalist*   *6 wks*

| 2 Jul | 77 | **I DON'T WANT TO PUT A HOLD ON YOU** | | |
| | | *EMI EMC 3184* .... | 37 | 6 wks |

FLOATERS   US, male vocal/instrumental group   8 wks

| 20 Aug 77 | FLOATERS   ABC ABCL 5229 .... | 17 | 8 wks |

FLOCK   UK, male vocal/instrumental group   2 wks

| 2 May 70 | FLOCK   CBS 63733 .... | 59 | 2 wks |

A FLOCK OF SEAGULLS
UK, male vocal/instrumental group   59 wks

17 Apr 82	A FLOCK OF SEAGULLS Jive HOP 201	32	44 wks
7 May 83	LISTEN Jive HIP 4	16	10 wks
1 Sep 84	THE STORY OF A YOUNG HEART Jive HIP 14	30	5 wks

FLOWERED UP   UK, male vocal/instrumental group   3 wks

| 7 Sep 91 | A LIFE WITH BRIAN   London 8282441 .... | 23 | 3 wks |

Eddie FLOYD   US, male vocalist   5 wks

| 29 Apr 67 | KNOCK ON WOOD   Stax 589–006 .... | 36 | 5 wks |

FLUKE   UK, male instrumental/vocal group   1 wk

| 23 Oct 93 | SIX WHEELS ON MY WAGON   Circa CIRCDX 27 ...... | 41 | 1 wk |

A FLUX OF PINK INDIANS
UK, male vocal/instrumental group   2 wks

| 5 Feb 83 | STRIVE TO SURVIVE CAUSING LEAST SUFFERING POSSIBLE   Spiderleg SDL 8 .... | 79 | 2 wks |

FLYING LIZARDS
UK, male/female vocal/instrumental group   3 wks

| 16 Feb 80 | FLYING LIZARDS   Virgin V 2150 .... | 60 | 3 wks |

FLYING PICKETS   UK, male vocal group   22 wks

| 17 Dec 83 | LIVE AT THE ALBANY EMPIRE   AVM AVMLP 0001 ... | 48 | 11 wks |
| 9 Jun 84 | LOST BOYS   10 DIX 4 .... | 11 | 11 wks |

FM   UK, male vocal/instrumental group   3 wks

| 20 Sep 86 | INDISCREET   Portrait PRT 26827 .... | 76 | 1 wk |
| 14 Oct 89 | TOUGH IT OUT   Epic 465589 1 .... | 34 | 2 wks |

FOCUS   Holland, male instrumental group   65 wks

11 Nov 72 ●	MOVING WAVES Polydor 2931 002	2	34 wks
2 Dec 72 ●	FOCUS 3 Polydor 2383 016	6	15 wks
20 Oct 73	FOCUS AT THE RAINBOW Polydor 2442 118	23	5 wks
25 May 74	HAMBURGER CONCERTO Polydor 2442 124	20	5 wks
9 Aug 75	FOCUS Polydor 2384 070	23	6 wks

F

133

Dan FOGELBERG US, male vocalist   3 wks

29 Mar 80   **PHOENIX**   Epic EPC 83317   42   3 wks

John FOGERTY US, male vocalist/instrumentalist – guitar   11 wks

16 Feb 85   **CENTERFIELD**   Warner Bros. 92–5203–1   48   11 wks

Ellen FOLEY US, female vocalist   3 wks

17 Nov 79   **NIGHT OUT**   Epic EPC 83718   68   1 wk
4 Apr 81   **SPIRIT OF ST. LOUIS**   Epic EPC 84809   57   2 wks

Jane FONDA US, female exercise instructor   51 wks

29 Jan   83 ● **JANE FONDA'S WORKOUT RECORD**   CBS 88581   7   47 wks
22 Sep   84   **JANE FONDA'S WORKOUT RECORD: NEW AND
                IMPROVED**   CBS 88640   60   4 wks

Wayne FONTANA and the MINDBENDERS
UK, male vocalist and male vocal/instrumental group   1 wk

20 Feb 65   **WAYNE FONTANA AND THE MINDBENDERS**
               Fontana TL 5230   18   1 wk

See also the Mindbenders.

F
134

Steve FORBERT US, male vocalist   3 wks

9 Jun 79   **ALIVE ON ARRIVAL**   Epic EPC 83308   56   1 wk
24 Nov 79   **JACK RABBIT SLIM**   Epic EPC 83879   54   2 wks

Clinton FORD UK, male vocalist   4 wks

26 May 62   **CLINTON FORD**   Oriole PS 40021   16   4 wks

Lita FORD US, female vocalist   4 wks

26 May 84   **DANCIN' ON THE EDGE**   Vertigo VERL 13   96   1 wk
23 Jun 90   **STILETTO**   RCA PL 82090   66   1 wk
25 Jan 92   **DANGEROUS CURVES**   RCA PD 90592   51   2 wks

Julia FORDHAM UK, female vocalist   33 wks

18 Jun 88   **JULIA FORDHAM**   Circa CIRCA 4   20   22 wks
21 Oct 89   **PORCELAIN**   Circa CIRCA 10   13   5 wks
2 Nov 91   **SWEPT**   Circa CIRCA 18   33   6 wks

FOREIGNER UK/US, male vocal/instrumental group   125 wks

26 Aug 78   **DOUBLE VISION**   Atlantic K 50476   32   5 wks
25 Jul 81 ● **4**   Atlantic K 50796   5   62 wks
18 Dec 82   **RECORDS**   Atlantic A 0999   58   11 wks
22 Dec 84 ★ **AGENT PROVOCATEUR**   Atlantic 78–1999–1   1   32 wks
19 Dec 87   **INSIDE INFORMATION**   Atlantic WX 143   64   7 wks
6 Jul 91   **UNUSUAL HEAT**   Atlantic WX 424   56   1 wk
2 May 92   **THE VERY BEST OF FOREIGNER**   Atlantic 7567805112 .   19   7 wks

49ers Italy, male producer – Gianfranco Bortolotti   5 wks

10 Mar 90   **THE 49ERS**   Fourth & Broadway BRLP 547   51   5 wks

FOSTER and ALLEN   *Ireland, male vocal duo*   *142 wks*

14 May 83	**MAGGIE** *Ritz RITZLP 0012*	72	6 wks
5 Nov 83	**I WILL LOVE YOU ALL OF MY LIFE** *Ritz RITZLP 0015*	71	6 wks
17 Nov 84	**THE VERY BEST OF FOSTER AND ALLEN**		
	Ritz RITZ LP TV 1	18	18 wks
29 Mar 86	**AFTER ALL THESE YEARS** *Ritz RITZLP 0032*	82	2 wks
25 Oct 86	**REMINISCING** *Stylus SMR 623*	11	15 wks
27 Jun 87	**LOVE SONGS – THE VERY BEST OF FOSTER AND**		
	ALLEN VOL 2 *Ritz RITZLP 0036*	92	1 wk
10 Oct 87	**REFLECTIONS** *Stylus SMR 739*	16	16 wks
30 Apr 88	**REMEMBER YOU'RE MINE** *Stylus SMR 853*	16	15 wks
28 Oct 89	**THE MAGIC OF FOSTER AND ALLEN** *Stylus SMR 989*	29	12 wks
9 Dec 89	**THE FOSTER AND ALLEN CHRISTMAS ALBUM**		
	Stylus SMR 995	40	4 wks
10 Nov 90	**SOUVENIRS** *Telstar STAR 2457*	15	12 wks
8 Dec 90	**THE CHRISTMAS COLLECTION** *Telstar STAR 2459* . . .	44	4 wks
2 Nov 91	**MEMORIES** *Telstar STAR 2527*	18	11 wks
31 Oct 92	**HEART STRINGS** *Telstar TCD 2608*	37	10 wks
23 Oct 93	**BY REQUEST** *Telstar TCD 2670*	14†	10 wks

FOTHERINGAY   *UK, male/female vocal/instrumental group*   *6 wks*

11 Jul 70	**FOTHERINGAY** *Island ILPS 9125*	18	6 wks

4 NON BLONDES
US, female/male vocal/instrumental group   *18 wks*

17 Jul 93 ●	**BIGGER, BETTER, FASTER, MORE!**		
	Interscope 7567921122	4	18 wks

4 OF US   *Ireland, male vocal/instrumental group*   *1 wk*

20 Mar 93	**MAN ALIVE** *Columbia 4723262*	61	1 wk

FOUR PENNIES   *UK, male vocal/instrumental group*   *5 wks*

7 Nov 64	**TWO SIDES OF FOUR PENNIES** *Philips BL 7642*	13	5 wks

FOUR SEASONS   *US, male vocal group*   *62 wks*

6 Jul 63	**SHERRY** *Stateside SL 10033*	20	1 wk
10 Apr 71	**EDIZIONE D'ORO** *Philips 6640–002*	11	7 wks
20 Nov 71	**THE BIG ONES** *Philips 6336–208*	37	1 wk
6 Mar 76	**THE FOUR SEASONS STORY** *Private Stock DAPS 1001* ..	20	8 wks
6 Mar 76	**WHO LOVES YOU** *Warner Bros. K 56179*	12	17 wks
20 Nov 76 ●	**GREATEST HITS** *K-Tel NE 942*	4	6 wks
21 May 88	**THE COLLECTION** *Telstar STAR 2320*	38	9 wks
7 Mar 92 ●	**THE VERY BEST OF FRANKIE VALLI AND THE FOUR**		
	SEASONS *PolyGram TV 5131192★*	7	13 wks

★ *Frankie Valli and the Four Seasons.*

4-SKINS   *UK, male vocal/instrumental group*   *4 wks*

17 Apr 82	**THE GOOD, THE BAD AND THE 4-SKINS** *Secret SEC 4*	80	4 wks

FOUR TOPS   *US, male vocal group*   *255 wks*

19 Nov 66 ●	**FOUR TOPS ON TOP** *Tamla Motown TML 11037*	9	23 wks
11 Feb 67 ●	**FOUR TOPS LIVE!** *Tamla Motown STML 11041*	4	72 wks
25 Nov 67 ●	**REACH OUT** *Tamla Motown STML 11056*	4	34 wks
20 Jan 68 ★	**GREATEST HITS** *Tamla Motown STML 11061*	1	67 wks

F

135

8 Feb 69		YESTERDAY'S DREAMS	*Tamla Motown STML 11087*	37	1 wk
27 Jun 70		STILL WATERS RUN DEEP	*Tamla Motown STML 11149* .	29	8 wks
29 May 71	●	MAGNIFICENT SEVEN	*Tamla Motown STML 11179★*	6	11 wks
27 Nov 71		FOUR TOPS' GREATEST HITS VOL. 2			
			Tamla Motown STML 11195	25	10 wks
10 Nov 73		THE FOUR TOPS STORY 1964–72			
			Tamla Motown TMSP 11241/2	35	5 wks
13 Feb 82		THE BEST OF THE FOUR TOPS	*K-Tel NE 1160*	13	13 wks
8 Dec 90		THEIR GREATEST HITS	*Telstar STAR 2437*	47	6 wks
19 Sep 92		THE SINGLES COLLECTION	*PolyGram TV 5157102*	11	5 wks

★ *Supremes and Four Tops.*

FOX   UK, *male/female vocal instrumental group*   8 wks

17 May 75	●	FOX	*GTO GTLP 001*	7	8 wks

Samantha FOX   UK, *female vocalist*   18 wks

26 Jul 86	TOUCH ME	*Jive HIP 39*	17	10 wks
1 Aug 87	SAMANTHA FOX	*Jive HIP 48*	22	6 wks
18 Feb 89	I WANNA HAVE SOME FUN	*Jive HIP 72*	46	2 wks

Bruce FOXTON   UK, *male vocalist*   4 wks

12 May 84	TOUCH SENSITIVE	*Arista 206 251*	68	4 wks

John FOXX   UK, *male vocalist*   17 wks

2 Feb 80	METAMATIX	*Metalbeat V 2146*	18	7 wks
3 Oct 81	THE GARDEN	*Virgin V 2194*	24	6 wks
8 Oct 83	THE GOLDEN SECTION	*Virgin V 2233*	27	3 wks
5 Oct 85	IN MYSTERIOUS WAYS	*Virgin V 2355*	85	1 wk

FRAGGLES   UK/US, *puppets*   4 wks

21 Apr 84	FRAGGLE ROCK	*RCA PL 70221*	38	4 wks

Peter FRAMPTON
UK, *male vocalist/instrumentalist – guitar*   49 wks

22 May 76	●	FRAMPTON COMES ALIVE	*A & M AMLM 63703*	6	39 wks
18 Jun 77		I'M IN YOU	*A & M AMLK 64039*	19	10 wks

Connie FRANCIS   US, *female vocalist*   31 wks

26 Mar 60		ROCK 'N' ROLL MILLION SELLERS	*MGM C 804*	12	1 wk
11 Feb 61		CONNIE'S GREATEST HITS	*MGM C 831*	16	3 wks
18 Jun 77	★	20 ALL TIME GREATS	*Polydor 2391 290*	1	22 wks
24 Apr 93		THE SINGLES COLLECTION	*PolyGram TV 5191312*	12	5 wks

FRANK AND WALTERS
Ireland, *male vocal/instrumental group*   1 wk

7 Nov 92	TRAINS, BOATS AND PLANES	*Setanta 8283692*	36	1 wk

FRANK BLACK   US, *male vocal/instrumental group*   3 wks

20 Mar 93	●	FRANK BLACK	*4AD CAD 3004CD*	9	3 wks

FRANKIE GOES TO HOLLYWOOD
UK, male vocal/instrumental group   80 wks

10 Nov 84 ★	**WELCOME TO THE PLEASUREDOME** ZTT ZTTIQ 1 .		**1**	58 wks
1 Nov 86 ●	**LIVERPOOL** ZTT ZTTIQ 8		**5**	13 wks
30 Oct 93 ●	**BANG! – THE GREATEST HITS OF FRANKIE GOES TO**			
	HOLLYWOOD ZTT 4509939122		**4†**	9 wks

Aretha FRANKLIN US, female vocalist   58 wks

12 Aug 67	**I NEVER LOVED A MAN** Atlantic 587–006		**36**	2 wks
13 Apr 68	**LADY SOUL** Atlantic 588–099		**25**	18 wks
14 Sep 68 ●	**ARETHA NOW** Atlantic 588–114		**6**	11 wks
18 Jan 86	**WHO'S ZOOMIN' WHO?** Arista 2072 02		**49**	12 wks
24 May 86	**THE FIRST LADY OF SOUL** Stylus SMR 8506		**89**	1 wk
8 Nov 86	**ARETHA** Arista 208 020		**51**	13 wks
3 Jun 89	**THROUGH THE STORM** Arista 209842		**46**	1 wk

Rodney FRANKLIN US, male instrumentalist – piano   2 wks

24 May 80	**YOU'LL NEVER KNOW** CBS 83812		**64**	2 wks

Liz FRASER – See Harold BUDD/Liz FRASER/Robin GUTHRIE/Simon RAYMOND

FRAZIER CHORUS
UK, male/female vocal/instrumental group   2 wks

20 May 89	**SUE** Virgin V 2578		**56**	1 wk
16 Mar 91	**RAY** Virgin VFC 2654		**66**	1 wk

FREDDIE and the DREAMERS
UK, male vocal/instrumental group   26 wks

9 Nov 63 ●	**FREDDIE AND THE DREAMERS** Columbia 33SX 1577 ..		**5**	26 wks

FREDERICK – See NINA and FREDERICK

FREE UK, male vocal/instrumental group   71 wks

11 Jul 70 ●	**FIRE AND WATER** Island ILPS 9120		**2**	18 wks
23 Jan 71	**HIGHWAY** Island ILPS 9138		**41**	10 wks
26 Jun 71 ●	**FREE LIVE!** Island ILPS 9160		**4**	12 wks
17 Jun 72 ●	**FREE AT LAST** Island ILPS 9192		**9**	9 wks
3 Feb 73 ●	**HEARTBREAKER** Island ILPS 9217		**9**	7 wks
16 Mar 74 ●	**THE FREE STORY** Island ISLD 4		**2**	6 wks
2 Mar 91 ●	**THE BEST OF FREE – ALL RIGHT NOW** Island ILPTV 2		**9**	9 wks

FREEEZ UK, male vocal/instrumental group   18 wks

7 Feb 81	**SOUTHERN FREEEZ** Beggars Banquet BEGA 22		**17**	15 wks
22 Oct 83	**GONNA GET YOU** Beggars Banquet BEGA 48		**46**	3 wks

FREHLEY'S COMET US, male vocal/instrumental group   1 wk

18 Jun 88	**SECOND SIGHT** Atlantic 781862 1		**79**	1 wk

FRESH PRINCE – See DJ JAZZY JEFF and FRESH PRINCE

Glenn FREY US, male vocalist   9 wks

6 Jul 85	**THE ALLNIGHTER** MCA MCF 3277		**31**	9 wks

F
137

FRIDA *Norway, female vocalist*   *8 wks*

18 Sep 82	**SOMETHING'S GOING ON** Epic EPC 85966	18	7 wks
20 Oct 84	**SHINE** Epic EPC 26178	67	1 wk

Dean FRIEDMAN *US, male vocalist*   *14 wks*

21 Oct 78	**WELL, WELL, SAID THE ROCKING CHAIR** Lifesong LSLP 6019	21	14 wks

Robert FRIPP *UK, male vocalist/instrumentalist – guitar*   *3 wks*

12 May 79	**EXPOSURE** Polydor EGLP 101	71	1 wk
17 Jul 93	**THE FIRST DAY** Virgin CDVX 2712★	21	2 wks

★ David Sylvian and Robert Fripp.

FRONT 242 *Belgium/US, male vocal/instrumental group*   *3 wks*

2 Feb 91	**TYRANNY FOR YOU** RRE RRE 011	49	1 wk
22 May 93	**06:21:03:11 UP EVIL** RRE RRE 021CD	44	1 wk
4 Sep 93	**05:22:09:12 OFF** RRE RRE 022CD	46	1 wk

FUGAZI *UK, male vocal/instrumental group*   *3 wks*

21 Sep 91	**STEADY DIET OF NOTHING** Dischord DISCHORD 60 ..	63	1 wk
19 Jun 93	**IN ON THE KILLTAKER** Dischord DIS 70CD	24	2 wks

FULL FORCE – See LISA LISA and CULT JAM with FULL FORCE

F
138

FUN BOY THREE *UK, male vocal/instrumental group*   *40 wks*

20 Mar 82 ●	**FUNBOY THREE** Chrysalis CHR 1383	7	20 wks
19 Feb 83	**WAITING** Chrysalis CHR 1417	14	20 wks

FUNK FEDERATION – See Arlene PHILLIPS

FUNKADELIC *US, male vocal/instrumental group*   *5 wks*

23 Dec 78	**ONE NATION UNDER A GROOVE** Warner Bros. K 56539	56	5 wks

FUNKY BUNCH – See MARKY MARK and the FUNKY BUNCH

FUREYS and Davey ARTHUR
Ireland/UK, male vocal/instrumental group   *38 wks*

8 May 82	**WHEN YOU WERE SWEET SIXTEEN** Ritz RITZLP 0004	99	1 wk
10 Nov 84	**GOLDEN DAYS** K-Tel ONE 1283	17	19 wks
26 Oct 85	**AT THE END OF THE DAY** K-Tel ONE 1310	35	11 wks
21 Nov 87	**FUREYS FINEST** Telstar HSTAR 2311	65	7 wks

FURIOUS FIVE – See GRANDMASTER FLASH and the FURIOUS FIVE

Billy FURY *UK, male vocalist*   *51 wks*

4 Jun 60	**THE SOUND OF FURY** Decca LF 1329	18	2 wks
23 Sep 61 ●	**HALFWAY TO PARADISE** Ace Of Clubs ACL 1083	5	9 wks
11 May 63 ●	**BILLY** Decca LK 4533	6	21 wks
26 Oct 63	**WE WANT BILLY** Decca LK 4548	14	2 wks
19 Feb 83	**HIT PARADE** Decca TAB 37	44	15 wks
26 Mar 83	**THE ONE AND ONLY** Polydor POLD 5069	54	2 wks

---

FUSE *Canada, male instrumentalist – keyboards, Richie Hawtin*   *1 wk*

19 Jun 93   **DIMENSION INTRUSION** *Warp WARPCD 12* . . . .   **63**   1 wk

---

FUTURE SOUND OF LONDON
UK, male instrumental duo   *1 wk*

18 Jul 92   **ACCELERATOR** *Jumpin' & Pumpin' CDTOT 2* . . . .   **75**   1 wk

FUZZBOX – See WE'VE GOT A FUZZBOX AND WE'RE GONNA USE IT

FYC – See FINE YOUNG CANNIBALS

Kenny G *US, male instrumentalist – saxophone*   *35 wks*

17 Mar 84   **G FORCE** *Arista 206 168* . . . .   **56**   5 wks
 8 Aug 87   **DUOTONES** *Arista 207 792* . . . .   **28**   5 wks
14 Apr 90   **MONTAGE** *Arista 210621* . . . .   **32**   7 wks
15 May 93 ● **BREATHLESS** *Arista 07822186462* . . . .   **4**   18 wks

Peter GABRIEL *UK, male vocalist*   *198 wks*

12 Mar 77 ● **PETER GABRIEL** *Charisma CDS 4006* . . . .   **7**   19 wks
17 Jun 78 ● **PETER GABRIEL** *Charisma CDS 4013* . . . .   **10**   8 wks
 7 Jun 80 ★ **PETER GABRIEL** *Charisma CDS 4019* . . . .   **1**   18 wks
18 Sep 82 ● **PETER GABRIEL** *Charisma PG 4* . . . .   **6**   16 wks
18 Jun 83 ● **PETER GABRIEL PLAYS LIVE** *Charisma PGDL 1* . . . . . .   **8**   9 wks
30 Apr 85   **BIRDY – MUSIC FROM THE FILM** *Charisma CAS 1167* .   **51**   3 wks
31 May 86 ★ **SO** *Virgin PG 5* . . . .   **1**   76 wks
17 Jun 89   **PASSION** *Virgin RWLP 1* . . . .   **29**   5 wks
 1 Dec 90   **SHAKING THE TREE – GOLDEN GREATS**
             Virgin PGTV 6 . . . .   **11**   15 wks
10 Oct 92 ● **US** *Realworld PGCD 7* . . . .   **2**   29 wks

First four albums are different.

GABRIELLE *UK, female vocalist*   *9 wks*

30 Oct 93 ● **FIND YOUR WAY** *Go.Beat 8284412* . . . .   **9†**   9 wks

GALAXY – See Phil FEARON and GALAXY

GALLAGHER and LYLE
UK, male vocal/instrumental duo   *44 wks*

28 Feb 76 ● **BREAKAWAY** *A & M AMLH 68348* . . . .   **6**   35 wks
29 Jan 77   **LOVE ON THE AIRWAYS** *A &M AMLH 64620* . . . .   **19**   9 wks

Rory GALLAGHER
UK, male vocalist/instrumentalist – guitar   *43 wks*

29 May 71   **RORY GALLAGHER** *Polydor 2383–044* . . . .   **32**   2 wks
 4 Dec 71   **DEUCE** *Polydor 2383–076* . . . .   **39**   1 wk
20 May 72 ● **LIVE IN EUROPE** *Polydor 2383 112* . . . .   **9**   15 wks
24 Feb 73   **BLUE PRINT** *Polydor 2383 189* . . . .   **12**   7 wks

17 Nov 73	**TATTOO** *Polydor 2383 230*	**32**	3 wks
27 Jul 74	**IRISH TOUR '74** *Polydor 2659 031*	**36**	2 wks
30 Oct 76	**CALLING CARD** *Chrysalis CHR 1124*	**32**	1 wk
22 Sep 79	**TOP PRIORITY** *Chrysalis CHR 1235*	**56**	4 wks
8 Nov 80	**STAGE STRUCK** Chrysalis CHR 1280	**40**	3 wks
8 May 82	**JINX** Chrysalis CHR 1359	**68**	5 wks

GALLIANO UK, *male/female vocal/instrumental group*   *3 wks*

20 Jun 92	**A JOYFUL NOISE UNTO THE CREATOR**		
	Talkin Loud 8480802	**28**	3 wks

GALLON DRUNK UK, *male vocal/instrumental group*   *1 wk*

13 Mar 93	**FROM THE HEART OF TOWN** *Clawfist HUNKACDL 005*	**67**	1 wk

James GALWAY UK, *male instrumentalist – flute*   *93 wks*

27 May 78	**THE MAGIC FLUTE OF JAMES GALWAY**		
	RCA Red Seal LRLI 5131	**43**	6 wks
1 Jul 78	**THE MAN WITH THE GOLDEN FLUTE**		
	RCA Red Seal LRLI 5127	**52**	3 wks
9 Sep 78 ●	**JAMES GALWAY PLAYS SONGS FOR ANNIE**		
	RCA Red Seal RL 25163	**7**	40 wks
15 Dec 79	**SONGS OF THE SEASHORE** *Solar RL 25253*	**39**	6 wks
31 May 80	**SOMETIMES WHEN WE TOUCH** *RCA PL 25296*★	**15**	14 wks
18 Dec 82	**THE JAMES GALWAY COLLECTION** *Telstar STAR 2224*	**41**	8 wks
8 Dec 84	**IN THE PINK** *RCA Red Seal RL 85315*★★	**62**	6 wks
28 Mar 87	**JAMES GALWAY AND THE CHIEFTAINS IN IRELAND**		
	RCA Red Seal RL 85798★★★	**32**	5 wks
17 Apr 93	**THE ESSENTIAL FLUTE OF JAMES GALWAY**		
	RCA Victor 74321133852	**30**	5 wks

★ *Cleo Laine and James Galway.*
★★ *James Galway and Henry Mancini with the National Philharmonic Orchestra.*
★★★ *James Galway and the Chieftains.*

G
140

GANG OF FOUR UK, *male vocal/instrumental group*   *9 wks*

13 Oct 79	**ENTERTAINMENT** *EMI EMC 3313*	**45**	3 wks
21 Mar 81	**SOLID GOLD** *EMI EMC 3364*	**52**	2 wks
29 May 82	**SONGS OF THE FREE** *EMI EMC 3412*	**61**	4 wks

GANG STARR US, *male rap group*   *3 wks*

26 Jan 91	**STEP IN THE ARENA** *Cooltempo ZCTLP 21*	**36**	3 wks

GAP BAND US, *male vocal/instrumental group*   *3 wks*

7 Feb 87	**GAP BAND 8** *Total Experience FL 89992*	**47**	3 wks

Art GARFUNKEL US, *male vocalist*   *58 wks*

13 Oct 73	**ANGEL CLARE** *CBS 69021*	**14**	7 wks
1 Nov 75 ●	**BREAKAWAY** *CBS 86002*	**7**	10 wks
18 Mar 78	**WATER MARK** *CBS 86054*	**25**	5 wks
21 Apr 79 ●	**FATE FOR BREAKFAST** *CBS 86082*	**2**	20 wks
19 Sep 81	**SCISSORS CUT** *CBS 85259*	**51**	3 wks
17 Nov 84	**THE ART GARFUNKEL ALBUM** *CBS 10046*	**12**	13 wks

See also Simon and Garfunkel.

Judy GARLAND US, *female vocalist*   *3 wks*

3 Mar 62	**JUDY AT CARNEGIE HALL** *Capitol W 1569*	**13**	3 wks

Errol GARNER US, male instrumentalist – piano   1 wk

| 14 Jul | 62 | CLOSE UP IN SWING Philips BBL 7579 .... | 20 | 1 wk |

David GATES US, male vocalist   4 wks

| 31 May | 75 | NEVER LET HER GO Elektra K 52012 .... | 32 | 1 wk |
| 29 Jul | 78 | GOODBYE GIRL Elektra K 52091 .... | 28 | 3 wks |

Marvin GAYE US, male vocalist   156 wks

16 Mar	68	GREATEST HITS Tamla Motown STML 11065	40	1 wk
22 Aug	70	GREATEST HITS Tamla Motown STML 11153*	60	4 wks
19 Jan	71 ●	DIANA AND MARVIN Tamla Motown STMA 8015**	6	43 wks
10 Nov	73	LET'S GET IT ON Tamla Motown STMA 8013	39	1 wk
15 May	76	I WANT YOU Tamla Motown STML 12025	22	5 wks
30 Oct	76	THE BEST OF MARVIN GAYE Tamla Motown STML 12042	56	1 wk
28 Feb	81	IN OUR LIFETIME Motown STML 12149	48	4 wks
29 Aug	81	DIANA AND MARVIN (re-issue) Motown STMS 5001** ..	78	2 wks
20 Nov	82 ●	MIDNIGHT LOVE CBS 85977	10	16 wks
12 Nov	83	GREATEST HITS Telstar STAR 2234	13	61 wks
15 Jun	85	DREAM OF A LIFETIME CBS 26239	46	4 wks
12 Nov	88	LOVE SONGS Telstar STAR 2331***	69	9 wks
2 Nov	90	LOVE SONGS Telstar STAR 2427	39	5 wks

* Marvin Gaye and Tammi Terrell.   ** Diana Ross and Marvin Gaye.
*** Marvin Gaye and Smokey Robinson.
The Greatest Hits albums are different.

GAYE BYKERS ON ACID
UK, male vocal/instrumental group   1 wk

| 14 Nov | 87 | DRILL YOUR OWN HOLE Virgin V 2478 .... | 95 | 1 wk |

Crystal GAYLE US, female vocalist   25 wks

21 Jan	78	WE MUST BELIEVE IN MAGIC United Artists UAG 30108	15	7 wks
23 Sep	78	WHEN I DREAM United Artists UAG 30169	25	8 wks
22 Mar	80 ●	THE CRYSTAL GAYLE SINGLES ALBUM United Artists UAG 30287	7	10 wks

Gloria GAYNOR US, female vocalist   17 wks

8 Mar	75	NEVER CAN SAY GOODBYE MGM 2315 321	32	8 wks
24 Mar	79	LOVE TRACKS Polydor 2391 385	31	7 wks
16 Aug	86	THE POWER OF GLORIA GAYNOR Stylus SMR 618 ..	81	2 wks

J. GEILS BAND US, male vocal/instrumental group   15 wks

| 27 Feb | 82 | FREEZE FRAME EMI America AML 3020 .... | 12 | 15 wks |

Bob GELDOF Ireland, male vocalist   7 wks

| 6 Dec | 86 | DEEP IN THE HEART OF NOWHERE Mercury BOBLP 1 | 79 | 1 wk |
| 4 Aug | 90 | THE VEGETARIANS OF LOVE Mercury 8462501 .... | 21 | 6 wks |

GENE LOVES JEZEBEL
UK, male vocal/instrumental group   5 wks

| 19 Jul | 87 | DISCOVER Beggars Banquet BEGA 73 .... | 32 | 4 wks |
| 24 Oct | 87 | HOUSE OF DOLLS Beggars Banquet BEGA 87 .... | 81 | 1 wk |

Georgie Fame *finds the way to bathe, read, smoke and wash his clothes all at the same time, while* **Barry Gibb** *reads a 1969 edition of the Financial Times with front-page news concerning the Beatles. (Pictorial Press)*

GENERATION X UK, male vocal/instrumental group   9 wks

8 Apr	78	GENERATION X Chrysalis CHR 1169	29	4 wks
17 Feb	79	VALLEY OF THE DOLLS Chrysalis CHR 1193	51	5 wks

GENESIS UK, male vocal/instrumental group   468 wks

14 Oct	72	FOXTROT Charisma CAS 1058	12	7 wks
11 Aug	73 ●	GENESIS LIVE Charisma CLASS 1	9	10 wks
20 Oct	73 ●	SELLING ENGLAND BY THE POUND		
		Charisma CAS 1074	3	21 wks
11 May	74	NURSERY CRYME Charisma CAS 1052	39	1 wk
7 Dec	74 ●	THE LAMB LIES DOWN ON BROADWAY		
		Charisma CGS 101	10	6 wks
28 Feb	76 ●	A TRICK OF THE TAIL Charisma CDS 4001	3	39 wks
15 Jan	77 ●	WIND AND WUTHERING Charisma CDS 4005	7	22 wks
29 Oct	77 ●	SECONDS OUT Charisma GE 2001	4	17 wks
15 Apr	78 ●	AND THEN THERE WERE THREE Charisma CDS 4010	3	32 wks
5 Apr	80 ★	DUKE Charisma CBR 101	1	30 wks
26 Sep	81 ★	ABACAB Charisma CBR 102	1	27 wks
12 Jun	82 ●	3 SIDES LIVE Charisma GE 2002	2	19 wks
15 Oct	83 ★	GENESIS Charisma GENLP 1	1	51 wks
31 Mar	84	NURSERY CRYME (re-issue) Charisma CHC 22	68	1 wk
21 Apr	84	TRESPASS Charisma CHC 12	98	1 wk
21 Jun	86 ★	INVISIBLE TOUCH Charisma GENLP 2	1	96 wks
23 Nov	91 ★	WE CAN'T DANCE Virgin GENLP 3	1	61 wks
28 Nov	92 ●	LIVE – THE WAY WE WALK VOL. 1: THE SHORTS		
		Virgin GENCD 4	3	18 wks
23 Jan	93 ★	LIVE – THE WAY WE WALK VOL. 2: THE LONGS		
		Virgin GENCD 5	1	9 wks

G
143

Jackie GENOVA UK, female exercise instructor   2 wks

21 May	83	WORK THAT BODY Island ILPS 9732	74	2 wks

Bobbie GENTRY US, female vocalist   2 wks

25 Oct	69	TOUCH 'EM WITH LOVE Capitol EST 155	21	1 wk
28 Feb	70	BOBBIE GENTRY AND GLEN CAMPBELL		
		Capitol ST 2928★	50	1 wk

★ Bobbie Gentry and Glen Campbell.

Lowell GEORGE US, male vocalist/instrumentalist – guitar   1 wk

21 Apr	79	THANKS BUT I'LL EAT IT HERE Warner Bros. K 56487	71	1 wk

Robin GEORGE UK, male vocal/instrumentalist – guitar   3 wks

2 Mar	85	DANGEROUS MUSIC Bronze BRON 554	65	3 wks

GEORGIA SATELLITES
US, male vocal/instrumental group   9 wks

7 Feb	87	GEORGIA SATELLITES Elektra 980 496–1	52	7 wks
2 Jul	88	OPEN ALL NIGHT Elektra EKT 47	39	2 wks

GERRY and the PACEMAKERS
UK, male vocal/instrumental group   29 wks

26 Oct	63 ●	HOW DO YOU LIKE IT? Columbia 33SX 1546	2	28 wks
6 Feb	65	FERRY CROSS THE MERSEY Columbia 33SX 1676	19	1 wk

Stan GETZ and Charlie BYRD
US, male instrumental duo – saxophone and guitar   *7 wks*

23 Feb 63	**JAZZ SAMBA** Verve SULP 9013	15	7 wks

Andy GIBB *UK, male vocalist*   *9 wks*

19 Aug 78	**SHADOW DANCING** RSO RSS 0001	15	9 wks

Barry GIBB *UK, male vocalist*   *2 wks*

20 Oct 84	**NOW VOYAGER** Polydor POLH 14	85	2 wks

Steve GIBBONS BAND
UK, male vocal/instrumental group   *3 wks*

22 Oct 77	**CAUGHT IN THE ACT** Polydor 2478 112	22	3 wks

Debbie GIBSON *US, female vocalist*   *52 wks*

30 Jan 88	**OUT OF THE BLUE** Atlantic WX 139	28	35 wks
11 Feb 89 ●	**ELECTRIC YOUTH** Atlantic WX 231	8	16 wks
30 Mar 91	**ANYTHING IS POSSIBLE** Atlantic WX 399	69	1 wk

Don GIBSON *US, male vocalist*   *10 wks*

22 Mar 80	**COUNTRY NUMBER ONE** Warwick WW 5079	13	10 wks

GIBSON BROTHERS
Martinique, male vocal/instrumental group   *3 wks*

30 Aug 80	**ON THE RIVIERA** Island ILPS 9620	50	3 wks

Johnny GILL *US, male vocalist*   *3 wks*

19 Jun 93	**PROVOCATIVE** Motown 5302062	41	3 wks

GILLAN *UK, male vocal/instrumental group*   *53 wks*

17 Jul 76	**CHILD IN TIME** Polydor 2490 136★	55	1 wk
20 Oct 79	**MR. UNIVERSE** Acrobat ACRO 3	11	6 wks
16 Aug 80 ●	**GLORY ROAD** Virgin V 2171	3	12 wks
25 Apr 81 ●	**FUTURE SHOCK** Virgin VK 2196	2	13 wks
7 Nov 81	**DOUBLE TROUBLE** Virgin VGD 3506	12	15 wks
2 Oct 82	**MAGIC** Virgin V 2238	17	6 wks

★ *Ian Gillan Band.*
See also Ian Gillan.

Ian GILLAN *UK, male vocalist*   *1 wk*

28 Jul 90	**NAKED THUNDER** Teldec 9031718991	63	1 wk

See also Gillan.

David GILMOUR *UK, male instrumentalist – guitar*   *18 wks*

10 Jun 78	**DAVID GILMOUR** Harvest SHVL 817	17	9 wks
17 Mar 84	**ABOUT FACE** Harvest SHSP 2400791	21	9 wks

Gordon GILTRAP *UK, male instrumentalist – guitar* *7 wks*

18 Feb	78	**PERILOUS JOURNEY** *Electric TRIX 4*	29	7 wks

GIPSY KINGS *France, male vocal/instrumental group* *49 wks*

15 Apr	89	**GIPSY KINGS** *Telstar STAR 2355*	16	29 wks
25 Nov	89	**MOSAIQUE** *Telstar STAR 2398*	27	13 wks
13 Jul	91	**ESTE MUNDO** *Columbia 4686481*	19	7 wks

GIRL *UK, male vocal/instrumental group* *6 wks*

9 Feb	80	**SHEER GREED** *Jet JETLP 224*	33	5 wks
23 Jan	82	**WASTED YOUTH** *Jet JETLP 238*	92	1 wk

GIRLS AT OUR BEST
UK, male/female vocal/instrumental group *3 wks*

7 Nov	81	**PLEASURE** *Happy Birthday RVLP 1*	60	3 wks

GIRLSCHOOL *UK, female vocal/instrumental group* *23 wks*

5 Jul	80	**DEMOLITION** *Bronze BRON 525*	28	10 wks
25 Apr	81	● **HIT 'N' RUN** *Bronze BRON 534*	5	6 wks
12 Jun	82	**SCREAMING BLUE MURDER** *Bronze BRON 541*	27	6 wks
12 Nov	83	**PLAY DIRTY** *Bronze BRON 548*	66	1 wk

Gary GLITTER *UK, male vocalist* *100 wks*

21 Oct	72	● **GLITTER** *Bell BELLS 216*	8	40 wks
16 Jun	73	● **TOUCH ME** *Bell BELLS 222*	2	33 wks
29 Jun	74	● **REMEMBER ME THIS WAY** *Bell BELLS 237*	5	14 wks
27 Mar	76	**GARY GLITTER'S GREATEST HITS** *Bell BELLS 262* ..	33	5 wks
14 Nov	92	**MANY HAPPY RETURNS – THE HITS** *EMI CDEMTV 68*	35	8 wks

GLITTER BAND *UK, male vocal/instrumental group* *17 wks*

14 Sep	74	**HEY** *Bell BELLS 241*	13	12 wks
3 May	75	**ROCK 'N' ROLL DUDES** *Bell BELLS 253*	17	4 wks
19 Jun	76	**GREATEST HITS** *Bell BELLS 264*	52	1 wk

GLOVE *UK, male vocal/instrumental group* *3 wks*

17 Sep	83	**BLUE SUNSHINE** *Wonderland SHELP 2*	35	3 wks

GO WEST *UK, male vocal/instrumental duo* *115 wks*

13 Apr	85	● **GO WEST/BANGS AND CRASHES** *Chrysalis CHR 1495* .	8	83 wks
6 Jun	87	**DANCING ON THE COUCH** *Chrysalis CDL 1550*	19	5 wks
14 Nov	92	**INDIAN SUMMER** *Chrysalis CDCHR 1964*	13	16 wks
16 Oct	93	● **ACES AND KINGS – THE BEST OF GO WEST** *Chrysalis CDCHR 6050*	5†	11 wks

Bangs And Crashes is an album of remixed versions of Go West tracks and some new material. From 31 May 1986 both records were available together as a double album.

GO-BETWEENS
Australia, male/female vocal/instrumental group *2 wks*

13 Jun	87	**TALLULAH** *Beggars Banquet BEGA 81*	91	1 wk
10 Sep	88	**16 LOVERS LANE** *Beggars Banquet BEGA 95*	81	1 wk

GODFATHERS UK, male vocal/instrumental group *3 wks*

13 Feb 88	**BIRTH SCHOOL WORK DEATH** Epic 460263 1	**80**	2 wks
20 May 89	**MORE SONGS ABOUT LOVE AND HATE** Epic 463394 1	**49**	1 wk

GOD MACHINE US, male vocal/instrumental group *1 wk*

20 Feb 93	**SCENES FROM THE SECOND STOREY** Fiction 5171562	**55**	1 wk

GODLEY and CREME UK, male vocal/instrumental duo *34 wks*

19 Nov 77	**CONSEQUENCES** Mercury CONS 017	**52**	1 wk
9 Sep 78	**L** Mercury 9109 611	**47**	2 wks
17 Oct 81	**ISMISM** Polydor POLD 5043	**29**	13 wks
29 Aug 87	● **CHANGING FACES – THE VERY BEST OF 10 C.C. AND GODLEY AND CREME** ProTV TGCLP 1★	**4**	18 wks

★ 10 C.C. and Godley and Creme.

GO-GO'S US, female vocal/instrumental group *3 wks*

21 Aug 82	**VACATION** IRS SP 70031	**75**	3 wks

Andrew GOLD US, male vocalist/instrumentalist – piano *7 wks*

15 Apr 78	**ALL THIS AND HEAVEN TOO** Asylum K 53072	**31**	7 wks

GOLDEN EARRING
Holland, male vocal/instrumental group *4 wks*

2 Feb 74	**MOONTAN** Track 2406 112	**24**	4 wks

Glen GOLDSMITH UK, male vocalist *9 wks*

23 Jul 88	**WHAT YOU SEE IS WHAT YOU GET** RCA PL 71750 .	**14**	9 wks

GOODBYE MR. MACKENZIE
UK, male/female vocal/instrumental group *4 wks*

22 Apr 89	**GOOD DEEDS AND DIRTY RAGS** Capitol EST 2089 ...	**26**	3 wks
16 Mar 91	**HAMMER AND TONGS** Radioactive RAR 10227	**61**	1 wk

GOODIES UK, male vocal group *11 wks*

8 Nov 75	**THE NEW GOODIES LP** Bradley's BRADL 1010	**25**	11 wks

Benny GOODMAN US, male instrumentalist – clarinet *1 wk*

3 Apr 71	**BENNY GOODMAN TODAY** Decca DDS 3	**49**	1 wk

Ron GOODWIN UK, orchestra *1 wk*

2 May 70	**LEGEND OF THE GLASS MOUNTAIN** Studio Two TWO 220	**49**	1 wk

GOOMBAY DANCE BAND
Germany/Montserrat, male/female vocal group *9 wks*

10 Apr 82	**SEVEN TEARS** Epic EPC 85702	**16**	9 wks

GOONS UK, male comedy group   31 wks

28 Nov 59	● BEST OF THE GOON SHOWS Parlophone PMC 1108	8	14 wks
17 Dec 60	BEST OF THE GOON SHOWS VOL. 2		
	Parlophone PMC 1129	12	6 wks
4 Nov 72	● LAST GOON SHOW OF ALL		
	BBC Radio Enterprises REB 142	8	11 wks

GORDON – See PETER and GORDON

Martin L. GORE
UK, male vocalist/instrumentalist – keyboards   1 wk

| 24 Jun 89 | COUNTERFEIT E.P.   Mute STUMM 67 .... | 51 | 1 wk |

Jaki GRAHAM UK, female vocalist   10 wks

| 14 Sep 85 | HEAVEN KNOWS   EMI JK 1 .... | 48 | 5 wks |
| 20 Sep 86 | BREAKING AWAY   EMI EMC 3514 .... | 25 | 5 wks |

GRAND PRIX UK, male vocal/instrumental group   2 wks

| 18 Jun 83 | SAMURAI   Chrysalis CHR 1430 .... | 65 | 2 wks |

GRANDMASTER FLASH and the FURIOUS FIVE US, male vocalist and male vocal group   20 wks

23 Oct 82	THE MESSAGE Sugar Hill SHLP 1007	77	3 wks
23 Jun 84	GREATEST MESSAGES Sugar Hill SHLP 5552	41	16 wks
23 Feb 85	THEY SAID IT COULDN'T BE DONE Elektra 9–60389–1.	95	1 wk

G

147

GRANDMASTER MELLE MEL US, male vocalist   5 wks

| 20 Oct 84 | WORK PARTY   Sugar Hill SHLP 5553 .... | 45 | 5 wks |

Amy GRANT US, female vocalist   15 wks

| 22 Jun 91 | HEART IN MOTION   A & M 3953211 .... | 25 | 15 wks |

David GRANT UK, male vocalist   7 wks

| 5 Nov 83 | DAVID GRANT   Chrysalis CHR 1448 .... | 32 | 6 wks |
| 18 May 85 | HOPES AND DREAMS   Chrysalis CHR 1483 .... | 96 | 1 wk |

Eddy GRANT Guyana, male vocalist/multi-instrumentalist   47 wks

30 May 81	CAN'T GET ENOUGH Ice ICELP 21	39	6 wks
27 Nov 82	● KILLER ON THE RAMPAGE Ice ICELP 3023	7	23 wks
17 Nov 84	ALL THE HITS K-Tel NE 1284	23	10 wks
1 Jul 89	WALKING ON SUNSHINE (THE BEST OF EDDY		
	GRANT) Parlophone PCSD 108	20	8 wks

GRANT LEE BUFFALO
US, male vocal/instrumental group   1 wk

| 10 Jul 93 | FUZZY   Slash 8283892 .... | 74 | 1 wk |

GRATEFUL DEAD US, male vocal/instrumental group   12 wks

19 Sep 70	WORKINGMAN'S DEAD Warner Bros. WS 1869	69	2 wks
3 Aug 74	GRATEFUL DEAD FROM THE MARS HOTEL		
	Atlantic K 59302	47	1 wk

1 Nov 75	**BLUES FOR ALLAH** *United Artists UAS 29895*	**45**	1 wk
4 Sep 76	**STEAL YOUR FACE** *United Artists UAS 60131/2*	**42**	1 wk
20 Aug 77	**TERRAPIN STATION** *Arista SPARTY 1016*	**30**	1 wk
19 Sep 87	**IN THE DARK** *Arista 208 564*	**57**	3 wks
18 Feb 89	**DYLAN AND THE DEAD** *CBS 4633811★*	**38**	3 wks

★ *Bob Dylan and the Grateful Dead.*

David GRAY and Tommy TYCHO
UK, male arrangers   *6 wks*

16 Oct 76	**ARMCHAIR MELODIES** *K-Tel NE 927*	**21**	6 wks

Alltrina GRAYSON – *See Wilton FELDER*

GREAT WHITE *US, male vocal/instrumental group*   *1 wk*

9 Mar 91	**HOOKED** *Capitol EST 2138*	**43**	1 wk

Al GREEN *US, male vocalist*   *25 wks*

26 Apr 75	**AL GREEN'S GREATEST HITS** *London SHU 8481*	**18**	16 wks
1 Oct 88	**HI LIFE – THE BEST OF AL GREEN** *K-Tel NE 1420* ...	**34**	7 wks
24 Oct 92	**AL** *Beechwood AGREECD 1*	**41**	2 wks

Peter GREEN *UK, male vocalist/instrumentalist – guitar*   *17 wks*

9 Jul 79	**IN THE SKIES** *Creole PULS 101*	**32**	13 wks
24 May 80	**LITTLE DREAMER** *PUK PULS 102*	**34**	4 wks

G
148

GREEN JELLY *US, male vocal/instrumental group*   *10 wks*

3 Jul 93	**CEREAL KILLER SOUNDTRACK** *Zoo 72445110382*	**18**	10 wks

GREEN ON RED *US, male vocal/instrumental group*   *1 wk*

26 Oct 85	**NO FREE LUNCH** *Mercury MERM 78*	**99**	1 wk

Dave GREENFIELD – *See Jean-Jacques BURNEL*

GREENSLADE *UK, male vocal/instrumental group*   *3 wks*

14 Sep 74	**SPYGLASS GUEST** *Warner Bros. K 56055*	**34**	3 wks

Christina GREGG *UK, female exercise instructor*   *1 wk*

27 May 78	**MUSIC 'N' MOTION** *Warwick WW 5041*	**51**	1 wk

Nanci GRIFFITH *US, female vocalist*   *19 wks*

28 Mar 88	**LITTLE LOVE AFFAIRS** *MCA MCF 3413*	**78**	1 wk
23 Sep 89	**STORMS** *MCA MCG 6066*	**38**	3 wks
28 Sep 91	**LATE NIGHT GRANDE HOTEL** *MCA MCA 10306*	**40**	5 wks
20 Mar 93	**OTHER VOICES/OTHER ROOMS** *MCA MCD 10796* ..	**18**	6 wks
13 Nov 93	**THE BEST OF NANCI GRIFFITH** *MCA MCD 10966* ...	**27**	4 wks

GROUNDHOGS *UK, male vocal/instrumental group*   *50 wks*

6 Jun 70 ●	**THANK CHRIST FOR THE BOMB** *Liberty LBS 83295* ..	**9**	13 wks
3 Apr 71 ●	**SPLIT** *Liberty LBG 83401*	**5**	27 wks
18 Mar 72 ●	**WHO WILL SAVE THE WORLD** *United Artists UAG 29237* ..	**8**	9 wks
13 Jul 74	**SOLID** *WWA WWA 004*	**31**	1 wk

Sir Charles GROVES – *See ROYAL PHILHARMONIC ORCHESTRA*

GTR   *UK, male vocal/instrumental group*   *4 wks*

19 Jul	86	**GTR** *Arista 207 716*	**41**	4 wks

---

GUILDFORD CATHEDRAL CHOIR   *UK, choir*   *4 wks*

10 Dec	66	**CHRISTMAS CAROLS FROM GUILDFORD CATHEDRAL** *MFP 1104*	**24**	4 wks

Record credits Barry Rose as conductor.

GUITAR CORPORATION
UK, male instrumental group   *5 wks*

15 Feb	92	**IMAGES** *Quality Television QTVCD 002*	**41**	5 wks

---

GUN   *UK, male vocal/instrumental group*   *14 wks*

22 Jul	89	**TAKING ON THE WORLD** *A & M AMA 7007*	**44**	10 wks
18 Apr	92	**GALLUS** *A & M 3953832*	**14**	4 wks

---

GUNS N' ROSES   *US, male vocal/instrumental group*   *339 wks*

1 Aug	87	● **APPETITE FOR DESTRUCTION** *Geffen WX 125*	**5**	131 wks
17 Dec	88	**G N' R LIES . . .** *Geffen WX 218*	**22**	41 wks
28 Sep	91	● **USE YOUR ILLUSION I** *Geffen GEF 24415*	**2**	81 wks
28 Sep	91	★ **USE YOUR ILLUSION II** *Geffen GEF 24420*	**1**	82 wks
4 Dec	93	● **THE SPAGHETTI INCIDENT?** *Geffen GED 24617*	**2†**	4 wks

---

GUNSHOT   *UK, male rap group*   *1 wk*

19 Jun	93	**PATRIOT GAMES** *Vinyl Solution STEAM 43CD*	**60**	1 wk

---

David GUNSON   *UK, male after dinner speaker*   *2 wks*

25 Dec	82	**WHAT GOES UP MIGHT COME DOWN** *Big Ben BB 0012*	**92**	2 wks

---

GURU   *US, male vocalist*   *2 wks*

29 May	93	**JAZZAMATAZZ** *Cooltempo CTCD 34*	**58**	2 wks

---

GURU JOSH   *UK, male producer*   *2 wks*

14 Jul	90	**INFINITY** *deConstruction PL 74701*	**41**	2 wks

---

G.U.S. (FOOTWEAR) BAND and the MORRISTOWN ORPHEUS CHOIR
UK, male instrumental group and male/female vocal group   *1 wk*

3 Oct	70	**LAND OF HOPE AND GLORY** *Columbia SCX 6406*	**54**	1 wk

---

Arlo GUTHRIE   *US, male vocalist*   *1 wk*

7 Mar	70	**ALICE'S RESTAURANT** *Reprise RSLP 6267*	**44**	1 wk

G

Gwen GUTHRIE US, *female vocalist* *14 wks*

23 Aug 86	**GOOD TO GO LOVER** Boiling Point POLD 5201	42	14 wks

Robin GUTHRIE – See Harold BUDD/Liz FRASER/Robin GUTHRIE/Simon RAYMOND

Buddy GUY US, *male vocalist/instrumentalist – guitar* *9 wks*

22 Jun 91	**DAMN RIGHT I'VE GOT THE BLUES** Silvertone ORELP 516	43	5 wks
13 Mar 93	**FEELS LIKE RAIN** Silvertone ORECD 525	36	4 wks

A GUY CALLED GERALD
UK, *male multi-instrumentalist* *1 wk*

14 Apr 90	**AUTOMANIKK** Subscape 4664821	68	1 wk

GUYS 'N' DOLLS UK, *male/female vocal group* *1 wk*

31 May 75	**GUYS 'N' DOLLS** Magnet MAG 5005	43	1 wk

GWENT CHORALE – See Bryn YEMM

Steve HACKETT UK, *male vocalist/instrumentalist – guitar 38 wks*

1 Nov 75	**VOYAGE OF THE ACOLYTE** Charisma CAS 1111	26	4 wks
6 May 78	**PLEASE DON'T TOUCH** Charisma CDS 4012	38	5 wks
26 May 79	**SPECTRAL MORNINGS** Charisma CDS 4017	22	11 wks
21 Jun 80 ●	**DEFECTOR** Charisma CDS 4018	9	7 wks
29 Aug 81	**CURED** Charisma CDS 4021	15	5 wks
30 Apr 83	**HIGHLY STRUNG** Charisma HACK 1	16	3 wks
19 Nov 83	**BAY OF KINGS** Lamborghini LMGLP 3000	70	1 wk
22 Sep 84	**TILL WE HAVE FACES** Lamborghini LMGLP 4000	54	2 wks

HADDAWAY Trinidad, *male vocalist* *5 wks*

23 Oct 93	**HADDAWAY – THE ALBUM** Logic 74321169222	19	5 wks

Sammy HAGAR US, *male vocalist/instrumentalist – guitar* *19 wks*

29 Sep 79	**STREET MACHINE** Capitol EST 11983	38	4 wks
22 Mar 80	**LOUD AND CLEAR** Capitol EST 25330	12	8 wks
7 Jun 80	**DANGER ZONE** Capitol EST 12069	25	3 wks
13 Feb 82	**STANDING HAMPTON** Geffen GEF 85456	84	2 wks
4 Jul 87	**SAMMY HAGAR** Geffen WX 114	86	2 wks

See also Hagar, Schon, Aaronson, Shrieve.

HAGAR, SCHON, AARONSON, SHRIEVE
US, *male vocal/instrumental group* *1 wk*

19 May 84	**THROUGH THE FIRE** Geffen GEF 25893	92	1 wk

See also Sammy Hagar.

Paul HAIG   UK, *male vocalist*   *2 wks*

22 Oct 83   **RHYTHM OF LIFE**   *Crepuscule ILPS 9742*   82   2 wks

HAIRCUT 100   UK, *male vocal/instrumental group*   *34 wks*

6 Mar 82 ● **PELICAN WEST**   *Arista HCC 100*   2   34 wks

Bill HALEY and his COMETS
US, *male vocal/instrumental group*   *5 wks*

18 May 68   **ROCK AROUND THE CLOCK**   *Ace Of Hearts AH 13*   34   5 wks

HALF MAN HALF BISCUIT
UK, *male vocal/instrumental group*   *14 wks*

8 Feb 86   **BACK IN THE DHSS**   *Probe Plus PROBE 4*   59   14 wks

Daryl HALL   US, *male vocalist*   *6 wks*

23 Aug 86   **THREE HEARTS IN THE HAPPY ENDING MACHINE**
                  RCA PL 87196   26   5 wks
23 Oct 93   **SOUL ALONE**   *Epic 4732912*   57   1 wk
See also Daryl Hall and John Oates.

Daryl HALL and John OATES   US, *male vocal duo*   *150 wks*

3 Jul 76   **HALL AND OATES**   *RCA Victor APLI 1144*   56   1 wk
18 Sep 76   **BIGGER THAN BOTH OF US**   *RCA Victor APLI 1467* . . .   25   7 wks
15 Oct 77   **BEAUTY ON A BACK STREET**   *RCA PL 12300*   40   2 wks
6 Feb 82 ● **PRIVATE EYES**   *RCA RCALP 6001*   8   21 wks
23 Oct 82   **H2O**   *RCA RCALP 6056*   24   35 wks
29 Oct 83   **ROCK 'N' SOUL (PART 1)**   *RCA PL 84858*   16   45 wks
27 Oct 84   **BIG BAM BOOM**   *RCA PL 85309*   28   13 wks
28 Sep 85   **LIVE AT THE APOLLO WITH DAVID RUFFIN AND**
                  EDDIE KENDRICK   *RCA PL 87035*   32   5 wks
18 Jun 88   **OOH YEAH!**   *RCA 208895*   52   3 wks
27 Oct 90   **CHANGE OF SEASON**   *Arista 210548*   44   2 wks
19 Oct 91 ● **THE BEST OF HALL AND OATES – LOOKING BACK**
                  Arista PL 90388   9   16 wks

See also Daryl Hall.

HALO JAMES   UK, *male vocal/instrumental group*   *4 wks*

14 Apr 90   **WITNESS**   *Epic 466761*   18   4 wks

HAMBURG STUDENTS' CHOIR
Germany, *male vocal group*   *6 wks*

17 Dec 60   **HARK THE HERALD ANGELS SING**   *Pye GGL 0023* . . .   11   6 wks

George HAMILTON IV   US, *male vocalist*   *11 wks*

10 Apr 71   **CANADIAN PACIFIC**   *RCA SF 8062*   45   1 wk
10 Feb 79   **REFLECTIONS**   *Lotus WH 5008*   25   9 wks
13 Nov 82   **SONGS FOR A WINTER'S NIGHT**   *Ronco RTL 2082*   94   1 wk

HAMMER – *See MC HAMMER*

Jan HAMMER
Czechoslovakia, male instrumentalist – keyboards　　　　*12 wks*

14 Nov 87	**ESCAPE FROM TV**　*MCA MCF 3407*	34	12 wks

Herbie HANCOCK
US, male vocalist/instrumentalist – keyboards　　　　*24 wks*

9 Sep 78	**SUNLIGHT**　*CBS 82240*	27	6 wks
24 Feb 79	**FEETS DON'T FAIL ME NOW**　*CBS 83491*	28	8 wks
27 Aug 83	**FUTURE SHOCK**　*CBS 25540*	27	10 wks

Tony HANCOCK　*UK, male comedian*　　　*42 wks*

9 Apr 60 ●	**THIS IS HANCOCK**　*Pye NPL 10845*	2	22 wks
12 Nov 60	**PIECES OF HANCOCK**　*Pye NPL 18054*	17	2 wks
3 Mar 62	**HANCOCK**　*Pye NPL 18068*	12	14 wks
14 Sep 63	**THIS IS HANCOCK (re-issue)**　*Pye Golden Guinea GGL 0206*	16	4 wks

Vernon HANDLEY – *See Nigel KENNEDY*

Bo HANNSON　*Sweden, multi-instrumentalist*　　　*2 wks*

18 Nov 72	**LORD OF THE RINGS**　*Charisma CAS 1059*	34	2 wks

HANOI ROCKS　*Finland/UK, male vocal/instrumental group*　*4 wks*

11 Jun 83	**BACK TO MYSTERY CITY**　*Lick LICLP 1*	87	1 wk
20 Oct 84	**TWO STEPS FROM THE MOVE**　*CBS 26066*	28	3 wks

John HANSON　*UK, male vocalist*　　　*12 wks*

23 Apr 60	**THE STUDENT PRINCE**　*Pye NPL 18046*	17	1 wk
2 Sep 61 ●	**THE STUDENT PRINCE/VAGABOND KING**		
	Pye GGL 0086	9	7 wks
10 Dec 77	**JOHN HANSON SINGS 20 SHOWTIME GREATS**		
	K-Tel NE 1002	16	4 wks

HAPPY MONDAYS　*UK, male vocal/instrumental group*　*48 wks*

27 Jan 90	**BUMMED**　*Factory FACT 220*	59	14 wks
17 Nov 90 ●	**PILLS 'N' THRILLS AND BELLYACHES**		
	Factory FACT 320	4	28 wks
12 Oct 91	**LIVE**　*Factory FACT 322*	21	3 wks
10 Oct 92	**... YES PLEASE!**　*Factory FACD 420*	14	3 wks

HAPPY PIANO – *See Brian SMITH and his HAPPY PIANO*

Paul HARDCASTLE
UK, male producer/instrumentalist – synthesizer　　　　*5 wks*

30 Nov 85	**PAUL HARDCASTLE**　*Chrysalis CHR 1517*	53	5 wks

Mike HARDING　*UK, male comedian*　　　*24 wks*

30 Aug 75	**MRS 'ARDIN'S KID**　*Rubber RUB 011*	24	6 wks
10 Jul 76	**ONE MAN SHOW**　*Philips 6625 022*	19	10 wks
11 Jun 77	**OLD FOUR EYES IS BACK**　*Philips 6308 290*	31	6 wks
24 Jun 78	**CAPTAIN PARALYTIC AND THE BROWN ALE**		
	COWBOY　*Philips 6641 798*	60	2 wks

HARDY – *See LAUREL and HARDY*

The first chart album by **Isaac Hayes** featured his Oscar-winning theme from the film Shaft.

Jimi Hendrix is shown backstage at London's Savile Theatre. (Pictorial Press)

Steve HARLEY and COCKNEY REBEL
UK, male vocalist and male vocal/instrumental group　　　*52 wks*

22 Jun	74 ●	**THE PSYCHOMODO** *EMI EMC 3033★*	**8**	20 wks
22 Mar	75 ●	**THE BEST YEARS OF OUR LIVES** *EMI EMC 3068*	**4**	19 wks
14 Feb	76	**TIMELESS FLIGHT** *EMI EMA 775*	**18**	6 wks
27 Nov	76	**LOVE'S A PRIMA DONNA** *EMI EMC 3156*	**28**	3 wks
30 Jul	77	**FACE TO FACE – A LIVE RECORDING** *EMI EMSP 320*	**40**	4 wks

★ *Cockney Rebel.*

Roy HARPER *UK, male vocalist/instrumentalist – guitar*　　*9 wks*

9 Mar	74	**VALENTINE** *Harvest SHSP 4027*	**27**	1 wk
21 Jun	75	**H.Q.** *Harvest SHSP 4046*	**31**	2 wks
12 Mar	77	**BULLINAMINGVASE** *Harvest SHSP 4060*	**25**	2 wks
16 Mar	85	**WHATEVER HAPPENED TO JUGULA?**		
		Beggars Banquet BEGA 60★	**44**	4 wks

★ *Roy Harper and Jimmy Page.*

Anita HARRIS *UK, female vocalist*　　*5 wks*

27 Jan	68	**JUST LOVING YOU** *CBS SBPG 63182*	**29**	5 wks

Emmylou HARRIS *US, female vocalist*　　*33 wks*

14 Feb	76	**ELITE HOTEL** *Reprise K 54060*	**17**	11 wks
29 Jan	77	**LUXURY LINER** *Warner Bros. K 56344*	**17**	6 wks
4 Feb	78	**QUARTER MOON IN A TEN CENT TOWN**		
		Warner Bros. K 56433	**40**	5 wks
29 Mar	80	**HER BEST SONGS** *K-Tel NE 1058*	**36**	3 wks
14 Feb	81	**EVANGELINE** *Warner Bros. K 56880*	**53**	4 wks
14 Mar	87	**TRIO** *Warner Bros 9254911★*	**60**	4 wks

★ *Dolly Parton/Emmylou Harris/Linda Ronstadt.*

H
154

Keith HARRIS, ORVILLE and CUDDLES
UK, male ventriloquist vocalist with dummies　　*1 wk*

4 Jun	83	**AT THE END OF THE RAINBOW** *BBC REH 465*	**92**	1 wk

George HARRISON
UK, male vocalist/instrumentalist – guitar　　*76 wks*

26 Dec	70 ●	**ALL THINGS MUST PASS** *Apple STCH 639*	**4**	24 wks
7 Jul	73 ●	**LIVING IN THE MATERIAL WORLD** *Apple PAS 10006* .	**2**	12 wks
18 Oct	75	**EXTRA TEXTURE (READ ALL ABOUT IT)**		
		Apple PAS 10009	**16**	4 wks
18 Dec	76	**THIRTY THREE AND A THIRD** *Dark Horse K 56319* ...	**35**	4 wks
17 Mar	79	**GEORGE HARRISON** *Dark Horse K 56562*	**39**	5 wks
13 Jun	81	**SOMEWHERE IN ENGLAND** *Dark Horse K 56870*	**13**	4 wks
14 Nov	87 ●	**CLOUD NINE** *Dark Horse WX 123*	**10**	23 wks

Jane HARRISON *UK, female operatic vocalist*　　*1 wk*

4 Feb	89	**NEW DAY** *Stylus SMR 869*	**70**	1 wk

Deborah HARRY *US, female vocalist*　　*53 wks*

8 Aug	81 ●	**KOO KOO** *Chrysalis CHR 1347★*	**6**	7 wks
29 Nov	86	**ROCKBIRD** *Chrysalis CHR 1540★*	**31**	11 wks
17 Dec	88	**ONCE MORE INTO THE BLEACH** *Chrysalis CJB 2★★* ...	**50**	4 wks

28 Oct 89	**DEF DUMB AND BLONDE** *Chrysalis CHR 1650*	**12**	7 wks
16 Mar 91 ●	**THE COMPLETE PICTURE – THE VERY BEST OF DEBORAH HARRY AND BLONDIE** *Chrysalis CHR 1817**★★*	**3**	22 wks
31 Jul 93	**DEBRAVATION** *Chrysalis CDCHR 6033*	**24**	2 wks

★Debbie Harry.
★★ Deborah Harry and Blondie.

Keef HARTLEY BAND
UK, male vocal/instrumental group   *3 wks*

5 Sep 70	**THE TIME IS NEAR** *Deram SML 1071*	**41**	3 wks

Richard HARVEY and FRIENDS
UK, male instrumental group   *1 wk*

6 May 89	**EVENING FALLS** *Telstar STAR 2350*	**72**	1 wk

HATFIELD AND THE NORTH
UK, male/female vocal/instrumental group   *1 wk*

29 Mar 75	**ROTTERS CLUB** *Virgin V 2030*	**43**	1 wk

Juliana HATFIELD THREE
US, female/male vocal/instrumental group   *1 wk*

14 Aug 93	**BECOME WHAT YOU ARE** *Mammoth 4509935292*	**44**	1 wk

Donny HATHAWAY – *See Roberta FLACK*

Chesney HAWKES *UK, male vocalist*   *8 wks*

13 Apr 91	**BUDDY'S SONG (film soundtrack)** *Chrysalis CHR 1812* ..	**18**	8 wks

Sophie B. HAWKINS *US, female vocalist*   *2 wks*

1 Aug 92	**TONGUES AND TAILS** *Columbia 4688232*	**46**	wks

Ted HAWKINS *US, male vocalist/instrumentalist – guitar*   *1 wk*

18 Apr 87	**HAPPY HOUR** *Windows On The World WOLP 2*	**82**	1 wk

HAWKWIND *UK, male vocal/instrumental group*   *101 wks*

6 Nov 71	**IN SEARCH OF SPACE** *United Artists UAS 29202*	**18**	19 wks
23 Dec 72	**DOREMI FASOL LATIDO** *United Artists UAS 29364*	**14**	5 wks
2 Jun 73 ●	**SPACE RITUAL ALIVE** *United Artists UAD 60037/8*	**9**	5 wks
21 Sep 74	**HALL OF THE MOUNTAIN GRILL** *United Artists UAG 29672*	**16**	5 wks
31 May 75	**WARRIOR ON THE EDGE OF TIME** *United Artists UAG 29766*	**13**	7 wks
24 Apr 76	**ROAD HAWKS** *United Artists UAK 29919*	**34**	4 wks
18 Sep 76	**ASTONISHING SOUNDS, AMAZING MUSIC** *Charisma CDS 4004*	**33**	5 wks
9 Jul 77	**QUARK STRANGENESS AND CHARM** *Charisma CDS 4008*	**30**	6 wks
21 Oct 78	**25 YEARS ON** *Charisma CD 4014★*	**48**	3 wks
30 Jun 79	**PXR 5** *Charisma CDS 4016*	**59**	5 wks
9 Aug 80	**LIVE 1979** *Bronze BRON 527*	**15**	7 wks
8 Nov 80	**LEVITATION** *Bronze BRON 530*	**21**	4 wks
24 Oct 81	**SONIC ATTACK** *RCA RCALP 5004*	**19**	5 wks
22 May 82	**CHURCH OF HAWKWIND** *RCA RCALP 9004*	**26**	6 wks

23 Oct 82	**CHOOSE YOUR MASQUES** *RCA RCALP 6055*	**29**	5 wks
5 Nov 83	**ZONES** *Flicknife SHARP 014*	**57**	2 wks
25 Feb 84	**HAWKWIND** *Liberty SLS 1972921*	**75**	1 wk
16 Nov 85	**CHRONICLE OF THE BLACK SWORD**		
	Flicknife SHARP 033	**65**	2 wks
14 May 88	**THE XENON CODEX** *GWR GWLP 26*	**79**	2 wks
6 Oct 90	**SPACE BANDITS** *GWR GWLP 103*	**70**	1 wk
23 May 92	**ELECTRIC TEPEE** *Essential ESSCD 181*	**53**	1 wk
6 Nov 93	**IT IS THE BUSINESS OF THE FUTURE TO BE**		
	DANGEROUS *Essential ESCDCD 196*	**75**	1 wk

* *Hawklords.*

Isaac HAYES *US, male vocalist/multi-instrumentalist*   *14 wks*

| 18 Dec 71 | **SHAFT** *Polydor 2659 007* .... | **17** | 13 wks |
| 12 Feb 72 | **BLACK MOSES** *Stax 2628 004* .... | **38** | 1 wk |

HAYSI FANTAYZEE *UK, male/female vocal duo*   *5 wks*

| 26 Feb 83 | **BATTLE HYMNS FOR CHILDREN SINGING** | | |
| | *Regard RGLP 6000* .... | **53** | 5 wks |

Justin HAYWARD *UK, male vocalist*   *35 wks*

29 Mar 75 ●	**BLUE JAYS** *Threshold THS 12*★	**4**	18 wks
5 Mar 77	**SONGWRITER** *Deram SDL 15*	**28**	5 wks
19 Jul 80	**NIGHT FLIGHT** *Decca TXS 138*	**41**	4 wks
19 Oct 85	**MOVING MOUNTAINS** *Towerbell TOWLP 15*	**78**	1 wk
28 Oct 89	**CLASSIC BLUE** *Trax MODEM 1040*★★	**47**	7 wks

* *Justin Hayward and John Lodge.*
** *Justin Hayward, Mike Batt and the London Philharmonic Orchestra.*

Lee HAZLEWOOD – *See Nancy SINATRA*

Jeff HEALEY BAND *US, male vocal/instrumental group*   *14 wks*

14 Jan 89	**SEE THE LIGHT** *Arista 209441*	**58**	7 wks
9 Jun 90	**HELL TO PAY** *Arista 210815*	**18**	6 wks
28 Nov 92	**FEEL THIS** *Arista 74321120872*	**72**	1 wk

HEART *US, female/male vocal/instrumental group*   *137 wks*

22 Jan 77	**DREAMBOAT ANNIE** *Arista ARTY 139*	**36**	8 wks
23 Jul 77	**LITTLE QUEEN** *Portrait PRT 82075*	**34**	4 wks
19 Jun 82	**PRIVATE AUDITION** *Epic EPC 85792*	**77**	2 wks
26 Oct 85	**HEART** *Capitol EJ 24-0372-1*	**19**	43 wks
6 Jun 87 ●	**BAD ANIMALS** *Capitol ESTU 2032*	**7**	56 wks
14 Apr 90 ●	**BRIGADE** *Capitol ESTU 2121*	**3**	20 wks
28 Sep 91	**ROCK THE HOUSE 'LIVE'** *Capitol ESTU 2154*	**45**	2 wks
11 Dec 93	**DESIRE WALKS ON** *Capitol CDEST 2216*	**32**	2 wks

Heart *changed label number during its chart run to Capitol LOVE 1.*

HEARTBREAKERS *US, male vocal/instrumental group*   *1 wk*

| 5 Nov 77 | **L.A.M.F.** *Track 2409 218* .... | **55** | 1 wk |

Ted HEATH AND HIS MUSIC
UK, conductor and orchestra   *5 wks*

| 21 Apr 62 | **BIG BAND PERCUSSION** *Decca PFM 24004* .... | **17** | 5 wks |

HEATWAVE *UK/US, male vocal/instrumental group*   *27 wks*

11 Jun 77	**TOO HOT TO HANDLE** *GTO GTLP 013*	46	2 wks
6 May 78	**CENTRAL HEATING** *GTO GTLP 027*	26	15 wks
14 Feb 81	**CANDLES** *GTO GTLP 047*	29	9 wks
23 Feb 91	**GANGSTERS OF THE GROOVE** *Telstar STAR 2434*	56	1 wk

HEAVEN 17 *UK, male vocal/instrumental group*   *128 wks*

26 Sep 81	**PENTHOUSE AND PAVEMENT** *Virgin V 2208*	14	76 wks
7 May 83 ●	**THE LUXURY GAP** *Virgin V 2253*	4	36 wks
6 Oct 84	**HOW MEN ARE** *B.E.F. V 2326*	12	11 wks
12 Jul 86	**ENDLESS** *Virgin TCVB/CDV 2383*	70	2 wks
29 Nov 86	**PLEASURE ONE** *Virgin V 2400*	78	1 wk
20 Mar 93	**HIGHER AND HIGHER – THE BEST OF HEAVEN 17**		
	Virgin CDV 2717	31	2 wks

HEAVY PETTIN' *UK, male vocal/instrumental group*   *4 wks*

29 Oct 83	**LETTIN' LOOSE** *Polydor HEPLP 1*	55	2 wks
13 Jul 85	**ROCK AIN'T DEAD** *Polydor HEPLP 2*	81	2 wks

HELLOWEEN *Germany, male vocal/instrumental group*   *9 wks*

17 Sep 88	**KEEPER OF THE SEVEN KEYS PART 2**		
	Noise International NUK 117	24	5 wks
15 Apr 89	**LIVE IN THE UK** *EMI EMC 3558*	26	2 wks
23 Mar 91	**PINK BUBBLES GO APE** *EMI EMC 3588*	41	2 wks

Jimi HENDRIX *US, male vocalist/instrumentalist – guitar* *228 wks*

27 May 67 ●	**ARE YOU EXPERIENCED** *Track 612–001★*	2	33 wks
16 Dec 67 ●	**AXIS: BOLD AS LOVE** *Track 613–003★*	5	16 wks
27 Apr 68 ●	**SMASH HITS** *Track 613–004★*	4	25 wks
18 May 68	**GET THAT FEELING** *London HA 8349★★*	39	2 wks
16 Nov 68 ●	**ELECTRIC LADYLAND** *Track 613–008/9★*	6	12 wks
4 Jul 70 ●	**BAND OF GYPSIES** *Track 2406–001*	6	30 wks
3 Apr 71 ●	**CRY OF LOVE** *Track 2408–101*	2	14 wks
28 Aug 71 ●	**EXPERIENCE** *Ember NR 5057*	9	6 wks
20 Nov 71	**JIMI HENDRIX AT THE ISLE OF WIGHT**		
	Track 2302 016	17	2 wks
4 Dec 71	**RAINBOW BRIDGE** *Reprise K 44159*	16	8 wks
5 Feb 72 ●	**HENDRIX IN THE WEST** *Polydor 2302 018*	7	14 wks
11 Dec 72	**WAR HEROES** *Polydor 2302 020*	23	3 wks
21 Jul 73	**SOUNDTRACK RECORDINGS FROM THE FILM 'JIMI**		
	HENDRIX' *Warner Bros. K 64017*	37	1 wk
29 Mar 75	**JIMI HENDRIX** *Polydor 2343 080*	35	4 wks
30 Aug 75	**CRASH LANDING** *Polydor 2310 398*	35	3 wks
29 Nov 75	**MIDNIGHT LIGHTNING** *Polydor 2310 415*	46	1 wk
14 Aug 82	**THE JIMI HENDRIX CONCERTS** *CBS 88592*	16	11 wks
19 Feb 83	**THE SINGLES ALBUM** *Polydor PODV 6*	77	4 wks
11 Mar 89	**RADIO ONE** *Castle Collectors CCSLP 212*	30	6 wks
3 Nov 90 ●	**CORNERSTONES 1967–1970** *Polydor 8472311*	5	16 wks
14 Nov 92	**THE ULTIMATE EXPERIENCE** *PolyGram TV 5172352* ..	25	17 wks

★ *Jimi Hendrix Experience.*
★★ *Jimi Hendrix and Curtis Knight.*

Don HENLEY *US, male vocalist*   *27 wks*

9 Mar 85	**BUILDING THE PERFECT BEAST** *Geffen GEF 25939* ..	14	11 wks
8 Jul 89	**THE END OF INNOCENCE** *Geffen WX 253*	17	16 wks

Band and Chorus of HER MAJESTY'S GUARDS DIVISION *UK, military band*   *4 wks*

22 Nov 75	**30 SMASH HITS OF THE WAR YEARS**		
	Warwick WW 5006	38	4 wks

HERD *UK, male vocal/instrumental group*   *1 wk*

24 Feb 68	**PARADISE LOST** *Fontana STL 5458*	38	1 wk

HERMAN'S HERMITS
UK, male vocal/instrumental group   *11 wks*

18 Sep 65	**HERMAN'S HERMITS** *Columbia 33SX 1727*	16	2 wks
25 Sep 71	**THE MOST OF HERMAN'S HERMITS** *MFP 5216*	14	5 wks
8 Oct 77	**GREATEST HITS** *K-Tel NE 1001*	37	4 wks

Nick HEYWARD *UK, male vocalist*   *13 wks*

29 Oct 83	● **NORTH OF A MIRACLE** *Arista NORTH 1*	10	13 wks

HI JACK *US, male vocal group*   *1 wk*

19 Oct 91	**THE HORNS OF JERICHO** *Warner Bros. 7599263861*	54	1 wk

HI TENSION *UK, male vocal/instrumental group*   *4 wks*

6 Jan 79	**HI TENSION** *Island ILPS 9564*	74	4 wks

John HIATT *US, male vocalist*   *2 wks*

7 Jul 90	**STOLEN MOMENTS** *A & M 3953101*	72	1 wk
11 Sep 93	**PERFECTLY GOOD GUITAR** *A & M 5401302*	67	1 wk

HIGH *UK, male vocal group*   *2 wks*

17 Nov 90	**SOMEWHERE SOON** *London 8282241*	59	2 wks

Benny HILL *UK, male vocalist*   *8 wks*

11 Dec 71	● **WORDS AND MUSIC** *Columbia SCX 6479*	9	8 wks

Vince HILL *UK, male vocalist*   *10 wks*

20 May 67	**EDELWEISS** *Columbia SCX 6141*	23	9 wks
29 Apr 78	**THAT LOVING FEELING** *K-Tel NE 1017*	51	1 wk

Steve HILLAGE *UK, male vocalist/instrumentalist – guitar*   *41 wks*

3 May 75	**FISH RISING** *Virgin V 2031*	33	3 wks
16 Oct 76	● **L** *Virgin V 2066*	10	12 wks
22 Oct 77	**MOTIVATION RADIO** *Virgin V 2777*	28	5 wks
29 Apr 78	**GREEN VIRGIN** *V 2098*	30	8 wks
17 Feb 79	**LIVE HERALD** *Virgin VGD 3502*	54	5 wks
5 May 79	**RAINBOW DOME MUSIC** *Virgin VR 1*	52	5 wks
27 Oct 79	**OPEN** *Virgin V 2135*	71	1 wk
5 Mar 83	**FOR TO NEXT** *Virgin V 2244*	48	2 wks

HIPSWAY *UK, male vocal/instrumental group*   *23 wks*

19 Apr 86	**HIPSWAY** *Mercury MERH 85*	42	23 wks

Roger HODGSON *UK, male vocalist*   *4 wks*

20 Oct 84	**IN THE EYE OF THE STORM** *A & M AMA 5004*	70	4 wks

H
158

Gerard HOFFNUNG   UK, male comedian   19 wks

| 3 Sep | 60 ● AT THE OXFORD UNION   Decca LF 1330 . . . . | 4 | 19 wks |

Susanna HOFFS   US, female vocalist   2 wks

| 6 Apr | 91   WHEN YOU'RE A BOY   Columbia 4672021 . . . . | 56 | 2 wks |

Christopher HOGWOOD – See ACADEMY OF ANCIENT MUSIC conducted by Christopher HOGWOOD

HOLE   US, female/male vocal/instrumental group   1 wk

| 12 Oct | 91   PRETTY ON THE INSIDE   City Slang E 04071 . . . . | 59 | 1 wk |

Billie HOLIDAY   US, female vocalist   10 wks

| 16 Nov 85 | THE LEGEND OF BILLIE HOLIDAY   MCA BHTV 1 . . . | 60 | 10 wks |

Jools HOLLAND   UK, male vocalist/instrumentalist – piano   1 wk

| 5 May 90 | WORLD OF HIS OWN   IRS EIRSA 1018 . . . . | 71 | 1 wk |

HOLLIES   UK, male vocal/instrumental group   150 wks

15 Feb	64 ● STAY WITH THE HOLLIES Parlophone PMC 1220	2	25 wks
2 Oct	65 ● HOLLIES Parlophone PMC 1261	8	14 wks
16 Jul	66 WOULD YOU BELIEVE Parlophone PMC 7008	16	8 wks
17 Dec	66 FOR CERTAIN BECAUSE Parlophone PCS 17011	23	7 wks
17 Jun	67 EVOLUTION Parlophone PCS 7022	13	10 wks
17 Aug	68 ★ GREATEST HITS Parlophone PCS 7057	1	27 wks
17 May	69 ● HOLLIES SING DYLAN Parlophone PCS 7078	3	7 wks
28 Nov 70	CONFESSIONS OF THE MIND Parlophone PCS 7117	30	5 wks
16 Mar 74	HOLLIES Polydor 2383 262	38	3 wks
19 Mar	77 ● HOLLIES LIVE HITS Polydor 2383 428	4	12 wks
22 Jul	78 ● 20 GOLDEN GREATS EMI EMTV 11	2	20 wks
1 Oct	88 ALL THE HITS AND MORE EMI EM 1301	51	5 wks
3 Apr	93 THE AIR THAT I BREATHE – THE BEST OF THE		
	HOLLIES EMI CDEMTV 74	15	7 wks

The two albums titled Hollies are different.

Laurie HOLLOWAY – See SOUTH BANK ORCHESTRA

Buddy HOLLY and the CRICKETS
US, male vocalist, male vocal/instrumental group   328 wks

2 May	59 ● BUDDY HOLLY STORY Coral LVA 9105	2	156 wks
15 Oct	60 ● BUDDY HOLLY STORY VOL. 2 Coral LVA 9127	7	14 wks
21 Oct	61 ● THAT'LL BE THE DAY Ace Of Hearts AH 3	5	14 wks
6 Apr	63 ● REMINISCING Coral LVA 9212	2	31 wks
13 Jun	64 ● BUDDY HOLLY SHOWCASE Coral LVA 9222	3	16 wks
26 Jun	65 HOLLY IN THE HILLS Coral LVA 9227	13	6 wks
15 Jul	67 ● BUDDY HOLLY'S GREATEST HITS		
	Ace Of Hearts AH 148	9	40 wks
12 Apr	69 GIANT MCA MUPS 371	13	1 wk
21 Aug	71 BUDDY HOLLY'S GREATEST HITS (re-issue)		
	Coral CP 8	32	6 wks
12 Jul	75 BUDDY HOLLY'S GREATEST HITS (2nd re-issue)		
	Coral CDLM 8007	42	3 wks
11 Mar	78 ★ 20 GOLDEN GREATS MCA EMTV 8	1	20 wks
8 Sep	84 GREATEST HITS (3rd re-issue) MCA MCL 1618	100	1 wk
18 Feb	89 ● TRUE LOVE WAYS Telstar STAR 2339	8	11 wks
20 Feb	93 ★ WORDS OF LOVE PolyGram TV 5144872	1	9 wks

Most albums feature the Crickets on at least some tracks. See also The Crickets.

H
159

John HOLT Jamaica, male vocalist   2 wks

1 Feb 75   **A THOUSAND VOLTS OF HOLT** *Trojan TRLS 75* .....   **42**   2 wks

HOME UK, male vocal/instrumental group   1 wk

11 Nov 72   **DREAMER** *CBS 67522* ....   **41**   1 wk

HONEYDRIPPERS
UK/US, male vocal/instrumental group   10 wks

1 Dec 84   **THE HONEYDRIPPERS VOLUME 1** *Es Paranza 790220* .   **56**   10 wks

John Lee HOOKER US, male vocalist   24 wks

4 Feb 67   **HOUSE OF THE BLUES** *Marble Arch MAL 663* ....   **34**   2 wks
11 Nov 89   **THE HEALER** *Silvertone ORELP 508* ....   **63**   8 wks
21 Sep 91 ● **MR LUCKY** *Silvertone ORELP 519* ....   **3**   10 wks
7 Nov 92   **BOOM BOOM** *Pointblank VPBCD 12* ....   **15**   4 wks

Mary HOPKIN UK, female vocalist   9 wks

1 Mar 69 ● **POSTCARD** *Apple SAPCOR 5* ....   **3**   9 wks

Bruce HORNSBY and the RANGE
US, male vocal/instrumental group   54 wks

H
160

13 Sep 86   **THE WAY IT IS** *RCA PL 89901* ....   **16**   26 wks
14 May 88   **SCENES FROM THE SOUTHSIDE** *RCA PL 86686* .....   **18**   18 wks
30 Jun 90   **A NIGHT ON THE TOWN** *RCA PL 82041* ....   **23**   7 wks
8 May 93   **HARBOR LIGHTS** *RCA 07863661142* ....   **32**   3 wks

HORSE UK, female/male vocal/instrumental group   4 wks

23 Jun 90   **THE SAME SKY** *Echo Chamber EST 2123* ....   **44**   2 wks
13 Nov 93   **GOD'S HOME MOVIE** *Oxygen MCD 10935* ....   **42**   2 wks

HORSLIPS Ireland, male vocal/instrumental group   3 wks

30 Apr 77   **THE BOOK OF INVASIONS – A CELTIC SYMPHONY**
           DJM DJF 20498 ....   **39**   3 wks

HOT CHOCOLATE UK, male vocal/instrumental group 122 wks

15 Nov 75   **HOT CHOCOLATE** *RAK SRAK 516* ....   **34**   7 wks
7 Aug 76   **MAN TO MAN** *RAK SRAK 522* ....   **32**   7 wks
20 Nov 76 ● **GREATEST HITS** *RAK SRAK 524* ....   **6**   35 wks
8 Apr 78   **EVERY 1'S A WINNER** *RAK SRAK 531* ....   **30**   8 wks
15 Dec 79 ● **20 HOTTEST HITS** *RAK EMTV 22* ....   **3**   19 wks
25 Sep 82   **MYSTERY** *RAK SRAK 549* ....   **24**   7 wks
21 Feb 87 ★ **THE VERY BEST OF HOT CHOCOLATE**
           RAK EMTV 42 ....   **1**   28 wks
20 Mar 93 ★ **THEIR GREATEST HITS** *EMI CDEMTV 73* ....   **1**   11 wks

HOT RODS – *See EDDIE and the HOT RODS*

HOTHOUSE FLOWERS
Ireland, male vocal/instrumental group   51 wks

18 Jun 88 ● **PEOPLE** *London LONLP 58* ....   **2**   19 wks
16 Jun 90 ● **HOME** *London 8281971* ....   **5**   21 wks
20 Mar 93 ● **SONGS FROM THE RAIN** *London 8283502* ....   **7**   11 wks

HOUND DOG and the MEGAMIXERS
UK, male producer   *9 wks*

1 Dec 90	**THE GREATEST EVER JUNIOR PARTY MEGAMIX**	
	Pop & Arts PATLP 201	**34** 9 wks

HOUSE OF LOVE   *UK, male vocal/instrumental group*   *14 wks*

10 Mar 90 ●	**HOUSE OF LOVE** *Fontana 8422931*	**8** 10 wks
10 Nov 90	**HOUSE OF LOVE** *Fontana 8469781*	**49** 1 wk
18 Jul 92	**BABE RAINBOW** *Fontana 5125492*	**34** 2 wks
3 Jul 93	**AUDIENCE WITH THE MIND** *Fontana 5148802*	**38** 1 wk

Identically titled albums are different.

HOUSE OF PAIN   *US, male rap group*   *1 wk*

21 Nov 92	**HOUSE OF PAIN** *XL XLCD 111*	**73** 1 wk

HOUSEMARTINS   *UK, male vocal/instrumental group*   *70 wks*

5 Jul 86 ●	**LONDON 0 HULL 4** *Go! Discs AGOLP 7*	**3** 41 wks
27 Dec 86	**HOUSEMARTINS' CHRISTMAS SINGLES BOX**	
	Go! Discs GOD 816	**84** 1 wk
3 Oct 87 ●	**THE PEOPLE WHO GRINNED THEMSELVES TO**	
	DEATH *Go! Discs AGOLP 9*	**9** 18 wks
21 May 88 ●	**NOW THAT'S WHAT I CALL QUITE GOOD!**	
	Go! Discs AGOLP 11	**8** 10 wks

Whitney HOUSTON   *US, female vocalist*   *249 wks*

14 Dec 85 ●	**WHITNEY HOUSTON** *Arista 206978*	**2** 119 wks
13 Jun 87 ★	**WHITNEY** *Arista 208141*	**1** 101 wks
17 Nov 90 ●	**I'M YOUR BABY TONIGHT** *Arista 211039*	**4** 29 wks

Steve HOWE   *UK, male vocalist/instrumentalist – guitar*   *6 wks*

15 Nov 75	**BEGINNINGS** *Atlantic K 50151*	**22** 4 wks
24 Nov 79	**STEVE HOWE ALBUM** *Atlantic K 50621*	**68** 2 wks

See also Anderson Bruford Wakeman Howe.

HUDDERSFIELD CHORAL SOCIETY
UK, choir   *14 wks*

13 Dec 86	**THE CAROLS ALBUM** *EMI EMTV 43*	**29** 4 wks

HUE AND CRY   *UK, male vocal/instrumental duo*   *74 wks*

7 Nov 87	**SEDUCED AND ABANDONED** *Circa CIRCA 2*	**22** 11 wks
10 Dec 88 ●	**REMOTE/THE BITTER SUITE** *Circa CIRCA 6*	**10** 48 wks
29 Jun 91 ●	**STARS CRASH DOWN** *Circa CIRCA 15*	**10** 9 wks
29 Aug 92	**TRUTH AND LOVE** *Fidelity FIDELCD 1*	**33** 2 wks
10 Apr 93	**LABOURS OF LOVE – THE BEST OF HUE AND CRY**	
	Circa HACCD 1	**27** 4 wks

Remote re-entered the chart on 16 Dec 89 when it was made available with the free album The Bitter Suite.

Alan HULL   *UK, male vocalist*   *3 wks*

28 Jul 73	**PIPEDREAM** *Charisma CAS 1069*	**29** 3 wks

HUMAN LEAGUE
UK, male/female vocal/instrumental group   233 wks

31 May 80	**TRAVELOGUE** *Virgin V 2160*	16	42 wks
22 Aug 81	**REPRODUCTION** *Virgin V 2133*	49	23 wks
24 Oct 81 ★	**DARE** *Virgin V 2192*	1	71 wks
17 Jul 82 ●	**LOVE AND DANCING** *Virgin OVED 6**	3	52 wks
19 May 84 ●	**HYSTERIA** *Virgin V 2315*	3	18 wks
20 Sept 86 ●	**CRASH** *Virgin V 2391*	7	6 wks
12 Nov 88 ●	**GREATEST HITS** *Virgin HLTV 1*	3	19 wks
22 Sep 90	**ROMANTIC?** *Virgin V 2624*	24	2 wks

* League Unlimited Orchestra.

HUMBLE PIE *UK, male vocal/instrumental group*   10 wks

6 Sep 69	**AS SAFE AS YESTERDAY IS** *Immediate IMSP 025*	32	1 wk
22 Jan 72	**ROCKING AT THE FILLMORE** *A & M AMLH 63506* ...	32	2 wks
15 Apr 72	**SMOKIN'** *A & M AMLS 64342*	28	5 wks
7 Apr 73	**EAT IT** *A & M AMLS 6004*	34	2 wks

Engelbert HUMPERDINCK *UK, male vocalist*   233 wks

20 May 67 ●	**RELEASE ME** *Decca SKL 4868*	6	58 wks
25 Nov 67 ●	**THE LAST WALTZ** *Decca SKL 4901*	3	33 wks
3 Aug 68 ●	**A MAN WITHOUT LOVE** *Decca SKL 4939*	3	45 wks
1 Mar 69 ●	**ENGELBERT** *Decca SKL 4985*	3	8 wks
6 Dec 69 ●	**ENGELBERT HUMPERDINCK** *Decca SKL 5030* ..	5	23 wks
11 Jul 70	**WE MADE IT HAPPEN** *Decca SKL 5054*	17	11 wks
18 Sep 71	**ANOTHER TIME, ANOTHER PLACE** *Decca SKL 5097* .	48	1 wk
26 Feb 72	**LIVE AT THE RIVIERA LAS VEGAS** *Decca TXS 105* ...	45	1 wk
21 Dec 74 ★	**ENGELBERT HUMPERDINCK – HIS GREATEST HITS** *Decca SKL 5198*	1	34 wks
4 May 85	**GETTING SENTIMENTAL** *Telstar STAR 2254*	35	10 wks
4 Apr 87	**THE ENGELBERT HUMPERDINCK COLLECTION** *Telstar STAR 2294*	35	9 wks

Ian HUNTER *UK, male vocalist*   26 wks

12 Apr 75	**IAN HUNTER** *CBS 80710*	21	15 wks
29 May 76	**ALL AMERICAN ALIEN BOY** *CBS 81310*	29	4 wks
5 May 79	**YOU'RE NEVER ALONE WITH A SCHIZOPHRENIC** *Chrysalis CHR 1214*	49	3 wks
26 Apr 80	**WELCOME TO THE CLUB** *Chrysalis CJT 6*	61	2 wks
29 Aug 81	**SHORT BACK AND SIDES** *Chrysalis CHR 1326*	79	2 wks

HURRAH! *UK, male vocal/instrumental group*   1 wk

28 Feb 87	**TELL GOD I'M HERE** *Kitchenware 208 201*	71	1 wk

HURRICANES – *See JOHNNY and the HURRICANES*

HÜSKER DÜ *US, male vocal/instrumental group*   1 wk

14 Feb 87	**WAREHOUSE: SONGS AND STORIES** *Warner Bros. 925 544-1*	72	1 wk

Phyllis HYMAN *US, female vocalist*   1 wk

20 Sep 86	**LIVING ALL ALONE** *Philadelphia International PHIL 4001* ..	97	1 wk

H
162

ICE CUBE US, male rapper

10 wks

28 Jul	90	**AMERIKKKA'S MOST WANTED**		
		Fourth & Broadway BRLP 551	48	5 wks
9 Mar	91	**KILL AT WILL** Fourth & Broadway BRLM 572	66	3 wks
5 Dec	92	**THE PREDATOR** Fourth & Broadway BRCD 592	73	1 wk
18 Dec	93	**LETHAL INJECTION** Fourth & Broadway BRCD 609	52	1 wk

ICEHOUSE
Australia/New Zealand, male vocal/instrumental group

7 wks

| 5 Mar | 83 | **LOVE IN MOTION** Chrysalis CHR 1390 .... | 64 | 6 wks |
| 2 Apr | 88 | **MAN OF COLOURS** Chrysalis CHR 1592 .... | 93 | 1 wk |

ICE-T US, male rapper

13 wks

21 Oct	89	**THE ICEBERG/FREEDOM OF SPEECH**		
		Warner Bros. WX 316	42	2 wks
25 May	91	**O.G.: ORIGINAL GANGSTER** Sire WX 412	38	4 wks
3 Apr	93	**HOME INVASION** Rhyme Syndicate RSYND 1	15	7 wks

ICICLE WORKS UK, male vocal/instrumental group

19 wks

31 Mar	84	**THE ICICLE WORKS** Beggars Banquet BEGA 50	24	6 wks
28 Sep	85	**THE SMALL PRICE OF A BICYCLE**		
		Beggars Banquet BEGA 61	55	3 wks
1 Mar	86	**SEVEN SINGLES DEEP** Beggars Banquet BEGA 71	52	2 wks
21 Mar	87	**IF YOU WANT TO DEFEAT YOUR ENEMY SING HIS**		
		SONG Beggars Banquet BEGA 78	28	4 wks
14 May	88	**BLIND** Beggars Banquet IWA 2	40	3 wks
5 Sep	92	**THE BEST OF THE ICICLE WORKS**		
		Beggars Banquet BEGA 124CD	60	1 wk

Billy IDOL UK, male vocalist

100 wks

8 Jun	85	● **VITAL IDOL** Chrysalis CUX 1502	7	34 wks
28 Sep	85	**REBEL YELL** Chrysalis CHR 1450	36	11 wks
1 Nov	86	● **WHIPLASH SMILE** Chrysalis CDL 1514	8	20 wks
2 Jul	88	● **IDOL SONGS: 11 OF THE BEST** Chrysalis BILTVD 1 ...	2	25 wks
12 May	90	**CHARMED LIFE** Chrysalis CHR 1735	15	8 wks
10 Jul	93	**CYBERPUNK** Chrysalis CDCHR 6000	20	2 wks

Frank IFIELD UK, male vocalist

83 wks

16 Feb	63	● **I'LL REMEMBER YOU** Columbia 33SX 1467	3	36 wks
21 Sep	63	● **BORN FREE** Columbia 33SX 1462	3	32 wks
28 Mar	64	● **BLUE SKIES** Columbia 55SX 1588	10	12 wks
19 Dec	64	● **GREATEST HITS** Columbia 33SX 1633	9	3 wks

Julio IGLESIAS Spain, male vocalist

116 wks

7 Nov	81	**DE NINA A MUJER** CBS 85063	43	5 wks
28 Nov	81	● **BEGIN THE BEGUINE** CBS 85462	5	28 wks
16 Oct	82	**AMOR** CBS 25103	14	14 wks
2 Jul	83	● **JULIO** CBS 10038	5	17 wks
1 Sep	84	**1100 BEL AIR PLACE** CBS 86308	14	14 wks
19 Oct	85	**LIBRA** CBS 26623	61	4 wks
3 Sep	88	**NON STOP** CBS 460990 1	33	14 wks
1 Dec	90	**STARRY NIGHT** CBS 4672841	27	20 wks

I-LEVEL UK, male vocal/instrumental group   4 wks

9 Jul	83	**I-LEVEL** *Virgin V 2270*	50	4 wks

IMAGINATION UK, male vocal group   122 wks

24 Oct	81	**BODY TALK** *R & B RBLP 1001*	20	53 wks
11 Sep	82	● **IN THE HEAT OF THE NIGHT** *R & B RBLP 1002*	7	29 wks
14 May	83	● **NIGHT DUBBING** *R & B RBDUB 1*	9	20 wks
12 Nov	83	**SCANDALOUS** *R & B RBLP 1004*	25	8 wks
12 Aug	89	● **IMAGINATION** *Stylus SMR 985*	7	12 wks

IMMACULATE FOOLS
UK, male vocal/instrumental group   2 wks

11 May	85	**HEARTS OF FORTUNE** *A & M AMA 5030*	65	2 wks

INCANTATION UK, male instrumental group   52 wks

11 Dec	82	● **CACHARPAYA (PANPIPES OF THE ANDES)** *Beggars Banquet BEGA 39*	9	26 wks
17 Dec	83	**DANCE OF THE FLAMES** *Beggars Banquet BEGA 49*	61	7 wks
28 Dec	85	**BEST OF INCANTATION – MUSIC FROM THE ANDES** *West Five CODA 19*	28	19 wks

INCOGNITO
France/UK, male/female vocal/instrumental group   14 wks

18 Apr	81	**JAZZ FUNK** *Ensign ENVY 504*	28	8 wks
27 Jul	91	**INSIDE LIFE** *Talkin Loud 8485461*	44	2 wks
4 Jul	92	**TRIBES VIBES AND SCRIBES** *Talkin Loud 5123632*	41	2 wks
6 Nov	93	**POSITIVITY** *Talkin Loud 5182602*	55	2 wks

INCREDIBLE STRING BAND
UK, male/female vocal/instrumental group   36 wks

21 Oct	67	**5,000 SPIRITS OR THE LAYERS OF THE ONION** *Elektra EUKS 257*	26	4 wks
6 Apr	68	● **HANGMAN'S BEAUTIFUL DAUGHTER** *Elektra EVKS7 258*	5	21 wks
20 Jul	68	**INCREDIBLE STRING BAND** *Elektra EKL 254*	34	3 wks
24 Jan	70	**CHANGING HORSES** *Elektra EKS 74057*	30	1 wk
9 May	70	**I LOOKED UP** *Elektra 2469–002*	30	4 wks
31 Oct	70	**U** *Elektra 2665–001*	34	2 wks
30 Oct	71	**LIQUID ACROBAT AS REGARDS THE AIR** *Island ILPS 9172*	46	1 wk

INFA RIOT UK, male vocal/instrumental group   4 wks

7 Aug	82	**STILL OUT OF ORDER** *Secret SEC 7*	42	4 wks

James INGRAM US, male vocalist   19 wks

31 Mar	84	**IT'S YOUR NIGHT** *Qwest 9239701*	25	17 wks
30 Aug	86	**NEVER FELT SO GOOD** *Qwest WX 44*	72	2 wks

INNER CIRCLE Jamaica, male vocal/instrumental group   2 wks

29 May	93	**BAD TO THE BONE** *Magnet 9031776772*	44	2 wks

INNER CITY US, male/female vocal/instrumental duo   40 wks

20 May	89 ●	**PARADISE** 10 DIX 81	**3**	31 wks
10 Feb	90	**PARADISE REMIXED** 10 XID 81	**17**	6 wks
11 Jul	92	**PRAISE** Ten 4718862	**52**	1 wk
15 May	93	**TESTAMENT 93** Ten CDOVD 438	**33**	2 wks

INNOCENCE UK, male/female vocal/instrumental group   20 wks

10 Nov	90	**BELIEF** Cooltempo CTLP 20	**24**	19 wks
31 Oct	92	**BUILD** Cooltempo CTCD 26	**66**	1 wk

INSPIRAL CARPETS UK, male vocal/instrumental group   30 wks

5 May	90 ●	**LIFE** Cow DUNG 8	**2**	21 wks
4 May	91 ●	**THE BEAST INSIDE** Cow DUNG 14	**5**	6 wks
17 Oct	92	**REVENGE OF THE GOLDFISH** Cow DUNG 19	**17**	3 wks

INSPIRATIONAL CHOIR US, male/female choir   4 wks

18 Jan	86	**SWEET INSPIRATION** Portrait PRT 10048	**59**	4 wks

INTI ILLIMANI-GUAMARY
Chile, male vocal/instrumental group – panpipes   7 wks

17 Dec	83	**THE FLIGHT OF THE CONDOR – ORIGINAL TV SOUNDTRACK** BBC REB 440	**62**	7 wks

INVISIBLE GIRLS – See Pauline MURRAY and the INVISIBLE GIRLS

INXS Australia, male vocal/instrumental group   211 wks

8 Feb	86	**LISTEN LIKE THIEVES** Mercury MERH 82	**48**	15 wks
28 Nov	87 ●	**KICK** Mercury MERH 114	**9**	103 wks
6 Oct	90 ●	**X** Mercury 8466681	**2**	44 wks
16 Nov	91	**LIVE BABY LIVE** Mercury 5105801	**8**	9 wks
15 Aug	92 ★	**WELCOME TO WHEREVER YOU ARE** Mercury 5125072	**1**	33 wks
13 Nov	93 ●	**FULL MOON, DIRTY HEARTS** Mercury 5186372	**3†**	7 wks

Tony IOMMI – See BLACK SABBATH

IQ UK, male vocal/instrumental group   1 wk

22 Jun	85	**THE WAKE** Sahara SAH 136	**72**	1 wk

IRON MAIDEN UK, male vocal/instrumental group   183 wks

26 Apr	80 ●	**IRON MAIDEN** EMI EMC 3330	**4**	15 wks
28 Feb	81	**KILLERS** EMI EMC 3357	**12**	8 wks
10 Apr	82 ★	**THE NUMBER OF THE BEAST** EMI EMC 3400	**1**	31 wks
28 May	83 ●	**PIECE OF MIND** EMI EMA 800	**3**	18 wks
15 Sep	84 ●	**POWERSLAVE** EMI POWER 1	**2**	13 wks
15 Jun	85	**IRON MAIDEN (re-issue)** Fame FA 41–3121–1	**71**	2 wks
26 Oct	85 ●	**LIVE AFTER DEATH** EMI RIP 1	**2**	14 wks
11 Oct	86 ●	**SOMEWHERE IN TIME** EMI EMC 3512	**3**	11 wks
20 Jun	87	**THE NUMBER OF THE BEAST (re-issue)** Fame FA 3178	**98**	1 wk
23 Apr	88 ★	**SEVENTH SON OF A SEVENTH SON** EMI EMD 1006 .	**1**	18 wks
24 Feb	90 ●	**RUNNING FREE/SANCTUARY** EMI IRN 1	**10**	4 wks
3 Mar	90 ●	**WOMEN IN UNIFORM/TWILIGHT ZONE** EMI IRN 2	**10**	3 wks
10 Mar	90 ●	**PURGATORY/MAIDEN JAPAN** EMI IRN 3	**5**	3 wks

The **Isley Brothers** are dressed in their late 60s finery.

Ice-T – The Original Gangster. (Virgin Records)

Former Real Madrid footballer **Julio Iglesias** gets back in goal with Manchester United's Gary Bailey.

17 Mar	90 ●	**RUN TO THE HILLS/THE NUMBER OF THE BEAST** *EMI IRN 4*	3	2 wks
24 Mar	90 ●	**FLIGHT OF ICARUS/THE TROOPER** *EMI IRN 5*	7	2 wks
31 Mar	90	**2 MINUTES TO MIDNIGHT/ACES HIGH** *EMI IRN 6* ..	11	2 wks
7 Apr	90 ●	**RUNNING FREE (LIVE)/RUN TO THE HILLS (LIVE)** *EMI IRN 7*	9	2 wks
14 Apr	90 ●	**WASTED YEARS/STRANGER IN A STRANGE LAND** *EMI IRN 8*	9	2 wks
21 Apr	90 ●	**CAN I PLAY WITH MADNESS/THE EVIL THAT MEN DO** *EMI IRN 9*	10	3 wks
28 Apr	90	**THE CLAIRVOYANT/INFINITE DREAMS (LIVE)** *EMI IRN 10*	11	2 wks
13 Oct	90 ●	**NO PRAYER FOR THE DYING** *EMI EMD 1017*	2	14 wks
23 May	92 ★	**FEAR OF THE DARK** *EMI CDEMD 1032*	1	5 wks
3 Apr	93 ◓	**A REAL LIVE ONE** *EMI CDEMD 1042*	3	4 wks
30 Oct	93	**A REAL DEAD ONE** *EMI CDEMD 1048*	12	3 wks
20 Nov	93	**LIVE AT DONNINGTON** *EMI CDDON 1*	23	1 wk

Entries from Feb to Apr 1990 are double 12 inch singles made ineligible for the singles chart by their retail price.

Gregory ISAACS *Jamaica, male vocalist*   6 wks

12 Sep	81	**MORE GREGORY** *Charisma PREX 9*	93	1 wk
4 Sep	82	**NIGHT NURSE** *Island ILPS 9721*	32	5 wks

Chris ISAAK *US, male vocalist*   35 wks

26 Jan	91 ●	**WICKED GAME** *Reprise WX 406*	3	30 wks
24 Apr	93	**SAN FRANCISCO DAYS** *Reprise 9362451162*	12	5 wks

ISLEY BROTHERS *US, male vocal/instrumental group*   24 wks

14 Dec	68	**THIS OLD HEART OF MINE** *Tamla Motown STML 11034*	23	6 wks
14 Aug	76	**HARVEST FOR THE WORLD** *Epic EPC 81268*	50	5 wks
14 May	77	**GO FOR YOUR GUNS** *Epic EPC 86027*	46	2 wks
24 Jun	78	**SHOWDOWN** *Epic EPC 86039*	50	1 wk
5 Mar	88	**GREATEST HITS** *Telstar STAR 2306*	41	10 wks

IT BITES *UK, male vocal/instrumental group*   12 wks

6 Sep	86	**THE BIG LAD IN THE WINDMILL** *Virgin V 2378*	35	5 wks
2 Apr	88	**ONCE AROUND THE WORLD** *Virgin V 2456*	43	3 wks
24 Jun	89	**EAT ME IN ST. LOUIS** *Virgin V 2591*	40	3 wks
31 Aug	91	**THANK YOU AND GOODNIGHT** *Virgin VGD 24233* ..	59	1 wk

IT'S A BEAUTIFUL DAY
US, male/female vocal/instrumental group   3 wks

23 May	70	**IT'S A BEAUTIFUL DAY** *CBS 63722*	58	1 wk
18 Jul	70	**MARRYING MAIDEN** *CBS 66236*	45	2 wks

IT'S IMMATERIAL *UK, male vocal/instrumental group*   3 wks

27 Sep	86	**LIFE'S HARD AND THEN YOU DIE** *Siren SIRENLP 4* ..	62	3 wks

Freddie JACKSON US, male vocalist   48 wks

18 May 85	**ROCK ME TONIGHT** *Capitol EJ 2440316–1*	27	22 wks
8 Nov 86	**JUST LIKE THE FIRST TIME** *Capitol EST 2023*	30	15 wks
30 Jul 88	**DON'T LET LOVE SLIP AWAY** *Capitol EST 2067*	24	9 wks
17 Nov 90	**DO ME AGAIN** *Capitol EST 2134*	48	2 wks

Janet JACKSON US, female vocalist   153 wks

5 Apr 86 ●	**CONTROL** *A & M AMA 5016*	8	72 wks
14 Nov 87	**CONTROL – THE REMIXES** *Breakout MIXLP 1*	20	14 wks
30 Sep 89 ●	**RHYTHM NATION 1814** *A & M AMA 3920*	4	43 wks
29 May 93 ★	**JANET** *Virgin CDV 2720*	1†	24 wks

Jermaine JACKSON US, male vocalist   12 wks

| 31 May 80 | **LET'S GET SERIOUS** *Motown STML 12127* | 22 | 6 wks |
| 12 May 84 | **DYNAMITE** *Arista 206 317* | 57 | 6 wks |

Joe JACKSON UK, male vocalist   106 wks

17 Mar 79	**LOOK SHARP** *A & M AMLH 64743*	40	11 wks
13 Oct 79	**I'M THE MAN** *A & M AMLH 64794*	12	16 wks
18 Oct 80	**BEAT CRAZY** *A & M AMLH 64837*	42	3 wks
4 Jul 81	**JUMPIN' JIVE** *A & M AMLH 68530★*	14	14 wks
3 Jul 82 ●	**NIGHT AND DAY** *A & M AMLH 64906*	3	27 wks
7 Apr 84	**BODY AND SOUL** *A & M AMLX 65000*	14	14 wks
5 Apr 86	**BIG WORLD** *A & M JWA 3*	41	5 wks
7 May 88	**LIVE 1980–1986** *A & M AMA 6706*	66	2 wks
29 Apr 89	**BLAZE OF GLORY** *A & M AMA 5249*	36	3 wks
15 Sep 90 ●	**STEPPING OUT – THE VERY BEST OF JOE JACKSON** *A & M 3970521*	7	9 wks
11 May 91	**LAUGHTER AND LUST** *Virgin America VUSLP 34*	41	2 wks

★ *Joe Jackson's Jumpin' Jive.*

Michael JACKSON US, male vocalist   740 wks

3 Jun 72	**GOT TO BE THERE** *Tamla Motown STML 11205*	37	5 wks
13 Jan 73	**BEN** *Tamla Motown STML 11220*	17	7 wks
29 Sep 79 ●	**OFF THE WALL** *Epic EPC 4500861*	5	176 wks
4 Jul 81	**BEST OF MICHAEL JACKSON** *Motown STMR 9009*	11	18 wks
18 Jul 81	**ONE DAY IN YOUR LIFE** *Motown STML 12158*	29	8 wks
11 Dec 82 ★	**THRILLER** *Epic EPC 85930*	1	173 wks
12 Feb 83	**E.T. THE EXTRA TERRESTRIAL** *MCA 7000*	82	2 wks
9 Jul 83 ★	**18 GREATEST HITS** *Telstar STAR 2232★*	1	58 wks
3 Dec 83	**MICHAEL JACKSON 9 SINGLE PACK** *Epic MJ 1*	66	3 wks
9 Jun 84 ●	**FAREWELL MY SUMMER LOVE** *Motown ZL 72227*	9	14 wks
15 Nov 86	**DIANA ROSS. MICHAEL JACKSON. GLADYS KNIGHT. STEVIE WONDER. THEIR VERY BEST BACK TO BACK** *PrioriTyV PTVR 2★★*	21	10 wks
12 Sep 87 ★	**BAD** *Epic EPC 4502901*	1	115 wks
31 Oct 87	**LOVE SONGS** *Telstar STAR 2298★★★*	12	24 wks
26 Dec 87	**THE MICHAEL JACKSON MIX** *Stylus SMR 745*	27	25 wks
30 Jul 88	**SOUVENIR SINGLES PACK** *Epic MJ 5*	91	1 wk
30 Nov 91 ★	**DANGEROUS** *Epic 4658021*	1	96 wks
29 Feb 92	**MOTOWN'S GREATEST HITS** *Motown 5300142*	53	2 wks
15 Aug 92	**TOUR SOUVENIR PACK** *Epic MJ 4*	32	3 wks

★ *Michael Jackson plus the Jackson Five.*
★★ *Diana Ross/Michael Jackson/Gladys Knight/Stevie Wonder.*
★★★ *Diana Ross and Michael Jackson.*
From 14 Jan 89, when multi-artist albums were excluded from the main chart, Love Songs was listed in the compilation albums chart. See also Various Artists – Telstar.

Millie JACKSON *US, female vocalist*　　　　　*7 wks*

18 Feb	84	**E.S.P.** *Sire 250382*	59	5 wks
6 Apr	85	**LIVE AND UNCENSORED** *Important TADLP 001*	81	2 wks

JACKSONS *US, male vocal group*　　　　　*140 wks*

21 Mar	70	**DIANA ROSS PRESENTS THE JACKSON FIVE**		
		Tamla Motown STML 11142★	16	4 wks
15 Aug	70	**ABC** *Tamla Motown STML 11153★*	22	6 wks
7 Oct	72	**GREATEST HITS** *Tamla Motown STML 11212★*	26	14 wks
18 Nov	72	**LOOKIN' THROUGH THE WINDOWS**		
		Tamla Motown STML 11214★	16	8 wks
16 Jul	77	**THE JACKSONS** *Epic EPC 86009*	54	1 wk
3 Dec	77	**GOIN' PLACES** *Epic EPC 86035*	45	1 wk
5 May	79	**DESTINY** *Epic EPC 83200*	33	7 wks
11 Oct	80	**TRIUMPH** *Epic EPC 86112*	13	16 wks
12 Dec	81	**THE JACKSONS** *Epic EPC 88562*	53	9 wks
9 Jul	83	★ **18 GREATEST HITS** *Telstar STAR 2232★★*	1	58 wks
21 Jul	84	● **VICTORY** *Epic EPC 86303*	3	13 wks
1 Jul	89	**2300 JACKSON ST** *Epic 463352 1*	39	3 wks

★ *Jackson Five.*
★★ *Michael Jackson plus the Jackson Five.*

JADE *US, female vocal group*　　　　　*3 wks*

29 May	93	**JADE TO THE MAX** *Giant 74321148002*	43	3 wks

Mick JAGGER *UK, male vocalist*　　　　　*20 wks*

16 Mar	85	● **SHE'S THE BOSS** *CBS 86310*	6	11 wks
26 Sep	87	**PRIMITIVE COOL** *CBS 460 123–1*	26	5 wks
20 Feb	93	**WANDERING SPIRIT** *Atlantic 7567824362*	12	4 wks

JAM *UK, male vocal/instrumental group*　　　　　*173 wks*

28 May	77	**IN THE CITY** *Polydor 2383 447*	20	18 wks
26 Nov	77	**THIS IS THE MODERN WORLD** *Polydor 2383 475*	22	5 wks
11 Nov	78	● **ALL MOD CONS** *Polydor POLD 5008*	6	17 wks
24 Nov	79	● **SETTING SONS** *Polydor POLD 5028*	4	19 wks
6 Dec	80	● **SOUND AFFECTS** *Polydor POLD 5035*	2	19 wks
20 Mar	82	★ **THE GIFT** *Polydor POLD 5055*	1	24 wks
18 Dec	82	● **DIG THE NEW BREED** *Polydor POLD 5075*	2	15 wks
27 Aug	83	**IN THE CITY (re-issue)** *Polydor SPELP 27*	100	1 wk
22 Oct	83	● **SNAP** *Polydor SNAP 1*	2	30 wks
13 Jul	91	● **GREATEST HITS** *Polydor 8495541*	2	19 wks
18 Apr	92	**EXTRAS** *Polydor 5131772*	15	4 wks
6 Nov	93	**LIVE JAM** *Polydor 5196672*	28	2 wks

JAMES *UK, male vocal/instrumental group*　　　　　*63 wks*

2 Aug	86	**STUTTER** *blanco y negro JIMLP 1*	68	2 wks
8 Oct	88	**STRIP MINE** *Sire JIMLP 2*	90	1 wk
16 Jun	90	● **GOLD MOTHER** *Fontana 8485951*	2	34 wks
29 Feb	92	● **SEVEN** *Fontana 5109322*	2	14 wks
9 Oct	93	● **LAID** *Fontana 5149432*	3†	12 wks

Rick JAMES *US, male vocalist*　　　　　*2 wks*

24 Jul	82	**THROWIN' DOWN** *Motown STML 12167*	93	2 wks

Wendy JAMES *UK, female vocalist*　　　　　*1 wk*

20 Mar	93	**NOW AIN'T THE TIME FOR YOUR TEARS**		
		MCA MCD 10800	43	1 wk

JAMIROQUAI *UK, male vocal/instrumental group* *21 wks*

26 Jun 93 ★ **EMERGENCY ON PLANET EARTH** *Sony S2 4740692* . . **1** 21 wks

JAN and DEAN *US, male vocal duo* *2 wks*

12 Jul 80 **THE JAN AND DEAN STORY** *K-Tel NE 1084* . . . . **67** 2 wks

JANE'S ADDICTION *US, male vocal/instrumental group* *2 wks*

8 Sep 90 **RITUAL DE LO HABITUAL** *Warner Bros. WX 306* . . . . . . **37** 2 wks

JAPAN *UK, male vocal/instrumental group* *136 wks*

9 Feb 80	**QUIET LIFE** *Ariola Hansa AHAL 8011*	**53**	8 wks
15 Nov 80	**GENTLEMEN TAKE POLAROIDS** *Virgin V 2180*	**45**	10 wks
26 Sep 81	**ASSEMBLAGE** *Hansa HANLP 1*	**26**	46 wks
28 Nov 81	**TIN DRUM** *Virgin V 2209*	**12**	50 wks
18 Jun 83 ●	**OIL ON CANVAS** *Virgin VD 2513*	**5**	14 wks
8 Dec 84	**EXORCISING GHOSTS** *Virgin VGD 3510*	**45**	8 wks

Jeff JARRATT and Don REEDMAN
UK, male producers *8 wks*

22 Nov 80 **MASTERWORKS** *K-Tel ONE 1093* . . . . **39** 8 wks

Jean-Michel JARRE
France, male instrumentalist/producer *226 wks*

20 Aug 77 ●	**OXYGENE** *Polydor 2310 555*	**2**	24 wks
16 Dec 78	**EQUINOXE** *Polydor POLD 5007*	**11**	26 wks
6 Jun 81 ●	**MAGNETIC FIELDS** *Polydor POLS 1033*	**6**	17 wks
15 May 82 ●	**THE CONCERTS IN CHINA** *Polydor PODV 3*	**6**	17 wks
12 Nov 83	**THE ESSENTIAL JEAN MICHEL JARRE** *Polystar PROLP 3*	**14**	29 wks
24 Nov 84	**ZOOLOOK** *Polydor POLH 15*	**47**	14 wks
12 Apr 86 ●	**RENDEZ-VOUS** *Polydor POLH 27*	**9**	37 wks
18 Jul 87	**IN CONCERT LYONS/HOUSTON** *Polydor POLH 36* . . .	**18**	15 wks
8 Oct 88 ●	**REVOLUTIONS** *Polydor POLH 45*	**2**	13 wks
14 Oct 89	**JARRE LIVE** *Polydor 841258 1*	**16**	4 wks
23 Jun 90	**WAITING FOR COUSTEAU** *Dreyfus 8436141*	**14**	10 wks
26 Oct 91	**IMAGES – THE BEST OF JEAN-MICHEL JARRE** *Dreyfus 5113061*	**14**	12 wks
5 Jun 93	**CHRONOLOGIE** *Polydor 5193732*	**11**	8 wks

Al JARREAU *US, male vocalist* *37 wks*

5 Sep 81	**BREAKING AWAY** *Warner Bros. K 56917*	**60**	8 wks
30 Apr 83	**JARREAU** *WEA International U 0070*	**39**	18 wks
17 Nov 84	**HIGH CRIME** *WEA 250807*	**81**	1 wk
13 Sep 86	**L IS FOR LOVER** *WEA International 253 080–1*	**45**	10 wks

JAZZY JEFF – *See DJ JAZZY JEFF and FRESH PRINCE*

JEFFERSON AIRPLANE
US/UK, female/male vocal/instrumental group *28 wks*

28 Jun 69	**BLESS ITS POINTED LITTLE HEAD** *RCA SF 8019*	**38**	1 wk
7 Mar 70	**VOLUNTEERS** *RCA SF 8076*	**34**	7 wks
2 Oct 71	**BARK** *Grunt FTR 1001*	**42**	1 wk
2 Sep 72	**LONG JOHN SILVER** *Grunt FTR 1007*	**30**	1 wk
31 Jul 76	**SPITFIRE** *Grunt RFL 1557★*	**30**	2 wks

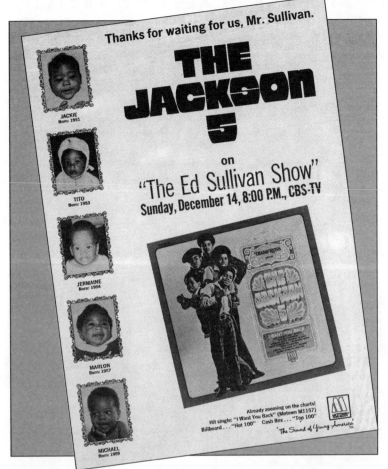

Thanks for waiting for us, Mr. Sullivan.

THE JACKSON 5

on
"The Ed Sullivan Show"
Sunday, December 14, 8:00 P.M., CBS-TV

JACKIE
Born: 1951

TITO
Born: 1953

JERMAINE
Born: 1954

MARLON
Born: 1957

MICHAEL
Born: 1959

Already zooming on the charts!
Hit single: "I Want You Back" (Motown M1157)
Billboard . . . "Hot 100"   Cash Box . . . "Top 100"
"The Sound of Young America"

This late 1969 advertisement promoted the first American network television appearance by
the *Jackson Five*.

Janet Jackson has her hands full of Billboard
Awards trophies. *(Pictorial Press)*

Michael Jackson had, by the end of 1993,
released 30 singles from four studio albums
over a 14-year period, giving the illusion of
high productivity.

9 Feb 80	**FREEDOM AT POINT ZERO** *Grunt FL 13452★*	22	11 wks
18 Jul 87	**NO PROTECTION** *Grunt FL 86413★★*	26	5 wks

★ *Jefferson Starship.*
★★ *Starship.*

JELLYBEAN *US, male instrumentalist/producer*   *35 wks*

31 Oct 87	**JUST VISITING THIS PLANET** *Chrysalis CHR 1569*	15	28 wks
3 Sep 88	**ROCKS THE HOUSE!** *Chrysalis CJB 1*	16	7 wks

JELLYFISH *US, male vocal/instrumental group*   *2 wks*

22 May 93	**SPILT MILK** *Charisma CDCUS 20*	21	2 wks

JESUS AND MARY CHAIN
UK, male vocal/instrumental group   *36 wks*

30 Nov 85	**PSYCHOCANDY** *blanco y negro BYN 7*	31	10 wks
12 Sep 87 ●	**DARKLANDS** *blanco y negro BYN 11*	5	7 wks
30 Apr 88 ●	**BARBED WIRE KISSES** *blanco y negro BYN 15*	9	7 wks
21 Oct 89	**AUTOMATIC** *blanco y negro BYN 20*	11	4 wks
4 Apr 92	**HONEY'S DEAD** *blanco y negro 9031765542*	14	5 wks
24 Jul 93	**THE SOUND OF SPEED** *blanco y negro 4509931052*	15	3 wks

JESUS JONES *UK, male vocal/instrumental group*   *31 wks*

14 Oct 89	**LIQUIDIZER** *Food FOODLP 3*	32	3 wks
9 Feb 91 ★	**DOUBT** *Food FOODLP 5*	1	24 wks
6 Feb 93 ●	**PERVERSE** *Food FOODCD 8*	6	4 wks

JESUS LOVES YOU
UK, male vocalist, Boy George   *1 wk*

13 Apr 91	**THE MARTYR MANTRAS** *More Protein CUMLP 1*	60	1 wk

See also Boy George.

JETHRO TULL *UK, male vocal/instrumental group*   *231 wks*

2 Nov 68 ●	**THIS WAS** *Island ILPS 9085*	10	22 wks
9 Aug 69 ★	**STAND UP** *Island ILPS 9103*	1	29 wks
9 May 70 ●	**BENEFIT** *Island ILPS 9123*	3	13 wks
3 Apr 71 ●	**AQUALUNG** *Island ILPS 9145*	4	21 wks
18 Mar 72 ●	**THICK AS A BRICK** *Chrysalis CHR 1003*	5	14 wks
15 Jul 72 ●	**LIVING IN THE PAST** *Chrysalis CJT 1*	8	11 wks
28 Jul 73	**A PASSION PLAY** *Chrysalis CHR 1040*	13	8 wks
2 Nov 74	**WAR CHILD** *Chrysalis CHR 1067*	14	4 wks
27 Sep 75	**MINSTREL IN THE GALLERY** *Chrysalis CHR 1082*	20	6 wks
31 Jan 76	**M.U. THE BEST OF JETHRO TULL** *Chrysalis CHR 1078*	44	5 wks
15 May 76	**TOO OLD TO ROCK 'N' ROLL TOO YOUNG TO DIE** *Chrysalis CHR 1111*	25	10 wks
19 Feb 77	**SONGS FROM THE WOOD** *Chrysalis CHR 1132*	13	12 wks
29 Apr 78	**HEAVY HORSES** *Chrysalis CHR 1175*	20	10 wks
14 Oct 78	**LIVE BURSTING OUT** *Chrysalis CJT 4*	17	8 wks
6 Oct 79	**STORM WATCH** *Chrysalis CDL 1238*	27	4 wks
6 Sep 80	**A** *Chrysalis CDL 1301*	25	5 wks
17 Apr 82	**BROADSWORD AND THE BEAST** *Chrysalis CDL 1380* .	27	19 wks
15 Sep 84	**UNDER WRAPS** *Chrysalis CDL 1461*	18	5 wks
2 Nov 85	**ORIGINAL MASTERS** *Chrysalis JTTV 1*	63	3 wks
19 Sep 87	**CREST OF A KNAVE** *Chrysalis CDL 1590*	19	10 wks
9 Jul 88	**20 YEARS OF JETHRO TULL** *Chrysalis TBOX 1*	78	1 wk
2 Sep 89	**ROCK ISLAND** *Chrysalis CHR 1708*	18	6 wks
14 Sep 91	**CATFISH RISING** *Chrysalis CHR 1886*	27	3 wks
26 Sep 92	**A LITTLE LIGHT MUSIC** *Chrysalis CCD 1954*	34	2 wks

JETS *UK, male vocal/instrumental group*   *6 wks*

10 Apr 82	**100 PERCENT COTTON** *EMI EMC 3399*	**30**	6 wks

JETS *US, male/female vocal/instrumental group*   *4 wks*

11 Apr 87	**CRUSH ON YOU** *MCA MCF 3312*	**57**	4 wks

Joan JETT and the BLACKHEARTS
US, female/male vocal/instrumental group   *7 wks*

8 May 82	**I LOVE ROCK 'N' ROLL** *Epic EPC 85686*	**25**	7 wks

JIVE BUNNY and the MASTERMIXERS
UK, male production/mixing group   *29 wks*

9 Dec 89 ●	**JIVE BUNNY – THE ALBUM** *Telstar STAR 2390*	**2**	22 wks
8 Dec 90	**IT'S PARTY TIME** *Telstar STAR 2449*	**23**	7 wks

JO BOXERS *UK, male vocal/instrumental group*   *5 wks*

24 Sep 83	**LIKE GANGBUSTERS** *RCA BOXXLP 1*	**18**	5 wks

Billy JOEL *US, male vocalist*   *309 wks*

25 Mar 78	**THE STRANGER** *CBS 82311*	**25**	40 wks
25 Nov 78 ●	**52ND STREET** *CBS 83181*	**10**	43 wks
22 Mar 80 ●	**GLASS HOUSES** *CBS 86108*	**9**	24 wks
10 Oct 81	**SONGS IN THE ATTIC** *CBS 85273*	**57**	3 wks
2 Oct 82	**NYLON CURTAIN** *CBS 85959*	**27**	8 wks
10 Sep 83 ●	**AN INNOCENT MAN** *CBS 25554*	**2**	94 wks
4 Feb 84	**COLD SPRING HARBOUR** *CBS 32400*	**95**	1 wk
23 Jun 84	**PIANO MAN** *CBS 32002*	**98**	1 wk
20 Jul 85 ●	**GREATEST HITS VOLUME I & VOLUME II** *CBS 88666*	**7**	39 wks
16 Aug 86	**THE BRIDGE** *CBS 86323*	**38**	10 wks
28 Nov 87	**KOHYEPT – LIVE IN LENINGRAD** *CBS 460 407–1*	**92**	1 wk
4 Nov 89 ●	**STORM FRONT** *CBS 4656581*	**5**	25 wks
14 Aug 93 ●	**RIVER OF DREAMS** *Columbia 4738722*	**3†**	20 wks

Elton JOHN *UK, male vocalist/instrumentalist – piano*   *763 wks*

23 May 70	**ELTON JOHN** *DJM DJLPS 406*	**11**	14 wks
16 Jan 71 ●	**TUMBLEWEED CONNECTION** *DJM DJLPS 410*	**6**	20 wks
1 May 71	**THE ELTON JOHN LIVE ALBUM 17-11-70** *DJM DJLPS 414*	**20**	2 wks
20 May 72	**MADMAN ACROSS THE WATER** *DJM DJLPH 420*	**41**	2 wks
3 Jun 72 ●	**HONKY CHATEAU** *DJM DJLPH 423*	**2**	23 wks
10 Feb 73 ★	**DON'T SHOOT ME I'M ONLY THE PIANO PLAYER** *DJM DJLPH 427*	**1**	42 wks
3 Nov 73 ★	**GOODBYE YELLOW BRICK ROAD** *DJM DJLPO 1001* .	**1**	84 wks
13 Jul 74 ★	**CARIBOU** *DJM DJLPH 439*	**1**	18 wks
23 Nov 74 ★	**ELTON JOHN'S GREATEST HITS** *DJM DJLPH 442*	**1**	84 wks
7 Jun 75 ●	**CAPTAIN FANTASTIC AND THE BROWN DIRT** **COWBOY** *DJM DJLPX 1*	**2**	24 wks
8 Nov 75 ●	**ROCK OF THE WESTIES** *DJM DJLPH 464*	**5**	12 wks
15 May 76 ●	**HERE AND THERE** *DJM DJLPH 473*	**6**	9 wks
6 Nov 76 ●	**BLUE MOVES** *Rocket ROSP 1*	**3**	15 wks
15 Oct 77 ●	**GREATEST HITS VOL. 2** *DJM DJH 20520*	**6**	24 wks
4 Nov 78 ●	**A SINGLE MAN** *Rocket TRAIN 1*	**8**	26 wks
20 Oct 79	**VICTIM OF LOVE** *Rocket HISPD 125*	**41**	3 wks
8 Mar 80	**LADY SAMANTHA** *DJM 22085*	**56**	2 wks
31 May 80	**21 AT 33** *Rocket HISPD 126*	**12**	13 wks
25 Oct 80	**THE VERY BEST OF ELTON JOHN** *K-Tel NE 1094* ...	**24**	13 wks

30 May	81	**THE FOX** *Rocket TRAIN 16*	**12**	12 wks
17 Apr	82	**JUMP UP** *Rocket HISPD 127*	**13**	12 wks
6 Nov	82	**LOVE SONGS** *TV Records TVA 3*	**39**	13 wks
11 Jun	83 ●	**TOO LOW FOR ZERO** *Rocket HISPD 24*	**7**	73 wks
30 Jun	84 ●	**BREAKING HEARTS** *Rocket HISPD 25*	**2**	23 wks
16 Nov	85 ●	**ICE ON FIRE** *Rocket HISPD 26*	**3**	23 wks
15 Nov	86	**LEATHER JACKETS** *Rocket EJLP 1*	**24**	9 wks
12 Sep	87	**LIVE IN AUSTRALIA** *Rocket EJBXL 1★*	**43**	7 wks
16 Jul	88	**REG STRIKES BACK** *Rocket EJLP 3*	**18**	6 wks
23 Sep	89 ★	**SLEEPING WITH THE PAST** *Rocket 8388391*	**1**	42 wks
10 Nov	90 ●	**THE VERY BEST OF ELTON JOHN** *Rocket 8469471*	**1**	91 wks
27 Jun	92 ●	**THE ONE** *Rocket 5123602*	**2**	18 wks
4 Dec	93 ●	**DUETS** *Rocket 5184782*	**5†**	4 wks

★ *Elton John and the Melbourne Symphony Orchestra.*
Live In Australia *reappeared in 1988 as EJLP 2; EJBXL 1 was the original 'de luxe' version.*

JOHNNY HATES JAZZ
UK, male vocal/instrumental group   *39 wks*

23 Jan	88 ★	**TURN BACK THE CLOCK** *Virgin V 2475*	**1**	39 wks

JOHNNY and the HURRICANES
US, male instrumental group   *5 wks*

3 Dec	60	**STORMSVILLE** *London HAI 2269*	**18**	1 wk
1 Apr	61	**BIG SOUND OF JOHNNY AND THE HURRICANES** *London HAK 2322*	**14**	4 wks

Holly JOHNSON *UK, male vocalist*   *17 wks*

J
174

6 May	89 ★	**BLAST** *MCA MCG 6042*	**1**	17 wks

Linton Kwesi JOHNSON *Jamaica, male poet*   *8 wks*

30 Jun	79	**FORCE OF VICTORY** *Island ILPS 9566*	**66**	1 wk
31 Oct	80	**BASS CULTURE** *Island ILPS 9605*	**46**	5 wks
10 Mar	84	**MAKING HISTORY** *Island ILPS 9770*	**73**	2 wks

Matt JOHNSON – *See The THE*

Paul JOHNSON *UK, male vocalist*   *3 wks*

4 Jul	87	**PAUL JOHNSON** *CBS 450640 1*	**63**	2 wks
16 Sep	89	**PERSONAL** *CBS 463284 1*	**70**	1 wk

Al JOLSON *US, male vocalist*   *11 wks*

14 Mar	81	**20 GOLDEN GREATS** *MCA MCTV 4*	**18**	7 wks
17 Dec	83	**THE AL JOLSON COLLECTION** *Ronco RON LP 5*	**67**	4 wks

JON and VANGELIS
UK, male vocalist and Greece, male instrumentalist – keyboards   *53 wks*

26 Jan	80 ●	**SHORT STORIES** *Polydor POLD 5030*	**4**	11 wks
11 Jul	81	**THE FRIENDS OF MR. CAIRO** *Polydor POLD 5039*	**17**	8 wks
23 Jan	82 ●	**THE FRIENDS OF MR. CAIRO (re-issue)** *Polydor POLD 5053*	**6**	15 wks
2 Jul	83	**PRIVATE COLLECTION** *Polydor POLH 4*	**22**	10 wks
11 Aug	84	**THE BEST OF JON AND VANGELIS** *Polydor POLH 6* ..	**42**	9 wks

See also Jon Anderson; Vangelis.

JONES – *See SMITH and JONES*

Aled JONES *UK, male chorister*   *140 wks*

27 Apr	85	●	VOICES FROM THE HOLY LAND *BBC REC 564★*	6	43 wks
29 Jun	85	●	ALL THROUGH THE NIGHT *BBC REH 569★*	2	43 wks
23 Nov	85		ALED JONES WITH THE BBC WELSH CHORUS *10/BBC AJ 1★*	11	10 wks
22 Feb	86		WHERE E'ER YOU WALK *10 DIX 21*	36	6 wks
12 Jul	86		PIE JESU *10 AJ 2*	25	16 wks
29 Nov	86		AN ALBUM OF HYMNS *Telstar STAR 2272*	18	11 wks
14 Mar	87		ALED (MUSIC FROM THE TV SERIES) *10 AJ 3*	52	6 wks
5 Dec	87		THE BEST OF ALED JONES *10 AJ 5*	59	5 wks

★ Aled Jones with the BBC Welsh Chorus.

Glenn JONES *US, male vocalist*   *1 wk*

31 Oct	87	GLENN JONES *Jive HIP 51*	62	1 wk

Grace JONES *US, female vocalist*   *80 wks*

30 Aug	80		WARM LEATHERETTE *Island ILPS 9592*	45	2 wks
23 May	81		NIGHTCLUBBING *Island ILPS 9624*	35	16 wks
20 Nov	82		LIVING MY LIFE *Island ILPS 9722*	15	22 wks
9 Nov	85		SLAVE TO THE RHYTHM *ZTT GRACE 1*	12	8 wks
14 Dec	85	●	ISLAND LIFE *Island GJ 1*	4	30 wks
29 Nov	86		INSIDE STORY *Manhattan MTL 1007*	61	2 wks

Howard JONES *UK, male vocalist*   *122 wks*

17 Mar	84	★	HUMAN'S LIB *WEA WX 1*	1	57 wks
8 Dec	84		THE 12" ALBUM *WEA WX 14*	15	33 wks
23 Mar	85	●	DREAM INTO ACTION *WEA WX 15*	2	25 wks
25 Oct	86	●	ONE TO ONE *WEA WX 68*	10	4 wks
1 Apr	89		CROSS THAT LINE *WEA WX 225*	64	1 wk
5 Jun	93		THE BEST OF HOWARD JONES *East West 4509927012* .	36	2 wks

Jack JONES *US, male vocalist*   *70 wks*

29 Apr	72	●	A SONG FOR YOU *RCA Victor SF 8228*	9	6 wks
3 Jun	72	●	BREAD WINNERS *RCA Victor SF 8280*	7	36 wks
7 Apr	73	●	TOGETHER *RCA Victor SF 8342*	8	10 wks
23 Feb	74	●	HARBOUR *RCA Victor APLI 0408*	10	5 wks
19 Feb	77		THE FULL LIFE *RCA Victor PL 12067*	41	5 wks
21 May	77	●	ALL TO YOURSELF *RCA TVL 2*	10	8 wks

Quincy JONES
US, male arranger/instrumentalist – keyboards   *41 wks*

18 Apr	81	THE DUDE *A & M AMLK 63721*	19	25 wks
20 Mar	82	THE BEST *A & M AMLH 68542*	41	4 wks
20 Jan	90	BACK ON THE BLOCK *Qwest WX 313*	26	12 wks

Rickie Lee JONES *US, female vocalist*   *39 wks*

16 Jun	79	RICKIE LEE JONES *Warner Bros. K 56628*	18	19 wks
8 Aug	81	PIRATES *Warner Bros. K 56816*	37	11 wks
2 Jul	83	GIRL AT HER VOLCANO *Warner Bros. 92–3805–1*	51	3 wks
13 Oct	84	THE MAGAZINE *Warner Bros. 925117*	40	4 wks
7 Oct	89	FLYING COWBOYS *Geffen WX 309*	50	2 wks

Tammy JONES *UK, female vocalist*   *5 wks*

12 Jul	75	LET ME TRY AGAIN *Epic EPC 80853*	38	5 wks

J
175

Elton John is shown shortly after
signing his contract with
Dick James Music in 1968.
(Pictorial Press)

James came into
flower in 1990.
(LFI)

Lenny Kravitz was a former member of the California Boys Choir. *(Pictorial Press)*

Tom JONES UK, male vocalist 421 wks

5 Jun	65	ALONG CAME JONES Decca LK 6693	11	5 wks
8 Oct	66	FROM THE HEART Decca LK 4814	23	8 wks
8 Apr	67 ●	GREEN GREEN GRASS OF HOME Decca SKL 4855	3	49 wks
24 Jun	67 ●	LIVE AT THE TALK OF THE TOWN Decca SKL 4874 ..	6	90 wks
30 Dec	67 ●	13 SMASH HITS Decca SKL 4909	5	49 wks
27 Jul	68 ★	DELILAH Decca SKL 4946	1	29 wks
21 Dec	68 ●	HELP YOURSELF Decca SKL 4982	4	9 wks
28 Jun	69 ●	THIS IS TOM JONES Decca SKL 5007	2	20 wks
15 Nov	69 ●	TOM JONES LIVE IN LAS VEGAS Decca SKL 5032	3	45 wks
25 Apr	70 ●	TOM Decca SKL 5045	4	18 wks
14 Nov	70 ●	I WHO HAVE NOTHING Decca SKL 5072	10	10 wks
29 May	71 ●	SHE'S A LADY Decca SKL 5089	9	7 wks
27 Nov	71	LIVE AT CAESAR'S PALACE Decca 1/1–1/2	27	5 wks
24 Jun	72	CLOSE UP Decca SKL 5132	17	4 wks
23 Jun	73	THE BODY AND SOUL OF TOM JONES Decca SKL 5162	31	1 wk
5 Jan	74	GREATEST HITS Decca SKL 5176	15	13 wks
22 Mar	75 ★	20 GREATEST HITS Decca TJD 1/11/2	1	21 wks
7 Oct	78	I'M COMING HOME Lotus WH 5001	12	9 wks
16 May	87	THE GREATEST HITS Telstar STAR 2296	16	12 wks
13 May	89	AT THIS MOMENT Jive TOMTV 1	34	3 wks
8 Jul	89	AFTER DARK Stylus SMR 978	46	4 wks
6 Apr	91	CARRYING A TORCH Dover ADD 20	44	4 wks
27 Jun	92 ●	THE COMPLETE TOM JONES The Hit Label 8442862 ...	8	6 wks

Janis JOPLIN US, female vocalist 7 wks

17 Apr	71	PEARL CBS 64188	50	1 wk
22 Jul	72	JANIS JOPLIN IN CONCERT CBS 67241	30	6 wks

Ronny JORDAN UK, male instrumentalist – guitar 6 wks

7 Mar	92	THE ANTIDOTE Island CID 9988	52	4 wks
9 Oct	93	THE QUIET REVOLUTION Island CID 8009	49	2 wks

JOURNEY US, male vocal/instrumental group 30 wks

20 Mar	82	ESCAPE CBS 85138	32	16 wks
19 Feb	83 ●	FRONTIERS CBS 25261	6	8 wks
6 Aug	83	EVOLUTION CBS 32342	100	1 wk
24 May	86	RAISED ON RADIO CBS 26902	22	5 wks

JOY DIVISION UK, male vocal/instrumental group 29 wks

26 Jul	80 ●	CLOSER Factory FACT 25	6	8 wks
30 Aug	80	UNKNOWN PLEASURES Factory FACT 10	71	1 wk
17 Oct	81 ●	STILL Factory FACT 40	5	12 wks
23 Jul	88 ●	1977–1980 SUBSTANCE Factory FAC 250	7	8 wks

JTQ with Noel McKOY
UK, male vocal/instrumental group 3 wks

1 May	93	SUPERNATURAL FEELING Big Life BLRCD 21	36	3 wks

JUDAS PRIEST UK, male vocal/instrumental group 78 wks

14 May	77	SIN AFTER SIN CBS 82008	23	6 wks
25 Feb	78	STAINED GLASS CBS 82430	27	5 wks
11 Nov	78	KILLING MACHINE CBS 83135	32	9 wks
6 Oct	79 ●	UNLEASHED IN THE EAST CBS 83852	10	8 wks
19 Apr	80 ●	BRITISH STEEL CBS 84160	4	17 wks
7 Mar	81	POINT OF ENTRY CBS 84834	14	5 wks
17 Jul	82	SCREAMING FOR VENGEANCE CBS 85941	11	9 wks

J

177

28 Jan	84	**DEFENDERS OF THE FAITH** *CBS 25713*	19	5 wks
19 Apr	86	**TURBO** *CBS 26641*	33	4 wks
13 Jun	87	**PRIEST LIVE** *CBS 450 639–1*	47	2 wks
28 May	88	**RAM IT DOWN** *CBS 461108 1*	24	5 wks
22 Sep	90	**PAINKILLER** *CBS 4672901*	26	2 wks
8 May	93	**METAL WORKS 73–93** *Columbia 4730502*	37	1 wk

JUDGE DREAD UK, *male vocalist* 14 wks

| 6 Dec | 75 | **BEDTIME STORIES** *Cactus CTLP 113* .... | 26 | 12 wks |
| 7 Mar | 81 | **40 BIG ONES** *Creole BIG 1* .... | 51 | 2 wks |

JUICY LUCY UK, *male vocal/instrumental group* 5 wks

| 18 Apr | 70 | **JUICY LUCY** *Vertigo VO 2* .... | 41 | 4 wks |
| 21 Nov | 70 | **LIE BACK AND ENJOY IT** *Vertigo 6360 014* .... | 53 | 1 wk |

JULUKA South Africa, *male/female vocal/instrumental group* 3 wks

| 23 Jul | 83 | **SCATTERLINGS** *Safari SHAKA 1* .... | 50 | 3 wks |

JUNGLE BROTHERS US, *male rap group* 3 wks

| 3 Feb | 90 | **DONE BY THE FORCES OF NATURE** *Eternal WX 332* . | 41 | 3 wks |

JUNIOR UK, *male vocalist* 14 wks

| 5 Jun | 82 | **JI** *Mercury MERS 3* .... | 28 | 14 wks |

Bert KAEMPFERT Germany, *orchestra* 104 wks

5 Mar	66	● **BYE BYE BLUES** *Polydor BM 84086*	4	22 wks
16 Apr	66	**BEST OF BERT KAEMPFERT** *Polydor 84–012*	27	1 wk
28 May	66	**SWINGING SAFARI** *Polydor LPHM 46–384*	20	15 wks
30 Jul	66	**STRANGERS IN THE NIGHT** *Polydor LPHM 84–053*	13	26 wks
4 Feb	67	**RELAXING SOUND OF BERT KAEMPFERT**		
		Polydor 583–501	33	3 wks
18 Feb	67	**BERT KAEMPFERT – BEST SELLER** *Polydor 583–551* ...	25	18 wks
29 Apr	67	**HOLD ME** *Polydor 184–072*	36	5 wks
26 Aug	67	**KAEMPFERT SPECIAL** *Polydor 236–207*	24	5 wks
19 Jun	71	**ORANGE COLOURED SKY** *Polydor 2310–091*	49	1 wk
5 Jul	80	**SOUNDS SENSATIONAL** *Polydor POLTB 10*	17	8 wks

KAJAGOOGOO UK, *male vocal/instrumental group* 23 wks

| 30 Apr | 83 | ● **WHITE FEATHERS** *EMI EMC 3433* .... | 5 | 20 wks |
| 26 May | 84 | **ISLANDS** *EMI KAJA 1* .... | 35 | 3 wks |

Nick KAMEN UK, *male vocalist* 7 wks

| 18 Apr | 87 | **NICK KAMEN** *WEA WX 84* .... | 34 | 7 wks |

KANE GANG UK, *male vocal/instrumental group* 12 wks

23 Feb	85	**THE BAD AND LOWDOWN WORLD OF THE KANE**		
		GANG *Kitchenware KWLP 2*	21	8 wks
8 Aug	87	**MIRACLE** *Kitchenware KWLP 7*	41	4 wks

Mick KARN *UK, male vocalist/instrumentalist – bass*   *4 wks*

20 Nov 82	**TITLES** *Virgin V 2249*	74	3 wks
28 Feb 87	**DREAMS OF REASON PRODUCE MONSTERS**	
	Virgin V 2389	89	1 wk

KATRINA and the WAVES
UK/US, female/male vocal/instrumental group   *7 wks*

| 8 Jun 85 | **KATRINA AND THE WAVES** *Capitol KTW 1* .... | 28 | 6 wks |
| 10 May 86 | **WAVES** *Capitol EST 2010* .... | 70 | 1 wk |

K.C. and the SUNSHINE BAND
US, male vocal/instrumental group   *17 wks*

30 Aug 75	**K.C. AND THE SUNSHINE BAND** *Jayboy JSL 9*	26	7 wks
1 Mar 80 ●	**GREATEST HITS** *TK TKR 83385*	10	6 wks
27 Aug 83	**ALL IN A NIGHT'S WORK** *Epic EPC 85847*	46	4 wks

KEEL *US, male vocal/instrumental group*   *2 wks*

| 17 May 86 | **THE FINAL FRONTIER** *Vertigo VERH 33* .... | 83 | 2 wks |

Howard KEEL *US, male vocalist*   *36 wks*

14 Apr 84 ●	**AND I LOVE YOU SO** *Warwick WW 5137*	6	19 wks
9 Nov 85	**REMINISCING – THE HOWARD KEEL COLLECTION**	
	Telstar STAR 2259	20	12 wks
28 Mar 88	**JUST FOR YOU** *Telstar STAR 2318*	51	5 wks

R. KELLY and PUBLIC ANNOUNCEMENT
US, male vocalist and dancers   *2 wks*

| 29 Feb 92 | **BORN INTO THE 90S** *Jive CHIP 123* .... | 67 | 1 wk |
| 27 Nov 93 | **12-PLAY** *Jive CHIP 144* .... | 69 | 1 wk |

Felicity KENDAL *UK, female exercise instructor*   *47 wks*

| 19 Jun 82 | **SHAPE UP AND DANCE (VOL. 1)** *Lifestyle LEG 1* ...... | 29 | 47 wks |

Eddie KENDRICK – *See Daryl HALL and John OATES*

Brian KENNEDY *Ireland, male vocalist*   *1 wk*

| 31 Mar 90 | **THE GREAT WAR OF WORDS** *RCA PL 74475* .... | 64 | 1 wk |

Nigel KENNEDY *UK, male instrumentalist – violin*   *116 wks*

1 Mar 86	**ELGAR VIOLIN CONCERTO** *EMI EMX 4120581***	97	1 wk
7 Oct 89 ●	**VIVALDI: FOUR SEASONS** *EMI NIGE 2***	3	81 wks
5 May 90	**MENDELSSOHN/BRUCH/SCHUBERT**	
	*HMV 7496631****	28	15 wks
6 Apr 91	**BRAHMS VIOLIN CONCERTO** *EMI NIGE 3*	16	12 wks
22 Feb 92	**JUST LISTEN ...** *EMI Classics CDNIGE 4*	56	1 wk
21 Nov 92	**BEETHOVEN: VIOLIN CONCERTO**	
	*EMI Classics CDC 7545742****	40	6 wks

★ *Nigel Kennedy with the London Philharmonic Orchestra, conducted by Vernon Handley.*
★★ *Nigel Kennedy with the English Chamber Orchestra.*
★★★ *Nigel Kennedy with Jeffrey Tate and the English Chamber Orchestra.*
★★★★ *Nigel Kennedy with Klaus Tennstedt and the North German Radio Symphony Orchestra.*

KENNY UK, male vocal/instrumental group   1 wk

17 Jan 76   **THE SOUND OF SUPER K** *RAK SRAK 518* . . . .   **56**   1 wk

Gerard KENNY US, male vocalist   4 wks

21 Jul 79   **MADE IT THROUGH THE RAIN** *RCA Victor PL 25218* .   **19**   4 wks

Nik KERSHAW UK, male vocalist   100 wks

10 Mar 84 ● **HUMAN RACING** *MCA MCF 3197* . . . .   **5**   61 wks
1 Dec 84 ● **THE RIDDLE** *MCA MCF 3245* . . . .   **8**   36 wks
8 Nov 86   **RADIO MUSICOLA** *MCA MCG 6016* . . . .   **47**   3 wks

Chaka KHAN US, female vocalist   44 wks

21 Apr 84   **STOMPIN' AT THE SAVOY** *Warner Bros. 923679★* . . . . . .   **64**   5 wks
20 Oct 84   **I FEEL FOR YOU** *Warner Bros. 925 162* . . . .   **15**   22 wks
9 Aug 86   **DESTINY** *Warner Bros. WX 45* . . . .   **77**   2 wks
3 Jun 89   **LIFE IS A DANCE – THE REMIX PROJECT**
        Warner Bros. WX 268 . . . .   **14**   15 wks

★ *Rufus and Chaka Khan.*

Aram KHATCHATURIAN/VIENNA PHILMARMONIC ORCHESTRA
Russia, male conductor/Austria, orchestra   15 wks

22 Jan 72   **SPARTACUS** *Decca SXL 6000* . . . .   **16**   15 wks

KIDS FROM FAME
US, male/female vocal/instrumental group   117 wks

24 Jul 82 ★ **KIDS FROM FAME** *BBC REP 447* . . . .   **1**   45 wks
16 Oct 82 ● **KIDS FROM FAME AGAIN** *RCA RCALP 6057* . . . .   **2**   21 wks
26 Feb 83 ● **THE KIDS FROM FAME LIVE** *BBC KIDLP 003* . . . .   **8**   28 wks
14 May 83   **THE KIDS FROM FAME SONGS** *BBC KIDLP 004* . . . . .   **14**   16 wks
20 Aug 83   **SING FOR YOU** *BBC KIDLP 005* . . . .   **28**   7 wks

KILLING JOKE UK, male vocal/instrumental group   30 wks

25 Oct 80   **KILLING JOKE** *Polydor EGMD 545* . . . .   **39**   4 wks
20 Jun 81   **WHAT'S THIS FOR** *Malicious Damage EGMD 550* . . . .   **42**   4 wks
8 May 82   **REVELATIONS** *Malicious Damage EGMD 3* . . . .   **12**   6 wks
27 Nov 82   **'HA' – KILLING JOKE LIVE** *EG EGMDT 4* . . . .   **66**   2 wks
23 Jul 83   **FIRE DANCES** *EG EGMD 5* . . . .   **29**   3 wks
9 Mar 85   **NIGHT TIME** *EG EGLP 61* . . . .   **11**   9 wks
22 Nov 86   **BRIGHTER THAN A THOUSAND SUNS** *EG EGLP 66* .   **54**   1 wk
9 Jul 88   **OUTSIDE THE GATE** *EG EGLP 73* . . . .   **92**   1 wk

KIMERA with the LONDON SYMPHONY ORCHESTRA Korea, female vocalist with UK, orchestra   4 wks

26 Oct 85   **HITS ON OPERA** *Stylus SMR 8505* . . . .   **38**   4 wks
See also London Symphony Orchestra.

KING UK, male vocal/instrumental group   32 wks

9 Feb 85 ● **STEPS IN TIME** *CBS 26095* . . . .   **6**   21 wks
23 Nov 85   **BITTER SWEET** *CBS 86320* . . . .   **16**   11 wks

B.B. KING US, male vocalist/instrumentalist – guitar   5 wks

25 Aug 79	**TAKE IT HOME** MCA MCF 3010	60	5 wks

Ben E. KING US, male vocalist   27 wks

1 Jul 67	**SPANISH HARLEM** Atlantic 590–001	30	3 wks
14 Mar 87	**STAND BY ME (THE ULTIMATE COLLECTION)**		
	Atlantic WX 90★	14	8 wks
20 Oct 90	**THE BEST OF BEN E. KING AND THE DRIFTERS**		
	Telstar STAR 2373★	15	16 wks

★ Ben E. King and the Drifters.

Carole KING US, female vocalist/instrumentalist – piano   102 wks

24 Jul 71 ●	**TAPESTRY** A & M AMLS 2025	4	90 wks
15 Jan 72	**MUSIC** A & M AMLH 67013	18	10 wks
2 Dec 72	**RHYMES AND REASONS** Ode 77016	40	2 wks

Evelyn KING US, female vocalist   9 wks

11 Sep 82	**GET LOOSE** RCA RCALP 3093	35	9 wks

Mark KING UK, male vocalist/instrumentalist – bass   2 wks

21 Jul 84	**INFLUENCES** Polydor MKLP 1	77	2 wks

K
181

Solomon KING US, male vocalist   1 wk

22 Jun 68	**SHE WEARS MY RING** Columbia SCX 6250	40	1 wk

KING CRIMSON UK, male vocal/instrumental group   53 wks

1 Nov 69 ●	**IN THE COURT OF THE CRIMSON KING**		
	Island ILPS 9111	5	18 wks
30 May 70 ●	**IN THE WAKE OF POSEIDON** Island ILPS 9127	4	13 wks
16 Jan 71	**LIZARD** Island ILPS 9141	30	1 wk
8 Jan 72	**ISLANDS** Island ILPS 9175	30	1 wk
7 Apr 73	**LARKS' TONGUES IN ASPIC** Island ILPS 9230	20	4 wks
13 Apr 74	**STARLESS AND BIBLE BLACK** Island ILPS 9275	28	2 wks
26 Oct 74	**RED** Island ILPS 9308	45	1 wk
10 Oct 81	**DISCIPLINE** EG EGLP 49	41	4 wks
26 Jun 82	**BEAT** EG EGLP 51	39	5 wks
31 Mar 84	**THREE OF A PERFECT PAIR** EG EGLP 55	30	4 wks

KING KURT UK, male vocal/instrumental group   5 wks

10 Dec 83	**OOH WALLAH WALLAH** Stiff SEEZ 52	99	1 wk
8 Mar 86	**BIG COCK** Stiff SEEZ 62	50	4 wks

KINGDOM COME US, male vocal/instrumental group   10 wks

28 Mar 88	**KINGDOM COME** Polydor KCLP 1	43	6 wks
13 May 89	**IN YOUR FACE** Polydor 839192 1	25	4 wks

KINGMAKER UK, male vocal/instrumental group   10 wks

19 Oct 91	**EAT YOURSELF WHOLE** Scorch CHR 1878	29	3 wks
29 May 93	**SLEEPWALKING** Scorch CDCHR 6014	15	7 wks

Redhead KINGPIN and the FBI *US, male vocalist* *3 wks*

9 Sep 89	**A SHADE OF RED** *10 DIX 85*	35	3 wks

The Choir of KING'S COLLEGE, CAMBRIDGE *UK, choir* *3 wks*

11 Dec 71	**THE WORLD OF CHRISTMAS** *Argo SPAA 104*	38	3 wks

KINGS OF SWING ORCHESTRA
Australia, orchestra *11 wks*

29 May 82	**SWITCHED ON SWING** *K-Tel ONE 1166*	28	11 wks

KING'S X *US, male vocal/instrumental group* *3 wks*

1 Jul 89	**GRETCHEN GOES TO NEBRASKA** *Atlantic WX 279* ...	52	1 wk
10 Nov 90	**FAITH HOPE LOVE** *Megaforce 756821451*	70	1 wk
28 Mar 92	**KING'S X** *Atlantic 7567805062*	46	1 wk

KINKS *UK, male vocal/instrumental group* *129 wks*

17 Oct 64 ●	**KINKS** *Pye NPL 18096*	3	25 wks
13 Mar 65 ●	**KINDA KINKS** *Pye NPL 18112*	3	15 wks
4 Dec 65 ●	**KINKS KONTROVERSY** *Pye NPL 18131*	9	12 wks
11 Sep 66 ●	**WELL RESPECTED KINKS** *Marble Arch MAL 612*	5	31 wks
5 Nov 66	**FACE TO FACE** *Pye NPL 18149*	12	11 wks
14 Oct 67	**SOMETHING ELSE** *Pye NSPL 18193*	35	2 wks
2 Dec 67 ●	**SUNNY AFTERNOON** *Marble Arch MAL 716*	9	11 wks
23 Oct 71	**GOLDEN HOUR OF THE KINKS** *Golden Hour GH 501* ..	21	4 wks
14 Oct 78	**20 GOLDEN GREATS** *Ronco RPL 2031*	19	6 wks
5 Nov 83	**KINKS GREATEST HITS – DEAD END STREET** *PRT KINK 1*	96	1 wk
16 Sep 89	**THE ULTIMATE COLLECTION** *Castle Communications CTVLP 001*	35	7 wks
18 Sep 93	**THE DEFINITIVE COLLECTION** *PolyGram TV 5164652*	18	4 wks

Kathy KIRBY *UK, female vocalist* *8 wks*

4 Jan 64	**16 HITS FROM STARS AND GARTERS** *Decca LK 5475* .	11	8 wks

KISS *US, male vocal/instrumental group* *67 wks*

29 May 76	**DESTROYER** *Casablanca CBSP 4008*	22	5 wks
25 Jun 76	**ALIVE!** *Casablanca CBSP 401*	49	2 wks
17 Dec 77	**ALIVE** *Casablanca CALD 5004*	60	1 wk
7 Jul 79	**DYNASTY** *Casablanca CALH 2051*	50	6 wks
28 Jun 80	**UNMASKED** *Mercury 6302 032*	48	3 wks
5 Dec 81	**THE ELDER** *Casablanca 6302 163*	51	3 wks
26 Jun 82	**KILLERS** *Casablanca CANL 1*	42	6 wks
6 Nov 82	**CREATURES OF THE NIGHT** *Casablanca CANL 4*	22	4 wks
8 Oct 83 ●	**LICK IT UP** *Vertigo VERL 9*	7	7 wks
6 Oct 84	**ANIMALISE** *Vertigo VERL 18*	11	4 wks
5 Oct 85	**ASYLUM** *Vertigo VERH 32*	12	3 wks
7 Nov 87 ●	**CRAZY NIGHTS** *Vertigo VERH 49*	4	14 wks
10 Dec 88	**SMASHES, THRASHES AND HITS** *Vertigo 836759 1*	62	2 wks
4 Nov 89	**HOT IN THE SHADE** *Fontana 838913 1*	35	2 wks
23 May 92 ●	**REVENGE** *Mercury 8480372*	10	3 wks
29 May 93	**ALIVE III** *Mercury 5148272*	24	2 wks

KISSING THE PINK
UK, male/female vocal/instrumental group *5 wks*

4 Jun 83	**NAKED** *Magnet KTPL 1001*	54	5 wks

K
182

KITCHENS OF DISTINCTION
UK, male vocal/instrumental group   2 wks

30 Mar 91	**STRANGE FREE WORLD** One Little Indian TPLP 19	**45**	1 wk
15 Aug 92	**DEATH OF COOL** One Little Indian TPLP 39CD	**72**	1 wk

Eartha KITT US, female vocalist   1 wk

11 Feb 61	**REVISITED** London HA 2296	**17**	1 wk

KLEEER US, male vocal/instrumental group   1 wk

6 Jul 85	**SEEEKRET** Atlantic 78–1254–1	**96**	1 wk

KLF
UK, male multi-instrumental/production duo with guest vocalists   46 wks

16 Mar 91	● **THE WHITE ROOM** KLF Communications JAMSLP 6	**3**	46 wks

Earl KLUGH – See George BENSON

KNACK US, male vocal/instrumental group   2 wks

4 Aug 79	**GET THE KNACK** Capitol EST 11948	**65**	2 wks

Curtis KNIGHT – See Jimi HENDRIX

Gladys KNIGHT and the PIPS
US, female vocalist/male vocal backing group   115 wks

31 May 75	**I FEEL A SONG** Buddah BDLP 4030	**20**	15 wks
28 Feb 76	● **THE BEST OF GLADYS KNIGHT AND THE PIPS** Buddah BDLH 5013	**6**	43 wks
16 Jul 77	**STILL TOGETHER** Buddah BDLH 5014	**42**	3 wks
12 Nov 77	● **30 GREATEST** K-Tel NE 1004	**3**	22 wks
4 Oct 80	**A TOUCH OF LOVE** K-Tel NE 1090	**16**	6 wks
4 Feb 84	**THE COLLECTION – 20 GREATEST HITS** Starblend NITE 1	**43**	5 wks
15 Nov 86	**DIANA ROSS. MICHAEL JACKSON. GLADYS KNIGHT. STEVIE WONDER. THEIR VERY BEST BACK TO BACK** PrioriTyV PTVR 2★	**21**	10 wks
27 Feb 88	**ALL OUR LOVE** MCA MCF 3409	**80**	1 wk
28 Oct 89	**THE SINGLES ALBUM** Polygram GKTV 1	**13**	10 wks

★ Diana Ross/Michael Jackson/Gladys Knight/Stevie Wonder.

KNIGHTSBRIDGE STRINGS UK, male orchestra   1 wk

25 Jun 60	**STRING SWAY** Top Rank BUY 017	**20**	1 wk

David KNOPFLER UK, male vocalist/instrumentalist – guitar 1 wk

19 Nov 83	**RELEASE** Peach River DAVID 1	**82**	1 wk

Mark KNOPFLER
UK, male vocalist/instrumentalist – guitar   25 wks

16 Apr 83	**LOCAL HERO (film soundtrack)** Vertigo VERL 4	**14**	11 wks
20 Oct 84	**CAL – MUSIC FROM THE FILM** Vertigo VERH 17	**65**	3 wks
24 Nov 90	**NECK AND NECK** CBS 4674351★	**41**	11 wks

★ Chet Atkins and Mark Knopfler.

Frankie KNUCKLES *US, male producer*   *2 wks*

17 Aug 91   **BEYOND THE MIX**   *Virgin America VUSLP 6* ....   **59**   2 wks

John KONGOS
South Africa, male vocalist/multi-instrumentalist   *2 wks*

15 Jan 72   **KONGOS**   *Fly HIFLY 7* ....   **29**   2 wks

KOOL AND THE GANG
US, male vocal/instrumental group   *115 wks*

21 Nov 81 ●	**SOMETHING SPECIAL** *De-Lite DSR 001*	**10**	20 wks
2 Oct 82	**AS ONE** *De-Lite DSR 3*	**49**	10 wks
7 May 83 ●	**TWICE AS KOOL** *De-Lite PROLP 2*	**4**	23 wks
14 Jan 84	**IN THE HEART** *De-Lite DSR 4*	**18**	23 wks
15 Dec 84	**EMERGENCY** *De-Lite DSR 6*	**47**	25 wks
12 Nov 88	**THE SINGLES COLLECTION** *De-Lite KGTV 1*	**28**	13 wks
27 Oct 90	**KOOL LOVE** *Telstar STAR 2435*	**50**	1 wk

KORGIS   *UK, male vocal/instrumental duo*   *4 wks*

26 Jul 80   **DUMB WAITERS**   *Rialto TENOR 104* ....   **40**   4 wks

KRAFTWERK   *Germany, male vocal/instrumental group*   *71 wks*

17 May 75 ●	**AUTOBAHN** *Vertigo 6360 620*	**4**	18 wks
20 May 78 ●	**THE MAN–MACHINE** *Capitol EST 11728*	**9**	13 wks
23 May 81	**COMPUTER WORLD** *EMI EMC 3370*	**15**	22 wks
6 Feb 82	**TRANS-EUROPE EXPRESS** *Capitol EST 11603*	**49**	7 wks
22 Jun 85	**AUTOBAHN (re-issue)** *Parlophone AUTO 1*	**61**	3 wks
15 Nov 86	**ELECTRIC CAFE** *EMI EMD 1001*	**58**	2 wks
22 Jun 91	**THE MIX** *EMI EM 1408*	**15**	6 wks

Billy J. KRAMER and the DAKOTAS
UK, male vocalist, male instrumental backing group   *17 wks*

16 Nov 63   **LISTEN TO BILLY J. KRAMER**   *Parlophone PMC 1209* ...   **11**   17 wks

Lenny KRAVITZ   *US, male vocalist*   *72 wks*

26 May 90	**LET LOVE RULE** *Virgin America VUSLP 10*	**56**	4 wks
13 Apr 91 ●	**MAMA SAID** *Virgin America VUSLP 31*	**8**	27 wks
13 Mar 93 ★	**ARE YOU GONNA GO MY WAY**		
	Virgin America CDVUS 60	**1†**	41 wks

Kris KRISTOFFERSON – See Rita COOLIDGE

KRIS KROSS   *US, male rap duo*   *8 wks*

27 Jun 92   **TOTALLY KROSSED OUT**   *Columbia 4714342* ....   **31**   8 wks

KROKUS   *Switzerland/Malta, male vocal/instrumental group*   *11 wks*

21 Feb 81	**HARDWARE** *Ariola ARL 5064*	**44**	4 wks
20 Feb 82	**ONE VICE AT A TIME** *Arista SPART 1189*	**28**	5 wks
16 Apr 83	**HEADHUNTER** *Arista 205 255*	**74**	2 wks

Charlie KUNZ   *US, male instrumentalist – piano*   *11 wks*

14 Jun 69 ●   **THE WORLD OF CHARLIE KUNZ**   *Decca SPA 15* ......   **9**   11 wks

L.A. GUNS *US, male/female vocal/instrumental group*   *4 wks*

5 Mar	88	**L.A. GUNS** *Vertigo VERH 55*		**73**	1 wk
30 Sep	89	**COCKED AND LOADED** *Vertigo 8385921*		**45**	2 wks
13 Jul	91	**HOLLYWOOD VAMPIRES** *Mercury 8496041*		**44**	1 wk

LA'S *UK, male vocal/instrumental group*   *19 wks*

13 Oct	90	**THE LA'S** *Go! Discs 8282021*	**30**	19 wks

Patti LaBELLE *US, female vocalist*   *17 wks*

24 May	86	**THE WINNER IN YOU** *MCA MCF 3319*	**30**	17 wks

LADYSMITH BLACK MAMBAZO
South Africa, male vocal group   *11 wks*

11 Apr	87	**SHAKA ZULU** *Warner Bros. WX 94*	**34**	11 wks

Cleo LAINE *UK, female vocalist*   *37 wks*

7 Jan	78	**BEST OF FRIENDS** *RCA RS 1094★*	**18**	22 wks
2 Dec	78	**CLEO** *Arcade ADEP 37*	**68**	1 wk
31 May	80	**SOMETIMES WHEN WE TOUCH** *RCA PL 25296★★*	**15**	14 wks

★ *Cleo Laine and John Williams*
★★ *Cleo Laine and James Galway.*

Frankie LAINE *US, male vocalist*   *29 wks*

24 Jun	61 ●	**HELL BENT FOR LEATHER** *Philips BBL 7468*	**7**	23 wks
24 Sep	77 ●	**THE VERY BEST OF FRANKIE LAINE**		
		Warwick PR 5032	**7**	6 wks

Greg LAKE *UK, male vocalist*   *3 wks*

17 Oct	81	**GREG LAKE** *Chrysalis CHR 1357*	**62**	3 wks

See also Emerson, Lake and Palmer; Emerson, Lake and Powell.

Annabel LAMB *UK, female vocalist*   *1 wk*

28 Apr	84	**THE FLAME** *A & M AMLX 68564*	**84**	1 wk

LAMBRETTAS
UK, male vocal/instrumental group   *8 wks*

5 Jul	80	**BEAT BOYS IN THE JET AGE** *Rocket TRAIN 10*	**28**	8 wks

LANDSCAPE *UK, male vocal/instrumental group*   *12 wks*

21 Mar	81	**FROM THE TEAROOMS OF MARS TO THE**		
		HELLHOLES OF URANUS *RCA RCALP 5003*	**13**	12 wks

Ronnie LANE UK, male vocal/instrumental group · 4 wks

17 Aug 74	**ANYMORE FOR ANYMORE** GM GML 1013★	....	**48**	1 wk
15 Oct 77	**ROUGH MIX** Polydor 2442147★★	....	**44**	3 wks

★ Ronnie Lane and the Band Slim Chance.
★★ Pete Townshend and Ronnie Lane.

k.d. lang Canada, female vocalist · 36 wks

28 Mar 92 ●	**INGENUE** Sire 7599268402	....	**3**	34 wks
13 Nov 93	**EVEN COW GIRLS GET THE BLUES** Sire 9362454332	..	**36**	2 wks

Thomas LANG UK, male vocalist · 1 wk

20 Feb 88	**SCALLYWAG JAZ** Epic 450996 1	....	**92**	1 wk

Mario LANZA US, male vocalist · 56 wks

6 Dec 58 ●	**THE STUDENT PRINCE/THE GREAT CARUSO** RCA RB 16113	....	**4**	21 wks
23 Jul 60 ●	**THE GREAT CARUSO** RCA RB 16112	....	**3**	15 wks
9 Jan 71	**HIS GREATEST HITS VOL. 1** RCA LSB 4000	....	**39**	1 wk
5 Sep 81	**THE LEGEND OF MARIO LANZA** K-Tel NE 1110	.....	**29**	11 wks
14 Nov 87	**A PORTRAIT OF MARIO LANZA** Stylus SMR 741	.....	**49**	8 wks

The Great Caruso side of the first album is a film soundtrack.

LARD UK, male vocal/instrumental group · 1 wk

6 Oct 90	**THE LAST TEMPTATION** Alternative Tentacles VIRUS 84	.	**69**	1 wk

James LAST Germany, male orchestra leader · 413 wks

15 Apr 67 ●	**THIS IS JAMES LAST** Polydor 104–678	....	**6**	48 wks
22 Jul 67	**HAMMOND A-GO-GO** Polydor 249–043	....	**27**	10 wks
26 Aug 67	**NON-STOP DANCING** Polydor 236–203	....	**35**	1 wk
26 Aug 67	**LOVE THIS IS MY SONG** Polydor 583–553	....	**32**	2 wks
22 Jun 68	**JAMES LAST GOES POP** Polydor 249–160	....	**32**	3 wks
8 Feb 69	**DANCING '68 VOL. 1** Polydor 249–216	....	**40**	1 wk
31 May 69	**TRUMPET A-GO-GO** Polydor 249–239	....	**13**	1 wk
9 Aug 69	**NON-STOP DANCING '69** Polydor 249–294	....	**26**	1 wk
24 Jan 70	**NON-STOP DANCING '69/2** Polydor 249/354	....	**27**	3 wks
23 May 70	**NON-STOP EVERGREENS** Polydor 249–370	....	**26**	1 wk
11 Jul 70	**CLASSICS UP TO DATE** Polydor 249–371	....	**44**	1 wk
11 Jul 70	**NON-STOP DANCING '70** Polydor 2371–04	....	**67**	1 wk
24 Oct 70	**VERY BEST OF JAMES LAST** Polydor 2371–054	....	**45**	4 wks
8 May 71	**NON-STOP DANCING '71** Polydor 2371–111	....	**21**	4 wks
26 Jun 71	**SUMMER HAPPENING** Polydor 2371–133	....	**38**	1 wk
18 Sep 71	**BEACH PARTY 2** Polydor 2371–211	....	**47**	1 wk
2 Oct 71	**YESTERDAY'S MEMORIES** Contour 2870–117	....	**17**	14 wks
16 Oct 71	**NON-STOP DANCING 12** Polydor 2371–141	....	**30**	3 wks
19 Feb 72	**NON-STOP DANCING 13** Polydor 2371–189	....	**32**	2 wks
4 Mar 72	**POLKA PARTY** Polydor 2371–190	....	**22**	3 wks
29 Apr 72	**JAMES LAST IN CONCERT** Polydor 2371–191	....	**13**	6 wks
24 Jun 72	**VOODOO PARTY** Polydor 2371–235	....	**45**	1 wk
16 Sep 72	**CLASSICS UP TO DATE VOL. 2** Polydor 184–061	....	**49**	1 wk
30 Sep 72	**LOVE MUST BE THE REASON** Polydor 2371–281	......	**32**	2 wks
27 Jan 73	**THE MUSIC OF JAMES LAST** Polydor 2683 010	....	**19**	12 wks
24 Feb 73	**JAMES LAST IN RUSSIA** Polydor 2371 293	....	**12**	9 wks
24 Feb 73	**NON-STOP DANCING VOL. 14** Polydor 2371–319	......	**27**	3 wks
28 Jul 73	**OLE** Polydor 2371 384	....	**24**	5 wks
1 Sep 73	**NON-STOP DANCING VOL. 15** Polydor 2371–376	......	**34**	2 wks
20 Apr 74	**NON-STOP DANCING VOL. 16** Polydor 2371–444	......	**43**	2 wks
29 Jun 74	**IN CONCERT VOL. 2** Polydor 2371–320	....	**49**	1 wk
23 Nov 74	**GOLDEN MEMORIES** Polydor 2371–472	....	**39**	2 wks
26 Jul 75 ●	**TEN YEARS NON-STOP JUBILEE** Polydor 2660–111	....	**5**	16 wks

2 Aug 75	VIOLINS IN LOVE *K-Tel /*	60	1 wk
22 Nov 75 ●	MAKE THE PARTY LAST *Polydor 2371–612*	3	19 wks
8 May 76	CLASSICS UP TO DATE VOL. 3 *2371–538*	54	1 wk
6 May 78	EAST TO WEST *Polydor 2630–092*	49	4 wks
14 Apr 79 ●	LAST THE WHOLE NIGHT LONG *Polydor PTD 001*	2	45 wks
23 Aug 80	THE BEST FROM 150 GOLD RECORDS *Polydor 2681 211*	56	3 wks
1 Nov 80	CLASSICS FOR DREAMING *Polydor POLTV 11*	12	18 wks
14 Feb 81	ROSES FROM THE SOUTH *Polydor 2372 051*	41	5 wks
21 Nov 81	HANSIMANIA *Polydor POLTV 14*	18	13 wks
28 Nov 81	LAST FOREVER *Polydor 2630 135*	88	2 wks
5 Mar 83	BLUEBIRD *Polydor POLD 5072*	57	3 wks
30 Apr 83	THE BEST OF MY GOLD RECORDS *Polydor PODV 7* ..	42	5 wks
30 Apr 83	NON-STOP DANCING '83 – PARTY POWER		
	Polydor POLD 5094	56	2 wks
3 Dec 83	THE GREATEST SONGS OF THE BEATLES		
	Polydor POLD 5119	52	8 wks
24 Mar 84	THE ROSE OF TRALEE AND OTHER IRISH		
	FAVOURITES *Polydor POLD 5131*	21	11 wks
13 Oct 84	PARADISE *Polydor POLD 5163*	74	2 wks
8 Dec 84	JAMES LAST IN SCOTLAND *Polydor POLD 5166*	68	9 wks
14 Sep 85	LEAVE THE BEST TO LAST *Polydor PROLP 7*	11	27 wks
18 Apr 87	BY REQUEST *Polydor POLH 34*	22	11 wks
26 Nov 88	DANCE DANCE DANCE *Polydor JLTV 1*	38	8 wks
14 Apr 90	CLASSICS BY MOONLIGHT *Polydor 8432181*	12	12 wks
15 Jun 91 ●	POP SYMPHONIES *Polydor 8494291*	10	11 wks
9 Nov 91	TOGETHER AT LAST *Delphine/Polydor 5115251★*	14	15 wks
12 Sep 92	VIVA ESPAÑA *PolyGram TV 5172202*	23	5 wks
20 Nov 93	JAMES LAST PLAYS ANDREW LLOYD WEBBER		
	Polydor 5199102	12†	6 wks

★ Richard Clayderman and James Last.

LATIN QUARTER
UK, male/female vocal/instrumental group   *3 wks*

L
187

1 Mar 86	MODERN TIMES *Rockin' Horse RHLP 1*	91	2 wks
6 Jun 87	MICK AND CAROLINE *Rockin' Horse 208 142*	96	1 wk

Cyndi LAUPER *US, female vocalist*   *57 wks*

18 Feb 84	SHE'S SO UNUSUAL *Portrait PRT 25792*	16	32 wks
11 Oct 86	TRUE COLORS *Portrait PRT 26948*	25	12 wks
1 Jul 89 ●	A NIGHT TO REMEMBER *Epic 462499 1*	9	12 wks
27 Nov 93	HAT FULL OF STARS *Epic 4730542*	56	1 wk

LAUREL and HARDY *UK/US, male comic duo*   *4 wks*

6 Dec 75	THE GOLDEN AGE OF HOLLYWOOD COMEDY		
	United Artists UAG 29676	55	4 wks

LAW *UK/US, male vocal/instrumental duo*   *1 wk*

6 Apr 91	THE LAW *Atlantic 7567821951*	61	1 wk

Joey LAWRENCE *US, male vocalist*   *3 wks*

31 Jul 93	JOEY LAWRENCE *EMI CDEMC 3657*	39	3 wks

Syd LAWRENCE *UK, orchestra*   *9 wks*

8 Aug 70	MORE MILLER AND OTHER BIG BAND MAGIC		
	Philips 6642 001	14	4 wks
25 Dec 71	SYD LAWRENCE WITH THE GLENN MILLER SOUND		
	Fontana SFL 13178	31	2 wks
25 Dec 71	MUSIC OF GLENN MILLER IN SUPER STEREO		
	Philips 6641–017	43	2 wks
26 Feb 72	SOMETHING OLD, SOMETHING NEW *Philips 6308 090*	34	1 wk

Ronnie LAWS
US, male vocalist/instrumentalist – saxophone   *1 wk*

17 Oct 81	**SOLID GROUND** *Liberty LBG 30336*	100	1 wk

Doug LAZY *US, male vocalist*   *1 wk*

10 Mar 90	**DOUG LAZY GETTIN' CRAZY** *Atlantic 7567820661*	65	1 wk

LEAGUE UNLIMITED ORCHESTRA – *See HUMAN LEAGUE*

LED ZEPPELIN
UK, male vocal/instrumental group   *438 wks*

12 Apr 69 ●	**LED ZEPPELIN** *Atlantic 588–171*	6	79 wks
8 Nov 69 ★	**LED ZEPPELIN 2** *Atlantic 588–198*	1	138 wks
7 Nov 70 ★	**LED ZEPPELIN 3** *Atlantic 2401–002*	1	40 wks
27 Nov 71 ★	**FOUR SYMBOLS** *Atlantic K 2401–012*	1	63 wks
14 Apr 73 ★	**HOUSES OF THE HOLY** *Atlantic K 50014*	1	13 wks
15 Mar 75 ★	**PHYSICAL GRAFFITI** *Swan Song SSK 89400*	1	27 wks
24 Apr 76 ★	**PRESENCE** *Swan Song SSK 59402*	1	14 wks
6 Nov 76 ★	**THE SONG REMAINS THE SAME** *Swan Song SSK 89402* .	1	15 wks
8 Sep 79 ★	**IN THROUGH THE OUT DOOR** *Swan Song SSK 59410* .	1	16 wks
4 Dec 82 ●	**CODA** *Swan Song A 0051*	4	7 wks
27 Oct 90 ●	**REMASTERS** *Atlantic ZEP 1*	10	23 wks
10 Nov 90	**LED ZEPPELIN** *Atlantic 7567821441*	48	2 wks
9 Oct 93	**BOXED SET II** *Atlantic 7567824772*	56	1 wk

Led Zeppelin 2 changed label/number to Atlantic K 40037 and Four Symbols changed to Atlantic K 50008 during their runs. The fourth Led Zeppelin album appeared in the chart under various guises: The Fourth Led Zeppelin Album, Runes, The New Led Zeppelin Album, Led Zeppelin 4 and Four Symbols. The two albums titled Led Zeppelin are different. (The 1990 entry was a boxed CD set of old and previously unreleased material.)

LEE – *See PETERS and LEE*

Brenda LEE *US, female vocalist*   *57 wks*

24 Nov 62	**ALL THE WAY** *Brunswick LAT 8383*	20	2 wks
16 Feb 63	**BRENDA – THAT'S ALL** *Brunswick LAT 8516*	13	9 wks
13 Apr 63 ●	**ALL ALONE AM I** *Brunswick LAT 8530*	8	20 wks
16 Jul 66	**BYE BYE BLUES** *Brunswick LAT 8649*	21	2 wks
1 Nov 80	**LITTLE MISS DYNAMITE** *Warwick WW 5083*	15	11 wks
7 Jan 84	**25TH ANNIVERSARY** *MCA MCLD 609*	65	4 wks
30 Mar 85	**THE VERY BEST OF BRENDA LEE** *MCA LETV 1*	16	9 wks

Peggy LEE *US, female vocalist*   *23 wks*

4 Jun 60 ●	**LATIN A LA LEE** *Capitol T 1290*	8	15 wks
11 Jun 60	**BEAUTY AND THE BEAT** *Capitol T 1219★*	16	6 wks
20 May 61	**BEST OF PEGGY LEE VOL. 2** *Brunswick LAT 8355*	18	1 wk
21 Oct 61	**BLACK COFFEE** *Ace of Hearts AH 5*	20	1 wk

★ *Peggy Lee and George Shearing.*

Raymond LEFEVRE *France, orchestra*   *9 wks*

7 Oct 67 ●	**RAYMOND LEFEVRE** *Major Minor MMLP 4*	10	7 wks
17 Feb 68	**RAYMOND LEFEVRE VOL. 2** *Major Minor SMLP 13*	37	2 wks

Tom LEHRER *US, male comic vocalist*   *26 wks*

8 Nov 58 ●	**SONGS BY TOM LEHRER** *Decca LF 1311*	7	19 wks
25 Jun 60 ●	**AN EVENING WASTED WITH TOM LEHRER**		
	Decca LK 4332	7	7 wks

LEMONHEADS *US, male vocal/instrumental group* — 22 wks

1 Aug	92	**IT'S A SHAME ABOUT RAY** *Atlantic 7567824602*	33	12 wks
23 Oct	93	● **COME ON FEEL THE LEMONHEADS** *Atlantic 7567825372*	5†	10 wks

Group was male/female for first album.

John LENNON *UK, male vocalist* — 297 wks

16 Jan	71	**JOHN LENNON AND THE PLASTIC ONO BAND** *Apple PCS 7124★*	11	11 wks
30 Oct	71	★ **IMAGINE** *Apple PAS 10004★★*	1	101 wks
14 Oct	72	**SOMETIME IN NEW YORK CITY** *Apple PCSP 716★★★* ..	11	6 wks
8 Dec	73	**MIND GAMES** *Apple PCS 7165*	13	12 wks
19 Oct	74	● **WALLS AND BRIDGES** *Apple PCTC 253*	6	10 wks
8 Mar	75	● **ROCK 'N' ROLL** *Apple PCS 7169*	6	28 wks
8 Nov	75	● **SHAVED FISH** *Apple PCS 7173*	8	29 wks
22 Nov	80	★ **DOUBLE FANTASY** *Geffen K 99131★★★★*	1	36 wks
20 Nov	82	★ **THE JOHN LENNON COLLECTION** *Parlophone EMTV 37*	1	42 wks
4 Feb	84	● **MILK AND HONEY** *Polydor POLH 5★★★★*	3	13 wks
8 Mar	86	**LIVE IN NEW YORK CITY** *Parlophone PCS 7031*	55	3 wks
22 Oct	88	**IMAGINE – MUSIC FROM THE MOTION PICTURE** *Parlophone PCSP 722*	64	6 wks

★ *John Lennon and the Plastic Ono Band.*
★★ *John Lennon and the Plastic Ono Band with the Flux Fiddlers.*
★★★ *John and Yoko Lennon with the Plastic Ono Band and Elephant's Memory.*
★★★★ *John Lennon and Yoko Ono.*
Imagine *changed its label credit to Parlophone PAS 10004 between its initial chart run and later runs.* Imagine
– Music From The Motion Picture *includes tracks by the Beatles. See also Beatles; Yoko Ono.*

Julian LENNON *UK, male vocalist* — 20 wks

3 Nov	84	**VALOTTE** *Charisma JLLP 1*	20	15 wks
5 Apr	86	**THE SECRET VALUE OF DAYDREAMING** *Charisma CAS 1171*	93	1 wk
5 Oct	91	**HELP YOURSELF** *Virgin V 2668*	42	4 wks

Annie LENNOX *UK, female vocalist* — 71 wks

18 Apr	92	★ **DIVA** *RCA PD 75326*	1	71 wks

Deke LEONARD
UK, male vocalist/instrumentalist – guitar — 1 wk

13 Apr	74	**KAMIKAZE** *United Artists UAG 29544*	50	1 wk

Paul LEONI *UK, male instrumentalist – pan flute* — 19 wks

24 Sep	83	**FLIGHTS OF FANCY** *Nouveau Music NML 1002*	17	19 wks

LEVEL 42 *UK, male vocal/instrumental group* — 223 wks

29 Aug	81	**LEVEL 42** *Polydor POLS 1036*	20	18 wks
10 Apr	82	**THE EARLY TAPES JULY–AUGUST 1980** *Polydor POLS 1064*	46	6 wks
18 Sep	82	**THE PURSUIT OF ACCIDENTS** *Polydor POLD 5067*	17	16 wks
3 Sep	83	● **STANDING IN THE LIGHT** *Polydor POLD 5110*	9	13 wks
13 Oct	84	**TRUE COLOURS** *Polydor POLH 10*	14	8 wks
6 Jul	85	**A PHYSICAL PRESENCE** *Polydor POLH 23*	28	5 wks
26 Oct	85	● **WORLD MACHINE** *Polydor POLH 25*	3	72 wks
28 Mar	87	● **RUNNING IN THE FAMILY** *Polydor POLH 42*	2	54 wks
1 Oct	88	● **STARING AT THE SUN** *Polydor POLH 50*	2	11 wks
18 Nov	89	● **LEVEL BEST** *Polydor LEVTV 1*	5	15 wks
14 Sep	91	● **GUARANTEED** *RCA PL 75005*	3	5 wks

L
189

LEVELLERS *UK, male vocal/instrumental group* *43 wks*

19 Oct	91	**LEVELLING THE LAND** *China WOL 1022*		14	29 wks
4 Sep	93 ●	**LEVELLERS** *China WOLCD 1034*		2	14 wks

LEVERT *UK, male vocal group* *1 wk*

29 Aug	87	**THE BIG THROWDOWN** *Atlantic 781773–1*		86	1 wk

LEVITATION *UK, male vocal/instrumental group* *1 wk*

16 May	92	**NEED FOR NOT** *Rough Trade R 2862*		45	1 wk

Huey LEWIS and the NEWS
US, male vocal/instrumental group *94 wks*

14 Sep	85	**SPORTS** *Chrysalis CHR 1412*		23	24 wks
20 Sep	86 ●	**FORE!** *Chrysalis CDL 1534*		8	52 wks
6 Aug	88	**SMALL WORLD** *Chrysalis CDL 1622*		12	8 wks
18 May	91	**HARD AT PLAY** *Chrysalis CHR 1847*		39	2 wks
21 Nov	92	**THE HEART OF ROCK 'N' ROLL – BEST OF HUEY LEWIS AND THE NEWS** *Chrysalis CDCHR 1934*		23	8 wks

Jerry Lee LEWIS *US, male vocalist/instrumentalist – piano* *6 wks*

2 Jun	62	**JERRY LEE LEWIS VOL. 2** *London HA 2440*		14	6 wks

L

190

Linda LEWIS *UK, female vocalist* *4 wks*

9 Aug	75	**NOT A LITTLE GIRL ANYMORE** *Arista ARTY 109*		40	4 wks

Ramsey LEWIS TRIO *US, male instrumental trio* *4 wks*

21 May	66	**HANG ON RAMSEY** *Chess CRL 4520*		20	4 wks

LFO *UK, male instrumental group* *2 wks*

3 Aug	91	**FREQUENCIES** *Warp WARPLP 3*		42	2 wks

LIGHT OF THE WORLD
UK, male vocal/instrumental group *1 wk*

24 Jan	81	**ROUND TRIP** *Ensign ENVY 14*		73	1 wk

Gordon LIGHTFOOT *Canada, male vocalist* *2 wks*

20 May	72	**DON QUIXOTE** *Reprise K 44166*		44	1 wk
17 Aug	74	**SUNDOWN** *Reprise K 54020*		45	1 wk

LIGHTNING SEEDS *UK, male vocalist* *3 wks*

10 Feb	90	**CLOUDCUCKOOLAND** *Ghetto GHETT 3*		50	2 wks
18 Apr	92	**SENSE** *Virgin CDV 2690*		53	1 wk

LIL LOUIS *US, male producer* *5 wks*

26 Aug	89	**FRENCH KISSES** *FFRR 828170 1*		35	5 wks

LIMAHL *UK, male vocalist*   *3 wks*

1 Dec 84	**DON'T SUPPOSE** *EMI PLML 1*	63	3 wks

Alison LIMERICK *UK, female vocalist*   *2 wks*

4 Apr 92	**AND STILL I RISE** *Arista 262365*	53	2 wks

LINDISFARNE
UK, male vocal/instrumental group   *118 wks*

30 Oct 71 ★	**FOG ON THE TYNE** *Charisma CAS 1050*	1	56 wks
15 Jan 72 ●	**NICELY OUT OF TUNE** *Charisma CAS 1025*	8	30 wks
30 Sep 72 ●	**DINGLY DELL** *Charisma CAS 1057*	5	10 wks
11 Aug 73	**LINDISFARNE LIVE** *Charisma CLASS 2*	25	6 wks
18 Oct 75	**FINEST HOUR** *Charisma CAS 1108*	55	1 wk
24 Jun 78	**BACK AND FOURTH** *Mercury 9109 609*	22	11 wks
9 Dec 78	**MAGIC IN THE AIR** *Mercury 6641 877*	71	1 wk
23 Oct 82	**SLEEPLESS NIGHT** *LMP GET 1*	59	3 wks

LINX *UK, male vocal/instrumental duo*   *23 wks*

28 Mar 81 ●	**INTUITION** *Chrysalis CHR 1332*	8	19 wks
31 Oct 81	**GO AHEAD** *Chrysalis CHR 1358*	35	4 wks

LIQUID GOLD
UK, male/female vocal/instrumental group   *3 wks*

16 Aug 80	**LIQUID GOLD** *Polo POLP 101*	34	3 wks

LISA – *See WENDY and LISA*

LISA LISA and CULT JAM with FULL FORCE
US, female vocalist with two US, male vocal/instrumental groups   *1 wk*

21 Sep 85	**LISA LISA AND CULT JAM WITH FULL FORCE** *CBS 26593*	96	1 wk

LITTLE ANGELS
UK, male vocal/instrumental group   *11 wks*

2 Mar 91	**YOUNG GODS** *Polydor 8478461*	17	6 wks
6 Feb 93 ★	**JAM** *Polydor 5176422*	1	5 wks

LITTLE FEAT *US, male vocal/instrumental group*   *19 wks*

6 Dec 75	**THE LAST RECORD ALBUM** *Warner Bros. K 56156*	36	3 wks
21 May 77 ●	**TIME LOVES A HERO** *Warner Bros. K 56349*	8	11 wks
11 Mar 78	**WAITING FOR COLUMBUS** *Warner Bros. K 66075*	43	1 wk
1 Dec 79	**DOWN ON THE FARM** *Warner Bros. K 56667*	46	3 wks
8 Aug 81	**HOY HOY** *Warner Bros. K 666100*	76	1 wk

LITTLE STEVEN
US, male vocalist/instrumentalist – guitar   *4 wks*

6 Nov 82	**MEN WITHOUT WOMEN** *EMI America 3027*★	73	2 wks
6 Jun 87	**FREEDOM NO COMPROMISE** *Manhattan MTL 1010*	52	2 wks

★ *Little Steven and the Disciples of Soul.*

L
191

The **Long Ryders** made the list for one week on the back of their minor hit single 'Looking For Lewis And Clark'.

Josef Locke got an unexpected second chart life with the popularity of the film about him, Hear My Song. *(Popperfoto)*

The **Levellers** surpassed the pack of labelmates and chart veterans Dogs D'Amour with their first hit. *(China Records)*

LITTLE VILLAGE *UK/US, male vocal/instrumental group* *4 wks*

| 29 Feb 92 | LITTLE VILLAGE *Reprise 7599267132* .... | 23 | 4 wks |

LIVING COLOR *US, male vocal/instrumental group* *22 wks*

| 15 Sep 90 | TIME'S UP *Epic 4669201* .... | 20 | 19 wks |
| 6 Mar 93 | STAIN *Epic 4728562* .... | 19 | 3 wks |

LIVING IN A BOX *UK, male vocal/instrumental group* *35 wks*

| 9 May 87 | LIVING IN A BOX *Chrysalis CDL 1547* .... | 25 | 19 wks |
| 8 Jul 89 | GATECRASHING *Chrysalis CDI 1676* .... | 21 | 16 wks |

LL COOL J *US, male rapper* *26 wks*

15 Feb 86	RADIO *Def Jam DEF 26745*	71	1 wk
13 Jun 87	BIGGER AND DEFFER *Def Jam 450 515–1*	54	19 wks
8 Jul 89	WALKING WITH A PANTHER *Def Jam 465112 1*	43	3 wks
13 Oct 90	MAMA SAID KNOCK YOU OUT *Def Jam 4673151*	49	2 wks
17 Apr 93	14 SHOTS TO THE DOME *Def Jam 4736782*	74	1 wk

Andrew LLOYD WEBBER
UK, male composer/producer *37 wks*

| 11 Feb 78 ● | VARIATIONS *MCA MCF 2824* .... | 2 | 19 wks |
| 23 Mar 85 ● | REQUIEM *HMV ALW 1* .... | 4 | 18 wks |

Variations features cellist Julian Lloyd Webber. Requiem credits Placido Domingo, Sarah Brightman, Paul Miles-Kingston, Winchester Cathedral Choir and the English Chamber Orchestra conducted by Lorin Maazel.

Julian LLOYD WEBBER *UK, male instrumentalist* *19 wks*

14 Sep 85	PIECES *Polydor PROLP 6*	59	5 wks
21 Feb 87	ELGAR CELLO CONCERTO *Philips 416 354–1*	94	1 wk
27 Oct 90	LLOYD WEBBER PLAYS LLOYD WEBBER		
	Philips 4322911	15	13 wks

First two albums credit the London Symphony Orchestra, third credits the Royal Philharmonic Orchestra. See also the London Symphony Orchestra; Andrew Lloyd Webber; Royal Philharmonic Orchestra.

Los LOBOS *US, male vocal/instrumental group* *9 wks*

| 6 Apr 85 | HOW WILL THE WOLF SURVIVE? *Slash SLMP 3* ...... | 77 | 6 wks |
| 7 Feb 87 | BY THE LIGHT OF THE MOON *Slash SLAP 13* .... | 77 | 3 wks |

Tone LOC *US, male rapper* *16 wks*

| 25 Mar 89 | LOC'ED AFTER DARK *Delicious BRLP 526* .... | 22 | 16 wks |

Josef LOCKE *Ireland, male vocalist* *20 wks*

28 Jun 69	THE WORLD OF JOSEF LOCKE TODAY *Decca SPA 21* .	29	1 wk
21 Mar 92 ●	HEAR MY SONG (THE BEST OF JOSEF LOCKE)		
	EMI CDGO 2034	7	17 wks
27 Jun 92	TAKE A PAIR OF SPARKLING EYES *EMI CDGO 2038* .	41	2 wks

John LODGE *UK, male vocalist/instrumentalist – guitar* *20 wks*

| 29 Mar 75 ● | BLUE JAYS *Threshold THS 12★* .... | 4 | 18 wks |
| 19 Feb 77 | NATURAL AVENUE *Decca TXS 120* .... | 38 | 2 wks |

★ Justin Hayward and John Lodge.

Nils LOFGREN
US, male vocalist/instrumentalist – guitar   *30 wks*

17 Apr	76 ●	**CRY TOUGH** *A & M AMLH 64573*	**8**	11 wks
26 Mar	77	**I CAME TO DANCE** *A & M AMLH 64628*	**30**	4 wks
5 Nov	77	**NIGHT AFTER NIGHT** *A & M AMLH 68439*	**38**	2 wks
26 Sep	81	**NIGHT FADES AWAY** *Backstreet MCF 3121*	**50**	3 wks
1 May	82	**A RHYTHM ROMANCE** *A & M AMLH 68543*	**100**	1 wk
6 Jul	85	**FLIP** *Towerbell TOWLP 11*	**36**	7 wks
5 Apr	86	**CODE OF THE ROAD** *Towerbell TOWDLP 17*	**86**	1 wk
27 Apr	91	**SILVER LINING** *Essential ESSLP 145*	**61**	1 wk

Johnny LOGAN *Ireland, male vocalist*   *1 wk*

22 Aug	87	**HOLD ME NOW** *CBS 451 073–1*	**83**	1 wk

LONDON BOYS *UK, male vocal duo*   *38 wks*

29 Jul	89 ●	**THE TWELVE COMMANDMENTS OF DANCE**		
		WEA WX 278	**2**	38 wks

LONDON PHILHARMONIC CHOIR
UK, choir   *20 wks*

3 Dec	60 ●	**THE MESSIAH** *Pye Golden Guinea GGL 0062★*	**10**	7 wks
13 Nov	76 ●	**SOUND OF GLORY** *Arcade ADEP 25★★*	**10**	10 wks
13 Apr	91	**PRAISE – 18 CHORAL MASTERPIECES**		
		Pop & Arts PATLP 301★★★	**54**	3 wks

★ *London Philharmonic Choir with the London Orchestra conducted by Peter Susskind.*
★★ *London Philharmonic Choir with the National Philharmonic Orchestra conducted by John Aldiss.*
★★★ *London Philharmonic Choir with the National Philharmonic Orchestra.*

LONDON PHILHARMONIC ORCHESTRA
UK, orchestra   *5 wks*

23 Apr	60	**RAVEL'S BOLERO** *London HAV 2189*	**15**	4 wks
8 Apr	61	**VICTORY AT SEA** *Pye GGL 0073*	**12**	1 wk

See also Nigel Kennedy; Ennio Morricone; Justin Hayward.

LONDON SYMPHONY ORCHESTRA
UK, orchestra   *181 wks*

18 Mar	72	**TOP TV THEMES** *Studio Two STWO 372*	**13**	7 wks
16 Dec	72 ●	**THE STRAUSS FAMILY** *Polydor 2659 014★*	**2**	21 wks
5 Jul	75	**MUSIC FROM 'EDWARD VII'** *Polydor 2659 041*	**52**	1 wk
21 Jan	78	**STAR WARS (film soundtrack)** *20th Century BTD 541*	**21**	12 wks
8 Jul	78 ●	**CLASSIC ROCK** *K-Tel ONE 1009*	**3**	39 wks
10 Feb	79	**CLASSIC ROCK – THE SECOND MOVEMENT**		
		K-Tel NE 1039	**26**	8 wks
5 Jan	80	**RHAPSODY IN BLACK** *K-Tel ONE 1063*	**34**	5 wks
1 Aug	81 ●	**CLASSIC ROCK – ROCK CLASSICS** *K-Tel ONE 1123* ..	**5**	23 wks
27 Nov	82	**THE BEST OF CLASSIC ROCK** *K-Tel ONE 1080*	**35**	11 wks
27 Aug	83	**ROCK SYMPHONIES** *K-Tel ONE 1243*	**40**	9 wks
16 Nov	85	**THE POWER OF CLASSIC ROCK** *Portrait PRT 10049* ...	**13**	15 wks
14 Nov	87	**CLASSIC ROCK COUNTDOWN** *CBS MOOD 3*	**32**	16 wks
18 Nov	89	**CLASSIC ROCK – THE LIVING YEARS** *CBS MOOD 9* .	**51**	6 wks
18 Jan	92	**WIND OF CHANGE – CLASSIC ROCK**		
		Columbia MOODCD 19★★	**24**	8 wks

★ *London Symphony Orchestra conducted by Cyril Ornadel.*
★★ *London Symphony Orchestra and the Royal Choral Society*
See also Michael Crawford; Kimera; Julian Lloyd Webber; Spike Milligan.

Trini Lopez (middle right) was one of the artists featured in an unfriendly 1965 Time cover story acknowledging 'that pervasive, durable phenomenon known as rock 'n' roll'.

LONDON WELSH MALE VOICE CHOIR
UK, male choir   *10 wks*

5 Sep	81	**SONGS OF THE VALLEYS** *K-Tel NE 1117*	61	10 wks

LONDONBEAT *UK/US, male vocal/instrumental group*   *6 wks*

13 Oct	90	**IN THE BLOOD** *AnXious ZL 74810*	34	6 wks

LONE JUSTICE *US, male/female vocal/instrumental group*   *5 wks*

6 Jul	85	**LONE JUSTICE** *Geffen GEF 26288*	49	2 wks
8 Nov	86	**SHELTER** *Geffen WX 73*	84	3 wks

LONE STAR *UK, male vocal/instrumental group*   *7 wks*

2 Oct	76	**LONE STAR** *Epic EPC 81545*	47	1 wk
17 Sep	77	**FIRING ON ALL SIX** *CBS 82213*	36	6 wks

LONG RYDERS *US, male vocal/instrumental group*   *1 wk*

16 Nov	85	**STATE OF OUR UNION** *Island ILPS 9802*	66	1 wk

Joe LONGTHORNE *UK, male vocalist – impersonator*   *30 wks*

3 Dec	88	**THE JOE LONGTHORNE SONGBOOK**		
		Telstar STAR 2353	16	12 wks
29 Jul	89	**ESPECIALLY FOR YOU** *Telstar STAR 2365*	22	10 wks
9 Dec	89	**THE JOE LONGTHORNE CHRISTMAS ALBUM**		
		Telstar STAR 2385	44	4 wks
13 Nov	93	**I WISH YOU LOVE** *EMI CDEMC 3662*	47	4 wks

LOOP *UK, male vocal/instrumental group*   *2 wks*

4 Feb	89	**FADE OUT** *Chapter 22 CHAPLP 34*	51	1 wk
3 Feb	90	**A GILDED ETERNITY** *Situation Two SITU 27*	39	1 wk

LOOSE ENDS
UK, male/female vocal/instrumental group   *41 wks*

21 Apr	84	**A LITTLE SPICE** *Virgin V 2301*	46	9 wks
20 Apr	85	**SO WHERE ARE YOU?** *Virgin V 2340*	13	13 wks
18 Oct	86	**ZAGORA** *Virgin V 2384*	15	8 wks
2 Jul	88	**THE REAL CHUCKEEBOO** *Virgin V 2528*	52	4 wks
22 Sep	90	**LOOK HOW LONG** *Ten DIX 94*	19	5 wks
19 Sep	92	**TIGHTEN UP VOL. 1** *Ten DIXCD 112*	40	2 wks

Trini LOPEZ *US, male vocalist*   *42 wks*

26 Oct	63	● **TRINI LOPEZ AT P.J.'S** *Reprise R 6093*	7	25 wks
25 Mar	67	● **TRINI LOPEZ IN LONDON** *Reprise RSLP 6238*	6	17 wks

Jeff LORBER
US, male vocalist/instrumentalist – keyboards   *2 wks*

18 May	85	**STEP BY STEP** *Club JABH 9*	97	2 wks

Sophia LOREN – *See Peter SELLERS*

Joe LOSS   UK, orchestra   10 wks

| 30 Oct 71 | **ALL-TIME PARTY HITS** MFP 5227 .... | 24 | 10 wks |

See also the George Mitchell Minstrels.

LOTUS EATERS   UK, male vocal/instrumental group   1 wk

| 16 Jun 84 | **NO SENSE OF SIN** Sylvan 206 263 .... | 96 | 1 wk |

James LOUGHRAN – See BBC SYMPHONY ORCHESTRA

Jacques LOUSSIER   France, male instrumentalist – piano   3 wks

| 30 Mar 85 | **THE BEST OF PLAY BACH** Start STL 1 .... | 58 | 3 wks |

LOVE   US, male vocal/instrumental group   8 wks

| 24 Feb 68 | **FOREVER CHANGES** Elektra EKS7 4013 .... | 24 | 6 wks |
| 16 May 70 | **OUT HERE** Harvest Show 3/4 .... | 29 | 2 wks |

Geoff LOVE   UK, orchestra   28 wks

7 Aug 71	**BIG WAR MOVIE THEMES** MFP 5171	11	20 wks
21 Aug 71	**BIG WESTERN MOVIE THEMES** MFP 5204	38	3 wks
30 Oct 71	**BIG LOVE MOVIE THEMES** MFP 5221	28	5 wks

See also Manuel and his Music of the Mountains.

Monie LOVE   UK, female rapper   3 wks

| 20 Oct 90 | **DOWN TO EARTH** Cooltempo CTLP 14 .... | 30 | 3 wks |

LOVE AND MONEY
UK, male vocal/instrumental group   2 wks

| 29 Oct 88 | **STRANGE KIND OF LOVE** Fontana SFLP 7 .... | 71 | 1 wk |
| 3 Aug 91 | **DOGS IN THE TRAFFIC** Fontana 8489931 .... | 41 | 1 wk |

LOVE/HATE   US, male vocal/instrumental group   5 wks

| 7 Mar 92 | **WASTED IN AMERICA** Columbia 4694532 .... | 20 | 4 wks |
| 24 Jul 93 | **LET'S RUMBLE** RCA 74321153112 .... | 24 | 1 wk |

Lene LOVICH   US, female vocalist   17 wks

| 17 Mar 79 | **STATELESS** Stiff SEEZ 7 .... | 35 | 11 wks |
| 2 Feb 80 | **FLEX** Stiff SEEZ 19 .... | 19 | 6 wks |

LOVIN' SPOONFUL
US/Canada, male vocal/instrumental group   11 wks

| 7 May 66 ● | **DAYDREAM** Pye NPL 28078 .... | 8 | 11 wks |

Nick LOWE   UK, male vocalist   17 wks

11 Mar 78	**THE JESUS OF COOL** Radar RAD 1	22	9 wks
23 Jun 79	**LABOUR OF LUST** Radar RAD 21	43	6 wks
20 Feb 82	**NICK THE KNIFE** F.Beat XXLP 14	99	2 wks

L
197

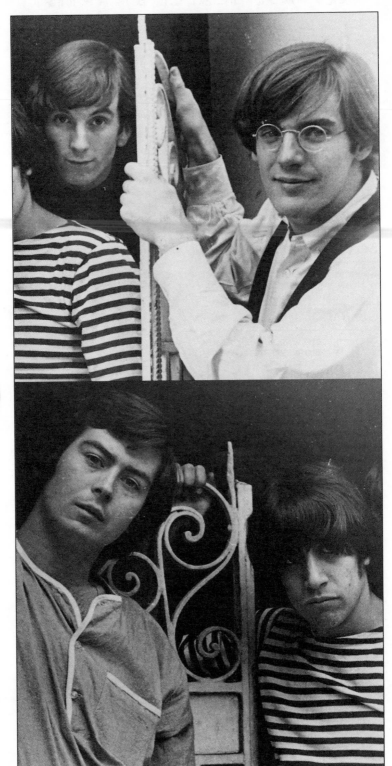

'Creeque Alley' by the Mamas and Papas includes references to Zal Yanovsky (bottom right) and John Sebastian (top right) of the **Lovin' Spoonful**.

L7   US, female vocal/instrumental group   6 wks

| 2 May 92 | **BRICKS ARE HEAVY** Slash 8283072 | 24 | 6 wks |

LULU   UK, female vocalist   7 wks

| 25 Sep 71 | **THE MOST OF LULU** MFP 5215 | 15 | 6 wks |
| 6 Mar 93 | **INDEPENDENCE** Dôme DOMECD 1 | 67 | 1 wk |

Bob LUMAN   US, male vocalist   1 wk

| 14 Jan 61 | **LET'S THINK ABOUT LIVING** Warner Bros. WM 4025 | 18 | 1 wk |

LURKERS   UK, male vocal/instrumental group   1 wk

| 1 Jul 78 | **FULHAM FALLOUT** Beggars Banquet BEGA 2 | 57 | 1 wk |

LUSH   UK, male/female vocal/instrumental group   3 wks

| 8 Feb 92● | **SPOOKY** 4AD CAD 2002CD | 7 | 3 wks |

LYLE – See GALLAGHER and LYLE

Vera LYNN   UK, female vocalist   15 wks

| 21 Nov 81 | **20 FAMILY FAVOURITES** EMI EMTV 28 | 25 | 12 wks |
| 9 Sep 89 | **WE'LL MEET AGAIN** Telstar STAR 2369 | 44 | 3 wks |

Jeff LYNNE   UK, male vocalist   4 wks

| 4 Aug 90 | **ARMCHAIR THEATRE** Reprise WX 347 | 24 | 4 wks |

Philip LYNOTT   Ireland, male vocalist   16 wks

| 26 Apr 80 | **SOLO IN SOHO** Vertigo 9102 038 | 28 | 6 wks |
| 14 Nov 87 | **SOLDIER OF FORTUNE – THE BEST OF PHIL LYNOTT AND THIN LIZZY** Telstar STAR 2300★ | 55 | 10 wks |

★ Phil Lynott and Thin Lizzy.
See also Midge Ure.

LYNYRD SKYNYRD   US, male vocal/instrumental group   19 wks

3 May 75	**NUTHIN' FANCY** MCA MCF 2700	43	1 wk
28 Feb 76	**GIMME BACK MY BULLETS** MCA MCF 2744	34	5 wks
6 Nov 76	**ONE MORE FOR THE ROAD** MCA MCPS 279	17	4 wks
12 Nov 77	**STREET SURVIVORS** MCA MCG 3525	13	4 wks
4 Nov 78	**SKYNYRD'S FIRST AND LAST** MCA MCG 3529	50	1 wk
9 Feb 80	**GOLD AND PLATINUM** MCA MCSP 308	49	4 wks

L
199

M PEOPLE UK, male/female vocal/instrumental group 13 wks

6 Mar 93	**NORTHERN SOUL** *Deconstruction 74321117772*	**53**	2 wks
16 Oct 93 ●	**ELEGANT SLUMMING** *Deconstruction 74321166782*	**2†**	11 wks

Lorin MAAZEL – *See Andrew LLOYD WEBBER*

MAC BAND featuring the McCAMPBELL BROTHERS US, male vocal group 3 wks

20 Aug 88	**THE MAC BAND** *MCA MCC 6032*	**61**	3 wks

Frankie McBRIDE Ireland, male vocalist 3 wks

17 Feb 68	**FRANKIE McBRIDE** *Emerald SLD 28*	**29**	3 wks

MACC LADS UK, male vocal/instrumental group 1 wk

7 Oct 89	**FROM BEER TO ETERNITY** *Hectic House HHLP 12*	**72**	1 wk

McCAMPBELL BROTHERS – *See MAC BAND featuring the McCAMPBELL BROTHERS*

Paul McCARTNEY
UK, male vocalist/multi-instrumentalist 522 wks

2 May 70 ●	**McCARTNEY** *Apple PCS 7102*	**2**	32 wks
5 Jun 71 ★	**RAM** *Apple PAS 10003★*	**1**	24 wks
18 Dec 71	**WILD LIFE** *Apple PCS 7142★★*	**11**	9 wks
19 May 73 ●	**RED ROSE SPEEDWAY** *Apple PCTC 251★★★*	**5**	16 wks
15 Dec 73 ★	**BAND ON THE RUN** *Apple PAS 10007★★★*	**1**	124 wks
21 Jun 75 ★	**VENUS AND MARS** *Apple PCTC 254★★*	**1**	29 wks
17 Apr 76 ●	**WINGS AT THE SPEED OF SOUND** *Apple PAS 10010★★* .	**2**	35 wks
15 Jan 77 ●	**WINGS OVER AMERICA** *Parlophone PAS 720★★*	**8**	22 wks
15 Apr 78 ●	**LONDON TOWN** *Parlophone PAS 10012★★*	**4**	23 wks
16 Dec 78 ●	**WINGS GREATEST HITS** *Parlophone PCTC 256★★*	**5**	32 wks
23 Jun 79 ●	**BACK TO THE EGG** *Parlophone PCTC 257★★*	**6**	15 wks
31 May 80 ★	**McCARTNEY II** *Parlophone PCTC 258*	**1**	18 wks
7 Mar 81	**McCARTNEY INTERVIEW** *EMI CHAT 1*	**34**	4 wks
8 May 82 ★	**TUG OF WAR** *Parlophone PCTC 259*	**1**	27 wks
12 Nov 83 ●	**PIPES OF PEACE** *Parlophone PCTC 1652301*	**4**	23 wks
3 Nov 84 ★	**GIVE MY REGARDS TO BROAD STREET**		
	Parlophone PCTC 2	**1**	21 wks
13 Sep 86 ●	**PRESS TO PLAY** *Parlophone PCSD 103*	**8**	6 wks
14 Nov 87 ●	**ALL THE BEST!** *Parlophone PMTV 1*	**2**	21 wks
17 Jun 89 ★	**FLOWERS IN THE DIRT** *Parlophone PCSD 106*	**1**	20 wks
17 Nov 90	**TRIPPING THE LIVE FANTASTIC** *Parlophone PCST 7346*	**17**	11 wks
1 Jun 91 ●	**UNPLUGGED – THE OFFICIAL BOOTLEG**		
	Parlophone PCSD 116	**7**	3 wks
12 Oct 91	**CHOBA B CCCP (THE RUSSIAN ALBUM)**		
	Parlophone CDPCSD 117	**63**	1 wk
13 Feb 93 ●	**OFF THE GROUND** *Parlophone CDPCSD 125*	**5**	4 wks
20 Nov 93	**PAUL IS LIVE** *Parlophone PDPCSD 147*	**34**	2 wks

★ *Paul and Linda McCartney.* ★★ *Wings.* ★★★ *Paul McCartney and Wings.*

Kirsty MacCOLL UK, female vocalist 20 wks

20 May 89	**KITE** *Virgin KMLP 1*	**34**	12 wks
6 Jul 91	**ELECTRIC LANDLADY** *Virgin V 2663*	**17**	8 wks

Van McCOY and the SOUL CITY SYMPHONY
US, orchestra   11 wks

5 Jul 75	**DISCO BABY** Avco 9109 004	**32**	11 wks

George McCRAE US, male vocalist   29 wks

3 Aug 74	**ROCK YOUR BABY** Jayboy JSL 3	**13**	28 wks
13 Sep 75	**GEORGE McCRAE** Jayboy JSL 10	**54**	1 wk

Ian McCULLOCH UK, male vocalist   4 wks

7 Oct 89	**CANDLELAND** WEA WX 303	**18**	3 wks
21 Mar 92	**MYSTERIO** East West 9031762642	**46**	1 wk

Michael McDONALD US, male vocalist   39 wks

22 Nov 86 ●	**SWEET FREEDOM: BEST OF MICHAEL McDONALD**		
	Warner Bros. WX 67	**6**	35 wks
26 May 90	**TAKE IT TO HEART** Reprise WX 285	**35**	4 wks

Bobby McFERRIN US, male vocalist   1 wk

29 Oct 88	**SIMPLE PLEASURES** Manhattan MTL 1018	**92**	1 wk

Kate and Anna McGARRIGLE
Canada, female vocal duo   4 wks

26 Feb 77	**DANCER WITH BRUISED KNEES** Warner Bros. K 56356 .	**35**	4 wks

Mary MacGREGOR US, female vocalist   1 wk

23 Apr 77	**TORN BETWEEN TWO LOVERS**		
	Ariola America AAS 1504	**59**	1 wk

McGUINNESS FLINT UK, male vocal/instrumental group 10 wks

23 Jan 71 ●	**McGUINNESS FLINT** Capitol EA–ST 22625	**9**	10 wks

Duff McKAGAN US, male vocalist/instrumentalist – bass 2 wks

9 Oct 93	**BELIEVE IN ME** Geffen GED 24605	**27**	2 wks

Maria McKEE US, female vocalist   6 wks

24 Jun 89	**MARIA McKEE** Geffen WX 270	**49**	3 wks
12 Jun 93	**YOU GOTTA SIN TO GET SAVED** Geffen GED 24508 ..	**26**	3 wks

Kenneth McKELLAR UK, male vocalist   10 wks

28 Jun 69	**THE WORLD OF KENNETH McKELLAR** Decca SPA 11	**27**	7 wks
31 Jan 70	**ECCO DI NAPOLI** Decca SKL 5018	**45**	3 wks

Craig McLACHLAN and CHECK 1–2
Australia, male vocal/instrumental group   11 wks

21 Jul 90 ●	**CRAIG McLACHLAN AND CHECK 1–2** Epic 4663471 ...	**10**	11 wks

Malcolm McLAREN UK, *male vocalist*   *40 wks*

4 Jun	83	**DUCK ROCK** *Charisma MMLP 1*		**18**	17 wks
26 May	84	**WOULD YA LIKE MORE SCRATCHIN'**			
		Charisma CLAM 1★		**44**	4 wks
29 Dec	84	**FANS** *Charisma MMDL 2*		**47**	8 wks
15 Jul	89	**WALTZ DANCING** *Epic 460736 1★★*		**30**	11 wks

★ *Malcolm McLaren and the World's Famous Supreme Team.*
★★ *Malcolm McLaren and the Bootzilla Orchestra.*

Mahavishnu John McLAUGHLIN – *See Carlos SANTANA; MAHAVISHNU ORCHESTRA*

Don McLEAN US, *male vocalist*   *89 wks*

11 Mar	72 ●	**AMERICAN PIE** *United Artists UAS 29285*		**3**	54 wks
17 Jun	72	**TAPESTRY** *United Artists UAS 29350*		**16**	12 wks
24 Nov	73	**PLAYIN' FAVORITES** *United Artists UAG 29528*		**42**	2 wks
14 Jun	80	**CHAIN LIGHTNING** *EMI International INS 3025*		**19**	9 wks
27 Sep	80 ●	**THE VERY BEST OF DON McLEAN**			
		United Artists UAG 30314		**4**	12 wks

Ian McNABB UK, *male vocalist*   *1 wk*

30 Jan	93	**TRUTH AND BEAUTY** *This Way Up 5143782*		**51**	1 wk

Rita MacNEIL Canada, *female vocalist*   *4 wks*

24 Nov	90	**REASON TO BELIEVE** *Polydor 8471061*		**32**	4 wks

M
202

Ian McSHANE UK, *male vocalist*   *7 wks*

21 Nov	92	**FROM BOTH SIDES NOW** *PolyGram TV 5176192*		**40**	7 wks

Ralph McTELL UK, *male vocalist*   *17 wks*

18 Nov	72	**NOT TILL TOMORROW** *Reprise K 44210*		**36**	1 wk
2 Mar	74	**EASY** *Reprise K 54013*		**31**	4 wks
15 Feb	75	**STREETS** *Warner Bros. K 56105*		**13**	12 wks

Christine McVIE UK, *female vocalist*   *4 wks*

11 Feb	84	**CHRISTINE McVIE** *Warner Bros. 92 5059*		**58**	4 wks

David McWILLIAMS UK, *male vocalist*   *9 wks*

10 Jun	67	**DAVID McWILLIAMS SINGS** *Major Minor MMLP 2*		**38**	2 wks
4 Nov	67	**DAVID McWILLIAMS VOL. 2** *Major Minor MMLP 10*		**23**	6 wks
9 Mar	68	**DAVID McWILLIAMS VOL. 3** *Major Minor MMLP 11*		**39**	1 wk

MADNESS UK, *male vocal/instrumental group*   *358 wks*

3 Nov	79 ●	**ONE STEP BEYOND** *Stiff SEEZ 17*		**2**	78 wks
4 Oct	80 ●	**ABSOLUTELY** *Stiff SEEZ 29*		**2**	46 wks
10 Oct	81 ●	**MADNESS 7** *Stiff SEEZ 39*		**5**	29 wks
1 May	82 ★	**COMPLETE MADNESS** *Stiff HIT-TV 1*		**1**	88 wks
13 Nov	82 ●	**THE RISE AND FALL** *Stiff SEEZ 46*		**10**	22 wks
3 Mar	84 ●	**KEEP MOVING** *Stiff SEEZ 53*		**6**	19 wks
12 Oct	85	**MAD NOT MAD** *Zarjazz JZLP 1*		**16**	9 wks
6 Dec	86	**UTTER MADNESS** *Zarjazz JZLP 2*		**29**	8 wks
7 May	88	**THE MADNESS** *Virgin V 2507*		**65**	1 wk
7 Mar	92 ★	**DIVINE MADNESS** *Virgin CDV 2692*		**1**	49 wks
14 Nov	92	**MADSTOCK** *Go! Discs 8283672*		**22**	9 wks

MADONNA US, female vocalist — 604 wks

11 Feb	84 ●	MADONNA/THE FIRST ALBUM Sire 923867	6	123 wks
24 Nov	84 ★	LIKE A VIRGIN Sire 925157	1	152 wks
12 Jul	86 ★	TRUE BLUE Sire WX 54	1	81 wks
28 Nov	87 ●	YOU CAN DANCE Sire WX 76	5	14 wks
1 Apr	89 ★	LIKE A PRAYER Sire WX 239	1	65 wks
2 Jun	90 ●	I'M BREATHLESS Sire WX 351	2	20 wks
24 Nov	90 ★	THE IMMACULATE COLLECTION Sire WX 370	1	111 wks
24 Oct	92 ●	EROTICA Maverick 9362450312	2	38 wks

From 22 Aug 85 Madonna was repackaged as The First Album *Sire WX 22.* Like A Virgin *changed label number to SIRE WX 20 during its chart run.*

MAGAZINE UK, male vocal/instrumental group — 24 wks

24 Jun	78	REAL LIFE Virgin V 2100	29	8 wks
14 Apr	79	SECONDHAND DAYLIGHT Virgin V 2121	38	8 wks
10 May	80	CORRECT USE OF SOAP Virgin V 2156	28	4 wks
13 Dec	80	PLAY Virgin V 2184	69	1 wk
27 Jun	81	MAGIC, MURDER AND THE WEATHER Virgin V 2200 .	39	3 wks

MAGIC BAND – See CAPTAIN BEEFHEART and his MAGIC BAND

MAGNA CARTA UK, male vocal/instrumental group — 2 wks

8 Aug	70	SEASONS Vertigo 6360 003	55	2 wks

M
203

MAGNUM UK, male vocal/instrumental group — 46 wks

16 Sep	78	KINGDOM OF MADNESS Jet JETLP 210	58	1 wk
19 Apr	80	MARAUDER Jet JETLP 230	34	5 wks
6 Mar	82	CHASE THE DRAGON Jet JETLP 235	17	7 wks
21 May	83	THE ELEVENTH HOUR Jet JETLP 240	38	4 wks
25 May	85	ON A STORYTELLER'S NIGHT FM WKFM LP 34	24	7 wks
4 Oct	86	VIGILANTE Polydor POLD 5198	24	5 wks
9 Apr	88 ●	WINGS OF HEAVEN Polydor POLD 5221	5	9 wks
21 Jul	90 ●	GOODNIGHT L.A. Polydor 8435681	9	5 wks
14 Sep	91	THE SPIRIT Polydor 5111691	50	1 wk
24 Oct	92	SLEEPWALKING Music For Nations CDMFN 143	27	2 wks

MAHAVISHNU ORCHESTRA
UK/US, male instrumental group — 14 wks

31 Mar	73	BIRDS OF FIRE CBS 65321	20	5 wks
28 Jul	73 ●	LOVE DEVOTION SURRENDER CBS 69037★	7	9 wks

★ Carlos Santana and Mahavishnu John McLaughlin.

MAI TAI Holland, female vocal group — 1 wk

6 Jul	85	HISTORY Virgin V 2359	91	1 wk

MAJESTICS UK, male/female vocal group — 4 wks

4 Apr	87	TUTTI FRUTTI BBC REN 629	64	4 wks

Tommy MAKEM – See CLANCY BROTHERS and Tommy MAKEM

Timmy MALLETT – See BOMBALURINA featuring Timmy MALLETT

Yngwie J. MALMSTEEN
Sweden, male instrumentalist – guitar   *11 wks*

21 May 88	**ODYSSEY** *Polydor POLD 5224*	**27**	7 wks
4 Nov 89	**TRIAL BY FIRE – LIVE IN LENINGRAD** *Polydor 839726 1*	**65**	1 wk
28 Apr 90	**ECLIPSE** *Polydor 8434611*	**43**	2 wks
29 Feb 92	**FIRE AND ICE** *Elektra 7559611372*	**57**	1 wk

MAMA'S BOYS *Ireland, male vocal/instrumental group*   *4 wks*

6 Apr 85	**POWER AND PASSION** *Jive HIP 24*	**55**	4 wks

MAMAS and PAPAS *US, male/female vocal group*   *61 wks*

25 Jun 66 ●	**THE MAMAS AND PAPAS** *RCA Victor RD 7803*	**3**	18 wks
28 Jan 67	**CASS, JOHN, MICHELLE, DENNY** *RCA Victor SF 7639* .	**24**	6 wks
24 Jun 67 ●	**MAMAS AND PAPAS DELIVER** *RCA Victor SF 7880*	**4**	22 wks
26 Apr 69 ●	**HITS OF GOLD** *Stateside S 5007*	**7**	2 wks
18 Jun 77 ●	**THE BEST OF THE MAMAS AND PAPAS** *Arcade ADEP 30*	**6**	13 wks

MAN *UK, male vocal/instrumental group*   *11 wks*

20 Oct 73	**BACK INTO THE FUTURE** *United Artists UAD 60053/4* ..	**23**	3 wks
25 May 74	**RHINOS WINOS AND LUNATICS** *United Artists UAG 29631*	**24**	4 wks
11 Oct 75	**MAXIMUM DARKNESS** *United Artists UAG 29872*	**25**	2 wks
17 Apr 76	**WELSH CONNECTION** *MCA MCF 2753*	**40**	2 wks

MANCHESTER BOYS CHOIR *UK, male choir*   *2 wks*

21 Dec 85	**THE NEW SOUND OF CHRISTMAS** *K-Tel ONE 1314* ..	**80**	2 wks

Henry MANCINI *US, orchestra/chorus*   *23 wks*

16 Oct 76	**HENRY MANCINI** *Arcade ADEP 24*	**26**	8 wks
30 Jun 84	**MAMMA** *Decca 411959★*	**96**	1 wk
8 Dec 84	**IN THE PINK** *RCA Red Seal RL 85315★★*	**62**	6 wks
13 Dec 86	**THE HOLLYWOOD MUSICALS** *CBS 4502581★★★*	**46**	8 wks

★ *Luciano Pavarotti with the Henry Mancini Orchestra.*
★★ *James Galway and Henry Mancini and the National Philharmonic Orchestra.*
★★★ *Johnny Mathis and Henry Mancini.*

MANFRED MANN
South Africa/UK, male vocal/instrumental group   *100 wks*

19 Sep 64 ●	**FIVE FACES OF MANFRED MANN** *HMV CLP 1731* ...	**3**	24 wks
23 Oct 65 ●	**MANN MADE** *HMV CLP 1911*	**7**	11 wks
17 Sep 66	**MANN MADE HITS** *HMV CLP 3559*	**11**	18 wks
29 Oct 66	**AS IS** *Fontana TL 5377*	**22**	4 wks
21 Jan 67	**SOUL OF MANN** *HMV CSD 3594*	**40**	1 wk
17 Jun 78	**WATCH** *Bronze BRON 507★*	**33**	6 wks
24 Mar 79	**ANGEL STATION** *Bronze BRON 516★*	**30**	8 wks
15 Sep 79 ●	**SEMI-DETACHED SUBURBAN** *EMI EMTV 19*	**9**	14 wks
26 Feb 83	**SOMEWHERE IN AFRIKA** *Bronze BRON 543★*	**87**	1 wk
18 Sep 86 ●	**THE ROARING SILENCE** *Bronze ILPS 9357★*	**10**	9 wks
23 Jan 93	**AGES OF MANN** *PolyGram TV 5143622*	**23**	4 wks

★ *Manfred Mann's Earth Band.*

The bare feet of **Paul McCartney**, first seen on an album cover in 1969 (the Beatles' Abbey Road), reappeared in 1993 on the front of Hope Of Deliverance.

In an excellent example of successful target marketing, five of the eight **Barry Manilow** hits released during 1979–83 were repackaged or retitled American material.

Manfred Mann gets suburban at his Blackheath home. (Pictorial Press)

MANHATTAN TRANSFER
US, male/female vocal group   *85 wks*

12 Mar	77		COMING OUT	Atlantic K 50291	12	20 wks
19 Mar	77		MANHATTAN TRANSFER	Atlantic K 50138	49	7 wks
25 Feb	78	●	PASTICHE	Atlantic K 50444	10	34 wks
11 Nov	78	●	LIVE	Atlantic K 50540	4	17 wks
17 Nov	79		EXTENSIONS	Atlantic K 50674	63	3 wks
18 Feb	84		BODIES AND SOULS	Atlantic 780104	53	4 wks

MANHATTANS   *US, male vocal group*   *3 wks*

14 Aug	76	MANHATTANS	CBS 81513	37	3 wks

MANIC STREET PREACHERS
UK, male vocal/instrumental group   *21 wks*

22 Feb	92		GENERATION TERRORISTS	Columbia 4710602	13	10 wks
3 Jul	93	●	GOLD AGAINST THE SOUL	Columbia 4640642	8	11 wks

Barry MANILOW   *US, male vocalist*   *333 wks*

23 Sep	78		EVEN NOW	Arista SPART 1047	12	28 wks
3 Mar	79	●	MANILOW MAGIC	Arista ARTV 2	3	151 wks
20 Oct	79		ONE VOICE	Arista SPART 1106	18	7 wks
29 Nov	80	●	BARRY	Arista DLART 2	5	34 wks
25 Apr	81		GIFT SET	Arista BOX 1	62	1 wk
3 Oct	81	●	IF I SHOULD LOVE AGAIN	Arista BMAN 1	5	26 wks
1 May	82	★	BARRY LIVE IN BRITAIN	Arista ARTV 4	1	23 wks
27 Nov	82	●	I WANNA DO IT WITH YOU	Arista BMAN 2	7	9 wks
8 Oct	83	●	A TOUCH MORE MAGIC	Arista BMAN 3	10	12 wks
1 Dec	84		2.00 AM PARADISE CAFE	Arista 206 496	28	6 wks
16 Nov	85		MANILOW	RCA PL 87044	40	6 wks
20 Feb	88		SWING STREET	Arista 208860	81	1 wk
20 May	89		SONGS TO MAKE THE WHOLE WORLD SING Arista 209927		20	4 wks
17 Mar	90		LIVE ON BROADWAY	Arista 303785	19	3 wks
30 Jun	90		SONGS 1975–1990	Arista 303868	13	7 wks
2 Nov	91		SHOWSTOPPERS	Arista 212091	53	3 wks
3 Apr	93		HIDDEN TREASURES	Arista 74321135682	36	7 wks
27 Nov	93		THE PLATINUM COLLECTION	Arista 74321175452	37†	5 wks

Aimee MANN   *US, female vocalist*   *1 wk*

18 Sep	93	WHATEVER	Imago 72787210172	39	1 wk

Roberto MANN   *UK, male orchestra leader*   *9 wks*

9 Dec	67	GREAT WALTZES	Deram SML 1010	19	9 wks

Shelley MANNE   *US, male instrumentalist – drums*   *1 wk*

18 Jun	60	MY FAIR LADY	Vogue LAC 12100	20	1 wk

MANOWAR   *US, male vocal/instrumental group*   *3 wks*

18 Feb	84	HAIL TO ENGLAND	Music For Nations MFN 19	83	2 wks
6 Oct	84	SIGN OF THE HAMMER	10 DIX 10	73	1 wk

M 206

MANTOVANI *UK, orchestra*   *151 wks*

21 Feb 59 ●	**CONTINENTAL ENCORES** *Decca LK 4298*	**4**	12 wks
18 Feb 61	**CONCERT SPECTACULAR** *Decca LK 4377*	**16**	2 wks
16 Apr 66 ●	**MANTOVANI MAGIC** *Decca LK 7949*	**3**	15 wks
15 Oct 66	**MR MUSIC – MANTOVANI** *Decca LK 4809*	**24**	3 wks
14 Jan 67 ●	**MANTOVANI'S GOLDEN HITS** *Decca SKL 4818*	**10**	43 wks
30 Sep 67	**HOLLYWOOD** *Decca SKL 4887*	**37**	1 wk
14 Jun 69 ●	**THE WORLD OF MANTOVANI** *Decca SPA 1*	**6**	31 wks
4 Oct 69 ●	**THE WORLD OF MANTOVANI VOL. 2** *Decca SPA 36* ..	**4**	19 wks
16 May 70	**MANTOVANI TODAY** *Decca SKL 5003*	**16**	8 wks
26 Feb 72	**TO LOVERS EVERYWHERE** *Decca SKL 5112*	**44**	1 wk
3 Nov 79 ●	**20 GOLDEN GREATS** *Warwick WW 5067*	**9**	13 wks
16 Mar 85	**MANTOVANI MAGIC** *Telstar STAR 2237★*	**52**	3 wks

★ *Mantovani Orchestra conducted by Roland Shaw.*

MANTRONIX *Jamaica/US, male vocal/instrumental duo*   *17 wks*

29 Mar 86	**THE ALBUM** *10 DIX 37*	**45**	3 wks
13 Dec 86	**MUSICAL MADNESS** *10 DIX 50*	**66**	3 wks
2 Apr 88	**IN FULL EFFECT** *10 DIX 74*	**39**	3 wks
17 Feb 90	**THIS SHOULD MOVE YA** *Capitol EST 2117*	**18**	6 wks
30 Mar 91	**THE INCREDIBLE SOUND MACHINE** *Capitol EST 2139*	**36**	2 wks

MANUEL and his MUSIC OF THE MOUNTAINS
UK, orchestra conductor Geoff Love   *38 wks*

10 Sep 60	**MUSIC OF THE MOUNTAINS** *Columbia 33SX 1212*	**17**	1 wk
7 Aug 71	**THIS IS MANUEL** *Studio Two STWO 5*	**18**	19 wks
31 Jan 76 ●	**CARNIVAL** *Studio Two TWO 337*	**3**	18 wks

See also Geoff Love.

Phil MANZANERA
UK, male vocalist/instrumentalist – guitar   *1 wk*

24 May 75	**DIAMOND HEAD** *Island ILPS 9315*	**40**	1 wk

MARC AND THE MAMBAS – *See Marc ALMOND*

MARILLION *UK, male vocal/instrumental group*   *153 wks*

26 Mar 83 ●	**SCRIPT FOR A JESTER'S TEAR** *EMI EMC 3429*	**7**	31 wks
24 Mar 84 ●	**FUGAZI** *EMI EMC 2400851*	**5**	20 wks
17 Nov 84 ●	**REAL TO REEL** *EMI JEST 1*	**8**	21 wks
29 Jun 85 ★	**MISPLACED CHILDHOOD** *EMI MRL 2*	**1**	41 wks
4 Jul 87 ●	**CLUTCHING AT STRAWS** *EMI EMD 1002*	**2**	15 wks
23 Jul 88	**B SIDES THEMSELVES** *EMI EMS 1295*	**64**	6 wks
10 Dec 88	**THE THIEVING MAGPIE** *EMI MARIL 1*	**25**	6 wks
7 Oct 89 ●	**SEASON'S END** *EMI EMD 1011 22*	**7**	4 wks
6 Jul 91 ●	**HOLIDAYS IN EDEN** *EMI EMD 1022*	**7**	7 wks
20 Jun 92	**A SINGLES COLLECTION 1982–1992** *EMI CDEMD 1033* .	**27**	2 wks

Yannis MARKOPOULOS *Greece, orchestra*   *8 wks*

26 Aug 78	**WHO PAYS THE FERRYMAN** *BBC REB 315*	**22**	8 wks

Marky MARK and the FUNKY BUNCH
US, male vocalist and dancers   *1 wk*

5 Oct 91	**MUSIC FOR THE PEOPLE** *Interscope 7567917371*	**61**	1 wk

M
207

Bob MARLEY and the WAILERS
Jamaica, male vocal/instrumental group   *374 wks*

4 Oct 75	**NATTY DREAD** *Island ILPS 9281*	43	5 wks
20 Dec 75	**LIVE** *Island ILPS 9376*	38	11 wks
8 May 76	**RASTAMAN VIBRATION** *Island ILPS 9383*	15	13 wks
11 Jun 77 ●	**EXODUS** *Island ILPS 9498*	8	56 wks
1 Apr 78 ●	**KAYA** *Island ILPS 9517*	4	24 wks
16 Dec 78	**BABYLON BY BUS** *Island ISLD 11*	40	11 wks
13 Oct 79	**SURVIVAL** *Island ILPS 9542*	20	6 wks
28 Jun 80 ●	**UPRISING** *Island ILPS 9596*	6	17 wks
28 May 83 ●	**CONFRONTATION** *Island ILPS 9760*	5	19 wks
19 May 84 ★	**LEGEND** *Tuff Gong BMWX 1*	1	204 wks
28 Jul 86	**REBEL MUSIC** *Island ILPS 9843*	54	3 wks
3 Oct 92 ●	**SONGS OF FREEDOM** *Tuff Gong TGCBX 1*	10	5 wks

Live *Island ILPS 9376 returned to the chart in 1981 under the title* Live At The Lyceum.

Neville MARRINER and the ACADEMY OF ST. MARTIN IN THE FIELDS
UK, male conductor with chamber orchestra   *6 wks*

6 Apr 85	**AMADEUS (film soundtrack)** *London LONDP 6*	64	6 wks

Bernie MARSDEN *UK, male vocalist/instrumentalist – guitar*   *2 wks*

5 Sep 81	**LOOK AT ME NOW** *Parlophone PCF 7217*	71	2 wks

M
208

Lena MARTELL *UK, female vocalist*   *71 wks*

25 May 74	**THAT WONDERFUL SOUND OF LENA MARTELL** *Pye SPL 18427*	35	2 wks
8 Jan 77	**THE BEST OF LENA MARTELL** *Pye NSPL 18506*	13	16 wks
27 May 78	**THE LENA MARTELL COLLECTION** *Ronco RTL 2028* ..	12	19 wks
20 Oct 79 ●	**LENA'S MUSIC ALBUM** *Pye N 123*	5	18 wks
19 Apr 80 ●	**BY REQUEST** *Ronco RTL 2046*	9	9 wks
29 Nov 80	**BEAUTIFUL SUNDAY** *Ronco RTL 2052*	23	7 wks

MARTHA and the MUFFINS
Canada, male/female vocal/instrumental group   *6 wks*

15 Mar 80	**METRO MUSIC** *DinDisc DID 1*	34	6 wks

MARTIKA *US, female vocalist*   *52 wks*

16 Sep 89	**MARTIKA** *CBS 463355 1*	11	37 wks
7 Sep 91	**MARTIKA'S KITCHEN** *Columbia 4671891*	15	15 wks

Dean MARTIN *US, male vocalist*   *25 wks*

13 May 61	**THIS TIME I'M SWINGING** *Capitol T 1442*	18	1 wk
25 Feb 67	**AT EASE WITH DEAN** *Reprise RSLP 6322*	35	1 wk
4 Nov 67	**WELCOME TO MY WORLD** *Reprise DBL 001*	39	1 wk
12 Oct 68	**GREATEST HITS VOL. 1** *Reprise RSLP 6301*	40	1 wk
22 Feb 69 ●	**BEST OF DEAN MARTIN** *Capitol ST 21194*	9	1 wk
22 Feb 69 ●	**GENTLE ON MY MIND** *Reprise RSLP 6330*	9	8 wks
27 Nov 71	**WHITE CHRISTMAS** *MFP 524★*	45	1 wk
13 Nov 76 ●	**20 ORIGINAL DEAN MARTIN HITS** *Reprise K 54066* ...	7	11 wks

★ *Nat 'King' Cole and Dean Martin.*

George MARTIN ORCHESTRA – *See* BEATLES

Juan MARTIN and the ROYAL PHILHARMONIC ORCHESTRA
Spain, male instrumentalist – guitar with UK, orchestra   9 wks

11 Feb 84	**SERENADE** *K-Tel NE 1267*	21	9 wks

See also Royal Philharmonic Orchestra.

John MARTYN UK, male vocalist/instrumentalist – guitar   25 wks

4 Feb 78	**ONE WORLD** *Island ILPS 9492*	54	1 wk
1 Nov 80	**GRACE AND DANGER** *Island ILPS 9560*	54	2 wks
26 Sep 81	**GLORIOUS FOOL** *Geffen K 99178*	25	7 wks
4 Sep 82	**WELL KEPT SECRET** *WEA K 99255*	20	7 wks
17 Nov 84	**SAPPHIRE** *Island ILPS 9779*	57	2 wks
8 Mar 86	**PIECE BY PIECE** *Island ILPS 9807*	28	4 wks
10 Oct 92	**COULDN'T LOVE YOU MORE** *Permanent PERMCD 9* ..	65	2 wks

Hank MARVIN UK, male vocalist/instrumentalist – guitar   21 wks

22 Nov 69	**HANK MARVIN** *Columbia SCX 6352*	14	2 wks
20 Mar 82	**WORDS AND MUSIC** *Polydor POLD 5054*	66	3 wks
31 Oct 92	**INTO THE LIGHT** *Polydor 5171482*	18	10 wks
20 Nov 93	**HEARTBEAT** *PolyGram TV 52132222*	23†	6 wks

See also Marvin, Welch and Farrar.

MARVIN, WELCH and FARRAR
UK, male vocal/instrumental group   4 wks

3 Apr 71	**MARVIN, WELCH AND FARRAR** *Regal Zonophone SRZA 8502*	30	4 wks

See also Hank Marvin.

MARY JANE GIRLS US, female vocal group   9 wks

28 May 83	**MARY JANE GIRLS** *Gordy STML 12189*	51	9 wks

Richard MARX US, male vocalist   34 wks

9 Apr 88	**RICHARD MARX** *Manhattan MTL 1017*	68	2 wks
20 May 89 ●	**REPEAT OFFENDER** *EMI-USA MTL 1043*	8	12 wks
16 Nov 91 ●	**RUSH STREET** *Capitol ESTU 2158*	7	20 wk

MARXMAN Ireland/UK, male rap group   1 wk

3 Apr 93	**33 REVOLUTIONS PER MINUTE** *Talkin Loud 5145382* ..	69	1 wk

MASSED WELSH CHOIRS UK, male voice choir   7 wks

9 Aug 69	**CYMANSA GANN** *BBC REC 53 M*	5	7 wks

MASSIVE ATTACK
UK, male/female vocal/instrumental group   16 wks

20 Apr 91	**BLUE LINES** *Wild Bunch WBRLP 1*	13	16 wks

MASTERMIXERS – *See JIVE BUNNY and the MASTERMIXERS*

MATCHBOX UK, male vocal/instrumental group   14 wks

2 Feb 80	**MATCHBOX** *Magnet MAG 5031*	44	5 wks
11 Oct 80	**MIDNITE DYNAMOS** *Magnet MAG 5036*	23	9 wks

M
209

Mireille MATHIEU *France, female vocalist*   *1 wk*

2 Mar 68	MIREILLE MATHIEU *Columbia SCX 6210*	39	1 wk

Johnny MATHIS *US, male vocalist*   *228 wks*

8 Nov 58 ●	WARM *Fontana TBA TFL 5015*	6	2 wks
24 Jan 59 ●	SWING SOFTLY *Fontana TBA TFL 5039*	10	1 wk
13 Feb 60 ●	RIDE ON A RAINBOW *Fontana TFL 5061*	10	2 wks
10 Dec 60 ●	RHYTHMS AND BALLADS OF BROADWAY *Fontana SET 101*	6	10 wks
17 Jun 61	I'LL BUY YOU A STAR *Fontana TFL 5143*	18	1 wk
16 May 70	RAINDROPS KEEP FALLING ON MY HEAD *CBS 63587*	23	10 wks
3 Apr 71	LOVE STORY *CBS 64334*	27	5 wks
9 Sep 72	FIRST TIME EVER I SAW YOUR FACE *CBS 64930* ...	40	3 wks
16 Dec 72	MAKE IT EASY ON YOURSELF *CBS 65161*	49	1 wk
8 Mar 75	I'M COMING HOME *CBS 65690*	18	11 wks
5 Apr 75	THE HEART OF A WOMAN *CBS 80533*	39	2 wks
26 Jul 75	WHEN WILL I SEE YOU AGAIN *CBS 80738*	13	10 wks
3 Jul 76	I ONLY HAVE EYES FOR YOU *CBS 81329*	14	12 wks
19 Feb 77	GREATEST HITS VOL. IV *CBS 86022*	31	5 wks
18 Jun 77 ★	THE JOHNNY MATHIS COLLECTION *CBS 10003*	1	40 wks
17 Dec 77	SWEET SURRENDER *CBS 86036*	55	1 wk
29 Apr 78 ●	YOU LIGHT UP MY LIFE *CBS 86055*	3	19 wks
26 Aug 78	THAT'S WHAT FRIENDS ARE FOR *CBS 86068*★	16	11 wks
7 Apr 79	THE BEST DAYS OF MY LIFE *CBS 86080*	38	5 wks
3 Nov 79	MATHIS MAGIC *CBS 86103*	59	4 wks
8 Mar 80 ★	TEARS AND LAUGHTER *CBS 10019*	1	15 wks
12 Jul 80	ALL FOR YOU *CBS 86115*	20	8 wks
19 Sep 81 ●	CELEBRATION *CBS 10028*	9	16 wks
15 May 82	FRIENDS IN LOVE *CBS 85652*	34	7 wks
17 Sep 83 ●	UNFORGETTABLE: A MUSICAL TRIBUTE TO NAT 'KING' COLE *CBS 10042*★★	5	16 wks
15 Sep 84	A SPECIAL PART OF ME *CBS 25475*	45	3 wks
13 Dec 86	THE HOLLYWOOD MUSICALS *CBS 4502581*★★★	46	8 wks

★ *Johnny Mathis and Deniece Williams.*
★★ *Johnny Mathis and Natalie Cole.*
★★★ *Johnny Mathis and Henry Mancini.*

MATT BIANCO *UK, male vocalist, Mark Riley*   *67 wks*

8 Sep 84	WHOSE SIDE ARE YOU ON *WEA WX 7*	35	39 wks
22 Mar 86	MATT BIANCO *WEA WX 35*	26	13 wks
9 Jul 88	INDIGO *WEA WX 181*	23	13 wks
2 Nov 90	THE BEST OF MATT BIANCO *East West WX 376*	49	2 wks

For first album, act was a UK/Poland, male/female vocal/instrumental group.

MATTHEWS' SOUTHERN COMFORT
UK, male vocal/instrumental group   *4 wks*

25 Jul 70	SECOND SPRING *Uni UNLS 112*	52	4 wks

MAX Q *Australia, male vocal/instrumental duo*   *1 wk*

4 Nov 89	MAX Q *Mercury 838942 1*	69	1 wk

Brian MAY *UK, male vocalist/instrumentalist – guitar*   *18 wks*

12 Nov 83	STAR FLEET PROJECT *EMI SFLT 1078061*★	35	4 wks
10 Oct 92 ●	BACK TO THE LIGHT *Parlophone CDPCSD 123*	6	14 wks

★ *Brian May and Friends.*

Simon MAY ORCHESTRA UK, orchestra   7 wks

| 27 Sep | 86 | SIMON'S WAY BBC REB 594 .... | 59 | 7 wks |

John MAYALL UK, male vocalist   115 wks

30 Jul	66 ●	BLUES BREAKERS Decca LK 4804★	6	17 wks
4 Mar	67 ●	A HARD ROAD Decca SKL 4853	10	19 wks
23 Sep	67 ●	CRUSADE Decca SKL 4890	8	14 wks
25 Nov	67	BLUES ALONE Ace Of Clubs SCL 1243	24	5 wks
16 Mar	68	DIARY OF A BAND VOL. 1 Decca SKL 4918	27	9 wks
16 Mar	68	DIARY OF A BAND VOL. 2 Decca SKL 4919	28	5 wks
20 Jul	68 ●	BARE WIRES Decca SKL 4945	3	17 wks
18 Jan	69	BLUES FROM LAUREL CANYON Decca SKL 4972	33	3 wks
23 Aug	69	LOOKING BACK Decca SKL 5010	14	7 wks
15 Nov	69	TURNING POINT Polydor 583-571	11	7 wks
11 Apr	70 ●	EMPTY ROOMS Polydor 583-580	9	8 wks
12 Dec	70	U.S.A. UNION Polydor 2425-020	50	1 wk
26 Jun	71	BACK TO THE ROOTS Polydor 2657-005	31	2 wks
17 Apr	93	WAKE UP CALL Silvertone ORECD 527	61	1 wk

★ John Mayall and Eric Clapton.

Curtis MAYFIELD US, male vocalist   2 wks

| 31 Mar | 73 | SUPERFLY Buddah 2318 065 .... | 26 | 2 wks |

MAZE featuring Frankie BEVERLY
US, male vocalist and male vocal/instrumental group   25 wks

7 May	83	WE ARE ONE Capitol EST 12262	38	6 wks
9 Mar	85	CAN'T STOP THE LOVE Capitol MAZE 1	41	12 wks
27 Sep	86	LIVE IN LOS ANGELES Capitol ESTSP 24	70	2 wks
16 Sep	89	SILKY SOUL Warner Bros. WX 301	43	5 wks

MAZZY STARR US, male/female vocal/instrumental duo   1 wk

| 9 Oct | 93 | SO TONIGHT THAT I MIGHT SEE Capitol CDEST 2206 | 68 | 1 wk |

MC HAMMER US, male rapper   67 wks

28 Jul	90 ●	PLEASE HAMMER DON'T HURT 'EM Capitol EST 2120	8	59 wks
6 Apr	91	LET'S GET IT STARTED Capitol EST 2140	46	2 wks
2 Nov	91	TOO LEGIT TO QUIT Capitol ESTP 26★	41	6 wks

★ Hammer.

MC TUNES UK, male rapper   3 wks

| 13 Oct | 90 | THE NORTH AT ITS HEIGHTS ZTT ZTT 3 .... | 26 | 3 wks |

Vaughn MEADER US, male comedian   8 wks

| 29 Dec | 62 | THE FIRST FAMILY London HAA 8048 .... | 12 | 8 wks |

MEAT LOAF US, male vocalist   624 wks

11 Mar	78 ●	BAT OUT OF HELL Cleveland International EPC 82419	9†	457 wks
12 Sep	81 ★	DEAD RINGER Epic EPC 83645	1	46 wks
7 May	83 ●	MIDNIGHT AT THE LOST AND FOUND Epic EPC 25243	7	23 wks
10 Nov	84 ●	BAD ATTITUDE Arista 206 619	8	16 wks

Madonna Ciccone (centre) was a cheerleader in high school. (Pictorial Press)

Meat Loaf looks as surprised as anyone that he motored back so strongly from chart hell. (Pictorial Press)

Freddie Mercury's posthumous number one single, 'Living On My Own', was a re-mix from his 1985 album, Mr Bad Guy. (Pictorial Press)

26 Jan	85 ●	**HITS OUT OF HELL** *Epic EPC 26156*	2†	59 wks
11 Oct	86	**BLIND BEFORE I STOP** *Arista 207 741*	28	6 wks
7 Nov	87	**LIVE AT WEMBLEY** *RCA 208599*	60	2 wks
18 Sep	93 ★	**BAT OUT OF HELL II – BACK INTO HELL**		
		Virgin CDV 2710	1†	15 wks

Hits Out Of Hell *changed catalogue number to Epic EPC 4504471 during its chart run.*

MECHANICS – *See MIKE and the MECHANICS*

Glenn MEDEIROS *US, male vocalist* *2 wks*

8 Oct	88	**NOT ME** *London LONLP 68*	63	2 wks

MEDICS – *See DOCTOR and the MEDICS*

MEGA CITY FOUR
UK, male vocal/instrumental group *3 wks*

17 Jun	89	**TRANZOPHOBIA** *Decoy DYL 3*	67	1 wk
7 Mar	92	**SEBASTOPOL RD** *Big Life MEGCD 1*	41	1 wk
22 May	93	**MAGIC BULLETS** *Big Life MEGCD 3*	57	1 wk

MEGADETH *US, male vocal/instrumental group* *17 wks*

26 Mar	88	**SO FAR SO GOOD ... SO WHAT!** *Capitol EST 2053* ...	18	5 wks
6 Oct	90 ●	**RUST IN PEACE** *Capitol EST 2132*	8	4 wks
18 Jul	92 ●	**COUNTDOWN TO EXTINCTION** *Capitol CDESTU 2175*	5	8 wks

MEL and KIM *UK, female vocal duo* *25 wks*

25 Apr	87 ●	**F.L.M.** *Supreme SU 2*	3	25 wks

See also Kim Appleby.

MELANIE *US, female vocalist* *69 wks*

19 Sep	70 ●	**CANDLES IN THE RAIN** *Buddah 2318–009*	5	27 wks
16 Jan	71	**LEFTOVER WINE** *Buddah 2318–011*	22	11 wks
29 May	71 ●	**GOOD BOOK** *Buddah 2322 001*	9	9 wks
8 Jan	72	**GATHER ME** *Buddah 2322 002*	14	14 wks
1 Apr	72	**GARDEN IN THE CITY** *Buddah 2318 054*	19	6 wks
7 Oct	72	**THE FOUR SIDES OF MELANIE** *Buddah 2659 013*	23	2 wks

MELBOURNE SYMPHONY ORCHESTRA – *See Elton JOHN*

John Cougar MELLENCAMP *US, male vocalist* *27 wks*

6 Nov	82	**AMERICAN FOOL** *Riva RVLP 16★*	37	6 wks
3 Mar	84	**UH-HUH** *Riva RIVL 1*	92	1 wk
3 Oct	87	**THE LONESOME JUBILEE** *Mercury MERH 109*	31	12 wks
27 May	89	**BIG DADDY** *Mercury MERH 838220 1*	25	4 wks
19 Oct	91	**WHENEVER WE WANTED** *Mercury 5101511*	39	2 wks
18 Sep	93	**HUMAN WHEELS** *Mercury 5180882*	37	2 wks

★ *John Cougar.*

MEN AT WORK
Australia, male vocal/instrumental group *71 wks*

15 Jan	83 ★	**BUSINESS AS USUAL** *Epic EPC 85669*	1	44 wks
30 Apr	83 ●	**CARGO** *Epic EPC 25372*	8	27 wks

M
213

MEN THEY COULDN'T HANG
UK, male vocal/instrumental group   *9 wks*

27 Jul 85	**NIGHT OF A THOUSAND CANDLES** *Imp FIEND 50* ..	**91**	2 wks
8 Nov 86	**HOW GREEN IS THE VALLEY** *MCA MCF 3337*	**68**	2 wks
23 Apr 88	**WAITING FOR BONAPARTE** *Magnet MAGL 5075*	**41**	2 wks
6 May 89	**SILVER TOWN** *Silvertone ORELP 503*	**39**	2 wks
1 Sep 90	**THE DOMINO CLUB** *Silvertone ORELP 512*	**53**	1 wk

MEN WITHOUT HATS
Canada, male vocal/instrumental group   *1 wk*

12 Nov 83	**RHYTHM OF YOUTH** *Statik STATLP 10*	**96**	1 wk

MEMBERS   *UK, male vocal/instrumental group*   *5 wks*

28 Apr 79	**AT THE CHELSEA NIGHTCLUB** *Virgin V 2120*	**45**	5 wks

Freddie MERCURY   *UK, male vocalist*   *56 wks*

11 May 85 ●	**MR BAD GUY** *CBS 86312*	**6**	23 wks
22 Oct 88	**BARCELONA** *Polydor POLH 44★*	**15**	8 wks
28 Nov 92 ●	**THE FREDDIE MERCURY ALBUM** *Parlophone CDPCSD 124*	**4†**	25 wks

★ *Freddie Mercury and Montserrat Caballe.*

MERCURY REV   *UK, male/female vocal/instrumental group*   *1 wk*

12 Jun 93	**BOCES** *Beggars Banquet BBQCD 140*	**43**	1 wk

MERLE and ROY   *UK, female/male vocal/instrumental duo*   *5 wks*

26 Sep 87	**REQUESTS** *Mynod Mawr RMBR 8713*	**74**	5 wks

MERSEYBEATS   *UK, male vocal/instrumental group*   *9 wks*

20 Jun 64	**THE MERSEYBEATS** *Fontana TL 5210*	**12**	9 wks

METALLICA   *US/Denmark, male vocal/instrumental group*   *83 wks*

11 Aug 84	**RIDE THE LIGHTNING** *Music For Nations MFN 27*	**87**	2 wks
15 Mar 86	**MASTER OF PUPPETS** *Music For Nations MFN 60*	**41**	4 wks
17 Sep 88 ●	**. . . AND JUSTICE FOR ALL** *Vertigo VERH 61*	**4**	6 wks
19 May 90	**THE GOOD THE BAD AND THE LIVE** *Vertigo 8754871*	**56**	1 wk
24 Aug 91 ★	**METALLICA** *Vertigo 5100221*	**1**	69 wks
11 Dec 93	**LIVE SHIT – BINGE AND PURGE** *Vertigo 5187250*	**54**	1 wk

Live Shit – Binge and Purge was a boxed set containing two CDs, 3 video cassettes and a book.

METEORS   *UK, male vocal/instrumental group*   *3 wks*

26 Feb 83	**WRECKIN' CREW** *I.D. NOSE 1*	**53**	3 wks

MEZZOFORTE   *Iceland, male instrumental group*   *10 wks*

5 Mar 83	**SURPRISE SURPRISE** *Steinar STELP 02*	**23**	9 wks
2 Jul 83	**CATCHING UP WITH MEZZOFORTE** *Steinar STELP 03* .	**95**	1 wk

M
214

George MICHAEL *UK, male vocalist* *129 wks*

14 Nov 87 ★	**FAITH** *Epic 4600001*	**1**	72 wks
15 Sep 90 ★	**LISTEN WITHOUT PREJUDICE VOL. 1** *Epic 4672951* ..	**1**	57 wks

Keith MICHELL *Australia, male vocalist* *12 wks*

9 Feb 80	**CAPTAIN BEAKY AND HIS BAND** *Polydor 238 3462* ...	**28**	12 wks

Bette MIDLER *US, female vocalist* *30 wks*

15 Jul 89	**BEACHES (film soundtrack)** *Atlantic 7819931*	**21**	9 wks
13 Jul 91 ●	**SOME PEOPLE'S LIVES** *Atlantic 7567821291*	**5**	11 wks
15 Feb 92	**FOR THE BOYS (film soundtrack)** *Atlantic 7567823292* ..	**75**	1 wk
30 Oct 93 ●	**EXPERIENCE THE DIVINE – GREATEST HITS**		
	Atlantic 7567824972	**3†**	9 wks

MIDNIGHT OIL *Australia, male vocal/instrumental group* *21 wks*

25 Jun 88	**DIESEL AND DUST** *CBS 4600051*	**19**	16 wks
10 Mar 90	**BLUE SKY MINING** *CBS 4656531*	**28**	3 wks
1 May 93	**EARTH AND SUN AND MOON** *Columbia 4736052*	**27**	2 wks

MIDNIGHT STAR
US, male/female vocal/instrumental group *6 wks*

2 Feb 85	**PLANETARY INVASION** *Solar MCF 3251*	**85**	2 wks
5 Jul 86	**HEADLINES** *Solar MCF 3322*	**42**	4 wks

MIGHTY LEMON DROPS
UK, male vocal/instrumental group *5 wks*

4 Oct 86	**HAPPY HEAD** *Blue Guitar AZLP 1*	**58**	2 wks
27 Feb 88	**THE WORLD WITHOUT END** *Blue Guitar AZLP 4*	**34**	3 wks

MIGHTY WAH *UK, male vocal/instrumental group* *11 wks*

18 Jul 81	**NAH-POO = THE ART OF BLUFF** *Eternal CLASSIC 1★* .	**33**	5 wks
4 Aug 84	**A WORD TO THE WISE GUY** *Beggars Banquet BEGA 54* .	**28**	6 wks

★ *Wah!*

MIKE and the MECHANICS
UK, male vocal/instrumental group *29 wks*

15 Mar 86	**MIKE AND THE MECHANICS** *WEA WX 49*	**78**	3 wks
26 Nov 88 ●	**THE LIVING YEARS** *WEA WX 203*	**2**	19 wks
27 Apr 91	**WORD OF MOUTH** *Virgin V 2662*	**11**	7 wks

See also Mike Rutherford.

Buddy MILES – *See SANTANA*

John MILES *UK, male vocalist/multi-instrumentalist* *25 wks*

27 Mar 76 ●	**REBEL** *Decca SKL 5231*	**9**	10 wks
26 Feb 77	**STRANGER IN THE CITY** *Decca TXS 118*	**37**	3 wks
1 Apr 78	**ZARAGON** *Decca TXS 126*	**43**	5 wks
21 Apr 79	**MORE MILES PER HOUR** *Decca TXS 135*	**46**	5 wks
29 Aug 81	**MILES HIGH** *EMI EMC 3374*	**96**	2 wks

Paul MILES-KINGSTON – *See Andrew LLOYD WEBBER*

M
215

Frankie MILLER UK, *male vocalist*   *1 wk*

14 Apr 79	**FALLING IN LOVE** *Chrysalis CHR 1220*	**54**	1 wk

Glenn MILLER US, *orchestra*   *74 wks*

28 Jan	61 ●	**GLENN MILLER PLAYS SELECTIONS FROM 'THE GLENN MILLER STORY' AND OTHER HITS** *RCA RD 27068 0023*	**10**	18 wks
5 Jul	69 ●	**THE BEST OF GLENN MILLER** *RCA International 1002* ..	**5**	14 wks
6 Sep	69	**NEARNESS OF YOU** *RCA International INTS 1019*	**30**	2 wks
25 Apr	70	**A MEMORIAL 1944–1969** *RCA GM 1*	**18**	17 wks
25 Dec	71	**THE REAL GLENN MILLER AND HIS ORCHESTRA PLAY THE ORIGINAL MUSIC OF THE FILM 'THE GLENN MILLER STORY' AND OTHER HITS** *RCA International INTS 1157*	**28**	2 wks
14 Feb	76	**A LEGENDARY PERFORMER** *RCA Victor DPM 2065* ...	**41**	5 wks
14 Feb	76	**A LEGENDARY PERFORMER VOL. 2** *RCA Victor CPL 11349*	**53**	2 wks
9 Apr	77 ●	**THE UNFORGETTABLE GLENN MILLER** *RCA Victor TVL 1*	**4**	8 wks
20 Mar	93	**THE ULTIMATE GLENN MILLER** *Bluebird 74321131372* .	**11**	6 wks

The Real Glenn Miller And His Orchestra Play . . . *is a re-titled re-issue of the first album.*

M
216

Steve MILLER BAND US, *male vocal/instrumental group* 50 wks

12 Jun	76	**FLY LIKE AN EAGLE** *Mercury 9286 177*	**11**	17 wks
4 Jun	77	**BOOK OF DREAMS** *Mercury 9286 456*	**12**	12 wks
19 Jun	82 ●	**ABRACADABRA** *Mercury 6302 204*	**10**	16 wks
7 May	83	**STEVE MILLER BAND LIVE!** *Mercury MERL 18*	**79**	2 wks
6 Oct	90	**THE BEST OF 1968–1973** *Capitol EST 2133*	**34**	3 wks

MILLICAN and NESBIT UK, *male vocal duo*   *24 wks*

23 Mar	74 ●	**MILLICAN AND NESBIT** *Pye NSPL 18428*	**3**	21 wks
4 Jan	75	**EVERYBODY KNOWS MILLICAN AND NESBIT** *Pye NSPL 18446*	**23**	3 wks

Spike MILLIGAN UK, *male comedian*   *5 wks*

25 Nov 61	**MILLIGAN PRESERVED** *Parlophone PMC 1152*	**11**	4 wks
18 Dec 76	**THE SNOW GOOSE** *RCA RS 1088★*	**49**	1 wk

★ *Spike Milligan with the London Symphony Orchestra.*
See also Harry Secombe, Peter Sellers and Spike Milligan; London Symphony Orchestra.

MILLI VANILLI France/Germany, *male duo*   *24 wks*

21 Jan	89 ●	**ALL OR NOTHING/2X2** *Cooltempo CTLP 11*	**6**	24 wks

All Or Nothing *was repackaged and available with a free re-mix album, 2X2, from 16 Oct 89 onwards.*

Mrs. MILLS UK, *female instrumentalist – piano*   *13 wks*

10 Dec 66	**COME TO MY PARTY** *Parlophone PMC 7010*	**17**	7 wks
28 Dec 68	**MRS. MILLS' PARTY PIECES** *Parlophone PCS 7066*	**32**	3 wks
13 Dec 69	**LET'S HAVE ANOTHER PARTY** *Parlophone PCS 7035* ..	**23**	2 wks
6 Nov 71	**I'M MIGHTY GLAD** *MFP 5225*	**49**	1 wk

MILLTOWN BROTHERS
UK, *male vocal/instrumental group*   *5 wks*

23 Mar 91	**SLINKY** *A & M 3953461*	**27**	5 wks

MINDBENDERS *UK, male vocal/instrumental group*   *4 wks*

25 Jun	66	**THE MINDBENDERS** *Fontana TL 5324*	28	4 wks

See also Wayne Fontana and the Mindbenders.

MINDFUNK *US, male vocal/instrumental group*   *1 wk*

15 May	93	**DROPPED** *Megaforce CDZAZ 3*	60	1 wk

Zodiac MINDWARP and the LOVE REACTION
UK, male vocal/instrumental group   *5 wks*

5 Mar	88	**TATTOOED BEAT MESSIAH** *Mercury ZODLP 1*	20	5 wks

MINISTRY *US, male vocal/instrumental group*   *5 wks*

25 Jul	92	**PSALM 69** *Sire 7599267272*	33	5 wks

Liza MINNELLI *US, female vocalist*   *26 wks*

7 Apr	73 ●	**LIZA WITH A 'Z'** *CBS 65212*	9	15 wks
16 Jun	73	**THE SINGER** *CBS 65555*	45	1 wk
21 Oct	89 ●	**RESULTS** *Epic 465511 1*	6	10 wks

MINIPOPS *UK, male/female vocal group*   *12 wks*

26 Dec	81	**MINIPOPS** *K-Tel NE 1102*	63	7 wks
19 Feb	83	**WE'RE THE MINIPOPS** *K-Tel ONE 1187*	54	5 wks

Dannii MINOGUE *Australia, female vocalist*   *21 wks*

15 Jun	91 ●	**LOVE AND KISSES** *MCA MCA 10340*	8	20 wks
16 Oct	93	**GET INTO YOU** *MCA MCD 10909*	52	1 wk

Kylie MINOGUE *Australia, female vocalist*   *144 wks*

16 Jul	88 ★	**KYLIE** *PWL HF 3*	1	67 wks
21 Oct	89 ★	**ENJOY YOURSELF** *PWL HF 9*	1	33 wks
24 Nov	90 ●	**RHYTHM OF LOVE** *PWL HF 18*	9	22 wks
26 Oct	91	**LET'S GET TO IT** *PWL HF 21*	15	12 wks
5 Sep	92 ★	**GREATEST HITS** *PWL International HFCD 25*	1	10 wks

MIRAGE *UK, male/female vocal/instrumental group*   *33 wks*

26 Dec	87 ●	**THE BEST OF MIRAGE JACK MIX '88** *Stylus SMR 746* .	7	15 wks
25 Jun	88 ●	**JACK MIX IN FULL EFFECT** *Stylus SMR 856*	7	12 wks
7 Jan	89	**ROYAL MIX '89** *Stylus SMR 871*	34	6 wks

MISSION *UK, male vocal/instrumental group*   *45 wks*

22 Nov	86	**GOD'S OWN MEDICINE** *Mercury MERH 102*	14	20 wks
4 Jul	87	**THE FIRST CHAPTER** *Mercury MISH 1*	35	4 wks
12 Mar	88 ●	**LITTLE CHILDREN** *Mercury MISH 2*	2	9 wks
17 Feb	90 ●	**CARVED IN SAND** *Mercury 8422511*	7	8 wks
2 Nov	90	**GRAINS OF SAND** *Mercury 8469371*	28	2 wks
4 Jul	92	**MASQUE** *Vertigo 5121212*	23	2 wks

MR. BIG *US, male vocal/instrumental group* *14 wks*

22 Jul	89	**MR. BIG** *Atlantic 781990 1*	60	1 wk
13 Apr	91	**LEAN INTO IT** *Atlantic 7567822091*	28	12 wks
2 Oct	93	**BUMP AHEAD** *Atlantic 7567824952*	61	1 wk

MR. BUNGLE *US, male vocal/instrumental group* *1 wk*

21 Sep	91	**MR BUNGLE** *London 8282671*	57	1 wk

MR. MISTER *US, male vocal/instrumental group* *24 wks*

15 Feb	86	● **WELCOME TO THE REAL WORLD** *RCA PL 89647* ...	6	24 wks

Joni MITCHELL *Canada, female vocalist* *113 wks*

6 Jun	70	● **LADIES OF THE CANYON** *Reprise RSLP 6376*	8	25 wks
24 Jul	71	● **BLUE** *Reprise K 44128*	3	18 wks
16 Mar	74	**COURT AND SPARK** *Asylum SYLA 8756*	14	11 wks
1 Feb	75	**MILES OF AISLES** *Asylum SYSP 902*	34	4 wks
27 Dec	75	**THE HISSING OF SUMMER LAWNS** *Asylum SYLA 8763*	14	10 wks
11 Dec	76	**HEJIRA** *Asylum K 53063*	11	5 wks
21 Jan	78	**DON JUAN'S RECKLESS DAUGHTER** *Asylum K 63003* .	20	7 wks
14 Jul	79	**MINGUS** *Asylum K 53091*	24	7 wks
4 Oct	80	**SHADOWS AND LIGHT** *Elektra K 62030*	63	3 wks
4 Dec	82	**WILD THINGS RUN FAST** *Geffen GEF 25102*	32	8 wks
30 Nov	85	**DOG EAT DOG** *Geffen GEF 26455*	57	3 wks
2 Apr	88	**CHALK MARK IN A RAIN STORM** *Geffen WX 141*	26	7 wks
9 Mar	91	**NIGHT RIDE HOME** *Geffen GEF 24302*	25	5 wks

George MITCHELL MINSTRELS
UK, male/female vocal group *240 wks*

26 Nov	60	★ **THE BLACK AND WHITE MINSTREL SHOW** *HMV CLP 1399*	1	90 wks
21 Oct	61	★ **ANOTHER BLACK AND WHITE MINSTREL SHOW** *HMV CLP 1460*	1	64 wks
20 Oct	62	★ **ON STAGE WITH THE GEORGE MITCHELL MINSTRELS** *HMV CLP 1599*	1	26 wks
2 Nov	63	● **ON TOUR WITH THE GEORGE MITCHELL MINSTRELS** *HMV CLP 1667*	6	18 wks
12 Dec	64	● **SPOTLIGHT ON THE GEORGE MITCHELL MINSTRELS** *HMV CLP 1803*	6	7 wks
4 Dec	65	● **MAGIC OF THE MINSTRELS** *HMV CLP 1917*	9	7 wks
26 Nov	66	**HERE COME THE MINSTRELS** *HMV CLP 3579*	11	11 wks
16 Dec	67	**SHOWTIME** *HMV CSD 3642*	26	2 wks
14 Dec	68	**SING THE IRVING BERLIN SONGBOOK** *Columbia SCX 6267*	33	1 wk
19 Dec	70	**THE MAGIC OF CHRISTMAS** *Columbia SCX 6431*	32	4 wks
19 Nov	77	● **30 GOLDEN GREATS** *EMI EMTV 7★*	10	10 wks

★ *George Mitchell Minstrels with the Joe Loss Orchestra.*

MOCK TURTLES *UK, male/female vocal/instrumental group* *4 wks*

25 May	91	**TURTLE SOUP** *Imaginary ILLUSION 012*	54	1 wk
27 Jul	91	**TWO SIDES** *Siren SRNLP31*	33	3 wks

MODERN EON *UK, male vocal/instrumental group* *1 wk*

13 Jun	81	**FICTION TALES** *DinDisc DID 11*	65	1 wk

MODERN LOVERS – *See Jonathan RICHMAN and the MODERN LOVERS*

MODERN ROMANCE UK, male vocal/instrumental group 13 wks

| 16 Apr 83 | TRICK OF THE LIGHT WEA X 0127 .... | 53 | 7 wks |
| 3 Dec 83 | PARTY TONIGHT Ronco RON LP 3 .... | 45 | 6 wks |

MODERN TALKING
Germany, male vocal/instrumental group   3 wks

| 11 Oct 86 | READY FOR ROMANCE RCA PL 71133 .... | 76 | 3 wks |

MOLLY HATCHET US, male vocal/instrumental group   1 wk

| 25 Jan 86 | DOUBLE TROUBLE – LIVE Epic EPC 88670 .... | 94 | 1 wk |

Zoot MONEY and the BIG ROLL BAND
UK, male vocalist and male instrumental backing group   3 wks

| 15 Oct 66 | ZOOT Columbia SX 6075 .... | 23 | 3 wks |

MONKEES US/UK, male vocal/instrumental group   101 wks

28 Jan	67 ★	THE MONKEES RCA Victor SF 7844	1	36 wks
15 Apr	67 ★	MORE OF THE MONKEES RCA Victor SF 7868	1	25 wks
8 Jul	67 ●	HEADQUARTERS RCA Victor SF 7886	2	19 wks
13 Jan	68 ●	PISCES, AQUARIUS, CAPRICORN & JONES LTD.		
		RCA Victor SF 7912	5	11 wks
28 Nov	81	THE MONKEES Arista DARTY 12	99	1 wk
15 Apr	89	HEY HEY IT'S THE MONKEES – GREATEST HITS		
		K-Tel NE 1432	12	9 wks

The two albums titled The Monkees *are different.*

MONOCHROME SET UK, male vocal/instrumental group 4 wks

| 3 May 80 | STRANGE BOUTIQUE Dindisc DID 4 .... | 62 | 4 wks |

Tony MONOPOLY Australia, male vocalist   4 wks

| 12 Jun 76 | TONY MONOPOLY BUK BULP 2000 .... | 25 | 4 wks |

Matt MONRO UK, male vocalist   15 wks

7 Aug 65	I HAVE DREAMED Parlophone PMC 1250	20	1 wk
17 Sep 66	THIS IS THE LIFE Capitol T 2540	25	2 wks
26 Aug 67	INVITATION TO THE MOVIES Capitol ST 2730	30	1 wk
15 Mar 80 ●	HEARTBREAKERS EMI EMTV 23	5	11 wks

MONTROSE US, male vocal/instrumental group   1 wk

| 15 Jun 74 | MONTROSE Warner Bros. K 46276 .... | 43 | 1 wk |

MONTY PYTHON'S FLYING CIRCUS
UK, male comedy group   33 wks

30 Oct 71	ANOTHER MONTY PYTHON RECORD		
	Charisma CAS 1049	26	3 wks
27 Jan 73	MONTY PYTHON'S PREVIOUS ALBUM		
	Charisma CAS 1063	39	3 wks
23 Feb 74	MATCHING TIE AND HANDKERCHIEF		
	Charisma CAS 1080	49	2 wks

M
219

27 Jul	74	**LIVE AT DRURY LANE** *Charisma CLASS 4*	**19**	8 wks
9 Aug	75	**MONTY PYTHON** *Charisma CAS 1003*	**45**	4 wks
24 Nov	79	**THE LIFE OF BRIAN** *Warner Bros. K 56751*	**63**	3 wks
18 Oct	80	**CONTRACTUAL OBLIGATION ALBUM**		
		Charisma CAS 1152	**13**	8 wks
16 Nov	91	**MONTY PYTHON SINGS** *Virgin MONT 1*	**62**	2 wks

MOODY BLUES UK, male vocal/instrumental group   310 wks

27 Jan	68	**DAYS OF FUTURE PASSED** *Deram SML 707*	**27**	16 wks
3 Aug	68 ●	**IN SEARCH OF THE LOST CHORD** *Deram SML 711* ..	**5**	32 wks
3 May	69 ★	**ON THE THRESHOLD OF A DREAM** *Deram SML 1035*	**1**	73 wks
6 Dec	69 ●	**TO OUR CHILDREN'S CHILDREN'S CHILDREN**		
		Threshold THS 1	**2**	44 wks
15 Aug	70 ★	**A QUESTION OF BALANCE** *Threshold THS 3*	**1**	19 wks
7 Aug	71 ★	**EVERY GOOD BOY DESERVES FAVOUR**		
		Threshold THS 5	**1**	21 wks
2 Dec	72 ●	**SEVENTH SOJOURN** *Threshold THS 7*	**5**	18 wks
16 Nov	74	**THIS IS THE MOODY BLUES** *Threshold MB 1/2*	**14**	18 wks
24 Jun	78 ●	**OCTAVE** *Decca TXS 129*	**6**	18 wks
10 Nov	79	**OUT OF THIS WORLD** *K-Tel NE 1051*	**15**	10 wks
23 May	81 ●	**LONG DISTANCE VOYAGER** *Threshold TXS 139*	**7**	19 wks
10 Sep	83	**THE PRESENT** *Threshold TXS 140*	**15**	8 wks
10 May	86	**THE OTHER SIDE OF LIFE** *Threshold POLD 5190*	**24**	6 wks
25 Jun	88	**SUR LA MER** *Polydor POLH 43*	**21**	5 wks
20 Jan	90	**GREATEST HITS** *Threshold 8406591*	**71**	1 wk
13 Jul	91	**KEYS OF THE KINGDOM** *Threshold 8494331*	**54**	2 wks

Christy MOORE Ireland, male vocalist   6 wks

4 May	91	**SMOKE AND STRONG WHISKEY** *Newberry CM 21*	**49**	3 wks
21 Sep	91	**THE CHRISTY MOORE COLLECTION**		
		East West WX 434	**69**	1 wk
6 Nov	93	**KING PUCK** *Equator ATLASCD 003*	**66**	2 wks

Dudley MOORE UK, male instrumentalist – piano   24 wks

4 Dec	65	**THE OTHER SIDE OF DUDLEY MOORE**		
		Decca LK 4732	**11**	9 wks
11 Jun	66	**GENUINE DUD** *Decca LK 4788*	**13**	10 wks
26 Jan	91	**ORCHESTRA!** *Decca 4308361★*	**38**	5 wks

* *Sir George Solti and Dudley Moore.*
See also Peter Cook and Dudley Moore.

Gary MOORE UK, male vocalist/instrumentalist – guitar   89 wks

3 Feb	79	**BACK ON THE STREETS** *MCA MCF 2853*	**70**	1 wk
16 Oct	82	**CORRIDORS OF POWER** *Virgin V 2245*	**30**	6 wks
18 Feb	84	**VICTIMS OF THE FUTURE** *10 DIX 2*	**12**	7 wks
13 Oct	84	**WE WANT MOORE!** *10 GMDL 1*	**32**	3 wks
14 Sep	85	**RUN FOR COVER** *10 DIX 16*	**12**	8 wks
12 Jul	86	**ROCKIN' EVERY NIGHT** *10 XID 1*	**99**	1 wk
14 Mar	87 ●	**WILD FRONTIER** *10 DIX 56*	**8**	14 wks
11 Feb	89	**AFTER THE WAR** *Virgin V 2575*	**23**	5 wks
7 Apr	90	**STILL GOT THE BLUES** *Virgin V 2612*	**13**	26 wks
21 Mar	92 ●	**AFTER HOURS** *Virgin CDV 2684*	**4**	13 wks
22 May	93 ●	**BLUES ALIVE** *Virgin CDVX 2716*	**8**	5 wks

Patrick MORAZ
Switzerland, male instrumentalist – keyboards   8 wks

10 Apr	76	**PATRICK MORAZ** *Charisma CDS 4002*	**28**	7 wks
23 Jul	77	**OUT IN THE SUN** *Charisma CDS 4007*	**44**	1 wk

MORDRED UK, male vocal/instrumental group   1 wk

16 Feb	91	**IN THIS LIFE** *Noise International NO 1591*	**70**	1 wk

M
220

Giorgio MORODER – *See Philip OAKEY and Giorgio MORODER*

Joseph MOROVITZ – *See SOUTH BANK ORCHESTRA*

Ennio MORRICONE *Italy, orchestra*   *15 wks*

2 May 81	**THIS IS ENNIO MORRICONE** *EMI THIS 33*	23	5 wks
9 May 81	**CHI MAI** *BBC REH 414*	29	6 wks
7 Mar 87	**THE MISSION (film soundtrack)** *Virgin V 2402★*	73	4 wks

★ *Ennio Morricone and the London Philharmonic Orchestra.*
See also London Philharmonic Orchestra.

Van MORRISON *UK, male vocalist*   *155 wks*

18 Apr 70	**MOONDANCE** *Warner Bros. WS 1835*	32	2 wks
11 Aug 73	**HARD NOSE THE HIGHWAY** *Warner Bros. K 46242*	22	3 wks
16 Nov 74	**VEEDON FLEECE** *Warner Bros. K 56068*	41	1 wk
7 May 77	**A PERIOD OF TRANSITION** *Warner Bros. K 56322*	23	5 wks
21 Oct 78	**WAVELENGTH** *Warner Bros. K 56526*	27	6 wks
8 Sep 79	**INTO THE MUSIC** *Vertigo 9120 852*	21	9 wks
20 Sep 80	**THE COMMON ONE** *Mercury 6302 021*	53	3 wks
27 Feb 82	**BEAUTIFUL VISION** *Mercury 6302 122*	31	14 wks
26 Mar 83	**INARTICULATE SPEECH OF THE HEART** *Mercury MERL 16*	14	8 wks
3 Mar 84	**LIVE AT THE GRAND OPERA HOUSE** *Mercury MERL 36*	47	4 wks
9 Feb 85	**A SENSE OF WONDER** *Mercury MERH 54*	25	5 wks
2 Aug 86	**NO GURU, NO METHOD, NO TEACHER** *Mercury MERH 94*	27	5 wks
19 Sep 87	**POETIC CHAMPIONS COMPOSE** *Mercury MERH 110* ..	26	6 wks
2 Jul 88	**IRISH HEARTBEAT** *Mercury MERH 124★*	18	7 wks
10 Jun 89	**AVALON SUNSET** *Polydor 839262 1*	13	14 wks
7 Apr 90 ●	**THE BEST OF VAN MORRISON** *Polydor 8419701*	4	31 wks
20 Oct 90 ●	**ENLIGHTENMENT** *Polydor 8471001*	5	14 wks
21 Sep 91 ●	**HYMNS TO THE SILENCE** *Polydor 8490261*	5	6 wks
27 Feb 93	**THE BEST OF VAN MORRISON VOL. 2** *Polydor 5177602*	31	3 wks
12 Jun 93 ●	**TOO LONG IN EXILE** *Exile 5192192*	4	9 wks

★ *Van Morrison and The Chieftains.*

MORRISSEY *UK, male vocalist*   *35 wks*

26 Mar 88 ★	**VIVA HATE** *HMV CSD 3787*	1	20 wks
27 Oct 90 ●	**BONA DRAG** *HMV CLP 3788*	9	4 wks
16 Mar 91 ●	**KILL UNCLE** *HMV CSD 3789*	8	4 wks
8 Aug 92 ●	**YOUR ARSENAL** *HMV CDCSD 3790*	4	5 wks
22 May 93	**BEETHOVEN WAS DEAF** *HMV CDSCD 3791*	13	2 wks

MORRISSEY MULLEN
UK, male vocal/instrumental duo   *11 wks*

18 Jul 81	**BADNESS** *Beggars Banquet BEGA 27*	43	5 wks
3 Apr 82	**LIFE ON THE WIRE** *Beggars Banquet BEGA 33*	47	5 wks
23 Apr 83	**IT'S ABOUT TIME** *Beggars Banquet BEGA 44*	95	1 wk

MORRISTOWN ORPHEUS CHOIR – *See G.U.S. (FOOTWEAR) BAND and the MORRISTOWN ORPHEUS CHOIR*

MOTHERS OF INVENTION
US, male vocal/instrumental group   *12 wks*

29 Jun 68	**WE'RE ONLY IN IT FOR THE MONEY** *Verve SVLP 9199*	32	5 wks
28 Mar 70	**BURNT WEENY SANDWICH** *Reprise RSLP 6370*	17	3 wks
3 Oct 70	**WEASELS RIPPED MY FLESH** *Reprise RSLP 2028*	28	4 wks

MOTLEY CRUE US, male vocal/instrumental group   24 wks

13 Jul	85	**THEATRE OF PAIN** Elektra EKT 8	36	3 wks
30 May	87	**GIRLS GIRLS GIRLS** Elektra EKT 39	14	11 wks
16 Sep	89 ●	**DR. FEELGOOD** Elektra EKT 59	4	7 wks
19 Oct	91	**DECADE OF DECADENCE** Elektra EKT 95	20	3 wks

MOTORHEAD UK, male vocal/instrumental group   102 wks

24 Sep	77	**MOTORHEAD** Chiswick WIK 2	43	5 wks
24 Mar	79	**OVERKILL** Bronze BRON 515	24	11 wks
27 Oct	79	**BOMBER** Bronze BRON 523	12	13 wks
8 Dec	79	**ON PARADE** United Artists LBR 1004	65	2 wks
8 Nov	80 ●	**ACE OF SPADES** Bronze BRON 531	4	16 wks
27 Jun	81 ★	**NO SLEEP TILL HAMMERSMITH** Bronze BRON 535 ...	1	21 wks
17 Apr	82 ●	**IRONFIST** Bronze BRNA 539	6	9 wks
26 Feb	83	**WHAT'S WORDS WORTH** Big Beat NED 2	71	2 wks
4 Jun	83	**ANOTHER PERFECT DAY** Bronze BRON 546	20	4 wks
15 Sep	84	**NO REMORSE** Bronze PROTV MOTOR 1	14	6 wks
9 Aug	86	**ORGASMATRON** GWR GWLP 1	21	4 wks
5 Sep	87	**ROCK 'N' ROLL** GWR GWLP 14	34	3 wks
15 Oct	88	**NO SLEEP AT ALL** GWR GWR 31	79	1 wk
2 Feb	91	**1916** Epic 4674811	24	4 wks
8 Aug	92	**MARCH OR DIE** Epic 4717232	60	1 wk

MOTORS UK, male vocal/instrumental group   6 wks

15 Oct	77	**THE MOTORS** Virgin V 2089	46	5 wks
3 Jun	78	**APPROVED BY THE MOTORS** Virgin V 2101	60	1 wk

M
222

MOTT THE HOOPLE
UK, male vocal/instrumental group   32 wks

2 May	70	**MOTT THE HOOPLE** Island ILPS 9108	66	1 wk
17 Oct	70	**MAD SHADOWS** Island ILPS 9119	48	2 wks
17 Apr	71	**WILD LIFE** Island ILPS 9144	44	2 wks
23 Sep	72	**ALL THE YOUNG DUDES** CBS 65184	21	4 wks
11 Aug	73 ●	**MOTT** CBS 69038	7	15 wks
13 Apr	74	**THE HOOPLE** CBS 69062	11	5 wks
23 Nov	74	**LIVE** CBS 69093	32	2 wks
4 Oct	75	**DRIVE ON** CBS 69154	45	1 wk

MOUNTAIN US/Canada, male vocal/instrumental group   4 wks

5 Jun	71	**NANTUCKET SLEIGHRIDE** Island ILPS 9148	43	1 wk
8 Jul	72	**THE ROAD GOES EVER ON** Island ILPS 9199	21	3 wks

Nana MOUSKOURI Greece, female vocalist   208 wks

7 Jun	69 ●	**OVER AND OVER** Fontana S 5511	10	105 wks
4 Apr	70 ●	**THE EXQUISITE NANA MOUSKOURI** Fontana STL 5536	10	25 wks
10 Oct	70	**RECITAL '70** Fontana 6312 003	68	1 wk
3 Apr	71	**TURN ON THE SUN** Fontana 6312 008	16	15 wks
29 Jul	72	**BRITISH CONCERT** Fontana 6651 003	29	11 wks
28 Apr	73	**SONGS FROM HER TV SERIES** Fontana 6312 036 ...	29	11 wks
28 Sep	74	**SPOTLIGHT ON NANA MOUSKOURI** Fontana 6641 197	38	6 wks
10 Jul	76 ●	**PASSPORT** Philips 9101 061	3	16 wks
22 Feb	86	**ALONE** Philips PHH 3	19	10 wks
8 Oct	88	**THE MAGIC OF NANA MOUSKOURI** Philips NMTV 1 .	44	8 wks

MOVE UK, male vocal/instrumental group   9 wks

13 Apr	68	**MOVE** Regal Zonophone SLPZ 1002	15	9 wks

Alison MOYET UK, female vocalist

142 wks

17 Nov 84 ★	**ALF**	CBS 26229	**1**	84 wks
18 Apr 87 ●	**RAINDANCING**	CBS 450 152–1	**2**	52 wks
4 May 91	**HOODOO**	Columbia 4682721	**11**	6 wks

MSG – See Michael SCHENKER GROUP

MTUME US, male/female vocal/instrumental group

1 wk

6 Oct 84	**YOU, ME AND HE** Epic EPC 26077	**85**	1 wk

MUD UK, male vocal/instrumental group

58 wks

28 Sep 74 ●	**MUD ROCK** RAK SRAK 508	**8**	35 wks
26 Jul 75 ●	**MUD ROCK VOL. 2** RAK SRAK 513	**6**	12 wks
1 Nov 75	**MUD'S GREATEST HITS** RAK SRAK 6755	**25**	6 wks
27 Dec 75	**USE YOUR IMAGINATION** Private Stock PVLP 1003	**33**	5 wks

MUDHONEY UK, male vocal/instrumental group

4 wks

31 Aug 91	**EVERY GOOD BOY DESERVES FUDGE** Subpop SP 18160	**34**	2 wks
17 Oct 92	**PIECE OF CAKE** Reprise 9362450902	**39**	2 wks

MUFFINS – See MARTHA and the MUFFINS

Gerry MULLIGAN and Ben WEBSTER
US, male instrumental duo – baritone and tenor sax

1 wk

24 Sep 60	**GERRY MULLIGAN MEETS BEN WEBSTER** HMV CLP 1373	**15**	1 wk

MUNGO JERRY UK, male vocal/instrumental group

14 wks

8 Aug 70	**MUNGO JERRY** Dawn DNLS 3008	**13**	6 wks
10 Apr 71	**ELECTRONICALLY TESTED** Dawn DNLS 3020	**14**	8 wks

MUPPETS US, puppets

45 wks

11 Jun 77 ★	**THE MUPPET SHOW** Pye NSPH 19	**1**	35 wks
25 Feb 78	**THE MUPPET SHOW VOL. 2** Pye NSPH 21	**16**	10 wks

Peter MURPHY UK, male vocalist

1 wk

26 Jul 86	**SHOULD THE WORLD FAIL TO FALL APART** Beggars Banquet BEGA 69	**82**	1 wk

Anne MURRAY Canada, female vocalist

10 wks

3 Oct 81	**VERY BEST OF ANNE MURRAY** Capitol EMTV 31	**14**	10 wks

Pauline MURRAY and the INVISIBLE GIRLS
UK, female vocalist with male vocal/instrumental group

4 wks

11 Oct 80	**PAULINE MURRAY AND THE INVISIBLE GIRLS** Elusive 2394 227	**25**	4 wks

MUSIC OF THE MOUNTAINS – See MANUEL and his MUSIC OF THE MOUNTAINS

M
223

MUSICAL YOUTH *UK, male vocal/instrumental group* *22 wks*

4 Dec 82	**THE YOUTH OF TODAY** *MCA YOULP 1*	**24**	22 wks

MUSIC STUDENTS – *See Ian DURY and the BLOCKHEADS*

MY BLOODY VALENTINE
UK, male/female vocal/instrumental group *2 wks*

23 Nov 91	**LOVELESS** *Creation CRELP 060*	**24**	2 wks

Alannah MYLES *Canada, female vocalist* *21 wks*

28 Apr 90 ●	**ALANNAH MYLES** *Atlantic 7819561*	**3**	21 wks

Jimmy NAIL *UK, male vocalist* *12 wks*

8 Aug 92 ●	**GROWING UP IN PUBLIC** *East West 4509901442*	**2**	12 wks

NAPALM DEATH *UK, male vocal/instrumental group* *2 wks*

15 Sep 90	**HARMONY OF CORRUPTION** *Earache MOSH 19*	**67**	1 wk
30 May 92	**UTOPIA BANISHED** *Earache MOSH 53CD*	**58**	1 wk

NARADA *US, male vocalist/instrumentalist/producer* *5 wks*

14 May 88	**DIVINE EMOTION** *Reprise WX 172*	**60**	5 wks

Graham NASH *UK, male vocalist* *13 wks*

26 Jun 71	**SONGS FOR BEGINNERS** *Atlantic 2401–011*	**13**	8 wks
13 May 72	**GRAHAM NASH AND DAVID CROSBY**		
	Atlantic K 50011★	**13**	5 wks

★ *Graham Nash and David Crosby.*
See also Crosby, Stills, Nash and Young.

Johnny NASH *US, male vocalist* *17 wks*

5 Aug 72	**I CAN SEE CLEARLY NOW** *CBS 64860*	**39**	6 wks
10 Dec 77	**JOHNNY NASH COLLECTION** *Epic EPC 10008*	**18**	11 wks

NASH THE SLASH
Canada, male vocalist/multi-instrumentalist *1 wk*

21 Feb 81	**CHILDREN OF THE NIGHT** *DinDisc DID 9*	**61**	1 wk

NATASHA *UK, female vocalist* *3 wks*

9 Oct 82	**CAPTURED** *Towerbell TOWLP 2*	**53**	3 wks

NATIONAL BRASS BAND UK, orchestra 10 wks

10 May 80	**GOLDEN MELODIES** K-Tel ONE 1075	**15**	10 wks

NATIONAL PHILHARMONIC ORCHESTRA – See LONDON PHILHARMONIC CHOIR;
James GALWAY; Henry MANCINI

NAUGHTY BY NATURE US, male rap group 2 wks

6 Mar 93	**19 NAUGHTY III** Big Life BLRCD 23	**40**	2 wks

NAZARETH UK, male vocal/instrumental group 51 wks

26 May 73	**RAZAMANAZ** Mooncrest CREST 1	**11**	25 wks
24 Nov 73 ●	**LOUD 'N' PROUD** Mooncrest CREST 4	**10**	7 wks
18 May 74	**RAMPANT** Mooncrest CREST 15	**13**	3 wks
13 Dec 75	**GREATEST HITS** Mountain TOPS 108	**54**	1 wk
3 Feb 79	**NO MEAN CITY** Mountain TOPS 123	**34**	9 wks
28 Feb 81	**THE FOOL CIRCLE** NEMS NEL 6019	**60**	3 wks
3 Oct 81	**NAZARETH LIVE** NEMS NELD 102	**78**	3 wks

NED'S ATOMIC DUSTBIN
UK, male vocal/instrumental group 8 wks

9 Feb 91	**BITE (import)** Rough Trade Germany RTD 14011831	**72**	1 wk
13 Apr 91 ●	**GOD FODDER** Furtive 4681121	**4**	5 wks
31 Oct 92	**ARE YOU NORMAL** Furtive 4726332	**13**	2 wks

Vince NEIL US, male vocalist 1 wk

8 May 93	**EXPOSED** Warner Bros 9362452602	**44**	1 wk

Bill NELSON UK, male vocalist/multi-instrumentalist 21 wks

24 Feb 79	**SOUND ON SOUND** Harvest SHSP 4095★	**33**	5 wks
23 May 81 ●	**QUIT DREAMING AND GET ON THE BEAM**		
	Mercury 6359 055	**7**	6 wks
3 Jul 82	**THE LOVE THAT WHIRLS (DIARY OF A THINKING**		
	HEART) Mercury WHIRL 3	**28**	4 wks
14 May 83	**CHIMERA** Mercury MERB 19	**30**	5 wks
3 May 86	**GETTING THE HOLY GHOST ACROSS**		
	Portrait PRT 26602	**91**	1 wk

★ Bill Nelson's Red Noise.

Phyllis NELSON US, female vocalist 10 wks

20 Apr 85	**MOVE CLOSER** Carrere CAL 203	**29**	10 wks

Shara NELSON UK, female vocalist 4 wks

2 Oct 93	**WHAT SILENCE KNOWS** Cooltempo CTCD 35	**22**	4 wks

NENA Germany, female/male vocal/instrumental group 5 wks

24 Mar 84	**NENA** Epic EPC 25925	**31**	5 wks

NESBIT – See MILLICAN and NESBIT

Robbie NEVIL *US, male vocalist*   *1 wk*

13 Jun 87   **C'EST LA VIE** *Manhattan MTL 1006* 93   1 wk

Aaron NEVILLE – *See Linda RONSTADT; NEVILLE BROTHERS*

NEVILLE BROTHERS
US, male vocal/instrumental group   *3 wks*

18 Aug 90   **BROTHER'S KEEPER** *A & M 3953121* 35   3 wks

NEW BOHEMIANS – *See Edie BRICKELL and the NEW BOHEMIANS*

NEW FAST AUTOMATIC DAFFODILS
UK, male vocal/instrumental group   *2 wks*

17 Nov 90   **PIGEON HOLE** *Play It Again Sam BIAS 185* 49   1 wk
24 Oct 92   **BODY EXIT MIND** *Play It Again Sam BIAS 205CD* 57   1 wk

NEW KIDS ON THE BLOCK *US, male vocal group 105 wks*

 9 Dec 89 ● **HANGIN' TOUGH** *CBS 4608741* 2   41 wks
30 Jun 90 ★ **STEP BY STEP** *CBS 4666861* 1   31 wks
 2 Nov 90 ● **NEW KIDS ON THE BLOCK** *CBS 4675041* 6   13 wks
15 Dec 90 ● **MERRY MERRY CHRISTMAS** *CBS 4659071* 13   5 wks
 2 Mar 91   **NO MORE GAMES – THE REMIX ALBUM**
             Columbia 4674941 15   11 wks
21 Dec 91   **H.I.T.S.** *Columbia 4694381* 50   4 wks

NEW MODEL ARMY *UK, male vocal/instrumental group   20 wks*

12 May 84   **VENGEANCE** *Abstract ABT 008* 73   5 wks
25 May 85   **NO REST FOR THE WICKED** *EMI NMAL 1* 22   3 wks
11 Oct 86   **THE GHOST OF CAIN** *EMI EMC 3516* 45   3 wks
18 Feb 89   **THUNDER AND CONSOLATION** *EMI EMC 3552* 20   3 wks
 6 Oct 90   **IMPURITY** *EMI EMC 3581* 23   2 wks
22 Jun 91   **RAW MELODY MEN** *EMI EMC 3595* 43   2 wks
10 Apr 93   **THE LOVE OF HOPELESS CAUSES** *Epic 4735622* 22   2 wks

NEW MUSIK *UK, male vocal/instrumental group*   *11 wks*

17 May 80   **FROM A TO B** *GTO GTLP 041* 35   9 wks
14 Mar 81   **ANYWHERE** *GTO GTLP 044* 68   2 wks

NEW ORDER *UK, male/female vocal/instrumental group*   *128 wks*

28 Nov 81   **MOVEMENT** *Factory FACT 50* 30   10 wks
14 May 83 ● **POWER, CORRUPTION AND LIES** *Factory FACT 75* ... 4   29 wks
25 May 85 ● **LOW-LIFE** *Factory FACT 100* 7   10 wks
11 Oct 86 ● **BROTHERHOOD** *Factory FACT 150* 9   5 wks
29 Aug 87 ● **SUBSTANCE** *Factory FACT 200* 3   37 wks
11 Feb 89 ★ **TECHNIQUE** *Factory FACT 275* 1   14 wks
22 Feb 92   **BBC RADIO 1 LIVE IN CONCERT**
             Windsong International WINCD 011 33   2 wks
15 May 93 ★ **REPUBLIC** *London 8284132* 1   19 wks
17 Jul 93   **SUBSTANCE (re-issue)** *London 5200082* 32   2 wks

NEW POWER GENERATION – *See PRINCE*

N
226

NEW SEEKERS UK, male/female vocal/instrumental group 49 wks

5 Feb	72	**NEW COLOURS** Polydor 2383 066		40	4 wks
1 Apr	72 ●	**WE'D LIKE TO TEACH THE WORLD TO SING**			
		Polydor 2883 103		2	25 wks
12 Aug	72	**NEVER ENDING SONG OF LOVE** Polydor 2383 126		35	4 wks
14 Oct	72	**CIRCLES** Polydor 2442 102		23	5 wks
21 Apr	73	**NOW** Polydor 2383 195		47	2 wks
30 Mar	74	**TOGETHER** Polydor 2383 264		12	9 wks

NEW WORLD THEATRE ORCHESTRA
UK, orchestra   1 wk

24 Dec	60	**LET'S DANCE TO THE HITS OF THE 30'S AND 40'S**		
		Pye Golden Guinea GGL 0026	20	1 wk

NEWCLEUS US, male vocal/instrumental group   2 wks

25 Aug	84	**JAM ON REVENGE** Sunnyview SVLP 6600	84	2 wks

Bob NEWHART US, male comedian   37 wks

1 Oct	60 ●	**BUTTON-DOWN MIND OF BOB NEWHART**		
		Warner Bros. WM 4010	2	37 wks

Anthony NEWLEY UK, male vocalist   14 wks

14 May	60	**LOVE IS A NOW AND THEN THING** Decca LK 4343 ..	19	2 wks
8 Jul	61 ●	**TONY** Decca LK 4406	5	12 wks

See also Anthony Newley, Peter Sellers, Joan Collins.

Anthony NEWLEY, Peter SELLERS, Joan COLLINS
UK, male/female comedians   10 wks

28 Sep	63 ●	**FOOL BRITANNIA** Ember CEL 902	10	10 wks

See also Anthony Newley; Peter Sellers.

NEWS – *See Huey LEWIS and the NEWS*

Olivia NEWTON-JOHN UK, female vocalist   99 wks

2 Mar	74	**MUSIC MAKES MY DAY** Pye NSPL 28186	37	3 wks
29 Jun	74	**LONG LIVE LOVE** EMI EMC 3028	40	2 wks
26 Apr	75	**HAVE YOU NEVER BEEN MELLOW** EMI EMC 3069 ..	37	2 wks
29 May	76	**COME ON OVER** EMI EMC 3124	49	4 wks
27 Aug	77	**MAKING A GOOD THING BETTER** EMI EMC 3192 ..	60	1 wk
21 Jan	78	**GREATEST HITS** EMI EMA 785	19	9 wks
9 Dec	78	**TOTALLY HOT** EMI EMA 789	30	9 wks
31 Oct	81	**PHYSICAL** EMI EMC 3386	11	22 wks
23 Oct	82 ●	**GREATEST HITS** EMI EMTV 36	8	38 wks
8 Mar	86	**SOUL KISS** Mercury MERH 77	66	3 wks
25 Jul	92	**BACK TO BASICS – THE ESSENTIAL COLLECTION**		
		1971–1992 Mercury 5126412	12	6 wks

NICE UK, male instrumental group   38 wks

13 Sep	69 ●	**NICE** Immediate IMSP 026	3	6 wks
27 Jun	70 ●	**FIVE BRIDGES** Charisma CAS 1014	2	21 wks
17 Apr	71 ●	**ELEGY** Charisma CAS 1030	5	11 wks

N
227

Paul NICHOLAS *UK, male vocalist*   *8 wks*

29 Nov 86   JUST GOOD FRIENDS   *K-Tel ONE 1334* ....   **30**   8 wks

Stevie NICKS *US, female vocalist*   *77 wks*

8 Aug 81   BELLA DONNA   *WEA K 99169* ....   **11**   16 wks
2 Jul   83   THE WILD HEART   *WEA 25–0071–1* ....   **28**   19 wks
14 Dec 85   ROCK A LITTLE   *Modern PCS 7300* ....   **30**   22 wks
10 Jun 89 ● THE OTHER SIDE OF THE MIRROR   *EMI EMD 1008* .   **3**   14 wks
14 Sep 91   TIMESPACE – THE BEST OF STEVIE NICKS
              EMI EMD 3595 ....   **15**   6 wks

Hector NICOL *UK, male vocalist*   *1 wk*

28 Apr 84   BRAVO JULIET   *Klub KLP 42* ....   **92**   1 wk

NICOLE *Germany, female vocalist*   *2 wks*

2 Oct 82   A LITTLE PEACE   *CBS 85011* ....   **85**   2 wks

NILSSON *US, male vocalist*   *43 wks*

29 Jan 72   THE POINT   *RCA Victor SF 8166* ....   **46**   1 wk
5 Feb   72 ● NILSSON SCHMILSSON   *RCA Victor SF 8242* ....   **4**   22 wks
19 Aug 72   SON OF SCHMILSSON   *RCA Victor SF 8297* ....   **41**   1 wk
28 Jul   73   A LITTLE TOUCH OF SCHMILSSON IN THE NIGHT
              RCA Victor SF 8371 ....   **20**   19 wks

NINA and FREDERICK *Denmark, female/male vocal duo 6 wks*

13 Feb 60 ● NINA AND FREDERICK   *Pye NPT 19023* ....   **9**   2 wks
29 Apr 61   NINA AND FREDERICK   *Columbia COL 1314* ....   **11**   4 wks

These two albums, although identically named, are different.

9 BELOW ZERO *UK, male vocal/instrumental group*   *12 wks*

14 Mar 81   DON'T POINT YOUR FINGER   *A & M AMLH 68521* ...   **56**   6 wks
20 Mar 82   THIRD DEGREE   *A & M AMLH 68537* ....   **38**   6 wks

NINE INCH NAILS *US, male vocal/instrumental group*   *4 wks*

12 Oct 91   PRETTY HATE MACHINE   *TVT ILPS 9973* ....   **67**   1 wk
17 Oct 92   BROKEN   *Island IMCD 8004* ....   **18**   3 wks

999 *UK, male vocal/instrumental group*   *1 wk*

25 Mar 78   **999**   *United Artists UAG 30199* ....   **53**   1 wk

NIRVANA *US, male vocal/instrumental group*   *134 wks*

5 Oct 91 ● NEVERMIND   *DGC DGC 24425* ....   **7** 103 wks
7 Mar 92   BLEACH   *Tupelo TUPCD 6* ....   **33**   7 wks
26 Dec 92   INCESTICIDE   *Geffen GED 24504* ....   **14**   10 wks
25 Sep 93 ★ IN UTERO   *Geffen GED 24536* ....   **1†**   14 wks

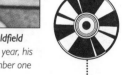

Although Tubular Bells *by* **Mike Oldfield** *preceded it on the chart by over a year, his* Hergest Ridge *actually got to number one first. (Redferns)*

The launch of **The Monkees** *was prefaced by teaser ads in industry publications.*

NOLANS *Ireland, female vocal group* — 84 wks

20 Jul	78 ●	**20 GIANT HITS** *Target TGS 502★*	**3**	12 wks
19 Jan	80	**NOLANS** *Epic EPC 83892*	**15**	13 wks
25 Oct	80	**MAKING WAVES** *Epic EPC 10023*	**11**	33 wks
27 Mar	82 ●	**PORTRAIT** *Epic EPC 10033*	**7**	10 wks
20 Nov	82	**ALTOGETHER** *Epic EPC 10037*	**52**	8 wks
17 Nov	84	**GIRLS JUST WANNA HAVE FUN** *Towerbell TOWLP 10* .	**39**	8 wks

★ *Nolan Sisters.*

NOMAD *UK, male/female vocal/instrumental duo* — 2 wks

22 Jun	91	**CHANGING CABINS** *Rumour RULP 100*	**48**	2 wks

NORTHSIDE *UK, male vocal/instrumental group* — 3 wks

29 Jun	91	**CHICKEN RHYTHMS** *Factory FACT 310*	**19**	3 wks

NOT THE 9 O'CLOCK NEWS CAST
UK/New Zealand, male/female comedians — 51 wks

8 Nov	80 ●	**NOT THE 9 O'CLOCK NEWS** *BBC REB 400*	**5**	23 wks
17 Oct	81 ●	**HEDGEHOG SANDWICH** *BBC REB 421*	**5**	24 wks
23 Oct	82	**THE MEMORY KINDA LINGERS** *BBC REF 453*	**63**	4 wks

NOTTING HILLBILLIES
UK, male vocal/instrumental group — 14 wks

17 Mar	90 ●	**MISSING . . . PRESUMED HAVING A GOOD TIME** *Vertigo 8426711*	**2**	14 wks

NU SHOOZ *US, male/female vocal duo* — 8 wks

14 Jun	86	**POOLSIDE** *Atlantic WX 60*	**32**	8 wks

NUCLEAR ASSAULT *US, male vocal/instrumental group* — 1 wk

7 Oct	89	**HANDLE WITH CARE** *Under One Flag FLAG 35*	**60**	1 wk

NUCLEUS *UK, male instrumental group* — 1 wk

11 Jul	70	**ELASTIC ROCK** *Vertigo 6360 006*	**46**	1 wk

Ted NUGENT *US, male vocalist/instrumentalist – guitar* — 14 wks

4 Sep	76	**TED NUGENT** *Epic EPC 81268*	**56**	1 wk
30 Oct	76	**FREE FOR ALL** *Epic EPC 81397*	**33**	2 wks
2 Jul	77	**CAT SCRATCH FEVER** *Epic EPC 82010*	**28**	5 wks
11 Mar	78	**DOUBLE LIVE GONZO** *Epic EPC 88282*	**47**	2 wks
14 Jun	80	**SCREAM DREAM** *Epic EPC 86111*	**37**	3 wks
25 Apr	81	**IN 10 CITIES** *Epic EPC 84917*	**75**	1 wk

Gary NUMAN *UK, male vocalist* — 139 wks

9 Jun	79 ★	**REPLICAS** *Beggars Banquet BEGA 7★*	**1**	31 wks
25 Aug	79	**TUBEWAY ARMY** *Beggars Banquet BEGA 4★*	**14**	10 wks

22 Sep	79 ★	THE PLEASURE PRINCIPLE *Beggars Banquet BEGA 10* ..	1	21 wks
13 Sep	80 ★	TELEKON *Beggars Banquet BEGA 19*	1	11 wks
2 May	81 ●	LIVING ORNAMENTS 1979–1980 *Beggars Banquet BOX 1* .	2	4 wks
2 May	81	LIVING ORNAMENTS 1979 *Beggars Banquet BEGA 24*	47	3 wks
2 May	81	LIVING ORNAMENTS 1980 *Beggars Banquet BEGA 25*	39	3 wks
12 Sep	81 ●	DANCE *Beggars Banquet BEGA 28*	3	8 wks
18 Sep	82 ●	I, ASSASSIN *Beggars Banquet BEGA 40*	8	6 wks
27 Nov	82	NEW MAN NUMAN – THE BEST OF GARY NUMAN		
		TV Records TVA 7	45	7 wks
24 Sep	83	WARRIORS *Beggars Banquet BEGA 47*	12	6 wks
6 Oct	84	THE PLAN *Beggars Banquet BEGA 55*	29	4 wks
24 Nov	84	BERSERKER *Numa NUMA 1001*	45	3 wks
13 Apr	85	WHITE NOISE - LIVE *Numa NUMAD 1002*	29	5 wks
28 Sep	85	THE FURY *Numa NUMA 1003*	24	5 wks
8 Nov	86	STRANGE CHARM *Numa NUMA 1005*	59	2 wks
3 Oct	87	EXHIBITION *Beggars Banquet BEGA 88*	43	3 wks
8 Oct	88	METAL RHYTHM *Illegal ILP 035*	48	2 wks
8 Jul	89	AUTOMATIC *Polydor 8395201★★*	59	1 wk
28 Oct	89	SKIN MECHANIC *IRS EIRSA 1019*	55	1 wk
30 Mar	91	OUTLAND *IRS EIRSA 1039*	39	1 wk
22 Aug	92	MACHINE AND SOUL *Numa NUMACD 1009*	42	1 wk
2 Oct	93	BEST OF GARY NUMAN 1978–83		
		Beggars Banquet BEGA 150CD	70	1 wk

★ *Tubeway Army.*
★★ *Sharpe and Numan.*

Living Ornaments 1979–1980 *is a boxed set of* Living Ornaments 1979 *and* Living Ornaments 1980.

N.W.A. *US, male rap group* 6 wks

30 Sep	89	STRAIGHT OUTTA COMPTON		
		Fourth & Broadway BRLP 534	41	4 wks
15 Jun	91	EFIL4ZAGGIN *Fourth & Broadway BRLP 562*	25	2 wks

Philip OAKEY and Giorgio MORODER
UK/Italy, male vocal/instrumental duo 5 wks

10 Aug	85	PHILIP OAKEY AND GIORGIO MORODER		
		Virgin V 2351	52	5 wks

OASIS *UK, male/female vocal group* 14 wks

28 Apr	84	OASIS *WEA WX 3*	23	14 wks

John OATES – *See Daryl HALL and John OATES*

OBITUARY *US, male vocal/instrumental group* 1 wk

18 Apr	92	THE END COMPLETE *Road Runner RC 92012*	52	1 wk

Billy OCEAN *UK, male vocalist* 119 wks

24 Nov	84 ●	SUDDENLY *Jive JIP 12*	9	59 wks
17 May	86	LOVE ZONE *Jive HIP 35*	2	32 wks
19 Mar	88 ●	TEAR DOWN THESE WALLS *Jive HIP 57*	3	13 wks
28 Oct	89 ●	GREATEST HITS *Jive BOTV 1*	4	15 wks

OCEANIC *UK, male/female vocal/instrumental group* 2 wks

4 Jul	92	THAT ALBUM BY OCEANIC *Dead Dead Good 4509900832*	49	2 wks

Des O'CONNOR UK, male vocalist   45 wks

7 Dec 68 ●	I PRETEND *Columbia SCX 6295*	....	8	10 wks
5 Dec 70	WITH LOVE *Columbia SCX 6417*	....	40	4 wks
2 Dec 72	SING A FAVOURITE SONG *Pye NSPL 18390*	....	25	6 wks
2 Feb 80	JUST FOR YOU *Warwick WW 5071*	....	17	7 wks
13 Oct 84	DES O'CONNOR NOW *Telstar STAR 2245*	....	24	14 wks
5 Dec 92	PORTRAIT *Columbia 4727302*	....	63	4 wks

Hazel O'CONNOR UK, female vocalist   45 wks

9 Aug 80 ●	BREAKING GLASS (film soundtrack)			
	A & M AMLH 64820	....	5	38 wks
12 Sep 81	COVER PLUS *Albion ALB 108*	....	32	7 wks

Sinéad O'CONNOR Ireland, female vocalist   77 wks

23 Jan 88	THE LION AND THE COBRA *Ensign CHEN 7*	....	27	20 wks
24 Mar 90 ★	I DO NOT WANT WHAT I HAVEN'T GOT			
	Ensign CHEN 14	....	1	51 wks
26 Sep 92 ●	AM I NOT YOUR GIRL *Ensign CCD 1952*	....	6	6 wks

Daniel O'DONNELL Ireland, male vocalist   59 wks

15 Oct 88	FROM THE HEART *Telstar STAR 2327*	....	56	12 wks
28 Oct 89	THOUGHTS OF HOME *Telstar STAR 2372*	....	43	10 wks
21 Apr 90	FAVOURITES *Ritz RITZLP 058*	....	75	1 wk
17 Nov 90	THE LAST WALTZ *Ritz RITZALP 058*	....	53	5 wks
9 Nov 91	THE VERY BEST OF DANIEL O'DONNELL			
	Ritz RITZBLD 700	....	34	14 wks
21 Nov 92	FOLLOW YOUR DREAM *Ritz RITZBCD 701*	....	17	9 wks
6 Nov 93	A DATE WITH DANIEL LIVE *Ritz RITZBCD 702*	.....	21†	8 wks

O
232

ODYSSEY US, male/female vocal group   32 wks

16 Aug 80	HANG TOGETHER *RCA PL 13526*	....	38	3 wks
4 Jul 81	I'VE GOT THE MELODY *RCA RCALP 5028*	....	29	7 wks
3 Jul 82	HAPPY TOGETHER *RCA RCALP 6036*	....	21	9 wks
20 Nov 82	THE MAGIC TOUCH OF ODYSSEY *Telstar STAR 2223* .		69	5 wks
26 Sep 87	THE GREATEST HITS *Stylus SMR 735*	....	26	8 wks

Esther and Abi OFARIM Israel, female/male vocal duo   24 wks

24 Feb 68 ●	2 IN 3 *Philips SBL 7825*	....	6	20 wks
12 Jul 69	OFARIM CONCERT – LIVE '69 *Philips XL 4*	....	29	4 wks

Mary O'HARA UK, female vocalist/instrumentalist – harp   12 wks

8 Apr 78	MARY O'HARA AT THE ROYAL FESTIVAL HALL			
	Chrysalis CHR 1159	....	37	3 wks
1 Dec 79	TRANQUILLITY *Warwick WW 5072*	....	12	9 wks

David OISTRAKH – *See Herbert VON KARAJAN*

Mike OLDFIELD UK, male multi-instrumentalist/vocalist   520 wks

14 Jul 73 ★	TUBULAR BELLS *Virgin V 2001*	....	1	271 wks
14 Sep 74 ★	HERGEST RIDGE *Virgin V 2013*	....	1	17 wks
8 Feb 75	THE ORCHESTRAL TUBULAR BELLS *Virgin V 2026*★ .		17	7 wks
15 Nov 75 ●	OMMADAWN *Virgin V 2043*	....	4	23 wks
20 Nov 76	BOXED *Virgin V BOX 1*	....	22	13 wks
9 Dec 78	INCANTATIONS *Virgin VDT 101*	....	14	17 wks
11 Aug 79	EXPOSED *Virgin VD 2511*	....	16	9 wks

8 Dec	79	**PLATINUM** *Virgin V 2141*	24	9 wks
8 Nov	80	**QE 2** *Virgin V 2181*	27	12 wks
27 Mar	82 ●	**FIVE MILES OUT** *Virgin V 2222*	7	27 wks
4 Jun	83 ●	**CRISES** *Virgin V 2262*	6	29 wks
7 Jul	84	**DISCOVERY** *Virgin V 2308*	15	16 wks
15 Dec	84	**THE KILLING FIELDS** *Virgin V 2328*	97	1 wk
2 Nov	85	**THE COMPLETE MIKE OLDFIELD** *Virgin MOC 1*	36	17 wks
10 Oct	87	**ISLANDS** *Virgin V 2466*	29	5 wks
22 Jul	89	**EARTH MOVING** *Virgin V 2610*	30	5 wks
9 Jun	90	**AMAROK** *Virgin V 2640*	49	2 wks
12 Sep	92 ★	**TUBULAR BELLS II** *WEA 4509906182*	1	30 wks
25 Sep	93 ●	**ELEMENTS – THE BEST OF MIKE OLDFIELD**		
		Virgin VTCD 18	5	10 wks

★ *Mike Oldfield with the Royal Philharmonic Orchestra.*

OMAR *UK, male vocalist*   12 wks

14 Jul	90	**THERE'S NOTHING LIKE THIS** *Kongo Dance KDLP 2* ..	54	4 wks
27 Jul	91	**THERE'S NOTHING LIKE THIS (re–issue)**		
		Talkin Loud 5100211	19	6 wks
24 Oct	92	**MUSIC** *Talkin Loud 5124012*	37	2 wks

ONE DOVE *UK, male/female vocal/instrumental group*   2 wks

25 Sep	93	**MORNING DOVE WHITE** *London 8283522*	30	2 wks

ONE HUNDRED & ONE STRINGS
Germany, orchestra   35 wks

26 Sep	59 ●	**GYPSY CAMPFIRES** *Pye GGL 0009*	9	7 wks
26 Mar	60	**SOUL OF SPAIN** *Pye GGL 0017*	17	1 wk
16 Apr	60 ●	**GRAND CANYON SUITE** *Pye GGL 0048*	10	1 wk
27 Aug	60 ★	**DOWN DRURY LANE TO MEMORY LANE**		
		Pye GGL 0061	1	21 wks
15 Oct	83	**MORNING, NOON AND NIGHT** *Ronco RTL 2094*	32	5 wks

The orchestra was American based for last album.

ONE WORLD *UK, male vocal/instrumental group*   3 wks

9 Jun	90	**ONE WORLD ONE VOICE** *Virgin V 2632*	27	3 wks

Alexander O'NEAL *US, male vocalist*   162 wks

1 Jun	85	**ALEXANDER O'NEAL** *Tabu TBU 26485*	19	18 wks
8 Aug	87 ●	**HEARSAY/ALL MIXED UP** *Tabu 4509361*	4	103 wks
17 Dec	88	**MY GIFT TO YOU** *Tabu 463152 1*	53	3 wks
2 Feb	91 ●	**ALL TRUE MAN** *Tabu 4658821*	2	16 wks
30 May	92 ●	**THIS THING CALLED LOVE – THE GREATEST HITS**		
		Tabu 4717142	4	18 wks
20 Feb	93	**LOVE MAKES NO SENSE** *Tabu 5495022*	14	4 wks

All Mixed Up, a re-mixed album of Hearsay, was listed with Hearsay from 15 Jul 89.

ONLY ONES *UK, male vocal/instrumental group*   8 wks

3 Jun	78	**THE ONLY ONES** *CBS 82830*	56	1 wk
31 Mar	79	**EVEN SERPENTS SHINE** *CBS 83451*	42	2 wks
3 May	80	**BABY'S GOT A GUN** *CBS 84089*	37	5 wks

Yoko ONO *Japan, female vocalist*   2 wks

20 Jun	81	**SEASON OF GLASS** *Geffen K 99164*	47	2 wks

See also John Lennon.

ONSLAUGHT UK, male vocal/instrumental group   2 wks

20 May 89   **IN SEARCH OF SANITY** London 828142 1 .... **46** 2 wks

ONYX US, male rap group   3 wks

4 Sep 93   **BACDAFUCUP** Columbia 4729802 .... **59** 3 wks

ORANGE JUICE UK, male vocal/instrumental group   18 wks

6 Mar 82   **YOU CAN'T HIDE YOUR LOVE FOREVER**
    Polydor POLS 1057 .... **21** 6 wks
20 Nov 82   **RIP IT UP** Holden Caulfield Universal POLS 1076 .... **39** 8 wks
10 Mar 84   **TEXAS FEVER** Polydor OJMLP 1 .... **34** 4 wks

ORB UK, male instrumental/production duo   16 wks

27 Apr 91   **ORB'S ADVENTURES BEYOND THE ULTRAWORLD**
    Big Life BLRDLP 5 .... **29** 5 wks
18 Jul 92 ★ **U.F. ORB** Big Life BLRCD 18 .... **1** 9 wks
4 Dec 93   **LIVE 93** Island CIDD 8022 .... **23** 2 wks

Roy ORBISON US, male vocalist   222 wks

8 Jun 63   **LONELY AND BLUE** London HAU 2342 .... **15** 8 wks
29 Jun 63   **CRYING** London HAU 2437 .... **17** 3 wks
30 Nov 63 ● **IN DREAMS** London HAU 8108 .... **6** 57 wks
25 Jul 64   **EXCITING SOUNDS OF ROY ORBISON** Ember NR 5013 **17** 2 wks
5 Dec 64 ● **OH PRETTY WOMAN** London HAU 8207 .... **4** 16 wks
25 Sep 65 ● **THERE IS ONLY ONE ROY ORBISON** London HAU 8252 **10** 12 wks
26 Feb 66   **THE ORBISON WAY** London HAU 8279 .... **11** 10 wks
24 Sep 66   **THE CLASSIC ROY ORBISON** London HAU 8297 ...... **12** 8 wks
22 Jul 67   **ORBISONGS** Monument SMO 5004 .... **40** 1 wk
30 Sep 67   **ROY ORBISON'S GREATEST HITS** Monument SMO 5007 **40** 1 wk
27 Jan 73   **ALL-TIME GREATEST HITS** Monument MNT 67290 .... **39** 3 wks
29 Nov 75 ★ **THE BEST OF ROY ORBISON** Arcade ADEP 19 .... **1** 20 wks
18 Jul 81   **GOLDEN DAYS** CBS 10026 .... **63** 1 wk
4 Jul 87   **IN DREAMS: THE GREATEST HITS** Virgin VGD 3514 . **86** 2 wks
29 Oct 88 ★ **THE LEGENDARY ROY ORBISON** Telstar STAR 2330 . **1** 38 wks
11 Feb 89 ● **MYSTERY GIRL** Virgin V 2576 .... **2** 23 wks
25 Nov 89   **A BLACK AND WHITE NIGHT** Virgin V 2601 .... **51** 3 wks
2 Nov 90   **BALLADS** Telstar STAR 2441 .... **38** 10 wks
28 Nov 92   **KING OF HEARTS** Virgin America CDVUS 58 .... **23** 4 wks

ORBITAL UK, male instrumental duo   4 wks

12 Oct 91   **ORBITAL** ffrr 8282481 .... **71** 1 wk
5 Jun 93   **ORBITAL** Internal TRUCD 2 .... **28** 2 wks
The identically titled albums are different.

ORCHESTRAL MANOEUVRES IN THE DARK
UK, male vocal/instrumental duo   219 wks

1 Mar 80   **ORCHESTRAL MANOEUVRES IN THE DARK**
    DinDisc DID 2 .... **27** 29 wks
1 Nov 80 ● **ORGANISATION** DinDisc DID 6 .... **6** 25 wks
14 Nov 81 ● **ARCHITECTURE AND MORALITY** DinDisc DID 12 ... **3** 39 wks
12 Mar 83 ● **DAZZLE SHIPS** Telegraph V 2261 .... **5** 13 wks
12 May 84 ● **JUNK CULTURE** Virgin V 2310 .... **9** 27 wks
29 Jun 85   **CRUSH** Virgin V 2349 .... **13** 12 wks
11 Oct 86   **THE PACIFIC AGE** Virgin V 2398 .... **15** 7 wks
12 Mar 88 ● **THE BEST OF O.M.D.** Virgin OMD 1 .... **2** 32 wks
18 May 91 ● **SUGAR TAX** Virgin V 2648 .... **3** 29 wks
26 Jun 93   **LIBERATOR** Virgin CDV 2715 .... **14** 6 wks

Group often known as O.M.D.

L'ORCHESTRE ELECTRONIQUE
UK, male synthesized orchestra   *1 wk*

29 Oct 83   **SOUND WAVES** *Nouveau Musique NML 1005* .... **75**   1 wk

ORCHESTRE NATIONALE DE LA RADIO DIFFUSION FRANÇAISE – *See Sir Thomas BEECHAM*

Cyril ORNADEL – *See LONDON SYMPHONY ORCHESTRA*

ORVILLE – *See Keith HARRIS, ORVILLE and CUDDLES*

Jeffrey OSBORNE *US, male vocalist*   *10 wks*

5 May 84   **STAY WITH ME TONIGHT** *A & M AMLX 64940* ...... **56**   7 wks
13 Oct 84   **DON'T STOP** *A & M AMA 5017* .... **59**   3 wks

Ozzy OSBOURNE *UK, male vocalist*   *57 wks*

20 Sep 80 ● **OZZY OSBOURNE'S BLIZZARD OF OZ** *Jet JETLP 234★*   **7**   8 wks
7 Nov 81   **DIARY OF A MADMAN** *Jet JETLP 237* .... **14** 12 wks
27 Nov 82   **TALK OF THE DEVIL** *Jet JETDP 401* .... **21**   6 wks
10 Dec 83   **BARK AT THE MOON** *Epic EPC 25739* .... **24**   7 wks
22 Feb 86 ● **THE ULTIMATE SIN** *Epic EPC 26404* .... **8**   10 wks
23 May 87   **TRIBUTE** *Epic 450 475–1* .... **13**   6 wks
22 Oct 88   **NO REST FOR THE WICKED** *Epic 462581 1* .... **23**   4 wks
17 Mar 90   **JUST SAY OZZY** *Epic 4659401* .... **69**   1 wk
19 Oct 91   **NO MORE TEARS** *Epic 4678591* .... **17**   3 wks

★ *Ozzy Osbourne's Blizzard Of Oz.*

OSIBISA *Ghana/Nigeria, male vocal/instrumental group*   *17 wks*

22 May 71   **OSIBISA** *MCA MDKS 8001* .... **11** 10 wks
5 Feb 72   **WOYAYA** *MCA MDKS 8005* .... **11**   7 wks

Donny OSMOND *US, male vocalist*   *104 wks*

23 Sep 72 ● **PORTRAIT OF DONNY** *MGM 2315 108* ....:.. **5**   43 wks
16 Dec 72 ● **TOO YOUNG** *MGM 2315 113* .... **7**   24 wks
26 May 73 ● **ALONE TOGETHER** *MGM 2315 210* .... **6**   19 wks
15 Dec 73 ● **A TIME FOR US** *MGM 2315 273* .... **4**   13 wks
8 Feb 75   **DONNY** *MGM 2315 314* .... **16**   4 wks
2 Oct 76   **DISCOTRAIN** *Polydor 2391 226* .... **59**   1 wk

See also Osmonds; Donny and Marie Osmond.

Donny and Marie OSMOND *US, male/female vocal duo* *19 wks*

2 Nov 74   **I'M LEAVING IT ALL UP TO YOU** *MGM 2315 307* .... **13** 15 wks
26 Jul 75   **MAKE THE WORLD GO AWAY** *MGM 2315 343* ...... **30**   3 wks
5 Jun 76   **DEEP PURPLE** *Polydor 2391 220* .... **48**   1 wk

See also Donny Osmond; Marie Osmond.

Little Jimmy OSMOND *US, male vocalist*   *12 wks*

17 Feb 73   **KILLER JOE** *MGM 2315 157* .... **20** 12 wks

Marie OSMOND *US, female vocalist*   *1 wk*

9 Feb 74   **PAPER ROSES** *MGM 2315 262* .... **46**   1 wk

See also Donny and Marie Osmond.

O
235

OSMONDS US, male vocal/instrumental group · · · · · · · · · · · 103 wks

18 Nov 72	**OSMONDS LIVE** MGM 2315 117	13	22 wks
16 Dec 72 ●	**CRAZY HORSES** MGM 2315 123	9	19 wks
25 Aug 73 ●	**THE PLAN** MGM 2315 251	6	25 wks
17 Aug 74 ●	**OUR BEST TO YOU** MGM 2315 300	5	20 wks
7 Dec 74	**LOVE ME FOR A REASON** MGM 2315 312	13	9 wks
14 Jun 75	**I'M STILL GONNA NEED YOU** MGM 2315 342	19	7 wks
10 Jan 76	**AROUND THE WORLD – LIVE IN CONCERT** MGM 2659 044	41	1 wk

See also Donny Osmond.

Gilbert O'SULLIVAN UK, male vocalist · · · · · · · · · · · 195 wks

25 Sep 71 ●	**HIMSELF** MAM 501	5	82 wks
18 Nov 72 ★	**BACK TO FRONT** MAM 502	1	64 wks
6 Oct 73 ●	**I'M A WRITER NOT A FIGHTER** MAMS 505	2	25 wks
26 Oct 74 ●	**STRANGER IN MY OWN BACK YARD** MAM MAMS 506	9	8 wks
18 Dec 76	**GREATEST HITS** MAM MAMA 2003	13	11 wks
12 Sep 81	**20 GOLDEN GREATS** K-Tel NE 1133	98	1 wk
11 May 91	**NOTHING BUT THE BEST** Castle Communications CTVLP 107	50	4 wks

John OTWAY and Wild Willy BARRETT
UK, male vocal/instrumental duo · · · · · · · · · · · 1 wk

1 Jul 78	**DEEP AND MEANINGLESS** Polydor 2382 501	44	1 wk

OUI 3 UK/US/Switzerland, male/female vocal/instrumental group · 3 wks

7 Aug 93	**OUI LOVE YOU** MCA MCD 10833	39	3 wks

OVERLORD X UK, male rapper · · · · · · · · · · · 1 wk

4 Feb 89	**WEAPON IS MY LYRIC** Mango Street ILPS 9924	68	1 wk

OZRIC TENTACLES UK, male instrumental/vocal group · 5 wks

31 Aug 91	**STRANGEITUDE** Dovetail DOVELP 3	70	1 wk
1 May 93	**JURASSIC SHIFT** Dovetail DOVECD 6	11	4 wks

PACEMAKERS – *See GERRY and the PACEMAKERS*

Jimmy PAGE UK, male instrumentalist – guitar · · · · · · · 14 wks

27 Feb 82	**DEATHWISH II (film soundtrack)** Swansong SSK 59415 ..	40	4 wks
16 Mar 85	**WHATEVER HAPPENED TO JUGULA?** Beggars Banquet BEGA 60★	44	4 wks
2 Jul 88	**OUTRIDER** Geffen WX 155	27	6 wks

★ *Roy Harper with Jimmy Page.*

Elaine PAIGE *UK, female vocalist* 142 wks

1 May 82	**ELAINE PAIGE** *WEA K 58385*		56	6 wks
5 Nov 83 ●	**STAGES** *K-Tel NE 1262*		2	48 wks
20 Oct 84	**CINEMA** *K-Tel NE 1282*		12	25 wks
16 Nov 85 ●	**LOVE HURTS** *WEA WX 28*		8	20 wks
29 Nov 86	**CHRISTMAS** *WEA WX 80*		27	6 wks
5 Dec 87	**MEMORIES – THE BEST OF ELAINE PAIGE** *Telstar STAR 2313*		14	15 wks
19 Nov 88	**THE QUEEN ALBUM** *Siren SRNLP 22*		51	8 wks
27 Apr 91	**LOVE CAN DO THAT** *RCA PL 74932*		36	4 wks
28 Nov 92	**THE BEST OF ELAINE PAIGE AND BARBARA DICKSON** *Telstar TCD 2632★*		22	9 wks
10 Apr 93	**ROMANCE AND THE STAGE** *RCA 74321136152*		71	1 wk

★ *Elaine Paige and Barbara Dickson.*

PALE FOUNTAINS *UK, male vocal/instrumental group* 3 wks

10 Mar 84	**PACIFIC STREET** *Virgin V 2274*		85	2 wks
16 Feb 85	**FROM ACROSS THE KITCHEN TABLE** *Virgin V 2333*		94	1 wk

PALE SAINTS *UK, male/female vocal/instrumental group* 3 wks

24 Feb 90	**THE COMFORTS OF MADNESS** *4AD CAD 0002*		40	2 wks
4 Apr 92	**IN RIBBONS** *4AD CAD 2004CD*		61	1 wk

PALLAS *UK, male vocal/instrumental group* 4 wks

25 Feb 84	**SENTINEL** *Harvest SHSP 2400121*		41	3 wks
22 Feb 86	**THE WEDGE** *Harvest SHVL 850*		70	1 wk

P
237

Robert PALMER *UK, male vocalist* 137 wks

6 Nov 76	**SOME PEOPLE CAN DO WHAT THEY LIKE** *Island ILPS 9420*		46	1 wk
14 Jul 79	**SECRETS** *Island ILPS 9544*		54	4 wks
6 Sep 80	**CLUES** *Island ILPS 9595*		31	8 wks
3 Apr 82	**MAYBE IT'S LIVE** *Island ILPS 9665*		32	6 wks
23 Apr 83	**PRIDE** *Island ILPS 9720*		37	9 wks
16 Nov 85 ●	**RIPTIDE** *Island ILPS 9801*		5	37 wks
9 Jul 88	**HEAVY NOVA** *EMI EMD 1007*		17	25 wks
11 Nov 89 ●	**ADDICTIONS VOLUME 1** *Island ILPS 9944*		7	17 wks
17 Nov 90 ●	**DON'T EXPLAIN** *EMI EMDX 1018*		9	20 wks
4 Apr 92	**ADDICTIONS VOL. 2** *Island CIDTV 4*		12	7 wks
31 Oct 92	**RIDIN' HIGH** *EMI CDEMD 1038*		32	3 wks

PANTERA *US, male vocal/instrumental group* 1 wk

7 Mar 92	**VULGAR DISPLAY OF POWER** *Atco 7567917582*		64	1 wk

PAPAS – *See MAMAS and PAPAS*

Vanessa PARADIS *France, female vocalist* 2 wks

7 Nov 92	**VANESSA PARADIS** *Remark 5139542*		45	2 wks

Mica PARIS *UK, female vocalist* 39 wks

3 Sep 88 ●	**SO GOOD** *Fourth & Broadway BRLP 525*		6	32 wks
27 Oct 90	**CONTRIBUTION** *Fourth & Broadway BRLP 558*		26	3 wks
26 Jun 93	**WHISPER A PRAYER** *Fourth & Broadway BRCD 591*		20	4 wks

PARIS ANGELS *Ireland, male vocal/instrumental duo* *2 wks*

| 17 Aug 91 | **SUNDEW** *Virgin V 2667* .... | 37 | 2 wks |

Graham PARKER and the RUMOUR
UK, male vocal/instrumental group *35 wks*

27 Nov 76	**HEAT TREATMENT** *Vertigo 6360 137*	52	2 wks
12 Nov 77	**STICK TO ME** *Vertigo 9102 017*	19	4 wks
27 May 78	**PARKERILLA** *Vertigo 6641 797*	14	5 wks
7 Apr 79	**SQUEEZING OUT SPARKS** *Vertigo 9102 030*	18	8 wks
7 Jun 80	**THE UP ESCALATOR** *Stiff SEEZ 23*	11	10 wks
27 Mar 82	**ANOTHER GREY AREA** *RCA RCALP 6029★*	40	6 wks

★ *Graham Parker.*

Ray PARKER Jr. *US, male vocalist* *7 wks*

| 10 Oct 87 | **AFTER DARK** *WEA WX 122* .... | 40 | 7 wks |

John PARR *UK, male vocalist* *2 wks*

| 2 Nov 85 | **JOHN PARR** *London LONLP 12* .... | 60 | 2 wks |

Alan PARSONS PROJECT
UK, male vocal/instrumental group *38 wks*

28 Aug 76	**TALES OF MYSTERY AND IMAGINATION** *Charisma CDS 4003*	56	1 wk
13 Aug 77	**I ROBOT** *Arista SPARTY 1016*	30	1 wk
10 Jun 78	**PYRAMID** *Arista SPART 1054*	49	4 wks
29 Sep 79	**EVE** *Arista SPARTY 1100*	74	1 wk
15 Nov 80	**THE TURN OF A FRIENDLY CARD** *Arista DLART 1* ..	38	4 wks
29 May 82	**EYE IN THE SKY** *Arista 204 666*	27	11 wks
26 Nov 83	**THE BEST OF THE ALAN PARSONS PROJECT** *Arista APP 1*	99	1 wk
3 Mar 84	**AMMONIA AVENUE** *Arista 206 100*	24	8 wks
23 Feb 85	**VULTURE CULTURE** *Arista 206 577*	40	5 wks
14 Feb 87	**GAUDI** *Arista 208 084*	66	2 wks

PARTISANS *UK, male vocal/instrumental group* *1 wk*

| 19 Feb 83 | **THE PARTISANS** *No Future PUNK 4* .... | 94 | 1 wk |

Dolly PARTON *US, female vocalist* *17 wks*

25 Nov 78	**BOTH SIDES** *Lotus WH 5006*	45	12 wks
7 Sep 85	**GREATEST HITS** *RCA PL 84422*	74	1 wk
14 Mar 87	**TRIO** *Warner Bros. 9254911★*	60	4 wks

★ *Dolly Parton/Emmylou Harris/Linda Ronstadt.*

PARTRIDGE FAMILY *US, male/female vocal group* *13 wks*

8 Jan 72	**UP TO DATE** *Bell SBLL 143*	46	2 wks
22 Apr 72	**THE PARTRIDGE FAMILY SOUND MAGAZINE** *Bell BELLS 206*	14	7 wks
30 Sep 72	**SHOPPING BAG** *Bell BELLS 212*	28	3 wks
9 Dec 72	**CHRISTMAS CARD** *Bell BELLS 214*	45	1 wk

PASADENAS *UK, male vocal group* *32 wks*

| 22 Oct 88 | ● **TO WHOM IT MAY CONCERN** *CBS 462877 1* .... | 3 | 21 wks |
| 7 Mar 92 | ● **YOURS SINCERELY** *Columbia 4712642* .... | 6 | 11 wks |

PASSIONS UK, male/female vocal/instrumental group   1 wk

3 Oct 81	**THIRTY THOUSAND FEET OVER CHINA**		
	Polydor POLS 1041	92	1 wk

Luciano PAVAROTTI Italy, male vocalist   225 wks

15 May 82	**PAVAROTTI'S GREATEST HITS** Decca D 2362	95	1 wk
30 Jun 84	**MAMMA** Decca 411959★	96	1 wk
9 Aug 86	**THE PAVAROTTI COLLECTION** Stylus SMR 8617	12	34 wks
16 Jul 88	**THE NEW PAVAROTTI COLLECTION LIVE!**		
	Stylus SMR 857	63	8 wks
17 Mar 90	★ **THE ESSENTIAL PAVAROTTI** Decca 4302101	1	72 wks
1 Sep 90	★ **IN CONCERT** Decca 4304331★★	1	70 wks
20 Jul 91	★ **ESSENTIAL PAVAROTTI II** Decca 4304701	1	28 wks
15 Feb 92	**PAVAROTTI IN HYDE PARK** Decca 4363202	19	7 wks
4 Sep 93	**TI AMO – PUCCINI'S GREATEST LOVE SONGS**		
	Decca 4250992	23	4 wks

★ Luciano Pavarotti with the Henry Mancini Orchestra.
★★ Luciano Pavarotti, Placido Domingo and José Carreras.

PAVEMENT US, male vocal/instrumental group   3 wks

25 Apr 92	**SLANTED AND ENCHANTED** Big Cat ABB 34CD	72	1 wk
3 Apr 93	**WESTING (BY MUSKET AND SEXTANT)**		
	Big Cat ABBCD 40	30	2 wks

Tom PAXTON US, male vocalist   10 wks

13 Jun 70	**NO. 6** Elektra 2469–003	23	5 wks
3 Apr 71	**THE COMPLEAT TOM PAXTON** Elektra EKD 2003	18	4 wks
1 Jul 72	**PEACE WILL COME** Reprise K 44182	47	1 wk

PEARL JAM US, male vocal/instrumental group   63 wks

7 Mar 92	**TEN** Epic 4688842	18	53 wks
23 Oct 93	● **VS** Epic 4745492	2†	10 wks

David PEASTON UK, male vocalist   1 wk

26 Aug 89	**INTRODUCING . . . DAVID PEASTON** Geffen 924228 1	66	1 wk

PEBBLES US, female vocalist   4 wks

14 May 88	**PEBBLES** MCA MCF 3418	56	4 wks

PEDDLERS UK, male vocal/instrumental group   16 wks

16 Mar 68	**FREE WHEELERS** CBS SBPG 63183	27	13 wks
7 Feb 70	**BIRTHDAY** CBS 63682	16	3 wks

Kevin PEEK UK, male instrumentalist – guitar   8 wks

21 Mar 81	**AWAKENING** Ariola ARL 5065	52	2 wks
13 Oct 84	**BEYOND THE PLANETS** Telstar STAR 2244★	64	6 wks

★ Kevin Peek and Rick Wakeman.
Beyond the Planets also features Jeff Wayne with narration by Patrick Allen.

Teddy PENDERGRASS US, male vocalist   8 wks

21 May 88	**JOY** Elektra 960775 1	45	8 wks

Pearl Jam dominated the 1993 MTV Awards with 'Jeremy' from Ten. *(Pictorial Press)*

Carl Perkins jams with Eric Clapton at New York City's Bottom Line. *(Pictorial Press)*

The **Pet Shop Boys** are shown during their first American performance in a Los Angeles club. *(Pictorial Press)*

PENETRATION UK, male/female vocal/instrumental group 8 wks

28 Oct	78	**MOVING TARGETS** *Virgin V 2109*	22	4 wks
6 Oct	79	**COMING UP FOR AIR** *Virgin V 2131*	36	4 wks

PENGUIN CAFE ORCHESTRA
UK, male instrumental group   5 wks

4 Apr	87	**SIGNS OF LIFE** *Edition EG EGED 50*	49	5 wks

Ce Ce PENISTON US, female vocalist   19 wks

8 Feb	92 ●	**FINALLY** *A & M 3971822*	10	19 wks

PENTANGLE UK, male/female vocal/instrumental group   39 wks

15 Jun	68	**THE PENTANGLE** *Transatlantic TRA 162*	21	9 wks
1 Nov	69 ●	**BASKET OF LIGHT** *Transatlantic TRA 205*	5	28 wks
12 Dec	70	**CRUEL SISTER** *Transatlantic TRA 228*	51	2 wks

PEPSI and SHIRLIE UK, female vocal duo   2 wks

7 Nov	87	**ALL RIGHT NOW** *Polydor POLH 38*	69	2 wks

Carl PERKINS US, male vocalist   3 wks

15 Apr	78	**OL' BLUE SUEDES IS BACK** *Jet UATV 30146*	38	3 wks

Steve PERRY US, male vocalist   2 wks

14 Jul	84	**STREET TALK** *CBS 25967*	59	2 wks

PESTALOZZI CHILDREN'S CHOIR
International, male/female vocal group   2 wks

26 Dec	81	**SONGS OF JOY** *K-Tel NE 1140*	65	2 wks

PET SHOP BOYS UK, male vocal/instrumental duo   297 wks

5 Apr	86 ●	**PLEASE** *Parlophone PSB 1*	3	82 wks
29 Nov	86	**DISCO** *EMI PRG 1001*	15	72 wks
19 Sep	87 ●	**ACTUALLY** *Parlophone PCSD 104*	2	59 wks
22 Oct	88 ●	**INTROSPECTIVE** *Parlophone PCS 7325*	2	39 wks
3 Nov	90 ●	**BEHAVIOUR** *Parlophone PCSD 113*	2	14 wks
16 Nov	91 ●	**DISCOGRAPHY** *Parlophone PMTV 3*	3	19 wks
9 Oct	93 ★	**VERY** *Parlophone CDPCSD 143*	1†	12 wks

PETER and GORDON UK, male vocal duo   1 wk

20 Jun	64	**PETER AND GORDON** *Columbia 33SX 1630*	18	1 wk

PETER, PAUL and MARY
US, male/female vocal/instrumental group   26 wks

4 Jan	64	**PETER PAUL AND MARY** *Warner Bros. WM 4064*	18	1 wk
21 Mar	64	**IN THE WIND** *Warner Bros. WM 8142*	11	19 wks
13 Feb	65	**IN CONCERT VOL. 1** *Warner Bros. WM 8158*	20	2 wks
5 Sep	70	**TEN YEARS TOGETHER** *Warner Bros. WS 2552*	60	4 wks

P
241

PETERS and LEE *UK, male/female vocal duo* *166 wks*

30 Jun 73 ★	**WE CAN MAKE IT** *Philips 6308 165*	**1**	55 wks
22 Dec 73 ●	**BY YOUR SIDE** *Philips 6308 192*	**9**	48 wks
21 Sep 74 ●	**RAINBOW** *Philips 6308 208*	**6**	27 wks
4 Oct 75 ●	**FAVOURITES** *Philips 9109 205*	**2**	32 wks
18 Dec 76	**INVITATION** *Philips 9101 027*	**44**	4 wks

Tom PETTY and the HEARTBREAKERS
US, male vocal/instrumental group *79 wks*

4 Jun 77	**TOM PETTY AND THE HEARTBREAKERS** *Shelter ISA 5014*	**24**	12 wks
1 Jul 78	**YOU'RE GONNA GET IT** *Island ISA 5017*	**34**	5 wks
17 Nov 79	**DAMN THE TORPEDOES** *MCA MCF 3044*	**57**	4 wks
23 May 81	**HARD PROMISES** *MCA MCF 3098*	**32**	5 wks
20 Nov 82	**LONG AFTER DARK** *MCA MCF 3155*	**45**	4 wks
20 Apr 85	**SOUTHERN ACCENTS** *MCA MCF 3260*	**23**	6 wks
2 May 87	**LET ME UP (I'VE HAD ENOUGH)** *MCA MCG 6014* ...	**59**	2 wks
8 Jul 89 ●	**FULL MOON FEVER** *MCA MCG 6034*★	**8**	16 wks
20 Jul 91 ●	**INTO THE GREAT WIDE OPEN** *MCA MCA 10317*	**3**	18 wks
13 Nov 93 ●	**GREATEST HITS** *MCA MCD 10964*	**10†**	7 wks

★ *Tom Petty.*

PHARCYDE *US, male rap group* *1 wk*

21 Aug 93	**BIZARRE RIDE II THE PHARCYDE** *Atlantic 756792222* .	**58**	1 wk

PhD *UK, male vocal/instrumental duo* *8 wks*

1 May 82	**PhD** *WEA K 99150*	**33**	8 wks

Barrington PHELOUNG
Australia, male conductor/arranger *53 wks*

2 Mar 91 ●	**INSPECTOR MORSE – MUSIC FROM THE TV SERIES** *Virgin Television VTLP 2*	**4**	30 wks
7 Mar 92	**INSPECTOR MORSE VOL. 2** *Virgin Television VTCD 14* ..	**18**	12 wks
16 Jan 93	**INSPECTOR MORSE VOL. 3** *Virgin Television VTCD 16* ..	**20**	11 wks

PHENOMENA *UK, male vocal/instrumental group* *2 wks*

6 Jul 85	**PHENOMENA** *Bronze PM 1*	**63**	2 wks

Arlene PHILLIPS *UK, female exercise instructor* *24 wks*

28 Aug 82	**KEEP IN SHAPE SYSTEM** *Supershape SUP 01*	**41**	23 wks
18 Feb 84	**KEEP IN SHAPE SYSTEM VOL. 2** *Supershape SUP 2*	**100**	1 wk

Keep In Shape System *features music by Funk Federation.*

PHOTOS *UK, male/female vocal/instrumental group* *9 wks*

21 Jun 80 ●	**THE PHOTOS** *CBS PHOTO 5*	**4**	9 wks

Edith PIAF *France, female vocalist* *5 wks*

26 Sep 87	**HEART AND SOUL** *Stylus SMR 736*	**58**	5 wks

PIGBAG   UK, male instrumental group   14 wks

| 13 Mar 82 | **DR HECKLE AND MR JIVE**   Y Y 17 .... | 18 | 14 wks |

PILOT   UK, male vocal/instrumental group   1 wk

| 31 May 75 | **SECOND FLIGHT**   EMI EMC 3075 .... | 48 | 1 wk |

Courtney PINE   UK, male instrumentalist – saxophone   13 wks

| 25 Oct 86 | **JOURNEY TO THE URGE WITHIN**   Island ILPS 9846 ... | 39 | 11 wks |
| 6 Feb 88 | **DESTINY'S SONGS**   Antilles AN 8275 .... | 54 | 2 wks |

PINK FAIRIES   UK, male vocal/instrumental group   1 wk

| 29 Jul 72 | **WHAT A BUNCH OF SWEETIES**   Polydor 2383 132 ..... | 48 | 1 wk |

PINK FLOYD   UK, male vocal/instrumental group   755 wks

19 Aug 67 ●	**PIPER AT THE GATES OF DAWN** Columbia SCX 6157 .	6	14 wks
13 Jul 68 ●	**SAUCERFUL OF SECRETS** Columbia SCX 6258	9	11 wks
28 Jun 69 ●	**MORE (film soundtrack)** Columbia SCX 6346	9	5 wks
15 Nov 69 ●	**UMMAGUMMA** Harvest SHDW 1/2	5	21 wks
24 Oct 70 ★	**ATOM HEART MOTHER** Harvest SHVL 781	1	23 wks
7 Aug 71	**RELICS** Starline SRS 5071	32	6 wks
20 Nov 71 ●	**MEDDLE** Harvest SHVL 795	3	82 wks
17 Jun 72 ●	**OBSCURED BY CLOUDS (film soundtrack)**		
	Harvest SHSP 4020	6	14 wks
31 Mar 73 ●	**THE DARK SIDE OF THE MOON** Harvest SHVL 804 ...	2	310 wks
19 Jan 74	**A NICE PAIR (double re-issue)** Harvest SHDW 403	21	20 wks
27 Sep 75 ★	**WISH YOU WERE HERE** Harvest SHVL 814	1	84 wks
19 Feb 77 ●	**ANIMALS** Harvest SHVL 815	2	33 wks
8 Dec 79 ●	**THE WALL** Harvest SHDW 411	3	51 wks
5 Dec 81	**A COLLECTION OF GREAT DANCE SONGS**		
	Harvest SHVL 822	37	10 wks
2 Apr 83 ★	**THE FINAL CUT** Harvest SHPF 1983	1	25 wks
19 Sep 87 ●	**A MOMENTARY LAPSE OF REASON** EMI EMD 1003 .	3	34 wks
3 Dec 88	**DELICATE SOUND OF THUNDER** EMI EQ 5009	11	12 wks

A Nice Pair *is a double re-issue of the first two albums.*

PIPS – *See Gladys KNIGHT and the PIPS*

PIRANHAS   UK, male vocal/instrumental group   3 wks

| 20 Sep 80 | **PIRANHAS**   Sire SRK 6098 .... | 69 | 3 wks |

PIRATES   UK, male vocal/instrumental group   3 wks

| 19 Nov 77 | **OUT OF THEIR SKULLS**   Warner Bros. K 56411 .... | 57 | 3 wks |

Gene PITNEY   US, male vocalist   73 wks

11 Apr 64 ●	**BLUE GENE** United Artists ULP 1061	7	11 wks
6 Feb 65	**GENE PITNEY'S BIG 16** Stateside SL 10118	12	6 wks
20 Mar 65	**I'M GONNA BE STRONG** Stateside SL 10120	15	2 wks
20 Nov 65	**LOOKIN' THRU THE EYES OF LOVE** Stateside SL 10148 .	15	5 wks
17 Sep 66	**NOBODY NEEDS YOUR LOVE** Stateside SL 10183	13	17 wks
4 Mar 67	**YOUNG WARM AND WONDERFUL** Stateside SSL 10194 .	39	1 wk
22 Apr 67	**GENE PITNEY'S BIG SIXTEEN** Stateside SSL 10199	40	1 wk
20 Sep 69 ●	**BEST OF GENE PITNEY** Stateside SSL 10286	8	9 wks
2 Oct 76 ●	**HIS 20 GREATEST HITS** Arcade ADEP 22	6	14 wks
20 Oct 90	**BACKSTAGE – THE GREATEST HITS AND MORE**		
	Polydor 8471191	17	7 wks

P
243

PIXIES *US, male/female vocal/instrumental group*   *22 wks*

29 Apr	89 ●	**DOOLITTLE**	*4AD CAD 905*	....	**8**	9 wks
25 Aug	90 ●	**BOSSANOVA**	*4AD CAD 0010*	....	**3**	8 wks
5 Oct	91 ●	**TROMPE LE MONDE**	*4AD CAD 1014*	....	**7**	5 wks

PJ HARVEY *UK, female/male vocal/instrumental group*   *11 wks*

11 Apr	92	**DRY**	*Too Pure PURECD 10*	....	**11**	5 wks
8 May	93 ●	**RID OF ME**	*Island CID 8002*	....	**3**	4 wks
30 Oct	93	**4-TRACK DEMOS**	*Island IMCD 170*	....	**19**	2 wks

Robert PLANT *UK, male vocalist*   *57 wks*

10 Jul	82 ●	**PICTURES AT ELEVEN**	*Swansong SSK 59418*	....	**2**	15 wks
23 Jul	83 ●	**THE PRINCIPLES OF MOMENTS**	*WEA 7901011*	....	**7**	14 wks
1 Jun	85	**SHAKEN 'N' STIRRED**	*Es Paranza 79–0265–1*	....	**19**	4 wks
12 Feb	88 ●	**NOW AND ZEN**	*Es Paranza WX 149*	....	**10**	7 wks
31 Mar	90	**MANIC NIRVANA**	*Es Paranza WX 339*	....	**15**	9 wks
5 Jun	93 ●	**FATE OF NATIONS**	*Es Paranza 5148672*	....	**6**	8 wks

PLASMATICS *US, male/female vocal/instrumental group*   *3 wks*

11 Oct	80	**NEW HOPE FOR THE WRETCHED**	*Stiff SEEZ 24*	.....	**55**	3 wks

PLASTIC ONO BAND – *See John LENNON*

PLATTERS *US, male/female vocal group*   *13 wks*

8 Apr	78 ●	**20 CLASSIC HITS**	*Mercury 9100 049*	....	**8**	13 wks

PLAYERS ASSOCIATION
US, male/female vocal/instrumental group   *4 wks*

17 Mar	79	**TURN THE MUSIC UP**	*Vanguard VSD 79421*	....	**54**	4 wks

PLAYN JAYN *UK, male vocal/instrumental group*   *1 wk*

1 Sep	84	**FRIDAY THE 13TH (AT THE MARQUEE CLUB)**			
		A & M JAYN 13	....	**93**	1 wk

PM DAWN *US, male rap duo*   *17 wks*

14 Sep	91 ●	**OF THE HEART OF THE SOUL AND OF THE CROSS**			
		Gee Street GEEA 7	....	**8**	12 wks
3 Apr	93 ●	**THE BLISS ALBUM...?**	*Gee Street GEED 9*	.... **9**	5 wks

POGUES *Ireland, male vocal/instrumental group*   *64 wks*

3 Nov	84	**RED ROSES FOR ME**	*Stiff SEEZ 55*	.... **89**	1 wk
17 Aug	85	**RUM, SODOMY AND THE LASH**	*Stiff SEEZ 58*	.... **13**	14 wks
30 Jan	88 ●	**IF I SHOULD FALL FROM GRACE WITH GOD**			
		Stiff NYR 1	....	**3**	16 wks
29 Jul	89 ●	**PEACE AND LOVE**	*WEA WX 247*	.... **5**	8 wks
13 Oct	90	**HELL'S DITCH**	*Pogue Mahone WX 366*	.... **12**	5 wks
12 Oct	91	**BEST OF THE POGUES**	*PM WX 430*	.... **11**	17 wks
11 Sep	93	**WAITING FOR HERB**	*PM 4509934632*	.... **20**	3 wks

Group was male/female for first two albums.

POINTER SISTERS *US, female vocal group* 88 wks

29 Aug 81	**BLACK AND WHITE** *Planet K 52300*	21	13 wks
5 May 84 ●	**BREAK OUT** *Planet PL 84705*	9	58 wks
27 Jul 85	**CONTACT** *Planet PL 85457*	34	7 wks
29 Jul 89	**JUMP – THE BEST OF THE POINTER SISTERS** *RCA PL 90319*	11	10 wks

POISON *US, male vocal/instrumental group* 37 wks

21 May 88	**OPEN UP AND SAY . . . AAH!** *Capitol EST 2059*	18	21 wks
21 Jul 90 ●	**FLESH AND BLOOD** *Enigma EST 2126*	3	11 wks
14 Dec 91	**SWALLOW THIS LIVE** *Capitol ESTU 2159*	52	2 wks
6 Mar 93	**NATIVE TONGUE** *Capitol CDSETU 2190*	20	3 wks

POLECATS *UK, male vocal/instrumental group* 2 wks

4 Jul 81	**POLECATS** *Vertigo 6359 057*	28	2 wks

POLICE *UK, male vocal/instrumental group* 349 wks

21 Apr 79 ●	**OUTLANDOS D'AMOUR** *A & M AMLH 68502*	6	96 wks
13 Oct 79 ★	**REGGATTA DE BLANC** *A & M AMLH 64792*	1	74 wks
11 Oct 80 ★	**ZENYATTA MONDATTA** *A & M AMLH 64831*	1	31 wks
10 Oct 81 ★	**GHOST IN THE MACHINE** *A & M AMLK 63730*	1	27 wks
25 Jun 83 ★	**SYNCHRONICITY** *A & M AMLX 63735*	1	48 wks
8 Nov 86 ★	**EVERY BREATH YOU TAKE – THE SINGLES** *A & M EVERY 1*	1	55 wks
10 Oct 92 ●	**GREATEST HITS** *A & M 5400302*	10	18 wks

Su POLLARD *UK, female vocalist* 3 wks

22 Nov 86	**SU** *K-Tel NE 1327*	86	3 wks

Iggy POP *US, male vocalist* 27 wks

9 Apr 77	**THE IDIOT** *RCA Victor PL 12275*	30	3 wks
4 Jun 77	**RAW POWER** *Embassy 31464★*	44	2 wks
1 Oct 77	**LUST FOR LIFE** *RCA PL 12488*	28	5 wks
19 May 79	**NEW VALUES** *Arista SPART 1092*	60	4 wks
16 Feb 80	**SOLDIER** *Arista SPART 1117*	62	2 wks
11 Oct 86	**BLAH-BLAH-BLAH** *A & M AMA 5145*	43	7 wks
2 Jul 88	**INSTINCT** *A & M AMA 5198*	61	1 wk
21 Jul 90	**BRICK BY BRICK** *Virgin America VUSLP 19*	50	2 wks
25 Sep 93	**AMERICAN CAESAR** *Virgin CDVUS 64*	43	1 wk

★ *Iggy and the Stooges.*

POP WILL EAT ITSELF
UK, male vocal/instrumental group 10 wks

13 May 89	**THIS IS THE DAY, THIS IS THE HOUR** *RCA PL 74141*	24	2 wks
2 Nov 90	**CURE FOR SANITY** *RCA PL 74828*	33	3 wks
19 Sep 92	**THE LOOKS OR THE LIFESTYLE** *RCA 74321102652* ..	15	3 wks
6 Mar 93	**WEIRD'S BAR AND GRILL** *RCA 74321133432*	44	1 wk
6 Nov 93	**16 DIFFERENT FLAVOURS OF HELL** *RCA 74321153172*	73	1 wk

PORNO FOR PYROS *US, male vocal/instrumental group* 3 wks

8 May 93	**PORNO FOR PYROS** *Warner Bros 9362452282*	13	3 wks

Nick PORTLOCK – *See ROYAL PHILHARMONIC ORCHESTRA*

Sandy POSEY US, *female vocalist* — 1 wk

11 Mar 67	**BORN A WOMAN** *MGM MGMCS 8035*	39	1 wk

Frank POURCEL France, *male orchestra leader* — 7 wks

20 Nov 71 ●	**THIS IS POURCEL** *Studio Two STWO 7*	8	7 wks

Cozy POWELL UK, *male instrumentalist – drums* — 8 wks

26 Jan 80	**OVER THE TOP** *Ariola ARL 5038*	34	3 wks
19 Sep 81	**TILT** *Polydor POLD 5047*	58	4 wks
28 May 83	**OCTOPUSS** *Polydor POLD 5093*	86	1 wk

See also Emerson, Lake and Powell.

Peter POWELL UK, *male exercise instructor* — 13 wks

20 Mar 82 ●	**KEEP FIT AND DANCE** *K-Tel NE 1167*	9	13 wks

POWER STATION UK/US, *male vocal/instrumental group* — 23 wks

6 Apr 85	**THE POWER STATION** *Parlophone POST 1*	12	23 wks

P
246

PRAYING MANTIS UK, *male vocal/instrumental group* — 2 wks

11 Apr 81	**TIME TELLS NO LIES** *Arista SPART 1153*	60	2 wks

PREFAB SPROUT
UK, *male/female vocal/instrumental group* — 100 wks

17 Mar 84	**SWOON** *Kitchenware KWLP 1*	22	7 wks
22 Jun 85	**STEVE McQUEEN** *Kitchenware KWLP 3*	21	35 wks
26 Mar 88 ●	**FROM LANGLEY PARK TO MEMPHIS** *Kitchenware KWLP 9*	5	24 wks
1 Jul 89	**PROTEST SONGS** *Kitchenware KWLP 4*	18	4 wks
8 Sep 90 ●	**JORDAN: THE COMEBACK** *Kitchenware KWLP 14*	7	17 wks
11 Jul 92 ●	**A LIFE OF SURPRISES – THE BEST OF PREFAB SPROUT** *Kitchenware 4718862*	3	13 wks

Elvis PRESLEY US, *male vocalist* — 1046 wks

8 Nov 58 ●	**ELVIS' GOLDEN RECORDS** *RCA RB 16069*	3	44 wks
8 Nov 58 ●	**KING CREOLE (film soundtrack)** *RCA RD 27086*	4	14 wks
4 Apr 59 ●	**ELVIS (ROCK 'N' ROLL NO. 1)** *HMV CLP 1093*	4	9 wks
8 Aug 59 ●	**A DATE WITH ELVIS** *RCA RD 27128*	4	15 wks
18 Jun 60 ★	**ELVIS IS BACK** *RCA RD 27171*	1	27 wks
18 Jun 60 ●	**ELVIS' GOLDEN RECORDS VOL. 2** *RCA RD 27159* ...	4	20 wks
10 Dec 60 ★	**G.I. BLUES (film soundtrack)** *RCA RD 27192*	1	55 wks
20 May 61 ●	**HIS HAND IN MINE** *RCA RD 27211*	3	25 wks
4 Nov 61 ●	**SOMETHING FOR EVERYBODY** *RCA RD 27224*	2	18 wks
9 Dec 61 ★	**BLUE HAWAII (film soundtrack)** *RCA RD 27238*	1	65 wks
7 Jul 62 ●	**POT LUCK** *RCA RD 27265*	1	25 wks
8 Dec 62 ●	**ROCK 'N' ROLL NO. 2** *RCA RD 7528*	3	17 wks
26 Jan 63 ●	**GIRLS! GIRLS! GIRLS! (film soundtrack)** *RCA RD 7534* .	2	21 wks
11 May 63 ●	**IT HAPPENED AT THE WORLD'S FAIR (film soundtrack)** *RCA RD 7565*	4	21 wks
28 Dec 63 ●	**FUN IN ACAPULCO (film soundtrack)** *RCA RD 7609* ..	9	14 wks
11 Apr 64 ●	**ELVIS' GOLDEN RECORDS VOL. 3** *RCA RD 7630*	6	13 wks
4 Jul 64 ●	**KISSIN' COUSINS (film soundtrack)** *RCA RD 7645*	5	17 wks
9 Jan 65	**ROUSTABOUT (film soundtrack)** *RCA RD 7678*	12	4 wks
1 May 65 ●	**GIRL HAPPY (film soundtrack)** *RCA RD 7714*	8	18 wks
25 Sep 65	**FLAMING STAR AND SUMMER KISSES** *RCA RD 7723.*	11	4 wks

Date			Title	Pos	Weeks
4 Dec	65	●	ELVIS FOR EVERYBODY *RCA RD 7782*	8	8 wks
15 Jan	66		HAREM HOLIDAY (film soundtrack) *RCA RD 7767* ...	11	5 wks
30 Apr	66		FRANKIE AND JOHNNY (film soundtrack)		
			RCA RD 7793	11	5 wks
6 Aug	66	●	PARADISE HAWAIIAN STYLE (film soundtrack)		
			RCA Victor RD 7810	7	9 wks
26 Nov	66		CALIFORNIA HOLIDAY (film soundtrack)		
			RCA Victor RD 7820	17	6 wks
8 Apr	67		HOW GREAT THOU ART *RCA Victor SF 7867*	11	14 wks
2 Sep	67		DOUBLE TROUBLE (film soundtrack)		
			RCA Victor SF 7892	34	1 wk
20 Apr	68		CLAMBAKE (film soundtrack) *RCA Victor SD 7917*	39	1 wk
3 May	69	●	ELVIS – NBC TV SPECIAL *RCA RD 8011*	2	26 wks
5 Jul	69	●	FLAMING STAR *RCA International INTS 1012*	2	14 wks
23 Aug	69	★	FROM ELVIS IN MEMPHIS *RCA SF 8029*	1	13 wks
28 Feb	70		PORTRAIT IN MUSIC (import) *RCA 558*	36	1 wk
14 Mar	70	●	FROM MEMPHIS TO VEGAS – FROM VEGAS TO		
			MEMPHIS *RCA SF 8080/1*	3	16 wks
1 Aug	70	●	ON STAGE *RCA SF 8128*	2	18 wks
5 Dec	70		ELVIS' GOLDEN RECORDS VOL. 1 (re-issue)		
			RCA SF 8129	21	11 wks
12 Dec	70		WORLDWIDE 50 GOLD AWARD HITS VOL. 1		
			RCA LPM 6401	49	2 wks
30 Jan	71		THAT'S THE WAY IT IS *RCA SF 8162*	12	41 wks
10 Apr	71	●	ELVIS COUNTRY *RCA SF 8172*	6	9 wks
24 Jul	71	●	LOVE LETTERS FROM ELVIS *RCA SF 8202*	7	5 wks
7 Aug	71	●	C'MON EVERYBODY *RCA International INTS 1286*	5	21 wks
7 Aug	71		YOU'LL NEVER WALK ALONE *RCA Camden CDM 1088*.	20	4 wks
25 Sep	71		ALMOST IN LOVE *RCA International INTS 1206*	38	2 wks
4 Dec	71	●	ELVIS' CHRISTMAS ALBUM *RCA International INTS 1126*.	7	5 wks
18 Dec	71		I GOT LUCKY *RCA International INTS 1322*	26	3 wks
27 May	72		ELVIS NOW *RCA Victor SF 8266*	12	8 wks
3 Jun	72		ROCK AND ROLL (re-issue of ROCK 'N' ROLL NO. 1)		
			RCA Victor SF 8233	34	4 wks
3 Jun	72		ELVIS FOR EVERYONE *RCA Victor SF 8232*	48	1 wk
15 Jul	72	●	ELVIS AT MADISON SQUARE GARDEN		
			RCA Victor SF 8296	3	20 wks
12 Aug	72		HE TOUCHED ME *RCA Victor SF 8275*	38	3 wks
24 Feb	73		ALOHA FROM HAWAII VIA SATELLITE		
			RCA Victor DPS 2040	11	10 wks
15 Sep	73		ELVIS *RCA Victor SF 8378*	16	4 wks
2 Mar	74		A LEGENDARY PERFORMER VOL. 1		
			RCA Victor CPLI 0341	20	3 wks
25 May	74		GOOD TIMES *RCA Victor APLI 0475*	42	1 wk
7 Sep	74		ELVIS PRESLEY LIVE ON STAGE IN MEMPHIS		
			RCA Victor APLI 0606	44	1 wk
22 Feb	75		PROMISED LAND *RCA Victor APLI 0873*	21	4 wks
14 Jun	75		TODAY *RCA Victor RS 1011*	48	1 wk
5 Jul	75	★	40 GREATEST HITS *Arcade ADEP 12*	1	38 wks
6 Sep	75		THE ELVIS PRESLEY SUN COLLECTION		
			RCA Starcall HY 1001	16	13 wks
19 Jun	76		FROM ELVIS PRESLEY BOULEVARD, MEMPHIS,		
			TENNESSEE *RCA Victor RS 1060*	29	5 wks
19 Feb	77		ELVIS IN DEMAND *RCA Victor PL 42003*	12	11 wks
27 Aug	77	●	MOODY BLUE *RCA PL 12428*	3	15 wks
3 Sep	77	●	WELCOME TO MY WORLD *RCA PL 12274*	7	9 wks
3 Sep	77		G.I. BLUES (re-issue) *RCA SF 5078*	14	10 wks
10 Sep	77		ELVIS' GOLDEN RECORDS VOL. 2 (re-issue)		
			RCA SF 8151	27	4 wks
10 Sep	77		HITS OF THE 70'S *RCA LPLI 7527*	30	4 wks
10 Sep	77		BLUE HAWAII (re-issue) *RCA SF 8145*	26	6 wks
10 Sep	77		ELVIS' GOLDEN RECORDS VOL. 3 (re-issue)		
			RCA SF 7630	49	2 wks
10 Sep	77		PICTURES OF ELVIS *RCA Starcall HY 1023*	52	1 wk
8 Oct	77		THE SUN YEARS *Charly SUN 1001*	31	2 wks
15 Oct	77		LOVING YOU *RCA PL 42358*	24	3 wks
19 Nov	77		ELVIS IN CONCERT *RCA PL 02578*	13	11 wks
22 Apr	78		HE WALKS BESIDE ME *RCA PL 12772*	37	1 wk
3 Jun	78		THE '56 SESSIONS VOL. 1 *RCA PL 42101*	47	4 wks
2 Sep	78		TV SPECIAL *RCA PL 42370*	50	2 wks
11 Nov	78		40 GREATEST HITS (re-issue) *RCA PL 42691*	40	14 wks
3 Feb	79		A LEGENDARY PERFORMER VOL. 3 *RCA PL 13082*.	43	3 wks
5 May	79		OUR MEMORIES OF ELVIS *RCA PL 13279*	72	1 wk
24 Nov	79	●	LOVE SONGS *K-Tel NE 1062*	4	13 wks

P

247

21 Jun 80	**ELVIS PRESLEY SINGS LIEBER AND STOLLER**			
	RCA International INTS 5031	32	5 wks
23 Aug 80	**ELVIS ARON PRESLEY** *RCA ELVIS 25*	21	4 wks
23 Aug 80	**PARADISE HAWAIIAN STYLE (re–issue)**		
	RCA International INTS 5037	53	2 wks
29 Nov 80 ●	**INSPIRATION** *K-Tel NE 1101*	6	8 wks
14 Mar 81	**GUITAR MAN** *RCA RCALP 5010*	33	5 wks
9 May 81	**THIS IS ELVIS PRESLEY** *RCA RCALP 5029*	47	4 wks
28 Nov 81	**THE ULTIMATE PERFORMANCE** *K-Tel NE 1141*	45	6 wks
13 Feb 82	**THE SOUND OF YOUR CRY** *RCA RCALP 3060*	31	12 wks
6 Mar 82	**ELVIS PRESLEY EP PACK** *RCA EP1*	97	1 wk
21 Aug 82	**ROMANTIC ELVIS/ROCKIN' ELVIS**		
	RCA RCALP 1000/1	62	5 wks
18 Dec 82	**IT WON'T SEEM LIKE CHRISTMAS WITHOUT YOU**		
	RCA INTS 5235	80	1 wk
30 Apr 83	**JAILHOUSE ROCK/LOVE IN LAS VEGAS**		
	RCA RCALP 9020	40	2 wks
20 Aug 83	**I WAS THE ONE** *RCA RCALP 3105*	83	1 wk
3 Dec 83	**A LEGENDARY PERFORMER VOL. 4** *RCA PL 84848* .	91	1 wk
7 Apr 84	**I CAN HELP** *RCA PL 89287*	71	3 wks
21 Jul 84	**THE FIRST LIVE RECORDINGS**		
	RCA International PG 89387	69	2 wks
26 Jan 85	**20 GREATEST HITS VOLUME 2**		
	RCA International NL 89168	98	1 wk
25 May 85	**RECONSIDER BABY** *RCA PL 85418*	92	1 wk
12 Oct 85	**BALLADS** *Telstar STAR 2264*	23	17 wks
29 Aug 87 ●	**PRESLEY – THE ALL TIME GREATEST HITS**		
	RCA PL 90100	4	22 wks
28 Jan 89	**STEREO '57 (ESSENTIAL ELVIS VOL. 2)** *RCA PL 90250*	60	2 wks
21 Jul 90	**HITS LIKE NEVER BEFORE (VOL. 3)** *RCA PL 90486* ..	71	1 wk
1 Sep 90	**THE GREAT PERFORMANCES** *RCA PL 82227*	62	1 wk
24 Aug 91	**COLLECTORS GOLD** *RCA PL 90574*	57	1 wk
22 Feb 92 ●	**FROM THE HEART – HIS GREATEST LOVE SONGS**		
	RCA PD 90642	4	18 wks

P
248

PRETENDERS
UK/US, female/male vocal/instrumental group   *136 wks*

19 Jan 80 ★	**PRETENDERS** *Real RAL 3*	1	35 wks
15 Aug 81 ●	**PRETENDERS II** *Real SRK 3572*	7	27 wks
21 Jan 84	**LEARNING TO CRAWL** *Real WX 2*	11	16 wks
1 Nov 86 ●	**GET CLOSE** *WEA WX 64*	6	28 wks
7 Nov 87 ●	**THE SINGLES** *WEA WX 135*	6	25 wks
26 May 90	**PACKED!** *WEA WX 346*	19	5 wks

---

PRETTY THINGS
UK, male vocal/instrumental group   *13 wks*

27 Mar 65 ●	**PRETTY THINGS** *Fontana TL 5239*	6	10 wks
27 Jun 70	**PARACHUTE** *Harvest SHVL 774*	43	3 wks

---

Alan PRICE
UK, male vocalist/instrumentalist – keyboards   *10 wks*

8 Jun 74 ●	**BETWEEN TODAY AND YESTERDAY**		
	Warner Bros. K 56032	9	10 wks

Charley PRIDE   *US, male vocalist*   *17 wks*

10 Apr 71	**CHARLEY PRIDE SPECIAL** *RCA SF 8171*	29	1 wk
28 May 77	**SHE'S JUST AN OLD LOVE TURNED MEMORY**		
	RCA Victor PL 12261	34	2 wks
3 Jun 78	**SOMEONE LOVES YOU HONEY** *RCA PL 12478*	48	2 wks
26 Jan 80 ●	**GOLDEN COLLECTION** *K-Tel NE 1056*	6	12 wks

The last two of the hat trick of number ones by **Prince** were both film soundtracks.
(Pictorial Press)

Queen are shown with the boys who played their junior versions in a promo video.
(Pictorial Press)

Maxi PRIEST *UK, male vocalist* — 35 wks

6 Dec 86	**INTENTIONS** *10 DIX 32*	96	1 wk
5 Dec 87	**MAXI** *10 DIX 64*	25	15 wks
15 Jul 90	**BONAFIDE** *10 DIX 92*	11	13 wks
9 Nov 91	**BEST OF ME** *10 DIX 111*	23	5 wks
14 Nov 92	**FE REAL** *10 DIXCD 113*	60	1 wk

PRIMAL SCREAM *UK, male vocal/instrumental group* — 18 wks

17 Oct 87	**SONIC FLOWER GROOVE** *Elevation ELV 2*	62	1 wk
5 Oct 91 ●	**SCREAMADELICA** *Creation CRELP 076*	8	17 wks

PRIMITIVES *UK, male/female vocal/instrumental group* — 13 wks

9 Apr 88 ●	**LOVELY** *RCA PL 71688*	6	10 wks
2 Sep 89	**LAZY 86–88** *Lazy 15*	73	1 wk
28 Oct 89	**PURE** *RCA PL 74252*	33	2 wks

PRIMUS *US, male vocal/instrumental group* — 1 wk

8 May 93	**PORK SODA** *Interscope 75679922572*	56	1 wk

P
250

PRINCE *US, male vocalist* — 353 wks

21 Jul 84 ●	**PURPLE RAIN – MUSIC FROM THE MOTION PICTURE** *Warner Bros. 9251101★*	7	86 wks
8 Sep 84	**1999** *Warner Bros. 923720*	30	21 wks
4 May 85 ●	**AROUND THE WORLD IN A DAY** *Warner Bros. 92-5286-1★*	5	20 wks
12 Apr 86 ●	**PARADE – MUSIC FROM 'UNDER THE CHERRY MOON'** *Warner Bros. WX 39★*	4	26 wks
11 Apr 87 ●	**SIGN 'O' THE TIMES** *Paisley Park WX 88*	4	32 wks
21 May 88 ★	**LOVESEXY** *Paisley Park WX 164*	1	30 wks
1 Jul 89 ★	**BATMAN** *Warner Bros. WX 281*	1	20 wks
1 Sep 90 ★	**GRAFFITI BRIDGE** *Paisley Park WX 361*	1	8 wks
24 Aug 91	**GETT OFF (import)** *Paisley Park 9401382*	33	3 wks
12 Oct 91 ●	**DIAMONDS AND PEARLS** *Paisley Park WX 432★★*	2	51 wks
17 Oct 92 ★	**SYMBOL** *Paisley Park 9362450372★★*	1	21 wks
25 Sep 93 ●	**THE HITS/THE B-SIDES** *Paisley Park 9362454402*	4	7 wks
25 Sep 93 ●	**THE HITS 1** *Paisley Park 9362454312*	5†	14 wks
25 Sep 93 ●	**THE HITS 2** *Paisley Park 9362454352*	5†	14 wks

★ *Prince and the Revolution.*
★★ *Prince and the New Power Generation.*

PRINCE CHARLES and the CITY BEAT BAND
US, male vocalist with male vocal/instrumental group — 1 wk

30 Apr 83	**STONE KILLERS** *Virgin V 2271*	84	1 wk

PRINCESS *UK, female vocalist* — 14 wks

17 May 86	**PRINCESS** *Supreme SU1*	15	14 wks

P.J. PROBY *US, male vocalist* — 3 wks

27 Feb 65	**I'M P.J. PROBY** *Liberty LBY 1235*	16	3 wks

PROCLAIMERS *UK, male vocal/instrumental duo* — 48 wks

9 May 87	**THIS IS THE STORY** *Chrysalis CHR 1602*	43	21 wks
24 Sep 88 ●	**SUNSHINE ON LEITH** *Chrysalis CHR 1668*	6	27 wks

PROCOL HARUM UK, male vocal/instrumental group   11 wks

19 Jul	69	**A SALTY DOG** *Regal Zonophone SLRZ 1009*	**27**	2 wks
27 Jun	70	**HOME** *Regal Zonophone SLRZ 1014*	**49**	1 wk
3 Jul	71	**BROKEN BARRICADES** *Island ILPS 9158*	**42**	1 wk
6 May	72	**A WHITER SHADE OF PALE/A SALTY DOG (double**		
		re-issue) *Fly Double Back TOOFA 7/8*	**26**	4 wks
6 May	72	**PROCOL HARUM IN CONCERT WITH THE**		
		EDMONTON SYMPHONY ORCHESTRA		
		Chrysalis CHR 1004	**48**	1 wk
30 Aug	75	**PROCOL'S NINTH** *Chrysalis CHR 1080*	**41**	2 wks

A Whiter Shade Of Pale/A Salty Dog is a double re-issue, although A Whiter Shade Of Pale *was not previously a hit. The Edmonton Symphony Orchestra is a Canadian orchestra.*

PRODIGY UK, male producer – Liam Howlett   25 wks

10 Oct	92	**EXPERIENCE** *XL XLCD 110*	**12**	25 wks

PROJECT D UK, male instrumentalist   18 wks

17 Feb	90	**THE SYNTHESIZER ALBUM** *Telstar STAR 2371*	**13**	11 wks
29 Sep	90	**THE SYNTHESIZER ALBUM 2** *Telstar STAR 2428*	**25**	7 wks

PROPAGANDA
Germany, male/female vocal/instrumental group   16 wks

13 Jul	85	**A SECRET WISH** *ZTT ZTTIQ 3*	**16**	12 wks
23 Nov	85	**WISHFUL THINKING** *ZTT ZTTIQ 20*	**82**	2 wks
9 Jun	90	**1234** *Virgin V 2625*	**46**	2 wks

Dorothy PROVINE US, female vocalist   49 wks

2 Dec	61 ●	**THE ROARING TWENTIES—SONGS FROM THE TV**		
		SERIES *Warner Bros. WM 4035*	**3**	42 wks
10 Feb	62 ●	**VAMP OF THE ROARING TWENTIES**		
		Warner Bros. WM 4053	**9**	7 wks

PSYCHEDELIC FURS UK, male vocal/instrumental group   38 wks

15 Mar	80	**PSYCHEDELIC FURS** *CBS 84084*	**18**	6 wks
23 May	81	**TALK TALK TALK** *CBS 84892*	**30**	9 wks
2 Oct	82	**FOREVER NOW** *CBS 85909*	**20**	6 wks
19 May	84	**MIRROR MOVES** *CBS 25950*	**15**	9 wks
14 Feb	87	**MIDNIGHT TO MIDNIGHT** *CBS 450 256–1*	**12**	4 wks
13 Aug	88	**ALL OF THIS AND NOTHING** *CBS 461101*	**67**	2 wks
18 Nov	89	**BOOK OF DAYS** *CBS 465982 1*	**74**	1 wk
13 Jul	91	**WORLD OUTSIDE** *East West WX 422*	**68**	1 wk

PUBLIC ENEMY US, male rap group   29 wks

30 Jul	88 ●	**IT TAKES A NATION OF MILLIONS TO HOLD US**		
		BACK *Def Jam 462415 1*	**8**	9 wks
28 Apr	90 ●	**FEAR OF A BLACK PLANET** *Def Jam 4662811*	**4**	10 wks
19 Oct	91 ●	**APOCALYPSE '91 – THE ENEMY STRIKES BLACK**		
		Def Jam 4687511	**8**	7 wks
3 Oct	92	**GREATEST MISSES** *Def Jam 4720312*	**14**	3 wks

PUBLIC IMAGE LTD. UK, male vocal/instrumental group   51 wks

23 Dec	78	**PUBLIC IMAGE** *Virgin V 2114*	**22**	11 wks
8 Dec	79	**METAL BOX** *Virgin METAL 1*	**18**	8 wks
8 Mar	80	**SECOND EDITION OF PIL** *Virgin VD 2512*	**46**	2 wks
22 Nov	80	**PARIS IN THE SPRING** *Virgin V 2183*	**61**	2 wks
18 Apr	81	**FLOWERS OF ROMANCE** *Virgin V 2189*	**11**	5 wks

8 Oct 83	**LIVE IN TOKYO** *Virgin VGD 3508*	**28** 6 wks
21 Jul 84	**THIS IS WHAT YOU WANT . . . THIS IS WHAT YOU GET** *Virgin V 2309*	**56** 2 wks
15 Feb 86	**ALBUM/CASSETTE** *Virgin V 2366*	**14** 6 wks
26 Sep 87	**HAPPY?** *Virgin V 2455*	**40** 2 wks
10 Jun 89	**9** *Virgin V 2588*	**36** 2 wks
10 Nov 90	**THE GREATEST HITS SO FAR** *Virgin V 2644*	**20** 3 wks
7 Mar 92	**THAT WHAT IS NOT** *Virgin CDV 2681*	**46** 2 wks

Gary PUCKETT and the UNION GAP
US, male vocalist, male vocal/instrumental group   *4 wks*

29 Jun 68	**UNION GAP** *CBS 63342*	**24** 4 wks

Q-TIPS *UK, male vocal/instrumental group*   *1 wk*

30 Aug 80	**Q-TIPS** *Chrysalis CHR 1255*	**50** 1 wk

Suzi QUATRO *US, female vocalist/instrumentalist – guitar*   *13 wks*

13 Oct 73	**SUZI QUATRO** *RAK SRAK 505*	**32** 4 wks
26 Apr 80 ●	**SUZI QUATRO'S GREATEST HITS** *RAK EMTV 24* ...	**4** 9 wks

QUEDO BRASS – *See CHAQUITO ORCHESTRA*

QUEEN *UK, male vocal/instrumental group*   *1061 wks*

23 Mar 74 ●	**QUEEN 2** *EMI EMA 767*	**5** 29 wks
30 Mar 74	**QUEEN** *EMI EMC 3006*	**24** 18 wks
23 Nov 74 ●	**SHEER HEART ATTACK** *EMI EMC 3061*	**2** 42 wks
13 Dec 75 ★	**A NIGHT AT THE OPERA** *EMI EMTC 103*	**1** 50 wks
25 Dec 76 ★	**A DAY AT THE RACES** *EMI EMTC 104*	**1** 24 wks
12 Nov 77 ●	**NEWS OF THE WORLD** *EMI EMA 784*	**4** 20 wks
25 Nov 78 ●	**JAZZ** *EMI EMA 788*	**2** 27 wks
7 Jul 79 ●	**LIVE KILLERS** *EMI EMSP 330*	**3** 27 wks
12 Jul 80 ★	**THE GAME** *EMI EMA 795*	**1** 18 wks
20 Dec 80 ●	**FLASH GORDON (film soundtrack)** *EMI EMC 3351*	**10** 15 wks
7 Nov 81 ★	**GREATEST HITS** *Parlophone EMYV 30*	**1** 406 wks
15 May 82 ●	**HOT SPACE** *EMI EMA 797*	**4** 19 wks
10 Mar 84 ●	**THE WORKS** *EMI EMC 240014*	**2** 93 wks
14 Jun 86 ★	**A KIND OF MAGIC** *EMI EU 3509*	**1** 63 wks
13 Dec 86 ●	**LIVE MAGIC** *EMI EMC 3519*	**3** 43 wks
3 Jun 89 ★	**THE MIRACLE** *Parlophone PCSD 107*	**1** 32 wks
16 Dec 89	**QUEEN AT THE BEEB** *Band Of Joy BOJLP 001*	**67** 1 wk
16 Feb 91 ★	**INNUENDO** *Parlophone PCSD 115*	**1** 37 wks
9 Nov 91 ★	**GREATEST HITS II** *Parlophone PMTV 2*	**1** 82 wks
6 Jun 92 ●	**LIVE AT WEMBLEY '86** *Parlophone CDPCSP 725*	**2** 15 wks

The Works *changed label number during its run to EMI WORK 1.*

QUEENSRYCHE *US, male vocal/instrumental group*   *8 wks*

29 Sep 84	**THE WARNING** *EMI America EJ 2402201*	**100** 1 wk
26 Jul 86	**RAGE FOR ORDER** *EMI America AML 3105*	**66** 1 wk
4 Jun 88	**OPERATION MINDCRIME** *Manhattan MTL 1023*	**58** 3 wks
22 Sep 90	**EMPIRE** *EMI-USA MTL 1058*	**13** 3 wks

QUIET RIOT US, *male vocal/instrumental group*   *1 wk*

4 Aug 84	**CONDITION CRITICAL**	*Epic EPC 26075*	**71**	1 wk

QUINTESSENCE
UK/Australia, *male vocal/instrumental group*   *6 wks*

27 Jun 70	**QUINTESSENCE** *Island ILPS 9128*		**22**	4 wks
3 Apr 71	**DIVE DEEP** *Island ILPS 9143*		**43**	1 wk
27 May 72	**SELF** *RCA Victor SF 8273*		**50**	1 wk

QUIREBOYS UK, *male vocal/instrumental group*   *17 wks*

10 Feb 90 ●	**A BIT OF WHAT YOU FANCY** *Parlophone PCS 7335*		**2**	15 wks
27 Mar 93	**BITTER SWEET AND TWISTED** *Parlophone CDPCSD 120*		**31**	2 wks

QUIVER – *See SUTHERLAND BROTHERS and QUIVER*

Harry RABINOWITZ – *See ROYAL PHILHARMONIC ORCHESTRA*

RACING CARS UK, *male vocal/instrumental group*   *6 wks*

19 Feb 77	**DOWNTOWN TONIGHT** *Chrysalis CHR 1099*		**39**	6 wks

RADIOHEAD UK, *male vocal/instrumental group*   *8 wks*

6 Mar 93	**PABLO HONEY** *Parlophone CDPCS 7360*		**25**	8 wks

Gerry RAFFERTY UK, *male vocalist*   *79 wks*

25 Feb 78 ●	**CITY TO CITY** *United Artists UAS 30104*		**6**	37 wks
2 Jun 79 ●	**NIGHT OWL** *United Artists UAK 30238*		**9**	24 wks
26 Apr 80	**SNAKES AND LADDERS** *United Artists UAK 30298*		**15**	9 wks
25 Sep 82	**SLEEPWALKING** *Liberty LBG 30352*		**39**	4 wks
21 May 88	**NORTH AND SOUTH** *London LONLP 55*		**43**	4 wks
13 Feb 93	**A WING AND A PRAYER** *A & M 5174952*		**73**	1 wk

RAGE AGAINST THE MACHINE
US, *male vocal/instrumental group*   *37 wks*

13 Feb 93	**RAGE AGAINST THE MACHINE** *Epic 4722242*		**17**	37 wks

RAGGA TWINS UK, *male vocal/instrumental duo*   *5 wks*

1 Jun 91	**REGGAE OWES ME MONEY**			
	Shut Up And Dance SUADLP 2		**26**	5 wks

RAH BAND UK, *male/female vocal/instrumental group*   *6 wks*

6 Apr 85	**MYSTERY** *RCA PL 70640*		**60**	6 wks

RAILWAY CHILDREN
UK, male vocal/instrumental group   3 wks

21 May 88	**RECURRENCE** *Virgin V 2525*	**96**	1 wk
16 Mar 91	**NATIVE PLACE** *Virgin V 2627*	**59**	2 wks

RAIN TREE CROW *UK, male vocal/instrumental group*   3 wks

20 Apr 91	**RAIN TREE CROW** *Virgin V 2659*	**24**	3 wks

RAINBOW *UK, male vocal/instrumental group*   163 wks

13 Sep 75	**RITCHIE BLACKMORE'S RAINBOW** *Oyster OYA 2001*★	**11**	6 wks
5 Jun 76	**RAINBOW RISING** *Polydor 2490 137*★	**11**	33 wks
30 Jul 77	● **ON STAGE** *Polydor 2657 016*	**7**	10 wks
6 May 78	● **LONG LIVE ROCK 'N' ROLL** *Polydor POLD 5002*	**7**	12 wks
18 Aug 79	● **DOWN TO EARTH** *Polydor POLD 5023*	**6**	37 wks
21 Feb 81	● **DIFFICULT TO CURE** *Polydor POLD 5036*	**3**	22 wks
8 Aug 81	**RITCHIE BLACKMORE'S RAINBOW (re-issue)**★		
	Polydor 2490 141	**91**	2 wks
21 Nov 81	**BEST OF RAINBOW** *Polydor POLDV 2*	**14**	17 wks
24 Apr 82	● **STRAIGHT BETWEEN THE EYES** *Polydor POLD 5056* ..	**5**	14 wks
17 Sep 83	**BENT OUT OF SHAPE** *Polydor POLD 5116*	**11**	6 wks
8 Mar 86	**FINYL VINYL** *Polydor PODV 8*	**31**	4 wks

★ *Ritchie Blackmore's Rainbow.*

R
254

RAIN PARADE *US, male vocal/instrumental group*   1 wk

29 Jun 85	**BEYOND THE SUNSET** *Island IMA 17*	**78**	1 wk

Bonnie RAITT
US, female vocalist/instrumentalist – guitar   8 wks

28 Apr 90	**NICK OF TIME** *Capitol EST 2095*	**51**	5 wks
6 Jul 91	**LUCK OF THE DRAW** *Capitol EST 2145*	**38**	3 wks

RAKIM – *See Eric B. and RAKIM*

RAMONES *US, male vocal/instrumental group*   28 wks

23 Apr 77	**LEAVE HOME** *Philips 9103 254*	**45**	1 wk
24 Dec 77	**ROCKET TO RUSSIA** *Sire 9103 255*	**60**	2 wks
7 Oct 78	**ROAD TO RUIN** *Sire SRK 6063*	**32**	2 wks
16 Jun 79	**IT'S ALIVE** *Sire SRK 26074*	**27**	8 wks
19 Jan 80	**END OF THE CENTURY** *Sire SRK 6077*	**14**	8 wks
26 Jan 85	**TOO TOUGH TO DIE** *Beggars Banquet BEGA 59*	**63**	3 wks
31 May 86	**ANIMAL BOY** *Beggars Banquet BEGA 70*	**38**	2 wks
10 Oct 87	**HALFWAY TO SANITY** *Beggars Banquet BEGA 89*	**78**	1 wk
19 Aug 89	**BRAIN DRAIN** *Chrysalis CHR 1725*	**75**	1 wk

RANGE – *See Bruce HORNSBY and the RANGE*

Shabba RANKS *UK, male rapper*   10 wks

22 Jun 91	**AS RAW AS EVER** *Epic 4681021*	**51**	2 wks
22 Aug 92	**ROUGH AND READY VOL. 1** *Epic 4714422*	**71**	2 wks
24 Apr 93	**X-TRA NAKED** *Epic 4723332*	**38**	6 wks

Roland RAT SUPERSTAR *UK, male rat vocalist*   3 wks

15 Dec 84	**THE CASSETTE OF THE ALBUM** *Rodent RATL 1001* ..	**67**	3 wks

RATT *US, male vocal/instrumental group*   *5 wks*

13 Jul	85	**INVASION OF YOUR PRIVACY** *Atlantic 78–1257–1*	50	2 wks
25 Oct	86	**DANCING UNDERCOVER** *Atlantic 781 683–1*	51	1 wk
12 Nov	88	**REACH FOR THE SKY** *Atlantic 781929*	82	1 wk
8 Sep	90	**DETONATOR** *Atlantic 7567821271*	55	1 wk

Mark RATTRAY *UK, male vocalist*   *8 wks*

8 Dec	90	**SONGS OF THE MUSICALS** *Telstar STAR 2458*	46	7 wks
10 Oct	92	**THE MAGIC OF THE MUSICALS**		
		Quality Television QTV 013★	55	1 wk

★ *Marti Webb and Mark Rattray.*

RAVEN *UK, male vocal/instrumental group*   *3 wks*

17 Oct	81	**ROCK UNTIL YOU DROP** *Neat NEAT 1001*	63	3 wks

Simon RAYMOND – *See Harold BUDD/Liz FRASER/Robin GUTHRIE/Simon RAYMOND*

Chris REA *UK, male vocalist*   *301 wks*

28 Apr	79	**DELTICS** *Magnet MAG 5028*	54	3 wks
12 Apr	80	**TENNIS** *Magnet MAG 5032*	60	1 wk
3 Apr	82	**CHRIS REA** *Magnet MAG 5040*	52	4 wks
18 Jun	83	**WATER SIGN** *Magnet MAGL 5048*	64	2 wks
21 Apr	84	**WIRED TO THE MOON** *Magnet MAGL 5057*	35	7 wks
25 May	85	**SHAMROCK DIARIES** *Magnet MAGL 5062*	15	14 wks
26 Apr	86	**ON THE BEACH** *Magnet MAGL 5069*	11	37 wks
26 Sep	87 ●	**DANCING WITH STRANGERS** *Magnet MAGL 5071*	2	46 wks
13 Aug	88	**ON THE BEACH (re-issue)** *WEA WX 191*	37	10 wks
29 Oct	88 ●	**NEW LIGHT THROUGH OLD WINDOWS**		
		WEA WX 200	5	49 wks
11 Nov	89 ★	**THE ROAD TO HELL** *WEA WX 317*	1	69 wks
9 Mar	91 ★	**AUBERGE** *9031735801*	1	37 wks
14 Nov	92 ●	**GOD'S GREAT BANANA SKIN** *East West 4509909952* ...	4	15 wks
13 Nov	93 ●	**ESPRESSO LOGIC** *East West 4509943112*	8†	7 wks

Eddi READER *UK, female vocalist*   *2 wks*

7 Mar	92	**MIRMAMA** *RCA PD 75156*	34	2 wks

REAL PEOPLE
UK, male vocal/instrumental group   *1 wk*

18 May	91	**THE REAL PEOPLE** *Columbia 4680841*	59	1 wk

REAL THING
UK, male vocal/instrumental group   *17 wks*

6 Nov	76	**REAL THING** *Pye NSPL 18507*	34	3 wks
7 Apr	79	**CAN YOU FEEL THE FORCE** *Pye NSPH 18601*	73	1 wk
10 May	80	**20 GREATEST HITS** *K-Tel NE 1073*	56	2 wks
12 Jul	86	**BEST OF THE REAL THING** *West Five NRT 1*	24	11 wks

REBEL MC *UK, male rapper*   *11 wks*

28 Apr	90	**REBEL MUSIC** *Desire LUVLP 5*	18	7 wks
13 Jul	91	**BLACK MEANING GOOD** *Desire LUVLP 12*	23	4 wks

REBEL ROUSERS – *See Cliff BENNETT and the REBEL ROUSERS*

R
255

R.E.M. captured two prizes at the 34th annual Grammy Awards, held in New York's Radio City Music Hall. Michael Stipes' cap reads 'White House Stop AIDS'. (Pictorial Press)

In 1968, the year after his death, **Otis Redding** had three titles in the chart simultaneously.

Ivan REBROFF   *USSR, male vocalist*   *4 wks*

16 Jun	90	**THE VERY BEST OF IVAN REBROFF** *BBC REB 778* ..	57	4 wks

RED BOX   *UK, male vocal/instrumental duo*   *4 wks*

6 Dec	86	**THE CIRCLE AND THE SQUARE** *Sire WX 79*	73	4 wks

RED HOT CHILI PEPPERS
US, male vocal/instrumental group   *40 wks*

12 Oct	91	**BLOOD SUGAR SEX MAGIK** *Warner Bros WX 441*	25	34 wks
17 Oct	92	**WHAT HITS!?** *EMI USA CDMTL 1071*	23	6 wks

RED HOUSE PAINTERS
US, male vocal/instrumental group   *2 wks*

5 Jun	93	**RED HOUSE PAINTERS** *4AD DAD 3008CD*	63	1 wk
30 Oct	93	**RED HOUSE PAINTERS** *4AD CAD 3016CD*	68	1 wk

The identically titled albums are different.

RED NOISE – *See Bill NELSON*

Sharon REDD   *US, female vocalist*   *5 wks*

23 Oct	82	**REDD HOTT** *Prelude PRL 25056*	59	5 wks

R
257

Otis REDDING   *US, male vocalist*   *215 wks*

19 Feb	66 ●	**OTIS BLUE** *Atlantic ATL 5041*	6	21 wks
23 Apr	66	**SOUL BALLADS** *Atlantic ATL 5029*	30	1 wk
23 Jul	66	**SOUL ALBUM** *Atlantic 587–011*	22	9 wks
21 Jan	67	**OTIS REDDING'S DICTIONARY OF SOUL** *Atlantic 588–050*	23	16 wks
21 Jan	67 ●	**OTIS BLUE (re-issue)** *Atlantic 587–036*	7	54 wks
29 Apr	67	**PAIN IN MY HEART** *Atlantic 587–042*	28	9 wks
1 Jul	67	**KING AND QUEEN** *Atlantic 589007★*	18	17 wks
10 Feb	68 ●	**HISTORY OF OTIS REDDING** *Volt S 418*	2	43 wks
30 Mar	68	**OTIS REDDING IN EUROPE** *Stax 589–016*	14	16 wks
1 Jun	68 ★	**DOCK OF THE BAY** *Stax 231–001*	1	15 wks
12 Oct	68	**IMMORTAL OTIS REDDING** *Atlantic 588–113*	19	8 wks
11 Sep	93	**DOCK OF THE BAY – THE DEFINITIVE COLLECTION (re-issue)** *Atlantic 9548317092*	50	6 wks

★ *Otis Redding and Carla Thomas.*

Helen REDDY   *Australia, female vocalist*   *27 wks*

8 Feb	75	**FREE AND EASY** *Capitol E–ST 11348*	17	9 wks
14 Feb	76 ●	**THE BEST OF HELEN REDDY** *Capitol E–ST 11467*	5	18 wks

REDSKINS   *UK, male vocal/instrumental duo*   *4 wks*

22 Mar	86	**NEITHER WASHINGTON, NOR MOSCOW** *Decca FLP 1*	31	4 wks

Dan REED NETWORK   *US, male vocal/instrumental group*   *6 wks*

4 Nov	89	**SLAM** *Mercury 8388681*	66	2 wks
27 Jul	91	**THE HEAT** *Mercury 8488551*	15	4 wks

Lou REED US, male vocalist   74 wks

21 Apr	73	**TRANSFORMER** *RCA Victor LSP 4807*	13	25 wks
20 Oct	73 ●	**BERLIN** *RCA Victor RS 1002*	7	5 wks
16 Mar	74	**ROCK 'N' ROLL ANIMAL** *RCA Victor APLI 0472*	26	1 wk
14 Feb	76	**CONEY ISLAND BABY** *RCA Victor RS 1035*	52	1 wk
3 Jul	82	**TRANSFORMER (re-issue)** *RCA INTS 5061*	91	2 wks
9 Jun	84	**NEW SENSATIONS** *RCA PL 84998*	92	1 wk
24 May	86	**MISTRIAL** *RCA PL 87190*	69	1 wk
28 Jan	89	**NEW YORK** *Sire WX 246*	14	22 wks
7 Oct	89	**RETRO** *RCA PL 90389*	29	5 wks
5 May	90	**SONGS FOR DRELLA** *Sire WX 345★*	22	5 wks
25 Jan	92 ●	**MAGIC AND LOSS** *Sire 7599266622*	6	6 wks

★ *Lou Reed and John Cale.*

Don REEDMAN – *See Jeff JARRATT and Don REEDMAN*

Jim REEVES US, male vocalist   391 wks

28 Mar	64 ●	**GOOD 'N' COUNTRY** *RCA Camden CDN 5114*	10	35 wks
9 May	64 ●	**GENTLEMAN JIM** *RCA RD 7541*	3	23 wks
15 Aug	64 ●	**A TOUCH OF VELVET** *RCA RD 7521*	8	9 wks
15 Aug	64	**INTERNATIONAL JIM REEVES** *RCA RD 7577*	11	15 wks
22 Aug	64	**HE'LL HAVE TO GO** *RCA RD 27176*	16	4 wks
29 Aug	64	**THE INTIMATE JIM REEVES** *RCA RD 27193*	12	4 wks
29 Aug	64 ●	**GOD BE WITH YOU** *RCA RD 7636*	10	10 wks
5 Sep	64 ●	**MOONLIGHT AND ROSES** *RCA RD 7639*	2	52 wks
19 Sep	64	**COUNTRY SIDE OF JIM REEVES** *RCA Camden CDN 5100*	12	5 wks
26 Sep	64	**WE THANK THEE** *RCA RD 7637*	17	3 wks
28 Nov	64 ●	**TWELVE SONGS OF CHRISTMAS** *RCA RD 7663*	3	17 wks
30 Jan	65 ●	**BEST OF JIM REEVES** *RCA RD 7666*	3	47 wks
10 Apr	65	**HAVE I TOLD YOU LATELY THAT I LOVE YOU** *RCA Camden CDN 5122*	12	5 wks
22 May	65	**THE JIM REEVES WAY** *RCA RD 7694*	16	4 wks
5 Nov	66 ●	**DISTANT DRUMS** *RCA Victor RD 7814*	2	34 wks
18 Jan	69	**A TOUCH OF SADNESS** *RCA SF 7978*	15	5 wks
5 Jul	69 ★	**ACCORDING TO MY HEART** *RCA International INTS 1013*	1	14 wks
23 Aug	69	**JIM REEVES AND SOME FRIENDS** *RCA SF 8022*	24	4 wks
29 Nov	69	**ON STAGE** *RCA SF 8047*	13	4 wks
26 Dec	70	**MY CATHEDRAL** *RCA SF 8146*	48	2 wks
3 Jul	71	**JIM REEVES WRITES YOU A RECORD** *RCA SF 8176* .	47	2 wks
7 Aug	71 ●	**JIM REEVES' GOLDEN RECORDS** *RCA International INTS 1070*	9	21 wks
14 Aug	71 ●	**THE INTIMATE JIM REEVES (re-issue)** *RCA International INTS 1256*	8	15 wks
21 Aug	71	**GIRLS I HAVE KNOWN** *RCA International INTS 1140*	35	5 wks
27 Nov	71 ●	**TWELVE SONGS OF CHRISTMAS (re-issue)** *RCA International INTS 1188*	3	6 wks
27 Nov	71	**A TOUCH OF VELVET (re-issue)** *RCA International INTS 1089*	49	2 wks
15 Apr	72	**MY FRIEND** *RCA SF 8258*	32	5 wks
20 Sep	75 ★	**40 GOLDEN GREATS** *Arcade ADEP 16*	1	25 wks
6 Sep	80	**COUNTRY GENTLEMAN** *K-Tel NE 1088*	53	4 wks
8 Aug	92 ●	**THE DEFINITIVE JIM REEVES** *Arcade ARC 94982*	9	10 wks

Vic REEVES UK, male vocalist   9 wks

16 Nov	91	**I WILL CURE YOU** *Sense SIGH 111*	16	9 wks

Neil REID UK, male vocalist   18 wks

5 Feb	72 ★	**NEIL REID** *Decca SKL 5122*	1	16 wks
2 Sep	72	**SMILE** *Decca SKL 5136*	47	2 wks

R.E.M. *US, male vocal/instrumental group*   255 wks

28 Apr	84	**RECKONING** *IRS A 7045*	91	2 wks
29 Jun	85	**FABLES OF THE RECONSTRUCTION** *IRS MIRF 1003*	35	3 wks
6 Sep	86	**LIFE'S RICH PAGEANT** *IRS MIRG 1014*	43	4 wks
16 May	87	**DEAD LETTER OFFICE** *IRS SP 70054*	60	2 wks
26 Sep	87	**DOCUMENT** *MCA MIRG 1025*	28	3 wks
29 Oct	88	**EPONYMOUS** *IRS MIRG 1038*	69	3 wks
19 Nov	88	**GREEN** *Warner Bros. WX 234*	27	20 wks
23 Mar	91 ★	**OUT OF TIME** *Warner Bros. WX 404*	1	136 wks
12 Oct	91 ●	**THE BEST OF R.E.M.** *IRS MIRH 1*	7	18 wks
10 Oct	92 ★	**AUTOMATIC FOR THE PEOPLE** *Warner Bros. 9362450552*	1†	64 wks

RENAISSANCE *UK, male/female vocal/instrumental group* 10 wks

21 Feb	70	**RENAISSANCE** *Island ILPS 9114*	60	1 wk
19 Aug	78	**A SONG FOR ALL SEASONS** *Warner Bros. K 56460*	35	8 wks
2 Jun	79	**AZUR D'OR** *Warner Bros. K 56633*	73	1 wk

RENATO *Italy, male vocalist*   14 wks

25 Dec	82	**SAVE YOUR LOVE** *Lifestyle LEG 9*	26	14 wks

RENEGADE SOUNDWAVE
UK, male vocal/instrumental group   1 wk

24 Mar	90	**SOUNDCLASH** *Mute STUMM 63*	74	1 wk

REO SPEEDWAGON
US, male vocal/instrumental group   36 wks

25 Apr	81 ●	**HI INFIDELITY** *Epic EPC 84700*	6	29 wks
17 Jul	82	**GOOD TROUBLE** *Epic EPC 85789*	29	7 wks

REVOLTING COCKS *US, male vocal/instrumental group* 1 wk

2 Oct	93	**LINGER FICKEN' GOOD** *Devotion CDDVN 22*	39	1 wk

REVOLUTION – *See PRINCE*

REZILLOS *UK, male/female vocal/instrumental group* 15 wks

5 Aug	78	**CAN'T STAND THE REZILLOS** *Sire WEA K 56530*	16	10 wks
28 Apr	79	**MISSION ACCOMPLISHED BUT THE BEAT GOES ON** *Sire SRK 6069*	30	5 wks

Charlie RICH *US, male vocalist*   28 wks

23 Mar	74 ●	**BEHIND CLOSED DOORS** *Epic 65716*	4	26 wks
13 Jul	74	**VERY SPECIAL LOVE SONGS** *Epic 80031*	34	2 wks

Richie RICH *UK, male vocalist*   1 wk

22 Jul	89	**I CAN MAKE YOU DANCE** *Gee St. GEEA 3*	65	1 wk

RICH KIDS *UK, male vocal/instrumental group*   1 wk

7 Oct	78	**GHOST OF PRINCES IN TOWERS** *EMI EMC 3263*	51	1 wk

R
259

Cliff RICHARD UK, male vocalist   731 wks

18 Apr	59 ●	**CLIFF** *Columbia 33SX 1147*	4	31 wks
14 Nov	59 ●	**CLIFF SINGS** *Columbia 33SX 1192*	2	36 wks
15 Oct	60 ●	**ME AND MY SHADOWS** *Columbia 33SX 1261*	2	33 wks
22 Apr	61 ●	**LISTEN TO CLIFF** *Columbia 33SX 1320*	2	28 wks
21 Oct	61 ★	**21 TODAY** *Columbia 33SX 1368*	1	16 wks
23 Dec	61 ★	**THE YOUNG ONES (film soundtrack)**		
		Columbia 33SX 1384	1	42 wks
29 Sep	62 ●	**32 MINUTES AND 17 SECONDS** *Columbia 33SX 1431* ...	3	21 wks
26 Jan	63 ★	**SUMMER HOLIDAY (film soundtrack)**		
		Columbia 33SX 1472	1	36 wks
13 Jul	63 ●	**CLIFF'S HIT ALBUM** *Columbia 33SX 1512*	2	19 wks
28 Sep	63 ●	**WHEN IN SPAIN** *Columbia 33SX 1541*	8	10 wks
11 Jul	64 ●	**WONDERFUL LIFE (film soundtrack)** *Columbia 33SX 1628*	2	23 wks
9 Jan	65	**ALADDIN (pantomime)** *Columbia 33SX 1676*	13	5 wks
17 Apr	65 ●	**CLIFF RICHARD** *Columbia 33SX 1709*	9	5 wks
14 Aug	65	**MORE HITS BY CLIFF** *Columbia 33SX 1737*	20	1 wk
8 Jan	66	**LOVE IS FOREVER** *Columbia 33SX 1769*	19	1 wk
21 May	66 ●	**KINDA LATIN** *Columbia SX 6039*	9	12 wks
17 Dec	66 ●	**FINDERS KEEPERS (film soundtrack)** *Columbia SX 6079* .	6	18 wks
7 Jan	67	**CINDERELLA (pantomime)** *Columbia 33SCX 6103*	30	6 wks
15 Apr	67	**DON'T STOP ME NOW . . .** *Columbia SCX 6133*	23	9 wks
11 Nov	67	**GOOD NEWS** *Columbia SCX 6167*	37	1 wk
1 Jun	68	**CLIFF IN JAPAN** *Columbia SCX 6244*	29	2 wks
16 Nov	68	**ESTABLISHED 1958** *Columbia SCX 6282*	30	4 wks
12 Jul	69 ●	**BEST OF CLIFF** *Columbia SCX 6343*	5	17 wks
27 Sep	69	**SINCERELY** *Columbia SCX 6357*	24	3 wks
12 Dec	70	**TRACKS 'N' GROOVES** *Columbia SCX 6435*	37	2 wks
23 Dec	72	**BEST OF CLIFF VOL. 2** *Columbia SCX 6519*	49	2 wks
19 Jan	74	**TAKE ME HIGH (film soundtrack)** *EMI EMC 3016*	41	4 wks
29 May	76 ●	**I'M NEARLY FAMOUS** *EMI EMC 3122*	5	21 wks
26 Mar	77 ●	**EVERY FACE TELLS A STORY** *EMI EMC 3172*	8	10 wks
22 Oct	77 ★	**40 GOLDEN GREATS** *EMI EMTV 6*	1	19 wks
4 Mar	78	**SMALL CORNERS** *EMI EMC 3219*	33	5 wks
21 Oct	78	**GREEN LIGHT** *EMI EMC 3231*	25	3 wks
17 Feb	79	**THANK YOU VERY MUCH – REUNION CONCERT AT**		
		THE LONDON PALLADIUM *EMI EMTV 15*	5	12 wks
15 Sep	79 ●	**ROCK 'N' ROLL JUVENILE** *EMI EMC 3307*	3	22 wks
13 Sep	80 ●	**I'M NO HERO** *EMI EMA 796*	4	12 wks
4 Jul	81 ★	**LOVE SONGS** *EMI EMTV 27*	1	43 wks
26 Sep	81 ●	**WIRED FOR SOUND** *EMI EMC 3377*	4	25 wks
4 Sep	82 ●	**NOW YOU SEE ME, NOW YOU DON'T** *EMI EMC 3415*	4	14 wks
21 May	83 ●	**DRESSED FOR THE OCCASION** *EMI EMC 3432*	7	17 wks
15 Oct	83 ●	**SILVER** *EMI EMC 1077871*	7	24 wks
14 Jul	84	**20 ORIGINAL GREATS** *EMI CRS 1*	43	6 wks
1 Dec	84	**THE ROCK CONNECTION** *EMI CLIF 2*	43	5 wks
26 Sep	87 ●	**ALWAYS GUARANTEED** *EMI EMD 1004*	5	25 wks
19 Nov	88 ★	**PRIVATE COLLECTION** *EMI CRTV 30*	1	26 wks
11 Nov	89 ●	**STRONGER** *EMI EMD 1012*	7	21 wks
17 Nov	90 ●	**FROM A DISTANCE . . . THE EVENT** *EMI CRTV 31* ..	3	15 wks
30 Nov	91 ●	**TOGETHER WITH CLIFF** *EMI EMD 1028*	10	7 wks
1 May	93 ●	**THE ALBUM** *EMI CDEMD 1043*	1†	12 wks

The Shadows featured on all or some of the tracks of all albums up to and including Aladdin *and the following subsequent albums:* More Hits By Cliff, Love Is Forever, Finders Keepers, Cinderella, Established 1958, Best Of Cliff, Best Of Cliff Vol. 2, 40 Golden Greats, Thank You Very Much, Love Songs *and* 20 Original Greats. Cliff *is credited to* Cliff Richard and the Drifters, *the original name used by the Shadows. See also the Shadows.*

Keith RICHARDS UK, male vocalist/instrumentalist – guitar   4 wks

15 Oct	88	**TALK IS CHEAP** *Virgin V 2554*	37	3 wks
31 Oct	92	**MAIN OFFENDER** *Virgin America CDVUS 59*	45	1 wk

Lionel RICHIE US, male vocalist   348 wks

27 Nov	82 ●	**LIONEL RICHIE** *Motown STMA 8037*	9	86 wks
29 Oct	83 ★	**CAN'T SLOW DOWN** *Motown STMA 8041*	1	154 wks
23 Aug	86 ●	**DANCING ON THE CEILING** *Motown ZL 72412*	2	53 wks
6 Jun	92 ★	**BACK TO FRONT** *Motown 5300182*	1	55 wks

Jonathan RICHMAN and the MODERN LOVERS
US, male vocal/instrumental group   3 wks

27 Aug 77   **ROCK 'N' ROLL WITH THE MODERN LOVERS**
            Beserkeley BSERK 9   . . . .   **50**   3 wks

RICHMOND STRINGS/MIKE SAMMES SINGERS
UK, orchestra/male/female vocal group   7 wks

19 Jan   76   **MUSIC OF AMERICA**   Ronco TRD 2016   . . . .   **18**   7 wks

Sviatoslav RICHTER – See Herbert VON KARAJAN

Frank RICOTTI ALL STARS
UK, male instrumental group   1 wk

26 Jun 93   **THE BEIDERBECKE COLLECTION**   Dormouse DM 20CD.   **73**   1 wk
★ This album first entered the chart on 24 Dec 88 as a compilation. See also Various Artists – TV and Radio
Soundtracks and Spin-Offs.

Nelson RIDDLE ORCHESTRA – See Shirley BASSEY; Linda RONSTADT; Kiri TE KANAWA

RIDE   UK, male vocal/instrumental group   10 wks

27 Oct 90   **NOWHERE**   Creation CRELP 074   . . . .   **11**   5 wks
21 Mar 92 ● **GOING BLANK AGAIN**   Creation CRECD 124   . . . .   **5**   5 wks

RIGHT SAID FRED   UK, male vocal/instrumental group   53 wks

28 Mar 93 ★ **UP**   Tug SNOGCD 1   . . . .   **1**   49 wks
13 Nov 93   **SEX AND TRAVEL**   Tug SNOGCD 2   . . . .   **35**   4 wks

RIGHTEOUS BROTHERS   US, male vocal duo   17 wks

1 Dec 90   **THE VERY BEST OF THE RIGHTEOUS BROTHERS**
           Verve 8472481   . . . .   **11**   17 wks

Mark RILEY – See MATT BIANCO

RIP RIG AND PANIC
UK/US, male/female vocal/instrumental group   3 wks

26 Jun 82   **I AM GOLD**   Virgin V 2228   . . . .   **67**   3 wks

Minnie RIPERTON   US, female vocalist   3 wks

17 May 75   **PERFECT ANGEL**   Epic EPC 80426   . . . .   **33**   3 wks

Angela RIPPON   UK, female exercise instructor   26 wks

17 Apr 82 ● **SHAPE UP AND DANCE (VOL. II)**   Lifestyle LEG 2   . . . . .   **8**   26 wks

RIVER CITY PEOPLE
UK, male/female vocal/instrumental group   10 wks

25 Aug 90   **SAY SOMETHING GOOD**   EMI EMCX 3561   . . . .   **23**   9 wks
2 Nov 91   **THIS IS THE WORLD**   EMI EMC 3611   . . . .   **56**   1 wk

RIVER DETECTIVES UK, male vocal/instrumental duo   *1 wk*

23 Sep	89	**SATURDAY NIGHT SUNDAY MORNING** WEA WX 2955	51	1 wk

David ROACH
UK, male vocalist/instrumentalist – saxophone   *1 wk*

14 Apr	84	**I LOVE SAX** *Nouveau Music NML 1006*	73	1 wk

ROACHFORD UK, male vocalist   *32 wks*

23 Jul	88	**ROACHFORD** *CBS 460630 1*	18	27 wks
18 May	91	**GET READY** *Columbia 4681361*	20	5 wks

ROBBIE – *See SLY and ROBBIE*

Marty ROBBINS US, male vocalist   *15 wks*

13 Aug	60	**GUNFIGHTER BALLADS** *Fontana TFL 5063*	20	1 wk
10 Feb	79 ●	**MARTY ROBBINS COLLECTION** *Lotus WH 5009*	5	14 wks

Paddy ROBERTS South Africa, male vocalist   *6 wks*

26 Sep	59 ●	**STRICTLY FOR GROWN-UPS** *Decca LF 1322*	8	5 wks
17 Sep	60	**PADDY ROBERTS TRIES AGAIN** *Decca LK 4358*	16	1 wk

R
262

B.A. ROBERTSON UK, male vocalist   *10 wks*

29 Mar	80	**INITIAL SUCCESS** *Asylum K 52216*	32	8 wks
4 Apr	81	**BULLY FOR YOU** *Asylum K 52275*	61	2 wks

Robbie ROBERTSON Canada, male vocalist   *14 wks*

14 Nov	87	**ROBBIE ROBERTSON** *Geffen WX 133*	23	14 wks
12 Oct	91	**STORYVILLE** *Geffen GEF 24303*	30	2 wks

Smokey ROBINSON US, male vocalist   *21 wks*

20 Jun	81	**BEING WITH YOU** *Motown STML 12151*	17	10 wks
12 Nov	88	**LOVE SONGS** *Telstar STAR 2331★*	69	9 wks
14 Nov	92	**THE GREATEST HITS** *PolyGram TV 5301212★★*	65	2 wks

★ *Marvin Gaye and Smokey Robinson.*
★★ *Smokey Robinson and the Miracles.*

Tom ROBINSON BAND
UK, male vocal/instrumental group   *23 wks*

3 Jun	78 ●	**POWER IN THE DARKNESS** *EMI EMC 3226*	4	12 wks
24 Mar	79	**TRB2** *EMI EMC 3296*	18	6 wks
29 Sep	84	**HOPE AND GLORY** *Castaway ZL 70483★*	21	5 wks

★ *Tom Robinson.*

ROCK GODDESS
UK, female vocal/instrumental group   *3 wks*

12 Mar	83	**ROCK GODDESS** *A & M AMLH 68554*	65	2 wks
29 Oct	83	**HELL HATH NO FURY** *A & M AMLX 68560*	84	1 wk

ROCKIN' BERRIES *UK, male vocal/instrumental group* 1 wk

| 19 Jun | 65 | **IN TOWN** *Pye NPL 38013* .... | 15 | 1 wk |

ROCKPILE *UK, male vocal/instrumental group* 5 wks

| 18 Oct | 80 | **SECONDS OF PLEASURE** *F-Beat XXLP 7* .... | 34 | 5 wks |

ROCKSTEADY CREW *US, male/female vocal group* 1 wk

| 16 Jun | 84 | **READY FOR BATTLE** *Charisma RSC LP1* .... | 73 | 1 wk |

ROCKWELL *US, male vocalist* 5 wks

| 25 Feb | 84 | **SOMEBODY'S WATCHING ME** *Motown ZL 72147* ..... | 52 | 5 wks |

Clodagh RODGERS *Ireland, female vocalist* 1 wk

| 13 Sep | 69 | **CLODAGH RODGERS** *RCA SF 8033* .... | 27 | 1 wk |

Paul RODGERS *UK, male vocalist* 7 wks

| 3 Jul | 93 ● | **MUDDY WATERS BLUES** *London 8284242* .... | 9 | 7 wks |

RODS *US, male vocal/instrumental group* 4 wks

| 24 Jul | 82 | **WILD DOGS** *Arista SPART 1196* .... | 75 | 4 wks |

R
263

Kenny ROGERS *US, male vocalist* 98 wks

18 Jun	77	**KENNY ROGERS** *United Artists UAS 30046*	14	7 wks
6 Oct	79	**THE KENNY ROGERS SINGLES ALBUM**		
		United Artists UAK 30263	12	22 wks
9 Feb	80 ●	**KENNY** *United Artists UAG 30273*	7	10 wks
31 Jan	81	**LADY** *Liberty LBG 30334*	40	5 wks
1 Oct	83	**EYES THAT SEE IN THE DARK** *RCA RCALP 6088* ...	53	19 wks
27 Oct	84	**WHAT ABOUT ME?** *RCA PL 85043*	97	1 wk
27 Jul	85 ●	**THE KENNY ROGERS STORY** *Liberty EMTV 39*	4	29 wks
25 Sep	93	**DAYTIME FRIENDS – THE VERY BEST OF KENNY**		
		ROGERS *EMI CDEMTV 79*	16	5 wks

ROLLING STONES *UK, male vocal/instrumental group* 694 wks

25 Apr	64 ★	**ROLLING STONES** *Decca LK 4805*	1	51 wks
23 Jan	65 ★	**ROLLING STONES NO. 2** *Decca LK 4661*	1	37 wks
2 Oct	65 ●	**OUT OF OUR HEADS** *Decca LK 4733*	2	24 wks
23 Apr	66 ★	**AFTERMATH** *Decca LK 4786*	1	28 wks
12 Nov	66 ●	**BIG HITS (HIGH TIDE AND GREEN GRASS)**		
		Decca TXS 101	4	43 wks
28 Jan	67 ●	**BETWEEN THE BUTTONS** *Decca SKL 4852*	3	22 wks
23 Dec	67 ●	**THEIR SATANIC MAJESTIES REQUEST** *Decca TXS 103*	3	13 wks
21 Dec	68 ●	**BEGGARS BANQUET** *Decca SKL 4955*	3	12 wks
27 Sep	69 ●	**THROUGH THE PAST DARKLY (BIG HITS VOL. 2)**		
		Decca SKL 5019	2	37 wks
20 Dec	69 ★	**LET IT BLEED** *Decca SKL 5025*	1	29 wks
19 Sep	70 ★	**'GET YOUR YA-YA'S OUT!'** *Decca SKL 5065*	1	15 wks
3 Apr	71 ●	**STONE AGE** *Decca SKL 5084*	4	7 wks
8 May	71 ★	**STICKY FINGERS** *Rolling Stones COC 59100*	1	25 wks
18 Sep	71	**GIMME SHELTER** *Decca SKL 5101*	19	5 wks
11 Mar	72	**MILESTONES** *Decca SKL 5098*	14	8 wks
10 Jun	72 ★	**EXILE ON MAIN STREET** *Rolling Stones COC 69100*	1	16 wks
11 Nov	72	**ROCK 'N' ROLLING STONES** *Decca SKL 5149*	41	1 wk

22 Sep	73	★	**GOAT'S HEAD SOUP**	*Rolling Stones COC 59101*	....	**1**	14 wks
2 Nov	74	●	**IT'S ONLY ROCK 'N' ROLL**	*Rolling Stones COC 59103*	..	**2**	9 wks
28 Jun	75		**MADE IN THE SHADE**	*Rolling Stones COC 59104*	....	**14**	12 wks
28 Jun	75		**METAMORPHOSIS**	*Decca SKL 5212*	....	**45**	1 wk
29 Nov	75	●	**ROLLED GOLD – THE VERY BEST OF THE ROLLING STONES**	*Decca ROST 1/2*	....	**7**	50 wks
8 May	76	●	**BLACK AND BLUE**	*Rolling Stones COC 59106*	....	**2**	14 wks
8 Oct	77	●	**LOVE YOU LIVE**	*Rolling Stones COC 89101*	....	**3**	8 wks
5 Nov	77	●	**GET STONED**	*Arcade ADEP 32*	....	**8**	15 wks
24 Jun	78	●	**SOME GIRLS**	*Rolling Stones CUN 39108*	....	**2**	25 wks
5 Jul	80	★	**EMOTIONAL RESCUE**	*Rolling Stones CUN 39111*	.....	**1**	18 wks
12 Sep	81	●	**TATTOO YOU**	*Rolling Stones CUNS 39114*	....	**2**	29 wks
12 Jun	82	●	**STILL LIFE (AMERICAN CONCERTS 1981)**	*Rolling Stones CUN 39115*	....	**4**	18 wks
31 Jul	82		**IN CONCERT (import)**	*Decca (Holland) 6640 037*	....	**94**	3 wks
11 Dec	82		**STORY OF THE STONES**	*K-Tel NE 1201*	....	**24**	12 wks
19 Nov	83	●	**UNDERCOVER**	*Rolling Stones CUN 1654361*	....	**3**	18 wks
7 Jul	84		**REWIND 1971–1984 (THE BEST OF THE ROLLING STONES)**	*Rolling Stones 4501991*	....	**23**	18 wks
5 Apr	86	●	**DIRTY WORK**	*Rolling Stones CUN 86321*	....	**4**	10 wks
23 Sep	89		**STEEL WHEELS**	*CBS 4657521*	....	**2**	18 wks
7 Jul	90	●	**HOT ROCKS 1964–1971**	*London 8201401*	....	**3**	16 wks
20 Apr	91	●	**FLASHPOINT**	*Rolling Stones 4681351*	....	**6**	7 wks
9 Oct	93		**HOT ROCKS 1964–1971**	*London 8201402*	....	**66**	2 wks
4 Dec	93		**JUMP BACK – THE BEST OF THE ROLLING STONES 1971–93**	*Virgin CDV 2726*	....	**16†**	4 wks

ROMAN HOLIDAY   *UK, male vocal/instrumental group*   *3 wks*

22 Oct	83	**COOKIN' ON THE ROOF**	*Jive HIP 9*	....	**31**	3 wks

RONDO VENEZIANO
UK, male/female orchestral group   *33 wks*

5 Nov	83	**VENICE IN PERIL**	*Ferroway RON 1*	....	**39**	13 wks
10 Nov	84	**THE GENIUS OF VENICE**	*Ferroway RON 2*	....	**60**	13 wks
9 Jul	88	**VENICE IN PERIL (re-issue)**	*Fanfare RON 1*	....	**34**	7 wks

Mick RONSON   *UK, male vocalist/instrumentalist – guitar*   *10 wks*

16 Mar	74	●	**SLAUGHTER ON TENTH AVENUE**	*RCA Victor APLI 0353*	....	**9**	7 wks
8 Mar	75		**PLAY DON'T WORRY**	*RCA Victor APLI 0681*	....	**29**	3 wks

Linda RONSTADT   *US, female vocalist*   *43 wks*

4 Sep	76	**HASTEN DOWN THE WIND**	*Asylum K 53045*	....	**32**	8 wks
25 Dec	76	**GREATEST HITS**	*Asylum K 53055*	....	**37**	9 wks
1 Oct	77	**SIMPLE DREAMS**	*Asylum K 53065*	....	**15**	5 wks
14 Oct	78	**LIVING IN THE USA**	*Asylum K 53085*	....	**39**	2 wks
8 Mar	80	**MAD LOVE**	*Asylum K 52210*	....	**65**	1 wk
28 Jan	84	**WHAT'S NEW**	*Asylum 96 0260★*	....	**31**	5 wks
19 Jan	85	**LUSH LIFE**	*Asylum 96–0387–1★*	....	**100**	1 wk
14 Mar	87	**TRIO**	*Warner Bros 9254911★★*	....	**60**	4 wks
11 Nov	89	**CRY LIKE A RAINSTORM – HOWL LIKE THE WIND**	*Elektra EKT 76*	....	**43**	8 wks

★ *Linda Ronstadt with the Nelson Riddle Orchestra.*
★★ *Dolly Parton/Emmylou Harris/Linda Ronstadt.*

ROSE MARIE   *UK, female vocalist*   *34 wks*

13 Apr	85	**ROSE MARIE SINGS JUST FOR YOU**	*A1 RMTV 1*	....	**30**	13 wks
24 May	86	**SO LUCKY**	*A1-Spartan RMLP 2*	....	**62**	3 wks
14 Nov	87	**SENTIMENTALLY YOURS**	*Telstar STAR 2302*	....	**22**	11 wks
19 Nov	88	**TOGETHER AGAIN**	*Telstar STAR 2333*	....	**52**	7 wks

ROSE ROYCE US, male/female vocal/instrumental group 62 wks

22 Oct	77	**IN FULL BLOOM** *Warner Bros. K 56394*	18	13 wks
30 Sep	78 ●	**STRIKES AGAIN** *Whitfield K 56257*	7	11 wks
22 Sep	79	**RAINBOW CONNECTION IV** *Atlantic K 56714*	72	2 wks
1 Mar	80 ★	**GREATEST HITS** *Whitfield K RRTV 1*	1	34 wks
13 Oct	84	**MUSIC MAGIC** *Streetwave MKL 2*	69	2 wks

See also compilation albums – Dino.

ROSE TATTOO Australia, male vocal/instrumental group 4 wks

26 Sep	81	**ASSAULT AND BATTERY** *Carrere CAL 127*	40	4 wks

Diana ROSS US, female vocalist 501 wks

24 Oct	70	**DIANA ROSS** *Tamla Motown SFTML 11159*	14	5 wks
19 Jun	71	**EVERYTHING IS EVERYTHING**		
		Tamla Motown STML 11178	31	3 wks
9 Oct	71 ●	**I'M STILL WAITING** *Tamla Motown STML 11193*	10	11 wks
9 Oct	71	**DIANA** *Tamla Motown STMA 8001*	43	1 wk
11 Nov	72	**GREATEST HITS** *Tamla Motown STMA 8006*	34	10 wks
1 Sep	73 ●	**TOUCH ME IN THE MORNING**		
		Tamla Motown STML 11239	7	35 wks
27 Oct	73	**LADY SINGS THE BLUES** *Tamla Motown TMSP 1131*	50	1 wk
19 Jan	74 ●	**DIANA AND MARVIN** *Tamla Motown STMA 8015★*	6	43 wks
2 Mar	74	**LAST TIME I SAW HIM** *Tamla Motown STML 11255*	41	1 wk
8 Jun	74	**LIVE** *Tamla Motown STML 11248*	21	8 wks
27 Mar	76 ●	**DIANA ROSS** *Tamla Motown STML 12022*	4	26 wks
7 Aug	76 ●	**GREATEST HITS 2** *Tamla Motown STML 12036*	2	29 wks
19 Mar	77	**AN EVENING WITH DIANA ROSS** *Motown TMSP 6005* .	52	1 wk
4 Aug	79	**THE BOSS** *Motown STML 12118*	52	2 wks
17 Nov	79 ●	**20 GOLDEN GREATS** *Motown EMTV 21*	2	29 wks
21 Jun	80	**DIANA** *Motown STMA 8033*	12	32 wks
28 Mar	81	**TO LOVE AGAIN** *Motown STML 12152*	26	10 wks
29 Aug	81	**DIANA AND MARVIN (re–issue)** *Motown STMS 5001★* ...	78	2 wks
7 Nov	81	**WHY DO FOOLS FALL IN LOVE** *Capitol EST 26733*	17	24 wks
21 Nov	81	**ALL THE GREAT HITS** *Motown STMA 8036*	21	31 wks
13 Feb	82	**DIANA ROSS** *Motown STML 12163*	43	6 wks
23 Oct	82	**SILK ELECTRIC** *Capitol EAST 27313*	33	12 wks
4 Dec	82 ●	**LOVE SONGS** *K-Tel NE 1200*	5	17 wks
19 Jul	83	**ROSS** *Capitol EST 1867051*	44	5 wks
24 Dec	83 ●	**PORTRAIT** *Telstar STAR 2238*	8	31 wks
6 Oct	84	**SWEPT AWAY** *Capitol ROSS 1*	40	5 wks
28 Sep	85	**EATEN ALIVE** *Capitol ROSS 2*	11	19 wks
15 Nov	86	**DIANA ROSS. MICHAEL JACKSON. GLADYS KNIGHT.**		
		STEVIE WONDER. THEIR VERY BEST BACK		
		TO BACK *PrioriTyV PTVR 2★★*	21	10 wks
30 May	87	**RED HOT RHYTHM 'N' BLUES** *EMI EMC 3532*	47	4 wks
31 Oct	87	**LOVE SONGS** *Telstar STAR 2298★★★*	12	24 wks
27 May	89	**WORKIN' OVERTIME** *EMI EMD 1009*	23	4 wks
25 Nov	89	**GREATEST HITS LIVE** *EMI EMDC 1001*	34	6 wks
14 Dec	91	**THE FORCE BEHIND THE POWER** *EMI EMD 1023* ..	11	31 wks
29 Feb	92	**MOTOWN'S GREATEST HITS** *Motown 5300132*	20	11 wks
24 Apr	93	**LIVE, STOLEN MOMENTS** *EMI CDEMD 1044*	45	2 wks
30 Oct	93 ●	**ONE WOMAN – THE ULTIMATE COLLECTION**		
		EMI CDONE 1	2†	9 wks
25 Dec	93	**CHRISTMAS IN VIENNA** *Sony Classical SK 53358★★★★* ...	71†	1 wk

★ *Diana Ross and Marvin Gaye.*
★★ *Diana Ross/Michael Jackson/Gladys Knight/Stevie Wonder.*
★★★ *Diana Ross and Michael Jackson.*
★★★★ *Placido Domingo, Diana Ross and José Carreras.*

The two Diana albums and the three Diana Ross titles are all different.
From 14 Jan 89, when multi-artist albums were excluded from the main chart, Love Songs by Diana Ross and Michael Jackson was listed in the compilation albums chart. See also Supremes; Various Artists – Telstar.

ROSTAL and SCHAEFER UK, male instrumental duo 2 wks

14 Jul	79	**BEATLES CONCERTO** *Parlophone PAS 10014*	61	2 wks

R
265

ALPHABETICALLY BY ARTIST

Mstilav ROSTROPOVICH – *see Herbert VON KARAJAN*

David Lee ROTH US, *male vocalist* — 30 wks

2 Mar	85	**CRAZY FROM THE HEAT** *Warner Bros. 92–5222–1*	91	2 wks
19 Jul	86	**EAT 'EM AND SMILE** *Warner Bros. WX 56*	28	9 wks
6 Feb	88	**SKYSCRAPER** *Warner Bros. 925671 1*	11	12 wks
26 Jan	91	● **A LITTLE AIN'T ENOUGH** *Warner Bros WX 403*	4	7 wks

Uli Jon ROTH and ELECTRIC SUN
Germany, male vocal/instrumental group — 2 wks

23 Feb	85	**BEYOND THE ASTRAL SKIES** *EMI ROTH 1*	64	2 wks

Thomas ROUND – *See June BRONHILL and Thomas ROUND*

Demis ROUSSOS Greece, *male vocalist* — 143 wks

22 Jun	74	● **FOREVER AND EVER** *Philips 6325 021*	2	68 wks
19 Apr	75	**SOUVENIRS** *Philips 6325 201*	25	18 wks
24 Apr	76	● **HAPPY TO BE** *Philips 9101 027*	4	34 wks
3 Jul	76	**MY ONLY FASCINATION** *Philips 6325 094*	39	6 wks
16 Apr	77	**THE MAGIC OF DEMIS ROUSSOS** *Philips 9101 131*	29	6 wks
28 Oct	78	**LIFE AND LOVE** *Philips 9199 873*	36	11 wks

ROXETTE Sweden, *male/female vocal/instrumental duo* — 118 wks

17 Jun	89	● **LOOK SHARP!** *EMI EMC 3557*	4	53 wks
13 Apr	91	● **JOYRIDE** *EMI EMD 1019*	2	48 wks
12 Sep	92	● **TOURISM** *EMI CDEMD 1036*	2	17 wks

**R
266**

ROXY MUSIC UK, *male vocal/instrumental group* — 397 wks

29 Jul	72	● **ROXY MUSIC** *Island ILPS 9200*	10	16 wks
7 Apr	73	● **FOR YOUR PLEASURE** *Island ILPS 9232*	4	27 wks
1 Dec	73	★ **STRANDED** *Island ILPS 9252*	1	17 wks
30 Nov	74	● **COUNTRY LIFE** *Island ILPS 9303*	3	10 wks
8 Nov	75	● **SIREN** *Island ILPS 9344*	4	17 wks
31 Jul	76	● **VIVA ROXY MUSIC** *Island ILPS 9400*	6	12 wks
19 Nov	77	**GREATEST HITS** *Polydor 2302 073*	20	11 wks
24 Mar	79	● **MANIFESTO** *Polydor POLH 001*	7	34 wks
31 May	80	★ **FLESH AND BLOOD** *Polydor POLH 002*	1	60 wks
5 Jun	82	★ **AVALON** *EG EGLP 50*	1	57 wks
19 Mar	83	**THE HIGH ROAD (import)** *EG EGMLP 1*	26	7 wks
12 Nov	83	**ATLANTIC YEARS 1973–1980** *EG EGLP 54*	23	25 wks
26 Apr	86	★ **STREET LIFE – 20 GREAT HITS** *EG EGTV 1★*	1	77 wks
19 Nov	88	● **THE ULTIMATE COLLECTION** *EG EGTV 2★*	6	27 wks

★ *Bryan Ferry and Roxy Music.*

ROYAL CHORAL SOCIETY – *See LONDON SYMPHONY ORCHESTRA*

ROYAL LIVERPOOL PHILHARMONIC ORCHESTRA – *See Carl DAVIS and the ROYAL
LIVERPOOL PHILHARMONIC ORCHESTRA*

ROYAL PHILHARMONIC ORCHESTRA
UK, *orchestra conducted by Louis Clark* — 117 wks

23 Dec	78	**CLASSIC GOLD VOL. 2** *Ronco RTD 42032*	31	4 wks
13 Jan	79	**CLASSICAL GOLD** *Ronco RTV 42020*	65	1 wk
19 Sep	81	● **HOOKED ON CLASSICS** *K-Tel ONE 1146*	4	43 wks
31 Jul	82	**CAN'T STOP THE CLASSICS – HOOKED ON CLASSICS 2** *K-Tel ONE 1173*	13	26 wks
9 Apr	83	**JOURNEY THROUGH THE CLASSICS – HOOKED ON CLASSICS 3** *K-Tel ONE 1226*	19	15 wks
8 Oct	83	**LOVE CLASSICS** *Nouveau Music NML 1003★*	30	9 wks
10 Dec	83	**THE BEST OF HOOKED ON CLASSICS** *K-Tel ONE 1266*	51	6 wks

26 May 84	**AS TIME GOES BY** *Telstar STAR 2240*★★	95	2 wks
26 Nov 88	**RHYTHM AND CLASSICS** *Telstar STAR 2344*	96	1 wk
22 Sep 90	**MUSIC FOR THE LAST NIGHT OF THE PROMS**		
	Cirrus TVLP 501★★★	39	4 wks
5 Oct 91	**SERIOUSLY ORCHESTRAL** *Virgin RPOLP 1*	31	6 wks

★ *Royal Philharmonic Orchestra conducted by Nick Portlock.*
★★ *Royal Philharmonic Orchestra conducted by Harry Rabinowitz.*
★★★ *Sir Charles Groves, Royal Philharmonic Orchestra and Chorus with Sarah Walker.*
See also Richard Clayderman; Julian Lloyd Webber; Juan Martin; Andy Williams.

ROZALLA *Zimbabwe, female vocalist* · 4 wks

4 Apr 92	**EVERYBODY'S FREE** *Pulse 8 PULSECD 3*	20	4 wks

RUBETTES *UK, male vocal/instrumental group* · 1 wk

10 May 75	**WE CAN DO IT** *State ETAT 001*	41	1 wk

David RUFFIN – *See Darryl HALL and John OATES*

Jimmy RUFFIN *US, male vocalist* · 10 wks

13 May 67	**THE JIMMY RUFFIN WAY** *Tamla Motown STML 11048* ..	32	6 wks
1 Jun 74	**GREATEST HITS** *Tamla Motown STML 11259*	41	4 wks

RUFUS *US, male instrumental group and female vocalist* · 7 wks

12 Apr 75	**RUFUSIZED** *ABC ABCL 5063*	48	2 wks
21 Apr 84	**STOMPIN' AT THE SAVOY** *Warner Bros. 923679*★	64	5 wks

★ *Rufus and Chaka Khan.*

RUMOUR – *See Graham PARKER and the RUMOUR*

Todd RUNDGREN *US, male vocalist* · 9 wks

29 Jan 77	**RA** *Bearsville K 55514*	27	6 wks
6 May 78	**HERMIT OF MINK HOLLOW** *Bearsville K 55521*	42	3 wks

RUN D.M.C. *US, male rap group* · 33 wks

26 Jul 86	**RAISING HELL** *Profile LONLP 21*	41	26 wks
4 Jun 88	**TOUGHER THAN LEATHER** *Profile LONLP 38*	13	5 wks
15 May 93	**DOWN WITH THE KING** *Profile FILECD 440*	44	2 wks

RUNRIG *UK, male vocal/instrumental group* · 27 wks

26 Nov 88	**ONCE IN A LIFETIME** *Chrysalis CHR 1695*	61	2 wks
7 Oct 89	**SEARCHLIGHT** *Chrysalis CHR 1713*	11	4 wks
22 Jun 91 ●	**THE BIG WHEEL** *Chrysalis CHR 1858*	4	15 wks
27 Mar 93 ●	**AMAZING THINGS** *Chrysalis CDCHR 2000*	2	6 wks

RUSH *Canada, male vocal/instrumental group* · 95 wks

8 Oct 77	**FAREWELL TO KINGS** *Mercury 9100 042*	22	4 wks
25 Nov 78	**HEMISPHERES** *Mercury 9100 059*	14	6 wks
26 Jan 80 ●	**PERMANENT WAVES** *Mercury 9100 071*	3	16 wks
21 Feb 81 ●	**MOVING PICTURES** *Mercury 6337 160*	3	11 wks
7 Nov 81 ●	**EXIT STAGE LEFT** *Mercury 6619 053*	6	14 wks
18 Sep 82 ●	**SIGNALS** *Mercury 6337 243*	3	9 wks
28 Apr 84 ●	**GRACE UNDER PRESSURE** *Vertigo VERH 12*	5	12 wks
9 Nov 85 ●	**POWER WINDOWS** *Vertigo VERH 31*	9	4 wks

21 Nov	87	● HOLD YOUR FIRE *Vertigo VERH 47*	**10**	4 wks
28 Jan	89	A SHOW OF HANDS *Vertigo 836346*	**12**	4 wks
9 Dec	89	PRESTO *Atlantic WX 327*	**27**	2 wks
13 Oct	90	CHRONICLES *Vertigo CBTV 1*	**42**	2 wks
14 Sep	91	● ROLL THE BONES *Atlantic WX 436*	**10**	4 wks
30 Oct	93	COUNTERPARTS *Atlantic 7567825282*	**14**	3 wks

Jennifer RUSH   *US, female vocalist* — 43 wks

16 Nov	85	● JENNIFER RUSH *CBS 26488*	**7**	35 wks
3 May	86	MOVIN' *CBS 26710*	**32**	5 wks
18 Apr	87	HEART OVER MIND *CBS 450 470–1*	**48**	3 wks

Patrice RUSHEN   *US, female vocalist* — 17 wks

1 May	82	STRAIGHT FROM THE HEART *Elektra K 52352*	**24**	14 wks
16 Jun	84	NOW *Elektra 960360*	**73**	3 wks

Brenda RUSSELL   *US, female vocalist* — 4 wks

23 Apr	88	GET HERE *A & M AMA 5178*	**77**	4 wks

Leon RUSSELL   *US, male vocalist* — 1 wk

3 Jul	71	LEON RUSSELL AND THE SHELTER PEOPLE *A & M AMLS 65003*	**29**	1 wk

Mike RUTHERFORD
UK, male vocalist/instrumentalist – guitar — 11 wks

23 Feb	80	SMALLCREEP'S DAY *Charisma CAS 1149*	**13**	7 wks
18 Sep	82	ACTING VERY STRANGE *WEA K 99249*	**23**	4 wks

See also Mike and the Mechanics.

RUTLES   *UK, male vocal/instrumental group* — 11 wks

15 Apr	78	THE RUTLES *Warner Bros. K 56459*	**12**	11 wks

RUTS   *UK, male vocal/instrumental group* — 10 wks

13 Oct	79	THE CRACK *Virgin V 2132*	**16**	6 wks
18 Oct	80	GRIN AND BEAR IT *Virgin V 2188★*	**28**	4 wks

★ *Ruts D.C.*

Robin S   *US, female vocalist* — 3 wks

4 Sep	93	SHOW ME LOVE *Champion CHAMPCD 1028*	**34**	3 wks

S EXPRESS   *UK, male/female vocal/instrumental group* — 9 wks

1 Apr	89	● ORIGINAL SOUNDTRACK *Rhythm King LEFTLP 8*	**5**	9 wks

SABRES OF PARADISE UK, male instrumental group   2 wks

23 Oct	93	**SABRESONIC** Warp WARPCD 16	29	2 wks

SAD CAFE UK, male vocal/instrumental group   36 wks

1 Oct	77	**FANX TA RA** RCA PL 25101	56	1 wk
29 Apr	78	**MISPLACED IDEALS** RCA PL 25133	50	1 wk
29 Sep	79 ●	**FACADES** RCA PL 25249	8	23 wks
25 Oct	80	**SAD CAFE** RCA SADLP 4	46	5 wks
21 Mar	81	**LIVE** RCA SAD LP 5	37	4 wks
24 Oct	81	**OLE** Polydor POLD 5045	72	2 wks

SADE UK, female vocalist   173 wks

28 Jul	84 ●	**DIAMOND LIFE** Epic EPC 26044	2	98 wks
16 Nov	85 ★	**PROMISE** Epic EPC 86318	1	31 wks
14 May	88 ●	**STRONGER THAN PRIDE** Epic 460497 1	3	17 wks
7 Nov	92 ●	**LOVE DELUXE** Epic 4726262	10	27 wks

SAILOR UK, male vocal/instrumental group   8 wks

7 Feb	76	**TROUBLE** Epic EPC 69192	45	8 wks

General SAINT – See Clint EASTWOOD and General SAINT

SAINT ETIENNE UK, male/female vocal/instrumental group   10 wks

26 Oct	91	**FOXBASE ALPHA** Heavenly HVNLP 1	34	3 wks
6 Mar	93 ●	**SO TOUGH** Heavenly HVNLP 6CD	7	7 wks

ST. PAUL'S BOYS' CHOIR UK, choir   8 wks

29 Nov	80	**REJOICE** K-Tel NE 1064	36	8 wks

Buffy SAINTE-MARIE Canada, female vocalist   2 wks

21 Mar	92	**COINCIDENCE (AND LIKELY STORIES)** Ensign CCD 1920	39	2 wks

Ryuichi SAKAMOTO
Japan, male composer/multi-instrumentalist   9 wks

3 Sep	83	**MERRY CHRISTMAS MR LAWRENCE (film soundtrack)** Virgin V 2276	36	9 wks

SALT–N–PEPA US, female rap group   63 wks

6 Aug	88	**A SALT WITH A DEADLY PEPA** ffrr FFRLP 3	19	27 wks
12 May	90	**BLACKS' MAGIC** ffrr 8281641	70	1 wk
6 Jul	91	**A BLITZ OF SALT-N-PEPA HITS** ffrr 8282491	70	2 wks
19 Oct	91 ●	**GREATEST HITS** ffrr 8282911	6	20 wks
25 Apr	93	**RAPPED IN REMIXES** ffrr 8282972	37	2 wks

SALVATION ARMY UK, brass band   5 wks

24 Dec	77	**BY REQUEST** Warwick WW 5038	16	5 wks

The **Shamen**'s Goode success extended to the album chart. (Pictorial Press)

Right Said Fred join Fred Schneider of the B-52's (second from right) at a New York City benefit for the Lifebeat Foundation. (Pictorial Press)

SAM and DAVE *US, male vocal duo* *20 wks*

21 Jan	67	**HOLD ON I'M COMIN'** *Atlantic 588–045*	35	7 wks
22 Apr	67	**DOUBLE DYNAMITE** *Stax 589–003*	28	5 wks
23 Mar	68	**SOUL MAN** *Stax 589–015*	32	8 wks

Richie SAMBORA *US, male vocalist/instrumentalist – guitar 3 wks*

14 Sep	91	**STRANGER IN THIS TOWN** *Mercury 8488951*	20	3 wks

Mike SAMMES SINGERS – *See RICHMOND STRINGS/Mike SAMMES SINGERS*

SAMSON *UK, male vocal/instrumental group* *6 wks*

26 Jul	80	**HEAD ON** *Gem GEMLP 108*	34	6 wks

David SANBORN *US, male instrumentalist – saxophone* *1 wk*

14 Mar	87	**A CHANGE OF HEART** *Warner Bros. 925 479–1*	86	1 wk

SANTANA *US, male vocal/instrumental group* *220 wks*

2 May	70	**SANTANA** *CBS 63815*	26	11 wks
28 Nov	70 ●	**ABRAXAS** *CBS 64807*	7	52 wks
13 Nov	71 ●	**SANTANA 3** *CBS 69015*	6	14 wks
26 Aug	72	**CARLOS SANTANA AND BUDDY MILES LIVE** *CBS 65142**	29	4 wks
29 Nov	72 ●	**CARAVANSERAI** *CBS 65299*	6	11 wks
28 Jul	73 ●	**LOVE DEVOTION SURRENDER** *CBS 69037***	7	9 wks
8 Dec	73 ●	**WELCOME** *CBS 69040*	8	6 wks
21 Sep	74	**GREATEST HITS** *CBS 69081*	14	15 wks
2 Nov	74	**ILLUMINATIONS** *CBS 69063****	40	1 wk
30 Nov	74	**BARBOLETTA** *CBS 69084*	18	5 wks
10 Apr	76	**AMIGOS** *CBS 86005*	21	9 wks
8 Jan	77	**FESTIVAL** *CBS 86020*	27	3 wks
5 Nov	77 ●	**MOONFLOWER** *CBS 88272*	7	27 wks
11 Nov	78	**INNER SECRETS** *CBS 86075*	17	16 wks
24 Mar	79	**ONENESS – SILVER DREAMS GOLDEN REALITY** *CBS 86037*****	55	4 wks
27 Oct	79	**MARATHON** *CBS 86098*	28	5 wks
20 Sep	80	**THE SWING OF DELIGHT** *CBS 22075*****	65	2 wks
18 Apr	81	**ZE BOP** *CBS 84946*	33	4 wks
14 Aug	82	**SHANGO** *CBS 85914*	35	7 wks
30 Apr	83	**HAVANA MOON** *CBS 25350*****	84	3 wks
23 Mar	85	**BEYOND APPEARANCES** *CBS 86307*	58	3 wks
15 Nov	86	**VIVA! SANTANA – THE VERY BEST** *K-Tel NE 1338* ..	50	8 wks
14 Jul	90	**SPIRITS DANCING IN THE FLESH** *CBS 4669131*	68	1 wk

★ *Carlos Santana and Buddy Miles.*
★★ *Carlos Santana and Mahavishnu John McLaughlin.*
★★★ *Carlos Santana and Alice Coltrane.*
★★★★ *Carlos Santana.*

Peter SARSTEDT *UK, male vocalist* *4 wks*

15 Mar	69 ●	**PETER SARSTEDT** *United Artists SULP 1219*	8	4 wks

Joe SATRIANI *US, male instrumentalist – guitar* *8 wks*

15 Aug	92	**THE EXTREMIST** *Epic 4716722*	13	6 wks
6 Nov	93	**TIME MACHINE** *Relativity 4745152*	32	2 wks

Telly SAVALAS *US, male vocalist* *10 wks*

22 Mar	75	**TELLY** *MCA MCF 2699*	12	10 wks

S
271

SAVOY BROWN *UK, male vocal/instrumental group*   *1 wk*

| 28 Nov 70 | **LOOKIN' IN** *Decca SKL 5066* .... | 50 | 1 wk |

SAXON *UK, male vocal/instrumental group*   *97 wks*

12 Apr	80 ●	**WHEELS OF STEEL** *Carrere CAL 115*	5	29 wks
15 Nov	80	**STRONG ARM OF THE LAW** *Carrere CAL 120*	11	13 wks
3 Oct	81 ●	**DENIM AND LEATHER** *Carrere CAL 128*	9	11 wks
22 May	82 ●	**THE EAGLE HAS LANDED** *Carrere CAL 157*	5	19 wks
26 Mar	83	**POWER AND THE GLORY** *Carrere CAL 147*	15	9 wks
11 Feb	84	**CRUSADER** *Carrere CAL 200*	18	7 wks
14 Sep	85	**INNOCENCE IS NO EXCUSE** *Parlophone SAXON 2*	36	4 wks
27 Sep	86	**ROCK THE NATIONS** *EMI EMC 3515*	34	3 wks
9 Apr	88	**DESTINY** *EMI EMC 3543*	49	2 wks

SAW DOCTORS *Ireland, male vocal/instrumental group*   *4 wks*

| 8 Jun | 91 | **IF THIS IS ROCK AND ROLL I WANT MY OLD JOB BACK** *Solid ROCK 7* .... | 69 | 2 wks |
| 31 Oct | 92 | **ALL THE WAY FROM TUAM** *Solid 4509911462* .... | 33 | 2 wks |

Leo SAYER *UK, male vocalist*   *236 wks*

5 Jan	74 ●	**SILVER BIRD** *Chrysalis CHR 1050*	2	22 wks
26 Oct	74 ●	**JUST A BOY** *Chrysalis CHR 1068*	4	14 wks
20 Sep	75 ●	**ANOTHER YEAR** *Chrysalis CHR 1087*	8	9 wks
27 Nov	76 ●	**ENDLESS FLIGHT** *Chrysalis CHR 1125*	4	66 wks
22 Oct	77 ●	**THUNDER IN MY HEART** *Chrysalis CDL 1154*	8	16 wks
2 Sep	78	**LEO SAYER** *Chrysalis CDL 1198*	15	25 wks
31 Mar	79 ★	**THE VERY BEST OF LEO SAYER** *Chrysalis CDL 1222* ..	1	37 wks
13 Oct	79	**HERE** *Chrysalis CDL 1240*	44	4 wks
23 Aug	80	**LIVING IN A FANTASY** *Chrysalis CDL 1297*	15	9 wks
8 May	82	**WORLD RADIO** *Chrysalis CDL 1345*	30	12 wks
12 Nov	83	**HAVE YOU EVER BEEN IN LOVE** *Chrysalis LEOTV 1* ..	15	18 wks
6 Mar	93	**ALL THE BEST** *Chrysalis CDCHR 1980*	26	4 wks

Alexei SAYLE *UK, male comedian*   *5 wks*

| 17 Mar | 84 | **THE FISH PEOPLE TAPES** *Island IMA 9* .... | 62 | 5 wks |

Boz SCAGGS *US, male vocalist*   *29 wks*

12 Mar	77	**SILK DEGREES** *CBS 81193*	37	24 wks
17 Dec	77	**DOWN TWO, THEN LEFT** *CBS 86036*	55	1 wk
3 May	80	**MIDDLE MAN** *CBS 86094*	52	4 wks

SCARS *UK, male vocal/instrumental group*   *3 wks*

| 18 Apr | 81 | **AUTHOR AUTHOR** *Pre PREX 5* .... | 67 | 3 wks |

SCHAEFER – *See ROSTAL and SCHAEFER*

Michael SCHENKER GROUP
Germany/UK, male vocal/instrumental group   *44 wks*

6 Sep	80 ●	**MICHAEL SCHENKER GROUP** *Chrysalis CHR 1302*	8	8 wks
19 Sep	81	**MICHAEL SCHENKER GROUP (re-issue)** *Chrysalis CHR 1336*	14	8 wks
13 Mar	82 ●	**ONE NIGHT AT BUDOKAN** *Chrysalis CTY 1375*	5	11 wks
23 Oct	82	**ASSAULT ATTACK** *Chrysalis CHR 1393*	19	5 wks

10 Sep	83	**BUILT TO DESTROY** *Chrysalis CHR 1441*	23	5 wks
23 Jun	84	**ROCK WILL NEVER DIE** *Chrysalis CUX 1470*	24	5 wks
24 Oct	87	**PERFECT TIMING** *EMI EMC 3539★*	65	2 wks

★ *MSG.*

SCHON – *See HAGAR, SCHON, AARONSON, SHRIEVE*

SCORPIONS   *Germany, male vocal/instrumental group*   *56 wks*

21 Apr	79	**LOVE DRIVE** *Harvest SHSP 4097*	36	11 wks
3 May	80	**ANIMAL MAGNETISM** *Harvest SHSP 4113*	23	6 wks
10 Apr	82	**BLACKOUT** *Harvest SHVL 823*	11	11 wks
24 Mar	84	**LOVE AT FIRST STING** *Harvest SHSP 2400071*	17	6 wks
29 Jun	85	**WORLD WIDE LIVE** *Harvest SCORP 1*	18	8 wks
14 May	88	**SAVAGE AMUSEMENT** *Harvest SHSP 4125*	18	6 wks
17 Nov	90	**CRAZY WORLD** *Vertigo 8469081*	27	7 wks
25 Sep	93	**FACE THE HEAT** *Mercury 5182802*	51	1 wk

SCOTLAND FOOTBALL WORLD CUP SQUAD 1974   *UK, male football team vocalists*   *9 wks*

25 May	74 ●	**EASY EASY** *Polydor 2383 282*	3	9 wks

Band of the SCOTS GUARDS   *UK, military band*   *2 wks*

28 Jun	69	**BAND OF THE SCOTS GUARDS** *Fontana SFXL 54*	25	2 wks

Jack SCOTT   *Canada, male vocalist*   *12 wks*

7 May	60 ●	**I REMEMBER HANK WILLIAMS** *Top Rank BUY 034* ...	7	11 wks
3 Sep	60	**WHAT IN THE WORLD'S COME OVER YOU** *Top Rank 25/024*	11	1 wk

SCREAMING BLUE MESSIAHS
UK, male vocal/instrumental group   *1 wk*

17 May	86	**GUN-SHY** *WEA WX 41*	90	1 wk

SCRITTI POLITTI   *UK, male vocal/instrumental group*   *37 wks*

11 Sep	82	**SONGS TO REMEMBER** *Rough Trade ROUGH 20*	12	7 wks
22 Jun	85 ●	**CUPID AND PSYCHE 85** *Virgin V 2350*	5	19 wks
18 Jun	88 ●	**PROVISION** *Virgin V 2515*	8	11 wks

SEAL   *UK, male vocalist*   *58 wks*

1 Jun	91 ★	**SEAL** *ZTT ZTT 9*	1	58 wks

SEARCHERS   *UK, male vocal/instrumental group*   *87 wks*

10 Aug	63 ●	**MEET THE SEARCHERS** *Pye NPL 18086*	2	44 wks
16 Nov	63 ●	**SUGAR AND SPICE** *Pye NPL 18089*	5	21 wks
30 May	64 ●	**IT'S THE SEARCHERS** *Pye NPL 18092*	4	17 wks
27 Mar	65 ●	**SOUNDS LIKE THE SEARCHERS** *Pye NPL 18111*	8	5 wks

SEBADOH   *US, male vocal/instrumental group*   *1 wk*

8 May	93	**BUBBLE AND SCRAPE** *Domino WIGCD 4*	63	1 wk

Jon SECADA *US, male vocalist* *11 wks*

5 Sep	92	**JON SECADA** *SBK SBKCD 19*	**20**	11 wks

Harry SECOMBE *UK, male vocalist* *61 wks*

31 Mar	62	**SACRED SONGS** *Philips RBL 7501*	**16**	1 wk
22 Apr	67 ●	**SECOMBE'S PERSONAL CHOICE** *Philips BETS 707*	**6**	13 wks
7 Aug	71	**IF I RULED THE WORLD** *Contour 6870 501*	**17**	20 wks
16 Dec	78 ●	**20 SONGS OF JOY** *Warwick WW 5052*	**8**	12 wks
5 Dec	81	**GOLDEN MEMORIES** *Warwick WW 5107★*	**46**	5 wks
13 Dec	86	**HIGHWAY OF LIFE** *Telstar STAR 2289*	**45**	5 wks
30 Nov	91	**YOURS SINCERELY** *Philips 5107321*	**46**	5 wks

★ *Harry Secombe and Moira Anderson.*

Harry SECOMBE, Peter SELLERS and Spike MILLIGAN *UK, male comedy group* *1 wk*

18 Apr	64	**HOW TO WIN AN ELECTION** *Philips AL 3464*	**20**	1 wk

See also Harry Secombe; Peter Sellers; Spike Milligan.

SECOND IMAGE *UK, male vocal/instrumental group* *1 wk*

30 Mar	85	**STRANGE REFLECTIONS** *MCA MCF 3255*	**100**	1 wk

SECRET AFFAIR *UK, male vocal/instrumental group* *15 wks*

1 Dec	79	**GLORY BOYS** *I-Spy 1*	**41**	8 wks
20 Sep	80	**BEHIND CLOSED DOORS** *I-Spy 2*	**48**	4 wks
13 Mar	82	**BUSINESS AS USUAL** *I-Spy 3*	**84**	3 wks

Neil SEDAKA *US, male vocalist* *68 wks*

1 Sep	73	**THE TRA-LA DAYS ARE OVER** *MGM 2315 248*	**13**	10 wks
22 Jun	74	**LAUGHTER IN THE RAIN** *Polydor 2383 265*	**17**	10 wks
23 Nov	74	**LIVE AT THE ROYAL FESTIVAL HALL** *Polydor 2383 299*	**48**	1 wk
1 Mar	75	**OVERNIGHT SUCCESS** *Polydor 2442 131*	**31**	6 wks
10 Jul	76 ●	**LAUGHTER AND TEARS – THE BEST OF NEIL SEDAKA TODAY** *Polydor 2383 399*	**2**	25 wks
2 Nov	91 ●	**TIMELESS – THE VERY BEST OF NEIL SEDAKA** *Polydor 5114421*	**10**	16 wks

SEEKERS *Australia, male/female vocal group* *268 wks*

3 Jul	65 ●	**A WORLD OF OUR OWN** *Columbia 33SX 1722*	**5**	36 wks
3 Jul	65	**THE SEEKERS** *Decca LK 4694*	**16**	1 wk
19 Nov	66 ●	**COME THE DAY** *Columbia SX 6093*	**3**	67 wks
25 Nov	67	**SEEKERS – SEEN IN GREEN** *Columbia SCX 6193*	**15**	10 wks
14 Sep	68 ●	**LIVE AT THE TALK OF THE TOWN** *Columbia SCX 6278*	**2**	29 wks
16 Nov	68 ★	**BEST OF THE SEEKERS** *Columbia SCX 6268*	**1**	125 wks

Bob SEGER and the SILVER BULLET BAND
US, male vocal/instrumental group *40 wks*

3 Jun	78	**STRANGER IN TOWN** *Capitol EAST 11698*	**31**	6 wks
15 Mar	80	**AGAINST THE WIND** *Capitol EAST 12041*	**26**	6 wks
26 Sep	81	**NINE TONIGHT** *Capitol ESTSP 23*	**24**	10 wks
8 Jan	83	**THE DISTANCE** *Capitol EST 12254*	**45**	10 wks
26 Apr	86	**LIKE A ROCK** *Capitol EST 2011*	**35**	6 wks
21 Sep	91	**THE FIRE INSIDE** *Capitol EST 2149*	**54**	2 wks

SELECTER *UK, male/female vocal/instrumental group*   *17 wks*

23 Feb	80 ●	**TOO MUCH PRESSURE** *2-Tone CDL TT 5002*	**5**	13 wks
7 Mar	81	**CELEBRATE THE BULLET** *Chrysalis CHR 1306*	**41**	4 wks

Peter SELLERS *UK, male vocalist*   *102 wks*

14 Feb	59 ●	**THE BEST OF SELLERS** *Parlophone PMD 1069*	**3**	47 wks
12 Dec	59 ●	**SONGS FOR SWINGING SELLERS** *Parlophone PMC 1111* .	**3**	37 wks
3 Dec	60 ●	**PETER AND SOPHIA** *Parlophone PMC 1131★*	**5**	18 wks

★ *Peter Sellers and Sophia Loren.*

SENSATIONAL ALEX HARVEY BAND
UK, male vocal/instrumental group   *42 wks*

26 Oct	74	**THE IMPOSSIBLE DREAM** *Vertigo 6360 112*	**16**	4 wks
10 May	75 ●	**TOMORROW BELONGS TO ME** *Vertigo 9102 003*	**9**	10 wks
23 Aug	75	**NEXT** *Vertigo 6360 103*	**37**	5 wks
27 Sep	75	**SENSATIONAL ALEX HARVEY BAND LIVE**		
		Vertigo 6360 122	**14**	7 wks
10 Apr	76	**PENTHOUSE TAPES** *Vertigo 9102 007*	**14**	7 wks
31 Jul	76	**SAHB STORIES** *Mountain TOPS 112*	**11**	9 wks

SENSELESS THINGS *UK, male vocal/instrumental group* *2 wks*

26 Oct	91	**THE FIRST OF TOO MANY** *Epic 4691571*	**66**	1 wk
13 Mar	93	**EMPIRE OF THE SENSELESS** *Epic 4735252*	**37**	1 wk

SEPULTURA *Brazil, male vocal/instrumental group*   *5 wks*

6 Apr	91	**ARISE** *Roadracer RO 93281*	**40**	2 wks
23 Oct	93	**CHAOS AD** *Roadrunner RR 90002*	**11**	3 wks

Taja SEVELLE *US, female vocalist*   *4 wks*

26 Mar	88	**TAJA SEVELLE** *Paisley Park WX 165*	**48**	4 wks

SEX PISTOLS *UK, male vocal/instrumental group*   *101 wks*

12 Nov	77 ★	**NEVER MIND THE BOLLOCKS HERE'S THE SEX**		
		PISTOLS *Virgin V 2086*	**1**	48 wks
10 Mar	79 ●	**THE GREAT ROCK 'N' ROLL SWINDLE**		
		Virgin VD 2410	**7**	33 wks
11 Aug	79 ●	**SOME PRODUCT – CARRI ON SEX PISTOLS**		
		Virgin VR 2	**6**	10 wks
16 Feb	80	**FLOGGING A DEAD HORSE** *Virgin V 2142*	**23**	6 wks
17 Oct	92 ●	**KISS THIS** *Virgin CDV 2702*	**10**	4 wks

SHADES OF RHYTHM
UK, male/female vocal/instrumental group   *3 wks*

17 Aug	91	**SHADES** *ZTT ZTT 8*	**51**	3 wk

SHADOWS *UK, male instrumental group*   *450 wks*

16 Sep	61 ★	**THE SHADOWS** *Columbia 33SX 1374*	**1**	57 wks
13 Oct	62 ★	**OUT OF THE SHADOWS** *Columbia 33SX 1458*	**1**	38 wks
22 Jun	63 ●	**GREATEST HITS** *Columbia 33SX 1522*	**2**	49 wks
9 May	64 ●	**DANCE WITH THE SHADOWS** *Columbia 33SX 1619* ...	**2**	27 wks
17 Jul	65 ●	**SOUND OF THE SHADOWS** *Columbia 33SX 1736*	**4**	17 wks

21 May	66 ●	SHADOW MUSIC *Columbia SX 6041*	5	17 wks
15 Jul	67 ●	JIGSAW *Columbia SCX 6148*	8	16 wks
24 Oct	70	SHADES OF ROCK *Columbia SCX 6420*	30	4 wks
13 Apr	74	ROCKIN' WITH CURLY LEADS *EMI EMA 762*	45	1 wk
11 May	74	GREATEST HITS (re-issue) *Columbia SCX 1522*	48	6 wks
29 Mar	75	SPECS APPEAL *EMI EMC 3066*	30	5 wks
12 Feb	77 ★	20 GOLDEN GREATS *EMI EMTV 3*	1	38 wks
15 Sep	79 ★	STRING OF HITS *EMI EMC 3310*	1	48 wks
26 Jul	80	ANOTHER STRING OF HITS *EMI EMC 3339*	16	8 wks
13 Sep	80	CHANGE OF ADDRESS *Polydor 2442 179*	17	6 wks
19 Sep	81	HITS RIGHT UP YOUR STREET *Polydor POLD 5046* ...	15	16 wks
25 Sep	82	LIFE IN THE JUNGLE/LIVE AT ABBEY ROAD		
		Polydor SHADS 1	24	6 wks
22 Oct	83	XXV *Polydor POLD 5120*	34	6 wks
17 Nov	84	GUARDIAN ANGEL *Polydor POLD 5169*	98	1 wk
24 May	86 ●	MOONLIGHT SHADOWS *Polydor PROLP 8*	6	19 wks
24 Oct	87	SIMPLY SHADOWS *Polydor SHAD 1*	11	17 wks
20 May	89	STEPPIN' TO THE SHADOWS *Polydor SHAD 30*	11	9 wks
16 Dec	89	AT THEIR VERY BEST *Polydor 8415201*	12	9 wks
13 Oct	90 ●	REFLECTION *Roll Over 8471201*	5	15 wks
16 Nov	91	THEMES AND DREAMS *Polydor 5113741*	21	11 wks
15 May	93	SHADOWS IN THE NIGHT *PolyGram TV 8437982*	22	4 wks

See also Cliff Richard.

SHAGGY *Jamaica, male vocalist*   *1 wk*

24 Jul	93	PURE PLEASURE *Greensleeves GRELCD 184*	67	1 wk

SHAKATAK *UK, male/female vocal/instrumental group*   *73 wks*

30 Jan	82	DRIVIN' HARD *Polydor POLS 1030*	35	17 wks
15 May	82 ●	NIGHT BIRDS *Polydor POLS 1059*	4	28 wks
27 Nov	82	INVITATIONS *Polydor POLD 5068*	30	11 wks
22 Oct	83	OUT OF THIS WORLD *Polydor POLD 5115*	30	4 wks
25 Aug	84	DOWN ON THE STREET *Polydor POLD 5148*	17	9 wks
23 Feb	85	LIVE! *Polydor POLH 21*	82	3 wks
22 Oct	88	THE COOLEST CUTS *K-Tel NE 1422*	73	1 wk

SHAKESPEAR'S SISTER
UK/US, female vocal/instrumental duo   *63 wks*

2 Sep	89 ●	SACRED HEART *London 828131 1*	9	8 wks
29 Feb	92 ●	HORMONALLY YOURS *London 8282262*	3	55 wks

SHAKIN' PYRAMIDS *UK, male vocal/instrumental group*   *4 wks*

4 Apr	81	SKIN 'EM UP *Cuba Libra V 2199*	48	4 wks

SHAKY – *See Shakin' STEVENS*

SHALAMAR *US, male/female vocal/instrumental group*   *121 wks*

27 Mar	82 ●	FRIENDS *Solar K 52345*	6	72 wks
11 Sep	82	GREATEST HITS *Solar SOLA 3001*	71	5 wks
30 Jul	83 ●	THE LOOK *Solar 960239*	7	20 wks
12 Apr	86 ●	THE GREATEST HITS *Stylus SMR 8615*	5	24 wks

The two Greatest Hits albums are different.

SHAM 69 *UK, male vocal/instrumental group*   *27 wks*

11 Mar	78	TELL US THE TRUTH *Polydor 2383 491*	25	8 wks
2 Dec	78	THAT'S LIFE *Polydor POLD 5010*	27	11 wks
29 Sep	79 ●	THE ADVENTURES OF THE HERSHAM BOYS		
		Polydor POLD 5025	8	8 wks

Jim Kerr led **Simple Minds** to four consecutive number ones, all of which were on top for just one week. (Redferns)

Frank Sinatra, star of the very first album chart, returned in glory in 1993, giving him the longest span of top five hits.

Sandie Shaw performed barefoot, but for bear feet she wore socks. (Pictorial Press)

SHAMEN *UK, male vocal/instrumental duo* — *45 wks*

2 Nov 90	**EN-TACT** *One Little Indian TPLP 22*		**31**	10 wks
28 Sep 91	**PROGENY** *One Little Indian TPLP 32*		**23**	2 wks
26 Sep 92 ●	**BOSS DRUM/DIFFERENT DRUM**			
	One Little Indian TPLP 42CD		**3†**	32 wks
20 Nov 93	**ON AIR** *Band Of Joy BOJCD 006*		**61**	1 wk

From 18 Dec 93 sales of Boss Drum *and the remix album,* Different Drum, *were amalgamated.*

Jimmy SHAND, HIS BAND AND GUESTS
UK, male instrumentalist – accordion, with male/female vocal/instrumental dance band — *2 wks*

24 Dec 83	**FIFTY YEARS ON WITH JIMMY SHAND** *Ross WGR 062*		97	2 wks

SHANICE *US, female vocalist* — *4 wks*

21 Mar 92	**INNER CHILD** *Motown 5300082*		**21**	4 wks

SHANNON *US, female vocalist* — *12 wks*

10 Mar 84	**LET THE MUSIC PLAY** *Club JABL 1*		**52**	12 wks

Del SHANNON *US, male vocalist* — *23 wks*

11 May 63 ●	**HATS OFF TO DEL SHANNON** *London HAX 8071*		**9**	17 wks
2 Nov 63	**LITTLE TOWN FLIRT** *London HAX 8091*		**15**	6 wks

Helen SHAPIRO *UK, female vocalist* — *25 wks*

10 Mar 62 ●	**TOPS WITH ME** *Columbia 33SX 1397*		**2**	25 wks

Feargal SHARKEY *UK, male vocalist* — *24 wks*

23 Nov 85	**FEARGAL SHARKEY** *Virgin V 2360*		**12**	20 wks
20 Apr 91	**SONGS FROM THE MARDI GRAS** *Virgin V 2642*		**27**	4 wks

SHARPE and NUMAN – *See Gary NUMAN*

Roland SHAW – *See MANTOVANI*

Sandie SHAW *UK, female vocalist* — *13 wks*

6 Mar 65 ●	**SANDIE** *Pye NPL 18110*		**3**	13 wks

George SHEARING *UK, male instrumentalist – piano* — *13 wks*

11 Jun 60	**BEAUTY AND THE BEAT** *Capitol T 1219★*		**16**	6 wks
20 Oct 62 ●	**NAT 'KING' COLE SINGS AND THE GEORGE**			
	SHEARING QUINTET PLAYS *Capitol W 1675★★*		**8**	7 wks

★ *Peggy Lee and George Shearing.*
★★ *Nat 'King' Cole and the George Shearing Quintet.*

SHEEP ON DRUGS
UK, male vocal/instrumental duo — *1 wk*

10 Apr 93	**GREATEST HITS** *Transglobal CID 8006*		**55**	1 wk

Pete SHELLEY UK, male vocalist   4 wks

| 2 Jul | 83 | **XL-1** Genetic XL 1 .... | 42 | 4 wks |

SHERRICK US, male vocalist   6 wks

| 29 Aug | 87 | **SHERRICK** Warner Bros. WX 118 .... | 27 | 6 wks |

Brendon SHINE Ireland, male vocalist   29 wks

12 Nov	83	**THE BRENDON SHINE COLLECTION** Play PLAYTV 1	51	12 wks
3 Nov	84	**WITH LOVE** Play PLAYTV 2	74	4 wks
16 Nov	85	**MEMORIES** Play PLAYTV 3	81	7 wks
18 Nov	89	**MAGIC MOMENTS** Stylus SMR 991	62	6 wks

SHIRLIE – See PEPSI and SHIRLIE

Michelle SHOCKED US, female vocalist   24 wks

10 Sep	88	**SHORT SHARP SHOCKED** Cooking Vinyl CVLP 1	33	19 wks
18 Nov	89	**CAPTAIN SWING** Cooking Vinyl 838878 1	31	3 wks
11 Apr	92	**ARKANSAS TRAVELER** London 5121892	46	2 wks

SHOP ASSISTANTS
UK, male/female vocal/instrumental group   1 wk

| 29 Nov | 86 | **SHOP ASSISTANTS** Blue Guitar AZLP 2 .... | 100 | 1 wk |

SHOWADDYWADDY
UK, male vocal/instrumental group   126 wks

7 Dec	74	● **SHOWADDYWADDY** Bell BELLS 248	9	19 wks
12 Jul	75	● **STEP TWO** Bell BELLS 256	7	17 wks
29 May	76	**TROCADERO** Bell SYBEL 8003	41	3 wks
25 Dec	76	● **GREATEST HITS** Arista ARTY 145	4	26 wks
3 Dec	77	**RED STAR** Arista SPARTY 1023	20	10 wks
9 Dec	78	★ **GREATEST HITS (1976–1978)** Arista ARTV 1	1	17 wks
10 Nov	79	● **CREPES AND DRAPES** Arista ARTV 3	8	14 wks
20 Dec	80	**BRIGHT LIGHTS** Arista SPART 1142	54	8 wks
7 Nov	81	**THE VERY BEST OF** Arista SPART 1178	33	11 wks
5 Dec	87	**THE BEST STEPS TO HEAVEN** Tiger SHTV 1	90	1 wk

SHRIEKBACK
UK, male vocal/instrumental group   1 wk

| 11 Aug | 84 | **JAM SCIENCE** Arista 206 416 .... | 85 | 1 wk |

SHRIEVE – See HAGAR, SCHON, AARONSON, SHRIEVE

SHUT UP AND DANCE
UK, male vocal/instrumental/sampling group   2 wks

| 27 Jun | 92 | **DEATH IS NOT THE END** | | |
| | | Shut Up And Dance SUADCD 005 .... | 38 | 2 wks |

SHY UK, male vocal/instrumental group   2 wks

| 11 Apr | 87 | **EXCESS ALL AREAS** RCA PL 71221 .... | 74 | 2 wks |

Labi SIFFRE *UK, male vocalist*   *2 wks*

| 24 Jul 71 | **SINGER AND THE SONG** *Pye NSPL 28147* .... | **47** | 1 wk |
| 14 Oct 72 | **CRYING, LAUGHING, LOVING, LYING** *Pye NSPL 28163* .... | **46** | 1 wk |

SILVER BULLET BAND – *See Bob SEGER and the SILVER BULLET BAND*

SIGUE SIGUE SPUTNIK
UK, male vocal/instrumental group   *7 wks*

| 9 Aug 86 | ● **FLAUNT IT** *Parlophone PCS 7305* .... | **10** | 6 wks |
| 15 Apr 89 | **DRESS FOR EXCESS** *Parlophone PCS 7328* .... | **53** | 1 wk |

SILENCERS *UK, male vocal/instrumental group*   *3 wks*

| 23 Mar 91 | **DANCE TO THE HOLY MAN** *RCA PL 74924* .... | **39** | 2 wks |
| 5 Jun 93 | **SECONDS OF PLEASURE** *RCA 74321141132* .... | **52** | 1 wk |

SILVER BULLET *UK, male vocal/instrumental duo*   *2 wks*

| 4 May 91 | **BRING DOWN THE WALLS NO LIMIT SQUAD** *Parlophone PCS 7350* .... | **38** | 2 wks |

SILVER CONVENTION
Germany/US, female vocal group   *3 wks*

| 25 Jun 77 | **SILVER CONVENTION: GREATEST HITS** *Magnet MAG 6001* .... | **34** | 3 wks |

SILVERFISH
US, male vocal/instrumental group   *1 wk*

| 27 Jun 92 | **ORGAN FAN** *Creation CRECD 118* .... | **65** | 1 wk |

Carly SIMON *US, female vocalist*   *61 wks*

20 Jan 73	● **NO SECRETS** *Elektra K 42127*	**3**	26 wks
16 Mar 74	**HOT CAKES** *Elektra K 52005*	**19**	9 wks
9 May 87	**COMING AROUND AGAIN** *Arista 208 140*	**25**	20 wks
3 Sep 88	**GREATEST HITS LIVE** *Arista 209196*	**49**	6 wks

Paul SIMON *US, male vocalist*   *261 wks*

26 Feb 72	★ **PAUL SIMON** *CBS 69007*	**1**	26 wks
2 Jun 73	● **THERE GOES RHYMIN' SIMON** *CBS 69035*	**4**	22 wks
1 Nov 75	● **STILL CRAZY AFTER ALL THESE YEARS** *CBS 86001* .	**6**	31 wks
3 Dec 77	● **GREATEST HITS, ETC.** *CBS 10007*	**6**	15 wks
30 Aug 80	**ONE-TRICK PONY** *Warner Bros. K 56846*	**17**	12 wks
12 Nov 83	**HEARTS AND BONES** *Warner Bros. 92–3942–1*	**34**	8 wks
13 Sep 86	★ **GRACELAND** *Warner Bros. WX 52*	**1**	101 wks
24 Jan 87	**GREATEST HITS, ETC. (re-issue)** *CBS 450 166–1*	**73**	2 wks
5 Nov 88	**NEGOTIATIONS AND LOVE SONGS 1971–1986** *Warner Bros. WX 223*	**17**	15 wks
27 Oct 90	★ **RHYTHM OF THE SAINTS** *Warner Bros WX 340*	**1**	28 wks
23 Nov 91	**THE CONCERT IN THE PARK – AUGUST 15TH 1991** *Warner Bros WX 448*	**60**	1 wk

See also Simon and Garfunkel.

SIMON and GARFUNKEL US, male vocal duo   1061 wks

16 Apr	66		SOUNDS OF SILENCE CBS 62690	13	104 wks
3 Aug	68	★	BOOKENDS CBS 63101	1	77 wks
31 Aug	68		PARSLEY, SAGE, ROSEMARY AND THYME CBS 62860	13	66 wks
26 Oct	68	●	THE GRADUATE (film soundtrack) CBS 70042	3	71 wks
9 Nov	68		WEDNESDAY MORNING 3 A.M. CBS 63370	24	6 wks
21 Feb	70	★	BRIDGE OVER TROUBLED WATER CBS 63699	1	303 wks
22 Jul	72	●	GREATEST HITS CBS 69003	2	283 wks
4 Apr	81		SOUNDS OF SILENCE (re-issue) CBS 32020	68	1 wk
21 Nov	81	●	THE SIMON AND GARFUNKEL COLLECTION CBS 10029	4	80 wks
20 Mar	82	●	THE CONCERT IN CENTRAL PARK Geffen GEF 96008	6	43 wks
30 Nov	91	●	THE DEFINITIVE SIMON AND GARFUNKEL Columbia MOODCD 21	8	27 wks

See also Paul Simon; Art Garfunkel.

Nina SIMONE US, female vocalist   12 wks

24 Jul	65	I PUT A SPELL ON YOU Philips BL 7671	18	3 wks
15 Feb	69	'NUFF SAID RCS SF 7979	11	1 wk
14 Nov	87	MY BABY JUST CARES FOR ME Charly CR 30217	56	8 wks

SIMPLE MINDS
UK, male vocal/instrumental group   *319 wks*

5 May	79		A LIFE IN THE DAY Zoom ZULP 1	30	6 wks
27 Sep	80		EMPIRES AND DANCE Arista SPART 1140	41	3 wks
12 Sep	81		SONS AND FASCINATIONS/SISTERS FEELINGS CALL Virgin V 2207	11	7 wks
27 Feb	82		CELEBRATION Arista SPART 1183	45	7 wks
25 Sep	82	●	NEW GOLD DREAM (81, 82, 83, 84) Virgin V 2230	3	52 wks
18 Feb	84	★	SPARKLE IN THE RAIN Virgin V 2300	1	57 wks
2 Nov	85	★	ONCE UPON A TIME Virgin V 2364	1	83 wks
6 Jun	87	★	LIVE IN THE CITY OF LIGHT Virgin V SMDL 1	1	26 wks
13 May	89	★	STREET FIGHTING YEARS Virgin MINDS 1	1	28 wks
20 Apr	91	●	REAL LIFE Virgin V 2660	2	25 wks
24 Oct	92	★	GLITTERING PRIZE 81–92 Virgin SMTVD 1	1	25 wks

SIMPLY RED
UK, male vocal/instrumental group   *371 wks*

26 Oct	85	●	PICTURE BOOK Elektra EKT 27	2	130 wks
21 Mar	87	●	MEN AND WOMEN WEA WX 85	2	56 wks
25 Feb	89	★	A NEW FLAME Elektra WX 242	1	84 wks
12 Oct	91	★	STARS East West WX 427	1	101 wks

SIMPSON – *See ASHFORD and SIMPSON*

SIMPSONS US, male/female cartoon group   30 wks

2 Feb	91	● THE SIMPSONS SING THE BLUES Geffen 7599243081 ..	6	30 wks

Joyce SIMS US, female vocalist   25 wks

9 Jan	88	● COME INTO MY LIFE London LONLP 47	5	24 wks
16 Sep	89	ALL ABOUT LOVE London 828129 1	64	1 wk

Kym SIMS US, female vocalist   2 wks

18 Apr	92	TOO BLIND TO SEE IT Atco 7567921042	39	2 wks

Frank SINATRA US, male vocalist   644 wks

8 Nov 58 ●	COME FLY WITH ME *Capitol LCT 6154*	2	18 wks
15 Nov 58 ●	SONGS FOR SWINGING LOVERS *Capitol LCT 6106* ...	8	8 wks
29 Nov 58 ●	FRANK SINATRA STORY *Fontana TFL 5030*	8	1 wk
13 Dec 58 ●	FRANK SINATRA SINGS FOR ONLY THE LONELY		
	Capitol LCT 6168	5	13 wks
16 May 59 ●	COME DANCE WITH ME *Capitol LCT 6179*	2	30 wks
22 Aug 59 ●	LOOK TO YOUR HEART *Capitol LCT 6181*	5	8 wks
11 Jun 60 ●	COME BACK TO SORRENTO *Fontana TFL 5082*	6	9 wks
29 Oct 60 ●	SWING EASY *Capitol W 587*	5	17 wks
21 Jan 61 ●	NICE 'N EASY *Capitol W 1417*	4	27 wks
15 Jul 61	SINATRA SOUVENIR *Fontana TFL 5138*	18	1 wk
19 Aug 61 ●	WHEN YOUR LOVER HAS GONE *Encore ENC 101*	6	10 wks
23 Sep 61 ●	SINATRA'S SWINGING SESSION *Capitol W 1491*	6	8 wks
28 Oct 61 ●	SINATRA SWINGS *Reprise R 1002*	8	8 wks
25 Nov 61 ●	SINATRA PLUS *Fontana SET 303*	7	9 wks
16 Dec 61 ●	RING-A-DING-DING *Reprise R 1001*	8	9 wks
17 Feb 62	COME SWING WITH ME *Capitol W 1594*	13	4 wks
7 Apr 62 ●	I REMEMBER TOMMY *Reprise R 1003*	10	12 wks
9 Jun 62 ●	SINATRA AND STRINGS *Reprise R 1004*	6	20 wks
27 Oct 62	GREAT SONGS FROM GREAT BRITAIN *Reprise R 1006*	12	9 wks
29 Dec 62	SINATRA WITH SWINGING BRASS *Reprise R 1005*	14	11 wks
23 Feb 63 ●	SINATRA – BASIE *Reprise R 1008★*	2	23 wks
27 Jul 63 ●	CONCERT SINATRA *Reprise R 1009*	8	18 wks
5 Oct 63 ●	SINATRA'S SINATRA *Reprise R 1010*	9	24 wks
19 Sep 64	IT MIGHT AS WELL BE SWING *Reprise R 1012*	17	4 wks
20 Mar 65	SOFTLY AS I LEAVE YOU *Reprise R 1013*	20	1 wk
22 Jan 66 ●	A MAN AND HIS MUSIC *Reprise R 1016*	9	19 wks
21 May 66	MOONLIGHT SINATRA *Reprise R 1018*	18	8 wks/
2 Jul 66 ●	STRANGERS IN THE NIGHT *Reprise R 1017*	4	18 wks
1 Oct 66 ●	SINATRA AT THE SANDS *Reprise RLP 1019*	7	18 wks
3 Dec 66	FRANK SINATRA SINGS SONGS FOR PLEASURE		
	MFP 1120	26	2 wks
25 Feb 67	THAT'S LIFE *Reprise RSLP 1020*	22	12 wks
7 Oct 67	FRANK SINATRA *Reprise RSLP 1022*	28	5 wks
19 Oct 68 ●	GREATEST HITS *Reprise RSLP 1025*	8	38 wks
7 Dec 68	BEST OF FRANK SINATRA *Capitol ST 21140*	17	10 wks
7 Jun 69 ●	MY WAY *Reprise RSLP 1029*	2	59 wks
4 Oct 69	A MAN ALONE *Reprise RSLP 1030*	18	7 wks
9 May 70	WATERTOWN *Reprise RSLP 1031*	14	9 wks
12 Dec 70 ●	GREATEST HITS VOL. 2 *Reprise RSLP 1032*	6	40 wks
5 Jun 71 ●	SINATRA AND COMPANY *Reprise RSLP 1033*	9	9 wks
27 Nov 71	FRANK SINATRA SINGS RODGERS AND HART		
	Starline SRS 5083	35	1 wk
8 Jan 72	MY WAY (re-issue) *Reprise K 44015*	35	1 wk
8 Jan 72	GREATEST HITS VOL. 2 *Reprise K 44018*	29	3 wks
1 Dec 73	OL' BLUE EYES IS BACK *Warner Bros. K 44249*	12	13 wks
17 Aug 74	SOME NICE THINGS I'VE MISSED *Reprise K 54020*	35	3 wks
15 Feb 75	THE MAIN EVENT (TV soundtrack) *Reprise K 54031* ...	30	2 wks
14 Jun 75	THE BEST OF OL' BLUE EYES *Reprise K 54042*	30	3 wks
19 Mar 77 ★	PORTRAIT OF SINATRA *Reprise K 64039*	1	18 wks
13 May 78 ●	20 GOLDEN GREATS *Capitol EMTV 10*	4	11 wks
18 Aug 84	L.A. IS MY LADY *Qwest 925145*	41	8 wks
22 Mar 86	NEW YORK NEW YORK (GREATEST HITS)		
	Warner Bros. WX 32	13	12 wks
4 Oct 86	THE FRANK SINATRA COLLECTION *Capitol EMTV 41.*	40	5 wks
6 Nov 93 ●	DUETS *Capitol CDEST 2218*	5†	8 wks

★ *Frank Sinatra and Count Basie.*

Nancy SINATRA US, female vocalist   15 wks

16 Apr 66	BOOTS *Reprise R 6202*	12	9 wks
18 Jun 66	HOW DOES THAT GRAB YOU *Reprise R 6207*	12	3 wks
10 Oct 70	NANCY'S GREATEST HITS *Reprise RSLP 6409*	39	3 wks

SINITTA US, female vocalist   23 wks

26 Dec 87	SINITTA! *Fanfare BOYLP 1*	34	19 wks
9 Dec 89	WICKED! *Fanfare FARE 2*	52	4 wks

SINFONIA OF LONDON – *See Howard BLAKE conducting the SINFONIA OF LONDON*

SIOUXSIE and the BANSHEES
UK, female/male vocal/instrumental group 117 wks

2 Dec	78	**THE SCREAM** *Polydor POLD 5009*	12	11 wks
22 Sep	79	**JOIN HANDS** *Polydor POLD 5024*	13	5 wks
16 Aug	80 ●	**KALEIDOSCOPE** *Polydor 2442 177*	5	6 wks
27 Jun	81 ●	**JU JU** *Polydor POLS 1034*	7	17 wks
12 Dec	81	**ONCE UPON A TIME** *Polydor POLS 1056*	21	26 wks
13 Nov	82	**A KISS IN THE DREAMHOUSE** *Polydor POLD 5064*	11	11 wks
3 Dec	83	**NOCTURNE** *Wonderland SHAH 1*	29	10 wks
16 Jun	84	**HYENA** *Wonderland SHELP 2*	15	6 wks
26 Apr	86	**TINDERBOX** *Wonderland SHELP 3*	13	6 wks
14 Mar	87	**THROUGH THE LOOKING GLASS** *Wonderland SHELP 4*	15	8 wks
17 Sep	88	**PEEP SHOW** *Wonderland SHELP 5*	20	5 wks
22 Jun	91	**SUPERSTITION** *Wonderland 8477311*	25	4 wks
17 Oct	92	**TWICE UPON A TIME – THE SINGLES** *Wonderland 5171602*	26	2 wks

SISTER SLEDGE *US, female vocal group* 58 wks

12 May	79 ●	**WE ARE FAMILY** *Atlantic K 50587*	7	39 wks
22 Jun	85	**WHEN THE BOYS MEET THE GIRLS** *Atlantic 78–1255–1*	19	11 wks
5 Dec	87	**FREAK OUT** *Telstar STAR 2319★*	72	3 wks
20 Feb	93	**THE VERY BEST OF SISTER SLEDGE 1973–1993** *Atlantic 9548318132*	19	5 wks

★ *Chic and Sister Sledge.*

SISTERHOOD
UK, male vocal/instrumental group 1 wk

26 Jul	86	**GIFT** *Merciful Release SIS 020*	90	1 wk

SISTERS OF MERCY
UK, male/female vocal/instrumental duo 42 wks

23 Mar	85	**FIRST AND LAST AND ALWAYS** *Merciful Release MR 337 L*	14	8 wks
28 Nov	87 ●	**FLOODLAND** *Merciful Release MR 441 L*	9	20 wks
2 Nov	90	**VISION THING** *Merciful Release*	11	4 wks
9 May	92 ●	**SOME GIRLS WANDER BY MISTAKE** *Merciful Release 9031764762*	5	5 wks
4 Sep	93	**GREATEST HITS VOL. 1** *Merciful Release 4509935792*	14	5 wks

Act was a male-only group for first album.

Peter SKELLERN *UK, male vocalist* 28 wks

9 Sep	78	**SKELLERN** *Mercury 9109 701*	48	3 wks
8 Dec	79	**ASTAIRE** *Mercury 9102 702*	23	20 wks
4 Dec	82	**A STRING OF PEARLS** *Mercury MERL 10*	67	5 wks

SKID ROW *UK, male vocal/instrumental group* 3 wks

17 Oct	70	**SKID** *CBS 63965*	30	3 wks

SKID ROW *US, male vocal/instrumental group* 25 wks

2 Sep	89	**SKID ROW** *Atlantic 781936 1*	30	16 wks
22 Jun	91 ●	**SLAVE TO THE GRIND** *Atlantic WX 423*	5	9 wks

SKIDS UK, male vocal/instrumental group 20 wks

17 Mar	79	SCARED TO DANCE *Virgin V 2116*	19	10 wks
27 Oct	79	DAYS IN EUROPA *Virgin V 2138*	32	5 wks
27 Sep	80 ●	THE ABSOLUTE GAME *Virgin V 2174*	9	5 wks

SKY UK/Australia, male instrumental group 202 wks

2 Jun	79 ●	SKY *Ariola ARLH 5022*	9	56 wks
26 Apr	80 ★	SKY 2 *Ariola ADSKY 2*	1	53 wks
28 Mar	81 ●	SKY 3 *Ariola ASKY 3*	3	23 wks
3 Apr	82 ●	SKY 4 - FORTHCOMING *Ariola ASKY 4*	7	22 wks
22 Jan	83	SKY FIVE LIVE *Ariola 302 171*	14	14 wks
3 Dec	83	CADMIUM *Ariola 205 885*	44	10 wks
12 May	84	MASTERPIECES – THE VERY BEST OF SKY *Telstar STAR 2241*	15	18 wks
13 Apr	85	THE GREAT BALLOON RACE *Epic EPC 26419*	63	6 wks

SKYY US, male vocal/instrumental group 1 wk

| 21 Jun | 86 | FROM THE LEFT SIDE *Capitol EST 2014* .... | 85 | 1 wk |

SLADE UK, male vocal/instrumental group 207 wks

8 Apr	72 ●	SLADE ALIVE *Polydor 2383 101*	2	58 wks
9 Dec	72 ★	SLAYED? *Polydor 2383 163*	1	34 wks
6 Oct	73 ★	SLADEST *Polydor 2442 119*	1	24 wks
23 Feb	74 ★	OLD NEW BORROWED AND BLUE *Polydor 2383 261* ..	1	16 wks
14 Dec	74 ●	SLADE IN FLAME *Polydor 2442 126*	6	18 wks
27 Mar	76	NOBODY'S FOOL *Polydor 2383 377*	14	4 wks
22 Nov	80	SLADE SMASHES *Polydor POLTV 13*	21	15 wks
21 Mar	81	WE'LL BRING THE HOUSE DOWN *Cheapskate SKATE 1*	25	4 wks
28 Nov	81	TILL DEAF US DO PART *RCA RCALP 6021*	68	2 wks
18 Dec	82	SLADE ON STAGE *RCA RCALP 3107*	58	3 wks
24 Dec	83	THE AMAZING KAMIKAZE SYNDROME *RCA PL 70116*	49	13 wks
9 Jun	84	SLADE'S GREATS *Polydor SLAD 1*	89	1 wk
6 Apr	85	ROGUES GALLERY *RCA PL 70604*	60	2 wks
30 Nov	85	CRACKERS – THE SLADE CHRISTMAS PARTY ALBUM *Telstar STAR 2271*	34	7 wks
9 May	87	YOU BOYZ MAKE BIG NOIZE *RCA PL 71260*	98	1 wk
23 Nov	91	WALL OF HITS *Polydor 5116121*	34	5 wks

SLAUGHTER US, male vocal/instrumental group 1 wk

| 23 May | 92 | THE WILD LIFE *Chrysalis CCD 1911* .... | 64 | 1 wk |

SLAYER US, male vocal/instrumental group 12 wks

2 May	87	REIGN IN BLOOD *Def Jam LONLP 34*	47	3 wks
23 Jul	88	SOUTH OF HEAVEN *London LONLP 63*	67	4 wks
6 Oct	90	SEASONS IN THE ABYSS *Def American 8468711*	18	3 wks
2 Nov	91	DECADE OF AGGRESSION LIVE *Def American 5106051* ..	29	2 wks

Percy SLEDGE US, male vocalist 4 wks

| 14 Mar | 87 | WHEN A MAN LOVES A WOMAN (THE ULTIMATE COLLECTION) *Atlantic WX 89* .... | 36 | 4 wks |

SLEIGHRIDERS UK, male vocal/instrumental group 1 wk

| 17 Dec | 83 | A VERY MERRY DISCO *Warwick WW 5136* .... | 100 | 1 wk |

Grace SLICK *US, female vocalist*   *6 wks*

31 May 80   **DREAMS** *RCA PL 13544* 28   6 wks

SLIK *UK, male vocal/instrumental group*   *1 wk*

12 Jun 76   **SLIK** *Bell SYBEL 8004* 58   1 wk

SLIM CHANCE – *See Ronnie LANE*

SLITS *UK, female vocal/instrumental group*   *5 wks*

22 Sep 79   **CUT** *Island ILPS 9573* 30   5 wks

SLOWDIVE *UK, male vocal/instrumental group*   *3 wks*

14 Sep 91   **JUST FOR A DAY** *Creation CRELP 094* 32   2 wks
12 Jun 93   **SOUVLAKI** *Creation CRECD 139* 51   1 wk

SLY and ROBBIE *Jamaica, male vocal/instrumental duo*   *5 wks*

9 May 87   **RHYTHM KILLERS** *Fourth & Broadway BRLP 512* 35   5 wks

SLY and the FAMILY STONE
US, male/female vocal/instrumental group   *2 wks*

5 Feb 72   **THERE'S A RIOT GOIN' ON** *Epic EPC 64613* 31   2 wks

SMALL FACES *UK, male vocal/instrumental group*   *66 wks*

14 May 66 ● **SMALL FACES** *Decca LK 4790* 3   25 wks
17 Jun 67   **FROM THE BEGINNING** *Decca LK 4879* 17   5 wks
1 Jul 67   **SMALL FACES** *Immediate IMSP 008* 12   17 wks
15 Jun 68 ★ **OGDEN'S NUT GONE FLAKE** *Immediate IMLP 012* 1   19 wks

The two albums titled Small Faces *are different.*

SMASHING PUMPKINS
US, male vocal/instrumental group   *12 wks*

31 Jul 93 ● **SIAMESE DREAM** *Hut CDHUT 11* 4   12 wks

Brian SMITH and his HAPPY PIANO
UK, male instrumentalist – piano   *1 wk*

19 Sep 81   **PLAY IT AGAIN** *Deram DS 047* 97   1 wk

Jimmy SMITH *US, male instrumentalist – organ*   *3 wks*

18 Jun 66   **GOT MY MOJO WORKING** *Verve VLP 912* 19   3 wks

Keely SMITH *US, female vocalist*   *9 wks*

16 Jan 65   **LENNON–McCARTNEY SONGBOOK** *Reprise R 6142* .. 12   9 wks

O.C. SMITH *US, male vocalist*   *1 wk*

17 Aug 68   **HICKORY HOLLER REVISITED** *CBS 63362* 40   1 wk

Patti SMITH GROUP
US, female/male vocal/instrumental group   *21 wks*

1 Apr 78	**EASTER** *Arista SPART 1043*	**16**	14 wks
19 May 79	**WAVE** *Arista SPART 1086*	**41**	6 wks
16 Jul 88	**DREAM OF LIFE** *Arista 209172★*	**70**	1 wks

★ *Patti Smith.*

Steven SMITH and FATHER
UK, male instrumental duo   *3 wks*

13 May 72	**STEVEN SMITH AND FATHER AND 16 GREAT SONGS** *Decca SKL 5128*	**17**	3 wks

SMITH and JONES   *UK, male comedy duo*   *8 wks*

15 Nov 86	**SCRATCH AND SNIFF** *10 DIX 51*	**62**	8 wks

SMITHS
UK, male vocal/instrumental group   *172 wks*

3 Mar 84 ●	**THE SMITHS** *Rough Trade ROUGH 61*	**2**	33 wks
24 Nov 84 ●	**HATFUL OF HOLLOW** *Rough Trade ROUGH 76*	**7**	46 wks
23 Feb 85 ★	**MEAT IS MURDER** *Rough Trade ROUGH 81*	**1**	13 wks
28 Jun 86 ●	**THE QUEEN IS DEAD** *Rough Trade ROUGH 96*	**2**	22 wks
7 Mar 87 ●	**THE WORLD WON'T LISTEN** *Rough Trade ROUGH 101* .	**2**	15 wks
30 May 87	**LOUDER THAN BOMBS (import)** *Rough Trade ROUGH 255*	**38**	5 wks
10 Oct 87 ●	**STRANGEWAYS HERE WE COME** *Rough Trade ROUGH 106*	**2**	17 wks
17 Sep 88 ●	**RANK** *Rough Trade ROUGH 126*	**2**	7 wks
29 Aug 92 ★	**BEST ... I** *WEA 4509903272*	**1**	9 wks
14 Nov 92	**BEST ... II** *WEA 4509904062*	**29**	5 wks

SMOKIE
UK, male vocal/instrumental group   *42 wks*

1 Nov 75	**SMOKIE/CHANGING ALL THE TIME** *RAK SRAK 517* .	**18**	5 wks
30 Apr 77 ●	**GREATEST HITS** *RAK SRAK 526*	**6**	22 wks
4 Nov 78	**THE MONTREUX ALBUM** *RAK SRAK 6757*	**52**	2 wks
11 Oct 80	**SMOKIE'S HITS** *RAK SRAK 540*	**23**	13 wks

SMURFS – *See FATHER ABRAHAM and the SMURFS*

SNAP   *US/Germany, male/female vocal/instrumental group*   *54 wks*

26 May 90 ●	**WORLD POWER** *Arista 210682*	**10**	39 wks
8 Aug 92 ●	**THE MADMAN'S RETURN** *Logic 262552*	**8**	15 wks

The Madman's Return *changed catalogue number to 74321128512 during its chart run.*

SNOOP DOGGY DOGG
US, male rapper   *3 wks*

11 Dec 93	**DOGGYSTYLE** *Death Row 6544922792*	**38†**	3 wks

SNOW   *Canada, male rapper*   *4 wks*

17 Apr 93	**12 INCHES OF SNOW** *East West America 7567922072*	**41**	4 wks

S

286

SOFT CELL *UK, male vocal/instrumental duo* *100 wks*

5 Dec	81 ●	**NON-STOP EROTIC CABARET**	*Some Bizzare BZLP 2* ..	5	46 wks
26 Jun	82 ●	**NON-STOP ECSTATIC DANCING**			
		Some Bizzare BZX 1012		6	18 wks
22 Jan	83 ●	**THE ART OF FALLING APART**	*Some Bizzare BIZL 3* ...	5	9 wks
31 Mar	84	**THE LAST NIGHT IN SODOM**	*Some Bizzare BIZL 6*	12	5 wks
20 Dec	86	**THE SINGLES ALBUM**	*Some Bizzare BZLP 3*	58	9 wks
1 Jun	91 ●	**MEMORABILIA–THE SINGLES**	*Mercury 8485121*	8	13 wks

SOFT MACHINE *UK, male vocal/instrumental group* *8 wks*

4 Jul	70	**THIRD** *CBS 66246*	18	6 wks
3 Apr	71	**FOURTH** *CBS 64280*	32	2 wks

SOLID SENDERS *UK, male vocal/instrumental group* *3 wks*

23 Sep	78	**SOLID SENDERS** *Virgin V 2105*	42	3 wks

Diane SOLOMON *UK, female vocalist* *6 wks*

9 Aug	75	**TAKE TWO** *Philips 6308 236*	26	6 wks

Sir George SOLTI – *See Dudley MOORE*

Jimmy SOMERVILLE *UK, male vocalist* *40 wks*

9 Dec	89	**READ MY LIPS** *London 8281661*	29	14 wks
24 Nov	90 ●	**THE SINGLES COLLECTION 1984–1990** *London 8282261* .	4	26 wks

SONIA *UK, female vocalist* *14 wks*

5 May	90 ●	**EVERYBODY KNOWS** *Chrysalis CHR 1734*	7	10 wks
19 Oct	91	**SONIA** *IQ ZL 751675*	33	2 wks
29 May	93	**BETTER THE DEVIL YOU KNOW** *Arista 74321149802* .	32	2 wks

SONIC BOOM *UK, male vocal/instrumental group* *1 wk*

17 Mar	90	**SPECTRUM** *Silvertone ORELP 56*	65	1 wk

SONIC YOUTH *US, male/female vocal/instrumental group* *10 wks*

29 Oct	88	**DAYDREAM NATION** *Blast First BFFP 34*	99	1 wk
4 Feb	89	**THE WHITEY ALBUM** *Blast First BFFP 28★*	63	1 wk
7 Jul	90	**GOO** *DGC 7599242971*	32	2 wks
4 May	91	**DIRTY BOOTS–PLUS 5 LIVE TRACKS**		
		DGC DGC 21634	69	1 wk
1 Aug	92 ●	**DIRTY** *DGC DGCD 24485*	6	5 wks

★ *Ciccone Youth.*

SONNY and CHER *US, male/female vocal duo* *20 wks*

16 Oct	65 ●	**LOOK AT US** *Atlantic ATL 5036*	7	13 wks
14 May	66	**THE WONDROUS WORLD OF SONNY AND CHER**		
		Atlantic 587–006	15	7 wks

See also Cher.

S.O.S. BAND *US, male/female vocal/instrumental group* *19 wks*

1 Sep	84	**JUST THE WAY YOU LIKE IT** *Tabu TBU 26058*	29	10 wks
17 May	86	**SANDS OF TIME** *Tabu TBU 26863*	15	9 wks

S
287

*The title of the debut album by the **Spin Doctors** suggested trouble for Superman at the very time he was being (temporarily) killed off in the comics. (Pictorial Press)*

__Bruce Springsteen__ and wife Patti take son Evan James to the streets. (Pictorial Press)

*The first artist to enter the US album chart at number one with a debut recording, **Snoop Doggy Dogg** originally drew attention as a guest vocalist on Dr. Dre's The Chronic.*

David SOUL US, *male vocalist* *51 wks*

27 Nov	76 ●	**DAVID SOUL** *Private Stock PVLP 1012*	**2**	28 wks
17 Sep	77 ●	**PLAYING TO AN AUDIENCE OF ONE**		
		Private Stock PVLP 1026	**8**	23 wks

SOUL ASYLUM US, *male vocal/instrumental group* *11 wks*

31 Jul	93	**GRAVE DANCERS UNION** *Columbia 4722532*	**52**	11 wks

SOUL CITY SYMPHONY – *See Van McCOY and the SOUL CITY SYMPHONY*

SOUL II SOUL
UK, *male/female vocal/instrumental group and male producer* *96 wks*

22 Apr	89 ★	**CLUB CLASSICS VOLUME ONE** *10 DIX 82*	**1**	60 wks
2 Jun	90 ★	**VOLUME II (A NEW DECADE)** *10 DIX 90*	**1**	20 wks
25 Apr	92 ●	**VOLUME III JUST RIGHT** *Ten DIXCD 100*	**3**	11 wks
27 Nov	93 ●	**VOLUME IV THE CLASSIC SINGLES 88–93**		
		Virgin CDV 2720	**10†**	5 wks

SOUNDGARDEN US, *male vocal/instrumental group* *2 wks*

25 Apr	92	**BADMOTORFINGER** *A & M 3953742*	**39**	2 wks

SOUNDS ORCHESTRAL UK, *orchestra* *1 wk*

12 Jun	65	**CAST YOUR FATE TO THE WIND** *Piccadilly NPL 38041*	**17**	1 wk

SOUNDTRACKS (films, TV etc) – *See VARIOUS ARTISTS*

SOUP DRAGONS UK, *male vocal/instrumental group* *17 wks*

7 May	88	**THIS IS OUR ART** *Sire WX 169*	**60**	1 wk
5 May	90 ●	**LOVEGOD** *Raw TV SOUPLP 2*	**7**	15 wks
16 May	92	**HOTWIRED** *Big Life BLRCD 15*	**74**	1 wk

SOUTH BANK ORCHESTRA UK, *orchestra* *6 wks*

2 Dec	78	**LILLIE** *Sounds MOR 516*	**47**	6 wks

This album was conducted by Joseph Morovitz and Laurie Holloway.

SOUTHERN DEATH CULT – *See CULT*

SPACE France, *male instrumental group* *9 wks*

17 Sep	77	**MAGIC FLY** *Pye NSPL 28232*	**11**	9 wks

SPACEMEN UK, *male instrumental group* *1 wk*

9 Mar	91	**RECURRING** *Fire FIRELP 23*	**46**	1 wk

SPANDAU BALLET UK, *male vocal/instrumental group* *250 wks*

14 Mar	81 ●	**JOURNEY TO GLORY** *Reformation CHR 1331*	**5**	29 wks
20 Mar	82	**DIAMOND** *Reformation CDL 1353*	**15**	18 wks
12 Mar	83 ★	**TRUE** *Reformation CDL 1403*	**1**	90 wks
7 Jul	84 ●	**PARADE** *Reformation CDL 1473*	**2**	39 wks
16 Nov	85 ●	**THE SINGLES COLLECTION** *Chrysalis SBTV 1*	**3**	49 wks

29 Nov 86 ●	**THROUGH THE BARRICADES**			
	Reformation CBS 450 259–1	**7**	19 wks
30 Sep 89	**HEART LIKE A SKY** *CBS 4633181*	**31**	3 wks
28 Sep 91	**THE BEST OF SPANDAU BALLET** *Chrysalis CHR 1894* ..	**44**	3 wks

SPARKS *US/UK, male vocal/instrumental group*   *42 wks*

1 Jun 74 ●	**KIMONO MY HOUSE** *Island ILPS 9272*	**4**	24 wks
23 Nov 74 ●	**PROPAGANDA** *Island ILPS 9312*	**9**	13 wks
18 Oct 75	**INDISCREET** *Island ILPS 9345*	**18**	4 wks
8 Sep 79	**NUMBER ONE IN HEAVEN** *Virgin V 2115*	**73**	1 wk

SPEAR OF DESTINY *UK, male vocal/instrumental group*   *35 wks*

23 Apr 83	**GRAPES OF WRATH** *Epic EPC 25318*	**62**	2 wks
28 Apr 84	**ONE EYED JACKS** *Burning Rome EPC 25836*	**22**	7 wks
7 Sep 85	**WORLD SERVICE** *Burning Rome EPC 26514*	**11**	7 wks
2 May 87	**OUTLAND** *10 DIX 59*	**16**	13 wks
16 May 87	**S.O.D. – THE EPIC YEARS** *Epic 450 872–1*	**53**	3 wks
22 Oct 88	**THE PRICE YOU PAY** *Virgin V 2549*	**37**	3 wks

Billie Jo SPEARS *US, female vocalist*   *28 wks*

11 Sep 76	**WHAT I'VE GOT IN MIND** *United Artists UAS 29955*	**47**	2 wks
19 May 79 ●	**THE BILLIE JO SPEARS SINGLES ALBUM**			
	United Artists UAK 30231	**7**	17 wks
21 Nov 81	**COUNTRY GIRL** *Warwick WW 5109*	**17**	9 wks

SPECIALS *UK, male instrumental group*   *79 wks*

3 Nov 79 ●	**SPECIALS** *2-Tone CDL TT 5001*	**4**	45 wks
4 Oct 80 ●	**MORE SPECIALS** *2-Tone CHR TT 5003*	**5**	19 wks
23 Jun 84	**IN THE STUDIO** *2-Tone CHR TT 5008★*	**34**	6 wks
7 Sep 91 ●	**THE SPECIALS SINGLES** *2-Tone CHRTT 5010*	**10**	9 wks

★ *Special A.K.A.*
Group was male only for the first two albums.

Phil SPECTOR *US, male producer*   *29 wks*

23 Dec 72	**PHIL SPECTOR'S CHRISTMAS ALBUM**			
	Apple SAPCOR 24	**21**	3 wks
15 Oct 77	**PHIL SPECTOR'S ECHOES OF THE 60'S**			
	Phil Spector International 2307 013	**21**	10 wks
25 Dec 82	**PHIL SPECTOR'S CHRISTMAS ALBUM (re–issue)**			
	Phil Spector International/Polydor 2307 005	**96**	2 wks
10 Dec 83	**PHIL SPECTOR'S GREATEST HITS/PHIL SPECTOR'S**			
	CHRISTMAS ALBUM (2nd re–issue) *Impression PSLP 1/2*	**19**	8 wks
12 Dec 87	**PHIL SPECTOR'S CHRISTMAS ALBUM (3rd re–issue)**			
	Chrysalis CDL 1625	**69**	6 wks

SPEEDY J *Holland, male producer – Jochem Paap*   *1 wk*

10 Jul 93	**GINGER** *Warp WARPCD 14*	**68**	1 wk

SPIDER *UK, male vocal/instrumental group*   *2 wks*

23 Oct 82	**ROCK 'N' ROLL GYPSIES** *RCA RCALP 3101*	**75**	1 wk
7 Apr 84	**ROUGH JUSTICE** *A & M AMLX 68563*	**96**	1 wk

SPIN DOCTORS *US, male vocal/instrumental group*   *34 wks*

20 Mar 93 ●	**POCKET FULL OF KRYPTONITE** *Epic 4682502*	**2†**	34 wks

SPINAL TAP *UK/US, male vocal/instrumental group* *2 wks*

11 Apr	92	**BREAK LIKE THE WIND** *MCA MCAD 10514*	51	2 wks

SPINNERS *UK, male vocal group* *24 wks*

5 Sep	70	**THE SPINNERS ARE IN TOWN** *Fontana 6309 014*	40	5 wks
7 Aug	71	**SPINNERS LIVE PERFORMANCE** *Contour 6870 502*	14	12 wks
13 Nov	71	**THE SWINGING CITY** *Philips 6382 002*	20	3 wks
8 Apr	72	**LOVE IS TEASING** *Columbia SCX 6493*	33	4 wks

SPIRIT *US, male vocal/instrumental duo* *2 wks*

18 Apr	81	**POTATO LAND** *Beggars Banquet BEGA 23*	40	2 wks

SPIRITUAL COWBOYS – *See Dave STEWART and the SPIRITUAL COWBOYS*

SPIRITUALIZED *UK, male vocal/instrumental group* *2 wks*

11 Apr	92	**LAZER GUIDED MELODIES** *Dedicated DEDCD 004*	27	2 wks

SPITTING IMAGE *UK, puppets* *3 wks*

18 Oct	86	**SPIT IN YOUR EAR** *Virgin V 2403*	55	3 wks

SPLIT ENZ *New Zealand/UK, male vocal/instrumental group* *9 wks*

30 Aug	80	**TRUE COLOURS** *A & M AMLH 64822*	42	8 wks
8 May	82	**TIME AND TIDE** *A & M AMLH 64894*	71	1 wk

SPOTNICKS *Sweden, male instrumental group* *1 wk*

9 Feb	63	**OUT-A-SPACE** *Oriole PS 40036*	20	1 wk

Dusty SPRINGFIELD *UK, female vocalist* *98 wks*

25 Apr	64	● **A GIRL CALLED DUSTY** *Philips BL 7594*	6	23 wks
23 Oct	65	● **EVERYTHING COMES UP DUSTY** *Philips RBL 1002* ...	6	12 wks
22 Oct	66	● **GOLDEN HITS** *Philips BL 7737*	2	36 wks
11 Nov	67	**WHERE AM I GOING** *Philips SBL 7820*	40	1 wk
21 Dec	68	**DUSTY . . . DEFINITELY** *Philips SBL 7864*	30	6 wks
2 May	70	**FROM DUSTY WITH LOVE** *Philips SBL 7927*	35	2 wks
4 Mar	78	**IT BEGINS AGAIN** *Mercury 9109 607*	41	2 wks
30 Jan	88	**DUSTY – THE SILVER COLLECTION**		
		Phonogram DUSTV 1	14	10 wks
7 Jul	90	**REPUTATION** *Parlophone PCSD 111*	18	6 wks

Rick SPRINGFIELD *Australia, male vocalist* *8 wks*

11 Feb	84	**LIVING IN OZ** *RCA PL 84660*	41	4 wks
25 May	85	**TAO** *RCA PL 85370*	68	3 wks
26 Mar	88	**ROCK OF LIFE** *RCA PL 86620*	80	1 wk

Bruce SPRINGSTEEN *US, male vocalist* *424 wks*

1 Nov	75	**BORN TO RUN** *CBS 69170*	17	50 wks
17 Jun	78	**DARKNESS ON THE EDGE OF TOWN** *CBS 86061*	16	40 wks
25 Oct	80	● **THE RIVER** *CBS 88510*	2	88 wks
2 Oct	82	● **NEBRASKA** *CBS 25100*	3	19 wks
16 Jun	84	★ **BORN IN THE USA** *CBS 86304*	1	128 wks

S

291

15 Jun	85	**THE WILD THE INNOCENT AND THE E STREET SHUFFLE** *CBS 32363*	33	12 wks
15 Jun	85	**GREETINGS FROM ASBURY PARK, N.J.** *CBS 32210* ..	41	10 wks
22 Nov	86 ●	**LIVE 1975–1985** *CBS 450 227–1★*	4	9 wks
17 Oct	87 ★	**TUNNEL OF LOVE** *CBS 460 270–1*	1	33 wks
4 Apr	92 ★	**HUMAN TOUCH** *Columbia 4714232*	1	17 wks
4 Apr	92 ●	**LUCKY TOWN** *Columbia 4714242*	2	11 wks
24 Apr	93 ●	**IN CONCERT – MTV PLUGGED** *Columbia 4738602*	4	7 wks

★ Bruce Springsteen and the E Street Band.

SPYRO GYRA *US, male instrumental group*   *23 wks*

14 Jul	79	**MORNING DANCE** *Infinity INS 2003*	11	16 wks
23 Feb	80	**CATCHING THE SUN** *MCA MCG 4009*	31	7 wks

SQUEEZE *UK, male vocal/instrumental group*   *121 wks*

28 Apr	79	**COOL FOR CATS** *A & M AMLH 68503*	45	11 wks
16 Feb	80	**ARGY BARGY** *A & M AMLH 64802*	32	15 wks
23 May	81	**EAST SIDE STORY** *A & M AMLH 64854*	19	26 wks
15 May	82	**SWEETS FROM A STRANGER** *A & M AMLH 64899* ...	20	7 wks
6 Nov	82 ●	**SINGLES–45'S AND UNDER** *A & M AMLH 68552*	3	29 wks
7 Sep	85	**COSI FAN TUTTI FRUTTI** *A & M AMA 5085*	31	7 wks
19 Sep	87	**BABYLON AND ON** *A & M AMA 5161*	14	8 wks
23 Sep	89	**FRANK** *A & M AMA 5278*	58	1 wk
7 Apr	90	**A ROUND AND A BOUT** *IRS DFCLP 1*	50	1 wk
7 Sep	91	**PLAY** *Reprise WX 428*	41	1 wk
23 May	92 ●	**GREATEST HITS** *A & M 3971812*	6	11 wks
25 Sep	93	**SOME FANTASTIC PLACE** *A & M 5401402*	26	4 wks

Chris SQUIRE *UK, male vocalist/instrumentalist – bass*   *7 wks*

6 Dec	75	**FISH OUT OF WATER** *Atlantic K 50203*	25	7 wks

STAGE CAST RECORDINGS – *See VARIOUS ARTISTS*

Lisa STANSFIELD *UK, female vocalist*   *86 wks*

2 Dec	89 ●	**AFFECTION** *Arista 210379*	2	31 wks
23 Nov	91 ●	**REAL LOVE** *Arista 212300*	3	49 wks
20 Nov	93 ●	**SO NATURAL** *Arista 74321172312*	6†	6 wks

Alvin STARDUST *UK, male vocalist*   *17 wks*

16 Mar	74 ●	**THE UNTOUCHABLE** *Magnet MAG 5001*	4	12 wks
21 Dec	74	**ALVIN STARDUST** *Magnet MAG 5004*	37	3 wks
4 Oct	75	**ROCK WITH ALVIN** *Magnet MAG 5007*	52	2 wks

Ed STARINK *US, male instrumentalist*   *11 wks*

27 Oct	90	**SYNTHESIZER GREATEST** *Arcade ARC 938101*	22	5 wks
9 Jan	93	**SYNTHESIZER GOLD** *Arcade ARC 3100012*	29	6 wks

Freddie STARR *UK, male vocalist*   *16 wks*

18 Nov	89 ●	**AFTER THE LAUGHTER** *Dover ADD 10*	10	9 wks
17 Nov	90	**THE WANDERER** *Dover ADD 17*	33	7 wks

Kay STARR *US, female vocalist*   *1 wk*

26 Mar	60	**MOVIN'** *Capitol/n n/1254*	16	1 wk

Never in Public

Record World, Award
for
The Most Promising Female Vocalist

The public put "I'd Rather Be An Old Man's
Sweetheart (Than A Young Man's Fool)"
on the charts: That's Candi's public.
When they hear "Never In Public" they'll
pass the word . . . and your sales to an
ever-growing Candi Staton public will go on
. . . and on . . . on Fame.
#1459
Produced by Rick Hall

Candi Staton was once married to Clarence Carter, but then her young heart ran free.

The first album by former Blue Zone vocalist
Lisa Stansfield went top ten and platinum in
both Britain and America. (Pictorial Press)

The **Stereo MCs** won Group and Album Of
The Year awards at the 1994 Brit's
ceremony.

Ringo STARR *UK, male vocalist* — *28 wks*

18 Apr	70 ●	SENTIMENTAL JOURNEY *Apple PCS 7101*	7	6 wks
8 Dec	73 ●	RINGO *Apple PCTC 252*	7	20 wks
7 Dec	74	GOODNIGHT VIENNA *Apple PMC 7168*	30	2 wks

STARSHIP – *See JEFFERSON AIRPLANE*

STARSOUND *Holland, disco aggregation* — *28 wks*

16 May	81 ★	STARS ON 45 *CBS 86132*	1	21 wks
19 Sep	81	STARS ON 45 VOL. 2 *CBS 85181*	18	6 wks
3 Apr	82	STARS MEDLEY *CBS 85651*	94	1 wk

STARTRAX *UK, disco aggregation* — *7 wks*

1 Aug	81	STARTRAX CLUB DISCO *Picksy KSYA 1001*	26	7 wks

Candi STATON *US, female vocalist* — *3 wks*

24 Jul	76	YOUNG HEARTS RUN FREE *Warner Bros. K 56259*	34	3 wks

S
294

STATUS QUO *UK, male vocal/instrumental group* — *432 wks*

20 Jan	73 ●	PILEDRIVER *Vertigo 6360 082*	5	37 wks
9 Jun	73	THE BEST OF STATUS QUO *Pye NSPL 18402*	32	7 wks
6 Oct	73 ★	HELLO *Vertigo 6360 098*	1	28 wks
18 May	74 ●	QUO *Vertigo 9102 001*	2	16 wks
1 Mar	75 ★	ON THE LEVEL *Vertigo 9102 002*	1	27 wks
8 Mar	75	DOWN THE DUSTPIPE *Golden Hour CH 604*	20	6 wks
20 Mar	76 ★	BLUE FOR YOU *Vertigo 9102 006*	1	30 wks
12 Mar	77 ●	LIVE *Vertigo 6641 580*	3	14 wks
26 Nov	77 ●	ROCKIN' ALL OVER THE WORLD *Vertigo 9102 014* ...	5	15 wks
11 Nov	78 ●	IF YOU CAN'T STAND THE HEAT *Vertigo 9102 027* ...	3	14 wks
20 Oct	79 ●	WHATEVER YOU WANT *Vertigo 9102 037*	3	14 wks
22 Mar	80 ●	12 GOLD BARS *Vertigo QUO TV 1*	3	48 wks
25 Oct	80 ●	JUST SUPPOSIN' *Vertigo 6302 057*	4	18 wks
28 Mar	81 ●	NEVER TOO LATE *Vertigo 6302 104*	2	13 wks
10 Oct	81	FRESH QUOTA *PRT DOW 2*	74	1 wk
24 Apr	82 ★	1982 *Vertigo 6302 169*	1	20 wks
13 Nov	82 ●●	FROM THE MAKERS OF . . . *Vertigo PROLP 1*	4	18 wks
3 Dec	83 ●	BACK TO BACK *Vertigo VERH 10*	9	22 wks
4 Aug	84	STATUS QUO LIVE AT THE NEC *Vertigo (Holland) 8189 471*	83	3 wks
1 Dec	84	12 GOLD BARS VOLUME 2 (AND 1) *Vertigo QUO TV 2*	12	18 wks
6 Sep	86 ●	IN THE ARMY NOW *Vertigo VERH 36*	7	23 wks
18 Jun	88	AIN'T COMPLAINING *Vertigo VERH 58*	12	5 wks
2 Dec	89	PERFECT REMEDY *Vertigo 842098 1*	49	2 wks
20 Oct	90 ●	ROCKING ALL OVER THE YEARS *Vertigo 8467971*	2	25 wks
5 Oct	91 ●	ROCK 'TIL YOU DROP *Vertigo 5103411*	10	7 wks
14 Nov	92	LIVE ALIVE QUO *Polydor 5173672*	37	1 wk

STEEL PULSE *UK, male vocal/instrumental group* — *18 wks*

5 Aug	78 ●	HANDSWORTH REVOLUTION *Island EMI ILPS 9502* ..	9	12 wks
14 Jul	79	TRIBUTE TO MARTYRS *Island ILPS 9568*	42	6 wks

STEELEYE SPAN
UK, male/female vocal instrumental group — *48 wks*

10 Apr	71	PLEASE TO SEE THE KING *B & C CAS 1029*	45	2 wks
14 Oct	72	BELOW THE SALT *Chrysalis CHR 1008*	43	1 wk
28 Apr	73	PARCEL OF ROGUES *Chrysalis CHR 1046*	26	5 wks
23 Mar	74	NOW WE ARE SIX *Chrysalis CHR 1053*	13	13 wks

15 Feb 75	**COMMONER'S CROWN** *Chrysalis CHR 1071*	21	4 wks
25 Oct 75 ●	**ALL AROUND MY HAT** *Chrysalis CHR 1091*	7	20 wks
16 Oct 76	**ROCKET COTTAGE** *Chrysalis CHR 1123*	41	3 wks

STEELY DAN *US, male vocal/instrumental group*   *82 wks*

30 Mar 74	**PRETZEL LOGIC** *Probe SPBA 6282*	37	2 wks
3 May 75	**KATY LIED** *ABC ABCL 5094*	13	6 wks
20 Sep 75	**CAN'T BUY A THRILL** *ABC ABCL 5024*	38	1 wk
22 May 76	**ROYAL SCAM** *ABC ABCL 5161*	11	13 wks
8 Oct 77 ●	**AJA** *ABC ABCL 5225*	5	10 wks
2 Dec 78	**GREATEST HITS** *ABC BLD 616*	41	18 wks
29 Nov 80	**GAUCHO** *MCA MCF 3090*	27	12 wks
3 Jul 82	**GOLD** *MCA MCF 3145*	44	6 wks
26 Oct 85	**REELIN' IN THE YEARS – THE VERY BEST OF STEELY DAN** *MCA DANTV 1*	43	5 wks
10 Oct 87	**DO IT AGAIN – THE VERY BEST OF STEELY DAN** *Telstar STAR 2297*	64	4 wks
20 Nov 93	**REMASTERED – THE BEST OF STEELY DAN** *MCA MCD 10967*	42	5 wks

Wout STEENHUIS *Holland, male instrumentalist – guitar*   *7 wks*

21 Nov 81	**HAWAIIAN PARADISE/CHRISTMAS** *Warwick WW 5106*	28	7 wks

Jim STEINMAN *US, male vocalist*   *24 wks*

9 May 81 ●	**BAD FOR GOOD** *Epic EPC 84361*	7	24 wks

Martin STEPHENSON and the DAINTEES
UK, male vocal/instrumental group   *11 wks*

17 May 86	**BOAT TO BOLIVIA** *Kitchenware KWLP 5*	85	3 wks
16 Apr 88	**GLADSOME, HUMOUR AND BLUE** *Kitchenware KWLP 8*	39	4 wks
19 May 90	**SALUTATION ROAD** *Kitchenware 8281981*	35	3 wks
25 Jul 92	**THE BOY'S HEART** *Kitchenware 8283242*	68	1 wk

STEPPENWOLF *Canada/US, male vocal/instrumental group* *20 wks*

28 Feb 70	**MONSTER** *Stateside SSL 5021*	43	4 wks
25 Apr 70	**STEPPENWOLF** *Stateside SSL 5020*	59	2 wks
4 Jul 70	**STEPPENWOLF LIVE** *Stateside SSL 5029*	16	14 wks

STEREO MCs *UK, male vocal/instrumental group*   *45 wks*

17 Oct 92 ●	**CONNECTED** *4th & B'way BRCD 589*	2	45 wks

STEREOLAB
UK/France, male/female vocal/instrumental group   *1 wk*

18 Sep 93	**TRANSIENT RANDOM NOISE BURSTS** *Duophonic Ultra High Frequency DUHFCD 02*	62	1 wk

Cat STEVENS *UK, male vocalist*   *259 wks*

25 Mar 67 ●	**MATTHEW AND SON** *Deram SML 1004*	7	16 wks
11 Jul 70	**MONA BONE JAKON** *Island ILPS 9118*	63	4 wks
28 Nov 70	**TEA FOR THE TILLERMAN** *Island ILPS 9135*	20	39 wks
2 Oct 71 ●	**TEASER AND THE FIRECAT** *Island ILPS 9154*	3	93 wks
7 Oct 72 ●	**CATCH BULL AT FOUR** *Island ILPS 9206*	2	27 wks
21 Jul 73 ●	**FOREIGNER** *Island ILPS 9240*	3	10 wks

6 Apr	74 ●	**BUDDAH AND THE CHOCOLATE BOX**		
		Island ILPS 9274	**3**	15 wks
19 Jul	75 ●	**GREATEST HITS** *Island ILPS 9310*	**2**	24 wks
14 May	77	**IZITSO** *Island ILPS 9451*	**18**	15 wks
3 Feb	90 ●	**THE VERY BEST OF CAT STEVENS** *Island CATV 1* ...	**4**	16 wks

Ray STEVENS   US, *male vocalist*   *8 wks*

26 Sep	70	**EVERYTHING IS BEAUTIFUL** *CBS 64074*	**62**	1 wk
13 Sep	75	**MISTY** *Janus 9109 401*	**23**	7 wks

Shakin' STEVENS   UK, *male vocalist*   *158 wks*

15 Mar	80	**TAKE ONE** *Epic EPC 83978*	**62**	2 wks
4 Apr	81 ●	**THIS OLE HOUSE** *Epic EPC 84985*	**2**	28 wks
8 Aug	81	**SHAKIN' STEVENS** *Hallmark/Pickwick SHM 3065*	**34**	5 wks
19 Sep	81 ★	**SHAKY** *Epic EPC 10027*	**1**	28 wks
9 Oct	82 ●	**GIVE ME YOUR HEART TONIGHT** *Epic EPC 10035* ...	**3**	18 wks
26 Nov	83	**THE BOP WON'T STOP** *Epic EPC 86301*	**21**	27 wks
17 Nov	84 ●	**GREATEST HITS** *Epic EPC 10047*	**8**	22 wks
16 Nov	85	**LIPSTICK POWDER AND PAINT** *Epic EPC 26646*	**37**	9 wks
31 Oct	87	**LET'S BOOGIE** *Epic 460 126–1*	**59**	7 wks
19 Nov	88	**A WHOLE LOTTA SHAKY** *Epic MOOD 5*	**42**	8 wks
20 Oct	90	**THERE'S TWO KINDS OF MUSIC: ROCK 'N' ROLL**		
		Telstar STAR 2454	**65**	2 wks
31 Oct	92	**THE EPIC YEARS** *Epic 4724222★*	**57**	2 wks

★ *Shaky.*

Al STEWART   UK, *male vocalist*   *20 wks*

11 Apr	70	**ZERO SHE FLIES** *CBS 63848*	**40**	4 wks
5 Feb	77	**YEAR OF THE CAT** *RCA RS 1082*	**38**	7 wks
21 Oct	78	**TIME PASSAGES** *RCA PL 25173*	**39**	1 wk
6 Sep	80	**24 CARAT** *RCA PL 25306*	**55**	6 wks
9 Jun	84	**RUSSIANS AND AMERICANS** *RCA PL 70307*	**83**	2 wks

Andy STEWART   UK, *male vocalist*   *2 wks*

3 Feb	62	**ANDY STEWART** *Top Rank 35–116*	**13**	2 wks

David A. STEWART   UK, *male vocalist/instrumentalist*   *7 wks*

7 Apr	90	**LILY WAS HERE (film soundtrack)** *Anxious ZL 74233* ...	**35**	5 wks
15 Sep	90	**DAVE STEWART AND THE SPIRITUAL COWBOYS**		
		RCA OB 74710★	**38**	2 wks

★ *Dave Stewart and the Spiritual Cowboys.*

Jermaine STEWART   US, *male vocalist*   *12 wks*

4 Oct	86	**FRANTIC ROMANTIC** *10 DIX 26*	**49**	4 wks
5 Mar	88	**SAY IT AGAIN** *Siren SRNLP 14*	**32**	8 wks

Rod STEWART   UK, *male vocalist*   *707 wks*

3 Oct	70	**GASOLINE ALLEY** *Vertigo 6360 500*	**62**	1 wk
24 Jul	71 ★	**EVERY PICTURE TELLS A STORY** *Mercury 6338 063* ..	**1**	81 wks
5 Aug	72 ★	**NEVER A DULL MOMENT** *Philips 6499 153*	**1**	36 wks
25 Aug	73 ★	**SING IT AGAIN ROD** *Mercury 6499 484*	**1**	30 wks
19 Oct	74 ★	**SMILER** *Mercury 9104 011*	**1**	20 wks
30 Aug	75 ★	**ATLANTIC CROSSING** *Warner Bros. K 56151*	**1**	88 wks
3 Jul	76 ★	**A NIGHT ON THE TOWN** *Riva RVLP 1*	**1**	47 wks
16 Jul	77	**BEST OF ROD STEWART** *Mercury 6643 030*	**18**	22 wks
19 Nov	77 ●	**FOOT LOOSE AND FANCY FREE** *Riva RVLP 5*	**3**	26 wks

21 Jan	78	**ATLANTIC CROSSING (re-issue)** *Riva RVLP 4*	60	1 wk
9 Dec	78 ●	**BLONDES HAVE MORE FUN** *Riva RVLP 8*	3	31 wks
10 Nov	79 ★	**GREATEST HITS** *Riva ROD TV 1*	1	74 wks
22 Nov	80 ●	**FOOLISH BEHAVIOUR** *Riva RVLP 11*	4	13 wks
14 Nov	81 ●	**TONIGHT I'M YOURS** *Riva RVLP 14*	8	21 wks
13 Nov	82	**ABSOLUTELY LIVE** *Riva RVLP 17*	35	5 wks
18 Jun	83 ●	**BODY WISHES** *Warner Bros. K 923 8771*	5	27 wks
23 Jun	84 ●	**CAMOUFLAGE** *Warner Bros. 925095*	8	17 wks
5 Jul	86 ●	**EVERY BEAT OF MY HEART** *Warner Bros. WX 53*	5	17 wks
4 Jun	88	**OUT OF ORDER** *Warner Bros. WX 152*	11	8 wks
25 Nov	89 ●	**THE BEST OF ROD STEWART** *Warner Bros. WX 314* ...	3	82 wks
6 Apr	91 ●	**VAGABOND HEART** *Warner Bros. WX 408*	2	27 wks
7 Nov	92	**THE BEST OF ROD STEWART AND THE FACES 1971–1975** *Mercury 5141802★*	58	1 wk
6 Mar	93 ●	**ROD STEWART, LEAD VOCALIST** *Warner Bros. 9362452582*	3	9 wks
5 Jun	93 ●	**UNPLUGGED ... AND SEATED** *Warner Bros. 9362452892* .	2†	23 wks

★ *Rod Stewart and the Faces.*
See also the Faces. Greatest Hits *changed label/number to* Warner Bros. K 56744 *during its chart run.*

STIFF LITTLE FINGERS
UK, male vocal/instrumental group   *57 wks*

3 Mar	79	**INFLAMMABLE MATERIAL** *Rough Trade ROUGH 1*	14	19 wks
15 Mar	80 ●	**NOBODY'S HEROES** *Chrysalis CHR 1270*	8	10 wks
20 Sep	80 ●	**HANX** *Chrysalis CHR 1300*	9	5 wks
25 Apr	81	**GO FOR IT** *Chrysalis CHX 1339*	14	8 wks
2 Oct	82	**NOW THEN** *Chrysalis CHR 1400*	24	6 wks
12 Feb	83	**ALL THE BEST** *Chrysalis CTY 1414*	19	9 wks

---

Curtis STIGERS *US, male vocalist*   *50 wks*

29 Feb	92 ●	**CURTIS STIGERS** *Arista 261953*	7	50 wks

---

Stephen STILLS *US, male vocalist*   *19 wks*

19 Dec	70	**STEPHEN STILLS** *Atlantic 2401 004*	30	1 wk
14 Aug	71	**STEPHEN STILLS 2** *Atlantic 2401 013*	22	3 wks
20 May	72	**MANASSAS** *Atlantic K 60021★*	30	5 wks
19 May	73	**DOWN THE ROAD** *Atlantic K 40440★*	33	2 wks
26 Jul	75	**STILLS** *CBS 69146*	31	1 wk
29 May	76	**ILLEGAL STILLS** *CBS 81330*	54	2 wks
9 Oct	76	**LONG MAY YOU RUN** *Reprise K 54081★★*	12	5 wks

★ *Stephen Stills' Manassas.*
★★ *Stills–Young Band.*
See also Crosby, Stills, Nash and Young.

STING *UK, male vocalist*   *181 wks*

29 Jun	85 ●	**THE DREAM OF THE BLUE TURTLES** *A & M DREAM 1*	3	64 wks
28 Jun	86	**BRING ON THE NIGHT** *A & M BRING 1*	16	12 wks
24 Oct	87 ★	**NOTHING LIKE THE SUN** *A & M AMA 6402*	1	47 wks
2 Feb	91 ★	**THE SOUL CAGES** *A & M 3964051*	1	16 wks
13 Mar	93 ●	**TEN SUMMONER'S TALES** *A & M 5400752*	2†	42 wks

---

STONE ROSES *UK, male vocal/instrumental group*   *51 wks*

13 May	89	**THE STONE ROSES** *Silvertone ORELP 502*	19	48 wks
1 Aug	92	**TURNS INTO STONE** *Silvertone ORECD 521*	32	3 wks

---

STONE TEMPLE PILOTS
US, male vocal/instrumental group   *8 wks*

4 Sep	93	**CORE** *Atlantic 7567824182*	27	8 wks

Ray Ragsdale found fame as **Ray Stevens** (centre).

In 1992 **Curtis Stigers** instantly became one of the biggest exports Idaho has known since potatoes. *(Pictorial Press)*

Sting is shown with Pele at the first Earth Day International Awards at the United Nations. *(Pictorial Press)*

STONE THE CROWS
UK, female/male vocal/instrumental group　　　　　　*3 wks*

| 7 Oct 72 | **ONTINUOUS PERFORMANCE** *Polydor 2391 043* .... | 33 | 3 wks |

STOOGES – *See Iggy POP*

STORYVILLE JAZZMEN – *See Bob WALLIS and his STORYVILLE JAZZMEN*

Izzy STRADLIN' and the JU JU HOUNDS
US, male vocal/instrumental group　　　　　　*1 wk*

| 24 Oct 92 | **IZZY STRADLIN' AND THE JU JU HOUNDS** | | |
| | *Geffen GED 24490* .... | 52 | 1 wk |

STRANGLERS *UK, male vocal/instrumental group*　　　*217 wks*

30 Apr 77 ●	**STRANGLERS IV (RATTUS NORVEGICUS)**		
	United Artists UAG 30045	4	34 wks
8 Oct 77 ●	**NO MORE HEROES** *United Artists UAG 30200*	2	19 wks
3 Jun 78 ●	**BLACK AND WHITE** *United Artists UAK 30222*	2	18 wks
10 Mar 79 ●	**LIVE (X CERT)** *United Artists UAG 30224*	7	10 wks
6 Oct 79 ●	**THE RAVEN** *United Artists UAG 30262*	4	8 wks
21 Feb 81 ●	**THEMENINBLACK** *Liberty LBG 30313*	8	5 wks
21 Nov 81	**LA FOLIE** *Liberty LBG 30342*	11	18 wks
25 Sep 82	**THE COLLECTION 1977–1982** *Liberty LBS 30353*	12	16 wks
22 Jan 83 ●	**FELINE** *Epic EPC 25237*	4	11 wks
17 Nov 84	**AURAL SCULPTURE** *Epic EPC 26220*	14	10 wks
20 Sep 86	**OFF THE BEATEN TRACK** *Liberty LBG 5001*	80	2 wks
8 Nov 86	**DREAMTIME** *Epic EPC 26648*	16	6 wks
20 Feb 88	**ALL LIVE AND ALL OF THE NIGHT** *Epic 465259*	12	6 wks
18 Feb 89	**THE SINGLES** *EMI EM 1314*	57	2 wks
17 Mar 90	**10** *Epic 4664831*	15	4 wks
1 Dec 90 ●	**GREATEST HITS 1977–1990** *Epic 4675411*	4	47 wks
19 Sep 92	**STRANGLERS IN THE NIGHT** *Psycho WOLCD 1030* ...	33	1 wk

STRAWBERRY SWITCHBLADE
UK, female vocal duo　　　　　　*4 wks*

| 13 Apr 85 | **STRAWBERRY SWITCHBLADE** *Korova KODE 11* ..... | 25 | 4 wks |

STRAWBS *UK, male vocal/instrumental group*　　　*31 wks*

21 Nov 70	**JUST A COLLECTION OF ANTIQUES AND CURIOS**		
	A & M AMLS 994	27	2 wks
17 Jul 71	**FROM THE WITCHWOOD** *A & M AMLH 64304*	39	2 wks
26 Feb 72	**GRAVE NEW WORLD** *A & M AMLH 68078*	11	12 wks
24 Feb 73 ●	**BURSTING AT THE SEAMS** *A & M AMLH 68144*	2	12 wks
27 Apr 74	**HERO AND HEROINE** *A & M AMLH 63607*	35	3 wks

STRAY CATS *US, male vocal/instrumental group*　　　*32 wks*

28 Feb 81 ●	**STRAY CATS** *Arista STRAY 1*	6	22 wks
21 Nov 81	**GONNA BALL** *Arista STRAY 2*	48	4 wks
3 Sep 83	**RANT 'N' RAVE WITH THE STRAY CATS**		
	Arista STRAY 3	51	5 wks
8 Apr 89	**BLAST OFF** *EMI MTL 1040*	58	1 wk

STREETWALKERS *UK, male vocal/instrumental group*　　　*6 wks*

| 12 Jun 76 | **RED CARD** *Vertigo 9102 010* .... | 16 | 6 wks |

Barbra STREISAND US, female vocalist   405 wks

22 Jan	66 ●	MY NAME IS BARBRA, TWO CBS BPG 62603	**6**	22 wks
4 Apr	70	GREATEST HITS CBS 63921	**44**	2 wks
17 Apr	71	STONEY END CBS 64269	**28**	2 wks
15 Jun	74	THE WAY WE WERE CBS 69057	**49**	1 wk
23 Jul	77	STREISAND SUPERMAN CBS 86030	**32**	9 wks
15 Jul	78	SONGBIRD CBS 86060	**50**	1 wk
17 Mar	79 ★	BARBRA STREISAND HITS VOL. 2 CBS 10012	**1**	30 wks
17 Nov	79	WET CBS 86104	**25**	13 wks
11 Oct	80 ★	GUILTY CBS 86122	**1**	82 wks
16 Jan	82 ★	LOVE SONGS CBS 10031	**1**	129 wks
19 Nov	83	YENTL (film soundtrack) CBS 86302	**21**	35 wks
27 Oct	84	EMOTION CBS 86309	**15**	12 wks
18 Jan	86 ●	THE BROADWAY ALBUM CBS 86322	**3**	16 wks
30 May	87	ONE VOICE CBS 450 890–1	**27**	7 wks
3 Dec	88	TILL I LOVED YOU CBS 462943 1	**29**	13 wks
25 Nov	89	A COLLECTION – GREATEST HITS . . . AND MORE CBS 465845 1	**22**	20 wks
10 Jul	93 ●	BACK TO BROADWAY Columbia 4738802	**4**	11 wks

STRINGS FOR PLEASURE UK, orchestra   1 wk

4 Dec	71	BEST OF BACHARACH MFP 1334	**49**	1 wk

Joe STRUMMER UK, male vocalist   1 wk

14 Oct	89	EARTHQUAKE WEATHER Epic 465347 1	**58**	1 wk

S
300

STYLE COUNCIL UK, male vocal/instrumental duo   94 wks

24 Mar	84 ●	CAFE BLEU Polydor TSCLP 1	**2**	38 wks
8 Jun	85 ★	OUR FAVOURITE SHOP Polydor TSCLP 2	**1**	22 wks
17 May	86 ●	HOME AND ABROAD Polydor TSCLP 3	**8**	8 wks
14 Feb	87 ●	THE COST OF LOVING Polydor TSCLP 4	**2**	7 wks
2 Jul	88	CONFESSIONS OF A POP GROUP Polydor TSCMC 5 ..	**15**	3 wks
18 Mar	89 ●	SINGULAR ADVENTURES OF THE STYLE COUNCIL Polydor TSCTV 1	**3**	15 wks
10 Jul	93	HERE'S SOME THAT GOT AWAY Polydor 5193722	**39**	1 wk

STYLISTICS US, male vocal group   142 wks

24 Aug	74	ROCKIN' ROLL BABY Avco 6466 012	**42**	3 wks
21 Sep	74	LET'S PUT IT ALL TOGETHER Avco 6466 013	**26**	14 wks
1 Mar	75	FROM THE MOUNTAIN Avco 9109 002	**36**	1 wk
5 Apr	75 ★	THE BEST OF THE STYLISTICS Avco 9109 003	**1**	63 wks
5 Jul	75 ●	THANK YOU BABY Avco 9109 005	**5**	23 wks
6 Dec	75	YOU ARE BEAUTIFUL Avco 9109 006	**26**	9 wks
12 Jun	76	FABULOUS Avco 9109 008	**21**	5 wks
18 Sep	76 ★	BEST OF THE STYLISTICS VOL. 2 H & L 9109 010 ...	**1**	21 wks
17 Oct	92	THE GREATEST HITS OF THE STYLISTICS Mercury 5129852	**34**	3 wks

STYX US, male vocal/instrumental group   24 wks

3 Nov	79	CORNERSTONE A & M AMLK 63711	**36**	8 wks
24 Jan	81 ●	PARADISE THEATER A & M AMLH 63719	**8**	8 wks
12 Mar	83	KILROY WAS HERE A & M AMLX 63734	**67**	6 wks
5 May	84	CAUGHT IN THE ACT A & M AMLM 66704	**44**	2 wks

SUEDE UK, male vocal/instrumental group   16 wks

10 Apr	93 ★	SUEDE Nude NUDE 1CD	**1**	16 wks

SUGAR *US, male vocal/instrumental group*   *16 wks*

19 Sep	92 ● **COPPER BLUE** *Creation CRECD 129*	**10**	11 wks
17 Apr	93 ● **BEASTER** *Creation CRECD 153*	**3**	5 wks

SUGARCUBES *Iceland, male/female vocal/instrumental group*   *14 wks*

7 May	88	**LIFE'S TOO GOOD** *One Little Indian TPLP 5*	**14**	6 wks
14 Oct	89	**HERE TODAY, TOMORROW, NEXT WEEK**		
		One Little Indian TPLP 15	**15**	3 wks
22 Feb	92	**STICK AROUND FOR JOY** *One Little Indian TPLP 30CD* .	**16**	4 wks
17 Oct	92	**IT'S IT** *One Little Indian TPLP 40CD*	**47**	1 wk

SUICIDAL TENDENCIES
UK, male vocal/instrumental group   *2 wks*

9 May	87	**JOIN THE ARMY** *Virgin V 2424*	**81**	1 wk
21 Jul	90	**LIGHTS ... CAMERA ... REVOLUTION** *Epic 4665691*	**59**	1 wk

SULTANS OF PING FC
Ireland, male vocal/instrumental group   *2 wks*

13 Feb	93	**CASUAL SEX IN THE CINEPLEX** *Rhythm King 4724952* .	**26**	2 wks

Donna SUMMER *US, female vocalist*   *196 wks*

31 Jan	76	**LOVE TO LOVE YOU BABY** *GTO GTLP 008*	**16**	9 wks
22 May	76	**A LOVE TRILOGY** *GTO GTLP 010*	**41**	10 wks
25 Jun	77 ●	**I REMEMBER YESTERDAY** *GTO GTLP 025*	**3**	23 wks
26 Nov	77	**ONCE UPON A TIME** *Casablanca CALD 5003*	**24**	13 wks
7 Jan	78 ●	**GREATEST HITS** *GTO GTLP 028*	**4**	18 wks
21 Oct	78	**LIVE AND MORE** *Casablanca CALD 5006*	**16**	16 wks
2 Jun	79	**BAD GIRLS** *Casablanca CALD 5007*	**23**	23 wks
10 Nov	79	**ON THE RADIO – GREATEST HITS VOLS. 1 & 2**		
		Casablanca CALD 5008	**24**	22 wks
1 Nov	80	**THE WANDERER** *Geffen K 99124*	**55**	2 wks
31 Jul	82	**DONNA SUMMER** *Warner Bros. K 99163*	**13**	16 wks
16 Jul	83	**SHE WORKS HARD FOR THE MONEY**		
		Mercury MERL 21	**28**	5 wks
15 Sep	84	**CATS WITHOUT CLAWS** *Warner Bros. 250806*	**69**	2 wks
25 Mar	89	**ANOTHER PLACE AND TIME** *Warner Bros. WX 219*	**17**	28 wks
24 Nov	90	**THE BEST OF DONNA SUMMER** *Warner Bros WX 397* .	**24**	9 wks

SUNDAYS *UK, male/female vocal/instrumental group*   *11 wks*

27 Jan	90 ●	**READING, WRITING AND ARITHMETIC**		
		Rough Trade ROUGH 148	**4**	8 wks
31 Oct	92	**BLIND** *Parlophone CDPCSD 121*	**15**	3 wks

SUNSCREEM *UK, male/female vocal/instrumental group*   *5 wks*

13 Feb	93	**03** *Sony S2 4722182*	**33**	5 wks

SUNSHINE BAND – *See KC and the SUNSHINE BAND*

SUPERTRAMP *UK/US, male vocal/instrumental group*   *174 wks*

23 Nov	74 ●	**CRIME OF THE CENTURY** *A & M AMLS 68258*	**4**	22 wks
6 Dec	75	**CRISIS? WHAT CRISIS?** *A & M AMLH 68347*	**20**	15 wks
23 Apr	77	**EVEN IN THE QUIETEST MOMENTS**		
		A & M AMLK 64634	**12**	22 wks
31 Mar	79 ●	**BREAKFAST IN AMERICA** *A & M AMLK 63708*	**3**	53 wks

4 Oct	80 ●	**PARIS** *A & M AMLM 66702*	**7**	17 wks
6 Nov	82 ●	**FAMOUS LAST WORDS** *A & M AMLK 63732*	**6**	16 wks
25 May	85	**BROTHER WHERE YOU BOUND** *A & M AMA 5014* ..	**20**	5 wks
18 Oct	86 ●	**THE AUTOBIOGRAPHY OF SUPERTRAMP**		
		A & M TRAMP 1	**9**	19 wks
31 Oct	87	**FREE AS A BIRD** *A & M AMA 5181*	**93**	1 wk
15 Aug	92	**THE VERY BEST OF SUPERTRAMP**		
		A & M TRACD 1992	**24**	4 wks

SUPREMES   *US, female vocal group*   222 wks

5 Dec	64 ●	**MEET THE SUPREMES** *Stateside SL 10109*	**8**	6 wks
17 Dec	66	**SUPREMES A GO-GO** *Tamla Motown STML 11039*	**15**	21 wks
13 May	67	**SUPREMES SING MOTOWN** *Tamla Motown STML 11047*	**15**	16 wks
30 Sep	67	**SUPREMES SING RODGERS AND HART**		
		Tamla Motown STML 11054	**25**	7 wks
20 Jan	68 ★	**GREATEST HITS** *Tamla Motown STML 11063*	**1**	60 wks
30 Mar	68 ●	**LIVE AT THE TALK OF THE TOWN**		
		Tamla Motown STML 11070	**6**	18 wks
20 Jul	68	**REFLECTIONS** *Tamla Motown STML 11073*	**30**	2 wks
25 Jan	69 ★	**DIANA ROSS AND THE SUPREMES JOIN THE**		
		TEMPTATIONS *Tamla Motown STML 11096★*	**1**	15 wks
1 Feb	69 ●	**LOVE CHILD** *Tamla Motown STML 11095*	**8**	6 wks
28 Jun	69	**TCB** *Tamla Motown STML 11110★*	**11**	12 wks
14 Feb	70	**TOGETHER** *Tamla Motown STML 11122★*	**28**	4 wks
29 May	71 ●	**MAGNIFICENT SEVEN** *Tamla Motown STML 11179★★* ...	**6**	11 wks
25 Sep	71	**TOUCH** *Tamla Motown STML 11189*	**40**	1 wk
17 Sep	77 ★	**20 GOLDEN GREATS** *Motown EMTV 5*	**1**	34 wks
21 Jan	89 ●	**LOVE SUPREME** *Motown ZL 72701*	**10**	9 wks

★ Diana Ross and the Supremes with the Temptations.
★★ Supremes and the Four Tops.
See also Diana Ross. All albums beginning with Greatest Hits, *with the exception of* Touch, *credit Diana Ross and the Supremes.*

SURVIVOR   *US, male vocal/instrumental group*   10 wks

21 Aug	82	**EYE OF THE TIGER** *Scotti Bros SCT 85845*	**12**	10 wks

Walter SUSSKIND – *See LONDON PHILHARMONIC CHOIR*

SUTHERLAND BROTHERS and QUIVER
UK, male vocal/instrumental group   11 wks

15 May	76	**REACH FOR THE SKY** *CBS 69191*	**26**	8 wks
9 Oct	76	**SLIPSTREAM** *CBS 81593*	**49**	3 wks

SWANS WAY
UK, male/female vocal/instrumental group   1 wk

3 Nov	84	**THE FUGITIVE KIND** *Balgier SWAN 1*	**88**	1 wk

Keith SWEAT   *US, male vocalist*   25 wks

16 Jan	88	**MAKE IT LAST FOREVER** *Elektra 960763 1*	**42**	21 wks
23 Jun	90	**I'LL GIVE ALL MY LOVE TO YOU** *Vintertainment EKT 60*	**47**	4 wks

SWEET   *UK, male vocal/instrumental group*   8 wks

18 May	74	**SWEET FANNY ADAMS** *RCA LPI 5038*	**27**	2 wks
22 Sep	84	**SWEET 16 – IT'S . . . IT'S . . . SWEET'S HITS**		
		Anagram GRAM 16	**49**	6 wks

*Brett Anderson was the front man of **Suede**, winners of the Mercury Music Prize in 1993. (LFI)*

SWERVEDRIVER *UK, male vocal/instrumental group*   *2 wks*

12 Oct 91	**RAISE** *Creation CRELP 093*	**44** 1 wk
9 Oct 93	**MEZCAL HEAD** *Creation CCRE 143*	**55** 1 wk

SWINGLE SINGERS *US/France, male/female vocal group 18 wks*

1 Feb 64	**JAZZ SEBASTIAN BACH** *Philips BL 7572*	**13** 18 wks

SWING OUT SISTER
UK, male/female vocal/instrumental group   *36 wks*

23 May 87 ★	**IT'S BETTER TO TRAVEL** *Mercury OUTLP 1*	**1** 21 wks
20 May 89 ●	**KALEIDOSCOPE WORLD** *Fontana 838293 1*	**3** 11 wks
16 May 92	**GET IN TOUCH WITH YOURSELF** *Fontana 5122412* ...	**27** 4 wks

SWV *US, female vocal group*   *16 wks*

17 Jul 93	**IT'S ABOUT TIME** *RCA 7863660742*	**17** 16 wks

SYBIL *US, female vocalist*   *12 wks*

5 Sep 87	**LET YOURSELF GO** *Champion CHAMP 1009*	**92** 1 wk
24 Feb 90	**WALK ON BY** *PWL HF 10*	**21** 5 wks
12 Jun 93	**GOOD 'N' READY** *PWL International HFCD 28*	**13** 6 wks

S
304

SYLVESTER *US, male vocalist*   *3 wks*

23 Jun 79	**MIGHTY REAL** *Fantasy FTA 3009*	**62** 3 wks

David SYLVIAN *UK, male vocalist*   *24 wks*

7 Jul 84 ●	**BRILLIANT TREES** *Virgin V 2290*	**4** 14 wks
13 Sep 86	**GONE TO EARTH** *Virgin VDL 1*	**24** 5 wks
7 Nov 87	**SECRETS OF THE BEEHIVE** *Virgin V 2471*	**37** 2 wks
2 Apr 88	**PLIGHT AND PREMONITION** *Virgin VE 11★*	**71** 1 wk
17 Jul 93	**THE FIRST DAY** *Virgin CDVX 2712★★*	**21** 2 wks

★ *David Sylvian and Holgar Czukay.*
★★ *David Sylvian and Robert Fripp.*

SYNTHPHONIC VARIATIONS
UK, session musicians   *1 wk*

1 Nov 86	**SEASONS** *CBS 450 149–1*	**84** 1 wk

SYSTEM 7 *UK, male/female instrumental/vocal group*   *3 wks*

20 Jun 92	**ALTITUDE** *Ten TENG 403*	**75** 1 wk
20 Mar 93	**777** *Big Life BFLCD 1*	**30** 2 wks

TAKE THAT UK, male vocal group   *71 wks*

5 Sep	92 ●	**TAKE THAT AND PARTY** *RCA 74321109*	**2**	61 wks
23 Oct	93 ★	**EVERYTHING CHANGES** *RCA 74321169262*	**1†**	10 wks

TALK TALK UK, male vocal/instrumental group   *84 wks*

24 Jul	82	**THE PARTY'S OVER** *EMI EMC 3431*	**21**	25 wks
25 Feb	84	**IT'S MY LIFE** *EMI EMC 2400021*	**35**	8 wks
1 Mar	86 ●	**THE COLOUR OF SPRING** *EMI EMC 3506*	**8**	21 wks
24 Sep	88	**SPIRIT OF EDEN** *Parlophone PCSD 105*	**19**	5 wks
9 Jun	90 ●	**THE VERY BEST OF TALK TALK – NATURAL HISTORY**		
		Parlophone PCSD 109	**3**	21 wks
6 Apr	91	**HISTORY REVISITED** *Parlophone PCS 7349*	**35**	2 wks
28 Sep	91	**LAUGHING STOCK** *Verve 8477171*	**26**	2 wks

TALKING HEADS
US/UK, male/female vocal/instrumental group   *229 wks*

25 Feb	78	**TALKING HEADS '77** *Sire 9103 328*	**60**	1 wk
29 Jul	78	**MORE SONGS ABOUT BUILDINGS AND FOOD**		
		Sire K 56531	**21**	3 wks
15 Sep	79	**FEAR OF MUSIC** *Sire SRK 6076*	**33**	5 wks
1 Nov	80	**REMAIN IN LIGHT** *Sire SRK 6095*	**21**	17 wks
10 Apr	82	**THE NAME OF THIS BAND IS TALKING HEADS**		
		Sire SRK 23590	**22**	5 wks
18 Jun	83	**SPEAKING IN TONGUES** *Sire K 923 8831*	**21**	12 wks
27 Oct	84	**STOP MAKING SENSE** *EMI TAH 1*	**37**	81 wks
29 Jun	85 ●	**LITTLE CREATURES** *EMI TAH 2*	**10**	65 wks
27 Sep	86 ●	**TRUE STORIES** *EMI EU 3511*	**7**	9 wks
26 Mar	88 ●	**NAKED** *EMI EMD 1005*	**3**	15 wks
24 Oct	92 ●	**ONCE IN A LIFETIME/SAND IN THE VASELINE**		
		EMI CDEQ 5010	**7**	16 wks

TANGERINE DREAM
Germany, male instrumental group   *77 wks*

20 Apr	74	**PHAEDRA** *Virgin V 2010*	**15**	15 wks
5 Apr	75	**RUBYCON** *Virgin V 2025*	**12**	14 wks
20 Dec	75	**RICOCHET** *Virgin V 2044*	**40**	2 wks
13 Nov	76	**STRATOSFEAR** *Virgin V 2068*	**39**	4 wks
23 Jul	77	**SORCERER (film soundtrack)** *MCA MCF 2806*	**25**	7 wks
19 Nov	77	**ENCORE** *Virgin VD 2506*	**55**	1 wk
1 Apr	78	**CYCLONE** *Virgin V 2097*	**37**	4 wks
17 Feb	79	**FORCE MAJEURE** *Virgin V 2111*	**26**	7 wks
7 Jun	80	**TANGRAM** *Virgin V 2147*	**36**	5 wks
18 Apr	81	**THIEF (film soundtrack)** *Virgin V 2198*	**43**	3 wks
19 Sep	81	**EXIT** *Virgin V 2212*	**43**	5 wks
10 Apr	82	**WHITE EAGLE** *Virgin V 2226*	**57**	5 wks
5 Nov	83	**HYPERBOREA** *Virgin V 2292*	**45**	2 wks
10 Nov	84	**POLAND** *Jive Electro HIP 22*	**90**	1 wk
26 Jul	86	**UNDERWATER SUNLIGHT** *Jive Electro HIP 40*	**97**	1 wk
27 Jun	87	**TYGER** *Jive Electro HIP 47*	**88**	1 wk

TANK UK, male vocal/instrumental group   *5 wks*

13 Mar	82	**FILTH HOUNDS OF HADES** *Kamaflage KAMLP 1*	**33**	5 wks

Bill TARMEY UK, male vocalist   5 wks

27 Nov 93 **A GIFT OF LOVE** *EMI CDEMC 3665* .... **25†** 5 wks

TASTE Ireland, male vocal/instrumental group   12 wks

7 Feb 70 **ON THE BOARDS** *Polydor 583–083* .... **18** 11 wks
9 Sep 72 **TASTE LIVE AT THE ISLE OF WIGHT** *Polydor 2383 120* **41** 1 wk

Jeffrey TATE – *See Nigel KENNEDY*

TAVARES US, male vocal group   15 wks

21 Aug 76 **SKY HIGH** *Capitol EST 11533* .... **22** 13 wks
1 Apr 78 **THE BEST OF TAVARES** *Capitol EST 11701* .... **39** 2 wks

Andy TAYLOR
UK, male vocalist/instrumentalist – guitar   1 wk

30 May 87 **THUNDER** *MCA MCG 6018* .... **61** 1 wk

James TAYLOR US, male vocalist   111 wks

21 Nov 70 ● **SWEET BABY JAMES** *Warner Bros. ES 1843* .... **7** 53 wks
29 May 71 ● **MUD SLIDE SLIM AND THE BLUE HORIZON**
    Warner Bros. WS 2561 .... **4** 41 wks
8 Jan 72 **SWEET BABY JAMES (re-issue)** *Warner Bros. K 46043* .... **34** 6 wks
18 Mar 72 **MUD SLIDE SLIM AND THE BLUE HORIZON (re-issue)**
    Warner Bros. K 46085 .... **49** 1 wk
9 Dec 72 **ONE MAN DOG** *Warner Bros. K 46185* .... **27** 5 wks
4 Apr 87 **CLASSIC SONGS** *CBS/WEA JTV 1* .... **53** 5 wks

Roger TAYLOR
UK, male vocalist/instrumentalist – drums   9 wks

18 Apr 81 **FUN IN SPACE** *EMI EMC 3369* .... **18** 5 wks
7 Jul 84 **STRANGE FRONTIER** *EMI RTA 1* .... **30** 4 wks

Kiri TE KANAWA New Zealand, female vocalist   48 wks

2 Apr 83 **CHANTS D'AUVERGNE VOL. 1** *Decca SXDL 7604★* .... **57** 1 wk
26 Oct 85 **BLUE SKIES** *London KTKT 1★★* .... **40** 29 wks
13 Dec 86 **CHRISTMAS WITH KIRI** *Decca PROLP 12* .... **47** 4 wks
17 Dec 88 **KIRI** *K-Tel NE 1424* .... **70** 3 wks
29 Feb 92 **THE ESSENTIAL KIRI** *Decca 4362862* .... **23** 10 wks
23 May 92 **KIRI SIDETRACKS – THE JAZZ ALBUM** *Philips 4340922* **73** 1 wk

★ *Kiri Te Kanawa with the English Chamber Orchestra.*
★★ *Kiri Te Kanawa with the Nelson Riddle Orchestra.*

TEARDROP EXPLODES
UK, male vocal/instrumental group   45 wks

18 Oct 80 **KILIMANJARO** *Mercury 6359 035* .... **24** 35 wks
5 Dec 81 **WILDER** *Mercury 6359 056* .... **29** 6 wks
14 Apr 90 **EVERYBODY WANTS TO SHAG THE TEARDROP**
    EXPLODES *Fontana 8424391 72* .... **72** 1 wk
15 Aug 92 **FLOORED GENIUS – THE BEST OF JULIAN COPE**
    Island CID 8000★ .... **22** 3 wks

★ *Julian Cope and the Teardrop Explodes.*

TEARS FOR FEARS UK, male vocal/instrumental duo *209 wks*

19 Mar	83 ★	**THE HURTING** *Mercury MERS 17*	**1**	65 wks
9 Mar	85 ●	**SONGS FROM THE BIG CHAIR** *Mercury MERH 58*	**2**	81 wks
7 Oct	89 ★	**THE SEEDS OF LOVE** *Fontana 838730 1*	**1**	30 wks
14 Mar	92 ●	**TEARS ROLL DOWN (GREATEST HITS 1982–1992)**		
		Fontana 5109392	**2**	26 wks
19 Jun	93 ●	**ELEMENTAL** *Mercury 5148752*	**5**	7 wks

Act was UK, male vocalist/instrumentalist for the last album.

TECHNOTRONIC
Belgium/UK, male/female vocal/instrumental group *62 wks*

6 Jan	90 ●	**PUMP UP THE JAM** *Swanyard SYRLP 1*	**2**	44 wks
2 Nov	90 ●	**TRIP ON THIS – REMIXES** *Telstar STAR 2461*	**7**	14 wks
15 Jun	91	**BODY TO BODY** *ARS 4683421*	**27**	4 wks

TEENAGE FANCLUB
UK, male vocal/instrumental group *12 wks*

7 Sep	91	**KING** *Creation CRELP 096*	**53**	2 wks
16 Nov	91	**BANDWAGONESQUE** *Creation CRELP 106*	**22**	7 wks
16 Oct	93	**THIRTEEN** *Creation CRECD 144*	**14**	3 wks

TELEVISION US, male vocal/instrumental group *17 wks*

26 Mar	77	**MARQUEE MOON** *Elektra K 52046*	**28**	13 wks
29 Apr	78 ●	**ADVENTURE** *Elektra K 52072*	**7**	4 wks

TEMPERANCE SEVEN
UK, male vocal/instrumental group *10 wks*

13 May	61	**TEMPERANCE SEVEN PLUS ONE** *Argo RG 11*	**19**	1 wk
25 Nov	61	**TEMPERANCE SEVEN 1961** *Parlophone PMC 1152*	**11**	9 wks

TEMPLE CHURCH CHOIR
UK, male vocal/instrumental group *3 wks*

16 Dec	61 ●	**CHRISTMAS CAROLS** *HMV CLP 1309*	**8**	3 wks

TEMPTATIONS US, male vocal group *139 wks*

24 Dec	66	**GETTING READY** *Tamla Motown STML 11035*	**40**	2 wks
11 Feb	67	**TEMPTATIONS GREATEST HITS**		
		Tamla Motown STML 11042	**26**	40 wks
22 Jul	67	**TEMPTATIONS LIVE** *Tamla Motown STML 11053*	**20**	4 wks
18 Nov	67	**TEMPTATIONS WITH A LOT OF SOUL**		
		Tamla Motown STML 11057	**19**	18 wks
25 Jan	69 ★	**DIANA ROSS AND THE SUPREMES JOIN THE**		
		TEMPTATIONS *Tamla Motown STML 11096★*	**1**	15 wks
28 Jun	69	**TCB** *Tamla Motown STML 11110★*	**11**	12 wks
20 Sep	69	**CLOUD NINE** *Tamla Motown STML 11109*	**32**	1 wk
14 Feb	70	**PUZZLE PEOPLE** *Tamla Motown STML 11133*	**20**	4 wks
14 Feb	70	**TOGETHER** *Tamla Motown STML 11122★*	**28**	4 wks
11 Jul	70	**PSYCHEDELIC SHACK** *Tamla Motown STML 11147*	**56**	1 wk
26 Dec	70	**GREATEST HITS VOL. 2** *Tamla Motown STML 11170*	**35**	12 wks
29 Apr	72	**SOLID ROCK** *Tamla Motown STML 11202*	**34**	2 wks
20 Jan	73	**ALL DIRECTIONS** *Tamla Motown STML 11218*	**19**	7 wks
7 Jul	73	**MASTERPIECE** *Tamla Motown STML 11229*	**28**	3 wks
8 Dec	84	**TRULY FOR YOU** *Motown ZL 72342*	**75**	5 wks
11 Apr	92 ●	**MOTOWN'S GREATEST HITS** *Motown 5300152*	**8**	9 wks

★ *Diana Ross and the Supremes with the Temptations.*

Take That cut a celebratory cake with disc jockey Neil Fox. *(Pictorial Press)*

Tina Turner is shown during October 1986, with Keith Richards. She was in the chart at the time with Break Every Rule. Keith already had.

The Voices you heard in 1991 belonged to **Kenny Thomas**. *(Pictorial Press)*

10 C.C. *UK, male vocal/instrumental group* 215 wks

1 Sep	73	**10 C.C.** UK UKAL 1005	**36**	5 wks
15 Jun	74 ●	**SHEET MUSIC** UK UKAL 1007	**9**	24 wks
22 Mar	75 ●	**THE ORIGINAL SOUNDTRACK** Mercury 9102 50Q	**4**	40 wks
7 Jun	75 ●	**GREATEST HITS OF 10 C.C.** Decca UKAL 1012	**9**	18 wks
31 Jan	76 ●	**HOW DARE YOU?** Mercury 9102 501	**5**	31 wks
14 May	77 ●	**DECEPTIVE BENDS** Mercury 9102 502	**3**	21 wks
10 Dec	77	**LIVE AND LET LIVE** Mercury 6641 698	**14**	15 wks
23 Sep	78 ●	**BLOODY TOURISTS** Mercury 9102 503	**3**	15 wks
6 Oct	79 ●	**GREATEST HITS 1972–1978** Mercury 9102 504	**5**	21 wks
5 Apr	80	**LOOK HERE** Mercury 9102 505	**35**	5 wks
15 Oct	83	**WINDOW IN THE JUNGLE** Mercury MERL 28	**70**	2 wks
29 Aug	87 ●	**CHANGING FACES – THE VERY BEST OF 10 C.C. AND GODLEY AND CREME** ProTV TGCLP 1*	**4**	18 wks

★ *10 C.C. and Godley and Creme.*

TEN CITY *US, male vocal/instrumental group* 12 wks

18 Feb	89	**FOUNDATION** Atlantic WX 249	**22**	12 wks

TEN POLE TUDOR *UK, male vocal/instrumental group* 8 wks

9 May	81	**EDDIE, OLD BOB, DICK & GARRY** Stiff SEEZ 31	**44**	8 wks

TEN SHARP *Holland, male vocal/instrumental duo* 2 wks

9 May	92	**UNDER THE WATER-LINE** Columbia 4690702	**46**	2 wks

10,000 MANIACS *US, female/male vocal/instrumental group* 12 wks

27 May	89	**BLIND MAN'S ZOO** Elektra EKT 57	**18**	8 wks
10 Oct	92	**OUR TIME IN EDEN** Elektra 7559613852	**33**	2 wks
6 Nov	93	**UNPLUGGED** Elektra 7559615692	**40**	2 wks

TEN YEARS AFTER *UK, male vocal/instrumental group* 73 wks

21 Sep	68	**UNDEAD** Deram SML 1023	**26**	7 wks
22 Feb	69 ●	**STONEDHENGE** Deram SML 1029	**6**	5 wks
4 Oct	69 ●	**SSSSH** Deram SML 1052	**4**	18 wks
2 May	70 ●	**CRICKLEWOOD GREEN** Deram SML 1065	**4**	27 wks
9 Jan	71 ●	**WATT** Deram SML 1078	**5**	12 wks
13 Nov	71	**SPACE IN TIME** Chrysalis CHR 1001	**36**	1 wk
7 Oct	72	**ROCK AND ROLL** Chrysalis CHR 1009	**27**	1 wk
28 Jul	73	**RECORDED LIVE** Chrysalis CHR 1049	**36**	2 wks

TENNILLE – *See CAPTAIN and TENNILLE*

TERRAPLANE *UK, male vocal/instrumental group* 1 wk

25 Jan	86	**BLACK AND WHITE** Epic EPC 26439	**74**	1 wk

Tammi TERRELL – *See Marvin GAYE*

TERRORVISION *UK, male vocal/instrumental group* 1 wk

15 May	93	**FORMALDEHYDE** Total Vegas VEGASCD 1	**75**	1 wk

TESLA *US, male vocal/instrumental group* 5 wks

11 Feb	89	**THE GREAT RADIO CONTROVERSY** Geffen WX 244 .	**34**	2 wks
2 Mar	91	**FIVE MAN ACOUSTICAL JAM** Geffen 9243111	**59**	1 wk
21 Sep	91	**PSYCHOTIC SUPPER** Geffen GEF 24424	**44**	2 wks

TESTAMENT US, male vocal/instrumental group   6 wks

28 May 88	THE NEW ORDER Megaforce 781849 1	81	1 wk
19 Aug 89	PRACTICE WHAT YOU PREACH Atlantic WX 297	40	2 wks
6 Oct 90	SOULS OF BLACK Megaforce 7567821431	35	2 wks
30 May 92	THE RITUAL Atlantic 7567823922	48	1 wk

TEXAS UK, male/female vocal/instrumental group   33 wks

25 Mar 89 ●	SOUTHSIDE Mercury 838171 1	3	27 wks
5 Oct 91	MOTHER'S HEAVEN Mercury 8485781	32	4 wks
13 Nov 93	RICK'S ROAD Vertigo 5182522	18	2 wks

THAT PETROL EMOTION
UK, male vocal/instrumental group   8 wks

10 May 86	MANIC POP THRILL Demon FIEND 70	84	2 wks
23 May 87	BABBLE Polydor TPE LP 1	30	3 wks
24 Sep 88	END OF MILLENNIUM PSYCHOSIS BLUES		
	Virgin V 2550	53	2 wks
21 Apr 90	CHEMICRAZY Virgin V 2618	62	1 wk

The THE UK, male vocal/instrumental group   51 wks

29 Oct 83	SOUL MINING Some Bizzare EPC 25525	27	5 wks
29 Nov 86	INFECTED Some Bizzare EPC 26770	14	30 wks
27 May 89 ●	MIND BOMB Epic 463319 1	4	9 wks
6 Feb 93 ●	DUSK Epic 4724682	2	4 wks
19 Jun 93	BURNING BLUE SOUL 4AD HAD 113CD	65	1 wk

Matt Johnson leads The The, which is an informal group of his studio guests and friends.

THEATRE OF HATE UK, male vocal/instrumental group 9 wks

| 13 Mar 82 | WESTWORLD Burning Rome TOH 1 .... | 17 | 6 wks |
| 18 Aug 84 | REVOLUTION Burning Rome TOH 2 .... | 67 | 3 wks |

THEN JERICO UK, male vocal/instrumental group   24 wks

| 3 Oct 87 | FIRST (THE SOUND OF MUSIC) London LONLP 26 ... | 35 | 7 wks |
| 4 Mar 89 ● | THE BIG AREA London 828122 1 .... | 4 | 17 wks |

THERAPY? UK, male vocal/instrumental group   4 wks

| 8 Feb 92 | PLEASURE DEATH Wiiija WIJ 11 .... | 52 | 1 wk |
| 14 Nov 92 | NURSE A & M 5400442 .... | 38 | 3 wks |

THEY MIGHT BE GIANTS
US, male vocal/instrumental duo   12 wks

| 7 Apr 90 | FLOOD Elektra EKT 68 .... | 14 | 12 wks |

THIN LIZZY
Ireland/UK/US, male vocal/instrumental group   239 wks

27 Sep 75	FIGHTING Vertigo 6360 121	60	1 wk
10 Apr 76 ●	JAILBREAK Vertigo 9102 008	10	50 wks
6 Nov 76	JOHNNY THE FOX Vertigo 9102 012	11	24 wks
1 Oct 77 ●	BAD REPUTATION Vertigo 9102 016	4	9 wks
17 Jun 78 ●	LIVE AND DANGEROUS Vertigo 6641 807	2	62 wks
5 May 79 ●	BLACK ROSE (A ROCK LEGEND) Vertigo 9102 032	2	21 wks

18 Oct	80 ●	**CHINA TOWN** *Vertigo 6359 030*	**7**	7 wks
11 Apr	81 ●	**ADVENTURES OF THIN LIZZY** *Vertigo LIZTV 1*	**6**	13 wks
5 Dec	81	**RENEGADE** *Vertigo 6359 083*	**38**	8 wks
12 Mar	83 ●	**THUNDER AND LIGHTNING** *Vertigo VERL 3*	**4**	11 wks
26 Nov	83	**LIFE** *Vertigo VERD 6*	**29**	6 wks
14 Nov	87	**SOLDIER OF FORTUNE – THE BEST OF PHIL LYNOTT**		
		AND THIN LIZZY *Telstar STAR 2300★*	**55**	10 wks
16 Feb	91 ●	**DEDICATION – THE VERY BEST OF THIN LIZZY**		
		Vertigo 8481921	**8**	17 wks

★ *Phil Lynott and Thin Lizzy.*

3RD BASS   *US, male rap group*   1 wk

20 Jul	91	**DERELICTS OF DIALECT** *Def Jam 4683171*	**46**	1 wk

THIRD EAR BAND   *UK, male instrumental group*   2 wks

27 Jun	70	**AIR, EARTH, FIRE, WATER** *Harvest SHVL 773*	**49**	2 wks

THIRD WORLD   *Jamaica, male vocal/instrumental group*   18 wks

21 Oct	78	**JOURNEY TO ADDIS** *Island ILPS 9554*	**30**	6 wks
11 Jul	81	**ROCKS THE WORLD** *CBS 85027*	**37**	9 wks
15 May	82	**YOU'VE GOT THE POWER** *CBS 85563*	**87**	3 wks

THIS MORTAL COIL
UK, male/female instrumental group   10 wks

20 Oct	84	**IT'LL END IN TEARS** *4AD CAD 411*	**38**	4 wks
11 Oct	86	**FILIGREE AND SHADOW** *4AD DAD 609*	**53**	3 wks
4 May	91	**BLOOD** *4AD DAD 1005*	**65**	3 wks

Carla THOMAS – *See Otis REDDING*

Kenny THOMAS   *UK, male vocalist*   28 wks

26 Oct	91 ●	**VOICES** *Cooltempo CTLP 24*	**3**	23 wks
25 Sep	93 ●	**WAIT FOR ME** *Cooltempo CTCD 36*	**10**	5 wks

Lillo THOMAS   *US, male vocalist*   7 wks

2 May	87	**LILLO** *Capitol EST 2031*	**43**	7 wks

Ray THOMAS   *UK, male vocalist*   3 wks

26 Jul	75	**FROM MIGHTY OAKS** *Threshold THS 16*	**23**	3 wks

Richard THOMPSON
UK, male vocalist/instrumentalist – guitar   7 wks

27 Apr	85	**ACROSS A CROWDED ROOM** *Polydor POLD 5175*	**80**	2 wks
18 Oct	86	**DARING ADVENTURES** *Polydor POLD 5202*	**92**	1 wk
29 Oct	88	**AMNESIA** *Capitol EST 2075*	**89**	1 wk
25 May	91	**RUMOUR AND SIGH** *Capitol EST 2142*	**32**	3 wks

THOMPSON TWINS
UK/New Zealand, male/female vocal/instrumental group   128 wks

13 Mar	82	**SET** *Tee TELP 2*	**48**	3 wks
26 Feb	83 ●	**QUICK STEP AND SIDE KICK** *Arista 204 924*	**2**	56 wks
25 Feb	84 ★	**INTO THE GAP** *Arista 205 971*	**1**	51 wks

T
311

28 Sep	85 ●	**HERE'S TO FUTURE DAYS** *Arista 207 164*	**5**	9 wks
2 May	87	**CLOSE TO THE BONE** *Arista 208 143*	**90**	1 wk
10 Mar	90	**GREATEST HITS** *Stylus SMR 92*	**23**	8 wks

George THOROGOOD and the DESTROYERS
US, male vocal/instrumental group   *1 wk*

2 Dec	78	**GEORGE THOROGOOD AND THE DESTROYERS** *Sonet SNTF 781*	**67**	1 wk

THOUSAND YARD STARE
UK, male vocal/instrumental group   *2 wks*

7 Mar	92	**HANDS ON** *Polydor 5130012*	**38**	2 wks

THREE DEGREES   *US, female vocal group*   *91 wks*

10 Aug	74	**THREE DEGREES** *Philadelphia International 65858*	**12**	22 wks
17 May	75 ●	**TAKE GOOD CARE OF YOURSELF** *Philadelphia International PIR 69137*	**6**	16 wks
24 Feb	79	**NEW DIMENSIONS** *Ariola ARLH 5012*	**34**	13 wks
3 Mar	79 ●	**A COLLECTION OF THEIR 20 GREATEST HITS** *Epic EPC 10013*	**8**	18 wks
15 Dec	79	**3D** *Ariola 3D 1*	**61**	7 wks
27 Sep	80 ●	**GOLD** *Ariola 3D 2*	**9**	15 wks

THROWING MUSES
US/UK, male/female vocal/instrumental group   *9 wks*

4 Feb	89	**HUNKPAPA** *4AD CAD 901*	**59**	1 wk
2 Mar	91	**THE REAL RAMONA** *4AD CAD 1002*	**26**	4 wks
22 Aug	92	**RED HEAVEN** *4AD CAD 2013CD*	**13**	3 wks
28 Nov	92	**THE CURSE** *4AD TAD 2019CD*	**74**	1 wk

THUNDER   *UK/US, male vocal/instrumental group*   *26 wks*

17 Mar	90	**BACKSTREET SYMPHONY** *EMI EMC 3570*	**21**	16 wks
5 Sep	92 ●	**LAUGHING ON JUDGEMENT DAY** *EMI CDEMD 1035* .	**2**	10 wks

TIFFANY   *US, female vocalist*   *27 wks*

27 Feb	88 ●	**TIFFANY** *MCA MCF 3415*	**5**	21 wks
17 Dec	88	**HOLD AN OLD FRIEND'S HAND** *MCA MCF 3437*	**56**	6 wks

TIGERTAILZ   *US, male vocal/instrumental group*   *2 wks*

7 Apr	90	**BEZERK** *Music For Nations MFN 96*	**36**	2 wks

TIGHT FIT   *UK, male/female vocal group*   *6 wks*

26 Sep	81	**BACK TO THE SIXTIES** *Jive HIP 1*	**38**	4 wks
4 Sep	82	**TIGHT FIT** *Jive HIP 2*	**87**	2 wks

TIJUANA BRASS – *See Herb ALPERT and the TIJUANA BRASS*

TIK and TOK   *UK, male vocal/instrumental duo*   *2 wks*

4 Aug	84	**INTOLERANCE** *Survival SUR LP 008*	**89**	2 wks

Tanita TIKARAM *UK, female vocalist* *59 wks*

24 Sep	88 ●	**ANCIENT HEART** *WEA WX 210*	**3**	48 wks
10 Feb	90 ●	**THE SWEET KEEPER** *East West WX 330*	**3**	7 wks
16 Feb	91	**EVERYBODY'S ANGEL** *East West WX 401*	**19**	4 wks

TILBROOK – *See DIFFORD and TILBROOK*

TIMBUK THREE *US, male/female vocal/instrumental duo* *4 wks*

14 Feb	87	**GREETINGS FROM TIMBUK THREE** *IRS MIRF 1015* ..	**51**	4 wks

TIME *US, male vocal/instrumental group* *1 wk*

28 Jul	90	**PANDEMONIUM** *Paisley Park WX 336*	**66**	1 wk

TIN MACHINE *US/UK, male vocal/instrumental group* *12 wks*

3 Jun	89 ●	**TIN MACHINE** *EMI-USA MTLS 1044*	**3**	9 wks
14 Sep	91	**TIN MACHINE II** *London 8282721*	**23**	3 wks

TINDERSTICKS *UK, male vocal/instrumental group* *1 wk*

23 Oct	93	**TINDERSTICKS** *This Way Up 5183064*	**56**	1 wk

TOM TOM CLUB *US, female/male vocal/instrumental group* *1 wk*

24 Oct	81	**TOM TOM CLUB** *Island ILPS 9686*	**78**	1 wk

TOMITA *Japan, male instrumentalist – synthesizer* *33 wks*

7 Jun	75	**SNOWFLAKES ARE DANCING** *RCA Red Seal ARL 1 0488*	**17**	20 wks
16 Aug	75	**PICTURES AT AN EXHIBITION** *RCA Red Seal ARL 1 0838*	**42**	5 wks
7 May	77	**HOLST: THE PLANETS** *RCA Red Seal RL 11919*	**41**	6 wks
9 Feb	80	**TOMITA'S GREATEST HITS** *RCA Red Seal RL 43076* ..	**66**	2 wks

TONGUE 'N' CHEEK
UK, male/female vocal/instrumental group *3 wks*

22 Sep	90	**THIS IS TONGUE 'N' CHEEK** *Syncopate SYLP 6006*	**45**	3 wks

TONY! TONI! TONE! *US, male vocal group* *1 wk*

2 Oct	93	**SONS OF SOUL** *Polydor 5149332*	**66**	1 wk

TOPOL *Israel, male vocalist* *1 wk*

11 May	85	**TOPOL'S ISRAEL** *BBC REH 529*	**80**	1 wk

Bernie TORME *UK, male vocalist/instrumentalist – guitar* *3 wks*

3 Jul	82	**TURN OUT THE LIGHTS** *Kamaflage KAMLP 2*	**50**	3 wks

Peter TOSH *Jamaica, male vocalist* *1 wk*

25 Sep	76	**LEGALIZE IT** *Virgin V 2061*	**54**	1 wk

T
313

TOTAL CONTRAST UK, male vocal/instrumental duo   3 wks

| 8 Mar 86 | **TOTAL CONTRAST** London LONLP 15 .... | 66 | 3 wks |

TOTO US, male vocal/instrumental group   39 wks

31 Mar 79	**TOTO** CBS 83148	37	5 wks
26 Feb 83 ●	**TOTO IV** CBS 85529	4	30 wks
17 Nov 84	**ISOLATION** CBS 86305	67	2 wks
20 Sep 86	**FAHRENHEIT** CBS 57091	99	1 wk
9 Apr 88	**THE SEVENTH ONE** CBS 460465 1	73	1 wk

TOURISTS UK, female/male vocal/instrumental group   18 wks

14 Jul 79	**THE TOURISTS** Logo GO 1018	72	1 wk
3 Nov 79	**REALITY EFFECT** Logo GO 1019	23	16 wks
22 Nov 80	**LUMINOUS BASEMENT** RCA RCALP 5001	75	1 wk

Pete TOWNSHEND
UK, male vocalist/instrumentalist – guitar   28 wks

21 Oct 72	**WHO CAME FIRST** Track 2408 201	30	2 wks
15 Oct 77	**ROUGH MIX** Polydor 2442147★	44	3 wks
3 May 80	**EMPTY GLASS** Atco K 50699	11	14 wks
3 Jul 82	**ALL THE BEST COWBOYS HAVE CHINESE EYES**		
	Atco K 50889	32	8 wks
30 Nov 85	**WHITE CITY** Atco 25–2392–1	70	1 wk

★ Pete Townshend and Ronnie Lane.

T
314

TOYAH UK, female vocalist   97 wks

14 Jun 80	**THE BLUE MEANING** Safari IEYA 666	40	4 wks
17 Jan 81	**TOYAH TOYAH TOYAH** Safari LIVE 2	22	14 wks
30 May 81 ●	**ANTHEM** Safari VOOR 1	2	46 wks
19 Jun 82 ●	**THE CHANGELING** Safari VOOR 9	6	12 wks
13 Nov 82	**WARRIOR ROCK – TOYAH ON TOUR** Safari TNT 1 ..	20	6 wks
5 Nov 83	**LOVE IS THE LAW** Safari VOOR 10	28	7 wks
25 Feb 84	**TOYAH! TOYAH! TOYAH!** K-Tel NE 1268	43	4 wks
3 Aug 85	**MINX** Portrait PRT 26415	24	4 wks

TOY DOLLS UK, male vocal/instrumental group   1 wk

| 25 May 85 | **A FAR OUT DISC** Volume VOLP 2 .... | 71 | 1 wk |

T'PAU UK, female/male vocal/instrumental group   85 wks

26 Sep 87 ★	**BRIDGE OF SPIES** Siren SIRENLP 8	1	59 wks
5 Nov 88 ●	**RAGE** Siren SRNLP 20	4	17 wks
22 Jun 91 ●	**THE PROMISE** Siren SRNLP 32	10	7 wks
27 Feb 93	**HEART AND SOUL – THE VERY BEST OF T'PAU**		
	Virgin TPAUD 1	35	2 wks

Ian TRACEY/LIVERPOOL CATHEDRALS' CHOIRS UK conductor with UK, male/female choirs   3 wks

| 21 Mar 92 | **YOUR FAVOURITE HYMNS** Virgin Classics 7912092 ..... | 62 | 3 wks |

TRACIE UK, female vocalist   2 wks

| 30 Jun 84 | **FAR FROM THE HURTING KIND** Respond RRL 502 ... | 64 | 2 wks |

TRAFFIC
UK, male vocal/instrumental group   37 wks

30 Dec 67 ● **MR. FANTASY** *Island ILP 9061*	**8**	16 wks
26 Oct 68 ● **TRAFFIC** *Island ILPS 9081 T*	**9**	8 wks
8 Aug 70 **JOHN BARLEYCORN MUST DIE** *Island ILPS 9116*	**11**	9 wks
24 Nov 73 **ON THE ROAD** *Island ISLD 2*	**40**	3 wks
28 Sep 74 **WHEN THE EAGLE FLIES** *Island ILPS 9273*	**31**	1 wk

TRANSGLOBAL UNDERGROUND
UK, male/female vocal/instrumental group   1 wk

30 Oct 93 **DREAM OF 100 NATIONS** *Nation NR 021CD*	**45**	1 wk

TRANSVISION VAMP
UK, male/female vocal/instrumental group   58 wks

15 Oct 88 ● **POP ART** *MCA MCF 3421*	**4**	32 wks
8 Jul 89 ★ **VELVETEEN** *MCA MCG 6050*	**1**	26 wks

TRASH CAN SINATRAS
UK, male vocal/instrumental group   2 wks

7 Jul 90 **CAKE** *Go! Discs 82820211*	**74**	1 wk
15 May 93 **I'VE SEEN EVERYTHING** *Go! Discs 8284082*	**50**	1 wk

TRAVELING WILBURYS
US/UK, male vocal/instrumental group   44 wks

5 Nov 88 **THE TRAVELING WILBURYS VOLUME 1** *Wilbury WX 224*	**16**	35 wks
10 Nov 90 **THE TRAVELING WILBURYS VOLUME 3** *Wilbury WX 384*	**14**	9 wks

Pat TRAVERS
US, male instrumentalist – guitar   3 wks

2 Apr 77 **MAKIN' MAGIC** *Polydor 2383 436*	**40**	3 wks

Randy TRAVIS *US, male vocalist*   2 wks

6 Aug 88 **OLD 8 x 10** *Warner Bros. WX 162*	**64**	2 wks

John TRAVOLTA *US, male vocalist*   6 wks

23 Dec 78 **SANDY** *Polydor POLD 5014*	**40**	6 wks

TREMELOES
UK, male vocal/instrumental group   7 wks

3 Jun 67 **HERE COME THE TREMELOES** *CBS SBPG 63017*	**15**	7 wks

Ralph TRESVANT *US, male vocalist*   3 wks

23 Feb 91 **RALPH TRESVANT** *MCA MCG 6120*	**37**	3 wks

T
315

T. REX UK, male vocal/instrumental group   216 wks

13 Jul	68	MY PEOPLE WERE FAIR AND HAD SKY IN THEIR HAIR BUT NOW THEY'RE CONTENT TO WEAR STARS ON THEIR BROWS Regal Zonophone SLRZ 1003★	15	9 wks
7 Jun	69	UNICORN Regal Zonophone S 1007★	12	3 wks
14 Mar	70	A BEARD OF STARS Regal Zonophone SLRZ 1013★	21	6 wks
16 Jan	71	T. REX Fly HIFLY 2	13	24 wks
7 Aug	71	THE BEST OF T. REX Flyback TON 2	21	7 wks
9 Oct	71 ★	ELECTRIC WARRIOR Fly HIFLY 6	1	44 wks
29 Mar	72 ★	PROPHETS, SEERS AND SAGES THE ANGELS OF THE AGES/MY PEOPLE WERE FAIR . . . Fly Doubleback 0037 TOOFA 3/4★	1	12 wks
20 May	72 ★	BOLAN BOOGIE Fly HIFLY 8	1	19 wks
5 Aug	72 ●	THE SLIDER EMI BLN 5001	4	18 wks
9 Dec	72	A BEARD OF STARS/UNICORN (re-issue) Cube TOOFA 9/10★	44	2 wks
31 Mar	73 ●	TANX EMI BLN 5002	4	12 wks
10 Nov	73	GREAT HITS EMI BLN 5003	32	3 wks
16 Mar	74	ZINC ALLOY AND THE HIDDEN RIDERS OF TOMORROW EMI BLNA 7751★★	12	3 wks
21 Feb	76	FUTURISTIC DRAGON EMI BLN 5004	50	1 wk
9 Apr	77	DANDY IN THE UNDERWORLD EMI BLN 5005	26	3 wks
30 Jun	79	SOLID GOLD EMI NUT 5	51	3 wks
12 Sep	81	T. REX IN CONCERT Marc ABOLAN 1	35	6 wks
7 Nov	81	YOU SCARE ME TO DEATH Cherry Red ERED 20★★★	88	1 wk
24 Sep	83	DANCE IN THE MIDNIGHT Marc On Wax MARCL 501★★★	83	3 wks
4 May	85 ●	BEST OF THE 20TH CENTURY BOY K-Tel NE 1297★★	5	21 wks
28 Sep	91 ●	THE ULTIMATE COLLECTION Telstar TCD 2539★★	4	16 wks

★ *Tyrannosaurus Rex.*   ★★ *Marc Bolan and T. Rex.*   ★★★ *Marc Bolan.*
Prophets . . ./My People . . . *is a double re-issue, although* Prophets *had not previously been a hit.*

316

A TRIBE CALLED QUEST US, male rap group   4 wks

19 May	90	PEOPLE'S INSTINCTIVE TRAVELS Jive HIP 96	54	2 wks
12 Oct	91	LOW END THEORY Jive HIP 117	58	1 wk
27 Nov	93	MIDNIGHT MARAUDERS Jive CHIP 143	70	1 wk

TRIFFIDS New Zealand, male vocal/instrumental group   1 wk

22 Apr	89	THE BLACK SWAN Island ILPS 9928	63	1 wk

TRIUMPH Canada, male vocal/instrumental group   8 wks

10 May	80	PROGRESSIONS OF POWER RCA PL 13524	61	5 wks
3 Oct	81	ALLIED FORCES RCA RCALP 6002	64	3 wks

TROGGS UK, male vocal/instrumental group   32 wks

30 Jul	66 ●	FROM NOWHERE . . . THE TROGGS Fontana TL 5355	6	16 wks
25 Feb	67 ●	TROGGLODYNAMITE Page One POL 001	10	11 wks
5 Aug	67	BEST OF THE TROGGS Page One FOR 001	24	5 wks

TROUBADOURS DU ROI BAUDOUIN
Zaire, male/female vocal group   1 wk

22 May	76	MISSA LUBA Philips SBL 7592	59	1 wk

TROUBLE FUNK US, male vocal/instrumental group   4 wks

8 Nov	86	SAY WHAT! Fourth & Broadway DCLP 101	75	2 wks
5 Sep	87	TROUBLE OVER HERE, TROUBLE OVER THERE Fourth & Broadway BRLP 513	54	2 wks

Robin TROWER
UK, male instrumentalist – guitar   *16 wks*

1 Mar	75	**FOR EARTH BELOW** *Chrysalis CHR 1073*	26	4 wks
13 Mar	76	**LIVE** *Chrysalis CHR 1089*	15	6 wks
30 Oct	76	**LONG MISTY DAYS** *Chrysalis CHR 1107*	31	1 wk
29 Oct	77	**IN CITY DREAMS** *Chrysalis CHR 1148*	58	1 wk
16 Feb	80	**VICTIMS OF THE FURY** *Chrysalis CHR 1215*	61	4 wks

TUBES *US, male vocal/instrumental group*   *7 wks*

4 Mar	78	**WHAT DO YOU WANT FROM LIFE** *A & M AMS 68460*	38	1 wk
2 Jun	79	**REMOTE CONTROL** *A & M AMLH 64751*	40	5 wks
4 Jun	83	**OUTSIDE INSIDE** *Capitol EST 12260*	77	1 wk

TUBEWAY ARMY – *See Gary Numan*

Ike and Tina TURNER
US, male instrumentalist – guitar and female vocalist   *1 wk*

1 Oct	66	**RIVER DEEP – MOUNTAIN HIGH** *London HAU 8298* ..	27	1 wk

See also Tina Turner.

Ruby TURNER *UK, female vocalist*   *19 wks*

18 Oct	86	**WOMEN HOLD UP HALF THE SKY** *Jive HIP 36*	47	11 wks
8 Oct	88	**THE MOTOWN SONGBOOK** *Jive HIP 58*	22	6 wks
17 Feb	90	**PARADISE** *Jive HIP 89*	74	2 wks

Tina TURNER *US, female vocalist*   *407 wks*

30 Jun	84 ●	**PRIVATE DANCER** *Capitol TINA 1*	2	147 wks
20 Sep	86 ●	**BREAK EVERY RULE** *Capitol EST 2018*	2	49 wks
2 Apr	88 ●	**LIVE IN EUROPE** *Capitol ESTD 1*	8	13 wks
30 Sep	89 ★	**FOREIGN AFFAIR** *Capitol ESTU 2103*	1	78 wks
12 Oct	91 ●	**SIMPLY THE BEST** *Capitol ESTV 1*	2†	92 wks
19 Jun	93 ★	**WHAT'S LOVE GOT TO DO WITH IT** (film soundtrack) *Parlophone CDPCSD 128*	1†	28 wks

See also Ike and Tina Turner.

TURTLES *US, male vocal/instrumental group*   *9 wks*

22 Jul	67	**HAPPY TOGETHER** *London HAU 8330*	18	9 wks

TWELFTH NIGHT
UK, male vocal/instrumental group   *2 wks*

27 Oct	84	**ART AND ILLUSION** *Music For Nations MFN 36*	83	2 wks

TWENTY 4 SEVEN
US/Holland/Germany/Italy, male/female vocal/instrumental group   *2 wks*

19 Jan	91	**STREET MOVES** *BCM BCM 3124*	69	2 wks

TWIGGY *UK, female vocalist*   *11 wks*

21 Aug	76	**TWIGGY** *Mercury 9102 600*	33	8 wks
30 Apr	77	**PLEASE GET MY NAME RIGHT** *Mercury 9102 601*	35	3 wks

T
317

TWISTED SISTER US, male vocal/instrumental group   20 wks

25 Sep 82	**UNDER THE BLADE** Secret SECX 9	70	3 wks
7 May 83	**YOU CAN'T STOP ROCK 'N' ROLL** Atlantic A 0074 ...	14	9 wks
16 Jun 84	**STAY HUNGRY** Atlantic 780156	34	5 wks
14 Dec 85	**COME OUT AND PLAY** Atlantic 78–1275–1	95	1 wk
25 Jul 87	**LOVE IS FOR SUCKERS** Atlantic WX 120	57	2 wks

2 IN A ROOM US, male vocal duo   1 wk

2 Mar 91	**WIGGLE IT** SBKLP 11	73	1 wk

2 UNLIMITED Holland, male/female vocal duo   22 wks

7 Mar 92	**GET READY** PWL Continental HFCD 23	37	3 wks
22 May 93 ★	**NO LIMITS** PWL Continental HFCD 27	1	19 wks

Tommy TYCHO – See David GRAY and Tommy TYCHO

TYGERS OF PAN TANG
UK, male vocal/instrumental group   20 wks

30 Aug 80	**WILD CAT** MCA MCF 3075	18	5 wks
18 Apr 81	**SPELLBOUND** MCA MCF 3104	33	4 wks
21 Nov 81	**CRAZY NIGHTS** MCA MCF 3123	51	3 wks
28 Aug 82	**THE CAGE** MCA MCF 3150	13	8 wks

Bonnie TYLER UK, female vocalist   75 wks

16 Apr 83 ★	**FASTER THAN THE SPEED OF NIGHT** CBS 25304 ...	1	45 wks
17 May 86	**SECRET DREAMS AND FORBIDDEN FIRE** CBS 86319	24	12 wks
29 Nov 86	**THE GREATEST HITS** Telstar STAR 2291	24	17 wks
21 May 88	**HIDE YOUR HEART** CBS 460125 1	78	1 wk

Judie TZUKE UK, female vocalist   61 wks

4 Aug 79	**WELCOME TO THE CRUISE** Rocket TRAIN 7	14	17 wks
10 May 80 ●	**SPORTS CAR** Rocket TRAIN 9	7	11 wks
16 May 81	**I AM PHOENIX** Rocket TRAIN 15	17	10 wks
17 Apr 82	**SHOOT THE MOON** Chrysalis CDL 1382	19	10 wks
30 Oct 82	**ROAD NOISE – THE OFFICIAL BOOTLEG**		
	Chrysalis CTY 1405	39	4 wks
1 Oct 83	**RITMO** Chrysalis CDL 1442	26	5 wks
15 Jun 85	**THE CAT IS OUT** Legacy LLP 102	35	3 wks
29 Apr 89	**TURNING STONES** Polydor 839087 1	57	1 wk

UB40 UK, male vocal/instrumental group   480 wks

6 Sep 80 ●	**SIGNING OFF** Graduate GRAD LP 2	2	71 wks
6 Jun 81 ●	**PRESENT ARMS** DEP International LP DEP 1	2	38 wks
10 Oct 81	**PRESENT ARMS IN DUB** DEP International LPS DEP 2 ..	38	7 wks
28 Aug 82	**THE SINGLES ALBUM** Graduate GRADLSP 3	17	8 wks
9 Oct 82 ●	**UB 44** DEP International LP DEP 3	4	8 wks
26 Feb 83	**UB 40 LIVE** DEP International LP DEP 4	44	5 wks
24 Sep 83 ★	**LABOUR OF LOVE** DEP International LP DEP 5	1	76 wks
20 Oct 84 ●	**GEFFREY MORGAN** DEP International DEP 6	3	14 wks
14 Sep 85	**BAGGARADDIM** DEP International LP DEP 10	14	23 wks
9 Aug 86 ●	**RAT IN THE KITCHEN** DEP International LP DEP 11	8	20 wks
7 Nov 87 ●	**THE BEST OF UB 40 VOL. 1** Virgin UBTV 1	3	106 wks
23 Jul 88	**UB40** DEP International LPDEP 13	12	12 wks
9 Dec 89 ●	**LABOUR OF LOVE II** DEP International LPDEP 14	3	69 wks
24 Jul 93 ★	**PROMISES AND LIES** DEP Int DEPCD 15	1†	23 wks

UFO *UK, male vocal/instrumental group*   48 wks

4 Jun	77	**LIGHTS OUT** *Chrysalis CHR 1127*	54	2 wks
15 Jul	78	**OBSESSION** *Chrysalis CDL 1182*	26	7 wks
10 Feb	79 ●	**STRANGERS IN THE NIGHT** *Chrysalis CJT 5*	8	11 wks
19 Jan	80	**NO PLACE TO RUN** *Chrysalis CDL 1239*	11	7 wks
24 Jan	81	**THE WILD THE WILLING AND THE INNOCENT**		
		Chrysalis CHR 1307	19	5 wks
20 Feb	82 ●	**MECHANIX** *Chrysalis CHR 1360*	8	6 wks
12 Feb	83	**MAKING CONTACT** *Chrysalis CHR 1402*	32	4 wks
3 Sep	83	**HEADSTONE – THE BEST OF UFO** *Chrysalis CTY 1437*	39	4 wks
16 Nov	85	**MISDEMEANOUR** *Chrysalis CHR 1518*	74	2 wks

UGLY KID JOE *US, male vocal/instrumental group*   37 wks

13 Jun	92 ●	**AS UGLY AS THEY WANNA BE** *Mercury 8688232*	9	13 wks
12 Sep	92	**AMERICA'S LEAST WANTED** *Vertigo 5125712*	11	24 wks

U.K. *UK, male vocal/instrumental group*   3 wks

27 May	78	**U.K.** *Polydor 2302 080*	43	3 wks

U.K. SUBS *UK, male vocal/instrumental group*   26 wks

13 Oct	79	**ANOTHER KIND OF BLUES** *Gem GEMLP 100*	21	6 wks
19 Apr	80	**BRAND NEW AGE** *Gem GEMLP 106*	18	9 wks
27 Sep	80 ●	**CRASH COURSE** *Gem GEMLP 111*	8	6 wks
21 Feb	81	**DIMINISHED RESPONSIBILITY** *Gem GEMLP 112*	18	5 wks

Tracey ULLMAN *UK, female vocalist*   22 wks

3 Dec	83	**YOU BROKE MY HEART IN 17 PLACES** *Stiff SEEZ 51*	14	20 wks
8 Dec	84	**YOU CAUGHT ME OUT** *Stiff SEEZ 56*	92	2 wks

ULTRA VIVID SCENE *US, male vocalist*   1 wk

19 May	90	**JOY 1967–1990** *4AD CAD 005*	58	1 wk

ULTRAMARINE *UK, male instrumental duo*   1 wk

4 Sep	93	**UNITED KINGDOMS** *blanco y negro 4509934252*	49	1 wk

ULTRAVOX *UK/Canada, male vocal/instrumental group*   225 wks

19 Jul	80 ●	**VIENNA** *Chrysalis CHR 1296*	3	72 wks
19 Sep	81 ●	**RAGE IN EDEN** *Chrysalis CDL 1338*	4	23 wks
23 Oct	82 ●	**QUARTET** *Chrysalis CDL 1394*	6	30 wks
22 Oct	83 ●	**MONUMENT – THE SOUNDTRACK** *Chrysalis CUX 1452*	9	15 wks
14 Apr	84 ●	**LAMENT** *Chrysalis CDL 1459*	8	26 wks
10 Nov	84 ●	**THE COLLECTION** *Chrysalis UTV 1*	2	53 wks
25 Oct	86 ●	**U-VOX** *Chrysalis CDL 1545*	9	6 wks

See also Midge Ure.

UNDERCOVER *UK, male vocal/instrumental group*   9 wks

5 Dec	92	**CHECK OUT THE GROOVE** *PWL International HFCD 26*	26	9 wks

UNDERTONES *UK, male vocal/instrumental group*   50 wks

19 May	79	**THE UNDERTONES** *Sire SRK 6071*	13	21 wks
26 Apr	80 ●	**HYPNOTISED** *Sire SRK 6088*	6	10 wks
16 May	81	**POSITIVE TOUCH** *Ardeck ARD 103*	17	6 wks

U
319

Zooropa returned **U2** to number one after
they had just missed with Achtung Baby.
(Pictorial Press)
UB40 had a real monster hit with their
1993 release, Promises And Lies. *(Pictorial
Press)*

The debut album by **Wet Wet Wet** *was number one immediately before the starter set from*
Johnny Hates Jazz, *but the Wets didn't dry up. (Pictorial Press)*

19 Mar 83	**THE SIN OF PRIDE** *Ardeck ARD 104*	**43**	5 wks
10 Dec 83	**ALL WRAPPED UP** *Ardeck ARD 1654281/3*	**67**	4 wks
14 Jun 86	**CHER O'BOWLIES: PICK OF UNDERTONES**		
	Ardeck EMS 1172	**96**	1 wk
25 Sep 93	**TEENAGE KICKS** *Castle Communications CTVCD 121*	**45**	3 wks

UNION UK, male instrumental group *6 wks*

26 Oct 91	**WORLD IN UNION** *Columbia 4690471*	**17**	6 wks

UNION GAP – *See Gary PUCKETT and the UNION GAP*

UNTOUCHABLES US, male vocal/instrumental group *7 wks*

13 Jul 85	**WILD CHILD** *Stiff SEEZ 57*	**51**	7 wks

Dawn UPSHAW (soprano)/LONDON SINFONIETTA/David ZINMAN (conductor)
US, female vocalist with UK orchestra and conductor *18 wks*

23 Jan 93 ●	**GORECKI SYMPHONY NO.3** *Elektra Nonsuch 7559792822*	**6**	18 wks

Midge URE UK, male vocalist *26 wks*

19 Oct 85 ●	**THE GIFT** *Chrysalis CHR 1508*	**2**	15 wks
10 Sep 88	**ANSWERS TO NOTHING** *Chrysalis CHR 1649*	**30**	3 wks
28 Sep 91	**PURE** *Arista 211922*	**36**	2 wks
6 Mar 93 ●	**IF I WAS: THE VERY BEST OF MIDGE URE**		
	Chrysalis CDCHR 1987	**10**	6 wks

If I Was: The Very Best Of Midge Ure *includes tracks by Ultravox, Visage, Band Aid and Phil Lynott.*

URIAH HEEP UK, male vocal/instrumental group *51 wks*

13 Nov 71	**LOOK AT YOURSELF** *Island ILPS 9169*	**39**	1 wk
10 Jun 72	**DEMONS AND WIZARDS** *Bronze ILPS 9193*	**20**	11 wks
2 Dec 72	**THE MAGICIAN'S BIRTHDAY** *Bronze ILPS 9213*	**28**	3 wks
19 May 73	**LIVE** *Island ISLD 1*	**23**	8 wks
29 Sep 73	**SWEET FREEDOM** *Island ILPS 9245*	**18**	3 wks
29 Jun 74	**WONDERWORLD** *Bronze ILPS 9280*	**23**	3 wks
5 Jul 75 ●	**RETURN TO FANTASY** *Bronze ILPS 9335*	**7**	6 wks
12 Jun 76	**HIGH AND MIGHTY** *Island ILPS 9384*	**55**	1 wk
22 Mar 80	**CONQUEST** *Bronze BRON 524*	**37**	3 wks
17 Apr 82	**ABOMINOG** *Bronze BRON 538*	**34**	6 wks
18 Jun 83	**HEAD FIRST** *Bronze BRON 545*	**46**	4 wks
6 Apr 85	**EQUATOR** *Portrait PRT 261414*	**79**	2 wks

USA FOR AFRICA
US, male/female vocal/instrumental group *5 wks*

25 May 85	**WE ARE THE WORLD** *CBS USAID F1*	**31**	5 wks

This album contains tracks by various artists in addition to the title track.

US3 UK, male instrumental duo *5 wks*

31 Jul 93	**HAND ON THE TORCH** *Capitol CDEST 2195*	**40**	5 wks

UTAH SAINTS UK, male instrumental/sampling/vocal duo *15 wks*

5 Jun 93 ●	**UTAH SAINTS** *ffrr 8283792*	**10**	15 wks

U.T.F.O. *US, male vocal group* — 1 wk

| 16 Mar 85 | **ROXANNE ROXANNE (6 track version)** | | |
| | *Streetwave 6 TRACK X KHAN 506* .... | **72** | 1 wk |

UTOPIA *UK, male vocal/instrumental group* — 3 wks

| 1 Oct 77 | **OOPS SORRY WRONG PLANET** *Bearsville K 53517* .... | **59** | 1 wk |
| 16 Feb 80 | **ADVENTURES IN UTOPIA** *Island ILPS 9602* .... | **57** | 2 wks |

U2 *Ireland, male vocal/instrumental group* — 854 wks

29 Aug 81	**BOY** *Island ILPS 9646*	**52**	31 wks
24 Oct 81	**OCTOBER** *Island ILPS 9680*	**11**	42 wks
12 Mar 83 ★	**WAR** *Island ILPS 9733*	**1**	147 wks
3 Dec 83 ●	**U2 LIVE: UNDER A BLOOD RED SKY** *Island IMA 3* ...	**2**	203 wks
13 Oct 84 ★	**THE UNFORGETTABLE FIRE** *Island U 25*	**1**	130 wks
27 Jul 85	**WIDE AWAKE IN AMERICA (import)** *Island 902791A* ...	**11**	16 wks
21 Mar 87 ★	**THE JOSHUA TREE** *Island U 26*	**1**	129 wks
20 Feb 88	**THE JOSHUA TREE SINGLES** *Island U2 PK 1*	**100**	1 wk
22 Oct 88 ★	**RATTLE AND HUM** *Island U2 7*	**1**	54 wks
30 Nov 91 ●	**ACHTUNG BABY** *Island U 28*	**2**	77 wks
17 Jul 93 ★	**ZOOROPA** *Island CIDU 29*	**1†**	24 wks

Steve VAI *UK, male vocalist* — 16 wks

| 2 Jun 90 ● | **PASSION AND WARFARE** *Food For Thought GRUB 17* ... | **8** | 10 wks |
| 7 Aug 93 | **SEX AND RELIGION** *Relativity 4729472★* .... | **17** | 6 wks |

★ *Vai.*

Frankie VALLI – *See FOUR SEASONS*

VAN DER GRAAF GENERATOR
UK, male vocal/instrumental group — 2 wks

| 25 Apr 70 | **THE LEAST WE CAN DO IS WAVE TO EACH OTHER** | | |
| | *Charisma CAS 1007* .... | **47** | 2 wks |

VAN HALEN *US/Holland, male vocal/instrumental group* — 95 wks

27 May 78	**VAN HALEN** *Warner Bros. K 56470*	**34**	11 wks
14 Apr 79	**VAN HALEN II** *Warner Bros. K 566116*	**23**	7 wks
5 Apr 80	**WOMEN AND CHILDREN FIRST** *Warner Bros. K 56793* .	**15**	7 wks
23 May 81	**FAIR WARNING** *Warner Bros. K 56899*	**49**	4 wks
1 May 82	**DIVER DOWN** *Warner Bros. K 57003*	**36**	5 wks
4 Feb 84	**1984** *Warner Bros. 92–3985*	**15**	23 wks
5 Apr 86	**5150** *Warner Bros. WS 5150*	**16**	18 wks
4 Jun 88	**OU812** *Warner Bros. WX 177*	**16**	12 wks
29 Jun 91	**FOR UNLAWFUL CARNAL KNOWLEDGE**		
	Warner Brothers WX 420	**12**	5 wks
6 Mar 93	**LIVE: RIGHT HERE RIGHT NOW** *Warner Bros 9362451982*	**24**	3 wks

Luther VANDROSS   *US, male vocalist*   *226 wks*

21 Jan	84	**BUSY BODY** *Epic EPC 25608*	42	8 wks
6 Apr	85	**THE NIGHT I FELL IN LOVE** *Epic EPC 26387*	19	10 wks
1 Nov	86 ●	**GIVE ME THE REASON** *Epic EPC 450134–1*	3	99 wks
21 Feb	87	**NEVER TOO MUCH** *Epic EPC 32807*	41	30 wks
4 Jul	87	**FOREVER, FOR ALWAYS, FOR LOVE** *Epic EPC 25013* .	23	16 wks
16 Apr	88	**BUSY BODY (re-issue)** *Epic 460183 1*	78	4 wks
29 Oct	88 ●	**ANY LOVE** *Epic 462908 1*	3	22 wks
11 Nov	89	**BEST OF LUTHER VANDROSS – BEST OF LOVE** *Epic 465801 1*	14	23 wks
25 May	91 ●	**POWER OF LOVE** *Epic 4680121*	9	9 wks
12 Jun	93	**NEVER LET ME GO** *Epic 4735982*	11	5 wks

VANGELIS   *Greece, male instrumentalist – keyboards*   *145 wks*

10 Jan	76	**HEAVEN AND HELL** *RCA Victor RS 1025*	31	7 wks
9 Oct	76	**ALBEDO 0.39** *RCA Victor RS 1080*	18	6 wks
18 Apr	81 ●	**CHARIOTS OF FIRE (film soundtrack)** *Polydor POLS 1026*	5	97 wks
5 May	84	**CHARIOTS OF FIRE (film soundtrack) (re-issue)** *Polydor POLD 5160*	39	10 wks
13 Oct	84	**SOIL FESTIVITIES** *Polydor POLH 11*	55	4 wks
30 Mar	85	**MASK** *Polydor POLH 19*	69	2 wks
22 Jul	89	**THEMES** *Polydor VGTV 1*	11	13 wks
24 Oct	92	**1492 – THE CONQUEST OF PARADISE (film soundtrack)** *East West 4509910142*	33	6 wks

See also Jon and Vangelis.

VANILLA ICE   *US, male rapper*   *23 wks*

15 Dec	90 ●	**TO THE EXTREME** *SBK SBKLP 9*	4	20 wks
6 Jul	91	**EXTREMELY LIVE** *SBK SBKLP 12*	35	3 wks

VANILLA FUDGE   *US, male vocal/instrumental group*   *3 wks*

4 Nov	67	**VANILLA FUDGE** *Atlantic 588–086*	31	3 wks

VAPORS   *UK, male vocal/instrumental group*   *6 wks*

7 Jun	80	**NEW CLEAR DAYS** *United Artists UAG 30300*	44	6 wks

VARDIS   *UK, male vocal/instrumental group*   *1 wk*

1 Nov	80	**100 MPH** *Logo MOGO 4012*	52	1 wk

Frankie VAUGHAN   *UK, male vocalist*   *20 wks*

5 Sep	59 ●	**FRANKIE VAUGHAN AT THE LONDON PALLADIUM** *Philips BDL 7330*	6	2 wks
4 Nov	67	**FRANKIE VAUGHAN SONGBOOK** *Philips DBL 001*	40	1 wk
25 Nov	67	**THERE MUST BE A WAY** *Columbia SCX 6200*	22	8 wks
12 Nov	77	**100 GOLDEN GREATS** *Ronco RTDX 2021*	24	9 wks

Sarah VAUGHAN   *US, female vocalist*   *1 wk*

20 Mar	60	**NO COUNT – SARAH** *Mercury MMC 14021*	19	1 wk

Stevie Ray VAUGHAN and DOUBLE TROUBLE
US, male vocal/instrumental group   *1 wk*

15 Jul	89	**IN STEP** *Epic 463395 1*	63	1 wk

V

323

VAUGHAN BROTHERS
US, male vocal/instrumental group *1 wk*

20 Oct	90	**FAMILY STYLE** *Epic 4670141*	**63**	1 wk

Bobby VEE *US, male vocalist* *73 wks*

24 Feb	62 ●	**TAKE GOOD CARE OF MY BABY** *London HAG 2428* ..	**7**	8 wks
31 Mar	62	**HITS OF THE ROCKIN' 50'S** *London HAG 2406*	**20**	1 wk
27 Oct	62 ●	**BOBBY VEE MEETS THE CRICKETS** *Liberty LBY 1086★* .	**2**	27 wks
12 Jan	63 ●	**A BOBBY VEE RECORDING SESSION** *Liberty LBY 1084*	**10**	11 wks
20 Apr	63 ●	**BOBBY VEE'S GOLDEN GREATS** *Liberty LBY 1112*	**10**	14 wks
5 Oct	63	**THE NIGHT HAS A THOUSAND EYES** *Liberty LIB 1139*	**15**	2 wks
19 Apr	80 ●	**THE BOBBY VEE SINGLES ALBUM** *United Artists UAG 30253*	**5**	10 wks

★ Bobby Vee and the Crickets.

Suzanne VEGA *US, female vocalist* *121 wks*

19 Oct	85	**SUZANNE VEGA** *A & M AMA 5072*	**11**	71 wks
9 May	87 ●	**SOLITUDE STANDING** *A & M SUZLP 2*	**2**	39 wks
28 Apr	90 ●	**DAYS OF OPEN HAND** *A & M 3952931*	**7**	7 wks
19 Sep	92	**99.9° F** *A & M 5400122*	**20**	4 wks

Rosie VELA *US, female vocalist* *11 wks*

31 Jan	87	**ZAZU** *A & M AMA 5016*	**20**	11 wks

VELVET UNDERGROUND
US, male/female vocal/instrumental group *5 wks*

23 Feb	85	**V.U.** *Polydor POLD 5167*	**47**	4 wks
12 Nov	93	**LIVE MCMXCIII** *Sire 9362454642*	**70**	1 wk

VENOM *UK, male vocal/instrumental group* *2 wks*

21 Apr	84	**AT WAR WITH SATAN** *Neat NEAT 1015*	**64**	1 wk
13 Apr	85	**POSSESSED** *Neat NEAT 1024*	**99**	1 wk

Anthony VENTURA ORCHESTRA
Switzerland, orchestra *4 wks*

20 Jan	79	**DREAM LOVER** *Lotus WH 5007*	**44**	4 wks

Tom VERLAINE *US, male vocalist* *1 wk*

14 Mar	87	**FLASH LIGHT** *Fontana SFLP 1*	**99**	1 wk

VERVE *UK, male vocal/instrumental group* *2 wks*

3 Jul	93	**A STORM IN HEAVEN** *Hut CDHUT 10*	**27**	2 wks

VIBRATORS *UK, male vocal/instrumental group* *7 wks*

25 Jun	77	**THE VIBRATORS** *Epic EPC 82907*	**49**	5 wks
29 Apr	78	**V2** *Epic EPC 82495*	**33**	2 wks

VICE SQUAD UK, male/female vocal/instrumental group 10 wks

| 24 Oct 81 | NO CAUSE FOR CONCERN Zonophone ZEM 103 ...... | 32 | 5 wks |
| 22 May 82 | STAND STRONG STAND PROUD Zonophone ZEM 104 . | 47 | 5 wks |

Sid VICIOUS UK, male vocalist 8 wks

| 15 Dec 79 | SID SINGS Virgin V 2144 .... | 30 | 8 wks |

VIENNA PHILHARMONIC ORCHESTRA – See Aram KHATCHATURIAN/VIENNA PHILHARMONIC ORCHESTRA

VIENNA SYMPHONY ORCHESTRA
Austria, orchestra 4 wks

| 4 Apr 87 | SYMPHONIC ROCK WITH THE VIENNA SYMPHONY ORCHESTRA Stylus SMR 730 .... | 43 | 4 wks |

VILLAGE PEOPLE US, male vocal group 29 wks

27 Jan 79	CRUISIN' Mercury 9109 614	24	9 wks
12 May 79	GO WEST Mercury 9109 621	14	19 wks
18 Dec 92	THE BEST OF THE VILLAGE PEOPLE Bell 4321178312 .	72	1 wk

Gene VINCENT US, male vocalist 2 wks

| 16 Jul 60 | CRAZY TIMES Capitol T 1342 .... | 12 | 2 wks |

Vinnie VINCENT US, male vocalist/instrumentalist – guitar 2 wks

| 28 May 88 | ALL SYSTEMS GO Chrysalis CHR 1626 .... | 51 | 2 wks |

Bobby VINTON US, male vocalist 2 wks

| 17 Nov 90 | BLUE VELVET Epic 4675701 .... | 67 | 2 wks |

VIOLENT FEMMES
US, male/female vocal/instrumental group 1 wk

| 1 Mar 86 | THE BLIND LEADING THE NAKED Slash SLAP 10 .... | 81 | 1 wk |

VIOLINSKI UK, male instrumental group 1 wk

| 26 May 79 | NO CAUSE FOR ALARM Jet JETLU 219 .... | 49 | 1 wk |

VISAGE UK, male vocal/instrumental group 58 wks

24 Jan 81	VISAGE Polydor 2490 157	13	29 wks
3 Apr 82 ●	THE ANVIL Polydor POLD 5050	6	16 wks
19 Nov 83	FADE TO GREY – THE SINGLES COLLECTION Polydor POLD 5117	38	11 wks
3 Nov 84	BEAT BOY Polydor POLH 12	79	2 wks

See also Midge Ure.

VIXEN US, female vocal/instrumental group 5 wks

| 8 Oct 88 | VIXEN Manhattan MTL 1028 .... | 66 | 1 wk |
| 18 Aug 90 | REV IT UP EMI USA MTL 1054 .... | 20 | 4 wks |

V
325

VOICE OF THE BEEHIVE
UK/US, male/female vocal/instrumental group   *26 wks*

2 Jul 88	**LET IT BEE** *London LONLP 57*	**13**	13 wks
24 Aug 91	**HONEY LINGERS** *London 8282591*	**17**	13 wks

Herbert VON KARAJAN *Austria, male conductor*   *9 wks*

26 Sep 70	**BEETHOVEN TRIPLE CONCERTO** *HMV ASD 2582* ..	**51**	2 wks
16 Apr 88	**THE ESSENTIAL KARAJAN**		
	Deutsche Grammophon HVKTV 1	**51**	5 wks
3 Aug 91	**HOLST: THE PLANETS** *Deutsche Grammophon 4352891* ...	**52**	2 wks

On the Beethoven concerto, the soloists were David Oistrakh (violin), Mstislav Rostropovich (cello) and Sviatoslav Richter (piano). Von Karajan conducted the Berlin Philharmonic Orchestra – Germany, orchestra.

VOW WOW *Japan/US, male vocal/instrumental group*   *1 wk*

18 Mar 89	**HELTER SKELTER** *Arista 209691*	**75**	1 wk

VOYAGE *UK/France, disco aggregation*   *1 wk*

9 Sep 78	**VOYAGE** *GTO GTLP 030*	**59**	1 wk

WAH! – *See MIGHTY WAH!*

John WAITE *UK, male vocalist*   *3 wks*

10 Nov 84	**NO BREAKS** *EMI America WAIT 1*	**64**	3 wks

Tom WAITS *US, male vocalist*   *19 wks*

8 Oct 83	**SWORDFISHTROMBONE** *Island ILPS 9762*	**62**	3 wks
19 Oct 85	**RAIN DOGS** *Island ILPS 9803*	**29**	5 wks
5 Sep 87	**FRANK'S WILD YEARS** *Island ITW 3*	**20**	5 wks
8 Oct 88	**BIG TIME** *Island ITW 4*	**84**	1 wk
19 Sep 92	**BONE MACHINE** *Island CID 9993*	**26**	3 wks
20 Nov 93	**THE BLACK RIDER** *Island CID 8021*	**47**	2 wks

WAILERS – *See Bob MARLEY and the WAILERS*

Rick WAKEMAN *UK, male instrumentalist – keyboards*   *129 wks*

24 Feb 73 ●	**THE SIX WIVES OF HENRY VIII** *A & M AMLH 64361* .	**7**	22 wks
18 May 74 ★	**JOURNEY TO THE CENTRE OF THE EARTH**		
	A & M AMLH 63621	**1**	30 wks
12 Apr 75 ●	**THE MYTHS AND LEGENDS OF KING ARTHUR AND**		
	THE KNIGHTS OF THE ROUND TABLE		
	A & M AMLH 64515 0022	**2**	28 wks
24 Apr 76 ●	**NO EARTHLY CONNECTION** *A & M AMLK 64583* ...	**9**	9 wks
12 Feb 77	**WHITE ROCK** *A & M AMLH 64614*	**14**	9 wks
3 Dec 77	**CRIMINAL RECORD** *A & M AMLK 64660*	**25**	5 wks
2 Jun 79	**RHAPSODIES** *A & M AMLX 68508*	**25**	10 wks

27 Jun	81	**1984** *Charisma CDS 4022*	**24**	9 wks
13 Oct	84	**BEYOND THE PLANETS** *Telstar STAR 2244★*	**64**	6 wks
16 May	87	**THE GOSPELS** *Stylus SMR 729*	**94**	1 wk

★ *Kevin Peek and Rick Wakeman.*
See also Anderson Bruford Wakeman Howe.

Scott WALKER *US, male vocalist*   *56 wks*

16 Sep	67	● **SCOTT** *Philips SBL 7816*	**3**	17 wks
20 Apr	68	★ **SCOTT 2** *Philips SBL 7840*	**1**	18 wks
5 Apr	69	● **SCOTT 3** *Philips S 7882*	**3**	4 wks
5 Jul	69	● **SONGS FROM HIS TV SERIES** *Philips SBL 7900*	**7**	3 wks
31 Mar	84	**CLIMATE OF HUNTER** *Virgin V 2303*	**60**	2 wks
25 Jan	92	● **NO REGRETS – THE BEST OF SCOTT WALKER AND THE WALKER BROTHERS** *Fontana 5108312★*	**4**	12 wks

★ *Scott Walker and the Walker Brothers.*
See also Walker Brothers.

WALKER BROTHERS *US, male vocal group*   *108 wks*

18 Dec	65	● **TAKE IT EASY** *Philips BL 7691*	**3**	36 wks
3 Sep	66	● **PORTRAIT** *Philips BL 7691*	**3**	23 wks
18 Mar	67	● **IMAGES** *Philips SBL 7770*	**6**	15 wks
16 Sep	67	● **WALKER BROTHERS' STORY** *Philips DBL 002*	**9**	19 wks
21 Feb	76	**NO REGRETS** *GTO GTLP 007*	**49**	3 wks
25 Jan	92	● **NO REGRETS – THE BEST OF SCOTT WALKER AND THE WALKER BROTHERS** *Fontana 5108312★*	**4**	12 wks

★ *Scott Walker and the Walker Brothers.*
See also Scott Walker.

W
327

Bob WALLIS and his STORYVILLE JAZZMEN
UK, male vocal/instrumental group   *1 wk*

11 Jun	60	**EVERYBODY LOVES SATURDAY NIGHT** *Top Rank BUY 023*	**20**	1 wk

Joe WALSH *US, male vocalist*   *20 wks*

17 Apr	76	**YOU CAN'T ARGUE WITH A SICK MIND** *Anchor ABCL 5156*	**28**	3 wks
10 Jan	78	**BUT SERIOUSLY FOLKS** *Asylum K 53081*	**16**	17 wks

WANG CHUNG *UK, male vocal/instrumental group*   *5 wks*

21 Apr	84	**POINTS ON THE CURVE** *Geffen GEF 25589*	**34**	5 wks

WAR – *See Eric BURDON and WAR*

Clifford T. WARD *UK, male vocalist*   *5 wks*

21 Jul	73	**HOME THOUGHTS** *Charisma CAS 1066*	**40**	3 wks
16 Feb	74	**MANTLE PIECES** *Charisma CAS 1077*	**42**	2 wks

Michael WARD *UK, male vocalist*   *3 wks*

5 Jan	74	**INTRODUCING MICHAEL WARD** *Philips 6308 189*	**26**	3 wks

WARLOCK *Germany, male/female vocal/instrumental group*   *2 wks*

14 Nov	87	**TRIUMPH AND AGONY** *Vertigo VERH 50*	**54**	2 wks

Jennifer WARNES US, female vocalist   12 wks

18 Jul	87	**FAMOUS BLUE RAINCOAT** RCA PL 90048	**33**	12 wks

WARRANT US, male vocal/instrumental group   1 wk

19 Sep	92	**DOG EAT DOG** Columbia 4720332	**74**	1 wk

Dionne WARWICK US, female vocalist   144 wks

23 May	64	**PRESENTING DIONNE WARWICK** Pye NPL 28037	**14**	10 wks
7 May	66 ●	**BEST OF DIONNE WARWICK** Pye NPL 28078	**8**	11 wks
4 Feb	67	**HERE WHERE THERE IS LOVE** Pye NPL 28096	**39**	2 wks
18 May	68 ●	**VALLEY OF THE DOLLS** Pye NSPL 28114	**10**	13 wks
23 May	70	**GREATEST HITS VOL. 1** Wand WNS 1	**31**	26 wks
6 Jun	70	**GREATEST HITS VOL. 2** Wand WNS 2	**28**	14 wks
30 Oct	82 ●	**HEARTBREAKER** Arista 204 974	**3**	33 wks
21 May	83	**THE COLLECTION** Arista DIONE 1	**11**	17 wks
29 Oct	83	**SO AMAZING** Arista 205 755	**60**	3 wks
23 Feb	85	**WITHOUT YOUR LOVE** Arista 206 571	**86**	2 wks
6 Jan	90 ●	**LOVE SONGS** Arista 410441	**6**	13 wks

WAS (NOT WAS)
US, male vocal/instrumental group   15 wks

9 Apr	88	**WHAT UP DOG?** Fontana SFLP 4	**47**	6 wks
21 Jul	90	**ARE YOU OKAY?** Fontana 8463511	**35**	6 wks
13 Jun	92	**HELLO DAD I'M IN JAIL** Fontana 5124642	**61**	3 wks

Geno WASHINGTON UK, male vocalist   51 wks

10 Dec	66 ●	**HAND CLAPPIN' – FOOT STOMPIN' – FUNKY BUTT – LIVE!** Piccadilly NPL 38026	**5**	38 wks
23 Sep	67 ●	**HIPSTERS, FLIPSTERS, AND FINGER POPPIN' DADDIES** Piccadilly NSPL 38032	**8**	13 wks

Grover WASHINGTON Jr
US, male instrumentalist – saxophone   10 wks

9 May	81	**WINELIGHT** Elektra K 52262	**34**	9 wks
19 Dec	81	**COME MORNING** Elektra K 52337	**98**	1 wk

W.A.S.P. US, male vocal/instrumental group   23 wks

8 Sep	84	**W.A.S.P.** Capitol EJ 2401951	**51**	2 wks
9 Nov	85	**THE LAST COMMAND** Capitol WASP 2	**48**	1 wk
8 Nov	86	**INSIDE THE ELECTRIC CIRCUS** Capitol EST 2025	**53**	3 wks
26 Sep	87	**LIVE IN THE RAW** Capitol EST 2040	**23**	4 wks
15 Apr	89 ●	**THE HEADLESS CHILDREN** Capitol EST 2087	**8**	10 wks
20 Jun	92	**THE CRIMSON IDOL** Parlophone CDPCSD 118	**21**	2 wks
6 Nov	93	**FIRST BLOOD ... LAST CUTS** Capitol CDESTFG 2217 ..	**69**	1 wk

WATERBOYS UK, male vocal/instrumental group   69 wks

16 Jun	84	**A PAGAN PLACE** Ensign ENCL 3	**100**	1 wk
28 Sep	85	**THIS IS THE SEA** Ensign ENCL 5	**37**	17 wks
29 Oct	88	**FISHERMAN'S BLUES** Ensign CHEN 5	**13**	19 wks
22 Sep	90 ●	**ROOM TO ROAM** Ensign CHEN 16	**5**	6 wks
11 May	91 ●	**BEST OF THE WATERBOYS '81–'91** Ensign CHEN 19	**2**	16 wks
5 Jun	93 ●	**DREAM HARDER** Geffen GED 24476	**5**	10 wks

WATERFRONT UK, male vocal/instrumental duo   3 wks

| 12 Aug 89 | **WATERFRONT** Polydor 837970 1 .... | **45** | 3 wks |

Roger WATERS
UK, male vocalist/instrumentalist – bass   25 wks

12 May 84	**THE PROS AND CONS OF HITCH-HIKING**		
	Harvest SHVL 240105	**13**	11 wks
27 Jun 87	**RADIO K.A.O.S.** EMI KAOS 1	**25**	7 wks
22 Sep 90	**THE WALL – LIVE IN BERLIN** Mercury 8466111	**27**	3 wks
19 Sep 92 ●	**AMUSED TO DEATH** Columbia 4687612	**8**	4 wks

Jody WATLEY US, female vocalist   4 wks

| 5 Sep 87 | **JODY WATLEY** MCA MCG 6024 .... | **62** | 2 wks |
| 27 May 89 | **LARGER THAN LIFE** MCA MCG 6044 .... | **39** | 2 wks |

WAVES – See KATRINA and the WAVES

WAX UK/US, male vocal/instrumental duo   3 wks

| 12 Sep 87 | **AMERICAN ENGLISH** RCA PL 71430 .... | **59** | 3 wks |

Jeff WAYNE US/UK, orchestra and cast   234 wks

| 1 Jul 78 ● | **WAR OF THE WORLDS** CBS 96000 .... | **5** | 232 wks |
| 3 Oct 92 | **SPARTACUS** Columbia 4720302 .... | **36** | 2 wks |

Both albums feature various artists but are commonly credited to Jeff Wayne, the creator and producer.

WAYSTED UK, male vocal/instrumental group   5 wks

| 8 Oct 83 | **VICES** Chrysalis CHR 1438 .... | **78** | 3 wks |
| 22 Sep 84 | **WAYSTED** Music For Nations MFN 31 .... | **73** | 2 wks |

WEATHER PROPHETS
UK, male vocal/instrumental group   2 wks

| 9 May 87 | **MAYFLOWER** Elevation ELV 1 .... | **67** | 2 wks |

WEATHER REPORT US, male instrumental group   12 wks

23 Apr 77	**HEAVY WEATHER** CBS 81775	**43**	6 wks
11 Nov 78	**MR. GONE** CBS 82775	**47**	3 wks
27 Feb 82	**WEATHER REPORT** CBS 85326	**88**	2 wks
24 Mar 84	**DOMINO THEORY** CBS 25839	**54**	1 wk

Marti WEBB UK, female vocalist   33 wks

16 Feb 80 ●	**TELL ME ON A SUNDAY** Polydor POLD 5031	**2**	23 wks
28 Sep 85	**ENCORE** Starblend BLEND 1	**55**	4 wks
6 Dec 86	**ALWAYS THERE** BBC REB 619	**65**	5 wks
10 Oct 92	**THE MAGIC OF THE MUSICALS**		
	Quality Television QTV 013★	**55**	1 wk

★ Marti Webb and Mark Rattray.

Ben WEBSTER – See Gerry MULLIGAN and Ben WEBSTER

W
329

WEDDING PRESENT
UK, male vocal/instrumental group   *18 wks*

24 Oct	87	**GEORGE BEST** *Reception LEEDS 001*	**47**	2 wks
23 Jul	88	**TOMMY** *Reception LEEDS 2*	**42**	3 wks
29 Apr	89	**UKRAINSKI VISTUIP V JOHNA PEELA** *RCA PL 74104* .	**22**	3 wks
4 Nov	89	**BIZZARO** *RCA PL 74302*	**22**	3 wks
8 Jun	91	**SEA MONSTERS** *RCA PL 75012*	**13**	3 wks
20 Jun	92	**HIT PARADE** *RCA PD 75343*	**22**	2 wks
16 Jan	93	**HIT PARADE 2** *RCA 74321127752*	**19**	2 wks

WEE PAPA GIRL RAPPERS *UK, female vocal duo*   *3 wks*

5 Nov	88	**THE BEAT, THE RHYME AND THE NOISE** *Jive HIP 67*	**39**	3 wks

Bert WEEDON *UK, male instrumentalist – guitar*   *26 wks*

16 Jul	60	**KING SIZE GUITAR** *Top Rank BUY 026*	**18**	1 wk
23 Oct	76 ★	**22 GOLDEN GUITAR GREATS** *Warwick WW 5019*	**1**	25 wks

WELCH – *See MARVIN, WELCH and FARRAR*

Paul WELLER *UK, male vocalist*   *22 wks*

12 Sep	92 ●	**PAUL WELLER** *Go! Discs 8283432*	**8**	7 wks
18 Sep	93 ●	**WILD WOOD** *Go! Discs 8284352*	**2†**	15 wks

WENDY and LISA *US, female vocal duo*   *7 wks*

10 Oct	87	**WENDY AND LISA** *Virgin V 2444*	**84**	2 wks
28 Mar	89	**FRUIT AT THE BOTTOM** *Virgin V 2580*	**45**	2 wks
4 Aug	90	**EROICA** *Virgin V 2633*	**33**	3 wks

WESTWORLD
UK/US, male/female vocal/instrumental group   *2 wks*

5 Sep	87	**WHERE THE ACTION IS** *RCA PL 71429*	**49**	2 wks

WET WET WET *UK, male vocal/instrumental group*   *145 wks*

3 Oct	87 ★	**POPPED IN SOULED OUT** *Precious JWWWL 1*	**1**	71 wks
19 Nov	88 ●	**THE MEMPHIS SESSIONS** *Precious JWWWL 2*	**3**	13 wks
11 Nov	89 ●	**HOLDING BACK THE RIVER** *Precious 842011 1*	**2**	26 wks
8 Feb	92 ★	**HIGH ON THE HAPPY SIDE** *Precious 5104272*	**1**	25 wks
29 May	93 ●	**LIVE AT THE ROYAL ALBERT HALL** *Precious 5147742★* .	**10**	4 wks
20 Nov	93 ●	**END OF PART ONE (THEIR GREATEST HITS)**		
		Precious 5184772	**4†**	6 wks

★ *Wet Wet Wet with the Wren Orchestra.*

WE'VE GOT A FUZZBOX AND WE'RE GONNA USE IT *UK, female vocal/instrumental group*   *6 wks*

26 Aug	89 ●	**BIG BANG** *WEA WX 282*	**5**	6 wks

WHAM! *UK, male vocal/instrumental duo*   *233 wks*

9 Jul	83 ★	**FANTASTIC** *Inner Vision IVL 25328*	**1**	116 wks
17 Nov	84 ★	**MAKE IT BIG** *Epic EPC 86311*	**1**	72 wks
19 Jul	86 ●	**THE FINAL** *Epic EPC 88681*	**2**	45 wks

CARON WHEELER UK, female vocalist   5 wks

13 Oct 90	**UK BLAK** *RCA PL 74751*	14	5 wks

WHISPERS US, male vocal group   9 wks

| 14 Mar 81 | **IMAGINATION** *Solar SOLA 7* .... | 42 | 5 wks |
| 6 Jun 87 | **JUST GETS BETTER WITH TIME** *Solar MCF 3381* ...... | 63 | 4 wks |

Alan WHITE UK, male instrumentalist – drums   4 wks

| 13 Mar 76 | **RAMSHACKLED** *Atlantic K 50217* .... | 41 | 4 wks |

Barry WHITE US, male vocalist   149 wks

9 Mar 74	**STONE GON'** *Pye NSPL 28186*	18	17 wks
6 Apr 74	**RHAPSODY IN WHITE** *Pye NSPL 28191*	50	1 wk
2 Nov 74 ●	**CAN'T GET ENOUGH** *20th Century BT 444*	4	34 wks
26 Apr 75	**JUST ANOTHER WAY TO SAY I LOVE YOU**		
	20th Century BT 466	12	15 wks
22 Nov 75	**GREATEST HITS** *20th Century BTH 8000*	18	12 wks
21 Feb 76	**LET THE MUSIC PLAY** *20th Century BT 502*	22	14 wks
9 Apr 77	**BARRY WHITE'S GREATEST HITS VOL. 2**		
	20th Century BTH 8001	17	7 wks
10 Feb 79	**THE MAN** *20th Century BT 571*	46	4 wks
21 Dec 85	**HEART AND SOUL** *K-Tel NE 1316*	34	10 wks
17 Oct 87	**THE RIGHT NIGHT AND BARRY WHITE**		
	Breakout AMA 5154	74	6 wks
2 Jul 88 ●	**THE COLLECTION** *Mercury BWTV 1*	5	29 wks

Karyn WHITE US, female vocalist   30 wks

| 11 Mar 89 | **KARYN WHITE** *Warner Bros. WX 235* .... | 20 | 27 wks |
| 21 Sep 91 | **RITUAL OF LOVE** *Warner Bros WX 411* .... | 31 | 3 wks |

Snowy WHITE UK, male vocalist/instrumentalist – guitar   5 wks

| 11 Feb 84 | **WHITE FLAMES** *Towerbell TOWLP 3* .... | 21 | 4 wks |
| 9 Feb 85 | **SNOWY WHITE** *Towerbell TOWLP 8* .... | 88 | 1 wk |

Tony Joe WHITE US, male vocalist   1 wk

| 26 Sep 70 | **TONY JOE** *CBS 63800* .... | 63 | 1 wk |

WHITE LION US, male vocal/instrumental group   3 wks

| 1 Jul 89 | **BIG GAME** *Atlantic WX 277* .... | 47 | 1 wk |
| 20 Apr 91 | **MANE ATTRACTION** *Atlantic WX 415* .... | 31 | 2 wks |

WHITESNAKE UK, male vocal/instrumental group   145 wks

18 Nov 78	**TROUBLE** *EMI International INS 3022*	50	2 wks
13 Oct 79	**LOVE HUNTER** *United Artists UAG 30264*	29	7 wks
7 Jun 80 ●	**READY AND WILLING** *United Artists UAG 30302*	6	15 wks
8 Nov 80 ●	**LIVE IN THE HEART OF THE CITY**		
	United Artists SNAKE 1	5	15 wks
18 Apr 81 ●	**COME AND GET IT** *Liberty LBG 30327*	2	23 wks
27 Nov 82 ●	**SAINTS 'N' SINNERS** *Liberty LBG 30354*	9	9 wks
11 Feb 84 ●	**SLIDE IT IN** *Liberty LBG 2400001*	9	7 wks
11 Apr 87 ●	**WHITESNAKE 1987** *EMI EMC 3528*	8	57 wks
25 Nov 89 ●	**SLIP OF THE TONGUE** *EMI EMD 1013*	10	10 wks

W
331

Slim WHITMAN US, male vocalist — *59 wks*

14 Dec 74	HAPPY ANNIVERSARY United Artists UAS 29670	44	2 wks
31 Jan 76 ★	THE VERY BEST OF SLIM WHITMAN		
	United Artists UAS 29898	1	17 wks
15 Jan 77 ★	RED RIVER VALLEY United Artists UAS 29993	1	14 wks
15 Oct 77 ●	HOME ON THE RANGE United Artists UATV 30102	2	13 wks
13 Jan 79	GHOST RIDERS IN THE SKY United Artists UATV 30202	27	6 wks
22 Dec 79	SLIM WHITMAN'S 20 GREATEST LOVE SONGS		
	United Artists UAG 30270	18	7 wks

Roger WHITTAKER Kenya, male vocalist — *110 wks*

28 Jun 70	I DON'T BELIEVE IN IF ANYMORE Columbia SCX 6404	23	1 wk
3 Apr 71	NEW WORLD IN THE MORNING Columbia SCX 6456 ..	45	2 wks
6 Sep 75 ●	THE VERY BEST OF ROGER WHITTAKER		
	Columbia SCX 6560	5	42 wks
15 May 76	THE SECOND ALBUM OF THE VERY BEST OF ROGER		
	WHITTAKER EMI EMC 3117	27	7 wks
9 Dec 78	ROGER WHITTAKER SINGS THE HITS		
	Columbia SCX 6601	52	5 wks
4 Aug 79	20 ALL TIME GREATS Polydor POLTV 8	24	9 wks
7 Feb 81	THE ROGER WHITTAKER ALBUM K-Tel NE 1105 ...	18	14 wks
27 Dec 86	SKYE BOAT SONG AND OTHER GREAT SONGS		
	Tembo TMB 113	89	1 wk
23 May 87	HIS FINEST COLLECTION Tembo RWTV 1	15	19 wks
23 Sep 89	HOME LOVIN' MAN Tembo RWTV 2	20	10 wks

WHO UK, male vocal/instrumental group — *203 wks*

25 Dec 65 ●	MY GENERATION Brunswick LAT 8616	5	11 wks
17 Dec 66 ●	A QUICK ONE Reaction 593–002	4	17 wks
13 Jan 68	THE WHO SELL-OUT Track 613–002	13	11 wks
7 Jun 69 ●	TOMMY Track 613–013/4	2	9 wks
6 Jun 70 ●	LIVE AT LEEDS Track 2406–001	3	21 wks
11 Sep 71 ★	WHO'S NEXT Track 2408–102	1	13 wks
18 Dec 71 ●	MEATY, BEATY, BIG AND BOUNCY Track 2406–006 ..	9	8 wks
17 Nov 73 ●	QUADROPHENIA Track 2647–013	2	13 wks
26 Oct 74 ●	ODDS AND SODS Track 2406–116	10	4 wks
23 Aug 75	TOMMY (film soundtrack) Track 2657–007	30	2 wks
18 Oct 75 ●	THE WHO BY NUMBERS Polydor 2490–129	7	6 wks
9 Oct 76 ●	THE STORY OF THE WHO Polydor 2683–069	2	18 wks
9 Sep 78 ●	WHO ARE YOU Polydor WHOD 5004	6	9 wks
30 Jun 79	THE KIDS ARE ALRIGHT Polydor 2675 174	26	13 wks
25 Oct 80	MY GENERATION (re-issue) Virgin V 2179	20	7 wks
28 Mar 81 ●	FACE DANCES Polydor WHOD 5037	2	9 wks
11 Sep 82	IT'S HARD Polydor WHOD 5066	11	6 wks
17 Nov 84	WHO'S LAST MCA WHO 1	48	4 wks
12 Oct 85	THE WHO COLLECTION Impression IMDP 4	44	6 wks
19 Mar 88 ●	WHO'S BETTER WHO'S BEST Polydor WTV 1	10	11 wks
19 Nov 88	THE WHO COLLECTION Stylus SMR 570	71	4 wks
24 Mar 90	JOIN TOGETHER Virgin VDT 102	59	1 wk

The two albums titled The Who Collection *are different.*

Jane WIEDLIN US, female vocalist — *3 wks*

| 24 Sep 88 | FUR Manhattan MTL 1029 .... | 48 | 3 wks |

WILD HORSES UK, male vocal/instrumental group — *4 wks*

| 26 Apr 80 | WILD HORSES EMI EMC 3324 .... | 38 | 4 wks |

Eugene WILDE US, male vocalist — *4 wks*

| 8 Dec 84 | EUGENE WILDE Fourth & Broadway BRLP 502 .... | 67 | 4 wks |

Kim WILDE   UK, *female vocalist*   *88 wks*

11 Jul	81 ●	KIM WILDE *RAK SRAK 544*	**3**	14 wks
22 May	82	SELECT *RAK SRAK 548*	**19**	11 wks
26 Nov	83	CATCH AS CATCH CAN *RAK SRAK 165408*	**90**	1 wk
17 Nov	84	TEASES AND DARES *MCA MCF 3250*	**66**	2 wks
18 May	85	THE VERY BEST OF KIM WILDE *RAK WILDE 1*	**78**	4 wks
15 Nov	86	ANOTHER STEP *MCA MCF 3339*	**73**	5 wks
25 Jun	88 ●	CLOSE *MCA MCG 6030*	**8**	38 wks
26 May	90	LOVE MOVES *MCA MCG 6088*	**37**	3 wks
30 May	92	LOVE IS *MCA MCAD 10625*	**21**	3 wks
25 Sep	93	THE SINGLES COLLECTION 1981–1993 *MCA MCD 10921*	**11**	7 wks

Another Step *changed label number to MCA KIML 1 during its chart run.*

WILDHEARTS   UK, *male vocal/instrumental group*   *1 wk*

11 Sep	93	EARTH VS THE WILDHEARTS *East West 4509932871* ..	**46**	1 wk

Colm WILKINSON   Ireland, *male vocalist*   *6 wks*

10 Jun	89	STAGE HEROES *RCA BL 74105*	**27**	6 wks

Alyson WILLIAMS   US, *female vocalist*   *21 wks*

25 Mar	89	RAW *Def Jam 463293 1*	**29**	21 wks

Andy WILLIAMS   US, *male vocalist*   *442 wks*

26 Jun	65 ●	ALMOST THERE *CBS BPG 62533*	**4**	46 wks
7 Aug	65	CAN'T GET USED TO LOSING YOU *CBS BPG 62146* ..	**16**	1 wk
19 Mar	66	MAY EACH DAY *CBS BPG 62658*	**11**	6 wks
30 Apr	66	GREAT SONGS FROM MY FAIR LADY *CBS BPG 62430*	**30**	1 wk
23 Jul	66	SHADOW OF YOUR SMILE *CBS 62633*	**24**	4 wks
29 Jul	67	BORN FREE *CBS SBPG 63027*	**22**	11 wks
11 May	68 ★	LOVE ANDY *CBS 63167*	**1**	22 wks
6 Jul	68 ●	HONEY *CBS 63311*	**4**	17 wks
26 Jul	69	HAPPY HEART *CBS 63614*	**22**	9 wks
27 Dec	69	GET TOGETHER WITH ANDY WILLIAMS *CBS 63800*	**13**	12 wks
24 Jan	70	ANDY WILLIAMS' SOUND OF MUSIC *CBS 63920*	**22**	10 wks
11 Apr	70 ★	GREATEST HITS *CBS 63920*	**1**	116 wks
20 Jun	70 ●	CAN'T HELP FALLING IN LOVE *CBS 64067*	**7**	48 wks
5 Dec	70 ●	ANDY WILLIAMS SHOW *CBS 64127*	**10**	6 wks
3 Apr	71 ★	HOME LOVING MAN *CBS 64286*	**1**	25 wks
31 Jul	71	LOVE STORY *CBS 64467*	**11**	11 wks
29 Apr	72	THE IMPOSSIBLE DREAM *CBS 67236*	**26**	3 wks
29 Jul	72	LOVE THEME FROM 'THE GODFATHER' *CBS 64869* .	**11**	16 wks
16 Dec	72	GREATEST HITS VOL. 2 *CBS 65151*	**23**	10 wks
22 Dec	73 ●	SOLITAIRE *CBS 65638*	**3**	26 wks
15 Jun	74 ●	THE WAY WE WERE *CBS 80152*	**7**	11 wks
11 Oct	75	THE OTHER SIDE OF ME *CBS 69152*	**60**	1 wk
28 Jan	78 ●	REFLECTIONS *CBS 10006*	**2**	17 wks
27 Oct	84	GREATEST LOVE CLASSICS *EMI ANDY 1★*	**22**	10 wks
7 Nov	92	THE BEST OF ANDY WILLIAMS *Dino DINCD 50*	**51**	3 wks

★ *Andy Williams and the Royal Philharmonic Orchestra.*

Deniece WILLIAMS   US, *female vocalist*   *23 wks*

21 May	77	THIS IS NIECEY *CBS 81869*	**31**	12 wks
26 Aug	78	THAT'S WHAT FRIENDS ARE FOR *CBS 86068★*	**16**	11 wks

★ *Johnny Mathis and Deniece Williams.*

W
333

Don WILLIAMS US, male vocalist
136 wks

10 Jul	76	**GREATEST HITS VOL. 1** *ABC ABCL 5147*	29	15 wks
19 Feb	77	**VISIONS** *ABC ABCL 5200*	13	20 wks
15 Oct	77	**COUNTRY BOY** *ABC ABCL 5233*	27	5 wks
5 Aug	78 ●	**IMAGES** *K-Tel NE 1033*	2	38 wks
5 Aug	78	**YOU'RE MY BEST FRIEND** *ABC ABCD 5127*	58	1 wk
4 Nov	78	**EXPRESSIONS** *ABC ABCL 5253*	28	8 wks
22 Sep	79	**NEW HORIZONS** *K-Tel NE 1048*	29	12 wks
15 Dec	79	**PORTRAIT** *MCA MCS 3045*	58	4 wks
6 Sep	80	**I BELIEVE IN YOU** *MCA MCF 3077*	36	5 wks
18 Jul	81	**ESPECIALLY FOR YOU** *MCA MCF 3114*	33	7 wks
17 Apr	82	**LISTEN TO THE RADIO** *MCA MCF 3135*	69	3 wks
23 Apr	83	**YELLOW MOON** *MCA MCF 3159*	52	1 wk
15 Oct	83	**LOVE STORIES** *K-Tel NE 1252*	22	13 wks
26 May	84	**CAFE CAROLINA** *MCA MCF 3225*	65	4 wks

Iris WILLIAMS UK, female vocalist
4 wks

22 Dec	79	**HE WAS BEAUTIFUL** *Columbia SCX 6627*	69	4 wks

John WILLIAMS UK, male instrumentalist – guitar
62 wks

3 Oct	70	**PLAYS SPANISH MUSIC** *CBS 72860*	46	1 wk
8 Feb	76	**RODRIGO: CONCERTO DE ARANJUEZ** *CBS 79369★* .	20	9 wks
7 Jan	78	**BEST OF FRIENDS** *RCA RS 1094★★*	18	22 wks
17 Jun	78	**TRAVELLING** *Cube HIFLY 27*	23	5 wks
30 Jun	79 ●	**BRIDGES** *Lotus WH 5015*	5	22 wks
4 Aug	79	**CAVATINA** *Cube HIFLY 32*	64	3 wks

★ *John Williams with the English Chamber Orchestra conducted by Daniel Barenboim.*
★★ *Cleo Laine and John Williams.*

John WILLIAMS US, male conductor
15 wks

25 Dec	82	**ET – THE EXTRATERRESTRIAL (film soundtrack)** *MCA MCF 3160*	47	10 wks
31 Jul	93	**JURASSIC PARK (film soundtrack)** *MCA MCD 10859* ..	42	5 wks

Vanessa WILLIAMS US, female vocalist
4 wks

25 Apr	92	**THE COMFORT ZONE** *Polydor 5112672*	24	4 wks

Wendy O. WILLIAMS US, female vocalist
1 wk

30 Jun	84	**W.O.W.** *Music For Nations MFN 24*	100	1 wk

Ann WILLIAMSON UK, female vocalist
13 wks

15 Feb	86	**PRECIOUS MEMORIES** *Emerald Gem ERTV 1*	16	9 wks
6 Feb	88	**COUNT YOUR BLESSINGS** *Emerald Gem ERTV 2*	58	4 wks

Sonny Boy WILLIAMSON
US, male vocalist/instrumentalist – guitar
1 wk

20 Jun	64	**DOWN AND OUT BLUES** *Pye NPL 28036*	20	1 wk

Bruce WILLIS US, male vocalist
28 wks

18 Apr	87 ●	**THE RETURN OF BRUNO** *Motown ZL 72571*	4	28 wks

Mari WILSON with the WILSATIONS
UK, female vocalist   9 *wks*

26 Feb 83	**SHOW PEOPLE** *Compact COMP 2*	24	9 wks

WILSON PHILLIPS *US, female vocal group*   38 *wks*

| 30 Jun 90 ● | **WILSON PHILLIPS** *SBK SBKLP 5* | 7 | 32 wks |
| 13 Jun 92 ● | **SHADOWS AND LIGHT** *SBK SBKCD 18* | 6 | 6 wks |

WIN *UK, male/female vocal/instrumental group*   1 *wk*

25 Apr 87	**UH! TEARS BABY** *Swampland LONLP 31*	51	1 wk

WINCHESTER CATHEDRAL CHOIR – *See Andrew Lloyd Webber*

WINDJAMMER *US, male vocal/instrumental group*   1 *wk*

25 Aug 84	**WINDJAMMER II** *MCA MCF 3231*	82	1 wk

WINGS – *See Paul McCartney*

Johnny WINTER *US, male/vocal instrumental group*   12 *wks*

16 May 70	**SECOND WINTER** *CBS 66321*	59	2 wks
31 Oct 70	**JOHNNY WINTER AND . . .** *CBS 64117*	29	4 wks
15 May 71	**JOHNNY WINTER AND LIVE** *CBS 64289*	20	6 wks

Ruby WINTERS *US, female vocalist*   16 *wks*

| 10 Jun 78 | **RUBY WINTERS** *Creole CRLP 512* | 27 | 7 wks |
| 23 Jun 79 | **SONGBIRD** *K-Tel NE 1045* | 31 | 9 wks |

Steve WINWOOD *UK, male vocalist*   120 *wks*

9 Jul 77	**STEVE WINWOOD** *Island ILPS 9494*	12	9 wks
10 Jan 81	**ARC OF A DIVER** *Island ILPS 9576*	13	20 wks
14 Aug 82 ●	**TALKING BACK TO THE NIGHT** *Island ILPS 9777*	6	13 wks
12 Jul 86 ●	**BACK IN THE HIGH LIFE** *Island ILPS 9844*	8	42 wks
7 Nov 87	**CHRONICLES** *Island SSW 1*	12	17 wks
2 Jul 88 ●	**ROLL WITH IT** *Virgin V 2532*	4	16 wks
17 Nov 90	**REFUGEES OF THE HEART** *Virgin V 2650*	26	3 wks

WIRE *UK, male vocal/instrumental group*   3 *wks*

7 Oct 78	**CHAIRS MISSING** *Harvest SHSP 4093*	48	1 wk
13 Oct 79	**154** *Harvest SHSP 4105*	39	1 wk
9 May 87	**THE IDEAL COPY** *Mute STUMM 42*	87	1 wk

WISHBONE ASH *UK, male vocal/instrumental group*   75 *wks*

23 Jan 71	**WISHBONE ASH** *MCA MKPS 2014*	34	2 wks
9 Oct 71	**PILGRIMAGE** *MCA MDKS 8004*	14	9 wks
20 May 72 ●	**ARGUS** *MCA MDKS 8006*	3	20 wks
26 May 73	**WISHBONE FOUR** *MCA MDKS 8011*	12	10 wks
30 Nov 74	**THERE'S THE RUB** *MCA MCF 2585*	16	5 wks
3 Apr 76	**LOCKED IN** *MCA MCF 2750*	36	2 wks
27 Nov 76	**NEW ENGLAND** *MCA MCG 3523*	22	3 wks
29 Oct 77	**FRONT PAGE NEWS** *MCA MCG 3524*	31	4 wks
28 Oct 78	**NO SMOKE WITHOUT FIRE** *MCA MCG 3528*	43	3 wks

W
335

2 Feb 80	**JUST TESTING** *MCA MCF 3052*	41	4 wks
1 Nov 80	**LIVE DATES II** *MCA MCG 4012*	40	3 wks
25 Apr 81	**NUMBER THE BRAVE** *MCA MCF 3103*	61	5 wks
16 Oct 82	**BOTH BARRELS BURNING** *A&M ASH 1*	22	5 wks

Bill WITHERS *US, male vocalist* — 10 wks

11 Feb 78	**MENAGERIE** *CBS 82265*	27	5 wks
15 Jun 85	**WATCHING YOU, WATCHING ME** *CBS 26200*	60	1 wk
17 Sep 88	**GREATEST HITS** *CBS 32343*	90	4 wks

WIZZARD *UK, male vocal/instrumental group* — 11 wks

19 May 73	**WIZZARD BREW** *Harvest SHSP 4025*	29	7 wks
17 Aug 74	**INTRODUCING EDDY AND THE FALCONS** *Warner Bros. K 52029*	19	4 wks

WOLFSBANE *UK, male vocal/instrumental group* — 3 wks

5 Aug 89	**LIVE FAST DIE FAST** *Def American 838486 1*	48	1 wk
20 Oct 90	**ALL HELL'S BREAKING LOOSE** *Def American 8469671* ..	48	1 wk
19 Oct 91	**DOWN FALL THE GOOD GUYS** *Def American 5104131* ..	53	1 wk

Bobby WOMACK *US, male vocalist* — 15 wks

28 Apr 84	**THE POET II** *Motown ZL 72205*	31	8 wks
28 Sep 85	**SO MANY RIVERS** *MCA MCF 3282*	28	7 wks

See also Wilton Felder.

WOMACK and WOMACK *US, male/female vocal duo* 52 wks

21 Apr 84	**LOVE WARS** *Elektra 960293*	45	13 wks
22 Jun 85	**RADIO M.U.S.I.C. MAN** *Elektra EKT 6*	56	2 wks
27 Aug 88 ●	**CONSCIENCE** *Fourth & Broadway BRLP 519*	4	37 wks

WOMBLES
UK, male vocalist/arranger/producer, Mike Batt under group name 55 wks

2 Mar 74	**WOMBLING SONGS** *CBS 65803*	19	17 wks
13 Jul 74	**REMEMBER YOU'RE A WOMBLE** *CBS 80191*	18	31 wks
21 Dec 74	**KEEP ON WOMBLING** *CBS 80526*	17	6 wks
8 Jan 77	**20 WOMBLING GREATS** *Warwick PR 5022*	29	1 wk

Stevie WONDER *US, male vocalist/multi-instrumentalist* 336 wks

7 Sep 68	**STEVIE WONDER'S GREATEST HITS** *Tamla Motown STML 11075*	25	10 wks
13 Dec 69	**MY CHERIE AMOUR** *Tamla Motown STML 11128*	17	2 wks
12 Feb 72	**GREATEST HITS VOL. 2** *Tamla Motown STML 11196*	30	4 wks
3 Feb 73	**TALKING BOOK** *Tamla Motown STMA 8007*	16	48 wks
1 Sep 73 ●	**INNERVISIONS** *Tamla Motown STMA 8011*	8	55 wks
17 Aug 74 ●	**FULFILLINGNESS' FIRST FINALE** *Tamla Motown STMA 8019*	5	16 wks
16 Oct 76 ●	**SONGS IN THE KEY OF LIFE** *Tamla Motown TMSP 6002*	2	54 wks
10 Nov 79 ●	**JOURNEY THROUGH THE SECRET LIFE OF PLANTS** *Motown TMSP 6009*	8	15 wks
8 Nov 80 ●	**HOTTER THAN JULY** *Motown STMA 8035*	2	55 wks
22 May 82 ●	**ORIGINAL MUSIQUARIUM 1** *Motown TMSP 6012*	8	17 wks
22 Sep 84 ●	**WOMAN IN RED** (film soundtrack) *Motown ZL 72285* ...	2	19 wks
24 Nov 84	**LOVE SONGS – 16 CLASSIC HITS** *Telstar STAR 2251* ..	20	10 wks
28 Sep 85 ●	**IN SQUARE CIRCLE** *Motown ZL 72005*	5	16 wks

15 Nov 86	**DIANA ROSS. MICHAEL JACKSON. GLADYS KNIGHT. STEVIE WONDER. THEIR VERY BEST BACK TO BACK** *PriotiTyV PTVR 2★*	21	10 wks
28 Nov 87	**CHARACTERS** *RCA ZL 72001*	33	4 wks
8 Jun 91	**JUNGLE FEVER (film soundtrack)** *Motown ZL 71750*	56	1 wk

★ *Diana Ross/Michael Jackson/Gladys Knight/Stevie Wonder.*

WONDER STUFF *UK, male vocal/instrumental group* 43 wks

27 Aug 88	**THE EIGHT LEGGED GROOVE MACHINE** *Polydor GONLP 1*	18	7 wks
14 Oct 89 ●	**HUP** *Polydor 841187 1*	5	8 wks
8 Jun 91 ●	**NEVER LOVED ELVIS** *Polydor 8472521*	3	23 wks
16 Oct 93 ●	**CONSTRUCTION FOR THE MODERN IDIOT** *Polydor 5198942*	4	5 wks

Roy WOOD *UK, male vocalist/multi-instrumentalist* 14 wks

18 Aug 73	**BOULDERS** *Harvest SHVL 803*	15	8 wks
24 Jul 82	**THE SINGLES** *Speed SPEED 1000*	37	6 wks

WOODENTOPS *UK, male vocal/instrumental group* 6 wks

12 Jul 86	**GIANT** *Rough Trade ROUGH 87*	35	4 wks
5 Mar 88	**WOODENFOOT COPS ON THE HIGHWAY** *Rough Trade ROUGH 127*	48	2 wks

Edward WOODWARD *UK, male vocalist* 12 wks

6 Jun 70	**THIS MAN ALONE** *DJM DJLPS 405*	53	2 wks
19 Aug 72	**THE EDWARD WOODWARD ALBUM** *Jam JAL 103*	20	10 wks

WORKING WEEK
UK, male/female vocal/instrumental group 10 wks

6 Apr 85	**WORKING NIGHTS** *Virgin V 2343*	23	9 wks
27 Sep 86	**COMPANEROS** *Virgin V 2397*	72	1 wk

WORLD OF TWIST *UK, male vocal/instrumental group* 1 wk

9 Nov 91	**QUALITY STREET** *Circa CIRCA 17*	50	1 wk

WORLD PARTY *Ireland/UK, male vocal/instrumental group* 22 wks

21 Mar 87	**PRIVATE REVOLUTION** *Chrysalis CHEN 4*	56	4 wks
19 May 90	**GOODBYE JUMBO** *Ensign CHEN 10*	36	10 wks
8 May 93 ●	**BANG!** *Ensign CDCHEN 33*	2	8 wks

WORLD'S FAMOUS SUPREME TEAM – *See Malcolm McLAREN*

WRECKLESS ERIC *UK, male vocalist* 5 wks

1 Apr 78	**WRECKLESS ERIC** *Stiff SEEZ 6*	46	1 wk
8 Mar 80	**BIG SMASH** *Stiff SEEZ 21*	30	4 wks

WREN ORCHESTRA – *See WET WET WET*

Klaus WUNDERLICH *Germany, male instrumentalist – organ* 19 wks

30 Aug 75	**THE HIT WORLD OF KLAUS WUNDERLICH** *Decca SPA 434*	27	8 wks
20 May 78	**THE UNIQUE KLAUS WUNDERLICH SOUND** *Decca DBC 5/5*	28	4 wks

W

337

26 May 79	THE FANTASTIC SOUND OF KLAUS WUNDERLICH		
	Lotus LH 5013	43	5 wks
17 Mar 84	ON THE SUNNY SIDE OF THE STREET		
	Polydor POLD 5133	81	2 wks

WURZELS UK, male vocal/instrumental group   29 wks

11 Mar 67	ADGE CUTLER AND THE WURZELS Columbia SX 6126★	38	4 wks
3 Jul 76	COMBINE HARVESTER One-Up OU 2138	15	20 wks
2 Apr 77	GOLDEN DELICIOUS EMI Note NTS 122	32	5 wks

★ Adge Cutler and the Wurzels.

WWF SUPERSTARS US/UK, male vocal group   5 wks

| 17 Apr 93 ● | WRESTLEMANIA – THE ALBUM   Arista 74321138062 | 10 | 5 wks |

Bill WYMAN UK, male vocalist/instrumentalist – bass   7 wks

| 8 Jun 74 | MONKEY GRIP   Rolling Stones COC 59102 | 39 | 1 wk |
| 10 Apr 82 | BILL WYMAN   A & M AMLH 68540 | 55 | 6 wks |

Tammy WYNETTE US, female vocalist   49 wks

17 May 75 ●	THE BEST OF TAMMY WYNETTE Epic EPC 63578	4	23 wks
21 Jun 75	STAND BY YOUR MAN Epic EPC 69141	13	7 wks
17 Dec 77 ●	20 COUNTRY CLASSICS CBS PR 5040	3	11 wks
4 Feb 78	COUNTRY GIRL MEETS COUNTRY BOY		
	Warwick PR 5039	43	3 wks
6 Jun 87	ANNIVERSARY – 20 YEARS OF HITS Epic 450 393–1	45	5 wks

X
338

X MAL DEUTSCHLAND
UK/Germany, male/female vocal/instrumental group   1 wk

| 7 Jul 84 | TOCSIN   4AD CAD 407 | 86 | 1 wk |

X-RAY SPEX UK, female/male vocal/instrumental group   14 wks

| 9 Dec 78 | GERM FREE ADOLESCENTS   EMI International INS 3023 | 30 | 14 wks |

XTC UK, male vocal/instrumental group   47 wks

11 Feb 78	WHITE MUSIC Virgin V 2095	38	4 wks
28 Oct 78	GO 2 Virgin V 2108	21	3 wks
1 Sep 79	DRUMS AND WIRES Virgin V 2129	34	7 wks
20 Sep 80	BLACK SEA Virgin V 2173	16	7 wks
20 Feb 82 ●	ENGLISH SETTLEMENT Virgin V 2223	5	11 wks
13 Nov 82	WAXWORKS – SOME SINGLES (1977–82) Virgin V 2251	54	3 wks
10 Sep 83	MUMMER Virgin V 2264	51	4 wks
27 Oct 84	THE BIG EXPRESS Virgin V 2325	38	2 wks
8 Nov 86	SKYLARKING Virgin V 2399	90	1 wk
11 Mar 89	ORANGES AND LEMONS Virgin V 2581	28	3 wks
9 May 92	NONSUCH Virgin CDV 2699	28	2 wks

Stevie Wonder meets former Supreme Court Chief Justice Earl Warren, head of the Warren Commission investigation into the assassination of President Kennedy.

Bobby Womack is shown in 1969, the year his first US hit album was in the charts, 15 years before he registered in the UK.

Not discouraged by the relative failure of her 1985 greatest hits album, **Kim Wilde** climbed 67 places higher with her 1993 anthology. (Pictorial Press)

It is 23 April, 1964, and the **Yardbirds** are boating on the Serpentine in Hyde Park. They seem to be indicating the size of fish that broke their reels, but in fact Eric Clapton (front left) was the one that got away. (Pictorial Press)

YARDBIRDS UK, male vocal/instrumental group   8 wks

23 Jul 66   **YARDBIRDS** Columbia SX 6063 ....   **20**   8 wks

YAZOO UK, female/male vocal/instrumental duo   83 wks

4 Sep 82 ● **UPSTAIRS AT ERIC'S** Mute STUMM 7 ....   **2**   63 wks
16 Jul 83 ★ **YOU AND ME BOTH** Mute STUMM 12 ....   **1**   20 wks

YAZZ UK, female vocalist   32 wks

26 Nov 88 ● **WANTED** Big Life YAZZLP 1 ....   **3**   32 wks

YELLO Switzerland, male vocal/instrumental duo   15 wks

21 May 83   **YOU GOTTA SAY YES TO ANOTHER EXCESS**
              Stiff SEEZ 48 ....   **65**   2 wks
6 Apr 85   **STELLA** Elektra EKT 1 ....   **92**   1 wk
4 Jul 87   **ONE SECOND** Mercury MERH 100 ....   **48**   3 wks
10 Dec 88   **FLAG** Mercury 836778 1 ....   **56**   7 wks
29 Jun 91   **BABY** Mercury 8487911 ....   **37**   2 wks

Bryn YEMM UK, male vocalist   14 wks

9 Jun 84   **HOW DO I LOVE THEE** Lifestyle LEG 17 ....   **57**   2 wks
7 Jul 84   **HOW GREAT THOU ART** Lifestyle LEG 15 ....   **67**   8 wks
22 Dec 84   **THE BRYN YEMM CHRISTMAS COLLECTION**
              Bay BAY 104 ....   **95**   2 wks
26 Oct 85   **MY TRIBUTE – BRYN YEMM INSPIRATIONAL ALBUM**
              Word WSTR 9665★ ....   **85**   2 wks

★ Bryn Yemm and the Gwent Chorale.

YES UK, male vocal/instrumental group   206 wks

1 Aug 70   **TIME AND A WORD** Atlantic 2400–006 ....   **45**   3 wks
3 Apr 71 ● **THE YES ALBUM** Atlantic 2400–101 ....   **7**   29 wks
4 Dec 71 ● **FRAGILE** Atlantic 2409–019 ....   **7**   17 wks
23 Sep 72 ● **CLOSE TO THE EDGE** Atlantic K 50012 ....   **4**   13 wks
26 May 73 ● **YESSONGS** Atlantic K 60045 ....   **7**   13 wks
22 Dec 73 ★ **TALES FROM TOPOGRAPHIC OCEANS**
              Atlantic K 80001 ....   **1**   15 wks
21 Dec 74 ● **RELAYER** Atlantic K 50096 ....   **4**   11 wks
29 Mar 75   **YESTERDAYS** Atlantic K 50048 ....   **27**   7 wks
30 Jul 77 ★ **GOING FOR THE ONE** Atlantic K 50379 ....   **1**   28 wks
7 Oct 78 ● **TORMATO** Atlantic K 50518 ....   **8**   11 wks
30 Aug 80 ● **DRAMA** Atlantic K 50736 ....   **2**   8 wks
10 Jan 81   **YESSHOWS** Atlantic K 60142 ....   **22**   9 wks
26 Nov 83   **90125** Atco 790125 ....   **16**   28 wks
29 Mar 86   **9012 LIVE: THE SOLOS** Atco 790 474–1 ....   **44**   3 wks
10 Oct 87   **BIG GENERATOR** Atco WEX 70 ....   **17**   5 wks
11 May 91 ● **UNION** Arista 211558 ....   **7**   6 wks

Dwight YOAKAM US, male vocalist/instrumentalist – guitar 4 wks

9 May 87   **HILLBILLY DELUXE** Reprise WX 106 ....   **51**   3 wks
13 Aug 88   **BUENAS NOCHES FROM A LONELY ROOM**
              Reprise WX 193 ....   **87**   1 wk

Faron YOUNG US, male vocalist   5 wks

28 Oct	72	**IT'S FOUR IN THE MORNING** *Mercury 6338 095*	27	5 wks

Neil YOUNG Canada, male vocalist   211 wks

31 Oct	70 ●	**AFTER THE GOLDRUSH** *Reprise RSLP 6383*	7	68 wks
4 Mar	72 ★	**HARVEST** *Reprise K 54005*	1	33 wks
27 Oct	73	**TIME FADES AWAY** *Warner Bros. K 54010*	20	2 wks
10 Aug	74	**ON THE BEACH** *Reprise K 54014*	42	2 wks
5 Jul	75	**TONIGHT'S THE NIGHT** *Reprise K 54040*	48	1 wk
27 Dec	75	**ZUMA** *Reprise K 54057*	44	2 wks
9 Oct	76	**LONG MAY YOU RUN** *Reprise K 54081★*	12	5 wks
9 Jul	77	**AMERICAN STARS 'N' BARS** *Reprise K 54088*	17	8 wks
17 Dec	77	**DECADE** *Reprise K 64037*	46	4 wks
28 Oct	78	**COMES A TIME** *Reprise K 54099*	42	3 wks
14 Jul	79	**RUST NEVER SLEEPS** *Reprise K 54105*	13	13 wks
1 Dec	79	**LIVE RUST** *Reprise K 64041*	55	3 wks
15 Nov	80	**HAWKS AND DOVES** *Reprise K 54109*	34	3 wks
14 Nov	81	**RE-AC-TOR** *Reprise K 54116*	69	3 wks
5 Feb	83	**TRANS** *Geffen GEF 25019*	29	5 wks
3 Sep	83	**EVERYBODY'S ROCKIN'** *Geffen GEF 25590*	50	3 wks
14 Sep	85	**OLD WAYS** *Geffen GEF 26377*	39	3 wks
2 Aug	86	**LANDING ON WATER** *Geffen 924 109–1*	52	2 wks
4 Jul	87	**LIFE** *Geffen WX 109*	71	1 wk
30 Apr	88	**THIS NOTE'S FOR YOU** *WEA WX 168*	56	3 wks
21 Oct	89	**FREEDOM** *Reprise WX 257*	17	5 wks
22 Sep	90	**RAGGED GLORY** *Reprise WX 374*	15	5 wks
2 Nov	91	**WELD** *Reprise 7599266711*	20	3 wks
14 Nov	92 ●	**HARVEST MOON** *Reprise 9362450572*	9	18 wks
23 Jan	93	**LUCKY THIRTEEN** *Geffen GED 24452*	69	1 wk
26 Jun	93 ●	**UNPLUGGED** *Reprise 9362453102*	4	12 wks

★ *Stills-Young Band.*
See also Crosby, Stills, Nash and Young.

Y
341

Paul YOUNG UK, male vocalist   225 wks

30 Jul	83 ★	**NO PARLEZ** *CBS 25521*	1	119 wks
6 Apr	85 ★	**THE SECRET OF ASSOCIATION** *CBS 26234*	1	49 wks
1 Nov	86 ●	**BETWEEN TWO FIRES** *CBS 450 150–1*	4	17 wks
16 Jun	90 ●	**OTHER VOICES** *CBS 4669171*	4	11 wks
14 Sep	91 ★	**FROM TIME TO TIME – THE SINGLES COLLECTION**		
		Columbia 4688251	1	27 wks
23 Oct	93	**THE CROSSING** *Columbia 4739282*	27	2 wks

YOUNG DISCIPLES
UK, male/female vocal/instrumental group   5 wks

31 Aug	91	**ROAD TO FREEDOM** *Talking Loud 5100971*	21	5 wks

YOUNG GODS Switzerland, male vocal/instrumental group   1 wk

15 Feb	92	**TV SKY** *Play It Again Sam BIAS 201CD*	54	1 wk

Sydney YOUNGBLOOD US, male vocalist   17 wks

28 Oct	89	**FEELING FREE** *Circa CIRCA 9*	23	17 wks

Y&T US, male vocal/instrumental group   15 wks

11 Sep	82	**BLACK TIGER** *A & M AMLH 64910*	53	8 wks
10 Sep	83	**MEAN STREAK** *A & M AMLX 64960*	35	4 wks
18 Aug	84	**IN ROCK WE TRUST** *A & M AMLX 65007*	33	3 wks

Frank ZAPPA US, male vocalist/multi-instrumentalist   55 wks

28 Feb	70	● HOT RATS *Reprise RSLP 6356*	9	27 wks
19 Dec	70	CHUNGA'S REVENGE *Reprise RSLP 2030*	43	1 wk
6 May	78	ZAPPA IN NEW YORK *Discreet K 69204*	55	1 wk
10 Mar	79	SHEIK YERBOUTI *CBS 88339*	32	7 wks
13 Oct	79	JOE'S GARAGE ACT 1 *CBS 86101*	62	3 wks
19 Jan	80	JOE'S GARAGE ACTS 2 & 3 *CBS 88475*	75	1 wk
16 May	81	TINSEL TOWN REBELLION *CBS 88516*	55	4 wks
24 Oct	81	YOU ARE WHAT YOU IS *CBS 88560*	51	2 wks
19 Jun	82	SHIP ARRIVING TOO LATE TO SAVE A DROWNING		
		WITCH *CBS 85804*	61	4 wks
18 Jun	83	THE MAN FROM UTOPIA *CBS 25251*	87	1 wk
27 Oct	84	THEM OR US *EMI FZD 1*	53	2 wks
30 Apr	88	GUITAR *Zappa ZAPPA 6*	82	2 wks

Lena ZAVARONI UK, female vocalist   5 wks

23 Mar	74	● MA *Philips 6308 201*	8	5 wks

ZOE UK, female vocalist   1 wk

7 Dec	91	SCARLET RED AND BLUE *M & G 5114431*	67	1 wk

ZUCCHERO Italy, male vocalist   4 wks

18 May	91	ZUCCHERO *A & M EVERY 1*	29	4 wks

Z.Z. TOP US, male vocal/instrumental group   200 wks

12 Jul	75	FANDANGO *London SHU 8482*	60	1 wk
8 Aug	81	EL LOCO *Warner Bros. K 56929*	88	2 wks
30 Apr	83	● ELIMINATOR *Warner Bros. W 3774*	3	135 wks
9 Nov	85	● AFTERBURNER *Warner Bros. WX 27*	2	40 wks
27 Oct	90	● RECYCLER *Warner Brothers WX 390*	8	7 wks
25 Apr	92	● GREATEST HITS *Warner Bros 7599268462*	5	15 wks

Various Artists

Compilation albums are listed alphabetically by label, for each label which has produced at least three hit compilations. Other hit compilations are listed together at the end of this section. Multi-artist Film Soundtracks, TV and Radio Soundtracks and Spin-Offs, Stage and Studio Cast Recordings, Anonymous Cover Versions and Miscellaneous albums are then listed alphabetically.

On 14 January 1989, the Compilation Albums chart was established, and all entries on this chart are listed in this section. A dotted line in each label listing indicates when the new chart began. Some albums will have entries both above and below the line, indicating that they appeared in the main chart before 14 January 1989, and the Compilation chart thereafter.

COMPILATIONS

A & M

2 May	87	**PRINCE'S TRUST TENTH ANNIVERSARY BIRTHDAY PARTY** *A & M AMA 3906*	76	3 wks
22 Aug	87	**THE PRINCE'S TRUST CONCERT 1987** *A & M PTA 1987*	44	3 wks
5 Dec	87	**SPECIAL OLYMPICS – A VERY SPECIAL CHRISTMAS** *A & M AMA 3911*	40	5 wks
23 Dec	89	**SPECIAL OLYMPICS – A VERY SPECIAL CHRISTMAS** *A & M AMA 3911*	19	1 wk
29 Sep	90 ★	**SLAMMIN'** *A & M SLAMM 1*	1	6 wks
20 Apr	91	**RAGE – MAKE SOME NOISE VOL 1** *A & M AMTV 1*	12	3 wks
29 Jun	91 ★	**WINGS OF LOVE** *A & M A & M 8455062*	1	21 wks

Arcade

29 Jul	72 ★	**20 FANTASTIC HITS** *Arcade 2891 001*	1	24 wks
29 Nov	72 ●	**20 FANTASTIC HITS VOL. 2** *Arcade 2891 002*	2	14 wks
7 Apr	73 ●	**40 FANTASTIC HITS FROM THE 50'S AND 60'S** *Arcade ADEP 3/4*	2	15 wks
26 May	73 ●	**20 FANTASTIC HITS VOL. 3** *Arcade ADEP 5*	3	8 wks
15 Nov	75 ●	**DISCO HITS '75** *Arcade ADEP 18*	5	11 wks
26 Mar	77	**ROCK ON** *Arcade ADEP 27*	16	10 wks
2 Jun	77	**RULE BRITANNIA** *Arcade ADEP 29*	56	1 wk
23 Feb	80	**FIRST LOVE** *Arcade ADEP 41*	58	2 wks
12 Jan	91	**POP CLASSICS – 28 CLASSIC TRACKS** *Arcade ARC 94421*	19	2 wks
30 Mar	91 ●	**SOFT METAL BALLADS** *Arcade ARC 933501*	5	10 wks
8 Jun	91 ●	**IT STARTED WITH A KISS** *Arcade ARC 910301*	9	8 wks
13 Jul	91 ●	**THE HEAT IS ON** *Arcade ARC 925401*	4	9 wks
31 Aug	91 ●	**DANCE CLASSICS VOL 1** *Arcade ARC 925501*	8	4 wks
31 Aug	91 ●	**DANCE CLASSICS VOL 2** *Arcade ARC 925511*	7	5 wks
21 Sep	91 ★	**GROOVY GHETTO** *Arcade ARC 925601*	1	6 wks
2 Nov	91	**GROOVY GHETTO – ALL THE RAGE** *Arcade ARC 925701*	15	2 wks
14 Dec	91	**CHRISTMAS LOVE SONGS** *Arcade ARC 948201*	11	6 wks
29 Feb	92 ●	**GROOVY GHETTO 2** *Arcade ARC 948102*	8	4 wks
4 Apr	92	**THE ESSENTIAL CHILL** *Arcade 948902*	16	2 wks
18 Jul	92 ●	**ONE LOVE – THE VERY BEST OF REGGAE** *Arcade ARC 94962*	7	6 wks
13 Feb	93 ●	**ROCK ROMANCE** *Arcade 3100032*	9	5 wks

Atlantic

2 Apr	66	**SOLID GOLD SOUL** *Atlantic ATL 5048*	12	27 wks
5 Nov	66	**MIDNIGHT SOUL** *Atlantic 587–021*	22	19 wks
14 Jun	69	**THIS IS SOUL** *Atlantic 643–301*	16	15 wks
25 Mar	72	**THE NEW AGE OF ATLANTIC** *Atlantic K 20024*	25	1 wk

VARIOUS ARTISTS

22 Jun	74	**ATLANTIC BLACK GOLD** *Atlantic K 40550*	23	7 wks
3 Apr	76	**BY INVITATION ONLY** *Atlantic K 60112*	17	6 wks
11 Apr	81	**CONCERTS FOR THE PEOPLE OF KAMPUCHEA**		
		Atlantic K 60153	39	2 wks
2 Feb	85	**THIS IS SOUL** *Atlantic SOUL 1*	78	7 wks
6 Jun	87 ●	**ATLANTIC SOUL CLASSICS** *Atlantic WX 105*	9	23 wks
18 Jun	88	**ATLANTIC SOUL BALLADS** *Atlantic WX 98*	84	2 wks

Beggars Banquet

21 Nov	81	**SLIP STREAM** *Beggars Banquet BEGA 31*	72	3 wks
15 May	82	**SEX SWEAT AND BLOOD** *Beggars Banquet BEGA 34*	88	1 wk
11 Sep	82	**THE BEST OF BRITISH JAZZ FUNK VOLUME 2**		
		Beggars Banquet BEGA 41	44	4 wks

Castle Communications

7 Jul	90 ●	**THE ULTIMATE 60s COLLECTION**		
		Castle Communications CTVLP 305	4	11 wks
12 Jan	91	**THE ULTIMATE BLUES COLLECTION**		
		Castle Communications CTVLP 206	14	6 wks
8 Aug	92 ●	**JAZZ ON A SUMMER'S DAY**		
		Castle Communications CTVCD 108	4	8 wks
10 Oct	92 ●	**BLOCKBUSTER! – THE SENSATIONAL 70s**		
		Castle Communications CTVCD 209	6	6 wks
5 Jun	93 ●	**ONE ORIGINAL STEP BEYOND**		
		Castle Communications CTVCD 115	7	5 wks
3 Jul	93	**MONSTER HITS OF DANCE**		
		Castle Communications CTVCD 220	13	3 wks
30 Oct	93	**GOING UNDERGROUND**		
		Castle Communications CTVCD 123	18	2 wks

CBS/Columbia

20 May	67	**THRILL TO THE SENSATIONAL SOUNDS OF SUPER**		
		STEREO *CBS PR 5*	20	30 wks
28 Jun	69	**THE ROCK MACHINE TURNS YOU ON** *CBS SPR 22* .	18	7 wks
28 Jun	69	**ROCK MACHINE I LOVE YOU** *CBS SPR 26*	15	5 wks
20 May	72 ●	**THE MUSIC PEOPLE** *CBS 66315*	10	9 wks
21 Oct	78 ●	**SATIN CITY** *CBS 10010*	10	11 wks
2 Jun	79	**THIS IS IT** *CBS 10014*	6	12 wks
19 Apr	80	**FIRST LADIES OF COUNTRY** *CBS 10018*	37	6 wks
21 Jun	80	**KILLER WATTS** *CBS KW1*	27	6 wks
4 Apr	81	**BITTER SUITE** *CBS 22082*	55	3 wks
16 Oct	82 ●	**REFLECTIONS** *CBS 10034*	4	91 wks
22 Oct	83	**IMAGINATIONS** *CBS 10044*	15	21 wks
20 Apr	85	**CLUB CLASSICS VOLUME 2** *CBS VAULT 2*	90	2 wks
14 Mar	87 ●	**MOVE CLOSER** *CBS MOOD 1*	4	19 wks
27 Jun	87	**THE HOLIDAY ALBUM** *CBS MOOD 2*	13	9 wks
30 Apr	88 ★	**NITE FLITE** *CBS MOOD 4*	1	26 wks
4 Mar	89 ●	**CHEEK TO CHEEK** *CBS MOOD 6*	2	32 wks
13 May	89 ★	**NITE FLITE 2** *CBS MOOD 8*	1	26 wks
30 Dec	89	**LAMBADA** *CBS 466055 1*	15	6 wks
24 Mar	90 ★	**JUST THE TWO OF US** *CBS MOOD 11*	1	37 wks
9 Jun	90 ★	**NITE FLITE 3 – BEING WITH YOU** *CBS MOOD 14* ...	3	11 wks
2 Feb	91 ★	**THINKING OF YOU** *Columbia MOOD 15*	1	23 wks
2 Feb	91 ●	**THE TREE AND THE BIRD** *Columbia 4678801*	9	3 wks
30 Mar	91	**EVERYBODY DANCE NOW** *Columbia 468501*	12	3 wks
20 Apr	91	**FREE SPIRIT – 17 CLASSIC ROCK BALLADS**		
		Columbia MOODS 16	4	23 wks
20 Apr	91 ●	**YOU'RE THE INSPIRATION** *Columbia MOOD 17*	10	5 wks
10 Aug	91	**SIMPLY . . . LOVE** *Columbia MOOD 17*	3	10 wks
17 Aug	91 ★	**THE SOUND OF THE SUBURBS** *Columbia MOOD 18* ..	1	25 wks
29 Feb	92	**THE SOUND OF THE CITY** *Columbia MOODCD 22*	11	5 wks
27 Jan	92 ●	**HARD FAX** *Columbia SETVCD 1*	3	6 wks
4 Jul	92	**THE BOYS ARE BACK IN TOWN**		
		Columbia MOODCD 23	11	6 wks
3 Oct	92 ●	**SOMETHING IN THE AIR** *Columbia SETVCD 2*	10	5 wks
31 Oct	92 ★	**THE ULTIMATE COUNTRY COLLECTION**		
		Columbia MOODCD 26	1	23 wks
21 Nov	92 ●	**HARD FAX 2 – TWICE THE VICE!** *Columbia SETVCD 3*	6	2 wks
29 May	93 ★	**ORIGINALS** *Columbia MOODCD 29*	1	21 wks
21 Aug	93 ●	**AFTER DARK** *Columbia SETVCD 5*	8	4 wks

VARIOUS ARTISTS

Champion
8 Nov 86	ULTIMATE TRAX VOLUME 1 *Champion CHAMP 103* ..	66	2 wks
7 Mar 87	ULTIMATE TRAX VOLUME 2 *Champion CHAMP 1005* .	50	2 wks
18 Jul 87	ULTIMATE TRAX 3 – BATTLE OF THE D.J.s		
	Champion CHAMP 1008	69	2 wks

Charm
21 Apr 90	PURE LOVERS VOL. 1 *Charm CLP 101*	14	4 wks
22 Sep 90	PURE LOVERS VOL. 2 *Charm CLP 102*	12	3 wks
6 Apr 91	PURE LOVERS VOL. 3 *Charm CLP 103*	16	2 wks
2 Nov 91	PURE LOVERS VOL. 4 *Charm CLP 104*	19	1 wk
25 Jul 92	JUST RAGGA *Charm CDCD 14*	17	1 wk
29 Aug 92	PURE LOVERS VOL. 5 *Charm CCDJS 105*	13	3 wks
27 Feb 93	JUST RAGGA VOL. III *Charm CRCD 16*	19	1 wk
1 May 93	PURE LOVERS VOL. 6 *Charm CCDJS 106*	17	1 wk

Cookie Jar
14 Dec 91 ●	STEAMIN' – HARDCORE 92 *Cookie Jar JARTV 1*	3	8 wks
21 Mar 92 ●	TECHNOSTATE *Cookie Jar JARCD 2*	2	9 wks
23 May 92 ★	THE RAVE GENER8TOR *Cookie Jar JARCD 3*	1	8 wks
5 Sep 92 ●	THE RAVE GENER8TOR 2 *Cookie Jar JARCD 4*	2	7 wks
28 Nov 92 ●	RAVE 92 *Cookie Jar JARCD 5*	3	11 wks
27 Mar 93 ●	UNDERGROUND VOL. 1 *Cookie Jar JARCD 6*	6	5 wks
7 Aug 93 ●	JAMMIN' *Cookie Jar JARCD 7*	7	5 wks
11 Sep 93	FULL ON DANCE *Cookie Jar JARCD 8*	12	2 wks
6 Nov 93 ●	SOUL BEAT *Cookie Jar JARCD 9*	8	2 wks
27 Nov 93 ●	FULL ON DANCE '93 *Cookie Jar JARCD 10*	3†	5 wks

Decca
8 Feb 64	READY STEADY GO *Decca LK 4577*	20	1 wk
28 Jun 69	THE WORLD OF BLUES POWER *Decca SPA 14*	24	6 wks
5 Jul 69	THE WORLD OF BRASS BANDS *Decca SPA 20*	13	11 wks
6 Sep 69 ●	THE WORLD OF HITS VOL. 2 *Decca SPA 35*	7	5 wks
20 Sep 69	THE WORLD OF PROGRESSIVE MUSIC (WOWIE ZOWIE) *Decca SPA 34*	17	2 wks
20 Sep 69	THE WORLD OF PHASE 4 STEREO *Decca SPA 32*	29	2 wks
7 Aug 71 ●	THE WORLD OF YOUR 100 BEST TUNES *Decca SPA 112*	10	22 wks
9 Oct 71 ●	THE WORLD OF YOUR 100 BEST TUNES VOL. 2 *Decca SPA 155*	9	13 wks
27 Sep 75	THE WORLD OF YOUR 100 BEST TUNES VOL. 10 *Decca SPA 400*	41	4 wks
13 Dec 75	THE TOP 25 FROM YOUR 100 BEST TUNES *Decca HBT 1112*	21	5 wks
26 Nov 83 ●	FORMULA 30 *Decca PROLP 4*	6	17 wks
1 Jun 91 ★	THE ESSENTIAL MOZART *Decca 4333231*	1	23 wks
16 Nov 91 ●	ESSENTIAL OPERA *Decca 4338221*	2	28 wks
26 Sep 92 ●	ESSENTIAL BALLET *Decca 4366582*	9	4 wks
12 Jun 93 ●	CLASSIC COMMERCIALS *Decca 4406382*	8	6 wks
6 Nov 93	ESSENTIAL OPERA 2 *Decca 4409472*	17	2 wks

Dino
2 Dec 89	THAT LOVING FEELING *Dino DINTV 5*	11	11 wks
3 Mar 90 ●	THAT LOVING FEELING VOL 2 *Dino DINTV 7*	5	24 wks
23 Jun 90 ●	LEATHER AND LACE *Dino DINTV 9*	3	8 wks
11 Aug 90 ●	THE SUMMER OF LOVE *Dino DINTV 10*	9	9 wks
6 Oct 90 ★	THAT LOVING FEELING VOL 3 *Dino DINTV 11*	1	29 wks
10 Nov 90	LEATHER AND LACE – THE SECOND CHAPTER *Dino DINTV 12*	14	4 wks
24 Nov 90 ●	ROCK 'N' ROLL LOVE SONGS *Dino DINTV 13*	4	25 wks
29 Dec 90	BACHARACH AND DAVID – THEY WRITE THE SONGS *Dino DINTV 16*	16	3 wks
9 Feb 91 ●	TRACKS OF MY TEARS (SMOKEY ROBINSON – WRITER AND PERFORMER) *Dino DINTV 17*	6	8 wks
30 Mar 91 ●	HARDCORE UPROAR *Dino DINTV 20*	2	9 wks
6 Apr 91 ●	THAT LOVING FEELING VOL 4 *Dino DINTV 18*	3	12 wks
1 Jun 91 ●	LOVE SUPREME *Dino DINTV 19*	4	5 wks
15 Jun 91 ★	THE RHYTHM DIVINE *Dino DINTV 22*	1	15 wks
13 Jul 91 ●	HARDCORE DANCEFLOOR *Dino DINTV 24*	2	10 wks
27 Jul 91 ●	CHIC AND ROSE ROYCE – THEIR GREATEST HITS SIDE BY SIDE *Dino DINTV 23*	8	6 wks
3 Aug 91 ●	LA FREEWAY *Dino DINTV 25*	6	7 wks
12 Oct 91 ●	WE WILL ROCK YOU *Dino DINTV 26*	3	6 wks
19 Oct 91 ●	THAT LOVING FEELING VOL 5 *Dino DINTV 28*	2	8 wks

VARIOUS ARTISTS

2 Nov 91 ★	**HARDCORE ECSTASY**	Dino DINTV 29	**1**	16 wks
2 Nov 91 ●	**THE RHYTHM DIVINE VOL 2**	Dino DINTV 27	**6**	5 wks
23 Nov 91 ●	**MORE ROCK 'N' ROLL LOVE SONGS**	Dino DINTV 30	**6**	20 wks
7 Dec 91 ●	**PARTY MIX**	Dino DINTV 32	**8**	9 wks
28 Dec 91 ★	**ESSENTIAL HARDCORE**	Dino DINTV 33	**1**	10 wks
14 Mar 92 ●	**HEAVENLY HARDCORE**	Dino DINCD 35	**2**	9 wks
28 Mar 92 ●	**BREAKING HEARTS**	Dino DINCD 34	**3**	10 wks
18 Apr 92 ●	**COLD SWEAT**	Dino DINCD 36	**2**	7 wks
2 May 92 ●	**HEARTLANDS**	Dino DINCD 37	**4**	11 wks
20 Jun 92 ●	**LET'S TALK ABOUT LOVE**	Dino DINCD 39	**3**	4 wks
11 Jul 92	**PRECIOUS**	Dino DINCD 38	**12**	2 wks
18 Jul 92 ●	**MIDNIGHT CRUISING**	Dino DINCD 37	**10**	4 wks
1 Aug 92 ●	**UNDER SPANISH SKIES**	Dino DINCD 41	**5**	7 wks
22 Aug 92 ●	**THE ORIGINALS!**	Dino DINCD 34	**8**	6 wks
29 Aug 92 ●	**TRANCE DANCE**	Dino DINCD 45	**7**	5 wks
19 Sep 92 ★	**SIXTIES BEAT**	Dino DINCD 42	**1**	13 wks
17 Oct 92 ★	**ENERGY RUSH**	Dino DINCD 53	**1**	6 wks
24 Oct 92 ●	**THE GREATEST VOICES**	Dino DINCD 44	**5**	6 wks
14 Nov 92	**SWING HITS**	Dino DINCD 46	**19**	1 wk
28 Nov 92	**ROCK 'N' ROLL IS HERE TO STAY**	Dino DINCD 48 ..	**14**	5 wks
12 Dec 92 ●	**ENERGY RUSH II**	Dino DINCD 55	**7**	4 wks
12 Dec 92 ●	**MEMORIES ARE MADE OF THIS**	Dino DINCD 55	**8**	8 wks
5 Dec 92 ●	**STOMPIN' PARTY**	Dino DINCD 52	**10**	7 wks
13 Feb 93 ★	**BLUES BROTHER SOUL SISTER**	Dino DINCD 56	**1†**	26 wks
30 Jan 93 ●	**ENERGY RUSH LEVEL 3**	Dino DINCD 57	**3**	6 wks
10 Apr 93 ★	**ENERGY RUSH PRESENTS DANCE HITS 93**			
		Dino DINCD 59	**1**	12 wks
5 Jun 93 ●	**ENERGY RUSH PHASE 4**	Dino DINCD 65	**2**	6 wks
10 Jul 93 ●	**HEART FULL OF SOUL**	Dino DINCD 63	**9**	8 wks
17 Jul 93 ●	**BLUES BROTHER SOUL SISTER VOL.2**	Dino DINCD 61	**8**	8 wks
24 Jul 93 ●	**ENERGY RUSH DANCE HITS 93 (2ND DIMENSION)**			
		Dino DINCD 62	**2**	8 wks
4 Sep 93 ●	**THAT LOVING FEELING VOL. VI**	Dino DINCD 64	**4**	8 wks
11 Sep 93 ●	**ENERGY RUSH FACTOR 5**	Dino DINCD 66	**3**	5 wks
18 Sep 93 ●	**RAVE GENERATION**	Dino DINCD 68	**2**	7 wks
25 Sep 93	**MORE THAN UNPLUGGED**	Dino DINCD 69	**11**	3 wks
16 Oct 93 ●	**ENERGY RUSH PRESENTS DANCE HITS OF THE YEAR**			
		Dino DINCD 70	**3†**	11 wks
16 Oct 93 ●	**PLANET ROCK**	Dino DINCD 67	**8**	2 wks
23 Oct 93 ●	**FUTURESHOCK – 20 FURIOUS DANCE TUNES**			
		Dino DINCD 71	**4**	4 wks
23 Oct 93	**COUNTRY WOMEN**	Dino DINCD 72	**11**	3 wks
27 Nov 93 ●	**AS TIME GOES BY**	Dino DINCD 77	**14†**	5 wks
4 Dec 93 ●	**THE VERY BEST OF THAT LOVING FEELING**			
		Dino DINCD 78	**3†**	4 wks
4 Dec 93 ●	**ENERGY RUSH – SAFE SIX**	Dino DINCD 74	**5†**	4 wks
4 Dec 93	**KEEP ON DANCING**	Dino DINCD 80	**14†**	4 wks
25 Dec 93	**LOVE IN THE SIXTIES**	Dino DINCD 81	**17†**	1 wk

DJ International

20 Sep 86	**THE HOUSE SOUND OF CHICAGO**			
		DJ International LONLP 22	**52**	12 wks
18 Apr 87	**THE HOUSE OF SOUND OF CHICAGO VOLUME 2**			
		DJ International LONLP 32	**38**	7 wks
31 Oct 87	**JACKMASTER VOLUME 1**	DJ International JACKLP 501 ...	**36**	4 wks
13 Feb 88	**JACKMASTER VOLUME 2**	DJ International JACKLP 502 ...	**38**	3 wks

Dover

4 Mar 89 ●	**AND ALL BECAUSE THE LADY LOVES . . .**	Dover ADD 6	**2**	10 wks
10 Feb 90 ●	**ALL BY MYSELF**	Dover ADD 12	**2**	15 wks
22 Sep 90 ●	**JUST SEVENTEEN – GET KICKIN'**	Dover ADD 16	**2**	6 wks
24 Nov 90 ●	**A TON OF HITS**	Dover ADD 19	**7**	8 wks
20 Apr 91 ●	**RED HOT METAL – 18 ROCK CLASSICS**	Dover ADD 21	**4**	6 wks
8 Jun 91	**ALL BY MYSELF 2**	Dover ADD 23	**13**	5 wks
14 Sep 91 ●	**MOMENTS IN SOUL**	Dover ADD 25	**2**	7 wks
16 May 92 ●	**THE GREATEST MOMENTS IN SOUL**	Dover CCD 33 .	**4**	7 wks

EMI

21 Jun 69	**IMPACT**	EMI STWO 2	**15**	14 wks
2 Jun 73 ★	**PURE GOLD**	EMI EMK 251	**1**	11 wks
18 Nov 78 ★	**DON'T WALK BOOGIE**	EMI EMTV 13	**1**	23 wks
21 Apr 79 ●	**COUNTRY LIFE**	EMI EMTV 16	**2**	14 wks
2 Jun 79	**KNUCKLE SANDWICH**	EMI International EMYV 18	**19**	6 wks

346

15 Dec	79	ALL ABOARD *EMI EMTX 101*	13	8 wks
23 Feb	80	METAL FOR MUTHAS *EMI EMC 3318*	16	7 wks
14 Jun	80	METAL FOR MUTHAS VOL. 2 *EMI EMC 3337*	58	1 wk
13 Mar	82	20 WITH A BULLET *EMI EMTV 32*	11	8 wks
26 May	84	● THEN CAME ROCK 'N' ROLL *EMI THEN 1*	5	15 wks
5 Mar	88	● UNFORGETTABLE *EMI EMTV 44*	5	21 wks
22 Oct	88	THE CLASSIC EXPERIENCE *EMI EMTVD 45*	27	12 wks
3 Dec	88	HELLO CHILDREN . . . EVERYWHERE *EMI EM 1307* .	59	5 wks
14 Jan	89	● THE CLASSIC EXPERIENCE *EMI EMTVD 45*	8	57 wks
28 Jan	89	UNFORGETTABLE *EMI EMTV 44*	18	1 wk
18 Mar	89	★ UNFORGETTABLE 2 *EMI EMTV 46*	1	15 wks
30 Sep	89	● IS THIS LOVE *EMI EMTV 47*	2	10 wks
18 Nov	89	● THE 80'S – ALBUM OF THE DECADE *EMI EMTVD 48*	1	12 wks
9 Dec	89	● IT'S CHRISTMAS *EMI EMTV 49*	2	16 wks
26 May	90	★ THE CLASSIC EXPERIENCE II *EMI EMTVD 50*	1	32 wks
4 Aug	90	● THE WILD ONE *EMI EMTV 52*	8	7 wks
20 Oct	90	★ MISSING YOU – AN ALBUM OF LOVE *EMI EMTV 53* .	1	18 wks
17 Nov	90	● TRULY UNFORGETTABLE *EMI EMTVD 55*	6	9 wks
1 Dec	90	THE BEST FROM THE MGM MUSICALS *EMI EMTV 56*	12	4 wks
16 Feb	91	● MISSING YOU 2 – AN ALBUM OF LOVE *EMI EMTV 57*	2	11 wks
11 May	91	● THE CLASSIC EXPERIENCE III *EMI EMTVD 59*	3	14 wks
26 Oct	91	● SEXUAL HEALING *EMI EMTV 60*	7	6 wks
30 Nov	91	A CLASSICAL CHRISTMAS *EMI EMTV 62*	14	7 wks
22 Feb	92	● TENDER LOVE – 17 ROMANTIC LOVE SONGS *EMI CDEMTV 64*	2	11 wks
22 Feb	92	● THE CLASSIC ROMANCE *EMI CDEMTV 63*	5	7 wks
22 Aug	92	● MAXIMUM RAVE *EMI CDEMTV 65*	2	9 wks
17 Oct	92	● WICKED!! *EMI CDEMTV 66*	2	5 wks
31 Oct	92	● SMASHIE AND NICEY PRESENT LET'S ROCK! *EMI CDEMTV 67*	8	4 wks
21 Nov	92	● IT'S CHRISTMAS TIME *EMI CDEMTV 69*	3†	12 wks
5 Dec	92	FOREVER *EMI CDEMTV 70*	17	2 wks
20 Feb	93	● SOUL MOODS *EMI CDEMTV 71*	4	8 wks
27 Mar	93	● CLASSIC EXPERIENCE IV *EMI CDEMTVD 72*	9	6 wks
3 Jul	93	INNA DANCEHALL STYLE *EMI CDEMTV 76*	11	4 wks
18 Sep	93	● BACK TO THE 70S *EMI CDEMTV 77*	8	6 wks
6 Nov	93	LET'S GO DISCO *EMI CDEMTV 78*	12	3 wks
27 Nov	93	IT TAKES TWO – LOVE'S GREATEST DUETS *EMI CDEMTV 80*	17	1 wk

EMI/Virgin/PolyGram

23 Feb	91	★ AWESOME! *EMI/Virgin/PolyGram EMTV 58*	1	12 wks
2 Nov	91	● AWESOME! 2 *EMI/Virgin/PolyGram EVP 1*	2	11 wks
25 Jan	92	★ THE ULTIMATE RAVE *EMI/Virgin/PolyGram CDEVP 2* ..	1	15 wks
30 Jan	93	● THE MEGA RAVE *EMI/Virgin/PolyGram CDEVP 3*	2	8 wks
13 Mar	93	● MEGA DANCE – THE POWER ZONE *EMI/Virgin/PolyGram CDEVP 4*	2	8 wks
10 Apr	93	● LOADED *EMI/Virgin/PolyGram CDEVP 5*	6	6 wks
17 Apr	93	● MEGA DANCE 2 – THE ENERGY ZONE *EMI/Virgin/PolyGram CDEVP 6*	3	6 wks

See also Now!

Epic

2 Jul	83	DANCE MIX – DANCE HITS VOL. 1 *Epic EPC 25564* ..	85	2 wks
24 Sep	83	DANCE MIX – DANCE HITS VOL. 2 *Epic DM 2*	51	3 wks
3 Mar	84	DANCE MIX – DANCE HITS VOL. 3 *Epic DM 3*	70	1 wk
3 Mar	84	ELECTRO SHOCK VOLTAGE *Epic VOLT 1*	73	1 wk
16 Jun	84	● AMERICAN HEARTBEAT *Epic EPC 10045*	4	22 wks
16 Jun	84	DANCE MIX – DANCE HITS VOL. 4 *Epic DM 4*	99	1 wk
8 Mar	86	● HITS FOR LOVERS *Epic EPC 10050*	2	14 wks
9 Nov	91	MELLOW MADNESS *Epic MOOD 20*	14	2 wks
18 Jul	92	● RED HOT + DANCE *Epic 4718212*	6	5 wks
29 Aug	92	● ROMANCING THE SCREEN *Epic 4719012*	5	11 wks

ffrr

30 Jan	88	THE HOUSE SOUND OF CHICAGO VOLUME 3 *ffrr FFRLP 1*	40	4 wks
27 Aug	88	THE HOUSE SOUND OF LONDON VOLUME 4 *ffrr FFRDP 4*	70	7 wks
1 Oct	88	BALEARIC BEATS VOLUME 1 *ffrr FFRLP 5*	58	2 wks

VARIOUS ARTISTS

Heart & Soul

28 Mar 87	**HEART OF SOUL VOLUME 1** *Mastersound HASL 001* ... **96**	1 wk
19 Aug 89 ●	**HEART AND SOUL** *Heart & Soul HASTV 1* **2**	12 wks
17 Feb 90 ●	**BODY AND SOUL – HEART AND SOUL II**	
	Heart & Soul 8407761 .... **2**	14 wks
4 Aug 90 ●	**HEART AND SOUL III – HEART FULL OF SOUL**	
	Heart & Soul 8450091 .... **4**	9 wks
16 Feb 91 ●	**SOUL REFLECTION** *Heart & Soul 8453341* **2**	12 wks

The Hit Label

27 Jun 92 ●	**Q THE BLUES** *The Hit Label AHLCD 1* **6**	5 wks
28 Nov 92	**BIG! DANCE HITS OF 92** *The Hit Label AHLCD 4* **11**	7 wks
5 Dec 92	**REMEMBER WHEN SINGERS COULD REALLY SING**	
	The Hit Label AHLCD 3 .... **16**	2 wks
10 Apr 93	**Q RHYTHM AND BLUES** *The Hit Label AHLCD 7* **14**	4 wks
8 May 93 ●	**THE LEGENDARY JOE BLOGGS DANCE ALBUM**	
	The Hit Label AHLCD 10 .... **3**	8 wks
31 Jul 93	**GET IT ON – GREATEST HITS OF THE 70S**	
	The Hit Label AHLCD 12 .... **12**	5 wks
30 Oct 93	**THE LEGENDARY JOE BLOGGS DANCE ALBUM 2**	
	The Hit Label AHLCD 13 .... **15**	2 wks
13 Nov 93	**IT MUST BE LOVE** *The Hit Label AHLCD 17* **11**	2 wks

Hits

1 Dec 84 ★	**THE HITS ALBUM** *CBS/WEA HITS 1* **1**	36 wks
13 Apr 85 ★	**HITS 2** *CBS/WEA HITS 2* **1**	21 wks
7 Dec 85 ●	**HITS 3** *CBS/WEA HITS 3* **2**	21 wks
29 Mar 86 ★	**HITS 4** *CBS/WEA/RCA/Arista HITS 4* **1**	21 wks
22 Nov 86 ★	**HITS 5** *CBS/WEA/RCA/Arista HITS 5* **1**	25 wks
25 Jul 87 ★	**HITS 6** *CBS/WEA/BMG HITS 6* **1**	19 wks
5 Dec 87 ●	**HITS 7** *CBS/WEA/BMG HITS 7* **2**	17 wks
30 Jul 88 ●	**HITS 8** *CBS/WEA/BMG HITS 8* **2**	13 wks
17 Dec 88 ●	**THE HITS ALBUM** *CBS/WEA/BMG HITS 9* **5**	4 wks
14 Jan 89 ●	**THE HITS ALBUM** *CBS/WEA/BMG HITS 9* **4**	7 wks
3 Jun 89 ★	**HITS 10** *CBS/WEA/BMG HITS 10* **1**	13 wks
2 Dec 89 ●	**MONSTER HITS** *CBS/WEA/BMG HITS 11* **2**	14 wks
11 Aug 90 ●	**SNAP IT UP – MONSTER HITS 2**	
	CBS/WEA/BMG HITS 12 .... **2**	10 wks
29 Dec 90 ●	**THE HIT PACK** *CBS/WEA/BMG COMPC 1* **2**	8 wks
10 Aug 91 ★	**THE HITS ALBUM** *CBS/WEA/BMG HITS 15* **1**	9 wks

Impression

16 Oct 82	**BEST FRIENDS** *Impression LP IMP 1* **28**	21 wks
3 Sep 83	**SUNNY AFTERNOON** *Impression LP IMP 2* **13**	8 wks
26 Nov 83	**PRECIOUS MOMENTS** *Impression LP IMP 3* **77**	5 wks
7 Apr 84	**ALWAYS AND FOREVER – THE COLLECTION**	
	Impression LP IMP 4 .... **24**	12 wks
21 Jul 84	**WIPEOUT – 20 INSTRUMENTAL GREATS**	
	Impression LP IMP 5 .... **37**	3 wks
28 Jul 84	**SUNNY AFTERNOON VOLUME TWO**	
	Impression LP IMP 7 .... **90**	1 wk
22 Dec 84	**FRIENDS AGAIN** *Impression LP IMP 8* **91**	1 wk

Island

26 Aug 67	**CLUB SKA '67** *Island ILP 956* **37**	19 wks
14 Jun 69	**YOU CAN ALL JOIN IN** *Island IWPS 2* **18**	10 wks
29 Mar 80	**CLUB SKA '67 (re-issue)** *Island IRSP 4* **53**	6 wks
16 Jun 84	**CREW CUTS** *Island IMA 11* **71**	4 wks
27 Oct 84	**CREW CUTS – LESSON 2** *Island IMA 14* **95**	2 wks
18 Jul 87 ●	**THE ISLAND STORY** *Island ISL 25* **9**	10 wks
3 Nov 90 ●	**HAPPY DAZE VOLUME 1** *Island ILPTV 1* **7**	4 wks
6 Apr 91 ●	**HAPPY DAZE VOLUME 2** *Island ILPTV 3* **17**	2 wks
30 Oct 93 ●	**REGGAE 93** *Island CIDTV 7* **5**	6 wks

Jack Trax

18 Jul 87	**JACK TRAX – THE FIRST ALBUM** *Jack Trax JTRAX 1* .. **83**	2 wks
3 Oct 87	**JACK TRAX – THE SECOND ALBUM** *Jack Trax JTRAX 2* **61**	2 wks
5 Mar 88	**JACK TRAX – THE FOURTH ALBUM** *Jack Trax JTRAX 4* **49**	4 wks

Jetstar

30 Mar 85	**REGGAE HITS VOLUME 1** *Jetstar JETLP 1001* **32**	11 wks
26 Oct 85	**REGGAE HITS VOLUME 2** *Jetstar JETLP 1002* **86**	2 wks

VARIOUS ARTISTS

4 Jun	88		**REGGAE HITS VOLUME 4** *Jetstar JETLP 1004*	**56**	7 wks
17 Dec	88		**REGGAE HITS VOLUME 5** *Jetstar JETLP 1005*	**96**	1 wk
5 Aug	89		**REGGAE HITS VOLUME 6** *Jetstar JETLP 1006*	**13**	6 wks
23 Dec	89		**REGGAE HITS VOLUME 7** *Jetstar JETLP 1007*	**13**	6 wks
30 Jun	90	●	**REGGAE HITS VOLUME 8** *Jetstar JETLP 1008*	**7**	5 wks
20 Jul	91	●	**REGGAE HITS VOLUME 10** *Jetstar JETLP 1010*	**6**	7 wks
18 Apr	92	●	**REGGAE HITS VOLUME 12** *Jetstar JECD 1012*	**5**	6 wks
28 Aug	93		**REGGAE HITS VOLUME 14** *Jetstar JECD 1014*	**13**	1 wk

K-Tel

10 Jun	72	★	**20 DYNAMIC HITS** *K-Tel TE 292*	**1**	28 wks
7 Oct	72	★	**20 ALL TIME HITS OF THE 50'S** *K-Tel NE 490*	**1**	22 wks
29 Nov	72	●	**25 DYNAMIC HITS VOL. 2** *K-Tel TE 291*	**2**	12 wks
2 Dec	72	★	**25 ROCKIN' & ROLLIN' GREATS** *K-Tel NE 493*	**1**	18 wks
31 Mar	73	★	**20 FLASHBACK GREATS OF THE SIXTIES**		
			K-Tel NE 494	**1**	11 wks
21 Apr	73	●	**BELIEVE IN MUSIC** *K-Tel TE 294*	**2**	8 wks
8 Nov	75		**GOOFY GREATS** *K-Tel NE 707*	**19**	7 wks
13 Dec	75	●	**40 SUPER GREATS** *K-Tel NE 708*	**9**	8 wks
31 Jan	76	●	**MUSIC EXPRESS** *K-Tel TE 702*	**3**	10 wks
10 Apr	76	●	**JUKE BOX JIVE** *K-Tel NE 709*	**3**	13 wks
17 Apr	76		**GREAT ITALIAN LOVE SONGS** *K-Tel NE 303* ...	**17**	14 wks
15 May	76	●	**HIT MACHINE** *K-Tel TE 713*	**4**	10 wks
5 Jun	76		**EUROVISION FAVOURITES** *K-Tel NE 712*	**44**	1 wk
2 Oct	76		**SUMMER CRUISING** *K-Tel NE 918*	**30**	1 wk
16 Oct	76	●	**COUNTRY COMFORT** *K-Tel NE 294*	**8**	12 wks
16 Oct	76	★	**SOUL MOTION** *K-Tel NE 930*	**1**	14 wks
4 Dec	76	●	**DISCO ROCKET** *K-Tel NE 948*	**3**	14 wks
11 Dec	76		**44 SUPERSTARS** *K-Tel NE 939*	**14**	10 wks
12 Feb	77	●	**HEARTBREAKERS** *K-Tel NE 954*	**2**	18 wks
19 Feb	77	●	**DANCE TO THE MUSIC** *K-Tel NE 957* ...	**5**	9 wks
7 May	77		**HIT ACTION** *K-Tel NE 993*	**15**	9 wks
29 Oct	77		**SOUL CITY** *K-Tel NE 1003*	**12**	7 wks
12 Nov	77	●	**FEELINGS** *K-Tel NE 1006*	**3**	24 wks
26 Nov	77	★	**DISCO FEVER** *K-Tel NE 1014*	**1**	20 wks
21 Jan	78		**40 NUMBER ONE HITS** *K-Tel NE 1008*	**15**	7 wks
4 Mar	78	●	**DISCO STARS** *K-Tel NE 1022*	**6**	8 wks
10 Jun	78	●	**DISCO DOUBLE** *K-Tel NE 1024*	**10**	6 wks
8 Jul	78		**ROCK RULES** *K-Tel RL 001*	**12**	11 wks
8 Jul	78		**THE WORLD'S WORST RECORD SHOW**		
			Yuk/K-Tel NE 1023	**47**	2 wks
19 Aug	78	●	**STAR PARTY** *K-Tel NE 1034*	**4**	9 wks
4 Nov	78	●	**EMOTIONS** *K-Tel NE 1035*	**2**	17 wks
25 Nov	78	●	**MIDNIGHT HUSTLE** *K-Tel NE 1037*	**2**	13 wks
20 Jan	79	★	**ACTION REPLAY** *K-Tel NE 1040*	**1**	14 wks
7 Apr	79		**DISCO INFERNO** *K-Tel NE 1043*	**11**	9 wks
5 May	79		**HI ENERGY** *K-Tel NE 1044*	**17**	7 wks
22 Sep	79		**HOT TRACKS** *K-Tel NE 1049*	**31**	8 wks
24 Nov	79	●	**NIGHT MOVES** *K-Tel NE 1065*	**10**	10 wks
24 Nov	79		**TOGETHER** *K-Tel NE 1053*	**35**	8 wks
12 Jan	80	●	**VIDEO STARS** *K-Tel NE 1066*	**5**	10 wks
26 Jan	80		**THE SUMMIT** *K-Tel NE 1067*	**17**	5 wks
29 Mar	80	●	**STAR TRACKS** *K-Tel NE 1070*	**6**	8 wks
26 Apr	80		**GOOD MORNING AMERICA** *K-Tel NE 1072*	**15**	12 wks
17 May	80		**HAPPY DAYS** *K-Tel ONE 1076*	**32**	6 wks
17 May	80	●	**MAGIC REGGAE** *K-Tel NE 1074*	**9**	17 wks
14 Jun	80	●	**HOT WAX** *K-Tel NE 1082*	**3**	10 wks
27 Sep	80	●	**MOUNTING EXCITEMENT** *K-Tel NE 1091*	**2**	8 wks
11 Oct	80	●	**THE LOVE ALBUM** *K-Tel NE 1062*	**6**	16 wks
25 Oct	80		**AXE ATTACK** *K-Tel NE 1100*	**15**	14 wks
15 Nov	80	●	**CHART EXPLOSION** *K-Tel NE 1103*	**6**	17 wks
3 Jan	81		**NIGHTLIFE** *K-Tel NE 1107*	**25**	9 wks
14 Feb	81		**HIT MACHINE** *K-Tel NE 1113*	**17**	6 wks
21 Mar	81		**RHYTHM 'N' REGGAE** *K-Tel NE 1115*	**42**	4 wks
25 Apr	81	●	**CHARTBUSTERS 81** *K-Tel NE 1118*	**3**	9 wks
2 May	81		**AXE ATTACK 2** *K-Tel NE 1120*	**31**	6 wks
23 May	81	●	**THEMES** *K-Tel NE 1122*	**6**	15 wks
29 Aug	81		**CALIFORNIA DREAMING** *K-Tel NE 1126*	**27**	11 wks
19 Sep	81		**DANCE DANCE DANCE** *K-Tel NE 1143*	**29**	4 wks
3 Oct	81		**THE PLATINUM ALBUM** *K-Tel NE 1134*	**32**	11 wks
10 Oct	81	●	**LOVE IS . . .** *K-Tel NE 1129*	**10**	15 wks
21 Nov	81	★	**CHART HITS 81** *K-Tel NE 1442*	**1**	17 wks

349

VARIOUS ARTISTS

9 Jan	82 ●	**MODERN DANCE** *K-Tel NE 1156*	**6**	10 wks
6 Feb	82 ●	**DREAMING** *K-Tel NE 1159*	**2**	12 wks
6 Mar	82 ●	**ACTION TRAX** *K-Tel NE 1162*	**2**	12 wks
1 May	82	**MIDNIGHT HOUR** *K-Tel NE 1157*	**98**	1 wk
3 Jul	82	**TURBO TRAX** *K-Tel NE 1176*	**17**	7 wks
4 Sep	82	**THE NO 1 SOUNDS OF THE SEVENTIES** *K-Tel NE 1172*	**83**	1 wk
11 Sep	82 ●	**CHARTBEAT/CHARTHEAT** *K-Tel NE 1180*	**2**	14 wks
30 Oct	82	**THE LOVE SONGS ALBUM** *K-Tel NE 1179*	**28**	8 wks
6 Nov	82	**CHART HITS '82** *K-Tel NE 1195*	**11**	17 wks
6 Nov	82	**DISCO DANCER** *K-Tel NE 1190*	**26**	8 wks
18 Dec	82	**STREETSCENE** *K-Tel NE 1183*	**42**	6 wks
15 Jan	83 ●	**VISIONS** *K-Tel ONE 1199*	**5**	21 wks
12 Feb	83	**HEAVY** *K-Tel NE 1203*	**46**	12 wks
5 Mar	83 ●	**HOTLINE** *K-Tel NE 1207*	**3**	9 wks
11 Jun	83 ●	**CHART STARS** *K-Tel NE 1225*	**7**	9 wks
20 Aug	83	**COOL HEAT** *K-Tel NE 1231*	**79**	3 wks
10 Sep	83 ●	**HEADLINE HITS** *K-Tel NE 1253*	**5**	6 wks
8 Oct	83 ●	**THE TWO OF US** *K-Tel NE 1222*	**3**	16 wks
8 Oct	83	**IMAGES** *K-Tel ONE 1254*	**33**	6 wks
12 Nov	83 ●	**CHART HITS '83 VOLS 1 AND 2** *K-Tel NE 1256*	**6**	11 wks
24 Mar	84	**NIGHT MOVES** *K-tel NE 1255*	**15**	11 wks
26 May	84 ●	**HUNGRY FOR HITS** *K-Tel NE 1272*	**4**	11 wks
23 Jun	84	**THE THEMES ALBUM** *K-Tel ONE 1257*	**43**	3 wks
28 Jul	84	**BREAKDANCE, YOU CAN DO IT** *K-Tel ONE 1276*	**18**	12 wks
12 Sep	84 ●	**ALL BY MYSELF** *K-Tel NE 1273*	**7**	16 wks
1 Dec	84	**HOOKED ON NUMBER ONES – 100 NON-STOP HITS** *K-Tel ONE 1285*	**25**	15 wks
2 Feb	85	**FOUR STAR COUNTRY** *K-Tel NE 1278*	**52**	6 wks
2 Mar	85	**MODERN LOVE** *K-Tel NE 1286*	**13**	7 wks
5 Oct	85	**EXPRESSIONS** *K-Tel NE 1307*	**11**	8 wks
9 Nov	85 ●	**ROCK ANTHEMS** *K-Tel NE 1309*	**10**	11 wks
9 Nov	85	**OVATION – THE BEST OF ANDREW LLOYD WEBBER** *K-Tel ONE 1311*	**34**	12 wks
12 Apr	86 ●	**HEART TO HEART** *K-Tel NE 1318*	**8**	15 wks
19 Apr	86	**ROCK ANTHEMS – VOLUME TWO** *K-Tel NE 1319* ...	**43**	9 wks
5 Jul	86	**RAP IT UP – RAP'S GREATEST HITS** *K-Tel NE 1324* .	**50**	4 wks
19 Jul	86	**DRIVE TIME USA** *K-Tel NE 1321*	**20**	8 wks
18 Oct	86	**DANCE HITS '86** *K-Tel NE 1344*	**35**	7 wks
1 Nov	86	**TOGETHER** *K-Tel NE 1345*	**20**	10 wks
7 Feb	87	**IMPRESSIONS** *K-Tel NE 1346*	**15**	14 wks
21 Mar	87	**RHYTHM OF THE NIGHT** *K-Tel NE 1348*	**36**	7 wks
21 Mar	87	**HITS REVIVAL** *K-Tel (Holland) KTLP 2351*	**63**	1 wk
13 Jun	87 ●	**FRIENDS AND LOVERS** *K-Tel NE 1352*	**10**	10 wks
27 Jun	87 ●	**HITS REVIVAL** *K-Tel NE 1363*	**10**	9 wks
17 Oct	87	**TRUE LOVE** *K-Tel NE 1359*	**38**	5 wks
31 Oct	87 ●	**FROM MOTOWN WITH LOVE** *K-Tel NE 1381*	**9**	9 wks
14 Nov	87	**ALWAYS** *K-Tel NE 1377*	**65**	5 wks
19 Dec	87	**WOW WHAT A PARTY** *K-Tel NE 1388*	**97**	2 wks
5 Mar	88	**HORIZONS** *K-Tel NE 1360*	**13**	10 wks
30 Apr	88	**HITS REVIVAL 2: REPLAY** *K-Tel NE 1405*	**45**	3 wks
14 May	88	**TSOP – THE SOUND OF PHILADELPHIA** *K-Tel NE 1406*	**26**	9 wks
11 Jun	88	**THE HITS OF HOUSE ARE HERE** *K-Tel NE 1419*	**12**	12 wks
15 Oct	88	**MOTOWN IN MOTION** *K-Tel NE 1410*	**28**	13 wks
15 Oct	88	**THE RETURN OF SUPERBAD** *K-Tel NE 1421*	**83**	4 wks
5 Nov	88	**THE LOVERS** *K-Tel NE 1426*	**50**	5 wks
26 Nov	88	**RAPPIN' UP THE HOUSE** *K-Tel NE 1428*	**43**	7 wks
		....		
14 Jan	89	**RAPPIN' UP THE HOUSE** *K-Tel NE 1428*	**19**	1 wk
4 Feb	89 ●	**FROM MOTOWN WITH LOVE** *K-Tel NE 1381*	**6**	7 wks
25 Mar	89 ●	**HIP HOUSE – THE DEEPEST BEATS IN TOWN** *K-Tel NE 1430*	**10**	5 wks
29 Jul	89 ●	**GLAM SLAM** *K-Tel NE 1434*	**5**	8 wks
23 Sep	89 ●	**LOVE HOUSE** *K-Tel NE 1446*	**5**	7 wks
30 Sep	89 ●	**ETERNAL LOVE** *K-Tel NE 1447*	**5**	7 wks
21 Oct	89 ●	**RAP ATTACK** *K-Tel NE 1450*	**6**	7 wks
25 Nov	89	**SEDUCTION** *K-Tel NE 1451*	**15**	4 wks
10 Mar	90	**CAN U FEEL IT? – THE CHAMPION LEGEND** *K-Tel ONE 1452*	**12**	3 wks
21 Apr	90 ●	**HOOKED ON COUNTRY** *K-Tel NE 1459*	**6**	12 wks

London

10 Jun	89 ●	**FFRR – SILVER ON BLACK** *London 8281551*	**8**	5 wks
11 Nov	89 ●	**DANCE DECADE – DANCE HITS OF THE 80's** *London DDTV 1*	**8**	7 wks

350

VARIOUS ARTISTS

16 Jun 90 ● **THE NORTHERN BEAT** _London 8409681_	4	8 wks
7 Jul 90 **MASSIVE 4** _London 8282101_	20	2 wks
8 Feb 92 ● **ONLY FOR THE HEADSTRONG** _London 8283032_	10	1 wk
20 Jun 92 **ONLY FOR THE HEADSTRONG II** _London 8283162_	18	1 wk

Mastercuts
28 Sep 91 **CLASSIC MELLOW MASTERCUTS** _Mastercuts CUTSLP 3_	18	2 wks
21 Mar 92 ● **CLASSIC NEW JACK SWING MASTERCUTS VOL. 1**		
Mastercuts CUTSCD 5	8	5 wks
16 May 92 **CLASSIC FUNK MASTERCUTS VOL. 1**		
Mastercuts CUTSCD 6	14	3 wks
4 Jul 92 **CLASSIC JAZZ FUNK MASTERCUTS VOL. 3**		
Mastercuts CUTSCD 7	18	1 wk
15 Aug 92 **CLASSIC MELLOW MASTERCUTS VOL. 2**		
Mastercuts CUTSCD 8	12	3 wks
6 Mar 93 **CLASSIC SALSOUL MASTERCUTS VOL. 1**		
Mastercuts CUTSCD 10	16	3 wks
24 Apr 93 **CLASSIC RARE GROOVE MASTERCUTS VOL. 1**		
Mastercuts CUTSCD 11	14	3 wks
22 May 93 **CLASSIC P-FUNK MASTERCUTS VOL. 1**		
Mastercuts CUTSCD 12	16	1 wk

Mercury
26 Nov 83 ● **FORMULA 30** _Mercury PROLP 4_	6	17 wks
14 Jun 86 **BEAT RUNS WILD** _Mercury WILD 1_	70	2 wks
1 Nov 86 **FORMULA 30 2** _Mercury PROLP 9_	80	3 wks
....		
26 Oct 91 ★ **TWO ROOMS – ELTON JOHN AND BERNIE TAUPIN**		
Mercury 8457491	1	21 wks

Needle
4 Jul 87 **DANCE MANIA VOLUME 1** _Needle DAMA 1_	46	4 wks
20 Feb 88 **MAD ON HOUSE VOLUME 1** _Needle MADD 1_	81	2 wks
14 May 88 **HOUSE HITS** _Needle HOHI 88_	25	8 wks

Nouveau Music
24 Sep 83 **CLASSIC THEMES** _Nouveau Music NML 1001_	61	2 wks
2 Jun 84 **ESSENTIAL DISCO AND DANCE** _Nouveau Music NML 1010_	96	1 wk
30 Mar 85 **DREAM MELODIES** _Nouveau Music NML 1013_	91	1 wk

Now!
10 Dec 83 ★ **NOW THAT'S WHAT I CALL MUSIC**		
EMI/Virgin NOW 1	1	50 wks
7 Apr 84 ★ **NOW THAT'S WHAT I CALL MUSIC 2**		
EMI/Virgin NOW 2	1	38 wks
11 Aug 84 ★ **NOW THAT'S WHAT I CALL MUSIC 3**		
EMI/Virgin NOW 3	1	30 wks
8 Dec 84 ● **NOW THAT'S WHAT I CALL MUSIC 4**		
EMI/Virgin NOW 4	2	43 wks
1 Jun 85 ● **NOW DANCE** _EMI/Virgin NOD 1_	3	14 wks
17 Aug 85 ★ **NOW THAT'S WHAT I CALL MUSIC 5**		
EMI/Virgin NOW 5	1	21 wks
30 Nov 85 ★ **NOW – THE CHRISTMAS ALBUM** _EMI/Virgin NOX 1_ ..	1	22 wks
7 Dec 85 ★ **NOW THAT'S WHAT I CALL MUSIC 6**		
EMI/Virgin NOW 6	1	40 wks
19 Jul 86 ● **NOW – THE SUMMER ALBUM** _EMI/Virgin SUMMER 1_ .	7	9 wks
23 Aug 86 ★ **NOW THAT'S WHAT I CALL MUSIC 7**		
EMI/Virgin NOW 7	1	21 wks
8 Nov 86 ● **NOW DANCE '86** _EMI/Virgin NOD 2_	2	13 wks
29 Nov 86 **NOW THAT'S WHAT I CALL MUSIC '86**		
EMI/Virgin/PolyGram CDNOW 86	65	4 wks
6 Dec 86 ★ **NOW THAT'S WHAT I CALL MUSIC 8**		
EMI/Virgin/PolyGram NOW 8	1	23 wks
4 Apr 87 ★ **NOW THAT'S WHAT I CALL MUSIC 9**		
EMI/Virgin/PolyGram NOW 9	1	26 wks
3 Oct 87 ● **NOW! SMASH HITS** _EMI/Virgin/PolyGram NOSH 1_	5	10 wks
5 Dec 87 ★ **NOW THAT'S WHAT I CALL MUSIC 10**		
EMI/Virgin/PolyGram NOW 10	1	21 wks
2 Apr 88 ★ **NOW THAT'S WHAT I CALL MUSIC 11**		
EMI/Virgin/PolyGram NOW 11	1	17 wks
23 Jul 88 ★ **NOW THAT'S WHAT I CALL MUSIC 12**		
EMI/Virgin/PolyGram NOW 12	1	17 wks
3 Dec 88 ★ **NOW THAT'S WHAT I CALL MUSIC 13**		
EMI/Virgin/PolyGram NOW 13	1	6 wks

VARIOUS ARTISTS

14 Jan	89 ★	**NOW THAT'S WHAT I CALL MUSIC 13**		
		EMI/Virgin/PolyGram NOW 13	1	15 wks
1 Apr	89 ★	**NOW THAT'S WHAT I CALL MUSIC 14**		
		EMI/Virgin/PolyGram NOW 14	1	18 wks
15 Jul	89 ★	**NOW DANCE '89** *EMI/Virgin NOD 3*	1	14 wks
26 Aug	89 ★	**NOW THAT'S WHAT I CALL MUSIC 15**		
		EMI/Virgin/PolyGram NOW 15	1	13 wks
2 Dec	89 ★	**NOW THAT'S WHAT I CALL MUSIC 16**		
		EMI/Virgin/PolyGram NOW 16	1	15 wks
10 Mar	90 ★	**NOW DANCE 901** *EMI/Virgin/PolyGram NOD 4*	1	14 wks
5 May	90 ★	**NOW THAT'S WHAT I CALL MUSIC 17**		
		EMI/Virgin/PolyGram NOW 17	1	15 wks
28 Jul	90 ★	**NOW DANCE 902** *EMI/Virgin/PolyGram NOD 5*	1	13 wks
10 Nov	90 ★	**NOW DANCE 903** *EMI/Virgin/PolyGram NOD 6*	1	9 wks
1 Dec	90 ★	**NOW THAT'S WHAT I CALL MUSIC 18**		
		EMI/Virgin/PolyGram NOW 18	1	18 wks
6 Apr	91 ★	**NOW THAT'S WHAT I CALL MUSIC 19**		
		EMI/Virgin/PolyGram NOW 19	1	16 wks
5 Oct	91 ★	**NOW DANCE 91** *EMI/Virgin/PolyGram NOD 7*	1	9 wks
30 Nov	91 ★	**NOW THAT'S WHAT I CALL MUSIC 20**		
		EMI/Virgin/PolyGram NOW 20	1	18 wks
25 Apr	92 ★	**NOW THAT'S WHAT I CALL MUSIC 21**		
		EMI/Virgin/PolyGram CDNOW 21	1	13 wks
8 Aug	92 ★	**NOW THAT'S WHAT I CALL MUSIC 22**		
		EMI/Virgin/PolyGram CDNOW 22	1	14 wks
14 Nov	92 ●	**NOW DANCE 92** *EMI/Virgin/PolyGram TCNOD 8*	3	11 wks
28 Nov	92 ★	**NOW THAT'S WHAT I CALL MUSIC 23**		
		EMI/Virgin/PolyGram CDNOW 23	1	18 wks
8 May	93 ★	**NOW THAT'S WHAT I CALL MUSIC 24**		
		EMI/Virgin/PolyGram CDNOW 24	1	13 wks
26 Jun	93 ★	**NOW DANCE 93** *EMI/Virgin/PolyGram CDNOD 9*	1	9 wks
14 Aug	93 ★	**NOW THAT'S WHAT I CALL MUSIC 25**		
		EMI/Virgin/PolyGram CDNOW 25	1	10 wks
4 Sep	93 ●	**NOW THAT'S WHAT I CALL MUSIC 1983**		
		EMI/Virgin/PolyGram CDNOW 1983	10	5 wks
4 Sep	93	**NOW THAT'S WHAT I CALL MUSIC 1984**		
		EMI/Virgin/PolyGram CDNOW 1984	13	4 wks
4 Sep	93	**NOW THAT'S WHAT I CALL MUSIC 1985**		
		EMI/Virgin/PolyGram CDNOW 1985	15	4 wks
4 Sep	93	**NOW THAT'S WHAT I CALL MUSIC 1986**		
		EMI/Virgin/PolyGram CDNOW 1986	16	2 wks
4 Sep	93	**NOW THAT'S WHAT I CALL MUSIC 1987**		
		EMI/Virgin/PolyGram CDNOW 1987	17	2 wks
25 Sep	93	**NOW THAT'S WHAT I CALL MUSIC 1988**		
		EMI/Virgin/PolyGram CDNOW 1988	20	1 wk
25 Sep	93	**NOW THAT'S WHAT I CALL MUSIC 1992**		
		EMI/Virgin/PolyGram CDNOW 1992	14	2 wks
9 Oct	93 ★	**NOW THAT'S WHAT I CALL MUSIC 1993**		
		EMI/Virgin/PolyGram CDNOW 1993	1	8 wks
30 Oct	93 ★	**NOW DANCE – THE BEST OF '93**		
		EMI/Virgin/PolyGram CDNOD 10	1	6 wks
27 Nov	93 ★	**NOW THAT'S WHAT I CALL MUSIC 26**		
		EMI/Virgin/PolyGram CDNOW 26	1†	5 wks

See also EMI/Virgin/PolyGram.

Philips

9 Mar	63 ●	**ALL STAR FESTIVAL** *Philips DL 99500*	4	19 wks
2 Jun	73 ●	**20 ORIGINAL CHART HITS** *Philips TV 1*	9	11 wks
2 Jun	73	**NICE 'N' EASY** *Philips 6441 076*	36	1 wk
6 Aug	77	**NEW WAVE** *Philips 5300 902*	11	12 wks

Polydor

10 Dec	66	**STEREO MUSICALE SHOWCASE** *Polydor 104450*	26	2 wks
9 Oct	71	**THE A–Z OF EASY LISTENING** *Polydor 2661 005*	24	4 wks
24 Feb	79	**20 OF ANOTHER KIND** *Polydor POLS 1006*	45	3 wks
19 May	79	**BOOGIE BUS** *Polydor 9198 174*	23	11 wks
3 May	80 ●	**CHAMPAGNE AND ROSES** *Polydor ROSTV 1*	7	14 wks
30 Aug	80	**I AM WOMAN** *Polydor WOMTV 1*	11	13 wks
11 Oct	80	**COUNTRY ROUND UP** *Polydor KOWTV 1*	64	3 wks
18 Oct	80	**MONSTERS OF ROCK** *Polydor 2488 810*	16	5 wks
6 Dec	80	**THE HITMAKERS** *Polydor HOPTV 1*	45	10 wks
4 Apr	81 ●	**ROLL ON** *Polydor REDTV 1*	3	13 wks

17 Oct	81	**MONSTER TRACKS** *Polydor HOPTV 2*		**20**	8 wks
12 Jan	85	**BREAKDANCE 2 – ELECTRIC BOOGALOO**			
		Polydor POLD 5168		**34**	20 wks
12 Nov	88 ●	**THE PREMIER COLLECTION** *Polydor ALWTV 1*		**3**	9 wks

14 Jan	89 ★	**THE PREMIER COLLECTION** *Polydor ALWTV 1*		**1**	53 wks
4 Feb	89 ★	**THE MARQUEE – 30 LEGENDARY YEARS**			
		Polydor MOTV 1		**1**	21 wks
31 Mar	90 ●	**SKINBEAT – THE FIRST TOUCH** *Polydor SKINL 101* ...		**6**	8 wks
18 Aug	90 ★	**KNEBWORTH – THE ALBUM** *Polydor 843912*		**1**	10 wks
5 Oct	91 ●	**ABSOLUTION – ROCK THE ALTERNATIVE WAY**			
		Polydor 8457471		**6**	5 wks

PolyGram TV

21 Mar	92 ★	**SOUL EMOTION** *PolyGram TV 5151882*		**1**	10 wks
2 May	92 ●	**COUNTRY MOODS** *PolyGram TV 5152992*		**2**	10 wks
6 Jun	92 ●	**POWER CUTS – ROCK'S GREATEST HITS**			
		PolyGram TV 5154152		**5**	9 wks
30 May	92 ●	**BEATS RHYMES AND BASSLINES – THE BEST OF RAP**			
		PolyGram TV 5153842		**7**	3 wks
20 Jun	92 ★	**MODERN LOVE** *PolyGram TV 5155182*		**1**	20 wks
18 Jul	92 ●	**DANCING ON SUNSHINE** *PolyGram TV 5155192*		**4**	11 wks
1 Aug	92 ●	**BLAME IT ON THE BOOGIE** *PolyGram TV 5155172*		**5**	8 wks
5 Sep	92 ●	**READING – THE INDIE ALBUM** *PolyGram TV 5156482* .		**5**	5 wks
27 Mar	93 ●	**COUNTRY ROADS** *PolyGram TV 5161002*		**3**	10 wks
17 Apr	93 ●	**MEGA-LO-MANIA** *PolyGram TV 5158132*		**8**	6 wks
8 May	93 ●	**MIDNIGHT MOODS – THE LIGHTER SIDE OF JAZZ**			
		PolyGram TV 5158162		**3**	8 wks
5 Jun	93 ●	**WOMAN TO WOMAN** *PolyGram TV 5161632*		**6**	10 wks
19 Jun	93 ●	**THE GIFT OF SONG** *PolyGram TV 5160582*		**7**	4 wks
26 Jun	93 ●	**SOUL INSPIRATION** *PolyGram TV 5162262*		**4**	7 wks
3 Jul	93 ●	**THE BLUES EXPERIENCE** *PolyGram TV 5162282*		**7**	6 wks
24 Jul	93 ●	**TEMPTED** *PolyGram TV 5163052*		**10**	4 wks
14 Aug	93 ●	**LEADERS OF THE PACK** *PolyGram TV 5163762*		**9**	6 wks
14 Aug	93	**ALL NIGHT LONG** *PolyGram TV 5163752*		**15**	3 wks
4 Sep	93 ●	**PROGRESSION** *PolyGram TV 5163982*		**9**	3 wks
2 Oct	93 ●	**'ROUND MIDNIGHT** *PolyGram TV 5164712*		**16**	2 wks
9 Oct	93 ●	**DISCO DIVA** *PolyGram TV 5164802*		**4**	5 wks

Pye

9 May	59 ●	**CURTAIN UP** *Pye Nixa BRTH 0059*		**4**	13 wks
23 Jun	62	**HONEY HIT PARADE** *Pye Golden Guinea GGL 0129*		**13**	7 wks
30 Nov	62	**ALL THE HITS BY ALL THE STARS**			
		Pye Golden Guinea GGL 0162		**19**	2 wks
7 Sep	63	**HITSVILLE** *Pye Golden Guinea GGL 0202*		**11**	6 wks
14 Sep	63	**THE BEST OF RADIO LUXEMBOURG**			
		Pye Golden Guinea GGL 0208		**14**	2 wks
23 Nov	63	**HITSVILLE VOL 2** *Pye Golden Guinea GGL 0233*		**20**	1 wk
4 Jan	64	**THE BLUES VOL 1** *Pye NPL 28030*		**15**	3 wks
22 Feb	64	**FOLK FESTIVAL OF THE BLUES (LIVE RECORDING)**			
		Pye NPL 28033		**16**	4 wks
30 May	64	**THE BLUES VOL 2** *Pye NPL 28035*		**16**	3 wks
10 Feb	68	**STARS OF '68** *Marble Arch MAL 762*		**23**	3 wks
16 Oct	71	**PYE CHARTBUSTERS** *Pye PCB 15000*		**36**	1 wk
18 Dec	71	**PYE CHARTBUSTERS VOL 2** *Pye PCB 15001*		**29**	3 wks

Quality Television

15 Feb	92 ●	**HIT THE DECKS VOL. 1 – BATTLE OF THE DJs**			
		Quality Television QTVCD 003		**3**	7 wks
4 Apr	92 ★	**ALL WOMAN** *Quality Television QTVCD 004*		**1**	15 wks
2 May	92 ●	**TEMPTATION** *Quality Television QTVCD 005*		**3**	8 wks
6 Jun	92 ●	**THE SOUND OF SKA** *Quality Television QTVCD 007*		**4**	6 wks
20 Jun	92 ●	**TO HAVE AND TO HOLD – THE WEDDING ALBUM**			
		Quality Television QTVCD 006		**7**	4 wks
4 Jul	92 ●	**HIT THE DECKS VOL. 2 – BATTLE OF THE DJs**			
		Quality Television QYVCD 008		**3**	6 wks
11 Jul	92 ●	**CELEBRATION – THE BEST OF REGGAE**			
		Quality Television QTVCD 0101		**5**	8 wks
18 Jul	92	**DANGER ZONE VOL. 1** *Quality Television QTVCD 009* ..		**17**	3 wks
12 Sep	92 ●	**THREE STEPS TO HEAVEN** *Quality Television QTVCD 011*		**6**	5 wks
10 Oct	92 ★	**ALL WOMAN 2** *Quality Television QTVCD 012*		**1**	7 wks
7 Nov	92 ●	**HIT THE DECKS III** *Quality Television QTVCD 017*		**3**	4 wks
7 Nov	92 ●	**THE POWER OF LOVE** *Quality Television QTVCD 015* ...		**4**	4 wks
21 Nov	92 ●	**RARE GROOVE** *Quality Television QTVCD 016*		**7**	14 wks

353

VARIOUS ARTISTS

16 Jan	93	**ALL WOMAN – THE COMPLETE WOMAN**		
		Quality Television QTVCD 019	19	1 wk
30 Jan	93 ●	**THE NASHVILLE DREAM** *Quality Television QTVCD 014*	10	3 wks
8 May	93 ●	**GLAM MANIA** *Quality Television MANIACD 1*	10	4 wks

React

22 Jun	91	**REACTIVATE VOLUME 1: BELGIAN TECHNO ANTHEMS**		
		React REACTLP	13	4 wks
5 Oct	91 ●	**REACTIVATE VOLUME 2: PHASERS ON FULL**		
		React REACTLP 2	9	4 wks
16 May	92	**REACTIVATE VOL. 4 – TECHNOVATION**		
		React REACTCD 6	16	2 wks
5 Sep	92	**REACTIVATE VOL. 5 – PURE TRANCE**		
		React REACTCD 10	18	2 wks

Ronco

21 Oct	72 ●	**20 STAR TRACKS** *Ronco PP 2001*	2	13 wks
23 Jun	73 ★	**THAT'LL BE THE DAY** *Ronco MR 2002/3*	1	8 wks
8 Nov	75	**BLAZING BULLETS** *Ronco RTI 2012*	17	8 wks
6 Dec	75	**GREATEST HITS OF WALT DISNEY** *Ronco RTD 2013* .	11	12 wks
13 Dec	75	**A CHRISTMAS GIFT** *Ronco P 12430*	39	5 wks
24 Jan	76 ●	**STAR TRACKIN' 76** *Ronco RTL 2014*	9	5 wks
8 Jan	77	**CLASSICAL GOLD** *Ronco RTD 42020*	24	12 wks
16 Jul	77	**SUPERGROUPS** *Ronco RTL 2023*	57	1 wk
26 Nov	77	**BLACK JOY** *Ronco RTL 2025*	26	13 wks
18 Mar	78 ●	**BOOGIE NIGHTS** *Ronco RTL 2027*	5	7 wks
18 Nov	78	**BOOGIE FEVER** *Ronco RTL 2034*	15	11 wks
9 Jun	79	**ROCK LEGENDS** *Ronco RTL 2037*	54	3 wks
3 Nov	79 ●	**ROCK 'N' ROLLER DISCO** *Ronco RTL 2040*	3	11 wks
8 Dec	79 ●	**PEACE IN THE VALLEY** *Ronco RTL 2043*	6	18 wks
22 Dec	79	**MILITARY GOLD** *Ronco RTD 42042*	62	3 wks
25 Oct	80	**STREET LEVEL** *Ronco RTL 2048*	29	5 wks
8 Nov	80 ●	**COUNTRY LEGENDS** *Ronco RTL 2050*	9	12 wks
15 Nov	80	**RADIOACTIVE** *Ronco RTL 2049*	13	9 wks
29 Nov	80	**SPACE INVADERS** *Ronco RTL 2051*	47	3 wks
6 Dec	80	**THE LEGENDARY BIG BANDS** *Ronco RTL 2047*	24	6 wks
9 May	81 ★	**DISCO DAZE AND DISCO NITES**		
		Ronco RTL 2056 A/B	1	23 wks
19 Sep	81 ●	**SUPER HITS 1 & 2** *Ronco RTL 2058 A/B*	2	17 wks
24 Oct	81	**COUNTRY SUNRISE/COUNTRY SUNSET**		
		Ronco RTL 2059 A/B	27	11 wks
14 Nov	81	**ROCK HOUSE** *Ronco RTL 2061*	44	4 wks
12 Dec	81	**MISTY MORNINGS** *Ronco RTL 2066*	44	5 wks
12 Dec	81	**MEMORIES ARE MADE OF THIS** *Ronco RTL 2062*	84	4 wks
26 Dec	81 ●	**HITS HITS HITS** *Ronco RTL 2063*	2	10 wks
24 Apr	82 ●	**DISCO UK & DISCO USA** *Ronco RTL 2073*	7	10 wks
15 May	82 ●	**CHARTBUSTERS** *Ronco RTL 2074*	3	10 wks
3 Jul	82 ●	**OVERLOAD** *Ronco RTL 2079*	10	8 wks
28 Aug	82	**SOUL DAZE/SOUL NITES** *Ronco RTL 2080*	25	10 wks
11 Sep	82 ●	**BREAKOUT** *Ronco RTL 2081*	4	8 wks
30 Oct	82	**MUSIC FOR THE SEASONS** *Ronco RTL 2075*	41	10 wks
27 Nov	82	**CHART WARS** *Ronco RTL 2086*	30	7 wks
27 Nov	82	**THE GREAT COUNTRY MUSIC SHOW**		
		Ronco RTD 2083	38	7 wks
18 Dec	82	**THE BEST OF BEETHOVEN/STRAUSS/**		
		TCHAIKOWSKY/MOZART (4 LPs) *Ronco RTL 2084* .	49	10 wks
25 Dec	82 ★	**RAIDERS OF THE POP CHARTS** *Ronco RTL 2088*	1	17 wks
19 Mar	83 ●	**CHART RUNNERS** *Ronco RTL 2090*	4	13 wks
21 May	83 ●	**CHART ENCOUNTERS OF THE HIT KIND**		
		Ronco RTL 2091	5	10 wks
18 Jun	83	**LOVERS ONLY** *Ronco RTL 2093*	12	13 wks
16 Jul	83	**HITS ON FIRE** *Ronco RTL 2095*	11	10 wks
17 Sep	83 ●	**THE HIT SQUAD – CHART TRACKING**		
		Ronco RON LP 1	4	9 wks
17 Sep	83	**THE HIT SQUAD – NIGHT CLUBBING**		
		Ronco RON LP 2	28	7 wks
12 Nov	83	**HIT SQUAD – HITS OF '83** *Ronco RON LP 4*	12	11 wks
17 Dec	83 ●	**GREEN VELVET** *Ronco RON LP 6*	6	17 wks
7 Jan	84	**CHART TREK VOLS. 1 & 2** *Ronco RON LP 8*	20	9 wks
21 Jan	84 ●	**SOMETIMES WHEN WE TOUCH** *Ronco RON LP 9*	8	14 wks
24 Mar	84	**BABY LOVE** *Ronco RON LP 11*	47	6 wks
7 Apr	84	**DREAMS AND THEMES** *Ronco RON LP 10*	75	2 wks

Green Velvet was re-issued on Telstar STAR 2252.

VARIOUS ARTISTS

Rumour

16 Sep 89	**WAREHOUSE RAVES** *Rumour RUMLD 101*	15	4 wks
31 Mar 90	**WAREHOUSE RAVES 3** *Rumour RUMLD 103*	12	5 wks
29 Sep 90	**WAREHOUSE RAVES 4** *Rumour RUMLD 104*	13	3 wks
11 May 91	**WAREHOUSE RAVES 5** *Rumour RUMLD 105*	18	1 wk
20 Jul 91	**BREAKS BASS AND BLEEPS** *Rumour RAID 504*	20	1 wk
21 Mar 92	**WAREHOUSE RAVES 6** *Rumour CDRUMD 106*	16	2 wks
18 Apr 92	**BREAKS, BASS AND BLEEPS** *Rumour CDRAID 507*	20	1 wk
27 Jun 92	**MOVIN' ON** *Rumour RULCD 300*	20	1 wk
29 Aug 92	**WAREHOUSE RAVES 7** *Rumour CDRUMD 107*	20	1 wk
26 Sep 92	**TRANCE** *Rumour CDRAID 508*	18	1 wk
24 Oct 92	**MOVIN' ON 2** *Rumour RULCD 301*	15	2 wks

Serious

7 Jun 86	**UPFRONT 1** *Serious UPFT 1*	17	10 wks
23 Aug 86	**UPFRONT 2** *Serious UPFT 2*	27	6 wks
1 Nov 86	**UPFRONT 3** *Serious UPFT 3*	37	5 wks
31 Jan 87	**UPFRONT 4** *Serious UPFT 4*	21	5 wks
28 Mar 87	**SERIOUS HIP-HOP 2** *Serious SHOP 2*	95	1 wk
28 Mar 87	**UPFRONT 5** *Serious UPFT 5*	21	6 wks
23 May 87	**UPFRONT 6** *Serious UPFT 6*	22	6 wks
4 Jul 87	**BEST OF HOUSE VOLUME 1** *Serious BEHO 1*	55	12 wks
15 Aug 87	**UPFRONT 7** *Serious UPFT 7*	31	4 wks
12 Sep 87	**BEST OF HOUSE VOLUME 2** *Serious BEHO 2*	30	7 wks
17 Oct 87	**HIP-HOP '87** *Serious HHOP 87*	81	1 wk
17 Oct 87	**UPFRONT 8** *Serious UPFT 8*	22	6 wks
14 Nov 87	**BEST OF HOUSE VOLUME 3** *Serious BEHO 3*	61	3 wks
12 Dec 87	**BEST OF HOUSE MEGAMIX** *Serious BOIT 1*	77	4 wks
19 Dec 87	**UPFRONT 9** *Serious UPFT 9*	92	1 wk
20 Feb 88	**DANCE MANIA VOLUME 2** *Serious DAMA 2*	59	2 wks
12 Mar 88	**BEST OF HOUSE VOLUME 4** *Serious BEHO 4*	27	8 wks
9 Apr 88	**UPFRONT 10** *Serious UPFT 10*	45	5 wks
14 May 88	**BEST OF HOUSE MEGAMIX VOLUME 2** *Serious BOIT 2*	73	2 wks
29 Oct 88	**ACID TRAX MEGAMIX VOLUME 1** *Serious DUIX 1*	93	1 wk
....	....		
18 Feb 89	**UPFRONT '89** *Serious UPFT 89*	15	1 wk

Smash Hits

29 Oct 88	**SMASH HITS PARTY '88** *Dover ADD 5*	12	11 wks
....	....		
14 Jan 89	**SMASH HITS PARTY '88** *Dover ADD 5*	12	5 wks
28 Oct 89 ★	**SMASH HITS PARTY '89** *Dover ADD 8*	1	14 wks
14 Jul 90 ●	**SMASH HITS – RAVE!** *Dover ADD 14*	1	10 wks
3 Nov 90 ●	**SMASH HITS 1990** *Dover ADD 18*	2	14 wks
25 May 91 ★	**SMASH HITS – MASSIVE!** *Dover ADD 24*	1	9 wks
26 Oct 91 ●	**SMASH HITS 1991** *Dover ADD 28*	3	16 wks
22 Aug 92 ●	**SMASH HITS – PARTY ON!** *Dover CCD 34*	9	5 wks
12 Dec 92 ●	**SMASH HITS '92** *Dover ADDCD 35*	5	8 wks
13 Nov 93 ●	**SMASH HITS '93 – 40 TOP CHARTIN' GROOVES** *Chrysalis CDCHR 6058*	4†	7 wks

Starblend

12 Nov 83	**IN TOUCH** *Starblend STD 9*	89	2 wks
23 Jun 84	**BROKEN DREAMS** *Starblend SLTD 1*	48	7 wks
27 Apr 85	**12 X 12 MEGA MIXES** *Starblend INCH 1*	77	2 wks
3 Aug 85	**AMERICAN DREAMS** *Starblend SLTD 12*	43	8 wks
21 Dec 85	**CHRISTMAS AT THE COUNTRY STORE** *Starblend NOEL 1*	94	1 wk
12 Jul 86	**DISCOVER COUNTRY/DISCOVER NEW COUNTRY** *Starblend DNC 1*	60	3 wks
16 Aug 86	**HEARTBREAKERS** *Starblend BLEND 3*	38	8 wks
20 Sep 86	**ABSOLUTE ROCK 'N' ROLL** *Starblend SLTD 15*	88	1 wk

Street Sounds

19 Feb 83	**STREET SOUNDS EDITION 2** *Street Sounds STSND 002* .	35	6 wks
23 Apr 83	**STREET SOUNDS EDITION 3** *Street Sounds STSND 003* .	21	5 wks
25 Jun 83	**STREET SOUNDS EDITION 4** *Street Sounds STSND 004* .	14	8 wks
13 Aug 83	**STREET SOUNDS EDITION 5** *Street Sounds STSND 005* .	16	8 wks
8 Oct 83	**STREET SOUNDS EDITION 6** *Street Sounds STSND 006* .	23	5 wks
22 Oct 83	**STREET SOUNDS ELECTRO 1** *Street Sounds ELCST 1* ..	18	8 wks
17 Dec 83	**STREET SOUNDS EDITION 7** *Street Sounds STSND 007* .	48	4 wks
7 Jan 84	**STREET SOUNDS ELECTRO 2** *Street Sounds ELCST 2* ..	49	7 wks
3 Mar 84	**STREET SOUNDS HI ENERGY 1** *Street Sounds HINRG 16*	71	1 wk

VARIOUS ARTISTS

10 Mar 84	**STREET SOUNDS CRUCIAL ELECTRO**			
	Street Sounds ELCST 999	24	10 wks
10 Mar 84	**STREET SOUNDS EDITION 8** *Street Sounds STSND 008* .	22	7 wks
7 Apr 84	**STREET SOUNDS ELECTRO 3** *Street Sounds ELCST 3* ...	25	9 wks
12 May 84	**STREET SOUNDS EDITION 9** *Street Sounds STSND 009* .	22	5 wks
9 Jun 84	**STREET SOUNDS ELECTRO 4** *Street Sounds ELCST 4* ...	25	9 wks
30 Jun 84	**STREET SOUNDS UK ELECTRO**			
	Street Sounds ELCST 1984	60	4 wks
21 Jul 84	**LET THE MUSIC SCRATCH** *Street Sounds MKL 1*	91	3 wks
11 Aug 84	**STREET SOUNDS CRUCIAL ELECTRO 2**			
	Street Sounds ELCST 1000	35	6 wks
18 Aug 84	**STREET SOUNDS EDITION 10** *Street Sounds STSND 010* .	24	6 wks
6 Oct 84	**STREET SOUNDS ELECTRO 5** *Street Sounds ELCST 5* ...	17	6 wks
10 Nov 84	**STREET SOUNDS EDITION 11** *Street Sounds STSND 011* .	48	4 wks
9 Mar 85	**STREET SOUNDS ELECTRO 6** *Street Sounds ELCST 6* ...	24	10 wks
9 Mar 85	**THE ARTISTS VOLUME 1** *Street Sounds ARTIS 1*	65	4 wks
18 May 85	**STREET SOUNDS ELECTRO 7** *Street Sounds ELCST 7* ..	12	7 wks
18 May 85	**STREET SOUNDS EDITION 12** *Street Sounds STSND 12* .	23	4 wks
13 Jul 85	**STREET SOUNDS ELECTRO 8** *Street Sounds ELCST 8* ...	23	5 wks
13 Jul 85	**THE ARTISTS VOLUME 2** *Street Sounds ARTIS 2*	45	4 wks
17 Aug 85	**STREET SOUNDS EDITION 13** *Street Sounds STSND 13* .	19	9 wks
17 Aug 85	**STREET SOUNDS NY VS LA BEATS**			
	Street Sounds ELCST 1001	65	4 wks
5 Oct 85	**STREET SOUNDS ELECTRO 9** *Street Sounds ELCST 9* ...	18	6 wks
12 Oct 85	**THE ARTISTS VOLUME 3** *Street Sounds ARTIS 3*	87	2 wks
16 Nov 85	**STREET SOUNDS EDITION 14** *Street Sounds STSND 14* .	43	3 wks
21 Dec 85	**STREET SOUNDS ELECTRO 10** *Street Sounds ELCST 10* .	72	6 wks
21 Dec 85	**STREET SOUNDS EDITION 15** *Street Sounds STSND 15* .	58	8 wks
29 Mar 86	**STREET SOUNDS HIP-HOP ELECTRO 11**			
	Street Sounds ELCST 11	19	5 wks
5 Apr 86	**STREET SOUNDS EDITION 16** *Street Sounds STSND 16* .	17	7 wks
21 Jun 86	**JAZZ JUICE 2** *Street Sounds SOUND 4*	96	1 wk
28 Jun 86	**STREET SOUNDS HIP-HOP ELECTRO 12**			
	Street Sounds ELCST 12	28	4 wks
19 Jul 86	**STREET SOUNDS EDITION 17** *Street Sounds STSND 17* ..	35	5 wks
6 Sep 86	**STREET SOUNDS HIP-HOP ELECTRO 13**			
	Street Sounds ELCST 13	23	5 wks
11 Oct 86	**STREET SOUNDS EDITION 18** *Street Sounds STSND 18* .	20	5 wks
11 Oct 86	**JAZZ JUICE 3** *Street Sounds SOUND 5*	88	1 wk
11 Oct 86	**STREET SOUNDS HIP-HOP ELECTRO 14**			
	Street Sounds ELCST 14	40	3 wks
15 Nov 86	**STREET SOUNDS HIP-HOP ELECTRO 15**			
	Street Sounds ELCST 15	46	2 wks
6 Dec 86	**STREET SOUNDS EDITION 19** *Street Sounds STSND 19* .	61	3 wks
24 Jan 87	**STREET SOUNDS ELECTRO 3** *Street Sounds ELCST 1002* .	41	3 wks
7 Feb 87	**STREET SOUNDS ANTHEMS VOLUME 1**			
	Street Sounds MUSIC 5	61	3 wks
14 Feb 87	**STREET SOUNDS EDITION 20** *Street Sounds STSND 20* .	25	4 wks
13 Jun 87	**STREET SOUNDS HIP-HOP ELECTRO 16**			
	Street Sounds ELCST 16	40	3 wks
4 Jul 87	**STREET SOUNDS DANCE MUSIC '87**			
	Street Sounds STSND 871	40	5 wks
15 Aug 87	**STREET SOUNDS HIP-HOP 17** *Street Sounds ELCST 17* .	38	3 wks
15 Aug 87	**JAZZ JUICE 5** *Street Sounds SOUND 8*	97	1 wk
12 Sep 87	**BEST OF WEST COAST HIP HOP** *Street Sounds MACA 1*	80	2 wks
12 Sep 87	**STREET SOUNDS '87 VOLUME 2**			
	Street Sounds STSND 872	47	3 wks
24 Oct 87	**STREET SOUNDS HIP-HOP 18** *Street Sounds ELCST 18* .	67	1 wk
12 Mar 88	**STREET SOUNDS HIP-HOP 20** *Street Sounds ELCST 20* .	39	4 wks
19 Mar 88	**STREET SOUNDS 88–1** *Street Sounds STSND 881*	73	2 wks
4 Jun 88	**STREET SOUNDS HIP-HOP 21** *Street Sounds ELCST 21* .	87	1 wk

Studio Two

21 Oct 67 ●	**BREAKTHROUGH** *Studio Two STWO 1*	2	11 wks
4 Sep 71	**TOTAL SOUND** *Studio Two STWO 4*	39	4 wks
30 Oct 71	**STUDIO TWO CLASSICS** *Studio Two STWO 6*	16	4 wks

Stylus

3 Aug 85	**THE MAGIC OF TORVILL AND DEAN** *Stylus SMR 8502*	35	9 wks
17 Aug 85	**NIGHT BEAT** *Stylus SMR 8501*	15	8 wks
24 Aug 85	**DISCO BEACH PARTY** *Stylus SMR 8503*	29	10 wks
14 Dec 85	**VELVET WATERS** *Stylus SMR 8507*	54	4 wks
28 Dec 85	**CHOICES OF THE HEART** *Stylus SMR 8511*	87	2 wks

8 Mar 86 ●	NIGHT BEAT 2 *Stylus SMR 8613*	7	9 wks
17 May 86	LET'S HEAR IT FROM THE GIRLS *Stylus SMR 8614* ...	17	10 wks
1 Nov 86	BLACK MAGIC *Stylus SMR 619*	26	9 wks
8 Nov 86 ●	HIT MIX '86 *Stylus SMR 624*	10	14 wks
22 Nov 86	CLASSICS BY CANDLELIGHT *Stylus SMR 620*	74	4 wks
14 Mar 87	BANDS OF GOLD – THE SWINGING SIXTIES		
	Stylus SMR 726	48	6 wks
21 Mar 87	BANDS OF GOLD – THE SENSATIONAL SEVENTIES		
	Stylus SMR 727	75	4 wks
28 Mar 87	BANDS OF GOLD – THE ELECTRIC EIGHTIES		
	Stylus SMR 728	82	1 wk
11 Jul 87 ●	SIXTIES MIX *Stylus SMR 733*	3	44 wks
24 Oct 87	HIT FACTORY *Stylus SMR 740*	18	17 wks
21 Nov 87	HIT MIX – HITS OF THE YEAR *Stylus SMR 744*	29	11 wks
2 Apr 88 ●	HIP HOP AND RAPPING IN THE HOUSE		
	Stylus SMR 852	5	13 wks
30 Apr 88	THE WORLDS OF FOSTER AND ALLEN		
	Stylus SMR 861	21	15 wks
7 May 88	SIXTIES MIX 2 *Stylus SMR 855*	14	20 wks
4 Jun 88	BACK ON THE ROAD *Stylus SMR 854*	29	11 wks
30 Jul 88 ●	THE GREATEST EVER ROCK 'N' ROLL MIX		
	Stylus SMR 858	8	15 wks
3 Sep 88 ●	RAP TRAX *Stylus SMR 859*	3	13 wks
1 Oct 88	RARE GROOVE MIX *Stylus SMR 863*	20	10 wks
17 Oct 88	THE GREATEST HITS OF HOUSE *Stylus SMR 867*	26	4 wks
22 Oct 88 ●	SOFT METAL *Stylus SMR 862*	7	12 wks
26 Nov 88	HIT MIX '88 *Stylus SMR 865*	48	7 wks
....			
14 Jan 89 ●	THE GREATEST HITS OF HOUSE *Stylus SMR 867*	5	9 wks
14 Jan 89 ●	SOFT METAL *Stylus SMR 862*	7	27 wks
14 Jan 89	HIT MIX '88 *Stylus SMR 865*	15	2 wks
14 Jan 89	THE WORLDS OF FOSTER AND ALLEN		
	Stylus SMR 861	16	3 wks
18 Feb 89 ●	BEAT THIS – 20 HITS OF RHYTHM KING		
	Stylus SMR 973	9	8 wks
11 Mar 89	NEW ROOTS *Stylus SMR 972*	18	1 wk
25 Mar 89 ●	HIP HOUSE *Stylus SMR 974*	3	8 wks
22 Apr 89 ●	THE SINGER AND THE SONG *Stylus SMR 975*	5	11 wks
27 May 89 ●	PRECIOUS METAL *Stylus SMR 976*	2	29 wks
24 Jun 89 ●	DON'T STOP THE MUSIC *Stylus SMR 977*	7	6 wks
15 Jul 89 ●	HOT SUMMER NIGHTS *Stylus SMR 980*	4	11 wks
19 Aug 89 ●	SUNSHINE MIX *Stylus SMP 986*	9	7 wks
26 Aug 89 ●	THE GREATEST EVER ROCK 'N' ROLL MIX		
	Stylus SMR 858	5	9 wks
2 Sep 89 ●	MIDNIGHT LOVE *Stylus SMR 981*	7	6 wks
16 Sep 89 ●	LEGENDS AND HEROES *Stylus SMR 987*	6	10 wks
21 Oct 89 ●	THE RIGHT STUFF – REMIX '89 *Stylus SMR 990*	2	11 wks
25 Nov 89	JUKE BOX JIVE MIX – ROCK 'N' ROLL GREATS		
	Stylus SMR 993	13	8 wks
30 Dec 89	WARE'S THE HOUSE *Stylus SMR 997*	15	1 wk
13 Jan 90 ★	PURE SOFT METAL *Stylus SMR 996*	1	23 wks
10 Mar 90 ●	RIGHT STUFF 2 – NOTHING BUT A HOUSEPARTY		
	Stylus SMR 998	2	15 wks
26 May 90 ●	SIXTIES MIX 3 *Stylus SMR 021*	4	9 wks
22 Oct 90 ●	MOMENTS IN SOUL *Stylus SMR 023*	9	2 wks

Tamla Motown

3 Apr 65	A COLLECTION OF TAMLA MOTOWN HITS		
	Tamla Motown TML 11001	16	4 wks
4 Mar 67	16 ORIGINAL BIG HITS – VOL. 4		
	Tamla Motown TML 11043	33	3 wks
17 Jun 67	TAMLA MOTOWN HITS VOL. 5		
	Tamla Motown TML 11050	11	40 wks
21 Oct 67 ●	BRITISH MOTOWN CHARTBUSTERS		
	Tamla Motown TML 11055	2	54 wks
10 Feb 68	MOTOWN MEMORIES *Tamla Motown TML 11064*	21	13 wks
24 Aug 68	TAMLA MOTOWN HITS VOL. 6		
	Tamla Motown STML 11074	32	2 wks
30 Nov 68 ●	BRITISH MOTOWN CHARTBUSTERS VOL. 2		
	Tamla Motown STML 11082	8	11 wks
25 Oct 69 ★	BRITISH MOTOWN CHARTBUSTERS VOL. 3		
	Tamla Motown STML 11121	1	93 wks
21 Feb 70	COLLECTION OF BIG HITS VOL. 8		
	Tamla Motown STML 11130	56	1 wk

24 Oct	70 ★	**MOTOWN CHARTBUSTERS VOL. 4**		
		Tamla Motown STML 11162	**1**	40 wks
17 Apr	71 ★	**MOTOWN CHARTBUSTERS VOL. 5**		
		Tamla Motown STML 11181	**1**	36 wks
23 Oct	71 ●	**MOTOWN CHARTBUSTERS VOL. 6**		
		Tamla Motown STML 11191	**2**	36 wks
26 Feb	72	**MOTOWN MEMORIES** *Tamla Motown STML 11200*	**22**	4 wks
18 Mar	72	**MOTOWN STORY** *Tamla Motown TMSP 1130*	**21**	8 wks
29 Nov	72 ●	**MOTOWN CHARTBUSTERS VOL. 7**		
		Tamla Motown STML 11215	**9**	16 wks
3 Nov	73 ●	**MOTOWN CHARTBUSTERS VOL. 8**		
		Tamla Motown STML 11246	**9**	15 wks
26 Oct	74	**MOTOWN CHARTBUSTERS VOL. 9**		
		Tamla Motown STML 11270	**14**	15 wks
1 Nov	75 ●	**MOTOWN GOLD** *Tamla Motown STML 12003*	**8**	35 wks
5 Nov	77	**MOTOWN GOLD VOL. 2** *Motown STML 12070*	**28**	4 wks
7 Oct	78 ●	**BIG WHEELS OF MOTOWN** *Motown EMTV 12*	**2**	18 wks
2 Feb	80 ★	**THE LAST DANCE** *Motown EMTV 20*	**1**	23 wks
2 Aug	80	**THE 20TH ANNIVERSARY ALBUM** *Motown TMSP 6010*	**53**	2 wks
21 May	88 ●	**MOTOWN DANCE PARTY** *Motown ZC 72700*	**3**	18 wks
19 May	90 ●	**MOTOWN DANCE PARTY 2** *Motown ZL 72703*	**10**	7 wks
6 Oct	90 ●	**SOUL DECADE: THE SIXTIES** *Motown ZL 74816*	**3**	10 wks
24 Oct	92 ●	**MOTOWN'S GREATEST LOVE SONGS** *Motown 5300062*	**5**	5 wks

Telstar

16 Oct	82 ●	**CHART ATTACK** *Telstar STAR 2221*	**7**	6 wks
6 Nov	82	**MIDNIGHT IN MOTOWN** *Telstar STAR 2222*	**34**	16 wks
18 Dec	82	**DIRECT HITS** *Telstar STAR 2226*	**89**	1 wk
8 Jan	83	**DANCIN' – 20 ORIGINAL MOTOWN MOVERS**		
		Telstar STAR 2225	**97**	1 wk
5 Feb	83	**INSTRUMENTAL MAGIC** *Telstar STAR 2227*	**68**	5 wks
30 Apr	83	**20 GREAT ITALIAN LOVE SONGS** *Telstar STAR 2230* ..	**28**	6 wks
4 Jun	83	**IN THE GROOVE – THE 12 INCH DISCO PARTY**		
		Telstar STAR 2228	**20**	12 wks
12 Nov	83	**ROOTS REGGAE 'N' REGGAE ROCK** *Telstar STAR 2233*	**34**	6 wks
19 Nov	83	**SUPERCHART '83** *Telstar STAR 2236*	**22**	9 wks
4 Feb	84 ●	**THE VERY BEST OF MOTOWN LOVE SONGS**		
		Telstar STAR 2239	**10**	22 wks
26 May	84	**DON'T STOP DANCING** *Telstar STAR 2242*	**11**	12 wks
13 Oct	84 ●	**HITS HITS HITS – 18 SMASH ORIGINALS**		
		Telstar STAR 2243	**6**	9 wks
8 Dec	84	**LOVE SONGS – 16 CLASSIC LOVE SONGS**		
		Telstar STAR 2246	**20**	12 wks
15 Dec	84 ●	**GREEN VELVET** *Telstar STAR 2252*	**10**	10 wks
7 Sep	85	**OPEN TOP CARS AND GIRLS IN T-SHIRTS**		
		Telstar STAR 2257	**13**	9 wks
16 Nov	85 ★	**THE GREATEST HITS OF 1985** *Telstar STAR 2269*	**1**	17 wks
16 Nov	85 ●	**THE LOVE ALBUM** *Telstar STAR 2268*	**7**	18 wks
30 Nov	85	**THE PRINCE'S TRUST COLLECTION** *Telstar STAR 2275*	**64**	5 wks
7 Dec	85	**PERFORMANCE – THE VERY BEST OF TIM RICE AND**		
		ANDREW LLOYD WEBBER *Telstar STAR 2262*	**33**	7 wks
7 Dec	85	**MORE GREEN VELVET** *Telstar STAR 2267*	**42**	5 wks
18 Dec	86 ●	**THE CHART** *Telstar STAR 2278*	**6**	12 wks
1 Nov	86	**ROCK LEGENDS** *Telstar STAR 2290*	**54**	7 wks
8 Nov	86	**LOVERS** *Telstar STAR 2279*	**14**	16 wks
8 Nov	86 ●	**THE GREATEST HITS OF 1986** *Telstar STAR 2286*	**8**	13 wks
22 Nov	86	**SIXTIES MANIA** *Telstar STAR 2287*	**19**	22 wks
6 Dec	86	**MOTOWN CHARTBUSTERS** *Telstar STAR 2283*	**25**	12 wks
28 Mar	87	**THE DANCE CHART** *Telstar STAR 2285*	**23**	8 wks
3 Oct	87	**TRACKS OF MY TEARS** *Telstar STAR 2295*	**27**	7 wks
21 Nov	87	**THE GREATEST HITS OF 1987** *Telstar STAR 2309*	**12**	11 wks
28 Nov	87	**DANCE MIX '87** *Telstar STAR 2314*	**39**	10 wks
28 Nov	87	**ALWAYS AND FOREVER** *Telstar STAR 2301*	**41**	10 wks
28 Nov	87	**SIXTIES PARTY MEGAMIX ALBUM** *Telstar STAR 2307*	**46**	7 wks
26 Dec	87 ●	**LIFE IN THE FAST LANE** *Telstar STAR 2315*	**10**	12 wks
26 Dec	87	**THE GREATEST LOVE** *Telstar STAR 2316*	**11**	40 wks
1 Oct	88	**. . . AND THE BEAT GOES ON** *Telstar STAR 2338*	**12**	8 wks
5 Nov	88	**THE HEART AND SOUL OF ROCK 'N' ROLL**		
		Telstar STAR 2351	**60**	6 wks
12 Nov	88	**THE LOVE ALBUM '88** *Telstar STAR 2332*	**51**	9 wks
19 Nov	88	**BEST OF HOUSE '88** *Telstar STAR 2347*	**33**	8 wks
19 Nov	88	**INSTRUMENTAL GREATS** *Telstar STAR 2341*	**79**	5 wks
19 Nov	88	**THE GREATEST HITS OF 1988** *Telstar STAR 2334*	**11**	8 wks

3 Dec	88		HYPERACTIVE *Telstar STAR 2328*	**78**	4 wks
3 Dec	88		BACK TO THE SIXTIES *Telstar STAR 2348*	**47**	6 wks
17 Dec	88		MORNING HAS BROKEN *Telstar STAR 2337*	**88**	2 wks
31 Dec	88		THE GREATEST LOVE 2 *Telstar STAR 2352*	**37**	2 wks
14 Jan	89		BEST OF HOUSE 1988 *Telstar STAR 2347*	**11**	5 wks
14 Jan	89		BACK TO THE SIXTIES *Telstar STAR 2348*	**14**	4 wks
14 Jan	89		LOVE SONGS *Telstar STAR 2298*	**18**	2 wks
14 Jan	89	●	THE GREATEST HITS OF 1988 *Telstar STAR 2334*	**8**	8 wks
14 Jan	89	●	THE GREATEST LOVE 2 *Telstar STAR 2352*	**3**	23 wks
14 Jan	89	●	THE GREATEST LOVE *Telstar STAR 2316*	**7**	31 wks
25 Feb	89	★	THE AWARDS *Telstar STAR 2346*	**1**	8 wks
4 Mar	89	★	DEEP HEAT *Telstar STAR 2345*	**1**	15 wks
22 Apr	89	●	DEEP HEAT – THE SECOND BURN *Telstar STAR 2356*	**2**	13 wks
15 Jul	89	●	PROTECT THE INNOCENT *Telstar STAR 2363*	**9**	9 wks
15 Jul	89		RHYTHM OF THE SUN *Telstar STAR 2362*	**12**	4 wks
22 Jul	89	●	THIS IS SKA *Telstar STAR 2366*	**6**	10 wks
22 Jul	89	●	DEEP HEAT 3 – THE THIRD DEGREE *Telstar STAR 2364*	**2**	13 wks
23 Sep	89	★	DEEP HEAT 4 – PLAY WITH FIRE *Telstar STAR 2388* ..	**1**	11 wks
11 Oct	89	●	THE GREATEST LOVE 3 *Telstar STAR 2384*	**4**	18 wks
14 Oct	89	●	MOTOWN HEARTBREAKERS *Telstar STAR 2343*	**4**	10 wks
18 Nov	89	●	NUMBER ONES OF THE EIGHTIES *Telstar STAR 2382* .	**2**	7 wks
18 Nov	89	●	THE GREATEST HITS OF 1989 *Telstar STAR 2389*	**4**	11 wks
18 Nov	89	●	THE GREATEST HITS OF THE 80s *Telstar STAR 2382* .	**2**	18 wks
25 Nov	89	●	DEEP HEAT 1989 – FIGHT THE FLAME		
			Telstar STAR 2380	**4**	17 wks
25 Nov	89	●	HEAVEN AND HELL *Telstar STAR 2361*	**9**	12 wks
9 Dec	89		SOFT ROCK *Telstar STAR 2397*	**15**	5 wks
3 Feb	90	★	DEEP HEAT 5 – FEED THE FEVER *Telstar STAR 2411* .	**1**	11 wks
3 Feb	90		NEW TRADITIONS *Telstar STAR 2399*	**13**	4 wks
10 Feb	90	●	MILESTONES – 20 ROCK OPERAS *Telstar STAR 2379* ..	**6**	11 wks
24 Feb	90	●	THE AWARDS 1990 *Telstar STAR 2368*	**3**	10 wks
17 Mar	90		PRODUCT 2378 *Telstar STAR 2378*	**16**	3 wks
31 Mar	90	★	DEEP HEAT 6 – THE SIXTH SENSE		
			Telstar STAR 2412	**1**	14 wks
12 May	90	●	GET ON THIS! – 30 DANCE HITS VOLUME 1		
			Telstar STAR 22420	**2**	12 wks
19 May	90	●	A NIGHT AT THE OPERA *Telstar STAR 2414*	**2**	12 wks
7 Jul	90	★	DEEP HEAT 7 – SEVENTH HEAVEN		
			Telstar STAR 2422	**1**	9 wks
18 Aug	90	●	MEGABASS *Telstar STAR 2425*	**1**	12 wks
25 Aug	90		MOLTEN METAL *Telstar STAR 2429*	**13**	5 wks
25 Aug	90	●	GET ON THIS!!! 2 *Telstar STAR 2424*	**3**	9 wks
15 Sep	90	●	COUNTRY'S GREATEST HITS *Telstar STAR 2433*	**9**	7 wks
27 Oct	90	●	DEEP HEAT 8 – THE HAND OF FATE		
			Telstar STAR 2447	**3**	5 wks
27 Oct	90	●	FINAL COUNTDOWN – BEST OF SOFT METAL		
			Telstar STAR 2431	**9**	6 wks
27 Oct	90	●	THE GREATEST LOVE 4 *Telstar STAR 2400*	**4**	19 wks
3 Nov	90	●	RAVE *Telstar STAR 2453*	**10**	4 wks
17 Nov	90	●	THE GREATEST HITS OF 1990 *Telstar STAR 2439*	**4**	14 wks
24 Nov	90	●	DEEP HEAT 90 *Telstar STAR 2438*	**3**	12 wks
24 Nov	90	●	THE MOTOWN COLLECTION *Telstar STAR 2375*	**8**	12 wks
1 Dec	90	●	60 NUMBER ONES OF THE SIXTIES *Telstar STAR 2432*	**7**	11 wks
8 Dec	90	●	MEGABASS 2 *Telstar STAR 2448*	**6**	8 wks
8 Dec	90	●	THE VERY BEST OF THE GREATEST LOVE		
			Telstar STAR 2443	**5**	17 wks
26 Jan	91	★	DEEP HEAT 9 – NINTH LIFE *Telstar STAR 2470*	**1**	7 wks
23 Feb	91	●	UNCHAINED MELODIES *Telstar STAR 2480*	**1**	20 wks
23 Mar	91		DON'T STOP – DOOWOP *Telstar STAR 2485*	**15**	4 wks
30 Mar	91	●	THIN ICE – THE FIRST STEP *Telstar STAR 2500*	**2**	9 wks
13 Apr	91		AFTER THE DANCE *Telstar STAR 2501*	**16**	3 wks
11 May	91	●	MASSIVE HITS *Telstar STAR 2505*	**2**	6 wks
18 May	91	●	UNCHAINED MELODIES II *Telstar STAR 2515*	**3**	8 wks
1 Jun	91	●	DEEP HEAT 10 – THE AWAKENING *Telstar STAR 2490*	**2**	7 wks
8 Jun	91	●	MEGABASS 3 *Telstar STAR 2483*	**3**	8 wks
22 Jun	91	●	FAST FORWARD *Telstar STAR 2502*	**4**	8 wks
3 Aug	91	★	THIN ICE 2 – THE SECOND SHIVER *Telstar STAR 2535*	**1**	9 wks
14 Sep	91	●	Q – THE ALBUM VOL 1 *Telstar STAR 2522*	**10**	4 wks
28 Sep	91	●	MAKE YOU SWEAT *Telstar STAR 2542*	**4**	6 wks
12 Oct	91	●	BORN TO BE WILD *Telstar STAR 2524*	**8**	5 wks
2 Nov	91	●	BURNING HEARTS *Telstar STAR 2492*	**7**	10 wks
9 Nov	91	●	BEST OF DANCE 91 *Telstar STAR 2537*	**2**	15 wks
16 Nov	91	●	THE GREATEST HITS OF 1991 *Telstar STAR 2536*	**4**	13 wks

23 Nov 91	● LOVE AT THE MOVIES *Telstar STAR 2545*	6	14 wks
23 Nov 91	PUNK AND DISORDERLY – NEW WAVE		
	Telstar STAR 2520	18	2 wks
30 Nov 91	CLASSICAL MASTERS *Telstar STAR 2549*	13	14 wks
19 Oct 91	● IN LOVE – GREATEST LOVE 5 *Telstar STAR 2510*	5	9 wks
7 Dec 91	LEGENDS OF SOUL – A WHOLE STACK OF SOUL		
	Telstar STAR 2489	15	10 wks
21 Dec 91	● DEEP HEAT 11 – SPIRIT OF ECSTASY		
	Telstar STAR 2555	3	8 wks
15 Feb 92	● KAOS THEORY *Telstar STAR 2562*	2	7 wks
15 Feb 92	● ALL THE BEST – LOVE DUETS VOL. 1		
	Telstar STAR 2557	5	6 wks
29 Feb 92	GOLD – 18 EPIC SPORTING ANTHEMS		
	Telstar TCD 2563	15	3 wks
7 Mar 92	★ THE ULTIMATE HARDCORE *Telstar TCD 2561*	1	10 wks
11 Apr 92	● CLUB FOR HEROES *Telstar TCD 2566*	3	9 wks
2 May 92	● KAOS THEORY 2 *Telstar STAR 2583*	2	8 wks
2 May 92	INDIE HITS *Telstar TCD 2578*	13	3 wks
9 May 92	FLIGHT OF THE CONDOR *Telstar TCD 2576*	11	6 wks
23 May 92	● GARAGE CITY *Telstar TCD 2584*	8	5 wks
6 Jun 93	● RAVING WE'RE RAVING *Telstar TCD 2567*	2	6 wks
18 Jul 92	★ KT3 – KAOS THEORY 3 *Telstar TCD 2593*	1	8 wks
1 Aug 92	● THE DIVAS OF DANCE *Telstar TCD 2592*	9	4 wks
8 Aug 92	● RAVE ALERT *Telstar TCD 2594*	2	10 wks
19 Sep 92	● BLUE EYED SOUL *Telstar TCD 2591*	4	6 wks
10 Oct 92	● KAOS THEORY 4 *Telstar TCD 2605*	2	5 wks
17 Oct 92	● RAVE NATION *Telstar TCD 2607*	2	6 wks
17 Oct 92	● MORE THAN LOVE *Telstar TCD 2606*	4	9 wks
7 Nov 92	★ THE BEST OF DANCE 92 *Telstar TCD 2610*	1	17 wks
14 Nov 92	● CLASSIC LOVE *Telstar TCD 2620*	4	15 wks
14 Nov 92	● THE GREATEST HITS OF 1992 *Telstar TCD 2611*	4	14 wks
21 Nov 92	ROCK 'N' ROLL HEARTBEATS *Telstar TCD 2628*	13	1 wk
21 Nov 92	MY GENERATION *Telstar TCD 2609*	16	1 wk
28 Nov 92	● THE GREATEST HITS OF DANCE *Telstar TCD 2616* ..	5	11 wks
19 Dec 92	SONIC SYSTEM *Telstar TCD 2624*	17	3 wks
23 Jan 93	MOVIE HITS *Telstar TCD 2615*	19	1 wk
6 Feb 93	IN LOVE – GREATEST LOVE 5 *Telstar TCD 2510*	12	2 wks
27 Feb 93	● COUNTRY LOVE *Telstar TCD 2645*	5	15 wks
20 Feb 93	★ HITS 93 VOL. 1 *Telstar TCD 2641*	1	15 wks
3 Apr 93	CLASSICAL MASTERS *Telstar TCD 2549*	18	1 wk
10 Apr 93	● DEEP HEAT 93 VOL. 1 *Telstar TCD 2651*	2	7 wks
29 May 93	● HITS 93 VOL. 2 *Telstar TCD 2661*	2	8 wks
12 Jun 93	THE PIG ATTRACTION FEATURING PINKY AND		
	PERKY *Telstar TCD 2668*	19	2 wks
26 Jun 93	★ 100% DANCE *Telstar TCD 2667*	1	15 wks
3 Jul 93	● RAGGA HEAT REGGAE BEAT *Telstar TCD 2666*	4	14 wks
17 Jul 93	● FRESH DANCE 93 *Telstar TCD 2665*	4	7 wks
14 Aug 93	● HITS 93 VOL. 3 *Telstar TCD 2680*	2	9 wks
18 Sep 93	★ DANCE ADRENALIN *Telstar TCD 2688*	1	7 wks
2 Oct 93	★ 100% DANCE VOL. 2 *Telstar TCD 2681*	1	9 wks
9 Oct 93	● LOVE IS RHYTHM *Telstar TCD 2683*	5	5 wks
9 Oct 93	COUNTRY LOVE *Telstar TCD 2682*	11	4 wks
6 Nov 93	★ THE BEST OF DANCE '93 *Telstar TCD 2662*	1†	8 wks
13 Nov 93	● THE GREATEST HITS OF 1993 *Telstar TCD 2663*	5†	7 wks
20 Nov 93	● HITS 93 VOL. 4 *Telstar CDHITS 934*	2	5 wks
20 Nov 93	THE ALL TIME GREATEST HITS OF DANCE		
	Telstar TCD 2679	11	4 wks
20 Nov 93	THE GREATEST LOVE 6 – WITH LOVE FROM ...		
	Telstar TCD 2686	16	4 wks
11 Dec 93	● 100% REGGAE *Telstar TCD 2659*	5†	3 wks
11 Dec 93	● 100% DANCE VOL. 3 *Telstar TCD 2705*	8†	3 wks
18 Dec 93	A HEART OF GOLD *Telstar TCD 2692*	11†	2 wks

Green Velvet *was a re-issue of Ronco RON LP 6.*

Towerbell

28 Sep 85	THE TV HITS ALBUM *Towerbell TVLP 3*	26	13 wks
8 Feb 86	● THE DANCE HITS ALBUM *Towerbell TVLP 8*	10	11 wks
15 Mar 86	THE CINEMA HITS ALBUM *Towerbell TVLP 9*	44	9 wks
12 Apr 86	THE TV HITS ALBUM TWO *Towerbell TVLP 10*	19	7 wks
17 May 86	SISTERS ARE DOIN' IT *Towerbell TVLP 11*	27	9 wks
7 Jun 86	TWO'S COMPANY *Towerbell TVLP 12*	51	5 wks
28 Jun 86	DANCE HITS II *Towerbell TVLP 13*	25	8 wks
2 Aug 86	THE ORIGINALS *Towerbell TBDLP 14*	15	9 wks
9 Aug 86	YOU'VE GOT TO LAUGH *Towerbell TVLP 15*	51	3 wks

Trax
17 Dec 88	**NOEL – CHRISTMAS SONGS AND CAROLS**			
	Trax TRXLP 701		89	2 wks

22 Jul 89	**DREAMS OF IRELAND** Trax MODEM 1035		19	1 wk
17 Feb 90 ●	**ROCK OF AMERICA** Trax MODEM 1036		7	6 wks
19 May 90 ●	**FREEDOM TO PARTY – FIRST LEGAL RAVE**			
	Trax MODEM 1048		4	10 wks
28 Jul 90 ●	**SUMMER CHART PARTY** Trax BWTX 1		9	6 wks
3 Nov 90	**FREEDOM 2 – THE ULTIMATE RAVE** Trax BWTX 4		16	2 wks
17 Nov 90	**KARAOKE PARTY** Trax BETX 5		20	1 wk
16 Mar 91 ●	**KARAOKE PARTY II** Trax TXTV 1		7	9 wks

Trojan
7 Aug 71	**TIGHTEN UP VOLUME 4** Trojan TBL 163		20	7 wks
21 Aug 71	**CLUB REGGAE** Trojan TBL 159		25	4 wks
16 Jun 84	**20 REGGAE CLASSICS** Trojan TRLS 222		89	1 wk

TV
2 Oct 82	**MODERN HEROES** TV TVA 1		24	7 wks
9 Oct 82	**ENDLESS LOVE** TV TV 2		26	8 wks
6 Nov 82	**FLASH TRACKS** TV PTVL 1		19	7 wks
25 Dec 82	**PARTY FEVER/DISCO MANIA** TV TVA 5		71	3 wks

2 Tone
26 Nov 83	**THIS ARE TWO TONE** 2 Tone CHRTT 5007		51	9 wks

5 Aug 89	**THE 2 TONE STORY** 2 Tone CHRTT 5009		16	5 wks
23 Oct 93 ●	**THE BEST OF 2 TONE** 2 Tone CDCHRTT 5012		10	4 wks

Urban
14 Nov 87	**URBAN CLASSICS** Urban URBLP 4		96	1 wk
24 Sep 88	**URBAN ACID** Urban URBLP 15		51	8 wks
8 Oct 88	**ACID JAZZ AND OTHER ILLICIT GROOVES**			
	Urban URBLP 16		86	3 wks

Vertigo
21 Jun 86	**HEAR 'N' AID** Vertigo VERH 35		50	2 wks
27 Aug 88 ★	**HOT CITY NIGHTS** Vertigo PROVTV 15		1	14 wks

4 Nov 89 ●	**ROCK CITY NIGHTS** Vertigo RCNTV 1		3	14 wks

Virgin
22 Nov 80	**CASH COWS** Virgin MILK 1		49	1 wk
17 Apr 82	**MUSIC OF QUALITY AND DISTINCTION (VOLUME 1)**			
	Virgin V 2219		25	6 wks
1 Jun 85	**MASSIVE** Virgin V 2346		61	3 wks

Virgin Television
19 Jan 91	**DANCE ENERGY** Virgin Television VTDLP 3		20	2 wks
1 Jun 91 ●	**DANCE ENERGY VOLUME 2** Virgin Television VTLP 4		6	5 wks
19 Oct 91 ●	**MOODS** Virgin Television VTLP 5		2	22 wks
30 Nov 91 ●	**DANCE ENERGY VOLUME 3** Virgin Television VTLP 6		10	6 wks
29 Feb 92 ●	**THREE MINUTE HEROES** Virgin Television VTCD 9		4	10 wks
16 May 92 ●	**MOODS 2** Virgin Television VTCD 12		3	8 wks
25 Jul 92 ●	**THE GREATEST DANCE ALBUM IN THE WORLD!**			
	Virgin Television VTCD 13		2	12 wks
31 Oct 92 ●	**NEW ROMANTIC CLASSICS** Virgin Television VTCD 15		7	5 wks
17 Jul 93 ★	**THE BEST DANCE ALBUM IN THE WORLD ... EVER!**			
	Virgin Television VTDCD 17		1	19 wks
23 Oct 93 ●	**THE SINGER AND THE SONG**			
	Virgin Television VTDCD 21		5	6 wks
20 Nov 93 ●	**THE BEST DANCE ALBUM IN THE WORLD ... EVER! 2**			
	Virgin Television VTDCD 22		3†	6 wks
4 Dec 93 ●	**THE BEST CHRISTMAS ... EVER!**			
	Virgin Television VTDCD 23		2†	4 wks

Vital Sounds
4 Jul 92	**RED HOT AND WHITE LABELS** Vital Sounds CDVIT 1		17	2 wks
26 Sep 92	**RED HOT AND WHITE 2** Vital Sounds CDVIT 2		13	2 wks
29 May 93	**STRICTLY RAGGA** Vital Sounds CDVIT 3		12	2 wks

Warner Bros.
25 Mar 78	**HOPE AND ANCHOR FRONT ROW FESTIVAL**			
	Warner Bros. K 66077		28	3 wks

361

VARIOUS ARTISTS

21 Jul 79 ★ **THE BEST DISCO ALBUM IN THE WORLD**		
Warner Bros. K 58062	**1**	17 wks

4 Aug 90 **NOBODY'S CHILD – ROMANIAN ANGEL APPEAL**		
Warner Bros. WX 353	**18**	3 wks
15 Aug 92 **BARCELONA GOLD** *Warner Bros. 9362450462*	**15**	2 wks

Warwick

29 Nov 75 **ALL-TIME PARTY HITS** *Warwick WW 5001*	**21**	8 wks
17 Apr 76 ● **INSTRUMENTAL GOLD** *Warwick WW 5012*	**3**	24 wks
29 May 76 **HAMILTON'S HOT SHOTS** *Warwick WW 5014*	**15**	5 wks
8 Jan 77 **SONGS OF PRAISE** *Warwick WW 5020*	**31**	2 wks
29 Jan 77 **HIT SCENE** *Warwick PR 5023*	**19**	5 wks
11 Mar 78 ● **FONZIE'S FAVOURITES** *Warwick WW 5037*	**8**	16 wks
25 Nov 78 **LOVE SONGS** *Warwick WW 5046*	**47**	7 wks
2 Dec 78 **BLACK VELVET** *Warwick WW 5047*	**72**	3 wks
31 Mar 79 **LEMON POPSICLE** *Warwick WW 5050*	**42**	6 wks
7 Apr 79 **COUNTRY PORTRAITS** *Warwick WW 5057*	**14**	10 wks
10 Nov 79 **20 SMASH DISCO HITS (THE BITCH)** *Warwick WW 5061*	**42**	5 wks
16 Feb 80 **COUNTRY GUITAR** *Warwick WW 5070*	**46**	3 wks
14 Nov 81 **DISCO EROTICA** *Warwick WW 5108*	**35**	8 wks
10 Apr 82 **PS I LOVE YOU** *Warwick WW 5121*	**68**	3 wks
6 Nov 82 **HITS OF THE SCREAMING 60'S** *Warwick WW 5124*	**24**	10 wks
22 Dec 84 **MERRY CHRISTMAS TO YOU** *Warwick WW 5141*	**64**	2 wks

————————— *Other Compilation Albums* —————————

10 Mar 62 **GREAT MOTION PICTURE THEMES** *HMV CLP 1508* .	**19**	1 wk
24 Aug 63 **THE MERSEY BEAT VOLUME 1** *Oriole PS 40047*	**17**	5 wks
16 May 64 **OUT CAME THE BLUES** *Ace of Hearts AH 72*	**19**	1 wk
11 Sep 66 **STARS CHARITY FANTASIA SAVE THE CHILDREN**		
FUND *SCF PL 145*	**6**	16 wks
8 Apr 67 ● **HIT THE ROAD STAX** *Stax 589005*	**10**	16 wks
11 May 68 **BLUES ANYTIME** *Immediate IMLP 014*	**40**	1 wk
4 Dec 71 **BREAKTHROUGH** *MFP 1334*	**49**	1 wk
22 Jan 72 ★ **CONCERT FOR BANGLADESH** *Apple STCX 3385*	**1**	13 wks
15 Mar 75 **SOLID SOUL SENSATIONS** *Disco Diamond DDLP 5001* ..	**30**	1 wk
16 Aug 75 **NEVER TOO YOUNG TO ROCK** *GTO GTLP 004*	**30**	5 wks
6 Dec 75 **SUPERSONIC** *Stallion SSM 001*	**21**	6 wks
31 Jan 76 **REGGAE CHARTBUSTERS 75** *Cactus CTLP 114*	**53**	1 wk
22 May 76 ● **A TOUCH OF COUNTRY** *Topaz TOC 1976*	**7**	7 wks
3 Jul 76 **GOLDEN FIDDLE AWARDS 1976** *Mountain TOPC 5002* .	**45**	2 wks
3 Jul 76 **A TOUCH OF CLASS** *Topaz TOC 1976*	**57**	1 wk
27 Nov 76 **ALL THIS AND WORLD WAR II** *Riva RVLP 2*	**23**	7 wks
16 Jul 77 **THE ROXY LONDON WC 2** *Harvest SHSP 4069*	**24**	5 wks
11 Mar 78 **STIFF'S LIVE STIFFS** *Stiff GET 1*	**28**	7 wks
28 Oct 78 **ECSTASY** *Lotus WH 5003*	**24**	6 wks
9 Dec 78 **STARS ON SUNDAY BY REQUEST**		
Curzon Sounds CSL 0081	**65**	3 wks
26 May 79 **A MONUMENT TO BRITISH ROCK** *Harvest EMTV 17* .	**13**	12 wks
9 Jun 79 **THAT SUMMER** *Arista SPART 1088*	**36**	8 wks
3 Nov 79 **MODS MAYDAY 79** *Arista FOUR 1*	**75**	1 wk
24 May 80 **PRECIOUS METAL** *MCA MCF 3069*	**60**	2 wks
14 Mar 81 **THE SOME BIZARRE ALBUM** *Some Bizzare BZLP 1*	**58**	1 wk
4 Apr 81 **REMIXTURE** *Champagne CHAMP 1*	**32**	5 wks
30 May 81 **STRENGTH THROUGH OI!** *Skin SKIN 1*	**51**	5 wks
31 Oct 81 **CARRY ON OI!** *Secret SEC 2*	**60**	4 wks
12 Dec 81 **LIVE AND HEAVY** *NEMS NEL 6020*	**100**	2 wks
19 Dec 81 **WE ARE MOST AMUSED** *Ronco/Charisma RTD 2067*	**30**	9 wks
27 Mar 82 ● **JAMES BOND'S GREATEST HITS** *Liberty EMTV 007* ...	**4**	13 wks
27 Mar 82 **PUNK AND DISORDERLY** *Abstract AABT 100*	**48**	8 wks
14 Aug 82 **SOWETO** *Rough Trade ROUGH 37*	**66**	3 wks
4 Sep 82 **PUNK AND DISORDERLY – FURTHER CHARGES**		
Anagram GRAM 001	**91**	2 wks
25 Sep 82 **OI OI THAT'S YOUR LOT** *Secret SEC 5*	**54**	4 wks
23 Oct 82 **STREET NOISE VOLUME 1** *Streetware STR 32234*	**51**	4 wks
14 May 83 **THE LAUGHTER AND TEARS COLLECTION**		
WEA LTC 1	**19**	16 wks
18 Jun 83 **TEARDROPS** *Ritz RITZSP 399*	**37**	6 wks
2 Jul 83 **WIRED FOR CLUBS (CLUB TRACKS VOLUME 1)**		
Club CLUBL 1001	**58**	4 wks
3 Sep 83 **COME WITH CLUB (CLUB TRACKS VOLUME 2)**		
Club CLUBL 002	**55**	2 wks

VARIOUS ARTISTS

15 Oct	83	**RESPOND PACKAGE – LOVE THE REASON**		
		Respond RRL 501	50	3 wks
26 Nov	83	**TWELVE INCHES OF PLEASURE** *Proto PROTO 1*	100	1 wk
16 Jun	84 ●	**EMERALD CLASSICS** *Stoic SRTV 1*	10	14 wks
21 Jul	84	**ROCKABILLY PSYCHOSIS AND THE GARAGE DISEASE**		
		Big Beat WIK 18	88	3 wks
11 Aug	84	**CHUNKS OF FUNK** *Loose End CHUNK 1*	46	5 wks
8 Sep	84	**RECORD SHACK PRESENTS – VOLUME ONE**		
		Record Shack RSTV 1	41	4 wks
8 Dec	84	**THE CHRISTMAS CAROL COLLECTION**		
		Fame WHS 413000	75	3 wks
16 Feb	85	**STARGAZERS** *Kasino KTV 1*	69	3 wks
6 Apr	85	**TOMMY BOY GREATEST BEATS** *Tommy Boy ILPS 9825*	44	6 wks
25 May	85 ●	**OUT NOW!** *Chrysalis/MCA OUTV 1*	2	16 wks
13 Jul	85	**KERRANG! KOMPILATION** *EMI/Virgin KER 1*	84	2 wks
24 Aug	85	**20 HOLIDAY HITS** *Creole CTV 1*	48	6 wks
19 Oct	85	**IQ6: ZANG TUMB TUUM SAMPLED** *ZTT IQ 6*	40	3 wks
26 Oct	85 ●	**OUT NOW! 2** *Chrysalis/MCA OUTV 2*	3	12 wks
16 Aug	86 ●	**THE HEAT IS ON** *Portrait PRT 10051*	9	12 wks
16 Aug	86	**SUMMER DAYS, BOOGIE NIGHTS** *Portrait PRT 10052* .	40	6 wks
18 Oct	86	**THE POWER OF LOVE** *West Five WEF 4*	33	7 wks
30 May	87	**THE SOLAR SYSTEM** *Solar MCG 3338*	70	1 wk
6 Jun	87	**CHICAGO JACKBEAT VOLUME 2** *Rhythm King LEFTLP 2*	67	2 wks
11 Jul	87	**LONELY IS AN EYESORE** *4AD CAD 703*	53	2 wks
1 Aug	87	**FIERCE** *Cooltempo CTLP 4*	37	6 wks
8 Aug	87	**KICK IT! – THE DEF JAM SAMPLER ALBUM**		
		Def Jam KICKIT 1	19	7 wks
24 Oct	87	**THE WORD** *Zomba HOP 217*	86	1 wk
26 Mar	88	**THE WORD VOLUME 2** *Jive HOP 220*	70	2 wks
9 Apr	88	**SERGEANT PEPPER KNEW MY FATHER**		
		NME PELP 100	37	8 wks
3 Sep	88	**HOUSE HALLUCINATIONS (PUMP UP LONDON)**		
		Breakout HOSA 9002	90	2 wks
8 Oct	88	**BROTHERS IN RHYTHM** *Ariola 303374*	35	5 wks
12 Nov	88	**THE HIT FACTORY VOLUME 2** *Fanfare/PWL HF 4*	16	9 wks
14 Jan	89	**THE HIT FACTORY VOLUME 2** *Fanfare/PWL HF 4*	13	3 wks
18 Feb	89	**CAPITOL CLASSICS VOLUME 1** *Capitol EMS 1316*	16	2 wks
15 Apr	89	**THE SONGS OF BOB DYLAN** *Start STDL 20*	13	5 wks
1 Jul	89	**THIS IS GARAGE** *Cooltempo CTLP 12*	18	2 wks
15 Jul	89 ●	**THE HIT FACTORY VOLUME 3** *Fanfare/PWL HF 8* ...	3	10 wks
23 Sep	89 ●	**JUST SEVENTEEN – HEARTBEATS** *Fanfare FARE 1* ...	3	6 wks
14 Oct	89 ●	**ITALIA – DANCE MUSIC FROM ITALY**		
		deConstruction 64289	4	6 wks
24 Mar	90	**EMERALD CLASSICS VOLUMES I & 11**		
		Westmoor WMTV 1	14	2 wks
7 Apr	90	**LET'S DANCE – SOUND OF THE SIXTIES PART 1**		
		Old Gold OG 1702	18	1 wk
21 Apr	90 ●	**THE EARTHQUAKE ALBUM**		
		Live Aid Armenia AIDLP 001	3	10 wks
16 Jun	90	**LOVERS FOR LOVERS VOLUME 3** *Business WBRLP 903*	18	1 wk
28 Jul	90	**NOTHING COMPARES TO THIS** *Parkfield PMLP 5020* ..	13	2 wks
13 Oct	90 ●	**ESSENTIAL CLASSICS** *Deutsche Grammophon 4315411*	6	9 wks
3 Nov	90 ●	**RED HOT AND BLUE** *Chrysalis CHR 1799*	6	3 wks
22 Dec	90	**CHRISTMAS GREATEST HITS** *Legends In LELP 501*	16	1 wk
16 Mar	91 ●	**PETER HETHERINGTON: SONGS FROM THE HEART**		
		Mawson And Wareham PHMC 2	10	3 wks
4 May	91 ●	**MARQUEE METAL** *Marquee 8454171*	5	6 wks
11 May	91 ●	**THE BEST OF INDIE TOP 20** *Beechwood BOTT 1*	10	3 wks
18 May	91	**SOUTHERN KNIGHTS** *Knight KTVLP 1*	13	2 wks
22 Jun	91 ●	**IT'S COOL** *Parlophone PCSTV 1*	3	7 wks
13 Jul	91 ★	**PURPLE RAINBOWS** *Polydor/EMI 8455341*	1	13 wks
14 Sep	91 ●	**XL RECORDINGS – THE SECOND CHAPTER**		
		XL XLLP 108	5	9 wks
28 Sep	91 ●	**THE POWER AND THE GLORY** *Vertigo 5103601*	2	9 wks
12 Oct	91	**I'M YOUR FAN – THE SONGS OF LEONARD COHEN**		
		East West WX 444	16	2 wks
9 Nov	91	**RAVE** *Reachin' REMULP 01*	18	2 wks
16 Nov	91	**R & S RECORDS – ORDER TO DANCE**		
		R & S RSLP 1	18	1 wk
18 Jan	92	**NOISE** *Jumpin' & Pumpin' CDTOT 3*	20	1 wk
1 Feb	92	**CLOSET CLASSICS VOL. 1** *More Protein CMMD 1*	20	1 wk
22 Feb	92	**SHUT UP AND DANCE**		
		Shut Up And Dance SUADCOMPCD 001	20	1 wk

VARIOUS ARTISTS

7 Mar 92	**THE REBIRTH OF COOL, TOO**	
	Fourth & Broadway BRCD 582	13 2 wks
28 Mar 92 ●	**LIVING CLASSICS** *Deutsche Grammophon 4356432*	7 5 wks
11 Apr 92	**RAVE 2 – STRICTLY HARDCORE** *Elevate ELVCD 02* ..	11 3 wks
11 Apr 92	**DISCOVER THE CLASSICS VOL. 1**	
	Imp Classics CDBOXD 21	15 3 wks
11 Apr 92	**DISCOVER THE CLASSICS VOL. 2**	
	Imp Classics CDBOXD 22	12 3 wks
25 Apr 92 ●	**THE THIRD CHAPTER** *XL XLCD 109*	6 8 wks
9 May 92	**VIRUS 100 – ALTERNATIVE TENTACLES**	
	Alternative Tentacles VIRUS 100CD	15 1 wk
16 May 92	**NOISE 2** *Jumpin' & Pumpin' CDTOT 4*	11 3 wks
13 Jun 92 ★	**EARTHRISE – THE RAINFOREST ALBUM** *ELF 5154192*	1 6 wks
27 Jun 92	**JUNGLE TEKNO** *Debut CDTOT 5*	18 1 wk
4 Jul 92 ●	**DANCE ENERGY – FEEL THE RHYTHM**	
	Parlophone CDPMTV 4	6 4 wks
11 Jul 92	**THE ULTIMATE OPERA COLLECTION** *Erato 2292457972*	14 5 wks
1 Aug 92	**HARDCORE DJs . . . TAKE CONTROL**	
	Perfecto 74321101812	15 4 wks
8 Aug 92	**RAVING MAD** *Elevate CDELV 01*	17 2 wks
19 Sep 92	**ILLEGAL RAVE** *Strictly Underground STHCCD 1*	20 1 wk
26 Sep 92	**VOLUME FOUR** *Worlds End V 4CD*	17 1 wk
21 Nov 92	**SENSUAL CLASSICS** *Teldec 4509900552*	19 2 wks
28 Nov 92 ●	**THE PREMIERE COLLECTION ENCORE**	
	Really Useful 5173362	2 11 wks
5 Dec 92	**TAKE 2: OPERA FAVOURITES/ORCHESTRAL CLASSICS**	
	Masterworks S2K 48226	18 3 wks
5 Dec 92	**FANTAZIA – THE FIRST TASTE** *Fantazia FANTA 001* .	13 5 wks
30 Jan 92 ●	**TALKIN LOUD TWO** *Talkin Loud 5159362*	6 3 wks
13 Feb 93 ●	**CELTIC HEART** *RCA 74321131662*	6 10 wks
27 Feb 93	**THE WIND DOWN ZONE** *Elevate CDELV 04*	17 3 wks
27 Feb 93	**FULL ON – A YEAR IN THE LIFE OF HOUSE**	
	Deconstruction 74321128032	18 2 wks
6 Mar 93	**AMBIENT DUB VOL. 2 – EARTH JUICE**	
	Beyond RABDCD 3	20 1 wk
13 Mar 93 ●	**D-FROST – 20 GLOBAL DANCE WARNINGS**	
	Touchdown CTVCD 114	8 4 wks
20 Mar 93	**YEAH YEAH YEAH YEAH/OUR TROUBLES YOUTH**	
	Catcall/Wiiija TUSS 001	12 2 wks
17 Apr 93	**DUB HOUSE DISCO 2000** *Guerilla GRCD 7*	18 1 wk
24 Apr 93	**WINNER'S CIRCLE** *Expansion CDEXP 2*	20 1 wk
1 May 93	**VOLUME SIX** *Volume 6VCD 6*	19 1 wk
8 May 93	**COWBOY COMPILATION** *Cowboy RODEOCD 1*	18 1 wk
15 May 93 ●	**THE REBIRTH OF COOL III**	
	Fourth & Broadway BRCD 590	9 4 wks
15 May 93	**UNIVERSE** *Universe VERSECD 1*	13 2 wks
29 May 93	**THE BEST OF ACID JAZZ VOL. 2** *Acid Jazz JAZIDCD 66*	16 1 wk
26 Jun 93	**DISCO INFERNO** *East West 9548319632*	17 1 wk
3 Jul 93 ●	**ON A REGGAE TIP** *Mango CIDTV 5*	3 9 wks
24 Jul 93	**FANTAZIA – TWICE AS NICE** *Fantazia FANTA 002CD* .	17 3 wks
11 Sep 93	**MINISTRY OF SOUND: THE SESSIONS VOL. 1**	
	Ministry Of Sound MINSTCD 1	16 2 wks
2 Oct 93	**TRANCE EUROPE EXPRESS** *Volume TEEXCD 1*	14 3 wks

364

FILM SOUNDTRACKS

8 Nov 58 ★	**SOUTH PACIFIC** *RCA RB 16065*	1 286 wks
8 Nov 58 ●	**THE KING AND I** *Capitol LCT 6108*	4 103 wks
8 Nov 58 ●	**OKLAHOMA** *Capitol LCT 6100*	4 90 wks
6 Dec 58 ●	**CAROUSEL** *Capitol LCT 6105*	8 15 wks
31 Jan 59 ●	**GIGI** *MGM C 770*	2 88 wks
10 Oct 59 ●	**PORGY AND BESS** *Philips ABL 3282*	7 5 wks
23 Jan 60 ●	**THE FIVE PENNIES** *London HAU 2189*	2 15 wks
7 May 60 ●	**CAN CAN** *Capitol W 1301*	2 31 wks
28 May 60	**PAL JOEY** *Capitol LCT 6148*	20 1 wk
23 Jul 60	**HIGH SOCIETY** *Capitol LCT 6116*	16 1 wk
5 Nov 60	**BEN HUR** *MGM C 802*	15 3 wks
21 Jan 61	**NEVER ON SUNDAY** *London HAT 2309*	17 1 wk
18 Feb 61 ●	**SONG WITHOUT END** *Pye GGL 30169*	9 10 wks
29 Apr 61 ●	**SEVEN BRIDES FOR SEVEN BROTHERS** *MGM C 853*	6 22 wks
3 Jun 61	**EXODUS** *RCA RD 27210*	17 1 wk
11 Nov 61	**GLENN MILLER STORY** *Ace Of Hearts AH 12*	12 7 wks

VARIOUS ARTISTS

24 Mar	62 ★	**WEST SIDE STORY** *Philips BBL 7530*	1	175 wks
28 Apr	62 ●	**IT'S TRAD DAD** *Columbia 33SX 1412*	3	21 wks
22 Sep	62	**THE MUSIC MAN** *Warner Bros. WB 4066*	14	9 wks
3 Nov	62	**PORGY AND BESS** *CBS APG 60002*	14	7 wks
15 Jun	63	**JUST FOR FUN** *Decca LK 4524*	20	2 wks
31 Oct	64 ●	**MY FAIR LADY** *CBS BPG 72237*	9	51 wks
31 Oct	64	**GOLDFINGER** *United Artists ULP 1076*	14	5 wks
16 Jan	65 ●	**MARY POPPINS** *HMV CLP 1794*	2	82 wks
10 Apr	65 ★	**SOUND OF MUSIC** *RCA RB 6616*	1	381 wks
30 Apr	66	**FUNNY GIRL** *Capitol W 2059*	19	3 wks
11 Sep	66 ●	**DR ZHIVAGO** *MGM C 8007*	3	106 wks
22 Jul	67	**CASINO ROYALE** *RCA Victor SF 7874*	35	1 wk
29 Jul	67	**A MAN AND A WOMAN** *United Artists SULP 1155*	31	11 wks
28 Oct	67 ●	**THOROUGHLY MODERN MILLIE** *Brunswick STA 8685* .	9	19 wks
9 Mar	68 ●	**THE JUNGLE BOOK** *Disney ST 3948*	5	51 wks
21 Sep	68	**STAR** *Stateside SSL 10233*	36	1 wk
12 Oct	68 ●	**THE GOOD, THE BAD AND THE UGLY**		
		United Artists SULP 1197	2	18 wks
23 Nov	68 ●	**OLIVER** *RCA Victor SB 6777*	4	107 wks
23 Nov	68	**CAMELOT** *Warner Bros. WS 1712*	37	1 wk
8 Feb	69 ●	**CHITTY CHITTY BANG BANG**		
		United Artists SULP 1200	10	4 wks
10 May	69	**FUNNY GIRL** *CBS 70044*	11	22 wks
14 Jun	69 ●	**2001 – A SPACE ODYSSEY** *MGM CS 8078*	3	67 wks
20 Dec	69 ●	**EASY RIDER** *Stateside SSL 5018*	2	67 wks
24 Jan	70	**JUNGLE BOOK (re-issue)** *Disney BVS 4041* (re-issue)	25	26 wks
7 Feb	70 ●	**PAINT YOUR WAGON** *Paramount SPFL 257*	2	102 wks
14 Mar	70	**HELLO DOLLY** *Stateside SSL 10292*	45	2 wks
18 Jul	70	**WOODSTOCK** *Atlantic 2662 001*	35	19 wks
24 Apr	71 ●	**LOVE STORY** *Paramount SPFL 267*	10	33 wks
12 Feb	72 ●	**CLOCKWORK ORANGE** *Warner Bros. K 46127*	4	46 wks
8 Apr	72	**FIDDLER ON THE ROOF** *United Artists UAD 60011/2* ...	26	2 wks
13 May	72	**2001 – A SPACE ODYSSEY (re-issue)** *MGM 2315 034* ...	20	2 wks
29 Nov	72	**SOUTH PACIFIC (re-issue)** *RCA Victor SB 2011* ...	25	2 wks
31 Mar	73	**CABARET** *Probe SPB 1052*	13	22 wks
14 Apr	73	**LOST HORIZON** *Bell SYBEL 8000*	36	3 wks
22 Sep	73	**JESUS CHRIST SUPERSTAR** *MCA MDKS 8012/3*	23	18 wks
23 Mar	74 ●	**THE STING** *MCA MCF 2537*	7	35 wks
27 Apr	74	**AMERICAN GRAFFITI** *MCA MCSP 253*	37	1 wk
8 Jun	74	**A TOUCH OF CLASS** *Philips 6612 040*	32	1 wk
5 Oct	74	**SUNSHINE** *MCA MCF 2566*	47	3 wks
5 Apr	75	**TOMMY** *Polydor 2657 014*	21	9 wks
31 Jan	76	**JAWS** *MCA MCF 2716*	55	1 wk
5 Mar	77	**MOSES** *Pye 28503*	43	2 wks
9 Apr	77 ★	**A STAR IS BORN** *CBS 86021*	1	54 wks
2 Jul	77	**THE BEST OF CAR WASH** *MCA MCF 2799*	59	1 wk
11 Mar	78 ★	**SATURDAY NIGHT FEVER** *RSO 2658 123*	1	65 wks
22 Apr	78 ●	**THE STUD** *Ronco RTD 2029*	2	19 wks
29 Apr	78	**CLOSE ENCOUNTERS OF THE THIRD KIND**		
		Arista DLART 2001	40	6 wks
6 May	78	**THE LAST WALTZ** *Warner Bros. K 66076*	39	4 wks
20 May	78	**THANK GOD IT'S FRIDAY** *Casablanca TGIF 100*	40	5 wks
27 May	78	**FM** *MCA MCSP 284*	37	7 wks
8 Jul	78 ★	**GREASE** *RSO RSD 2001*	1	47 wks
12 Aug	78	**SGT PEPPER'S LONELY HEARTS CLUB BAND**		
		A & M AMLZ 66600	38	2 wks
7 Oct	78	**CONVOY** *Capitol EST 24590*	52	1 wk
30 Jun	79	**THE WORLD IS FULL OF MARRIED MEN**		
		Ronco RTD 2038	25	9 wks
14 Jul	79	**THE WARRIORS** *A & M AMLH 64761*	53	7 wks
6 Oct	79	**QUADROPHENIA** *Polydor 2625 037*	23	16 wks
5 Jan	80	**THE SECRET POLICEMAN'S BALL** *Island ILPS 9601* ...	33	6 wks
9 Feb	80	**SUNBURN** *Warwick RTL 2044*	45	7 wks
16 Feb	80	**GOING STEADY** *Warwick WW 5078*	25	10 wks
8 Mar	80	**THE ROSE** *Atlantic K 50681*	68	1 wk
7 Jun	80	**THE GREAT ROCK 'N' ROLL SWINDLE** *Virgin V 2168*	16	11 wks
19 Jul	80 ●	**XANADU** *Jet JET LX 526*	2	17 wks
16 Aug	80 ●	**CAN'T STOP THE MUSIC** *Mercury 6399 051*	9	8 wks
6 Sep	80 ★	**FAME** *RSO 2479 253*	1	25 wks
14 Feb	81 ●	**DANCE CRAZE** *2-Tone CHRTT 5004*	5	15 wks
12 Dec	81	**THE SECRET POLICEMAN'S OTHER BALL**		
		Springtime HAHA 6003	69	4 wks
20 Mar	82	**THE SECRET POLICEMAN'S OTHER BALL (THE**		
		MUSIC) *Springtime HAHA 6004*	29	5 wks

VARIOUS ARTISTS

17 Jul	82	THE SOUND OF MUSIC (re-issue) *RCA Ints 5134*	98	1 wk
4 Sep	82	ROCKY III *Liberty LBG 30351*	42	7 wks
4 Sep	82	ANNIE *CBS 70219*	83	2 wks
11 Sep	82	BRIMSTONE AND TREACLE *A & M AMLH 64915*	67	3 wks
12 Feb	83	AN OFFICER AND A GENTLEMAN *Island ISTA 3*	40	14 wks
25 Jun	83	RETURN OF THE JEDI *RSO RSD 5023*	85	5 wks
2 Jul	83 ●	FLASHDANCE *Casablanca CANH 5*	9	30 wks
1 Oct	83	STAYING ALIVE *RSO RSBG 3*	14	8 wks
21 Apr	84 ●	FOOTLOOSE *CBS 70246*	7	25 wks
21 Apr	84	AGAINST ALL ODDS *Virgin V 2313*	29	10 wks
16 Jun	84 ●	BREAKDANCE *Polydor POLD 5147*	6	29 wks
7 Jul	84	BEAT STREET *Atlantic 780154*	30	13 wks
18 Aug	84	ELECTRIC DREAMS *Virgin V 2318*	46	7 wks
29 Sep	84	GHOSTBUSTERS *Arista 206 559*	24	25 wks
16 Feb	85	BEVERLY HILLS COP *MCA MCF 3253*	24	32 wks
22 Jun	85	A VIEW TO A KILL *Parlophone BOND 1*	81	1 wk
11 Jan	86	BACK TO THE FUTURE *MCA MCF 3285*	66	8 wks
1 Feb	86	MISTRAL'S DAUGHTER *Carrere CAL 221*	53	3 wks
1 Feb	86 ●	ROCKY IV *Scotti Brothers SCT 70272*	3	22 wks
5 Apr	86	ABSOLUTE BEGINNERS *Virgin V 2386*	19	9 wks
26 Apr	86	OUT OF AFRICA *MCA MCF 3310*	81	2 wks
5 Jul	86	LABYRINTH *EMI America AML 3104*	38	2 wks
11 Oct	86 ●	TOP GUN *CBS 70296*	4	46 wks
11 Apr	87	THE BLUES BROTHERS *Atlantic K 50715*	59	26 wks
2 May	87	PLATOON *WEA WX 95*	90	2 wks
18 Jul	87	BEVERLY HILLS COP 2 *MCA MCF 3383*	71	5 wks
1 Aug	87	THE LIVING DAYLIGHTS *Warner Bros. WX 111*	57	6 wks
1 Aug	87 ●	WHO'S THAT GIRL *Sire WX 102*	4	25 wks
22 Aug	87	LA BAMBA *London LONLP 36*	24	15 wks
3 Oct	87	FULL METAL JACKET *Warner Bros. 925 613–1*	60	4 wks
31 Oct	87 ●	DIRTY DANCING *RCA BL 86408*	4	63 wks
16 Jan	88	FLASHDANCE (re-issue) *Mercury PRICE 111*	93	2 wks
20 Feb	88	CRY FREEDOM *MCA MCG 6029*	73	2 wks
14 May	88 ●	MORE DIRTY DANCING *RCA BL 86965*	3	27 wks
24 Sep	88 ●	BUSTER *Virgin V 2544*	6	16 wks
22 Oct	88	GOOD MORNING VIETNAM *A & M AMA 3913*	50	10 wks
14 Jan	89 ●	BUSTER *Virgin V 2544*	2	36 wks
14 Jan	89 ★	DIRTY DANCING *RCA BL 86408*	1	144 wks
21 Jan	89 ●	GOOD MORNING VIETNAM *A & M AMA 3913*	7	29 wks
21 Jan	89 ●	THE BLUES BROTHERS *Atlantic K 50715*	4	78 wks
28 Jan	89 ★	THE LOST BOYS *Atlantic 7817671*	1	59 wks
4 Feb	89 ●	COCKTAIL *Elektra EKT 54*	2	15 wks
4 Feb	89	MORE DIRTY DANCING *RCA BL 86965*	14	17 wks
18 Mar	89	SCANDAL *Parlophone PCS 7331*	13	3 wks
22 Apr	89 ●	TOP GUN *CBS 70296*	4	34 wks
13 May	89	DIRTY DANCING – LIVE IN CONCERT *RCA BL 90336*	19	2 wks
15 Jul	89	LICENCE TO KILL *MCA MCG 6051*	17	2 wks
22 Jul	89	GHOSTBUSTERS 2 *MCA MCG 6056*	15	4 wks
10 Mar	90	THE DELINQUENTS *PWL HF 11*	16	1 wk
26 May	90 ●	PRETTY WOMAN *EMI USA MTL 1052*	2	71 wks
23 Jun	90 ●	TEENAGE MUTANT NINJA TURTLES *SBK SBKLP 6*	6	18 wks
11 Aug	90 ●	DAYS OF THUNDER *Epic 4671591*	4	15 wks
27 Oct	90	GHOST *Milan A 620*	15	4 wks
2 Feb	91 ●	ROCKY V *Capitol EST 2137*	9	9 wks
2 Mar	91 ●	GREASE (re-issue) *Polydor 8179981*	8	11 wks
23 Mar	91	THE GODFATHER III *Columbia 4678131*	19	1 wk
27 Apr	91	NEW JACK CITY *Giant 7599244091*	16	5 wks
1 Jun	91 ●	MERMAIDS *Epic 467874*	6	15 wks
27 Jul	91 ●	ROBIN HOOD – PRINCE OF THIEVES *Polydor 5110502*	3	14 wks
18 Jan	92 ●	BILL AND TED'S BOGUS JOURNEY *Interscope 7567917252*	3	8 wks
29 Feb	92	MY GIRL *Epic 4692134*	13	7 wks
30 May	92 ●	WAYNE'S WORLD *Reprise 7599258052*	5	11 wks
12 Sep	92 ●	THE BEST OF JAMES BOND – 30TH ANNIVERSARY *EMI CDBOND 007*	2	11 wks
19 Sep	92	MO' MONEY *Perspective 3610042*	16	1 wk
14 Nov	92	BOOMERANG *LaFace 73008260062*	17	2 wks
28 Nov	92 ★	THE BODYGUARD *Arista 07822186992*	1†	57 wks
30 Jan	93	SISTER ACT *Hollywood HWDCD 29*	14	4 wks
13 Feb	93 ●	BRAM STOKER'S DRACULA *Columbia 4727462*	10	6 wks
20 Mar	93	RESERVOIR DOGS *MCA MCD 10793*	16	1 wk
5 Jun	93	INDECENT PROPOSAL *MCA MCD 10863*	13	3 wks
24 Jul	93	THE LAST ACTION HERO *Columbia 4739902*	16	6 wks
18 Sep	93	SLIVER *Virgin CDVMMX 11*	20	1 wk

16 Oct	93 ●	SLEEPLESS IN SEATTLE *Epic 4735942*	**10**	6 wks
16 Oct	93	JUDGEMENT NIGHT *Epic 4741832*	**16**	2 wks
20 Nov	93 ●	THE VERY BEST OF DISNEY *Pickwick DISCD 471*	**4†**	6 wks

During its chart run, West Side Story changed label and number from Philips BBL 7530 to CBS BPG 62058.

STAGE CAST RECORDINGS

These albums still qualify for inclusion on the main chart, not the Compilation Albums chart.

8 Nov	58 ●	MY FAIR LADY (BROADWAY) *Philips RBL 1000*	**2**	129 wks
24 Jan	59 ●	WEST SIDE STORY (BROADWAY) *Philips BBL 7277* ...	**3**	27 wks
26 Mar	60 ●	AT THE DROP OF A HAT (LONDON)		
		Parlophone PMC 1033	**9**	1 wk
26 Mar	60 ●	FINGS AIN'T WOT THEY USED TO BE (LONDON)		
		Decca LK 4346	**5**	11 wks
2 Apr	60 ●	FLOWER DRUM SONG (BROADWAY)		
		Philips ABL 3302	**2**	27 wks
7 May	60 ●	FOLLOW THAT GIRL (LONDON) *HMV CLP 1366*	**5**	9 wks
21 May	60 ●	MOST HAPPY FELLA (BROADWAY) *Philips BBL 7374* .	**6**	13 wks
21 May	60	MAKE ME AN OFFER (LONDON) *HMV CLP 1333*	**18**	1 wk
28 May	60 ●	FLOWER DRUM SONG (LONDON) *HMV CLP 1359* ...	**10**	3 wks
9 Jul	60	MOST HAPPY FELLA (LONDON) *HMV CLP 1365*	**19**	1 wk
30 Jul	60	WEST SIDE STORY (BROADWAY) *Philips SBBL 504* ...	**14**	1 wk
10 Sep	60 ●	OLIVER (LONDON) *Decca LK 4359*	**4**	91 wks
11 Mar	61	KING KONG (SOUTH AFRICA) *Decca LK 4392*	**12**	8 wks
6 May	61 ●	MUSIC MAN (LONDON) *JMH CLP 1444*	**8**	13 wks
24 Jun	61 ●	SOUND OF MUSIC (BROADWAY) *Philips ABL 3370* ...	**4**	19 wks
22 Jul	61	BYE-BYE BIRDIE (LONDON) *Philips ABL 3385*	**17**	3 wks
22 Jul	61	BEYOND THE FRINGE (LONDON)		
		Parlophone PMC 1145	**13**	17 wks
29 Jul	61 ●	SOUND OF MUSIC (LONDON) *HMV CLP 1453*	**4**	68 wks
9 Sep	61 ●	STOP THE WORLD I WANT TO GET OFF (LONDON)		
		Decca LK 4408	**8**	14 wks
14 Jul	62 ●	BLITZ (LONDON) *HMV CLP 1569*	**7**	21 wks
18 May	63	HALF A SIXPENCE (LONDON) *Decca LK 4521*	**20**	2 wks
3 Aug	63	PICKWICK (LONDON) *Philips AL 3431*	**12**	10 wks
4 Jan	64	MY FAIR LADY (BROADWAY) *CBS BPG 68001*	**19**	1 wk
22 Feb	64	AT THE DROP OF ANOTHER HAT (LONDON)		
		Parlophone PMC 1216	**12**	11 wks
3 Oct	64 ●	CAMELOT (BROADWAY) *CBS APG 60001*	**10**	12 wks
16 Jan	65	CAMELOT (LONDON) *HMV CLP 1756*	**19**	1 wk
11 Mar	67 ●	FIDDLER ON THE ROOF (LONDON)		
		CBS SBPG 70030	**4**	50 wks
28 Dec	68 ●	HAIR (LONDON) *Polydor 583–043*	**3**	94 wks
30 Aug	69	OLIVER (LONDON) (re-issue) *Decca SPA 30*	**23**	4 wks
6 Sep	69	HAIR (BROADWAY) *RCA SF 7959*	**29**	3 wks
19 Feb	72	GODSPELL (LONDON) *Bell BELLS 203*	**25**	17 wks
18 Nov	78	EVITA (LONDON) *MCA MCF 3257*	**24**	18 wks
1 Aug	81 ●	CATS (LONDON) *Polydor CATX 001*	**6**	26 wks
6 Nov	82	MACK AND MABEL (BROADWAY)		
		MCA MCL 1728	**38**	7 wks
7 Aug	84	STARLIGHT EXPRESS (LONDON)		
		Starlight/Polydor LNER 1	**21**	9 wks
15 Feb	86	LES MISERABLES (LONDON)		
		First Night ENCORE 1	**72**	4 wks
21 Feb	87 ★	THE PHANTOM OF THE OPERA (LONDON)		
		Polydor PODV 9/Really Useful PODV 3	**1**	141 wks
16 Sep	89 ★	ASPECTS OF LOVE (LONDON) *Polydor 841126 1*	**1**	29 wks
24 Feb	90 ●	MISS SAIGON (LONDON) *Geffen WX329*	**4**	11 wks
29 Jun	91	FIVE GUYS NAMED MOE (LONDON)		
		First Night CAST 23	**59**	1 wk
31 Aug	91 ★	JOSEPH AND THE AMAZING TECHNICOLOR		
		DREAMCOAT (LONDON) *Really Useful 511301*	**1**	38 wks
10 Apr	93	THE NEW STARLIGHT EXPRESS (LONDON)		
		Really Useful 5190412	**42**	2 wks
11 Sep	93	SUNSET BOULEVARD (LONDON)		
		Really Useful 5197672	**11**	4 wks
2 Oct	93	GREASE (LONDON) *Epic 4746322*	**20**	3 wks

The Really Useful label was given credit midway through The Phantom of the Opera's chart run.

367

STUDIO CAST RECORDINGS

These albums still qualify for inclusion in the main chart, not the Compilation Albums chart.

25 Jun 60	**SHOWBOAT** *HMV CLP 1310*	12	1 wk
8 Feb 72 ●	**JESUS CHRIST SUPERSTAR** *MCA MKPS 2011/2*	6	20 wks
22 Jan 77 ●	**EVITA** *MCA MCX 503*	4	35 wks
17 Jun 78	**WHITE MANSIONS** *A & M AMLX 64691*	51	3 wks
10 Nov 84 ●	**CHESS** *RCA PL 70500*	10	16 wks
18 May 85	**WEST SIDE STORY** *Deutsche Grammophon 41525*	11	32 wks
2 Nov 85	**CHESS PIECES** *Telstar STAR 2274*	87	3 wks
10 May 86	**WEST SIDE STORY – HIGHLIGHTS**		
	Deutsche Grammophon 45963	72	6 wks
17 May 86	**DAVE CLARK'S 'TIME'** *EMI AMPH 1*	21	6 wks
11 Oct 86 ●	**SOUTH PACIFIC** *CBS SM 42205*	5	24 wks
27 Jun 87	**MATADOR** *Epic VIVA 1*	26	5 wks
21 Nov 87	**MY FAIR LADY** *DECCA MFL 1*	41	12 wks
10 Oct 92	**THE KING AND I** *Philips 4380072*	57	2 wks
10 Apr 93	**LEONARD BERNSTEIN'S WEST SIDE STORY**		
	IMG IMGCD 1801	33	5 wks

TV and RADIO SOUNDTRACKS and SPIN-OFFS

TV and RADIO SOUNDTRACKS (for example, the *Doctor Who* albums) qualify for the main artist album chart.

13 Dec 58 ●	**OH BOY!** *Parlophone PMC 1072*	9	14 wks
4 Mar 61 ●	**HUCKLEBERRY HOUND** *Pye GGL 004*	10	12 wks
28 Feb 63	**THAT WAS THE WEEK THAT WAS**		
	Parlophone PMC 1197	11	9 wks
28 Mar 64	**STARS FROM STARS AND GARTERS** *Pye GGL 0252* .	17	2 wks
4 Nov 72	**THE BBC 1922–1972 (TV AND RADIO EXTRACTS)**		
	BBC 50	16	7 wks
4 Jan 75	**BBC TV'S BEST OF TOP OF THE POPS**		
	Super Beeb BELP 001	21	5 wks
10 Apr 76 ★	**ROCK FOLLIES** *Island ILPS 9362*	1	15 wks
22 Oct 77	**10 YEARS OF HITS – RADIO ONE** *Super Beeb BEDP 002*	39	3 wks
8 Apr 78 ●	**PENNIES FROM HEAVEN** *World Records SH 266*	10	17 wks
1 Jul 78	**MORE PENNIES FROM HEAVEN** *World Records SH 267* .	31	4 wks
15 Dec 79	**FAWLTY TOWERS** *BBC REB 377*	25	10 wks
7 Feb 81	**FAWLTY TOWERS VOLUME 2** *BBC REB 405*	26	7 wks
14 Feb 81	**HITCHHIKERS GUIDE TO THE GALAXY VOLUME 2**		
	Original ORA 54	47	4 wks
1 Aug 81	**MUSIC OF COSMOS** *RCA RCALP 5032*	43	10 wks
21 Nov 81	**BRIDESHEAD REVISITED** *Chrysalis CDL 1367*	50	12 wks
23 Oct 82	**ON THE AIR – 60 YEARS OF BBC THEME MUSIC**		
	BBC REF 454	85	3 wks
26 Nov 83	**REILLY ACE OF THEMES** *Red Bus BUSLP 1004*	54	6 wks
4 Feb 84	**AUF WIEDERSEHEN PET** *Towerbell AUF 1*	21	6 wks
18 Feb 84	**THE TUBE** *K-Tel NE 1261*	30	6 wks
8 Sep 84	**SONG AND DANCE** *RCA BL 70480*	46	4 wks
18 May 85	**VICTORY IN EUROPE – BROADCASTS FROM BBC**		
	CORRESPONDENTS *BBC REC 562*	61	1 wk
28 Sep 85	**THE TV HITS ALBUM** *Towerbell TVLP 3*	26	13 wks
26 Oct 85	**MIAMI VICE** *BBC/MCA REMV 584*	11	9 wks
16 Nov 85	**THE EASTENDERS SING-A-LONG ALBUM**		
	BBC REB 586	33	10 wks
23 Nov 85	**TELLY HITS – 16 TOP TV THEMES** *Stylus BBSR 508* ..	34	6 wks
15 Feb 86 ●	**JONATHAN KING'S ENTERTAINMENT U.S.A.**		
	Stylus SMR 6812	6	11 wks
12 Apr 86	**THE TV HITS ALBUM TWO** *Towerbell TVLP 10*	19	7 wks
5 Jul 86	**TELLY HITS 2** *Stylus BBSR 616*	68	2 wks
18 Oct 86	**THE VERY BEST OF ENTERTAINMENT U.S.A.**		
	VOLUME 2 *Priority UPTVR 1*	44	4 wks
1 Nov 86	**SIMON BATES – OUR TUNE** *Polydor PROLP 10*	58	5 wks

VARIOUS ARTISTS

26 Dec	86 ●	**THE SINGING DETECTIVE** *BBC REN 608*	10	24 wks
27 Jun	87	**THE ROCK 'N' ROLL YEARS 1956–59** *BBR REN 631* . .	80	2 wks
27 Jun	87	**THE ROCK 'N' ROLL YEARS 1960–63** *BBC REN 632* . .	84	1 wk
27 Jun	87	**THE ROCK 'N' ROLL YEARS 1964–67** *BBC REN 633* . .	71	2 wks
27 Jun	87	**THE ROCK 'N' ROLL YEARS 1968–71** *BBC REN 634* . .	77	1 wk
3 Oct	87	**MOONLIGHTING** *MCA MCF 3386*	50	6 wks
17 Oct	87	**MIAMI VICE 2** *MCA MCG 6019*	71	4 wks
28 Nov	87	**THE CHART SHOW – DANCE HITS '87** *Chrysalis ADD 1*	39	6wks
26 Mar	88	**THE CHART SHOW – ROCK THE NATION**		
		Dover ADD 2	16	8 wks
1 Oct	88 ●	**MOONLIGHTING 2** *WEA WX 202*	5	9 wks
1 Oct	88	**MIAMI VICE 3** *MCA MCG 6033*	95	1 wk
8 Oct	88 ●	**ONES ON 1** *BBC REF 693*	10	7 wks
24 Dec	88	**THE BEIDERBECKE COLLECTION** *Dormouse DM 20* . .	89	2 wks
. . . .				
14 Jan	89	**THE BEIDERBECKE COLLECTION** *Dormouse DM 20* . .	14	5 wks
20 May	89 ●	**THE CHART SHOW – ROCK THE NATION 2**		
		Dover ADD 4	8	4 wks
3 Jun	89 ●	**THE CHART SHOW – DANCE MASTERS** *Dover ADD 7*	4	7 wks
17 Jun	89 ●	**RAY MOORE – A PERSONAL CHOICE** *BBC STAR 2352*	7	4 wks
23 Sep	89	**TV TUNES** *K-Tel NE 1429*	17	3 wks
17 Feb	90 ●	**PENNIES FROM HEAVEN** *BBC REF 768*	8	13 wks
16 Feb	91 ●	**BRITS 1991 – THE MAGIC OF BRITISH MUSIC**		
		Telstar/BPI STAR 2481	7	6 wks
21 Sep	91	**THE OLD GREY WHISTLE TEST – BEST OF THE TEST**		
		Windsong International OGWTLP 1	13	3 wks
30 Jan	92 ●	**THE BEST OF THE CLASSICAL BITS**		
		Philips/PolyGram TV 4381662	7	10 wks
22 Feb	92 ★	**THE AWARDS 1992** *PolyGram TV 5152072*	1	9 wks
27 Jun	92 ★	**HEARTBEAT** *Columbia 4719002*	1	14 wks
18 Jul	92	**DOCTOR WHO: THE EVIL OF THE DALEKS**		
		BBC ZBBC 1303	72	1 wk
25 Jul	92 ●	**32 ONES ON ONE – RADIO 1'S 25TH BIRTHDAY**		
		Connoisseur Collection ONECD 32	8	10 wks
17 Oct	92	**BEST OF CAPITAL GOLD** *The Hit Label AHLCD 2*	20	1 wk
28 Nov	92	**GLADIATORS** *PolyGram TV 5158772*	11	10 wks
13 Feb	93 ●	**HEAD OVER HEELS** *Telstar TCD 2649*	3	9 wks
20 Feb	93 ●	**THE AWARDS 1993** *PolyGram TV 5160752*	3	7 wks
13 Mar	93 ●	**LIPSTICK ON YOUR COLLAR** *PolyGram TV 51608642* .	2	13 wks
17 Apr	93 ●	**THE CHART SHOW ULTIMATE ROCK ALBUM**		
		The Hit Label AHLCD 9	5	11 wks
3 Jul	93	**ROADSHOW HITS** *Connoisseur Collection RSHCD 20*	18	2 wks
7 Aug	93 ●	**THE BIG BREAKFAST ALBUM** *Arcade ARC 3100082* . . .	8	5 wks
14 Aug	93	**DOCTOR WHO – THE POWER OF THE DALEKS**		
		BBC ZBBC 1433	71	1 wk
18 Sep	93	**DOCTOR WHO – THE PARADISE OF DEATH**		
		BBC ZBBC 1494	48	1 wk
2 Oct	93 ●	**THE CHART SHOW... ULTIMATE ROCK 2**		
		The Hit Label AHLCD 13	10	3 wks
23 Oct	93	**TALES FROM THE CITY** *PolyGram TV 5165152*	17	2 wks
20 Nov	93	**RETURN OF THE GLADIATORS** *PolyGram TV 5165172*	20	1 wk

ANONYMOUS COVER VERSIONS

29 Feb	64	**BEATLEMANIA** *Top Six TSL 1*	19	1 wk
7 Aug	71	**HOT HITS 5** *MFP 5208*	48	1 wk
7 Aug	71 ★	**HOT HITS 6** *MFP 5214*	1	7 wks
7 Aug	71	**TOP OF THE POPS VOL. 17** *Hallmark SHM 740*	16	3 wks
7 Aug	71 ★	**TOP OF THE POPS VOL. 18** *Hallmark SHM 745*	1	12 wks
7 Aug	71	**MILLION SELLER HITS** *MFP 5203*	46	2 wks
21 Aug	71	**SMASH HITS SUPREMES STYLE** *MFP 5184*	36	3 wks
2 Oct	71 ●	**TOP OF THE POPS VOL. 19** *Hallmark SHM 750*	3	9 wks
23 Oct	71 ●	**HOT HITS 7** *MFP 5236*	3	9 wks
6 Nov	71	**SMASH HITS COUNTRY STYLE** *MFP 5228*	38	1 wk
13 Nov	71 ★	**TOP OF THE POPS VOL. 20** *Hallmark SHM 739*	1	8 wks
27 Nov	71	**NON STOP 20 VOL. 4** *Plexium PXMS 1006*	35	2 wks
4 Dec	71	**SMASH HITS 71** *MFP 5229*	21	3 wks
11 Dec	71 ●	**HOT HITS 8** *MFP 5243*	2	4 wks
27 Sep	75	**40 SINGALONG PUB SONGS** *K-Tel NE 509*	21	7 wks
6 Nov	76	**FORTY MANIA** *Ronco RDT 2018*	21	6 wks

VARIOUS ARTISTS

MISCELLANEOUS

12 Sep	70	**EDINBURGH MILITARY TATTOO 1970**		
		Waverley SZLP 2121	34	4 wks
18 Sep	71	**EDINBURGH MILITARY TATTOO 1971**		
		Waverley SZLP 2128	44	1 wk
11 Dec	71	**ELECTRONIC ORGANS TODAY** *Ad-Rhythm ADBS 1* ..	48	1 wk
8 Dec	73 ●	**MUSIC FOR A ROYAL WEDDING** *BBC REW 163*	7	6 wks
27 Dec	75	**STRINGS OF SCOTLAND** *Philips 6382 108*	50	1 wk
8 Aug	81 ★	**THE OFFICIAL BBC ALBUM OF THE ROYAL WEDDING**		
		BBC REP 413	1	11 wks
3 Jul	82	**JOHN PAUL II – THE PILGRIM POPE** *BBC REB 445* ..	71	4 wks
9 Aug	86	**ROYAL WEDDING** *BBC REP 596*	55	1 wk
28 Dec	91	**TRIVIAL PURSUIT – THE MUSIC MASTER GAME**		
		Telstar STAC 2550	20	1 wk

HIT ALBUMS

ALPHABETICALLY BY TITLE

For the first time in *The Guinness Book of British Hit Albums*, we have listed all albums alphabetically, together with the name of the recording act and the year the album first hit the chart. For 'Various Artists' albums the label is listed in brackets, to help you locate the album in the main section. All albums with the same title are, obviously, different. When two or more albums have the same title, they are listed alphabetically by recording artist.

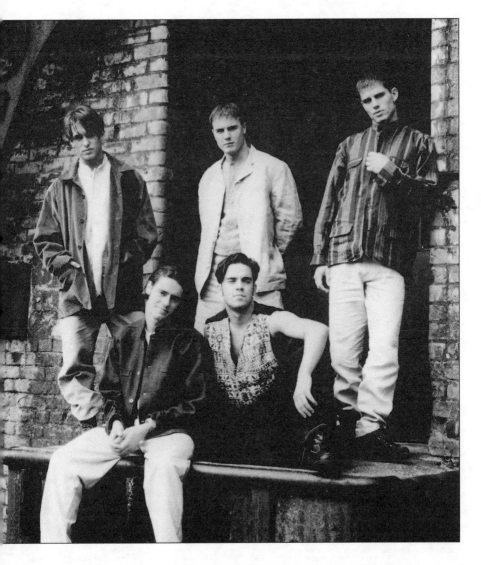

Take That *rewrote chart history when they became the first group to score four number one singles from one album (Everything Changes)*

380

HIT ALBUMS

FACTS AND FEATS

Meat Loaf's Bat Out Of Hell *has overtaken Fleetwood Mac's* Rumours *to become the album with the most weeks on chart in history.*

MOST WEEKS ON CHART

The following table lists the 164 recording acts that have spent 150 weeks or more on the British albums chart from the first chart on 8 Nov 1958 up to and including the chart of 25 Dec 1993. It is, of course, possible for an act to be credited with two or more chart weeks in the same week if the act has more than one album on the chart in any one week.

Beatles	1116
Queen	1061
Simon & Garfunkel	1061
Dire Straits	1058
Elvis Presley	1046
David Bowie	889
U2	854
Fleetwood Mac	766
Elton John	763
Pink Floyd	755
Michael Jackson	740

(includes 58 weeks with Jackson Five, 10 weeks with Diana Ross, Gladys Knight and Stevie Wonder, and 24 weeks with Diana Ross)

Phil Collins	739
Cliff Richard	731
Rod Stewart	707
Rolling Stones	694
Frank Sinatra	644

(includes 23 weeks with Count Basie)

Meatloaf	624
Madonna	605
Abba	584
Bob Dylan	568

(includes 3 weeks with the Grateful Dead)

Carpenters	564
Beach Boys	547
Neil Diamond	536
Paul McCartney/Wings	522
Mike Oldfield	520
Diana Ross	501

(includes 45 weeks with Marvin Gaye, 10 weeks with Michael Jackson, Gladys Knight and Stevie Wonder, and 24 weeks with Michael Jackson)

UB40	480
Genesis	468
Shadows	450
Andy Williams	442
Led Zeppelin	438
Status Quo	432
Eric Clapton	431

(includes 1 week as Derek & the Dominoes, 17 weeks with John Mayall and 105 weeks with Cream)

Bruce Springsteen	424
Eurythmics	423
Tom Jones	421

James Last	412

(includes 15 weeks with Richard Clayderman)

Tina Turner	407

(plus 1 week with Ike and Tina Turner)

Barbra Streisand	405
Roxy Music	397

(includes 104 weeks with Bryan Ferry)

Jim Reeves	391
The Sound of Music (Original Soundtrack)	382
Bob Marley and the Wailers	374
Simply Red	371
Electric Light Orchestra	370
Duran Duran	366
Madness	358
Prince	353
Police	349
Lionel Richie	348
Guns N' Roses	339
Stevie Wonder	336

(includes 10 weeks with Diana Ross, Gladys Knight and Michael Jackson)

Barry Manilow	333
Buddy Holly and the Crickets	328

(Crickets + 7 alone; + 27 with Bobby Vee)

Simple Minds	318
Herb Alpert	312
Moody Blues	310
Billy Joel	309
Chris Rea	301
John Lennon	297
Pet Shop Boys	297
Eagles	293
Blondie	292

(includes 26 with Debbie Harry)

South Pacific (Original Soundtrack)	288
Cream	287

(includes 105 weeks with Eric Clapton)

Johnny Cash	285
Erasure	284
Deep Purple	274
Shirley Bassey	273
Bryan Ferry	272

(includes 104 weeks with Roxy Music)

George Benson	270

(includes 6 weeks with Earl Klugh)

FACTS AND FEATS

David Essex	158	Five Star	153
Shakin' Stevens	158	Marillion	153
Marvin Gaye	156	Janet Jackson	152
(includes 45 weeks with Diana Ross, 9 weeks with Smokey Robinson and 4 weeks with Tammi Terrell)		Mantovani	151
		Adam and the Ants/Adam Ant	150
Depeche Mode	155	Daryl Hall and John Oates	150
Van Morrison	154	Hollies	150

Donny Osmond has racked up 104 weeks as a solo act, 103 as part of the Osmonds, and 19 with his sister Marie, a total of **226** weeks.

Alison Moyet has been on the chart for 142 weeks as a soloist and 83 as half of Yazoo, a total of **225** weeks.

Steve Winwood has clocked up 120 weeks on the chart as a solo act, 47 weeks as a member of the Spencer Davis Group, 37 playing in Traffic and 10 as part of Blind Faith, a total of **214** weeks.

Graham Nash has had 8 weeks on the chart as a soloist, 5 weeks as half of a duo with David Crosby, 14 weeks as one third of Crosby Stills and Nash, 79 weeks as one quarter of Crosby, Stills, Nash and Young and 106 weeks as one fifth of the Hollies, a total of **212** weeks.

Vangelis has had 145 weeks of chart life as a soloist and 53 more as half of Jon and Vangelis, a total of **198** weeks.

The Royal Philharmonic Orchestra have enjoyed 113 weeks on the chart, plus 25 more with Richard Clayderman, 13 with Julian Lloyd Webber, 10 with Andy Williams, 9 with Juan Martin and 4 with Sir Charles Groves and Sarah Jackson, a total of **174** weeks.

Jimmy Somerville has 40 solo chart weeks, 74 as a member of the Communards and 59 as part of Bronski Beat, a total of **173** weeks.

Placido Domingo has clocked up 57 chart weeks as a soloist, 70 with José Carreras and Luciano Pavarotti, 21 with John Denver, 18 on Andrew Lloyd Webber's *Requiem*, 3 with José Carreras and Montserrat Caballe, and 1 with José Carreras and Diana Ross, a total of **170** weeks.

Dionne Warwick has 144 solo chart weeks, and 19 more on Stevie Wonder's soundtrack album, *Woman In Red*. This is a total of **163** weeks.

David Sylvian has 21 solo weeks on chart, 2 in partnership with Robert Fripp, 1 with Holgar Czukay, 136 as a member of Japan and 3 with Rain Tree Crow, a total of **163** weeks.

New Order have notched up 128 weeks, and three quarters of the group have spent a further 29 weeks on the chart as Joy Division, a total of **157** weeks.

Boy George has 6 solo weeks, 1 as Jesus Loves You and 149 more as lead vocalist with Culture Club, a total of **156** weeks.

Nat 'King' Cole has 118 weeks of solo chart action, plus 7 with the George Shearing Quintet and 1 with Dean Martin. He is also the uncredited duettist with his daughter on her 29-week chart resident *Unforgettable – With Love* album, a total of **155** weeks.

Scott Walker has charted for 44 weeks as a solo artist, 96 weeks as a Walker Brother and 12 weeks on an album of both his and the Walker Brothers' hits, a total of **152** weeks.

Roger Taylor

Queen spent their 1062nd week on the album chart in the week ending 15 January 1994, to break the tie for second place on the all time list.

There are 14 people who have been on the albums charts for over 1000 weeks in total, if we count their solo albums and albums by groups of which they were fully paid-up members. They are, in order:

Paul McCartney	1638 weeks	Freddie Mercury	1117 weeks
John Lennon	1413 weeks	Mark Knopfler	1092 weeks
Paul Simon	1322 weeks	Brian May	1079 weeks
George Harrison	1249 weeks	Roger Taylor	1070 weeks
Phil Collins	1207 weeks	John Deacon	1061 weeks
Ringo Starr	1144 weeks	John Illsley	1058 weeks
Art Garfunkel	1119 weeks	Elvis Presley	1046 weeks

MOST WEEKS ON CHART IN A YEAR

There have been **54** instances of one act clocking up 100 or more chart weeks in one year, including – most recently – both Queen and Guns N' Roses in 1992. Dire Straits' record score in 1986 is the equivalent of four albums on the chart every week throughout the year.

217	Dire Straits	1986
198	David Bowie	1983
182	David Bowie	1973
177	Bruce Springsteen	1985
168	U2	1985
167	Simon and Garfunkel	1970
158	Dire Straits	1985
136	Michael Jackson	1984
135	Tom Jones	1968
131	Phil Collins	1985
128	Queen	1992
127	Madonna	1987
126	U2	1987
125	Johnny Cash	1970
125	Madonna	1986
123	Michael Jackson	1983
122	Beatles	1970
121	Otis Redding	1968
121	Guns N' Roses	1992
117	Queen	1987
116	Beach Boys	1968
116	Police	1980
116	Dire Straits	1984
116	Michael Jackson	1988
115	Jim Reeves	1964
115	Moody Blues	1970
113	Phil Collins	1986
112	Bob Dylan	1965
112	Abba	1978
112	Electric Light Orchestra	1979
111	Andy Williams	1971
109	George Mitchell Minstrels	1962
108	Pink Floyd	1977
107	David Bowie	1974
107	Dire Straits	1983
107	Queen	1986
107	Fleetwood Mac	1988
106	Carpenters	1974
106	Abba	1977
105	Elton John	1975
105	Duran Duran	1983
104	Beatles	1964
104	Simon and Garfunkel	1973
104	Beatles	1974
103	Four Tops	1968
102	Led Zeppelin	1970
102	Simon and Garfunkel	1971
102	Human League	1982
101	Herb Alpert	1967
101	Simon and Garfunkel	1974
100	Simon and Garfunkel	1975
100	Blondie	1979
100	U2	1984
100	Pet Shop Boys	1988

406

Simon and Garfunkel have racked up 100 chart weeks in a year five times. Dire Straits have done it four times, in consecutive years (1983–86 inclusive). The Beatles, David Bowie, Michael Jackson, U2 and Queen have topped the century in three years, while Abba, Phil Collins and Madonna have done it twice.

MOST WEEKS ON CHART IN EACH CHART YEAR

1958	Elvis Presley	16*
1959	Frank Sinatra	56*
1960	Elvis Presley	51
1961	Elvis Presley	91*
1962	George Mitchell Minstrels	109*
1963	Cliff Richard	72
1964	Jim Reeves	115*
1965	Bob Dylan	112
1966	Beach Boys	95
1967	Herb Alpert	101
1968	Tom Jones	135*
1969	Seekers	66
1970	Simon and Garfunkel	167*
1971	Andy Williams	111
1972	Cat Stevens	89
1973	David Bowie	182*
1974	David Bowie	107

1975	Elton John 105	1984	Michael Jackson 136
1976	Demis Roussos 84	1985	Bruce Springsteen 177
1977	Pink Floyd 108	1986	Dire Straits 217*
1978	Abba 112	1987	Madonna 127
1979	Electric Light	1988	Michael Jackson 116
	Orchestra 112	1989	Guns N' Roses 85
1980	Police 116	1990	Phil Collins 85
1981	Barry Manilow 92	1991	Michael Bolton 63
1982	Human League 102	1992	Queen 128
1983	David Bowie 198*	1993	R.E.M. 97

(*denotes record annual total at the time)

In 1960, the soundtrack album *South Pacific* was on the chart for all 53 chart weeks of the year, a total greater than that of the year's individual champion, Elvis Presley.

Elvis Presley and David Bowie have each been the year's chart champions three times and Michael Jackson has won it twice. No other act has been chart champion more than once.

Only six acts have chart careers featuring newly recorded hit albums over more than 30 years. They are Frank Sinatra (1958–93), Cliff Richard (1959–93), Adam Faith (1960–93), the Shadows (1961–93), the London Philharmonic Choir (1960–91) and Shirley Bassey (1961–93).

Jim Reeves (Pictorial Press)

MOST WEEKS ON CHART IN 1992

128 Queen
121 Guns N' Roses
77 Simply Red
76 Enya
73 U2
71 Michael Jackson
70 R.E.M.
63 Commitments
60 Nirvana
58 Genesis

MOST WEEKS ON CHART IN 1993

97 R.E.M.
68 Bon Jovi
65 Abba
62 Tina Turner
61 Guns N' Roses
61 Nirvana
58 Eric Clapton
58 Meat Loaf
57 U2
54 Take That

The success of Queen, in the wake of Freddie Mercury's death, was unsurprising. A flood of Queen albums came back onto the chart. What was more surprising was the heavy metal influx, led by Guns N' Roses with their two *Use Your Illusion* albums. They enjoyed their best chart year in terms of weeks, but still could not repeat their pole position of 1989. R.E.M. were the only survivors from the top ten album acts of 1991, while the Commitments became the first act created for a film (as opposed to television) to have such long-lasting album success.

R.E.M. completed their climb towards domination of the album charts, with a clear margin of 29 weeks over their nearest rival, the revitalised Bon Jovi. This was the biggest annual winning margin since Dire Straits were 92 weeks clear of Madonna in 1986. Three other acts, Guns N' Roses, U2 and Nirvana, held on to top ten places from 1992: for U2 it was the eighth year in the past ten that they had been one of the top album acts. The year's comeback stars were Meat Loaf, whose *Bat Out Of Hell II* was the year's biggest-selling album, and Abba, whose two hits collections pushed them back into the top ten for the first time since 1980. For Eric Clapton, for almost a quarter of a century a significant album seller, it was his first time as one of the top ten chart acts of the year. Take That, the teenybop sensation of the year, showed that they could sell albums as well as singles – a sign that augured well for their future.

MOST WEEKS ON CHART BY ONE ALBUM

This is a list of all the albums that have spent a total of 100 weeks or more on the chart to the end of 1993.

Bat Out Of Hell *Meat Loaf* 457
Rumours *Fleetwood Mac* 443
Greatest Hits *Queen* 406
The Sound Of Music *Original Film Soundtrack* 382
Dark Side Of The Moon *Pink Floyd* 310

FACTS AND FEATS

410

Of these albums, only *Bat Out Of Hell*, *The Beatles 1962–1966* and *The Beatles 1967–1970* were on the chart at the end of 1993. *Stars* reappeared in the first chart of 1994.

Five of the nine Dire Straits albums released to the end of 1991 are in this list. Three albums each by the Beatles, Phil Collins, Simon and Garfunkel, Michael Jackson, Madonna and U2 have spent over 100 weeks on the chart, as well as two each by David Bowie, Duran Duran, Electric Light Orchestra, Fleetwood Mac, Whitney Houston and Simply Red. Paul Simon, John Lennon and Paul McCartney each feature on four albums which have enjoyed at least 100 weeks of chart life.

The sales of a record are not necessarily reflected in the length of its chart run. *Off The Wall* and *Thriller* have both had longer chart runs than Michael Jackson's best seller in Britain, *Bad*, while Dire Straits' biggest seller, *Brothers in Arms*, still has some way to go before its chart life overtakes that of *Makin' Movies*.

Dirty Dancing Original Film Soundtrack spent 63 weeks on the main chart up to the beginning of 1989, and a further 144 weeks on the compilations chart to the end of 1991, a total of **207 weeks** of chart action. *The Blues Brothers* Original Film Soundtrack spent 26 weeks on the main chart up to the beginning of 1989, and a further 77 weeks on the compilations chart, a total of **103 weeks** of chart action.

No other album has totalled over 100 weeks on the Compilation Albums chart, nor by a combination of appearances on the two charts.

The leading performers on the Compilation Albums chart in its first five years of existence are:

Dirty Dancing *Original Film Soundtrack* 144
The Blues Brothers *Original Film Soundtrack* 77
Pretty Woman *Original Film Soundtrack* 71
The Lost Boys *Original Film Soundtrack* 59
The Bodyguard *Original Soundtrack* 57
The Classic Experience *Various Artists* 57

MOST HIT ALBUMS

An album is a hit even if it spends only one week at number 100. Double, treble and quadruple albums count as only one hit. Re-issues do not count as a new hit.

95	Elvis Presley	25	Beatles
59	James Last	25	Shadows
	(includes 1 with Richard Clayderman)	25	Andy Williams
51	Frank Sinatra	24	Jethro Tull
	(includes 1 with Count Basie)	24	Paul McCartney/Wings
48	Cliff Richard	23	Iron Maiden
38	Rolling Stones	23	Tom Jones
37	Bob Dylan	23	Gary Numan/Tubeway Army
	(includes 1 with Grateful Dead)		*(includes 1 with Sharpe and Numan)*
36	Diana Ross	23	Rod Stewart
	(includes 1 with Marvin Gaye, 1 with Michael Jackson, 1 with Placido Domingo and José Carreras and 1 with Gladys Knight, Stevie Wonder & Michael Jackson; plus 13 as a Supreme)		*(includes 1 with the Faces)*
		22	Hawkwind
			(includes 1 as Hawklords)
		21	Eric Clapton
32	Elton John		*(includes 1 as Derek and the Dominoes, 1 with John Mayall and 1 with Cream)*
31	Shirley Bassey		
29	David Bowie	21	Deep Purple
29	Neil Diamond	21	Jimi Hendrix
27	Johnny Mathis		*(includes 1 with Curtis Knight)*
	(includes 1 with Natalie Cole, 1 with Deniece Williams and 1 with Henry Mancini)	21	Who
		20	Marc Bolan/T. Rex/ Tyrannosaurus Rex
27	Jim Reeves	20	Van Morrison
26	Beach Boys	20	Queen
26	Status Quo	20	Santana
26	Neil Young		*(Carlos Santana 3 more with various other partners)*
	(includes 1 with Stills-Young Band; plus 3 with Crosby, Stills, Nash and Young)	19	Black Sabbath

411

19	Mike Oldfield
19	Roy Orbison
18	Genesis
18	Michael Jackson
	(includes 1 with Diana Ross, Gladys Knight and Stevie Wonder, 1 with Diana Ross and 1 with Jackson Five)
18	Barry Manilow
17	Cure
17	Stranglers
17	Barbra Streisand
16	Herb Alpert
16	Carpenters
16	Johnny Cash
16	Alice Cooper
16	Elvis Costello
	(includes 1 as the Costello Show)
16	John Denver
	(includes 1 with Placido Domingo)
16	David Essex
16	Kiss
16	Moody Blues
16	Pink Floyd
16	Slade
16	Tangerine Dream
16	Temptations
	(includes 3 with Diana Ross and the Supremes)
16	Stevie Wonder
	(includes 1 with Diana Ross, Gladys Knight and Michael Jackson)
16	Yes
15	Foster and Allen
15	Motorhead
15	Supremes
	(includes 1 with Four Tops, 3 with the Temptations)
14	Abba
14	Bee Gees
14	Fleetwood Mac
14	London Symphony Orchestra
14	John Mayall
	(includes 1 with Eric Clapton)
14	Prince
14	Roxy Music
	(includes 2 with Bryan Ferry)
14	Rush
14	Donna Summer
14	UB40
14	Don Williams
13	Joan Armatrading
13	George Benson
	(includes 1 with Earl Klugh)
13	Barbara Dickson
	(includes 1 with Elaine Paige)
13	Hollies

13	Jean-Michel Jarre
13	Billy Joel
13	Judas Priest
13	Led Zeppelin
13	Joni Mitchell
13	Chris Rea
13	Siouxsie and the Banshees
13	Thin Lizzy
	(includes 1 with Phil Lynott)
13	Wishbone Ash
12	AC/DC
12	Mr. Acker Bilk
	(includes 2 with Chris Barber and 1 with Chris Barber and Kenny Ball)
12	Elkie Brooks
12	Max Bygraves
12	Richard Clayderman
	(includes 1 with James Last)
12	Placido Domingo
	(includes 1 with John Denver, 1 with Luciano Pavarotti and José Carreras, 1 with José Carreras and Montserrat Caballe and 1 with Diana Ross and José Carreras)
12	Electric Light Orchestra
12	Everly Brothers
	(Phil Everly + 1 solo)
12	Fall
12	Four Tops
	(includes 1 with Supremes)
12	Marvin Gaye
	(includes 1 with Smokey Robinson, 1 with Diana Ross and 1 with Tammi Terrell)
12	Jacksons
	(4 as Jackson Five, including one with Michael Jackson, 8 as Jacksons)
12	Kinks
12	John Lennon/Plastic Ono Band
12	Mantovani
12	Bob Marley and the Wailers
12	Public Image Ltd
12	Leo Sayer
12	Bruce Springsteen
12	Squeeze
12	Shakin' Stevens
12	10 C.C.
	(includes 1 with Godley and Creme)
12	Uriah Heep
12	Frank Zappa
11	Ray Conniff
11	Chris De Burgh
11	Val Doonican
11	Doors
11	Hall and Oates
	(Daryl Hall + 1 solo)

412

11	Buddy Holly and the Crickets (Crickets + 1 with Bobby Vee and 1 solo)	10	Peter Gabriel
		10	Rory Gallagher
		10	Bert Kaempfert
11	Engelbert Humperdinck	10	King Crimson
11	Joe Jackson	10	Magnum
11	Jam	10	Marillion
11	Level 42	10	Nana Mouskouri
11	Madness	10	Orchestral Manoeuvres in the Dark
11	Manfred Mann (7 as Manfred Mann, 4 as Manfred Mann's Earth Band)	10	Elaine Paige (includes 1 with Barbara Dickson)
11	George Mitchell Minstrels	10	Alan Parsons Project
11	Gary Moore	10	Tom Petty and the Heartbreakers
11	Olivia Newton-John		
11	Robert Palmer	10	Gene Pitney
11	Rainbow	10	Otis Redding (includes 1 with Carla Thomas)
11	Simple Minds		
11	Steely Dan	10	Lou Reed (includes 1 with John Cale)
11	U2		
11	Dionne Warwick	10	R.E.M.
11	Barry White	10	Royal Philharmonic Orchestra
11	XTC	10	Showaddywaddy
10	Barclay James Harvest	10	Paul Simon
10	Byrds	10	Simon and Garfunkel (Art Garfunkel + 6 solo; Paul Simon + 10 solo)
10	Nat 'King' Cole (includes 1 with George Shearing and 1 with Dean Martin)		
		10	Smiths
10	Cream (includes 1 with Eric Clapton)	10	Cat Stevens
		10	Supertramp
10	Depeche Mode	10	Talking Heads
10	Eurythmics	10	Van Halen
10	Brian Ferry (includes 2 with Roxy Music)	10	Roger Whittaker
		10	Kim Wilde

413

Marc Almond has six solo hit albums to his credit, six more as vocalist with Soft Cell and two as Marc and the Mambas, a total of 14.

Ginger Baker has had one hit as leader of Ginger Baker's Air Force, one as co-general in the Baker-Gurvitz Army, eight as drummer with Cream and one more as part of the *Cream of Eric Clapton*, a total of 11.

Jack Bruce has one solo hit album, eight as bassist with Cream and one more as part of the *Cream of Eric Clapton*, a total of ten.

David Cassidy has had six hit albums and four more as part of the Partridge Family, a total of ten.

David Crosby has had one solo hit album, one as half of Graham Nash and David Crosby, two as one third of Crosby Stills and Nash, three as one quarter of Crosby Stills Nash and Young, and six more as part of the Byrds, a total of 12 hit albums.

Emerson Lake and Palmer have had nine hit albums, Emerson Lake and Powell one more, and Greg Lake one on his own.

Deborah Harry has had three solo hit albums, seven as lead vocalist of Blondie and two more billed as Deborah Harry and Blondie, totalling 12.

Don Henley has two solo hit albums to go with eight as a member of the Eagles, a total of ten.

Mark Knopfler has had two solo hit albums to go with eight Dire Straits hits, one Notting Hillbillies good time and a duet with Chet Atkins, total 12.

Graham Nash has had one solo hit album, one with David Crosby, two with Crosby Stills and Nash, three with Crosby Stills Nash and Young and eight as one of the Hollies, a total of 15.

Donny Osmond has had six solo hit album, three more with Marie Osmond and seven as one of the Osmonds, a total of 16.

Lionel Richie has four solo hit albums and features as lead vocalist on eight of the Commodores' hit albums, a total of 12.

Harry Secombe has had six solo hit albums, one with Moira Anderson, and four with Peter Sellers and Spike Milligan, three as the Goons; a total of 11.

Stephen Stills has four solo hit albums, two as leader of Stephen Stills' Manassas, two as part of Crosby Stills and Nash, three as one quarter of Crosby Stills Nash and Young, and one as half of the Stills-Young Band, giving him a share in 12 hit albums.

Midge Ure has had four solo hit albums, one as a member of Slik, seven as part of Ultravox and four involved with Visage, a total of 16.

Vangelis has amassed seven solo hit albums, plus four more with Jon Anderson, making 11 hit albums in all.

Rick Wakeman has hit the charts nine times, plus once more with Kevin Peek and again with Anderson Bruford Wakeman Howe, a total of 11 hit albums. He was also part of Yes for nine of their hit albums.

Scott Walker has had five solo hit albums and five more as part of the Walker Brothers, as well as one which is a combination of his own solo hits and the group's hits, a total of 11.

Steve Winwood has had seven solo hit albums, three more as lead vocalist of the Spencer Davis Group, five with Traffic and one with Blind Faith, a total of 16.

Steve Winood (Pictorial Press)

MOST TOP TEN HIT ALBUMS

The rules for this category are the same as for Most Hit Albums, except that the album must have made the top ten for at least one week.

36	Elvis Presley
32	Cliff Richard
29	Rolling Stones
29	Frank Sinatra
	(includes 1 with Count Basie)
24	Bob Dylan
21	David Bowie
19	Elton John
19	Paul McCartney/Wings
18	Beatles
18	Iron Maiden
18	Queen
18	Status Quo
18	Rod Stewart
	(+ 1 with the Faces)
15	Genesis
14	Beach Boys
14	Jim Reeves
13	Pink Floyd
13	Who
12	Tom Jones
12	Prince
11	Elvis Costello
11	Led Zeppelin
11	Roxy Music
	(includes 2 with Bryan Ferry)
11	Shadows
	(+ 16 with Cliff Richard)
10	Depeche Mode
10	Andy Williams
10	Yes
9	Abba
9	Black Sabbath
9	Eric Clapton
	(includes 1 with Cream and 1 with John Mayall)
9	Cure
9	Deep Purple
9	Dire Straits
9	Fleetwood Mac
9	Jimi Hendrix
9	Buddy Holly and the Crickets
	(Crickets + 1 with Bobby Vee)
9	Johnny Mathis
	(includes 1 with Natalie Cole)
9	Diana Ross
	(includes 1 with Marvin Gaye)
9	UB40
8	AC/DC
8	Bee Gees

8	Kate Bush
8	Carpenters
8	Cream
	(includes 1 with Eric Clapton)
8	Bryan Ferry
	(includes 2 with Roxy Music)
8	Madonna
8	Moody Blues
8	Rush
8	Smiths
	(Morrissey + 4 solo)
8	Bruce Springsteen
8	Stranglers
8	Supremes
	(includes 1 with the Four Tops, 1 with the Temptations)
8	10 C.C.
	(includes 1 with Godley and Creme)
8	Thin Lizzy
8	Stevie Wonder
7	Blondie
	(includes 1 listed as Deborah Harry and Blondie; Debbie Harry + 1 solo)
7	Marc Bolan/T. Rex/ Tyrannosaurus Rex
7	Neil Diamond
7	Duran Duran
7	Electric Light Orchestra
7	Emerson Lake and Palmer
7	Eurythmics
7	Peter Gabriel
7	Jam
7	John Lennon/Plastic Ono Band
7	Madness
7	Marillion
7	George Mitchell Minstrels
7	Mike Oldfield
7	Police
7	Simon and Garfunkel
	(Paul Simon + 6 solo, Art Garfunkel + 2 solo)
7	Simple Minds
7	Cat Stevens
7	U2
7	Ultravox
7	Whitesnake
6	Shirley Bassey
6	Acker Bilk
	(includes 2 with Chris Barber and 1 with Chris Barber and Kenny Ball)
6	Phil Collins

6	Russ Conway	5	Culture Club
6	Four Tops	5	Chris de Burgh
	(includes 1 with Supremes)	5	John Denver
6	Free	5	Val Doonican
6	Hollies	5	Eagles
6	Engelbert Humperdinck	5	Echo and the Bunnymen
6	Michael Jackson	5	Duane Eddy
	(includes 1 with Jacksons)	5	Erasure
6	Jethro Tull	5	Everly Brothers
6	Billy Joel	5	Human League
6	Level 42		*(includes 1 as League Unlimited*
6	Barry Manilow		*Orchestra)*
6	Mantovani	5	INXS
6	Bob Marley and the Wailers	5	Jean-Michel Jarre
6	Meatloaf	5	Jack Jones
6	New Order	5	Kinks
6	Gary Numan/Tubeway Army	5	James Last
6	Roy Orbison	5	John Mayall
6	Orchestral Manoeuvres In The		*(includes 1 with Eric Clapton)*
	Dark	5	Rainbow
6	Pet Shop Boys	5	Santana
6	Chris Rea		*(Carlos Santana + 1 with Mahavishnu*
6	Leo Sayer		*John McLaughlin)*
6	Paul Simon	5	Showaddywaddy
	(+ 7 with Simon and Garfunkel)	5	Slade
6	Barbra Streisand	5	Spandau Ballet
6	Tina Turner	5	Style Council
6	Wet Wet Wet	5	Supertramp
5	Herb Alpert	5	Tears For Fears
5	Joan Armatrading	5	Bobby Vee
5	Big Country		*(includes 1 with the Crickets)*
5	Max Bygraves	5	Scott Walker
5	Belinda Carlisle		*(includes 1 with the Walker Brothers)*
5	Johnny Cash	5	Walker Brothers
5	Randy Crawford		*(includes 1 with Scott Walker)*
5	Cult	5	Paul Young

Cher has had four solo top ten hits and one more with Sonny and Cher, a total of five.

Depeche Mode are the act with the best 100% top ten album record, with ten top ten hits out of ten releases. **Dire Straits** have hit the top ten with each one of their nine albums.

Billy Joel

FACTS AND FEATS

MOST HITS WITHOUT A TOP TEN HIT

Only seven acts have had ten or more hit albums without ever reaching the top ten. They are **Tangerine Dream** (16 hits), **Foster and Allen** (15 hits), **Public Image Ltd.** (12 hits), **Doors** (11 hits), **Barclay James Harvest** (10 hits), **Alan Parsons Project** (10 hits), and **Van Halen** (10 hits). The Alan Parsons Project has never even hit the top twenty, their most successful album being their eighth hit, *Ammonia Avenue*, which reached number 24 in 1984.

James Last has hit the top ten only five times out of 59 chart entries, a hit-making career which includes a run of 31 consecutive hit albums (his second to 32nd hits inclusive) which all missed the top ten. **Neil Young** clocked up 20 consecutive hit albums between top ten hits, a gap of just over 20 years. **Hawkwind** have hit the charts 19 times since their last brief taste of top ten glory in 1973.

There were 57 hit compilation albums on the **Street Sounds** label, totalling 269 weeks on the charts, but the highest placing for any of them was 12, achieved by *Street Sounds Electro 7* in March 1985.

MOST HITS WITHOUT A NUMBER ONE HIT

59	James Last (*who has had one no. 2 hit*)
31	Shirley Bassey (*who has had one no. 2 hit*)
22	Hawkwind (*who have had one no. 9 hit*)
20	Santana (*who have had two no. 6 hits; Carlos Santana has made 3 hit albums with other partners, none of which hit the top*)
21	Jimi Hendrix (*who has had two no. 2 hits*)
18	Van Morrison (*who has had one no. 4 hit*)
17	Stranglers (*who have had two no. 2 hits*)
16	Herb Alpert (*who has had one no. 2 hit*)
16	Johnny Cash (*who has had one no. 2 hit*)
16	John Denver (*who has had one no. 2 hit*)
16	David Essex (*who has had one no. 2 hit*)
16	Kiss (*who have had one no. 4 hit*)
16	Tangerine Dream (*who have had one no. 12 hit*)
15	Elvis Costello (*who has had two no. 2 hits*)
15	Foster and Allen (*who have had one no. 11 hit*)
15	Stevie Wonder (*whose had three no. 2 hits*)

MOST ALBUMS ON THE CHART IN ONE WEEK

Dire Straits' record total of 217 weeks on the chart in one year (1986) is the equivalent of an average of four albums in the top 100 in every week of the year. Only five artists in the history of the albums chart have charted seven albums in one week, as follows:

14 albums in a chart of	60	Elvis Presley	10 Sep 1977
12 albums in a chart of	60	Elvis Presley	17 Sep 1977
11 albums in a chart of	60	Elvis Presley	1 Oct 1977
11 albums in a chart of	60	Elvis Presley	8 Oct 1977

10 albums in a chart of 100	David Bowie	16 July 1983
9 albums in a chart of 60	Elvis Presley	24 Sep 1977
9 albums in a chart of 100	David Bowie	11 Jun 1983
9 albums in a chart of 100	David Bowie	9 Jul 1983
8 albums in a chart of 20	Jim Reeves	26 Sep 1964
8 albums in a chart of 100	David Bowie	27 Aug 1983
7 albums in a chart of 20	Jim Reeves	29 Aug 1964
7 albums in a chart of 20	Jim Reeves	5 Sep 1964
7 albums in a chart of 20	Jim Reeves	3 Oct 1964
7 albums in a chart of 20	Jim Reeves	10 Oct 1964
7 albums in a chart of 60	Elvis Presley	15 Oct 1977
7 albums in a chart of 75	U2	13 Jun 1992
7 albums in a chart of 100	David Bowie	14 May 1983
7 albums in a chart of 100	David Bowie	21 May 1983
7 albums in a chart of 100	David Bowie	28 May 1983
7 albums in a chart of 100	David Bowie	4 Jun 1983
7 albums in a chart of 100	David Bowie	18 Jun 1983
7 albums in a chart of 100	David Bowie	30 Jul 1983
7 albums in a chart of 100	David Bowie	20 Aug 1983
7 albums in a chart of 100	Bruce Springsteen	15 Jun 1985
	(nine consecutive weeks) to	10 Aug 1985

Of all these instances, only Elvis Presley on 10 Sep 1977 and Bruce Springsteen for four weeks from 6 Jul 1985 held the top spot. The most complete chart domination was by Jim Reeves on 26 Sep 1964, when he accounted for 40% of the albums chart. Bruce Springsteen's achievement in the summer of 1985 is the only example of an artist who has released as many as seven albums charting *all* his albums at once. In 1986, Dire Straits charted all six of their albums (one of which was a double album) for a total of twelve weeks. For seven of those weeks they held the no. 1 spot.

4|8

Bruce Springsteen (Pictorial Press)

LEAST SUCCESSFUL CHART ACT

Between 8 Aug 1981 and 14 Jan 1989, when the chart was a top 100, eight acts achieved the minor distinction of a chart career consisting of only one week at no. 100. These acts, in chronological order, were:

17 Oct 81	Ronnie Laws	Solid Ground
17 Dec 83	Sleighriders	A Very Merry Disco
11 Feb 84	Europeans	Live
30 Jun 84	Wendy O. Williams	WOW
30 Mar 85	Second Image	Strange Reflections
12 Oct 85	Alien Sex Fiend	Maximum Security
29 Nov 86	Shop Assistants	Shop Assistants
3 Oct 87	Bolshoi	Lindy's Party

There is also a compilation album which lasted at no. 100 for just 1 week:

26 Nov 83	Various Artists	Twelve Inches Of Pleasure

Before 8 Aug 1981 and since 14 Jan 1989, 23 acts achieved the slightly less negative ultimate of one week of chart life on the bottom rung of a smaller chart:

			Chart Size
11 Jun 60	Bob Wallis and his Storyville Jazzmen	Everybody Loves Saturday Night	20
18 Jun 60	Shelley Manne	My Fair Lady	20
25 Jun 60	Knightsbridge Strings	String Sway	20
17 Dec 60	Big Ben Banjo Band	More Minstrel Melodies	20
24 Dec 60	New World Theatre Orchestra	Let's Dance To The Hits Of The 30s and 40s	20
14 Jul 62	Erroll Garner	Close Up In Swing	20
9 Feb 63	Spotnicks	Out-A-Space	20
18 Apr 64	Harry Secombe, Peter Sellers & Spike Milligan	How To Win An Election	20
20 Jun 64	Sonny Boy Williamson	Down And Out Blues	20
29 Jul 67	Manitas de Plata	Flamenco Guitar	40
22 Jun 68	Solomon King	She Wears My Ring	40
17 Aug 68	O.C. Smith	Hickory Holler Revisited	40
28 Feb 70	Bobbie Gentry & Glen Campbell	Bobbie Gentry And Glen Campbell	50
20 Jun 70	Moira Anderson	These Are My Songs	50
28 Nov 70	Savoy Brown	Lookin' In	50
13 Apr 74	Deke Leonard	Kamikaze	50
1 Apr 78	Culture	Two Sevens Clash	60
30 Sep 78	Cerrone	Supernature	60
18 Mar 89	Vow Wow	Helter Skelter	75
16 Jul 91	Fishbone	The Reality Of My Surroundings	75
18 Jul 92	Future Sound of London	Accelerator	75
15 May 93	Terrorvision	Formaldehyde	75
5 Jun 93	Dodgy	The Dodgy Album	75

Harry Secombe, Peter Sellers and Spike Milligan, and Bobbie Gentry and Glen Campbell have all charted with solo albums. Moira Anderson has also enjoyed chart success in duet with Harry Secombe.

419

Five compilation albums have also spent just one week at the bottom of the smaller charts, as follows:

28 May 60	*Pal Joey Original Film Soundtrack*	20
23 Nov 63	*Hitsville Volume 2*	20
8 Feb 64	*Ready Steady Go!*	20
11 May 68	*Blues Anytime*	40
3 Nov 79	*Mods Mayday 79*	75

The Adicts spent one week at no. 99 with their only hit album, *The Sound of Music* and one week on the bottom rung, no. 75, with their only hit single, *Bad Boy*. This is the nearest to the ultimate least successful chart double so far.

Since the establishment of a separate top 20 compilations albums chart, there have been 17 albums which have spent just one week on the bottom rung:

23 Dec 89	*Reggae Hits Volume 7*	20
17 Nov 90	*Karaoke Party*	20
20 Jul 91	*Breaks Bass and Bleeps*	20
28 Dec 91	*Trivial Pursuit – The Music Master Game*	20
18 Jan 92	*Noise*	20
1 Feb 92	*Closet Classics Volume 1*	20
22 Feb 92	*Shut Up And Dance*	20
18 Apr 92	*Breaks Bass and Bleeps*	20
27 Jun 92	*Movin' On*	20
29 Aug 92	*Warehouse Raves 7*	20
19 Sep 92	*Illegal Rave*	20
17 Oct 92	*The Best Of Capital Gold*	20
6 Mar 93	*Ambient Dub Volume 2 – Earth Juice*	20
24 Apr 93	*Winner's Circle*	20
18 Sep 93	*Sliver (Original Soundtrack)*	20
25 Sep 93	*Now! That's What I Call Music 1988*	20
20 Nov 93	*The Return Of The Gladiators*	20

The two albums entitled *Breaks Bass and Bleeps* are different albums, both issued on the same label, Rumour.

Elvis Presley (Pictorial Press)

THE NUMBER ONE ALBUMS
8 NOVEMBER 1958–28 DECEMBER 1993

There have been 475 albums which have topped the charts in the 33 years since it was first compiled. In the first ten years of the albums charts, only 44 albums headed the lists, but over the past two years there have been 49 new chart-topping albums. The full list is as follows:

		Weeks
8 Nov 58	South Pacific *Film Soundtrack (RCA)*	70
12 Mar 60	The Explosive Freddy Cannon *Freddy Cannon (Top Rank)*	1
19 Mar 60	South Pacific *Film Soundtrack (RCA)*	19
30 Jul 60	Elvis Is Back *Elvis Presley (RCA)*	1
6 Aug 60	South Pacific *Film Soundtrack (RCA)*	5
10 Sep 60	Down Drury Lane To Memory Lane *101 Strings (Pye)*	5
15 Oct 60	South Pacific *Film Soundtrack (RCA)*	13
14 Jan 61	GI Blues *Elvis Presley (RCA)*	7
4 Mar 61	South Pacific *Film Soundtrack (RCA)*	1
11 Mar 61	GI Blues *Elvis Presley (RCA)*	3
1 Apr 61	South Pacific *Film Soundtrack (RCA)*	1
8 Apr 61	GI Blues *Elvis Presley (RCA)*	12
1 Jul 61	South Pacific *Film Soundtrack (RCA)*	4
29 Jul 61	Black And White Minstrel Show	
	George Mitchell Minstrels (HMV)	4
26 Aug 61	South Pacific *Film Soundtrack (RCA)*	1
2 Sep 61	Black and White Minstrel Show	
	George Mitchell Minstrels (HMV)	1
9 Sep 61	South Pacific *Film Soundtrack (RCA)*	1
16 Sep 61	Black And White Minstrel Show	
	George Mitchell Minstrels (HMV)	1
23 Sep 61	The Shadows *Shadows (Columbia)*	4
21 Oct 61	Black And White Minstrel Show	
	George Mitchell Minstrels (HMV)	1
28 Oct 61	The Shadows *Shadows (Columbia)*	1
4 Nov 61	21 Today *Cliff Richard (Columbia)*	1
11 Nov 61	Another Black And White Minstrel Show	
	George Mitchell Minstrels (HMV)	8
6 Jan 62	Blue Hawaii *Elvis Presley (RCA)*	1
13 Jan 62	The Young Ones *Cliff Richard (Columbia)*	6
24 Feb 62	Blue Hawaii *Elvis Presley (RCA)*	17
23 Jun 62	West Side Story *Film Soundtrack (Philips/CBS)*	5
28 Jul 62	Pot Luck *Elvis Presley (RCA)*	5
1 Sep 62	West Side Story *Film Soundtrack (CBS)*	1
8 Sep 62	Pot Luck *Elvis Presley (RCA)*	1
15 Sep 62	West Side Story *Film Soundtrack (CBS)*	1
22 Sep 62	The Best Of Ball, Barber And Bilk	
	Kenny Ball, Chris Barber and Acker Bilk (Pye)	1
29 Sep 62	West Side Story *Film Soundtrack (CBS)*	3
20 Oct 62	The Best Of Ball, Barber And Bilk	
	Kenny Ball, Chris Barber and Acker Bilk (Pye)	1
27 Oct 62	Out Of The Shadows *Shadows (Columbia)*	3
17 Nov 62	West Side Story *Film Soundtrack (CBS)*	1
24 Nov 62	Out Of The Shadows *Shadows (Columbia)*	1

421

1 Dec 62	On Stage With The Black And White Minstrels	
	George Mitchell Minstrels (HMV)	2
15 Dec 62	West Side Story *Film Soundtrack (CBS)*	1
22 Dec 62	Out Of The Shadows *Shadows (Columbia)*	1
29 Dec 62	Black And White Minstrel Show	
	George Mitchell Minstrels (HMV)	2
12 Jan 63	West Side Story *Film Soundtrack (CBS)*	1
19 Jan 63	Out Of The Shadows *Shadows (Columbia)*	2
2 Feb 63	Summer Holiday *Cliff Richard and the Shadows (Columbia)*	14
11 May 63	Pleae Please Me *Beatles (Parlophone)*	30
7 Dec 63	With The Beatles *Beatles (Parlophone)*	21
2 May 64	Rolling Stones *Rolling Stones (Decca)*	12
25 Jul 64	A Hard Day's Night *Beatles (Parlophone)*	21
19 Dec 64	Beatles For Sale *Beatles (Parlophone)*	7
6 Feb 65	Rolling Stones No. 2 *Rolling Stones (Decca)*	3
27 Feb 65	Beatles For Sale *Beatles (Parlophone)*	1
6 Mar 65	Rolling Stones No. 2 *Rolling Stones (Decca)*	6
17 Apr 65	Freewheelin' Bob Dylan *Bob Dylan (CBS)*	1
24 Apr 65	Rolling Stones No. 2 *Rolling Stones (Decca)*	1
1 May 65	Beatles For Sale *Beatles (Parlophone)*	3
22 May 65	Freewheelin' Bob Dylan *Bob Dylan (CBS)*	1
29 May 65	Bring It All Back Home *Bob Dylan (CBS)*	1
5 Jun 65	The Sound Of Music *Soundtrack (RCA)*	10
14 Aug 65	Help *Beatles (Parlophone)*	9
16 Oct 65	The Sound Of Music *Soundtrack (RCA)*	10
25 Dec 65	Rubber Soul *Beatles (Parlophone)*	9
19 Feb 66	The Sound Of Music *Soundtrack (RCA)*	10
30 Apr 66	Aftermath *Rolling Stones (Decca)*	8
25 Jun 66	The Sound Of Music *Soundtrack (RCA)*	7
13 Aug 66	Revolver *Beatles (Parlophone)*	7
1 Oct 66	The Sound Of Music *Soundtrack (RCA)*	18
4 Feb 67	Monkees *Monkees (RCA)*	7
25 Mar 67	The Sound Of Music *Soundtrack (RCA)*	7
13 May 67	More Of The Monkees *Monkees (RCA)*	1
20 May 67	The Sound Of Music *Soundtrack (RCA)*	1
27 May 67	More Of The Monkees *Monkees (RCA)*	1
3 Jun 67	The Sound Of Music *Soundtrack (RCA)*	1
10 Jun 67	Sergeant Pepper's Lonely Hearts Club Band	
	Beatles (Parlophone)	23
18 Nov 67	The Sound Of Music *Soundtrack (RCA)*	1
25 Nov 67	Sergeant Pepper's Lonely Hearts Club Band	
	Beatles (Parlophone)	1
2 Dec 67	The Sound Of Music *Soundtrack (RCA)*	3
23 Dec 67	Sergeant Pepper's Lonely Hearts Club Band	
	Beatles (Parlophone)	2
6 Jan 68	Val Doonican Rocks But Gently *Val Doonican (Pye)*	3
27 Jan 68	The Sound Of Music *Soundtrack (RCA)*	1
3 Feb 68	Sergeant Pepper's Lonely Hearts Club Band	
	Beatles (Parlophone)	1
10 Feb 68	Greatest Hits *Four Tops (Tamla Motown)*	1
17 Feb 68	Greatest Hits *Diana Ross and the Supremes (Tamla Motown)*	3
9 Mar 68	John Wesley Harding *Bob Dylan (CBS)*	10

18 May 68	Scott 2 Scott Walker (Philips)	1
25 May 68	John Wesley Harding Bob Dylan (CBS)	3
15 Jun 68	Love Andy Andy Williams (CBS)	1
22 Jun 68	Dock Of The Bay Otis Redding (Stax)	1
29 Jun 68	Ogden's Nut Gone Flake Small Faces (Immediate)	6
10 Aug 68	Delilah Tom Jones (Decca)	1
17 Aug 68	Bookends Simon and Garfunkel (CBS)	5
21 Sep 68	Delilah Tom Jones (Decca)	1
28 Sep 68	Bookends Simon and Garfunkel (CBS)	2
12 Oct 68	Greatest Hits Hollies (Parlophone)	6
23 Nov 68	The Sound Of Music Soundtrack (RCA)	1
30 Nov 68	Greatest Hits Hollies (Parlophone)	1
7 Dec 68	The Beatles Beatles (Apple)	7
25 Jan 69	Best Of The Seekers Seekers (Columbia)	1
1 Feb 69	The Beatles Beatles (Apple)	1
8 Feb 69	Best Of The Seekers Seekers (Columbia)	1
15 Feb 69	Diana Ross And The Supremes Join The Temptations	
	Diana Ross/Supremes/Temptations (Tamla Motown)	4
15 Mar 69	Goodbye Cream (Polydor)	2
29 Mar 69	Best Of The Seekers Seekers (Columbia)	2
12 Apr 69	Goodbye Cream (Polydor)	1
19 Apr 69	Best Of The Seekers Seekers (Columbia)	1
26 Apr 69	Goodbye Cream (Polydor)	1
3 May 69	Best Of The Seekers Seekers (Columbia)	1
10 May 69	On The Threshold Of A Dream Moody Blues (Deram)	2
24 May 69	Nashville Skyline Bob Dylan (CBS)	4
21 Jun 69	His Orchestra, His Chorus, His Singers, His Sound	
	Ray Conniff (CBS)	3
12 Jul 69	According To My Heart Jim Reeves (RCA International)	4
9 Aug 69	Stand Up Jethro Tull (Island)	3
30 Aug 69	From Elvis In Memphis Elvis Presley (RCA)	1
6 Sep 69	Stand Up Jethro Tull (Island)	2
20 Sep 69	Blind Faith Blind Faith (Polydor)	2
4 Oct 69	Abbey Road Beatles (Apple)	11
20 Dec 69	Let It Bleed Rolling Stones (Decca)	1
27 Dec 69	Abbey Road Beatles (Apple)	6
7 Feb 70	Led Zeppelin 2 Led Zeppelin (Atlantic)	1
14 Feb 70	Motown Chartbusters Vol. 3 Various (Tamla Motown)	1
21 Feb 70	Bridge Over Troubled Water Simon and Garfunkel (CBS)	13
23 May 70	Let It Be Beatles (Parlophone)	3
13 Jun 70	Bridge Over Troubled Water Simon and Garfunkel (CBS)	4
11 Jul 70	Self Portrait Bob Dylan (CBS)	1
18 Jul 70	Bridge Over Troubled Water Simon and Garfunkel (CBS)	5
22 Aug 70	Question Of Balance Moody Blues (Threshold)	3
12 Sep 70	Cosmo's Factory Creedence Clearwater Revival (Liberty)	1
19 Sep 70	Get Your Ya-Yas Out Rolling Stones (Decca)	2
3 Oct 70	Bridge Over Troubled Water Simon and Garfunkel (CBS)	1
10 Oct 70	Paranoid Black Sabbath (Vertigo)	1
17 Oct 70	Bridge Over Troubled Water Simon and Garfunkel (CBS)	1
24 Oct 70	Atom Heart Mother Pink Floyd (Harvest)	1
31 Oct 70	Motown Chartbusters Vol. 4 Various (Tamla Motown)	1
7 Nov 70	Led Zeppelin 3 Led Zeppelin (Atlantic)	3
28 Nov 70	New Morning Bob Dylan (CBS)	1
5 Dec 70	Greatest Hits Andy Williams (CBS)	1

423

12 Dec 70   Led Zeppelin 3 *Led Zeppelin (Atlantic)* 1
19 Dec 70   Greatest Hits *Andy Williams (CBS)* 4

16 Jan 71† Bridge Over Troubled Water *Simon and Garfunkel (CBS)* 11
† This includes 8 weeks at number one when charts were not published due to a
postal strike.
 3 Apr 71   Home Loving Man *Andy Williams (CBS)* 2
17 Apr 71   Motown Chartbusters Vol. 5 *Various (Tamla Motown)* 3
 8 May 71   Sticky Fingers *Rolling Stones (Rolling Stones)* 4
 5 Jun 71   Ram *Paul and Linda McCartney (Apple)* 2
19 Jun 71   Sticky Fingers *Rolling Stones (Rolling Stones)* 1
26 Jun 71   Tarkus *Emerson, Lake and Palmer (Island)* 1
 3 Jul 71   Bridge Over Troubled Water *Simon and Garfunkel (CBS)* 5
 7 Aug 71   Hot Hits 6 *Various (MFP)* 1
14 Aug 71   Every Good Boy Deserves Favour *Moody Blues (Threshold)* 1
21 Aug 71   Top Of The Pops Vol. 18 *Various (Hallmark)* 3
11 Sep 71   Bridge Over Troubled Water *Simon and Garfunkel (CBS)* 1
18 Sep 71   Who's Next *Who (Track)* 1
25 Sep 71   Fireball *Deep Purple (Harvest)* 1
 2 Oct 71   Every Picture Tells A Story *Rod Stewart (Mercury)* 4
30 Oct 71   Imagine *John Lennon/Plastic Ono Band (Apple)* 2
13 Nov 71   Every Picture Tells A Story *Rod Stewart (Mercury)* 2
27 Nov 71   Top Of The Pops Vol. 20 *Various (Hallmark)* 1
 4 Dec 71   Four Symbols *Led Zeppelin (Atlantic)* 2
18 Dec 71   Electric Warrior *T. Rex (Fly)* 6

29 Jan 72   Concert For Bangladesh *Various (Apple)* 1
 5 Feb 72   Electric Warrior *T. Rex (Fly)* 2
19 Feb 72   Neil Reid *Neil Reid (Decca)* 3
11 Mar 72   Harvest *Neil Young (Reprise)* 1
18 Mar 72   Paul Simon *Paul Simon (CBS)* 1
25 Mar 72   Fog On The Tyne *Lindisfarne (Charisma)* 4
22 Apr 72   Machine Head *Deep Purple (Purple)* 2
 6 May 72   Prophets, Seers And Sages And The Angels Of The Ages/My
            People Were Fair And Had Sky In Their Hair But Now
            They're Content To Wear Stars On Their Brows
            Tyrannosaurus Rex (Fly Double Back) 1
13 May 72   Machine Head *Deep Purple (Purple)* 1
20 May 72   Bolan Boogie *T. Rex (Fly)* 3
10 Jun 72   Exile On Main Street *Rolling Stones (Rolling Stones)* 1
17 Jun 72   20 Dynamic Hits *Various (K-Tel)* 8
12 Aug 72   20 Fantastic Hits *Various (Arcade)* 5
16 Sep 72   Never A Dull Moment *Rod Stewart (Philips)* 2
30 Sep 72   20 Fantastic Hits *Various (Arcade)* 1
 7 Oct 72   20 All Time Hits Of The Fifties *Various (K-Tel)* 8
 2 Dec 72   25 Rockin' And Rollin' Greats *Various (K-Tel)* 3
23 Dec 72   20 All Time Hits Of The Fifties *Various (K-Tel)* 3

13 Jan 73   Slayed? *Slade (Polydor)* 1
20 Jan 73   Back To Front *Gilbert O'Sullivan (MAM)* 1
27 Jan 73   Slayed? *Slade (Polydor)* 2
10 Feb 73   Don't Shoot Me, I'm Only The Piano Player *Elton John (DJM)* .. 6
24 Mar 73   Billion Dollar Babies *Alice Cooper (Warner Bros.)* 1
31 Mar 73   20 Flashback Great Hits Of The Sixties *Various (K-Tel)* 2
14 Apr 73   Houses Of The Holy *Led Zeppelin (Atlantic)* 2
28 Apr 73   Ooh La La *Faces (Warner Bros.)* 1
 5 May 73   Aladdin Sane *David Bowie (RCA Victor)* 5

9 Jun 73	Pure Gold *Various (EMI)*	3
30 Jun 73	That'll Be The Day *Various (Ronco)*	7
18 Aug 73	We Can Make It *Peters and Lee (Philips)*	2
1 Sep 73	Sing It Again *Rod Stewart (Mercury)*	3
22 Sep 73	Goat's Head Soup *Rolling Stones (Rolling Stones)*	2
6 Oct 73	Sladest *Slade (Polydor)*	3
27 Oct 73	Hello *Status Quo (Vertigo)*	1
3 Nov 73	Pin Ups *David Bowie (RCA)*	5
8 Dec 73	Stranded *Roxy Music (Island)*	1
15 Dec 73	Dreams Are Nothin' More Than Wishes *David Cassidy (Bell)*	1
22 Dec 73	Goodbye Yellow Brick Road *Elton John (DJM)*	2
5 Jan 74	Tales From Topographic Oceans *Yes (Atlantic)*	2
19 Jan 74	Sladest *Slade (Polydor)*	1
26 Jan 74	And I Love You So *Perry Como (RCA)*	1
2 Feb 74	The Singles 1969–73 *Carpenters (A & M)*	4
2 Mar 74	Old, New, Borrowed And Blue *Slade (Polydor)*	1
9 Mar 74	The Singles 1969–73 *Carpenters (A & M)*	11
25 May 74	Journey To The Centre Of The Earth *Rick Wakeman (A & M)*	1
1 Jun 74	The Singles 1969–73 *Carpenters (A & M)*	1
8 Jun 74	Diamond Dogs *David Bowie (RCA)*	4
6 Jul 74	The Singles 1969–73 *Carpenters (A & M)*	1
13 Jul 74	Caribou *Elton John (DJM)*	2
27 Jul 74	Band On The Run *Wings (Apple)*	7
14 Sep 74	Hergest Ridge *Mike Oldfield (Virgin)*	3
5 Oct 74	Tubular Bells *Mike Oldfield (Virgin)*	1
12 Oct 74	Rollin' *Bay City Rollers (Bell)*	1
19 Oct 74	Smiler *Rod Stewart (Mercury)*	1
26 Oct 74	Rollin' *Bay City Rollers (Bell)*	1
2 Nov 74	Smiler *Rod Stewart (Mercury)*	1
9 Nov 74	Rollin' *Bay City Rollers (Bell)*	2
23 Nov 74	Elton John's Greatest Hits *Elton John (DJM)*	11
8 Feb 75	His Greatest Hits *Engelbert Humperdinck (Decca)*	3
1 Mar 75	On The Level *Status Quo (Vertigo)*	2
15 Mar 75	Physical Graffiti *Led Zeppelin (Swansong)*	1
22 Mar 75	20 Greatest Hits *Tom Jones (Decca)*	4
19 Apr 75	The Best Of The Stylistics *Stylistics (Avco)*	2
3 May 75	Once Upon A Star *Bay City Rollers (Bell)*	3
24 May 75	The Best Of The Stylistics *Stylistics (Avco)*	5
28 Jun 75	Venus And Mars *Wings (Apple)*	1
5 Jul 75	Horizon *Carpenters (A & M)*	2
19 Jul 75	Venus And Mars *Wings (Apple)*	1
26 Jul 75	Horizon *Carpenters (A & M)*	3
16 Aug 75	The Best Of The Stylistics *Stylistics (Avco)*	2
30 Aug 75	Atlantic Crossing *Rod Stewart (Warner Bros.)*	5
4 Oct 75	Wish You Were Here *Pink Floyd (Harvest)*	1
11 Oct 75	Atlantic Crossing *Rod Stewart (Warner Bros.)*	2
25 Oct 75	40 Golden Greats *Jim Reeves (Arcade)*	3
15 Nov 75	We All Had Doctors' Papers *Max Boyce (EMI)*	1
22 Nov 75	40 Greatest Hits *Perry Como (K-Tel)*	5
27 Dec 75	A Night At The Opera *Queen (EMI)*	2
10 Jan 76	40 Greatest Hits *Perry Como (K-Tel)*	1
17 Jan 76	A Night At The Opera *Queen (EMI)*	2
31 Jan 76	The Best Of Roy Orbison *Roy Orbison (Arcade)*	1
7 Feb 76	The Very Best Of Slim Whitman *Slim Whitman (United Artists)*	6

425

20 Mar 76	Blue For You *Status Quo (Vertigo)*	3
10 Apr 76	Rock Follies *TV Soundtrack (Island)*	2
24 Apr 76	Presence *Led Zeppelin (Swansong)*	1
1 May 76	Rock Follies *TV Soundtrack (Island)*	1
8 May 76	Greatest Hits *Abba (Epic)*	9
10 Jul 76	A Night On The Town *Rod Stewart (Riva)*	2
24 Jul 76	20 Golden Greats *Beach Boys (Capitol)*	10
2 Oct 76	Best Of The Stylistics Vol. 2 *Stylistics (H & L)*	1
9 Oct 76	Stupidity *Dr Feelgood (United Artists)*	1
16 Oct 76	Greatest Hits *Abba (Epic)*	2
30 Oct 76	Soul Motion *Various (K-Tel)*	2
13 Nov 76	The Song Remains The Same *Led Zeppelin (Swansong)*	1
20 Nov 76	22 Golden Guitar Greats *Bert Weedon (Warwick)*	1
27 Nov 76	20 Golden Greats *Glen Campbell (Capitol)*	6
8 Jan 77	Day At The Races *Queen (EMI)*	1
15 Jan 77	Arrival *Abba (Epic)*	1
22 Jan 77	Red River Valley *Slim Whitman (United Artists)*	4
19 Feb 77	20 Golden Greats *Shadows (EMI)*	6
2 Apr 77	Portrait *Frank Sinatra (Reprise)*	2
16 Apr 77	Arrival *Abba (Epic)*	9
18 Jun 77	Live At The Hollywood Bowl *Beatles (Parlophone)*	1
25 Jun 77	The Muppet Show *Muppets (Pye)*	1
2 Jul 77	A Star Is Born *Soundtrack (CBS)*	2
16 Jul 77	Johnny Mathis Collection *Johnny Mathis (CBS)*	4
13 Aug 77	Going For The One *Yes (Atlantic)*	2
27 Aug 77	20 All Time Greats *Connie Francis (Polydor)*	2
10 Sep 77	Elvis Presley's 40 Greatest Hits *Elvis Presley (Arcade)*	1
17 Sep 77	20 Golden Greats	
	Diana Ross and the Supremes (Tamla Motown)	7
5 Nov 77	40 Golden Greats *Cliff Richard (EMI)*	1
12 Nov 77	Never Mind The Bollocks Here's The Sex Pistols	
	Sex Pistols (Virgin)	2
26 Nov 77	The Sound Of Bread *Bread (Elektra)*	2
10 Dec 77	Disco Fever *Various (K-Tel)*	6
21 Jan 78	The Sound Of Bread *Bread (Elektra)*	1
28 Jan 78	Rumours *Fleetwood Mac (Warner Bros.)*	1
4 Feb 78	The Album *Abba (Epic)*	7
25 Mar 78	20 Golden Greats *Buddy Holly/Crickets (MCA)*	3
15 Apr 78	20 Golden Greats *Nat King Cole (Capitol)*	3
6 May 78	Saturday Night Fever *Various (RSO)*	18
9 Sep 78	Night Flight To Venus *Boney M (Atlantic/Hansa)*	4
7 Oct 78	Grease *Soundtrack (RSO)*	13
6 Jan 79	Greatest Hits *Showaddywaddy (Arista)*	2
26 Jan 79	Don't Walk – Boogie *Various (EMI)*	3
10 Feb 79	Action Replay *Various (K-Tel)*	1
17 Feb 79	Parallel Lines *Blondie (Chrysalis)*	4
17 Mar 79	Spirits Having Flown *Bee Gees (RSO)*	2
31 Mar 79	Greatest Hits Vol. 2 *Barbra Streisand (CBS)*	4
28 Apr 79	The Very Best Of Leo Sayer *Leo Sayer (Chrysalis)*	3
19 May 79	Voulez-Vous *Abba (Epic)*	4
16 Jun 79	Discovery *Electric Light Orchestra (Jet)*	5
21 Jul 79	Replicas *Tubeway Army (Beggars Banquet)*	1
28 Jul 79	The Best Disco Album In The World *Various (Warner Bros.)*	6

8 Sep 79   In Through The Out Door Led Zeppelin (Swansong) 2
22 Sep 79   The Pleasure Principle Gary Numan (Beggars Banquet) I
29 Sep 79   Oceans Of Fantasy Boney M (Atlantic/Hansa) I
6 Oct 79   The Pleasure Principle Gary Numan (Beggars Banquet) I
13 Oct 79* Eat To The Beat Blondie (Chrysalis) I
13 Oct 79* Reggatta De Blanc Police (A & M) 4
* Two charts published this week because of a change in chart collation.
10 Nov 79   Tusk Fleetwood Mac (Warner Bros.) I
17 Nov 79   Greatest Hits Vol. 2 Abba (Epic) 3
8 Dec 79   Greatest Hits Rod Stewart (Riva) 5

12 Jan 80   Greatest Hits Vol. 2 Abba (Epic) I
19 Jan 80   Pretenders Pretenders (Real) 4
16 Feb 80   The Last Dance Various (Motown) 2
1 Mar 80   String Of Hits Shadows (EMI) 3
22 Mar 80   Tears And Laughter Johnny Mathis (CBS) 2
5 Apr 80   Duke Genesis (Charisma) 2
19 Apr 80   Greatest Hits Rose Royce (Whitfield) 2
3 May 80   Sky 2 Sky (Ariola) 2
17 May 80   The Magic Of Boney M Boney M (Atlantic/Hansa) 2
31 May 80   McCartney II Paul McCartney (Parlophone) 2
14 Jun 80   Peter Gabriel Peter Gabriel (Charisma) 2
28 Jun 80   Flesh And Blood Roxy Music (Polydor) I
5 Jul 80   Emotional Rescue Rolling Stones (Rolling Stones) 2
19 Jul 80   The Game Queen (EMI) 2
2 Aug 80   Deepest Purple Deep Purple (Harvest) I
9 Aug 80   Back In Black AC/DC (Atlantic) 2
23 Aug 80   Flesh And Blood Roxy Music (Polydor) 3
13 Sep 80   Telekon Gary Numan (Beggars Banquet) I
20 Sep 80   Never For Ever Kate Bush (EMI) I
27 Sep 80   Scary Monsters And Supercreeps David Bowie (RCA) 2
11 Oct 80   Zenyatta Mondatta Police (A & M) 4
8 Nov 80   Guilty Barbra Streisand (CBS) 2
22 Nov 80   Super Trouper Abba (Epic) 9

24 Jan 81   Kings Of The Wild Frontier Adam and the Ants (CBS) 2
7 Feb 81   Double Fantasy John Lennon (Geffen) 2
21 Feb 81   Face Value Phil Collins (Virgin) 3
14 Mar 81   Kings Of The Wild Frontier Adam and the Ants (CBS) 10
23 May 81   Stars On 45 Starsound (CBS) 5
27 Jun 81   No Sleep Til Hammersmith Motorhead (Bronze) I
4 Jul 81   Disco Daze & Disco Nites Various (Ronco) I
11 Jul 81   Love Songs Cliff Richard (EMI) 5
15 Aug 81   The Official BBC Album Of The Royal Wedding
            Soundtrack (BBC) 2
29 Aug 81   Time Electric Light Orchestra (Jet) 2
12 Sep 81   Dead Ringer Meat Loaf (Epic) 2
26 Sep 81   Abacab Genesis (Charisma) 2
10 Oct 81   Ghost In The Machine Police (A & M) 3
31 Oct 81   Dare Human League (Virgin) I
7 Nov 81   Shaky Shakin' Stevens (Epic) I
14 Nov 81   Greatest Hits Queen (EMI) 4
12 Dec 81   Chart Hits '81 Various (K-Tel) I
19 Dec 81   The Visitors Abba (Epic) 3

9 Jan 82   Dare Human League (Virgin) 3
30 Jan 82   Love Songs Barbra Streisand (CBS) 7

20 Mar 82	The Gift *Jam (Polydor)*	1
27 Mar 82	Love Songs *Barbra Streisand (CBS)*	2
10 Apr 82	The Number Of The Beast *Iron Maiden (EMI)*	2
24 Apr 82	1982 *Status Quo (Vertigo)*	1
1 May 82	Barry Live In Britain *Barry Manilow (Arista)*	1
8 May 82	Tug Of War *Paul McCartney (Parlophone)*	2
22 May 82	Complete Madness *Madness (Stiff)*	2
5 Jun 82	Avalon *Roxy Music (Polydor)*	1
12 Jun 82	Complete Madness *Madness (Stiff)*	1
19 Jun 82	Avalon *Roxy Music (Polydor)*	2
3 Jul 82	The Lexicon Of Love *ABC (Neutron)*	3
24 Jul 82	=The Lexicon Of Love *ABC (Neutron)*	1
	=Fame *Original Soundtrack (RSO)*	1
31 Jul 82	Fame *Original Soundtrack (RSO)*	1
7 Aug 82	Kids From Fame *Kids from Fame (BBC)*	8
2 Oct 82	Love Over Gold *Dire Straits (Vertigo)*	4
30 Oct 82	Kids From Fame *Kids from Fame (BBC)*	4
27 Nov 82	The Singles – The First Ten Years *Abba (Epic)*	1
4 Dec 82	The John Lennon Collection *John Lennon (Parlophone)*	6
15 Jan 83	Raiders Of The Pop Charts *Various Artists (Ronco)*	2
29 Jan 83	Business As Usual *Men At Work (Epic)*	5
5 Mar 83	Thriller *Michael Jackson (Epic)*	1
12 Mar 83	War *U2 (Island)*	1
19 Mar 83	Thriller *Michael Jackson (Epic)*	1
26 Mar 83	The Hurting *Tears For Fears (Mercury)*	1
2 Apr 83	The Final Cut *Pink Floyd (Harvest)*	2
16 Apr 83	Faster Than The Speed Of Night *Bonnie Tyler (CBS)*	1
23 Apr 83	Let's Dance *David Bowie (EMI America)*	3
14 May 83	True *Spandau Ballet (Reformation)*	1
21 May 83	Thriller *Michael Jackson (Epic)*	5
25 Jun 83	Synchronicity *Police (A & M)*	2
9 Jul 83	Fantastic! *Wham! (Inner Vision)*	2
23 Jul 83	You And Me Both *Yazoo (Mute)*	2
6 Aug 83	The Very Best Of The Beach Boys *Beach Boys (Capitol)*	2
20 Aug 83	18 Greatest Hits *Michael Jackson plus the Jackson Five (Telstar)*	3
10 Sep 83	The Very Best Of The Beach Boys *Beach Boys (Capitol)*	1
17 Sep 83	No Parlez *Paul Young (CBS)*	1
24 Sep 83	Labour Of Love *UB 40 (DEP International)*	1
1 Oct 83	No Parlez *Paul Young (CBS)*	2
15 Oct 83	Genesis *Genesis (Charisma/Virgin)*	1
22 Oct 83	Colour By Numbers *Culture Club (Virgin)*	3
12 Nov 83	Can't Slow Down *Lionel Richie (Motown)*	1
19 Nov 83	Colour By Numbers *Culture Club (Virgin)*	2
3 Dec 83	Seven And The Ragged Tiger *Duran Duran (EMI)*	1
10 Dec 83	No Parlez *Paul Young (CBS)*	1
17 Dec 83	Now! That's What I Call Music *Various Artists (EMI/Virgin)*	4
14 Jan 84	No Parlez *Paul Young (CBS)*	1
21 Jan 84	Now! That's What I Call Music *Various Artists (EMI/Virgin)*	1
28 Jan 84	Thriller *Michael Jackson (Epic)*	1
4 Feb 84	Touch *Eurythmics (RCA)*	2
18 Feb 84	Sparkle In The Rain *Simple Minds (Virgin)*	1
25 Feb 84	Into The Gap *Thompson Twins (Arista)*	3
17 Mar 84	Human's Lib *Howard Jones (WEA)*	2
31 Mar 84	Can't Slow Down *Lionel Richie (Motown)*	2

14 Apr 84	Now! That's What I Call Music 2 *Various Artists (EMI/Virgin)*	5
19 May 84	Legend *Bob Marley and the Wailers (Island)*	12
11 Aug 84	Now! That's What I Call Music 3 *Various Artists (EMI/Virgin)*	8
6 Oct 84	Tonight *David Bowie (EMI America)*	1
13 Oct 84	The Unforgettable Fire *U2 (Island)*	2
27 Oct 84	Steel Town *Big Country (Mercury)*	1
3 Nov 84	Give My Regards To Broad Street *Paul McCartney (Parlophone)*	1
10 Nov 84	Welcome To The Pleasure Dome *Frankie Goes To Hollywood (ZTT)*	1
17 Nov 84	Make It Big *Wham! (Epic)*	2
1 Dec 84	The Hits Album/The Hits Tape *Various Artists (CBS/WEA)*	7
19 Jan 85	Alf *Alison Moyet (CBS)*	1
26 Jan 85	Agent Provocateur *Foreigner (Atlantic)*	3
16 Feb 85	Born In The U.S.A. *Bruce Springsteen (CBS)*	1
23 Feb 85	Meat Is Murder *Smiths (Rough Trade)*	1
2 Mar 85	No Jacket Required *Phil Collins (Virgin)*	5
6 Apr 85	The Secret Of Association *Paul Young (CBS)*	1
13 Apr 85	The Hits Album 2/The Hits Tape 2 *Various Artists (CBS/WEA)*	6
25 May 85	Brothers In Arms *Dire Straits (Vertigo)*	2
8 Jun 85	Our Favourite Shop *Style Council (Polydor)*	1
15 Jun 85	Boys And Girls *Bryan Ferry (EG)*	2
29 Jun 85	Misplaced Childhood *Marillion (EMI)*	1
6 Jul 85	Born In The U.S.A. *Bruce Springsteen (CBS)*	4
3 Aug 85	Brothers In Arms *Dire Straits (Vertigo)*	2
17 Aug 85	Now! That's What I Call Music 5 *Various Artists (EMI/Virgin)*	5
21 Sep 85	Like A Virgin *Madonna (Sire)*	1
28 Sep 85	Hounds Of Love *Kate Bush (EMI)*	2
12 Oct 85	Like A Virgin *Madonna (Sire)*	1
19 Oct 85	Hounds Of Love *Kate Bush (EMI)*	1
26 Oct 85	The Love Songs *George Benson (K-Tel)*	1
2 Nov 85	Once Upon A Time *Simple Minds (Virgin)*	1
9 Nov 85	The Love Songs *George Benson (K-Tel)*	1
16 Nov 85	Promise *Sade (Epic)*	2
30 Nov 85	The Greatest Hits Of 1985 *Various Artists (Telstar)*	1
7 Dec 85	Now! That's What I Call Music 6 *Various Artists (EMI/Virgin)*	2
21 Dec 85	Now! – The Christmas Album *Various Artists (EMI/Virgin)*	2
4 Jan 86	Now! That's What I Call Music 6 *Various Artists (EMI/Virgin)*	2
18 Jan 86	Brothers In Arms *Dire Straits (Vertigo)*	10
29 Mar 86	Hits 4 *Various Artists (CBS/WEA/RCA Ariola)*	4
26 Apr 86	Street Life – 20 Great Hits *Bryan Ferry/Roxy Music (EG)*	5
31 May 86	So *Peter Gabriel (Virgin)*	2
14 Jun 86	A Kind Of Magic *Queen (EMI)*	1
21 Jun 86	Invisible Touch *Genesis (Charisma)*	3
12 Jul 86	True Blue *Madonna (Sire)*	6
23 Aug 86	Now! That's What I Call Music 7 *Various Artists (EMI/Virgin)*	5
27 Sep 86	Silk And Steel *Five Star (Tent)*	1
4 Oct 86	Graceland *Paul Simon (Warner Bros.)*	5
8 Nov 86	Every Breath You Take – The Singles *Police (A & M)*	2
22 Nov 86	Hits 5 *Various Artists (CBS/WEA/RCA Ariola)*	2
6 Dec 86	Now! That's What I Call Music 8 *Various Artists (EMI/Virgin)*	6
17 Jan 87	The Whole Story *Kate Bush (EMI)*	2
31 Jan 87	Graceland *Paul Simon (Warner Bros.)*	3

429

21 Feb 87	Phantom Of The Opera *Original London Cast (Polydor)*	3
14 Mar 87	The Very Best Of Hot Chocolate *Hot Chocolate (RAK)*	1
21 Mar 87	The Joshua Tree *U2 (Island)*	2
4 Apr 87	Now! That's What I Call Music 9	
	Various Artists (EMI/Virgin/Phonogram)	5
9 May 87	Keep Your Distance *Curiosity Killed The Cat (Mercury)*	2
23 May 87	It's Better To Travel *Swing Out Sister (Mercury)*	2
6 Jun 87	Live In The City Of Light *Simple Minds (Virgin)*	1
13 Jun 87	Whitney *Whitney Houston (Arista)*	6
25 Jul 87	Introducing The Hardline According To Terence Trent	
	D'Arby *Terence Trent D'Arby (CBS)*	1
1 Aug 87	Hits 6 *Various Artists (CBS/WEA/BMG)*	4
29 Aug 87	Hysteria *Def Leppard (Bludgeon Riffola)*	1
5 Sep 87	Hits 6 *Various Artists (CBS/WEA/BMG)*	1
12 Sep 87	Bad *Michael Jackson (Epic)*	5
17 Oct 87	Tunnel Of Love *Bruce Springsteen (CBS)*	1
24 Oct 87	Nothing Like The Sun *Sting (A & M)*	1
31 Oct 87	Tango In The Night *Fleetwood Mac (Warner Bros.)*	2
14 Nov 87	Faith *George Michael (Epic)*	1
21 Nov 87	Bridge Of Spies *T'Pau (Siren)*	1
28 Nov 87	When You Need Somebody *Rick Astley (RCA)*	1
5 Dec 87	Now! That's What I Call Music 10	
	Various Artists (EMI/Virgin/Polygram)	6
16 Jan 88	Popped In Souled Out *Wet Wet Wet (Precious)*	1
23 Jan 88	Turn Back The Clock *Johnny Hates Jazz (Virgin)*	1
30 Jan 88	Introducing The Hardline According To Terence Trent	
	D'Arby *Terence Trent D'Arby (CBS)*	8
26 Mar 88	Viva Hate *Morrissey (HMV)*	1
2 Apr 88	Now! That's What I Call Music 11	
	Various Artists(EMI/Virgin/Polygram)	3
23 Apr 88	Seventh Son Of A Seventh Son *Iron Maiden (EMI)*	1
30 Apr 88	The Innocents *Erasure (Mute)*	1
7 May 88	Tango In The Night *Fleetwood Mac (Warner Bros.)*	2
21 May 88	Lovesexy *Prince (Paisley Park)*	1
28 May 88	Tango In The Night *Fleetwood Mac (Warner Bros.)*	1
4 Jun 88	Nite Flite *Various Artists (CBS)*	4
2 Jul 88	Tracy Chapman *Tracy Chapman (Elektra)*	3
23 Jul 88	Now! That's What I Call Music 12	
	Various Artists (EMI/Virgin/Polygram)	5
27 Aug 88	Kylie *Kylie Minogue (PWL)*	4
24 Sep 88	Hot City Nights *Various Artists (Vertigo)*	1
1 Oct 88	New Jersey *Bon Jovi (Vertigo)*	2
15 Oct 88	Flying Colours *Chris De Burgh (A & M)*	1
22 Oct 88	Rattle And Hum *U2 (Island)*	1
29 Oct 88	Money And Nothing *Dire Straits (Vertigo)*	3
19 Nov 88	Kylie *Kylie Minogue (PWL)*	2
3 Dec 88	Now! That's What I Call Music 13	
	Various Artists (EMI/Virgin/Polygram)	3
24 Dec 88	Private Collection *Cliff Richard (EMI)*	2
7 Jan 89	Now! That's What I Call Music 13	
	Various Artists (EMI/Virgin/Polygram)	1

(From 14 January 1989, compilation albums were excluded from the main chart)

14 Jan 89	The Innocents *Erasure (Mute)*	1

21 Jan 89	The Legendary Roy Orbison *Roy Orbison (Telstar)*	3
11 Feb 89	Technique *New Order (Factory)*	1
18 Feb 89	The Raw And The Cooked *Fine Young Cannibals (London)*	1
25 Feb 89	A New Flame *Simply Red (Elektra)*	4
25 Mar 89	Anything For You	
	Gloria Estefan and Miami Sound Machine (Epic)	1
1 Apr 89	Like A Prayer *Madonna (Sire)*	2
15 Apr 89	When The World Knows Your Name *Deacon Blue (CBS)*	2
29 Apr 89	A New Flame *Simply Red (Elektra)*	1
6 May 89	Blast *Holly Johnson (MCA)*	1
13 May 89	Street Fighting Years *Simple Minds (Virgin)*	1
20 May 89	Ten Good Reasons *Jason Donovan (PWL)*	2
3 Jun 89	The Miracle *Queen (Parlophone)*	1
10 Jun 89	Ten Good Reasons *Jason Donovan (PWL)*	2
24 Jun 89	Flowers In The Dirt *Paul McCartney (Parlophone)*	1
1 Jul 89	Batman *Prince (Warner Bros.)*	1
8 Jul 89	Velveteen *Transvision Vamp (MCA)*	1
15 Jul 89	Club Classics Volume One *Soul II Soul (10)*	1
22 Jul 89	A New Flame *Simply Red (Elektra)*	2
5 Aug 89	Cuts Both Ways *Gloria Estefan (Epic)*	6
16 Sep 89	Aspects Of Love *Original London Cast (Polydor)*	1
23 Sep 89	We Too Are One *Eurythmics (RCA)*	1
30 Sep 89	Foreign Affair *Tina Turner (Capitol)*	1
7 Oct 89	The Seeds Of Love *Tears For Fears (Fontana)*	1
14 Oct 89	Crossroads *Tracy Chapman (Elektra)*	1
21 Oct 89	Enjoy Yourself *Kylie Minogue (PWL)*	1
28 Oct 89	Wild! *Erasure (Mute)*	2
11 Nov 89	The Road To Hell *Chris Rea (WEA)*	3
2 Dec 89	. . . But Seriously *Phil Collins (Virgin)*	8
27 Jan 90	Colour *Christians (Island)*	1
3 Feb 90	. . . But Seriously *Phil Collins (Virgin)*	7
24 Mar 90	I Do Not Want What I Haven't Got *Sinead O'Connor (Ensign)*	1
31 Mar 90	Changesbowie *David Bowie (EMI)*	1
7 Apr 90	Only Yesterday *Carpenters (A & M)*	2
21 Apr 90	Behind The Mask *Fleetwood Mac (Warner Brothers)*	1
28 Apr 90	Only Yesterday *Carpenters (A & M)*	5
2 Jun 90	Vol II (1990 A New Decade) *Soul II Soul (10)*	3
23 Jun 90	The Essential Pavarotti *Luciano Pavarotti (Decca)*	1
30 Jun 90	Step By Step *New Kids On The Block (CBS)*	1
7 Jul 90	The Essential Pavarotti *Luciano Pavarotti (Decca)*	3
28 Jul 90	Sleeping With The Past *Elton John (Rocket)*	5
1 Sep 90	Graffiti Bridge *Prince (Paisley Park)*	1
8 Sep 90	In Concert	
	Luciano Pavarotti, Placido Domingo and José Carreras (Decca)	1
15 Sep 90	Listen Without Prejudice Vol. 1 *George Michael (Epic)*	1
22 Sep 90	In Concert	
	Luciano Pavarotti, Placido Domingo and José Carreras (Decca)	4
20 Oct 90	Some Friendly *Charlatans (Situation Two)*	1
27 Oct 90	The Rhythm Of The Saints *Paul Simon (Warner Brothers)*	2
10 Nov 90	The Very Best Of Elton John *Elton John (Rocket)*	2
24 Nov 90	The Immaculate Collection *Madonna (Sire)*	9
26 Jan 91	MCMXC AD *Enigma (Virgin International)*	1
2 Feb 91	The Soul Cages *Sting (A & M)*	1
9 Feb 90	Doubt *Jesus Jones (Food)*	1

431

16 Feb 91	Innuendo Queen (Parlophone)	2
2 Mar 91	Circle Of One Oleta Adams (Fontana)	1
9 Mar 91	Auberge Chris Rea (East West)	1
16 Mar 91	Spartacus Farm (Produce)	1
23 Mar 91	Out Of Time R.E.M. (Warner Brothers)	1
30 Mar 91	Greatest Hits Eurythmics (RCA)	9
1 Jun 91	Seal Seal (ZTT)	3
22 Jun 91	Greatest Hits Eurythmics (RCA)	1
29 Jun 91	Love Hurts Cher (Geffen)	6
10 Aug 91	The Essential Pavarotti II Luciano Pavarotti (Decca)	2
24 Aug 91	Metallica Metallica (Vertigo)	1
31 Aug 91	Joseph And The Amazing Technicolour Dreamcoat	
	Jason Donovan/Original London Cast (Really Useful)	2
14 Sep 91	From Time To Time – The Singles Collection	
	Paul Young (Columbia)	1
21 Sep 91	On Every Street Dire Straits (Vertigo)	1
28 Sep 91	Use Your Illusion II Guns N' Roses (Geffen)	1
5 Oct 91	Waking Up The Neighbours Bryan Adams (A & M)	1
12 Oct 91	Stars Simply Red (East West)	2
26 Oct 91	Chorus Erasure (Mute)	1
2 Nov 91	Stars Simply Red (East West)	1
9 Nov 91	Greatest Hits II Queen (Parlophone)	1
16 Nov 91	Shepherd Moons Enya (WEA)	1
23 Nov 91	We Can't Dance Genesis (Virgin)	1
30 Nov 91	Dangerous Michael Jackson (Epic)	1
7 Dec 91	Greatest Hits II Queen (Parlophone)	4
4 Jan 92	Stars Simply Red (East West)	5
8 Feb 92	High On The Happy Side Wet Wet Wet (Precious)	2
22 Feb 92	Stars Simply Red (East West)	3
14 Mar 92	Divine Madness Madness (Virgin)	3
4 Apr 92	Human Touch Bruce Springsteen (Columbia)	1
11 Apr 92	Adrenalize Def Leppard (Bludgeon Riffola)	1
18 Apr 92	Diva Annie Lennox (RCA)	1
25 Apr 92	Up Right Said Fred (Tug)	1
2 May 92	Wish Cure (Fiction)	1
9 May 92	Stars Simply Red (East West)	1
16 May 92	1992 – The Love Album	
	Carter The Unstoppable Sex Machine (Chrysalis)	1
23 May 92	Fear Of The Dark Iron Maiden (EMI)	1
30 May 92	Michael Ball Michael Ball (Polydor)	1
6 Jun 92	Back To Front Lionel Richie (Motown)	6
18 Jul 92	U.F. Orb Orb (Big Life)	1
25 Jul 92	The Greatest Hits 1966–1992 Neil Diamond (Columbia)	3
15 Aug 92	Welcome To Whoever You Are INXS (Mercury)	1
22 Aug 92	We Can't Dance Genesis (Virgin)	1
29 Aug 92	Best ... 1 Smiths (WEA)	1
5 Sep 92	Greatest Hits Kylie Minogue (PWL)	1
12 Sep 92	Tubular Bells II Mike Oldfield (WEA)	2
26 Sep 92	The Best Of Belinda Volume 1 Belinda Carlisle (Virgin)	1
3 Oct 92	Gold – Greatest Hits Abba (Polydor)	1
10 Oct 92	Automatic For The People R.E.M. (Warner Brothers)	1
17 Oct 92	Symbol Prince (Paisley Park)	1
24 Oct 92	Glittering Prize 81–92 Simple Minds (Virgin)	3
14 Nov 92	Keep The Faith Bon Jovi (Jambco)	1

432

21 Nov 92   Cher's Greatest Hits 1965–1992 *Cher (Geffen)* 1
28 Nov 92   Pop! The First 20 Hits *Erasure (Mute)* 2
12 Dec 92   Cher's Greatest Hits 1965–1992 *Cher (Geffen)* 6

23 Jan 93   Live – The Way We Walk Volume II – The Longs
        Genesis (Virgin) 2
6 Feb 93   Jam *Little Angels (Polydor)* 1
13 Feb 93   Pure Cult *Cult (Beggars Banquet)* 1
20 Feb 93   Words Of Love *Buddy Holly and the Crickets (Polygram)* 1
27 Feb 93   Walthamstow *East 17 (London)* 1
6 Mar 93   Diva *Annie Lennox (RCA)* 1
13 Mar 93   Are You Gonna Go My Way *Lenny Kravitz (Virgin)* 2
27 Mar 93   Their Greatest Hits *Hot Chocolate (EMI)* 1
3 Apr 93   Songs Of Faith And Devotion *Depeche Mode (Mute)* 1
10 Apr 93   Suede *Suede (Nude)* 1
17 Apr 93   Black Tie White Noise *David Bowie (Arista)* 1
24 Apr 93   Automatic For The People *R.E.M. (Warner Brothers)* 1
1 May 93   The Album *Cliff Richard (EMI)* 1
8 May 93   Automatic For The People *R.E.M. (Warner Brothers)* 1
15 May 93   Republic *New Order (London)* 1
22 May 93   Automatic For The People *R.E.M. (Warner Brothers)* 1
29 May 93   Janet *Janet Jackson (Virgin)* 2
12 Jun 93   No Limits *2 Unlimited (PWL Continental)* 1
19 Jun 93   What's Love Got To Do With It *Tina Turner (Parlophone)* 1
26 Jun 93   Emergency On Planet Earth *Jamiroquai (Sony)* 3
17 Jul 93   Zooropa *U2 (Island)* 1
24 Jul 93   Promises And Lies *UB40 (DEP International)* 7
11 Sep 93   Music Box *Mariah Carey (Columbia)* 1
18 Sep 93   Bat Out Of Hell II – Back Into Hell *Meat Loaf (Virgin)* 1
25 Sep 93   In Utero *Nirvana (Geffen)* 1
2 Oct 93   Bat Out Of Hell II – Back Into Hell *Meat Loaf (Virgin)* 1
9 Oct 93   Very *Pet Shop Boys (Parlophone)* 1
16 Oct 93   Bat Out Of Hell II – Back Into Hell *Meat Loaf (Virgin)* 1
23 Oct 93   Everything Changes *Take That (RCA)* 1
30 Oct 93   Bat Out Of Hell II – Back Into Hell *Meat Loaf (Virgin)* 3
20 Nov 93   Both Sides *Phil Collins (Virgin)* 1
27 Nov 93   Bat Out Of Hell II – Back Into Hell *Meat Loaf (Virgin)* 5

Since 14 January 1989, the albums charts have been split into a Top 75 'Artist Albums' and a Top 20 'Compilation Albums'. The 87 number one hits on the Compilation Albums are as follows:

14 Jan 89   Now! That's What I Call Music 13 *(EMI/Virgin/Polygram)* 1
21 Jan 89   The Premiere Collection *(Really Useful/Polydor)* 2
4 Feb 89   The Marquee – Thirty Legendary Years *(Polydor)* 4
4 Mar 89   The Awards *(Telstar)* 1
11 Mar 89   The Premiere Collection *(Really Useful/Polydor)* 1
18 Mar 89   Deep Heat *(Telstar)* 1
25 Mar 89   Unforgettable 2 *(EMI)* 1
1 Apr 89   Now! That's What I Call Music 14 *(EMI/Virgin/Polygram)* 7
20 May 89   Nite Flite 2 *(CBS)* 2
3 Jun 89   The Hits Album 10 *(CBS/WEA/BMG)* 6
15 Jul 89   Now! Dance '89 *(EMI/Virgin)* 6
26 Aug 89   Now! That's What I Call Music 15 *(EMI/Virgin/Polygram)* 5
30 Sep 89   Deep Heat 4 – Play With Fire *(Telstar)* 5

4 Nov 89	Smash Hits Party '89 *(Dover)*	3
25 Nov 89	The 80s – The Album Of The Decade *(EMI)*	1
2 Dec 89	Now! That's What I Call Music 16 *(EMI/Virgin/Polygram)*	7
20 Jan 90	Pure Soft Metal *(Stylus)*	2
3 Feb 90	Deep Heat 5 – Feed The Fever *(Telstar)*	2
17 Feb 90	Pure Soft Metal *(Stylus)*	3
10 Mar 90	Now Dance 901 *(EMI/Virgin/Polygram)*	4
7 Apr 90	Deep Heat 6 – The Sixth Sense *(Telstar)*	2
21 Apr 90	Just The Two Of Us *(CBS)*	2
5 May 90	Now! That's What I Call Music 17 *(EMI/Virgin/Polygram)*	5
9 Jun 90	The Classic Experience II *(EMI)*	4
7 Jul 90	Deep Heat 7 – Seventh Heaven *(Telstar)*	1
14 Jul 90	Smash Hits – Rave! *(Dover)*	2
28 Jul 90	Now Dance 902 *(EMI/Virgin/Polygram)*	3
18 Aug 90	Knebworth – The Album *(Polydor)*	2
1 Sep 90	Megabass *(Telstar)*	4
29 Sep 90	Slammin' *(A & M)*	1
6 Oct 90	That Loving Feeling Vol. 3 *(Dino)*	3
27 Oct 90	Missing You – An Album Of Love *(EMI)*	3
17 Nov 90	Now Dance 903 *(EMI/Virgin/Polygram)*	2
1 Dec 90	Now! That's What I Call Music 18 *(EMI/Virgin/Polygram)*	7
19 Jan 91	Dirty Dancing *(Original Soundtrack) (RCA)*	2
2 Feb 91	Deep Heat – The Ninth Life *(Telstar)*	2
16 Feb 91	The Lost Boys *(Original Soundtrack) (Atlantic)*	1
23 Feb 91	Awesome!! *(EMI)*	3
16 Mar 91	Unchained Melodies *(Telstar)*	3
6 Apr 91	Now! That's What I Call Music 19 *(EMI/Virgin/Polygram)*	5
11 May 91	Thinking Of You *(Columbia)*	2
25 May 91	Smash Hits – Massive *(Dover)*	2
8 Jun 91	The Essential Mozart *(Decca)*	1
15 Jun 91	The Rhythm Divine *(Dino)*	1
22 Jun 91	The Essential Mozart *(Decca)*	1
29 Jun 91	Wings Of Love *(A & M)*	5
3 Aug 91	Thin Ice 2 – The Second Shiver *(Telstar)*	1
10 Aug 91	Purple Rainbows *(Polydor)*	1
17 Aug 91	The Hits Album *(Sony/BMG)*	2
31 Aug 91	The Sound Of The Suburbs *(Columbia)*	3
21 Sep 91	Groovy Ghetto *(Arcade)*	2
5 Oct 91	Now! Dance 91 *(EMI/Virgin/Polygram)*	3
26 Oct 91	Two Rooms – Elton John & Bernie Taupin *(Mercury)*	1
2 Nov 91	Hardcore Ecstasy *(Dino)*	4
30 Nov 91	Now! That's What I Call Music 20 *(EMI/Virgin/Polygram)*	7
18 Jan 92	Essential Hardcore *(Dino)*	1
25 Jan 92	The Ultimate Rave *(EMI/Virgin/Polygram)*	4
22 Feb 92	The Awards 1992 *(Polygram TV)*	2
7 Mar 92	The Ultimate Hardcore *(Telstar)*	2
21 Mar 92	Soul Emotion *(Polygram)*	3
11 Apr 92	All Woman *(Quality Television)*	2
25 Apr 92	Now! That's What I Call Music 21 *(EMI/Virgin/Polygram)*	5
30 May 92	The Rave Gener8tor *(Cookie Jar)*	2
13 Jun 92	Earthrise – The Rainforest Album *(ELF)*	1
20 Jun 92	Modern Love *(Polygram)*	1
27 Jun 92	Heartbeat *(Columbia)*	4

434

25 Jul 92	KT3 – The Kaos Theory *(Telstar)*	2
8 Aug 92	Now! That's What I Call Music 22 *(EMI/Virgin/Polygram)*	8
3 Oct 92	Sixties Beat *(Dino)*	1
10 Oct 92	All Woman 2 *(Quality Television)*	1
17 Oct 92	Energy Rush *(Dino)*	2
31 Oct 92	The Ultimate Country Collection *(Columbia)*	1
7 Nov 92	The Best Of Dance '92 *(Telstar)*	1
14 Nov 92	The Ultimate Country Collection *(Columbia)*	1
21 Nov 92	The Best Of Dance '92 *(Telstar)*	1
28 Nov 92	Now! That's What I Call Music 23 *(EMI/Virgin/Polygram)*	5
2 Jan 93	The Bodyguard *(Original Soundtrack) (Arista)*	8
27 Feb 93	Hits '93 Volume 1 *(Telstar/BMG)*	3
20 Mar 93	The Bodyguard *(Original Soundtrack) (Arista)*	2
3 Apr 93	Blues Brother Soul Sister *(Dino)*	1
10 Apr 93	Energy Rush Presents Dance Hits '93 *(Dino)*	3
1 May 93	The Bodyguard *(Original Soundtrack) (Arista)*	1
8 May 93	Now! That's What I Call Music 24 *(EMI/Virgin/Polygram)*	6
19 Jun 93	Originals *(Columbia)*	1
26 Jun 93	Now! Dance '93 *(EMI/Virgin/Polygram)*	2
10 Jul 93	100% Dance *(Telstar)*	1
17 Jul 93	The Best Dance Album In The World ... Ever! *(Virgin)*	4
14 Aug 93	Now! That's What I Call Music 25 *(EMI/Virgin/Polygram)*	5
18 Sep 93	Dance Adrenalin *(Telstar)*	2
2 Oct 93	100% Dance Volume 2 *(Telstar)*	2
16 Oct 93	Now! 1993 *(EMI/Virgin/Polygram)*	1
23 Oct 93	100% Dance Volume 2 *(Telstar)*	2
6 Nov 93	Now! Dance – The Best Of '93 *(EMI/Virgin/Polygram)*	1
13 Nov 93	The Best Of Dance '93 *(Telstar)*	2
27 Nov 93	Now! That's What I Call Music 26 *(EMI/Virgin/Polygram)*	5

All albums were, of course, credited to 'Various Artists'.

435

Whitney Houston in The Bodyguard. *(Warner Bros.)*

MOST NUMBER ONE ALBUMS

12	Beatles	4	Shadows
9	Abba	4	Status Quo
9	Rolling Stones	3	Boney M
8	David Bowie	3	Kate Bush
8	Led Zeppelin	3	Carpenters
8	Queen	3	Deep Purple
7	Genesis	3	Eurythmics
7	Paul McCartney/Wings	3	Iron Maiden
7	Cliff Richard	3	John Lennon
7	Rod Stewart	3	Kylie Minogue
6	Bob Dylan	3	George Mitchell Minstrels
6	Elton John	3	Moody Blues
6	Elvis Presley	3	Gary Numan/Tubeway Army
5	Police	3	Mike Oldfield
5	Simple Minds	3	Pink Floyd
5	U2	3	Diana Ross and the Supremes
4	Phil Collins		*(includes 1 with the Temptations)*
4	Dire Straits	3	Paul Simon
4	Erasure		*(+ 2 with Simon and Garfunkel)*
4	Fleetwood Mac	3	Slade
4	Michael Jackson	3	Bruce Springsteen
	(includes 1 with Jacksons)	3	Barbra Streisand
4	Madonna	3	T. Rex
4	Prince	3	Andy Williams
4	Roxy Music	3	Paul Young
	(1 with Bryan Ferry)		

Bryan Ferry has had one solo number one to go with the four Roxy Music chart toppers, on all of which he sang lead and on one of which he was given equal billing with Roxy Music (it featured several solo Ferry tracks).

Sting has had two solo number one albums as well as five as lead singer of the Police.

Morrissey has had one solo number one hit album and two as a member of the Smiths.

George Michael has had two solo chart-topping albums and two more as half of Wham!

Luciano Pavarotti has had two number one albums as a soloist, plus one in collaboration with José Carreras and Placido Domingo.

MOST WEEKS AT NUMBER ONE

163	Beatles	15	Police
115	Cast of South Pacific Film Soundtrack	15	Barbra Streisand
70	Cast of The Sound of Music Film Soundtrack	14	Diana Ross and the Supremes (include 4 with the Temptations)
50	Abba	14	Led Zeppelin
49	Elvis Presley	13	Beach Boys
48	Simon and Garfunkel	13	Cher
43	Rolling Stones	13	Cast of Grease Film Soundtrack
30	Cliff Richard		
29	Carpenters	13	Eurythmics
28	Elton John	13	Meat Loaf
27	Rod Stewart	13	Roxy Music (includes 5 with Bryan Ferry)
24	Phil Collins		
22	David Bowie	13	Broadway cast of West Side Story
22	Dire Straits		
22	Bob Dylan	12	Adam and the Ants
21	Shadows (+ 22 weeks backing Cliff Richard)	12	Genesis
		12	Kids from 'Fame'
20	Queen	12	Bob Marley and the Wailers
19	Madonna	12	T. Rex
19	George Mitchell Minstrels	11	Luciano Pavarotti (includes 5 with José Carreras and Placido Domingo)
19	Simply Red		
18	Saturday Night Fever Film Soundtrack		
		11	Paul Simon
17	Michael Jackson (includes 3 with Jackson Five)	10	John Lennon
		10	Stylistics
16	Paul McCartney/Wings	10	Slim Whitman

List excludes individual appearances on compilations and soundtracks, except where the soundtrack is credited to one artist, for example Elvis Presley's Blue Hawaii.

437

MOST WEEKS AT NUMBER ONE IN A CALENDAR YEAR

Only five acts have spent more than 20 weeks on top of the charts in any one year. Two of these were film soundtrack casts. The feat has not been achieved since 1970.

52	Cast of South Pacific	1959
45	Cast of South Pacific	1960
40	Beatles	1964
34	Beatles	1963
30	Cast of The Sound Of Music	1966
26	Beatles	1967
24	Elvis Presley	1962
	Simon and Garfunkel	1970
22	Elvis Presley	1961
20	Cast of The Sound Of Music	1965

MOST NUMBER ONE ALBUMS IN A CALENDAR YEAR

Only two acts have achieved the feat of getting three albums to number one in one year. They are:

1965 Beatles
(Beatles For Sale, Help, Rubber Soul)
1972 T. Rex
(Electric Warrior, Prophets Seers . . ./My People Were Fair . . . , Bolan Boogie)

The second of T. Tex's three number ones was a re-issued double album of Tyrannosaurus Rex material, so Marc Bolan's achievement could be considered even better than the Beatles, whose chart-topping albums were all single discs.

Sixteen acts have had two or more number one hits in a year, as follows:

5 times	Beatles	(1963, 1964, 1965, 1969, 1970)
4 times	Abba	(1979, 1980, 1981, 1982)
3 times	Elton John	(1973, 1974, 1990)
2 times	Bob Dylan	(1965, 1970)
	Led Zeppelin	(1970, 1976)
	George Mitchell Minstrels	(1961, 1962)
Once	David Bowie	(1973)
	Erasure	(1989)
	Monkees	(1967)
	Gary Numan/Tubeway Army	(1979)
	Mike Oldfield	(1974)
	Elvis Presley	(1962)
	Queen	(1991)
	Slade	(1973)
	T. Rex	(1972)
	Andy Williams	(1971)

In 1981 and 1993, Phil Collins had number one hits as a soloist and as part of Genesis. In 1983 Michael Jackson hit the top with *Thriller* and also with a Greatest Hits package featuring tracks by the Jackson Five as well as some solo tracks by Michael. In 1990 Luciano Pavarotti was on top of the charts with *The Essential Pavarotti* and, seven weeks later, *In Concert* with José Carreras and Placido Domingo.

SELF-REPLACEMENT AT THE TOP

Only three acts have ever knocked themselves off the top of the charts. They are:

BEATLES: .... *With The Beatles* replaced *Please Please Me* on 7 Dec 63
BEATLES: .... *Beatles for Sale* replaced *A Hard Day's Night* on 19 Dec 64
BOB DYLAN: .... *Bringing It All Back Home* replaced *Freewheelin' Bob Dylan* on 29 May 65
MIKE OLDFIELD: .... *Tubular Bells* replaced *Hergest Ridge* on 5 Oct 74

On 7 Aug 82 *Kids From Fame* replaced *Fame* at the top, but the TV spin-off featured an entirely different cast from the album soundtrack.

Hergest Ridge was released after *Tubular Bells* but got to number one first. Bob Dylan had two top ten hit albums released between *Freewheelin'* and *Bringing It All Back Home*.

MOST WEEKS AT NUMBER ONE BY AN ALBUM IN TOTAL

115	South Pacific	Film Soundtrack
70	The Sound Of Music	Film Soundtrack
41	Bridge Over Troubled Water	Simon and Garfunkel
30	Please Please Me	Beatles
27	Sergeant Pepper's Lonely Hearts Club Band	Beatles
22	GI Blues	Elvis Presley (Film Soundtrack)
21	With The Beatles	Beatles
21	A Hard Day's Night	Beatles (Film Soundtrack)
18	Blue Hawaii	Elvis Presley (Film Soundtrack)
18	Saturday Night Fever	Film Soundtrack
17	Abbey Road	Beatles
17	The Singles 1969–1973	Carpenters
15	. . . But Seriously	Phil Collins
14	Brothers In Arms	Dire Straits
14	Summer Holiday	Cliff Richard and the Shadows (Film Soundtrack)
13	John Wesley Harding	Bob Dylan
13	Grease	Film Soundtrack
13	West Side Story	Film Soundtrack
12	Kings Of The Wild Frontier	Adam and the Ants
12	The Kids From 'Fame'	Kids From Fame
12	Legend	Bob Marley and the Wailers
12	The Rolling Stones	Rolling Stones
12	Stars	Simply Red
11	Greatest Hits	Abba
11	Bat Out Of Hell II – Back Into Hell	Meat Loaf
11	Beatles For Sale	Beatles
11	Elton John's Greatest Hits	Elton John
11	20 All Time Hits Of The Fifties	Various Artists
10	Arrival	Abba
10	20 Golden Greats	Beach Boys
10	Greatest Hits	Eurythmics
10	Rolling Stones No. 2	Rolling Stones

The Bodyguard (Original Soundtrack) has spent 11 weeks at number one in the Compilation Albums chart.

MOST CONSECUTIVE WEEKS AT NUMBER ONE BY ONE ALBUM

```
70  South Pacific  Film Soundtrack.....................................................from 8 Nov 58
30  Please Please Me  Beatles ......................................................from 11 May 63
23  Sergeant Pepper's Lonely Hearts Club Band  Beatles .........from 10 Jun 67
21  With The Beatles  Beatles ........................................................from 7 Dec 63
21  A Hard Day's Night  Beatles ...................................................from 25 Jul 64
19  South Pacific  Film Soundtrack .............................................from 19 Mar 60
18  The Sound Of Music  Film Soundtrack....................................from 1 Oct 66
18  Saturday Night Fever  Film Soundtrack..................................from 6 May 78
17  Blue Hawaii  Elvis Presley ......................................................from 24 Feb 62
14  Summer Holiday  Cliff Richard and the Shadows.....................from 2 Feb 63
13  South Pacific  Film Soundtrack ..............................................from 15 Oct 60
13  Bridge Over Troubled Water  Simon and Garfunkel...........from 21 Feb 70
13  Grease  Film Soundtrack ..........................................................from 7 Oct 78
12  GI Blues  Elvis Presley ..............................................................from 8 Apr 61
12  Rolling Stones  Rolling Stones .................................................from 2 May 64
12  Legend  Bob Marley and the Wailers ....................................from 19 May 84
11  Abbey Road  Beatles ..............................................................from 4 Oct 69
11  Bridge Over Troubled Water  Simon and Garfunkel ............from 16 Jan 71
11  The Singles 1969–1973  Carpenters .....................................from 9 Mar 74
11  Elton John's Greatest Hits  Elton John ..................................from 23 Nov 74
10  The Sound Of Music  Film Soundtrack....................................from 5 Jun 65
10  The Sound Of Music  Film Soundtrack...................................from 16 Oct 65
10  The Sound Of Music  Film Soundtrack ..................................from 19 Feb 66
10  John Wesley Harding  Bob Dylan............................................from 9 Mar 68
10  20 Golden Greats  Beach Boys...............................................from 24 Jul 76
10  Kings Of The Wild Frontier  Adam and the Ants .................from 14 Mar 81
10  Brothers In Arms  Dire Straits ...............................................from 18 Jan 86
```

The run of 11 weeks by *Bridge Over Troubled Water* includes 8 weeks at no. 1 when charts were not published because of a postal strike.

No album has spent more than 8 consecutive weeks at number one in the Compilation Albums chart, a record shared by *The Bodyguard (Original Soundtrack)* and *Now! That's What I Call Music 22.*

GAP BETWEEN SPELLS AT NUMBER ONE

13 albums have returned to number one more than ten weeks after dropping from the top. Two albums have done this twice. The longest gaps between spells at number one are:

```
45 wks  Diva  Annie Lennox......................................25 Apr 92 to 6 Mar 93
41 wks  The Sound of Music  (Original Soundtrack).....3 Feb 68 to 23 Nov 68
38 wks  We Can't Dance  Genesis.................30 Nov 91 to 22 Aug 92
31 wks  Thriller  Michael Jackson...........................25 Jun 83 to 28 Jan 84
27 wks  Automatic For The People  R.E.M. ........17 Oct 92 to 24 Apr 93
25 wks  Tango In The Night  Fleetwood Mac ..............14 Nov 87 to 7 May 88
23 wks  The Sound Of Music  (Original Soundtrack)..10 Jun 67 to 18 Nov 67
22 wks  Brothers In Arms  Dire Straits................17 Aug 85 to 18 Jan 86
```

19 wks   Can't Slow Down *Lionel Richie*.........................19 Nov 83 to 31 Mar 84
19 wks   Born in the U.S.A. *Bruce Springsteen* ....23 Feb 85 to 6 Jul 85
13 wks   Bridge Over Troubled Water *Simon and Garfunkel*
                                                            3 Apr 71 to 3 Jul 71
12 wks   South Pacific *(Original Soundtrack)* ....8 Apr 65 to 1 Jul 61
12 wks   Bridge Over Troubled Water *Simon and Garfunkel*
                                                  24 Oct 70 to 16 Jan 71
12 wks   Graceland *Paul Simon* ....8 Nov 86 to 31 Jan 87
11 wks   A New Flame *Simply Red* ....6 May 89 to 22 Jul 89

Between *Diva's* first and second weeks at number one, 26 other albums topped the chart.

The longest span of any record's run at the top, from its first week of chart supremacy to its last, is 3 years 177 days, achieved by *The Sound Of Music (Original Soundtrack)* between 5 June 1965 and 29 November 1968. *South Pacific (Original Soundtrack)* topped the first chart of all, on 8 November 1958, and enjoyed its final stint at number one on 9 Sep 1961, a total span at the top of 2 years 311 days.

LONGEST CLIMB TO NUMBER ONE

Four albums have taken more than one year to climb from their original date of chart entry to the number one position on the regular chart, as follows:

3 years 298 days ....(from 13 Jul 68 to 6 May 72)
Tyrannosaurus Rex......*My People Were Fair And Had Sky In Their Hair, But Now They're Content To Wear Stars On Their Brows*

2 years 67 days ....(from 5 Jul 75 to 10 Sep 77)
Elvis Presley.....................*40 Greatest Hits*

1 year 321 days ....(from 6 Sep 80 to 24 Jul 82)
Original Soundtrack ....*Fame*

1 year 83 days ....(from 14 Jul 73 to 5 Oct 74)
Mike Oldfield ....*Tubular Bells*

Ten other albums have taken 30 weeks or more to reach the top, as follows:

Rumours	Fleetwood Mac	49 weeks
The Freewheelin' Bob Dylan	Bob Dylan..	48 weeks
Sleeping With The Past	Elton John	44 weeks
Like A Virgin	Madonna	44 weeks
Circle Of One	Oleta Adams	40 weeks
Black And White Minstrel Show	George Mitchell Minstrels	36 weeks
Born In The USA	Bruce Springsteen	36 weeks
Greatest Hits	Andy Williams..	35 weeks
Band On The Run	Wings	33 weeks
And I Love You So	Perry Como	30 weeks

Tyrannosaurus Rex hit number one with the longest titled album ever to hit the top only after it was re-released in 1972 as a double album with *Prophets, Seers, Sages And The Angels Of The Ages*. Presley's album hit the top in the period immediately following his death. *Tubular Bells* spent 11 weeks at number two before replacing its follow-up at the very top, and *Rumours* remained 32 weeks in the top ten before hitting the number one slot. *The Freewheelin' Bob Dylan* climbed to the top during its seventh chart run. Oleta Adams became the first chart act ever to re-enter the charts at number one, 38 weeks after an original 2-week run for *Circle Of One*, during which it peaked at number 49.

The soundtrack album of the film *Dirty Dancing* came on to the main chart on 31 Oct 1987, before the formation of the Compilation Albums chart. It spent 63 weeks on the main chart without ever climbing higher than number four, before being switched to the Compilations chart on 14 Jan 1989. On 19 January 1991, 3 years and 80 days after its first entry on the main chart and 2 years and 5 days after it first came on to the Compilations chart, it topped the Compilation Albums chart for the first time.

MOST CONSECUTIVE NUMBER ONE HIT ALBUMS

Twenty-two different acts have hit the very top of the albums chart with three or more consecutive official album releases, as follows:

8 Abba .... (From 1976 to 1982: *Greatest Hits* to *The Singles – The First Ten Years* inclusive)

8 Led Zeppelin .... (From 1970 to 1979: *Led Zeppelin 2* to *In Through The Out Door* inclusive)

7 Beatles .... (from 1963 to 1966: *Please Please Me* to *Revolver* inclusive)

6 Rod Stewart .... (From 1971 to 1976: *Every Picture Tells A Story* to *A Night On The Town* inclusive)

5 Police .... (From 1979 to 1986: *Reggatta De Blanc* to *Every Breath You Take – The Singles* inclusive)

5 Rolling Stones .... (From 1969 to 1973: *Let It Bleed* to *Goat's Head Soup*. Their last two official releases on Decca and their first three on Rolling Stones Records)

4 Beatles .... (from 1967 to 1970: *Sergeant Pepper's Lonely Hearts Club Band* to *Let It Be*. During this run *Magical Mystery Tour* (import) and *Yellow Submarine* hit the charts, but cannot be considered part of the official sequence of Beatles albums)

4 Bob Dylan .... (From 1968 to 1970: *John Wesley Harding* to *New Morning* inclusive)

4 Erasure .... (from 1988 to 1992: *The Innocents* to *Pop! The First 20 Hits*)

4 Elton John .... (From 1973 to 1975: *Don't Shoot Me, I'm Only The Piano Player* to *Elton John's Greatest Hits* inclusive)

4 Simple Minds .... (From 1984 to 1989: *Sparkle In The Rain* to *Street Fighting Years* inclusive. Each album spent only one week at the top of the charts)

3 Boney M .... (From 1978 to 1980: *Night Flight To Venus*, *Oceans Of Fantasy* and *The Magic Of Boney M*)

3 David Bowie. .... (From 1973 to 1974: *Aladdin Sane*, *Pin-Ups* and *Diamond Dogs*)

3 Dire Straits .... (From 1985 to 1991: *Brothers In Arms*, *Money For Nothing* and *On Every Street*)

3 Genesis ....(From 1983 to 1991: *Genesis*, *Invisible Touch* and *We Can't Dance*. These were three consecutive official releases, although their 1970 album *Trespass* charted for the first time between the success of *Genesis* and *Invisible Touch*)

3 Michael Jackson .....(From 1982 to 1991: *Thriller*, *Bad* and *Dangerous*. No fewer than five other albums under the Jackson name hit the charts during this hat-trick, but there is no doubt that these were three consecutive official releases by Jacko)

3 George Mitchell ....(From 1961 to 1963, the first album chart hat-trick:
Minstrels   *The Black And White Minstrel Show*, *Another Black And White Minstrel Show* and *On Stage With The George Mitchell Minstrels*)

3 Gary Numan ....(From 1979 to 1980: *Replicas*, *The Pleasure Principle* and *Telekon*. *Tubeway Army* was released before *Replicas*, even though it hit the charts later)

3 Prince ....(From 1988 to 1991: *Lovesexy*, *Batman* and *Graffiti Bridge*)

3 Queen ....(From 1989 to 1991: *Miracle*, *Innuendo* and *Greatest Hits Vol. 2*)

3 Slade ....(From 1973 to 1974: *Slayed?*, *Sladest* and *Old New Borrowed And Blue*)

3 T. Rex ....(From 1971 to 1972: *Electric Warrior*, *Prophets Seers And Sages The Angels Of The Ages/My People Were Fair And Had Sky In Their Hair But Now They're Content To Wear Stars On Their Brows* and *Bolan Boogie*. The second of the three was a double album reissue, but it had never been issued in that format, and one half of the double album had never been a hit before)

3 U2 ....(From 1984 to 1988: *The Unforgettable Fire*, *The Joshua Tree* and *Rattle And Hum*)

STRAIGHT IN AT NUMBER ONE

After the first chart on 8 Nov 1958, no album made its chart debut at number one until the Beatles' fifth album, *Help!*, did so on 14 Aug 1965. However, it is now a routine event in the albums chart, so much so that, of 49 number one hit albums in 1992 and 1993, 43 came on to the charts at number one. Eighteen acts have achieved this feat at least three times, as follows:

8	David Bowie	5	Police	4	Elton John
6	Genesis	5	Simple Minds	4	Paul McCartney
6	Rolling Stones	5	U2	4	Prince
5	Abba	4	Phil Collins	4	Queen
5	Beatles	4	Dire Straits	3	Madonna
5	Led Zeppelin	4	Erasure	3	Status Quo

Phil Collins has therefore achieved the feat ten times, six times with Genesis and four times solo. Paul McCartney has done it nine times, five times with the Beatles and four times solo.

THE TOP TWENTY ALBUMS ACTS

A table showing the comparative achievements of the 20 most-charted album acts of all time.

ACT	Year First Charted	Total Weeks	Total Hits	Top Tens	No. Ones	Most-charted Album
Beatles	1963	1116	25	18	12	Sgt. Pepper's Lonely Hearts Club Band (172 wks)
Queen	1974	1061	20	18	8	Greatest Hits (406 wks)
Simon & Garfunkel	1966	1061	10	7	2	Bridge Over Troubled Water (303 wks)
Dire Straits	1978	1058	9	9	4	Makin' Movies (249 wks)
Elvis Presley	1958	1046	95	36	6	Blue Hawaii (71 wks)
David Bowie	1972	889	29	21	8	The Rise And Fall Of Ziggy Stardust And The Spiders From Mars (172 wks)
U2	1981	854	11	7	5	Live Under A Blood Red Sky (203 wks)
Fleetwood Mac	1968	766	14	9	4	Rumours (443 wks)
Elton John	1970	763	32	19	6	Very Best Of Elton John (91 wks)
Pink Floyd	1967	755	16	13	3	Dark Side Of The Moon (310 wks)
Michael Jackson	1972	740	18	6	4	Off The Wall (176 wks)
Phil Collins	1981	739	6	6	4	Face Value (274 wks)
Cliff Richard	1959	731	48	32	7	Love Songs (43 wks)
Rod Stewart	1970	707	23	18	7	Atlantic Crossing (89 wks)
Rolling Stones	1964	694	38	29	9	Rolling Stones (51 wks)
Frank Sinatra	1958	644	51	29	1	My Way (59 wks)
Meat Loaf	1978	624	8	6	2	Bat Out Of Hell (457 wks)
Madonna	1984	605	8	8	4	Like A Virgin (152 wks)
Abba	1974	584	14	9	9	Greatest Hits (130 wks)
Bob Dylan	1964	568	37	24	6	Greatest Hits (82 wks)

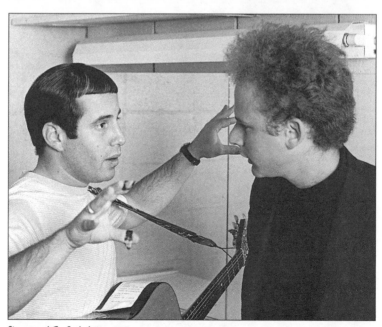

Simon and Garfunkel (Pictorial Press)

FACTS AND FEATS

Over the past two years since *British Hit Albums (5)* was published, Abba have climbed back into the top 20 acts, at the expense of the Carpenters, who slip to number 21. Madonna has also climbed into the top 20 for the first time, displacing the Beach Boys. All the top acts have appeared in the charts over the past two years, although Fleetwood Mac only appeared on the chart for one week. Queen have added most to their total in 1992 and 1993, a further 171 weeks, which moved them up from fifth to joint second on the overall weeks on chart listing.

Apart from Queen, U2 and Elton John have both climbed three places within the top 20 since the end of 1991, and Michael Jackson, with the help of albums recorded with other acts, has climbed from number 20 to number 11. Bob Dylan has fallen four places and Phil Collins three.

Both Elvis Presley and Frank Sinatra featured in the very first albums chart. The most recent arrival in the charts of any of the top 20 acts is by Madonna, whose first album chart action came in the week ending 11 February 1984.

Of the 20 leading acts, ten are British, seven are American, one is a transatlantic mixture (Fleetwood Mac), one is Swedish and one is Irish. There are ten male solo acts, but only one female soloist. Christine McVie and Stevie Nicks of Fleetwood Mac, and Agnetha Fältskog and Frida Lyngstad of Abba add to the female element of the top acts.

If we look at the top acts on the basis of the average number of weeks each album has spent in the charts (i.e. total weeks divided by total hits), eight acts prove to have spent an average of more than one year on the charts with each album:

Phil Collins .... 123.2 weeks on chart per album
Dire Straits .... 117.6 weeks on chart per album
Simon and Garfunkel .... 106.1 weeks on chart per album
Meat Loaf .... 78.0 weeks on chart per album
U2 .... 77.6 weeks on chart per album
Madonna .... 75.6 weeks on chart per album
Fleetwood Mac .... 54.7 weeks on chart per album
Queen .... 53.0 weeks on chart per album

At the other end of the scale, each album hit by Elvis Presley has lasted on average only 11 weeks on the chart, each Frank Sinatra hit lasts only 12.6 weeks, and each Cliff Richard album hangs around for no more than 15.2 weeks. Bob Dylan (15.4 weeks) and the Rolling Stones (18.3 weeks) are the only other acts to average fewer than 20 weeks of chart action per hit.

Ranking acts purely on the basis of weeks on chart is not a perfect solution, but in the case of the albums chart, overall success equates far more closely with chart life than on the singles charts. Long-running chart successes are what both the performers and their record companies are looking for. This chart is not meant to reflect total sales, but merely the relative chart success of the biggest album acts in British chart history.

THE GUINNESS BOOK OF TOP 40 CHARTS

The Guinness Book of Top 40 Charts presents popular music's lifeline through the years. The 700-plus pages feature every chart for every week from 10 March 1960, plus a detailed breakdown of the smaller charts of the 1950s.

- What was the number one single in the week you were born?
- Was the summer of '67 all legend has made it out to be?
- What single was at the top the week the Beatles first hit the Top 40?
- Who were the artists the Sex Pistols were shaking up when they first pogoed into the Top 40 in late 1976?

These questions and a host of others are answered in **The Guinness Book of Top 40 Charts**. (ISBN: 0–85112–541–7)

THE GUINNESS BOOK OF BRITISH HIT SINGLES

The Guinness Book of British Hit Singles, now a million seller, is Britain's most popular and critically acclaimed pop and rock book. The 9th edition gives the lowdown on every hit single since the charts began in 1952 and lists each one under both act name and song title.

Packed with more facts, feats, features and photos than ever before, **The Guinness Book of British Hit Singles** is a must for rock and pop fans of all ages. (ISBN: 0–85112526–3)

THE GUINNESS HITS QUIZ 2

The Guinness Hits Quiz 2 is a collection of brain-busting quizzes, anagrams and acrostics covering the whole spectrum of the pop music scene. It is ideal for journeys and get togethers, and indispensible for the pub quiz.

The Guinness Hits Quiz 2 was described by Q magazine as the book where 'the compilers really know their stuff and, as a result, there is something for everyone'. (ISBN: 0–85112–712–6)

ALSO FROM GUINNESS

THE GUINNESS BOOK OF NUMBER ONE HITS

Revealing the who, why, when and where of every chart topper, **The Guinness Book of Number One Hits** includes the date each hit reached the summit and the length of its duration on chart. (ISBN: 0–85112–769–X)

THE GUINNESS UK TOP 1000 SINGLES

The Guinness UK Top 1000 Singles is now in its second edition and presents Paul Gambaccini, Tim Rice and Jo Rice's ranking of the biggest UK hits of the rock era, based on chart positions achieved and sustained. Illustrated throughout it also lists the Top 40 chart hits of each year.
(ISBN: 0–85112–712–6)

Guinness Publishing also distribute the Billboard US chart statistics books.

A full listing of all GRR Publications and Guinness Publishing titles, including **Hits of the 80s** and **The Guinness Encyclopedia of Popular Music** (in four volumes), is contained in a catalogue available from:

The Marketing Department, Guinness Publishing, 33 London Road, Enfield, Middlesex, EN2 6DJ.

THE AUTHORS

When **Paul Gambaccini** was six, Bill Haley and His Comets changed the course of popular music with 'Rock Around The Clock'. With this edition *British Hit Albums* is six, and Paul is hoping something similarly cataclysmic will happen. In the meantime he is proudly polishing the gold disc he received for breaking Gorecki's *Symphony No. 3* on his Classic FM programme, showing everyone who is interested his near mint copies of Carl Barks' first issues of *Donald Duck* and *Walt Disney's Comics And Stories*, and trying to get people interested in his reference tome *Television's Greatest Hits*.

From 1992 to 1994 much of the work **Tim Rice** has done has been with the Walt Disney organisation. He contributed songs to the animated feature film *Aladdin*, one of which, 'A Whole New World', co-written with Alan Menken, won both a Golden Globe and an Oscar. He has also written lyrics for all the songs for the animated film *The Lion King*, to be released in 1994, with music by Elton John, and several songs with Alan Menken for the 1994 stage production of Disney's *Beauty And The Beast.*

Since the publication of *British Hit Albums* 5, **Jonathan Rice** has not only bought a few good albums (and some bad ones), but has also written two books that have been best sellers in their own fields (in one case, a very sparsely populated field). *Curiosities Of Cricket* kept everybody happy except Jonathan's bank manager, but *Keeping Up Appearances – Hyacinth Bucket's Book Of Etiquette For The Socially Less Fortunate* did so well that for several weeks at the end of 1993 it was outselling even *British Hit Singles*.